INDIANS OF MIDDLE AMERICA

AN INTRODUCTION TO THE ETHNOLOGY OF MEXICO, CENTRAL AMERICA, AND THE CARIBBEAN

By Robert B. Taylor

Kansas State University

Lifeway Books

Las Cruces, New Mexico

To: Floris, Mark, Linnea, and Gwen

Library of Congress Catalog Card Number: 89-63278

ISBN 0-9624522-3-8

Second Printing

Copyright© 1989 by Robert B. Taylor

Published by: Lifeway Books
                P.O. Box 8434
                Las Cruces, N.M. 88006

Cover photo credits:

Tarahumara man in traditional dress, photo taken near San Javier:
   Arizona State Museum, University of Arizona, Catalog No. C9188, Helga Teiwes, photographer

Zapotec woman shaping a tortilla: Robert B. Taylor, photographer

TABLE OF CONTENTS

MAPS

ABOUT THIS BOOK

This is a multi-purpose work on the native peoples of Mexico, Guatemala and the other Central American countries, and the nations of the Caribbean islands. It is designed primarily to introduce classroom students and general readers to the cultures of representative native American societies who survived the arrival of the Spanish long enough for observers to provide us with a picture of their cultures. Many of the groups remain today, living lives much different from those of their pre-Conquest ancestors but, also, diverse from today's national cultures.

As they have in the past, Indian cultures continue to influence heavily the lives and events of modern Middle American nations, and a knowledge of the contemporary and past cultures of Indian Middle America is essential to an adequate understanding of the region. This introduction provides beginners with both a general picture of Middle America's native cultures and knowledge of a variety of lifeways of specific Indian communities and tribes.

There have been and continue to be different kinds of cultures in Middle America. This work deals with (1) the gathering and hunting tribes of the deserts and mountains of northern Mexico, (2) the horticultural tribes of northwestern Mexico, (3) the Mesoamerican tribes of southern Mexico and Guatemala, and (4) the cultures of lower Central America and the Caribbean islands. (See map 1.) It provides a general view of each cultural area and describes the lifeways of representative groups for each--seven Mesoamerican groups and three groups for each of the other three types.

Some will be surprised to find most of this work written in the past tense, even if the time level involved is the 1980s and the group was still practicing the described customs at the time of publication. This is to avoid the misunderstanding that too commonly results from anthropological use of the "ethnographic present." In some cases we are reasonably certain only that most of the customs described were in force at the time of publication. The rapid pace of modern change does not allow anyone but a trained observer sufficiently familiar with the group's current situation to specify which customs continue and which are gone or nearly so. Also, many who read cultural descriptions long after publication tend to interpret present tense writing as indicating a custom described is current. It seems most accurate and least misleading to specify time levels and treat them as past, not in the sense of having disappeared but as lived during a specified past. When there is basis for it, a chapter includes statements about the likely durability of the cultural situations described.

Observers of the world's various social scenes find that people often acquire knowledge of the lifeways of different human groups without developing the perspectives necessary to avoid misinterpreting that knowledge. Many who read this book have had little or no exposure to the perspectives of cultural anthropology and closely similar social sciences, so an additional purpose of this volume is to supply basic perspectives, using the customs of Middle American Indian groups to illustrate them. This use of cultural description as a foundation for expounding sociocultural perspectives is one of this book's strong points, as a number who have used it have testified. Ethnocentrism and cultural relativism as alternative ways of responding to alien lifeways, cultures as systems of customs that are part of larger systems, the roles of various kinship arrangements in peoples' lives, the different ways groups respond to pressures to change their customs, the considerable technological knowledge and skill of peasant and tribal groups, and basic linguistic processes are examples of the many conceptual areas explored. For nonspecialists and beginners, then, this treatise provides both a knowledge of native American lifeways in Middle America and appreciation of principles of human relations exemplified in those lifeways.

The volume will also be useful to more advanced students and specialists as a handbook or reference work. Cultural anthropologists specializing in other parts of the world may find it useful for reviewing the cultures of Middle America. And even those specializing in Middle America, as they do with other sources, may refer to the summaries of the cultures of specific groups to refresh their memories, locate bibliographic references, or learn more about cultures they may not have had occasion to concentrate on.

Instructors may choose to eliminate some chapters so they can require the study of full-length ethnographies. If

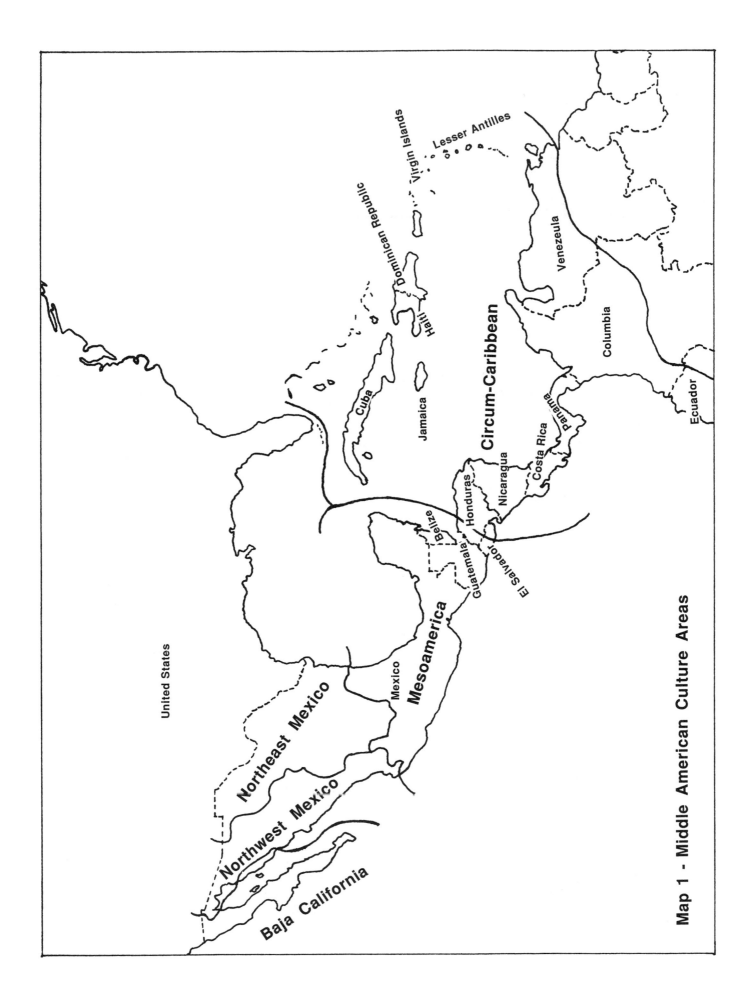

Map 1 - Middle American Culture Areas

this is done, it is possible for students to get a general picture of any culture described in this volume by reading the preliminary summary description that begins each chapter.

Each cultural summary has been reviewed by a scholar familiar with the group in question--either an anthropologist with field experience in the community or tribe or a scholar who is familiar with ethnohistorical sources on the group. In this connection, I wish to express special appreciation to Homer Aschmann, Thomas Bowen, Harold E. Driver, Thomas R. McGuire, John G. Kennedy, Joseph E.

Grimes, George Pierre Castile, Hugo G. Nutini, Michael Kearney, A. Richard Diebold, Jr., R. Jon McGee, Sol Tax, Douglas Brintnall, Mary Helms, Samuel M. Wilson, and James Howe. While the chapters have been greatly improved by their suggestions, the responsibility for any errors or other weaknesses is indisputedly mine. My familiarity with Middle America comes from field study in a Zapotec community in Oaxaca, research in libraries in Mexico and the United States, and years of teaching Middle American ethnography to undergraduate anthropology students at Kansas State University.

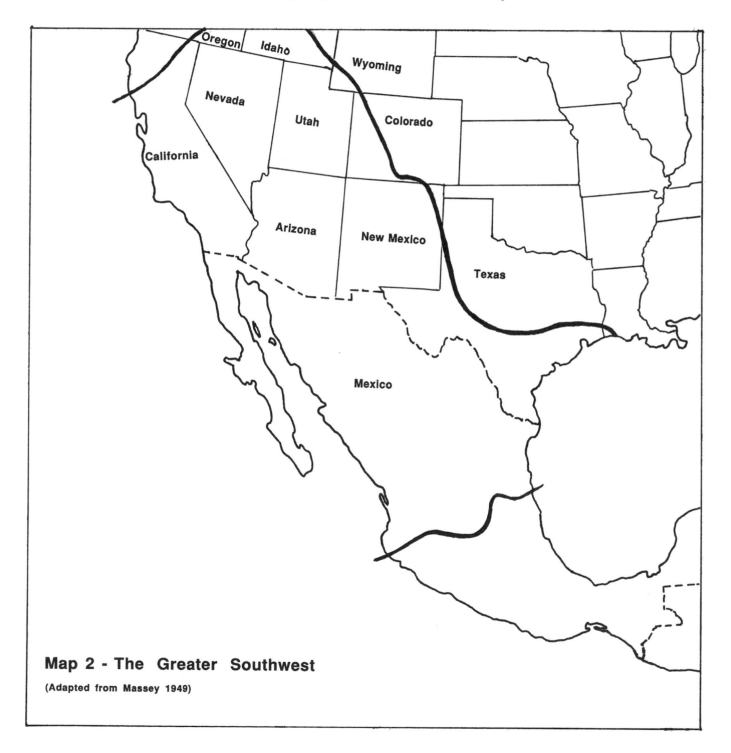

Map 2 - The Greater Southwest

(Adapted from Massey 1949)

PART I   GATHERER-HUNTERS OF NORTHERN MEXICO

CHAPTER 1

GATHERER-HUNTERS OF BAJA CALIFORNIA AND NORTHEAST MEXICO

Anthropologists have developed considerable appreciation for gathering and hunting lifeways. At one time many scholars supposed groups depending on wild plants and animals lived on the edge of starvation constantly, barely keeping body and soul together in spite of a dawn to dark quest for food. But field studies have shown that gatherer-hunters are among the leisured peoples of the world. In times of abundance it is not unusual for them to obtain all they need and want within a short period, leaving them with large blocks of time for visiting, ceremonies, sleeping, or whatever else they want to do. Researchers have also come to realize more fully the adaptability of gatherer-hunters, a trait that seems to stem from the need to be flexible in the face of changing resource availability from season to season and year to year. In addition, they have developed greater levels of appreciation for the observational skills of gatherer-hunters, who are frequently fine folk biologists aware of nuances of their habitat that escape the so-called civilized person.

Gatherer-hunters are one of two major types of people formerly common in the southwestern United States and northern Mexico. The other type is horticultural society, and it is the horticulturalists who must work so hard for a living that they enjoy relatively little leisure.

Earlier anthropologists thought of the Arizona-New Mexico country as a distinct area which, like other culture areas, was a region of cultures resembling one another more than they did any outside the area. But subsequent research revealed cultures like those of Arizona and New Mexico in neighboring regions, including northern Mexico. In 1943 Ralph Beals proposed a Greater Southwest culture area, and in 1954 Paul Kirchoff recommended that the Greater Southwest include (1) Arizona and New Mexico, (2) the vast inland area of desert and mountains that covers Nevada, Utah, and portions of neighboring states, (3) all of California but the northwestern part, (4) the coastal area of southern Texas, and (5) northern Mexico (including the Baja California peninsula) down to the Sinaloa River on the west coast and the Pánuco River on the east. It is apparent on the accompanying map (see map 2) that this joins the northern half of Mexico culturally with a large part of the United States. All of these subdivisions of the Greater Southwest share the two cultural types mentioned earlier: (1) a gathering lifeway supplemented by hunting and (2) a farming or horticultural lifeway.

Archaeological evidence indicates that the gathering of vegetable foods in combination with hunting and/or fishing was once the only subsistence combination throughout the region. Farming developed later in those spots where river water or run-off from rains provided sufficient moisture. The result was a region, especially in much of Arizona, New Mexico, and northwestern Mexico, dotted with horticultural oases. The gathering-hunting cultures continued over large areas, and in Mexico this includes the Baja California peninsula, a coastal stretch in northwestern Mexico, and most of north central and northeastern Mexico (see map 3).

The gatherer-hunter type of culture, sometimes called the Desert Culture, was characterized by a constellation of widely found features. These include a number of complex techniques for securing and processing a large variety of wild plants. Beals states that the core of the complex consists of three basic features: ways of rendering plant substances edible by leaching out the inedible matter, the seed beater and seed collecting tray, and the dominance of tree products that store well—such as piñon nuts, mesquite beans, or acorns (Beals 1943b:195). In addition to these three core features Beals and/or Kirchoff mention means for effectively utilizing small rodents, small nomadic bands with a patrilineal tendency, the ceremonial importance of puberty, strong witchcraft and magic, male nakedness, the wearing of front and back aprons by women, long hair, a skin or fur cap for men, blankets of intertwined strips of rabbit skin, coned or domed huts, the earth oven, the receiving of visions without a quest for them, and peaceableness. Though not all groups manifest all of these features, they are widespread among the Greater Southwest gatherer-hunters.

Anthropologists have long agreed that natural habitat does not determine just what a culture is like, since rather different cultures have been found in the same environment. But they grant that there are many important relationships between a culture and habitat characteristics and that one of the main reasons for resemblances among cultures may be similarities in the land and climate throughout the region in which they are found. Many anthropologists, in fact, specialize in the study of habitat-culture relationships.

It is no surprise to find terrain and climate rather similar throughout the country of the southwestern gatherer-hunters. Above all, it is arid, which means the people rely on the kinds of plants that can survive extended dry periods. The scarcity of water, relatively warm temperatures, and long distances from one kind of plant food to another have a variety of effects on the cultures. Many of these are noted in later discussions of specimen Indian lifeways.

The gatherer-hunters of Baja California and the western coast of the Mexican mainland lived in the Sonoran Desert, which also extends into southern Arizona, southwestern New Mexico, and southeastern California. Sonoran Desert topography is variable, including coastal and inland plains, hills, and low and high mountains. Vegetation is rich, with the large variety of succulent plants including the giant saguaro and cardón cacti and many smaller varieties. The Sonoran Desert is also rich in animal life.

The Chihuahuan Desert extends through much of north central Mexico and into southern New Mexico and Texas. Vast plains, large undrained basins, groups of limestone hills, and mountain ranges alternate with one another. There are fewer cacti than in the Sonoran Desert but more grasses. There are also fewer animal forms. The great Sierra Madre Oriental separates the Chihuahuan Desert from the coastal plain of northeastern Mexico, which is also arid.

Driver divides the gatherer-hunters of Mexico into two culture areas—Baja California, which includes the Seri of the mainland coast as well as the tribes of the peninsula, and Northeastern Mexico, which embraces the tribes of north central and northeastern Mexico (Driver 1961:17-18). There are various cultural differences between the two stemming from the differences between the Sonoran and Chihuahuan Deserts. But the similarities may far outweigh the differences, and there is too little cultural information about the Indians of northeastern/north central Mexico to make it very useful to separate it culturally from Baja California. The problem of determining culture areas and their boundaries is frequently troublesome, especially when information is limited so severely.

It is also difficult when data are scarce to determine what cultural and linguistic groups occupied various areas and which were subgroups of larger units. The difficulty becomes evident when we compare tribal maps prepared by different scholars. The differences among maps manifest guesses based on the best information available about what groups were where and how much territory they occupied. In the northern part of Baja California the Diegueño (approx. dee-eh-GWEHN-yoh) Indians lived on both sides of the Mexico-United States border, including San Diego county in California state. They lived within the semi-desert area of southern California and a large portion of northwestern Baja California. The Cocopa (approx. koh-KOH-pah) Indians of the northeastern part of Baja California are not included here because they were horticulturalists. The Diegueño called themselves Tipai (approx. TEE-pie) or "people," which explains why some tribal maps label them Tipai instead of Diegueño. But they apparently did not differentiate themselves sharply from all neighboring societies. In the summer of 1920 anthropologist Leslie Spier spent twelve days collecting information on Diegueño customs from one man over eighty years of age, producing the largest single body of information we have on the culture (Spier 1923).

The Akwa'ala (approx. ah-kwah-AH-lah) and the Kiliwa (approx. kee-LEE-wah) have sometimes been included as Diegueño, but they are treated separately here. The Akwa'ala called themselves Paipai, and were located to the southeast of the Diegueño. Anthropologists E. W. Gifford and Robert Lowie interviewed an aged Akwa'ala shaman from Mexico in 1921 and 1922, collecting a small amount of information on the social organization and religion. Only a few Akwa'ala were left in Mexico at the time Gifford and Lowie talked with the shaman.

The Kiliwa were located to the east of the Akwa'ala, south of the Cocopa. They have persisted in larger numbers and with less cultural change than neighboring groups and were studied by Meigs during the 1930s (Meigs 1939). They have remembered enough of their culture to make possible a recent film showing their hunting and gathering techniques.

To the south of the Diegueño, Akwa'ala and Kiliwa were the Cochimí (approx. koh-chee-MEE), who lived within the Sonoran Desert region of Baja California. The Ñakipa (approx. nyah-KEE-pah), located just to the south of the southwestern Diegueño territory, have been included with the Cochimí, but they did not live in the Sonoran Desert, and their language allies them with the northern groups. The Cochimí resided in a more difficult habitat than those to the north and south, and their culture was less elaborated. The Cochimí gathering-hunting bands were ranged over the width of the peninsula for some four hundred miles. They became extinct probably several decades before 1900, and no anthropologists interviewed even one. What we know of their culture has come from searches of the reports of the Jesuit missionaries who worked among them (Aschmann, 1959, 1966).

The Waicuru (or Guaicuru) (approx. y-KOO-roo) is the major culture south of the Cochimí. To the east and south of the Waicuru was a tribe or group of tribes known as the Cora (approx. KOH-rah). There is a brief description from the hand of Father Napoli of one of the Cora tribes (Napoli 1970[1721]). These Cora are not to be confused with the Cora of mainland Mexico, who were agricultural. Finally, the Pericú (approx. peh-ree-KOO) Indians were located at the very tip of the peninsula.

Across the Gulf of California along a portion of the Sonora coast lived the widely known Seri (approx. SEH-ree) Indians. Unlike the Indians of the peninsula they managed to survive as a group, and enough of their earlier

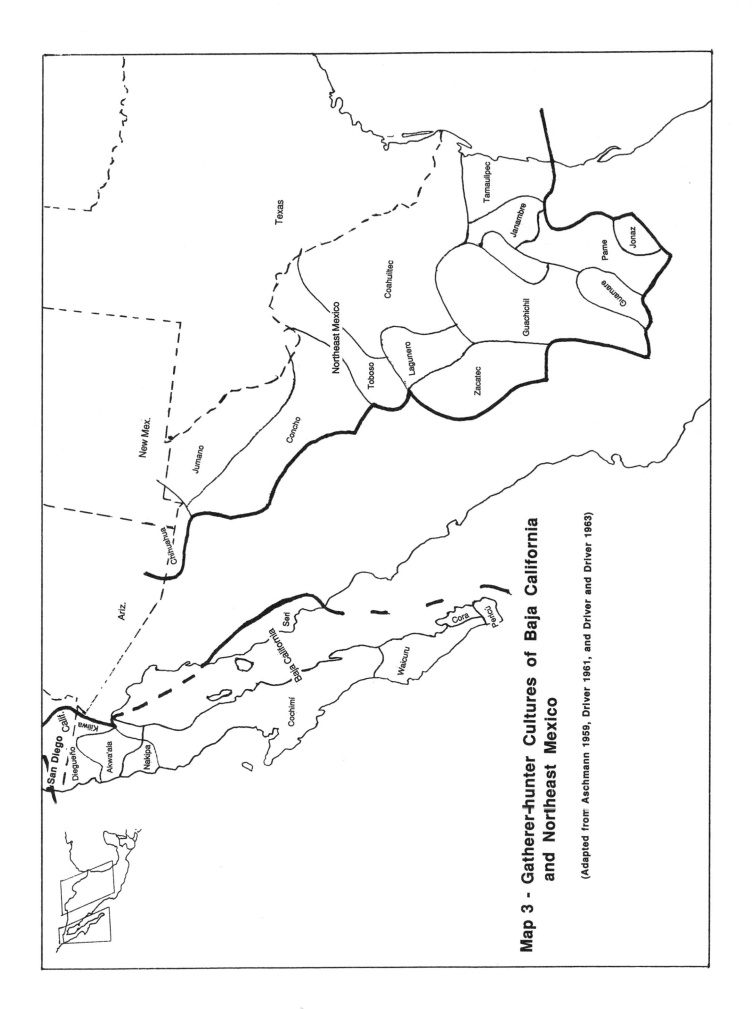

Map 3 - Gatherer-hunter Cultures of Baja California and Northeast Mexico

(Adapted from Aschmann 1959, Driver 1961, and Driver and Driver 1963)

customs endured to make it possible to refer to Seri culture into the twentieth century. For a long time the Seri were troubled little by the Spanish, but when they finally clashed with ranchers and other intruders, they fought back and were eventually crushed. The Spanish supposed they would soon die out, but small bands persisted along the remote coast and grew in numbers, taking what they wanted from Mexican culture but rejecting much as well.

The Indians just inland from the Seri and to the north and south were horticultural. But in the vast regions beyond the Sierra Madre range of western Mexico there were gathering-hunting groups even less well-known than the Baja Californians. This is one of the regions where cultural maps drawn by various scholars differ greatly. For many of the groups referred to in the ethnohistorical records it is probably impossible to know whether they were linguistically and culturally distinct tribes or local subdivisions given special prominence because they came to the notice of the Spanish. The Jumano (approx. hoo-MAH-noh) (including the Suma) apparently lived mostly in Mexico but also in adjacent areas of southwestern New Mexico and southwestern Texas. South of them the Concho (approx. KOHN-choh) were a major group or collection of groups generally recognized in the literature. To the east and somewhat to the south of the Concho were the Toboso (approx. toh-BOH-soh) people. To the south of the Toboso a Lagunero (approx. lah-goo-NEH-roh) group is often recognized as distinct, though some maps omit the Lagunero. The Zacatec (approx. SAH-kah-tehk) lie to the south of the Lagunero. Over a large territory extending from Toboso country to the coast of Texas and the northeastern corner of Mexico were many autonomous bands collectively known as Coahuiltec (approx. kwa-weel-TEHK), and to the south of them along the coast and extending inland some distance were the Tamaulipec (approx. tah-mow-lee-PEHK). South of the Coahuiltec in the interior were the Guachichil (approx. wah-chee-CHEEL), the Guamare (approx. wah-MAH-reh), the Pame (approx. PAH-meh), the Janambre (approx. hah-NAHM-breh), and the Jonaz (approx. hoh-NAHS). Horticulture has been reported for some of these groups, but gathering and hunting prevailed.

The gatherer-hunters of north central and northeastern Mexico often have been known by the widely used term Chichimec (approx. CHEE-chee-mehk) (Chichimeca in Spanish). Before the Spanish came the agricultural civilizations south of them had serious trouble from time to time with invading Chichimec groups. Some of the agricultural Indians from time to time tried to civilize neighboring Chichimec, which is probably one reason some of them were reported to be engaged in horticulture. The Spanish found most of the Chichimec especially hostile and otherwise difficult to cope with.

Chapter 2

THE COCHIMI OF CENTRAL BAJA CALIFORNIA

In the area now covered by northwestern Mexico the gathering-hunting lifeway prevailed throughout the peninsula of Baja California, along a stretch of mainland coast on the opposite side of the Gulf of California, and on some of the islands of the Gulf and the Pacific Ocean. The groups in the peninsula's northern portion were culturally similar to those in the southern part of the state of California. In fact, Murdock includes the Cahuilla, Chumash, Gabrieleño, Luiseño, Serrano, Tubatulabal, Kamia and Kawaiisu of Southern California in a Peninsula Culture Area along with those of the peninsula itself (Murdock 1975:109). The cultures of the northern and southern ends of the peninsula were somewhat more elaborate than those of the Central Desert, which reflects the richer habitats of those areas. Fishing was important to many living along or near a seacoast.

Anthropologists often have difficulty establishing the boundaries of the social units whose cultures they study. Sometimes it is easy to identify a society as a political entity with a distinctive lifeway and a consciousness of themselves as having their own culture. But the Cochimí (approx. koh-chee-MEE) and similar peoples lived in widely scattered nomadic communities of fluctuating size and membership and had little or no concept of themselves as a society of communities distinct from others. One can safely refer to a Cheyenne tribe, since the Cheyenne of the North American high plains were conscious of their unity and had a tribal government. But the Cochimí consisted only of a number of scattered families and small bands speaking various dialects and languages that have come to be called Cochimí. The lifeways of the various Cochimí groups were similar enough to one another and different enough from those of adjacent groups that outsiders viewed them as a unit.

No scientific descriptions of Cochimí physical characteristics are available, but they apparently were similar to many of the Indians of the Mexican mainland. Their skin color was dark brown, darker than some other Amerindian groups, and they had little body hair. They were of short to medium stature, certainly shorter than the tall people of the North American plains, and they may have been more heav-ily built than some, including the tall, slender Seri of the Sonoran coast. The dark skin resulted partly from going without clothing and living mostly in the open in a habitat with little shade. The men nearly always went without clothing, and the women wore very little. The Cochimí moved so frequently they thought it unprofitable to construct dwellings regularly, and those built were basically for protection from wind.

Of course, the Cochimí spent much of their time hunting game and collecting the various wild plants and small animals of the desert and seacoasts, but they also had time to handcraft the relatively few material objects they wanted, to conduct initiation rituals for their maturing young people, to watch their shamans conduct healings and other ceremonies, and to engage in intercommunity activities such as festivals, wrestling, and fighting. The Cochimí were flexible about the frequency and duration of nonproductive activities, largely because of the variable nature of their many food resources. It is impossible to know how many Cochimí there were before the whites arrived, but, after a consideration of many variables, Aschmann concluded there may have been about 21,000 people in the aboriginal territories of the Central Desert missions (1959:178).

Ethnohistory

The definitive synthesis on the geography, history and culture of the Central Desert is geographer Homer Aschmann's *The Central Desert of Baja California* (1959). The Cochimí Indians, who occupied most of the Central Desert, have been extinct for well over a century, and the culture was largely destroyed by Christian missionary enterprise half a century earlier. Aschmann has carefully investigated the available sources, the letters written by the Jesuit missionary-explorers who lived among the Cochimí for up to two or three decades (Aschmann 1965). A number of the more readily available accounts have been compiled from the missionaries' reports, but some fail to distinguish the cultures of different parts of the peninsula from one another. Aschmann has translated documents that deal primarily with the Cochimí of the central portion of the Central Desert (1966:14).

Ethnohistory is an interdisciplinary field that studies the cultural past by examining and interpreting the writings of missionaries, colonists, explorers and others who came into contact with now defunct cultures trained observers were unable to study. The difficulties are many. Documents are scattered among various museums, libraries and personal collections around the world. Often the authenticity or authorship of a writing is in question, and each must be evaluated in the light of its author's situation and biases. One of the documents on the Cochimí exists in at least two slightly different copies, each credited to a different author. One copy of the *Descripción de la California,* which forms a chapter of a manuscript by Pedro Alonso O'Crouley, is credited by O'Crouley to Jesuit missionary Padre Norberto Ducrue. The other copy is credited to Padre Fernando Consag. One of the two wrote the original, and both copies have been altered by copying mistakes and editing. Whoever wrote it had been in extended contact with the Cochimí at one of the Central Desert Jesuit missions (Aschmann 1966:16). The other document is a continuation of the first, its title being *Addiciones a las noticias contenidas in la compendiosa de lo descuvierto y conocido de la California.* My description of Cochimí culture relies on Aschmann's 1959 synthesis and his 1966 translations of the *Descripción* and the *Addiciones.* Since it was prepared another early document has been published, which enriches the existing information on the peninsula cultures. This is *Historia Natural y Crónica de la Antiqua California* (1973) by Fr. Miguel del Barco. Some of Del Barco's contribution is available in English under the title, *Ethnology and Linguistics of Baja California* (Del Barco 1981).

Cochimí Country

The portion of Baja California between roughly 27 and 30 degrees north latitude lies within the Sonoran Desert. The Sonoran geographic province includes most of Baja California, an area around the head of the Gulf of California, part of southeastern California state, most of southern Arizona, and much of northwestern Mexico. It is easy for an untrained observer to distinguish the Sonoran from adjacent deserts by its vegetation alone. It is far richer than the Chihuahuan Desert to the east, the Great Basin Desert to the north, and the Mohave Desert of interior southern California. Many are impressed by the forests of succulent plants, notably the large columnar cacti such as the *saguaro, cardón,* organ pipe cactus, and the *senita.* There are also the prickly pear, the various *chollas,* and the barrel cactus. Many kinds

of both evergreen and deciduous shrubs are present, and a variety of small trees mingle with the shrubbery and the cacti.

In spite of very low rainfall the Sonoran region has two rainy seasons rather than one, with a large number of ephemeral plants associated with them. The summer and winter rains frequently come in deluges that flood the desert suddenly with sheets of water that wash away the vegetal litter that would otherwise remain to form humus-rich soils. The plant life in the low areas is, of course, different from that of higher elevations, since it benefits from the moisture and litter deposited. There is also a heavy accumulation of salts in places where flood waters stand and evaporate. The Sonoran region is generally hot, with great temperature differences between night and day. The topography varies from plains to low mountains.

In the central portion of the peninsula of Baja California, where the Cochimí lived, it is generally much drier than many other parts of the Sonoran Desert. Also, the eastern coastal strip is more like the coast of the state of Sonora

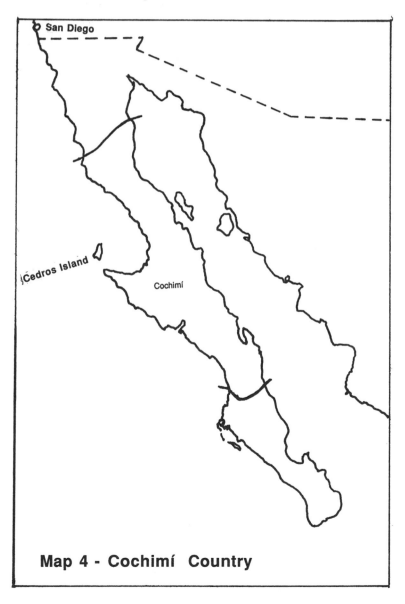

San Diego

Cedros Island

Cochimí

Map 4 - Cochimí Country

than the rest of the central area. Nevertheless, the vegetation shows the characteristic Sonoran diversity. The saguaro is absent, as it is in the rest of Baja California, but the other kinds of cacti are there along with several species of *agave* (century plants), mesquite trees, *palo verde* trees, ironwood trees, *palo blanco* trees, the wild fig tree, sweet acacia, elephant tree, yucca, piñon pine, fan palm, blue palm, *jojoba,* brittlebush, creosote bush, salt bush, bursage, burro bush, *torote,* Arizona grape, and a variety of seed plants. Mammals, also abundant, include deer, bighorn sheep, pronghorn antelope, cougars, coyotes, wildcats, badgers, gray foxes, kit foxes, rabbits, racoons, ring-tailed cats, squirrels, chipmunks, mice, kangaroo rats, and more. Jaguars and peccaries (wild pigs or *javelinas*) are absent. Chuckawallas, chameleons, rattlesnakes and a variety of other reptiles are plentiful. Along the beaches and in the coastal waters pismo clams, rock mussels, abalone, *langosta,* sea lions, sea otters, and turtles are among the many life forms. Birds include brown pelicans, frigate birds, cormorants, brants, many kinds of ducks, turkey vultures, gila woodpeckers, red-tailed hawks, osprey, *caracaras,* sparrow hawks, quails, herons, egrets, gulls, doves, roadrunners, scrub jays, ravens, cactus wrens, mockingbirds, shrikes, orioles, cardinals, house finches, and many more. Unlike some other deserts the Sonoran Desert is rich in plant and animal life.

Language

Linguists place the Cochimí language in the Hokan or Hokaltecan phylum and the Yuman family of languages (Mason 1977:78). Cochimí and closely related languages are known as Peninsular Yuman, since they are significantly different from the Yuman languages farther north. The Cochimí, then, are simply those who spoke dialects of Peninsular Yuman sufficiently different from other Peninsular Yuman dialects to justify treating them as a separate unit. Cochimí is primarily a linguistic term.

The linguistic situation in the Central Desert was like that in many other parts of the world in that neighboring groups spoke similar dialects and usually could communicate with one another in spite of vocabulary and pronunciation differences. But anyone who traveled a considerable distance through the 400 mile long Cochimí region would find the slightly varying dialects increasingly hard to understand. Neighboring dialects were mutually intelligible, but the cumulative effect of gradual variation was that Cochimí Indians in locations remote from one another would not be able to communicate effectively. A comparable situation exists in Western Europe. Although the official forms of Dutch and German are mutually unintelligible, there is no sharp break between local speech forms, and neighboring communities from one end of the Dutch-German speech community to the other speak mutually intelligible dialects (Bloomfield 1933:44).

On some linguistic maps two Peninsula languages, Borjeño and Ignacieño, are indicated for the Central Desert. This reflects certain evidence that some have interpreted to indicate two major Cochimí dialects, but Aschmann stresses linguistic continuity and gradual dialectical variation among the Cochimí (1959:54-55).

Clothing and Personal Appearance

Cochimí men went without clothing a good deal of the time, though they ornamented themselves and sometimes used headwear and footwear. The women usually wore front-and-back aprons suspended from a fiber belt. The front apron was usually of loose fibers or strings of the bamboo-like *carrizo* joints, which hung to some point along the upper leg or, in some groups, to the knees (Aschmann 1966:95). The back apron was a square of deer or other skin, which was large enough for them to sit on.

When the people desired protection from the cold, they added cloaks or capes. The most common type, especially in the interior, was a blanket made by tying together cords of rabbit skin with the fur still on. This was virtually identical to the rabbit skin blankets fashioned throughout the Great Basin (Nevada, Utah and adjacent areas) and other parts of the Greater Southwest. Long cords of furred skin were made from a rabbit hide by cutting on a spiral, then stretching and twisting the resulting strips. A sufficient number of these could be laid side by side and woven together or tied with fibers to make a fur blanket about three by six feet. The same techniques were sometimes used for skins of foxes, deer, or seals. Coastal groups made cloaks of different shapes and sizes by sewing together skins of seals, sea otters, or pelicans.

Both sexes were barefooted most of the time, but they apparently used simple deerskin sandals for long journeys. They attached two cords to the front of the skin sole, passed them between the big and second toe, and tied them together in back above the heel. They secured the back part of the sole with two cords drawn forward and tied across the instep.

The Cochimí ornamented themselves with headbands and collars made by piercing small shells or drilling holes in bits of mother-of-pearl and tying them together. The women sometimes added grass to their headbands, and the men might add feathers. The men also pierced their ears and nasal septums with sharp stones. Apparently they also pierced the lower lip sometimes. They expanded the openings in the ear lobes by inserting increasingly larger objects over an extended period. The men would insert a hollow reed in the opening and carry small objects in it. They inserted various objects of ornament in the nasal septum. The women wore snoods of fine netting and at times small seed-collecting baskets as hats. One observer reported that the Cochimí tattooed linear designs on young girls' faces with either a sharp stone or a barrel cactus spine with earth or charcoal for color. Both sexes painted their bodies extensively, especially for ceremonial occasions. They used various kinds of powdered minerals mixed with animal fat or plant gums.

The Cochimí sometimes bathed in the ocean, but there was only enough water for drinking in most locations. To wash their faces and, sometimes, their bodies they caught their urine with their hands and applied it immediately to the skin. Cultural difference is nicely illustrated for Americans by the fact that Cochimí men squatted to urinate, while the women stood (Aschmann 1966:90).

Houses and Other Structures

Cochimí families often camped in the open, especially if they expected to move on soon, which was common. One observer indicated that a family might change its location as often as a hundred times a year. When a family desired shelter, they built a windbreak of brush or rock arranged in the shape of a crescent. It might be around six feet across, three feet high at its center, and slope to ground level at its points. When the people wanted greater warmth they kept a fire going in front of the windbreak, and the family slept between the crescent and the fire. Sleeping between a fire and a windbreak is found in many gathering-hunting societies. Sometimes the Cochimí dug and occupied a pit one or two feet deep, either within a crescent or without a windbreak. They also used caves and rock shelters as winter dwellings sometimes, with fires near the entrances. Although a Cochimí family might be by itself at times, several families usually camped near one another.

Livelihood

The Cochimí hunted and fished, but they were basically gatherers of plant foods. The Central Desert produced a fair variety of readily available items appearing at different seasons to provide a balanced diet for most of the year. These items include the century plant (agave or maguey) and related forms, fruits and stem parts from the several kinds of large cacti, seeds from several leguminous trees and shrubs, seeds and other parts of various herbaceous plants, grass and sedge seeds, fruit and seeds from palm trees, edible roots, and the seeds and fruits of several other kinds of plants. The variety is evident, as is the importance of many kinds of seeds.

It is something of a fashion among those attempting to justify a certain kind of diet to suggest we should include large amounts of the types of food eaten by our prehistoric ancestors. They reason that we evolved bodies best equipped to utilize the kinds of foods available to our ancestors over hundreds of thousands of years and that it is a mistake to consume large quantities of foods our systems have not evolved to use effectively. One writer supported his view that we should avoid grains on the grounds that our ancestors were meat-eating hunters. But anthropological data on nineteenth and twentieth century gatherer-hunters indicates that gathering has usually been far more important than hunting and that wild grains sometimes formed an impor-

tant part of the diet. Meat was often a highly valued but secondary food. If the evolution-based argument is relevant to the question of what kinds of foods we should eat it would seem to indicate that humans have eaten a great variety of kinds of foods and that grains were often important.

The Cochimí used ways of collecting and processing plant foods similar to those of other groups around the world and, especially, those of the Greater Southwest. Fruit was often obtained with picking poles, roots were dug with sharpened sticks of wood or bone, and flat, coiled baskets were used to collect small seeds from herbs and grasses. Coiled baskets were especially useful because seeds knocked from their hulls lodge between the coils. Some foods were stored for winter use. Spring was the time of shortage, especially if there had been inadequate winter rains. But there were less desirable foods they could fall back on until the more valued ones appeared.

The agave, often known in Mexico as *maguey,* was especially important to the Cochimí. The *Agave americana* is popularly known as the century plant. The broad, thick, fleshy leaves, often several feet long in the large varieties, curve upward and outward from a trunkless rosette at ground level and end in spiny points. The Cochimí used the buds in season, but the rosette's heart, normally indigestible, was available at all times and could be made edible by prolonged roasting. The agave hearts served admirably when other foods were in short supply. They flourished in many well-drained areas, but their distribution was somewhat uneven, and the supply was not unlimited. The Indians frequently had to travel some distance from water to reach a clump of agave, and the roasting took so long that a woman would have to carry the bulky hearts back to camp to prepare them.

A fairly popular idea has been that so-called primitives are so in tune with nature that they do no damage to the habitat, but the truth is that human activity almost inevitably deteriorates the environment. The Cochimí, however necessary it might have been, were eradicating the agave from the areas nearest water sites, thereby increasing their difficulty of finding it during times of water and food shortage. Agaves apparently have become more abundant in the Central Desert since the extinction of the Cochimí.

The Cochimí collected the agave bud just as it began to sprout and roasted it for several hours on an open fire to produce a sugary, fibrous mass considered quite tasty. The women obtained the hearts by slicing through the plant just below ground level with a special cutting stake and, then, cutting off the large leaves and the central spike. They carried them to camp in nets and roasted them in a pit of hot stones. They placed the hearts among the stones, covered them with earth, and baked them from 12 to 48 hours. The time probably depended on the species. After taking the roasted hearts from the pit, the Cochimí tore off strips of the sweet, fibrous material and chewed them. Apparently, the agave hearts of some species cannot be made edible, and the Cochimí knew which were which. When water was unavailable the Cochimí sometimes chewed agave leaves for the juice, which made it possible for them to survive in waterless places for several days.

The organ pipe cactus (*Lemairiocerus thurberi*), which has also been called *pitahaya dulce,* is a columnar cactus of special seasonal importance to the people of the southern part of the Central Desert. It produces fruit in profusion, perhaps for a month or two, during the late summer and early fall. Although the crop might fail in wet summers, at other times its abundance made it possible for several Cochimí bands to assemble in one place for relatively large scale social and religious events. The organ pipe cactus consists of a set of vertically ribbed stems thinner and shorter than those of the giant cacti like the cardón and the saguaro, and the Cochimí could often pick the soft, juicy, spine-covered fruits directly from the tops of the stems or reach them with short sticks. They used a special pole for picking fruit from the tallest stems. It was made from the bamboo-like reed known as carrizo and had a wood or bone stick with a hooked tip attached to the end. After the Cochimí had secured the fruit, they brushed the spines off with leaves.

The cardón (*Pachycereus pringlei*), similar to and even larger than the saguaro, is another vertically-ribbed columnar cactus. But it was more important to the Cochimí than the organ pipe cactus and more valued for its seeds than its fruit. The people extracted the tiny black seeds from the small fruits, dried or toasted them, and either ate them whole or ground them. Apparently the seeds were of major importance to the northern Cochimí, who lived beyond the range of the organ pipe cactus. The spines on the cardón's trunk could be removed and became scarce enough as the plant aged that the people could sometimes climb the occasionally 35 foot high, three foot in diameter giants to get at the fruit.

The *pitahaya agria* (*Machaerocereus gummosus*) was found in all parts of Cochimí country, and the people valued it greatly for its excellent flavor. Its yield was limited, however, and many of the fruits were taken by birds before the people got to them. The senita or *garambullo* (*Lophocereus schottii*) cactus was eaten during the time of shortage just before other cacti ripened, but the Cochimí cared little for it. The fruit of the nopal or prickly pear (*Opuntia spp.*) was also eaten during times of scarcity. The thick, flat, oval leaves may also be viewed as forming the stems of the plant, since they link themselves to one another, edge to edge, as the plant grows. The people sometimes removed the links when young and still tender and baked or stewed them. They used the reddish date-seed-sized fruits of the *viznaga (Ferocactus wislizeni),* a barrel cactus, and the seeds, too. These ripened in midsummer just before the organ pipe cactus fruits. The pitahaya agria, senita, prickly pear, and viznaga were important mainly as stop-gap or supplementary foods. In addition to seeds from cactus fruit various species of the genera *Amaranthus* and *Chenopodium* were evidently major sources of edible seeds. The amaranth, also important to the ancient Aztecs, is a tall herb topped by large clusters containing a profusion of tiny

seeds. The chenopodiums are the various goosefoot and pigweed herbs. The amaranths produce after the summer rains and the chenopodiums following the winter rains. The Cochimí used seeds from several other kinds of herbs as well.

The seeds of various trees were even more important. Those of the palo verde trees (*Cercidium sonorae* and perhaps *Cercidium terreyanum*) were probably the most important. These trees produce bean-sized seeds in pods. Apparently a single specimen could produce enough for a Cochimí family, and the seeds were stored for winter use. The palo verdes do not produce every year, however, and they may bear at different times, depending on the unreliable rains. If the seeds were ready in late spring they were an especially helpful addition, since this was often a time of food scarcity. Mesquite trees *(Prosopis juliflora)* were abundant, but the Cochimí evidently made much less use of them than other Sonoran desert groups. The Cochimí also used the seeds of the palo blanco tree *(Lysiloma candida).*

The Central Desert people roasted the various kinds of seeds, usually by shaking them about in a flat basket with live coals. The roasting popped them open, and the people used the flat, coiled baskets to winnow them. After getting rid of the hulls this way they ground the kernels and either ate the resulting flour or made it into cakes.

The Cochimí also ate a few kinds of roots, though it has not been possible to identify them with certainty (Aschmann 1959:88). One may have been the root of the *zaya* (*Amoreuxia sp.*), since modern Central Desert residents use it some. The Indians also ate raw the roots of certain water reeds and flags.

Reportedly, at least some groups of Cochimí valued palm fruits highly and tied sticks to the palm trunks to make it easier to climb them. The palms native to the area are *Washingtonia robusta* and *Erythea armata.* The people also used fruit from the *datilillo (Yucca valida),* which produces in September and October if the rainfall is sufficient. In late spring and midsummer a white-barked fig tree *(Ficus palmeri)* yields appreciable quantities of small figs, providing another food that may have helped the people through the late spring time of scarcity.

The Cochimí also ate the seeds of the jojoba shrub (*Simmondsia californica*) and several other unidentified plants. Pine nuts, the seeds of the piñon pine *(Pinus muricata)*, were used only by the Cochimí of Cedros Island, which lies off the Pacific coast of the Central Desert. The seeds and fruits of several other trees and shrubs of the Central Desert were undoubtedly used by the Cochimí, even though the missionaries did not provide information on them.

In times of adequate rain the trees and other plants yielded their seeds and fruits abundantly and temporary water holes filled. The improved water supply enabled people to travel far enough from their main camps to reach the patches of grass and shrubs and the groves of trees to harvest the produce. In times of extended dryness the stands of agave were almost the only food source, but these might be so remote from dependable water sources that it would be risky to travel to them. As in other parts of the Sonoran Desert the Indians had to be deeply concerned about the availability of water.

The Cochimí also ate insects and their larvae, spiders, lizards, snakes, rats, mice, and the like. Although most of these seldom sit still for picking like plants, they are most accurately included as gathered rather than hunted items. They were taken mainly by the women and children in the course of collecting plant foods, while the hunting of larger animals was a separate male enterprise. In this way the Cochimí were like gatherer-hunters everywhere. The plants comprised the bulk of the collected items. The small animal life also was scarcest at the same time as plants, since their occurrence also depended on an adequate supply of moisture.

Ordinarily, small animal forms were either roasted on open coals or, if small enough, toasted in a basket. The smallest animals were eaten whole, while larger ones, such as some of the lizards, would be eaten only after the insides were removed. The people considered small animals sufficiently roasted when they extended their legs from the effects of the heat (Aschmann 1966:79).

The Cochimí gathered certain finger-sized grubs and, after removing their insides, braided them into strings and roasted them over live coals. They also saved the strings to give as gifts or to eat at fiestas. They ate tarantulas and other spiders as available. In moist years great numbers of a certain kind of spider congregated in piles that looked like heaps of hair. The Cochimí would grab the heaps in their hands and mash them with stones for eating.

Most modern North Americans feel that eating insects, spiders, and snakes is repulsive and risky. Most probably also regard it as a sign of inherent inferiority, lack of discrimination, or evidence of desperation. They react this way mainly because they have learned as members of American society that such items are unfit for food. They are doing what is natural to all humans as they confront the customs of other cultures. Their perception and evaluation of those customs reflects the concepts and values of their own culture, a type of reaction anthropologists have referred to as *ethnocentrism* (Taylor 1980:37). The reaction is ethnocentric in that it is based upon or centers around their own culture. Had the same people been brought up in Cochimí society, they would accept snakes, insects, and spiders as natural and desirable foods. Actually, those who have studied the question find that insects and spiders may be both highly nutritious and tasty, even by North American and European standards.

This may also be viewed as an instance of the power of one's culture. It matters little to most that insects are nutritious and can taste good. What we have learned from the teachings and reactions of other members of our society holds sway over our minds and emotions. Culturally learned ideas can become so deeply ingrained that we think they must have been genetically implanted. Some undoubtedly feel that the only way one could eat insects and the like would be by biologically inheriting different tastes and in-clinations as well as different digestive systems. Insects and their ilk seem like unnatural foods. The evidence that food preferences are learned (and unlearned) is so abundant, however, that cultural learning must be accepted as the source of most of our food likes and dislikes.

Cochimí women also collected various kinds of shellfish if they lived near or were able to travel to a coast. In spite of the fact that the people got more of their food from collecting shellfish than fishing, no one described their tools or techniques.

Cochimí hunting modes apparently were rather ineffective, and large animals constituted a rather uncertain food source. Deer and, perhaps, antelope were the most important game animals. An observer has reported that most of the men of a camp would cooperate to take a single animal. Typically, they stalked it at length, wounded it with an arrow, and ran it down. They had the greatest success with antelopes when the animals retreated to the mountains for protection against winter wind and cold. Normally, the antelopes were too fast to be hunted, but in the mountains they were unable to escape so easily among the rocks and precipices. When an animal had been killed, some of the men butchered it while others made a fire. The *Addiciones* (Aschmann 1966:78) states that they removed the contents of the paunch and stuffed it with the liver and other viscera and roasted the stuffed paunch and the intestines for eating at the kill site. The men divided the meat and carried it back to their camp. The hide went to the one who killed the animal and was used for sandals, women's clothing, and the like first. The balance was cut in strips, dried, and eaten. The people also ate the bones. They ground the harder bones on grinding stones.

The main hunting weapon around the world is the bow and arrow. No detailed description of Cochimí bows and arrows is available, but they apparently were not especially powerful. As noted earlier, the deer were usually wounded and run down rather than killed or disabled by the arrow. Sources also mention slings, nets, and snares for the Cochimí. The Indians also hunted rabbits and may have used the latter devices to take them.

The Cochimí had a rather unusual way of eating meat or plant portions, which was known in Spanish as the *maroma*. They tied a chunk of meat, usually, to a cord of agave fiber or human hair, chewed it slightly, swallowed it, and then pulled it from the stomach through the esophagus with a pop. They repeated this until the portion was about to fall from the cord. They maintained this was a distinctively human way of eating, since animals swallowed their food only once.

Europeans inevitably react to such a custom ethnocentrically. One observer thought it must have been due to the scarcity of meat, and all certainly regarded it as unnatural. An alternative to ethnocentric reactions is *cultural relativism*—perceiving and understanding a custom by discovering how it relates to other customs in the culture in which it exists and functions. Unfortunately, the missionaries failed to take this approach, but Aschmann suggests it had social and perhaps symbolic relationships (1959). Descriptions say that eight or ten people would form a circle and take turns swallowing and withdrawing a chunk of meat until the cord and meat fell apart. Modern investigators would probe beyond this point to find out how this sharing functioned in relation to social, religious, economic, and other socially standardized customs. The Kiliwa to the north of the Cochimí also practiced the maroma, and one Kiliwa indicated to investigator Ralph Michelson that it reflected the conviction that a proper meal should include both animal and vegetable components (Aschmann, personal communication). When there was almost no meat the people resorted to the maroma.

Cochimí living along or near a coast also fished, either from the shore or from a *balsa*. The balsa was a raft made by tying three bundles of canes or reeds together to form a cigar-shaped craft several yards long. The operator knelt at the balsa's center and wielded a double-bladed paddle. The people fished with hook and line mostly from the balsa, but they also used harpoons and two-pronged fish spears. They made fish hooks of deer horn, and the Cochimí of Cedros Island, at least, used the hooked thorns of the barrel cactus. Along the shores of estuaries and shallow bays both men and women used nets effectively. The women made the relatively small nets from twisted threads made from the thick, fibrous leaves of the agave. Plant poisons were also used. A plant or its root was ground up and placed in the water, paralyzing and killing the fish. This method of taking fish is widely spread around the world.

The Indians also hunted sea otters and sea lions regularly. They were either caught on rocky ledges or approached on a balsa or by swimming as they floated asleep at the water's surface. The Cochimí also valued the giant green sea turtles and took them easily by harpooning and overturning them.

Tribal societies are ethnocentrically regarded as improvident because they may feast in times of abundance rather than preserving food for times of scarcity. This overlooks their lack of techniques for effectively preserving many of their foods and also the fact that they store foods, such as seeds and nuts, that do not spoil rapidly.

The Cochimí and other groups in the Greater Southwest stored pitahaya seeds by the so- called "second harvest." Many of the seeds pass through the body without being digested, so the Cochimí prepared a storage area by laying down a bed of either flat rocks or dry plants, and there they would defecate. When they wanted to eat the seeds they pulverized the dried feces with their hands and winnowed the powder from the seeds by means of their flat, coiled baskets. Then they roasted the seeds in the basket as they would any other seed (Aschmann 1966:88).

Crafts, Tools, and Techniques

The commonest ways of making fire are percussion, rubbing the end of one piece of wood along a groove in another piece, sawing a withe or piece of wood across another one, and twirling a stick with one end of it in a depression in another piece of wood. The last, known as the *fire drill*, is widely found, and the Cochimí used it. Some groups have developed special devices for twirling the wooden drill, but the Cochimí turned it between the palms of the hands.

Water was scarce in Cochimí country. Aschmann estimated that there was an average of one water source for every hundred square miles (1959:48). Of course, these were not evenly distributed, and the Cochimí often felt they had to leave a spring farther behind than was completely safe. Evidently, they sometimes miscalculated and died of thirst. They tried to cope with this danger by using moisture-laden plants, carrying water with them or, along the coast, digging a pit in which brackish water would collect. They had no pottery to carry water in, and none of their baskets appear to have been shaped for carrying liquids. Sometimes they carried water in a turtle bladder or the intestine of a large animal. Without the large clay pots like those of the mainland Seri and some other desert groups the Cochimí were unable to store large quantities of water.

The Central Desert Indians coiled baskets so tightly that some of them were practically water tight, but they apparently made only the shallow baskets for working with seeds. The basketry coils were basically bundles of flexible splints prepared by slitting the twigs or branches of certain shrubs. The Cochimí manipulated the bundles of splints into a spiral by wrapping each of them with another splint, which they inserted through the previously made coil at frequent intervals to bind them tightly together. One observer reported that the men made the baskets, though the women used and repaired them.

The people transported many of their possessions in net bags made of agave fiber or some other material. They often suspended the bag full of objects from a pole. For small objects they used smaller bags having a much tighter weave and placed them within the large net bags. Evidently, the small bags were well made and nicely decorated.

The Central Desert contains an abundance of stone objects, though many of them were made by ancient peoples. The Cochimí used stones for arrows, scraping skins, working wood, pulverizing seeds, and other purposes. Not many of them are highly worked, and no one has left an adequate description of Cochimí stone techniques. They used stone scraper planes in crafting wooden tablets used by shamans.

Social Organization and Relationships

The Cochimí household was usually the nuclear family, that is, the parents and their children. The missionaries noted very few cases of *polygyny* (more than one wife), but *monogamy* was general. Apparently there were a few cases of *levirate,* the marriage of a widow to her deceased husband's brother. A Cochimí nearly always took his or her spouse from a group other than the band of families that normally camped together, so it may be that the people practiced band *exogamy*—exogamy being the anthropological term for marrying someone from a group other than one's own. Tribal societies generally consider the relationships a marriage establishes between groups more important than those between the bride and groom, and this was undoubtedly true of the Cochimí. Usually the parents and other near relatives have a lot to say about who marries whom in tribal societies.

Kinship was clearly very important in Cochimí culture, but details are scarce. A number of other Sonoran tribes, such as the Kiliwa in the northern part of the peninsula and the Seri of the Mexican mainland, are alleged by some to have had clans—groups of relatives who regarded themselves as having descended from a remote common ancestor. If so, the Cochimí may have had clans, too. Clans are frequently strongly exogamous, and the missionaries were impressed with the strength of Cochimí rules against marrying certain relatives. Recent scholarship, however, indicates that the total environmental-cultural situation for the Seri, gatherer-hunters who lived across the Gulf of California from the Cochimí, was such that they probably did not have clans. Undoubtedly, the same arguments would apply for the Cochimí.

The missionaries remarked on how hard Cochimí women worked as compared with the men and ethnocentrically interpreted this in terms of European notions of male authority. But there is evidence that the women were not under the men's thumbs. Since their contribution to the food supply was a good deal more important than that of the men, their position was relatively good. In fact, it has been reported that the women took the lead in proposing marriage and dominated Cochimí family life. There also is a report of a Cochimí band led by a headwoman. It is most accurate to view Cochimí husband and wife as economic partners, the women being the gatherers and householders, while the men hunted, exercised political and ceremonial responsibilities, and assisted in the gathering as needed.

Anthropologists with a strongly evolutionary orientation have classified cultures by *level of sociocultural integration* (Steward 1955; Sahlins and Service 1960). They distinguish among levels according to the prevailing means of organization or integration in the society. They see *band level* cultures as essentially familial. Band societies organize their lives, make their decisions, and carry out those decisions primarily within the context of relationships within and among families. Obviously, the course of life within the nuclear family is governed extensively by interaction between spouses as well as the parents' influence over their children as they care for their physical and developmental needs. In addition, the families that make up a band society relate to one another and cooperate through kinship ties and by residing together. The decisions and actions resulting from these intrafamilial and interfamilial relationships are also the people's political, economic, religious, ritual, educational, and aesthetic decisions and actions. Negatively stated, few if any individuals in a band society are charged

with specialized responsibility for these just mentioned aspects of life. Familial integration occurs in virtually all societies, but it is the prevailing and practically only integration mechanism in band societies.

Band communities prevail among gatherer-hunters, and most such societies practice familial sociocultural integration. Some Cochimí groups may have varied slightly in the direction of more complex integration modes, but they, too, were largely familial. Several Cochimí families camped near one another most of the time, forming the camp or nomadic band. In some places there were twenty to fifty nuclear family households moving about and camping together, and the total population of the Cochimí community seems to have ranged from 50 to 200 people. Evidence indicates that bands that became small tended to combine with others and that those that became too large tended to divide. Each Cochimí appears to have identified strongly with a particular band in spite of these changes.

These Cochimí bands were communities in the sense that they were residence units in which the member individuals and families could carry out most of the activities thought important and necessary for daily life. This is possible because a community has a relatively complete culture, that is, its lifeway includes technological, economic, social, political, religious, recreational, and aesthetic customs in sufficient balance for the people to live well-rounded lives within its arena.

The families making up the nomadic Cochimí bands were related to one another. Normally, the families of brothers would belong to the same community, and their parents and, at times, even some of the brothers' younger unmarried children would still be in the band. Other band families might well be those of cousins. Kinship was clearly important in the band's composition, even though it was a residential unit. The bands tended to be exogamous and were strongly *patrilocal*. The patrilocal residence rule requires or recommends that a bride take up residence with her husband's family, neighborhood, or community. Accordingly, a Cochimí band included women who had grown up in a band other than that of their husbands. Some have suggested gathering-hunting communities are so often patrilocal because hunting is a more cooperative activity than gathering. Supposedly, there would be a strong tendency for related men—brothers and male cousins who have grown up hunting together—to remain together.

Data are too scarce to make possible a balanced treatment of Cochimí responses to the stages of the biological life cycle. Many societies have numerous pregnancy taboos. They have been reported for Cochimí neighbors, so it seems likely that the Cochimí had such avoidances. One missionary to Baja California said that women returned to work immediately after birth while a husband would lie in the shade as though undone by the birth experience. The notion of a husband's involvement in childbirth and a recovery period for him is known as the *couvade* and, in this case, may have existed only in a group or groups south of the Cochimí.

Aschmann assembled evidence that infant mortality was high among the Cochimí (1959:133). Infanticide occurred, too. Since a mother's gathering provided a large part of the family food, caring for more than one child at a time was extremely difficult. Sometimes a mother would leave a small infant in camp all day with an elderly woman so she could more freely search for food. Mothers probably nursed their children for two or three years, as in many other cultures, and at weaning transferred them directly from the breast to foods such as parched seed flour, roasted agave hearts, and shellfish. Weaning is a traumatic experience in many societies, and Aschmann suggests it must have been especially difficult for Central Desert children.

The missionaries failed to explore modes of child rearing and their possible relationships to Cochimí personality. Children remained dependent on their parents until around ten and were definitely independent economically by twelve or fourteen years of age. Reportedly, age grading was important among the Cochimí, but there is no direct evidence of *age sets*, the associations composed of members who remain together through a portion or all of their lives without membership changes. Above the level of economic dependence was a category of young people who, though independent, had not been initiated into adulthood.

There were initiation ceremonies at puberty for both boys and girls. The boys were put under the tutelage of a shaman, who kept them separated from the community for several days with little to eat, if anything, and little to drink. It is said they were subjected to hunger and thirst to keep them from being big eaters, idle talkers, impudent toward elders, or shameless (Aschmann 1966:93). The boys' noses and ears were pierced at this time, which was necessary for them to be considered men. Then they were qualified to marry and participate in the religious ceremonies. Among some Cochimí, when a young man took his first deer, the other men placed him on the ground beside it, skinned it, and placed the skin over the boy.

At first menstruation a Cochimí girl was assigned a sponsor and, under a shaman's direction, subjected to isolation, hunger and thirst, and other ritual impositions. The first day the initiators took her to a secluded place, where they required her to rest. The second day the sponsor carried her to a specially prepared smoky fire and placed her on it for a thorough smoking. They used a large number of branches in the fire, including the trunk of a tree alleged to have medicinal qualities. Then they returned her to her place of seclusion for several more days. In the afternoons the women had her run a prescribed route through the countryside, and they sang songs to her during the night. Also, the sponsor made a run to a neighboring camp to notify them of the initiation and tell them how glad they were to have another woman. Though the missionaries did not say, there is little doubt that the rituals were intended to prepare the young woman for her all important career as a foodgetter. After the ceremonies were over initiates of both sexes were expected to wash themselves in their warm urine frequently, which was supposed to keep them from being big eaters (Aschmann 1966:94).

Puberty ceremonies are one kind of *passage rites*, rituals that mark a major change in a person's status. Helping the person adjust to the changed status is a major function of such rites. The initiates are acquainted with the new roles they are to perform and in various ways motivated to perform them well. In a more general sense the rituals validate and reinforce socially important values, as the Cochimí boys' initiation illustrates, and they help bind the members of the society together and release the tension the initiates may feel in connection with their role changes. These things can be accomplished effectively by detaching people from the roles of their previous status but preventing them for a time from assuming their new roles. During the period of social and physical isolation instruction can be especially effective and the initiate deeply impressed with the significance of the change. This liminal or threshold interlude is a widespread feature of passage rites (V. Turner 1974:231).

Illness may strike at any point in the life cycle, and shamanistic healing was a major kind of response in Cochimí and many other cultures. In addition to standard shamanistic practices some Cochimí shamans used plant and other substances of alleged medicinal value. Tobacco juice might be applied to wounds, and a poultice could be made by boiling and thereby thickening cactus juice. A half-roasted chunk of cactus might also be applied to a tooth or elsewhere to relieve pain. Injury, disease, and death resulted from a variety of circumstances. People sometimes died of rattlesnake bites. There are reports of illness and death from gastrointestinal disorders, and people are said to have died from diarrhea from eating large quantities of poorly ripened seeds. Apparently, thirsty Cochimí have died from drinking too much water in a short time following a long period without it. Sometimes there were gathering or hunting accidents. Certain plant delicacies were available only in places difficult to reach, and Cochimí sometimes fell and injured or killed themselves trying to obtain them. They seldom died in battles between bands.

Supernatural techniques may have accounted for some deaths, and certainly so in the people's eyes. Shamans sometimes used their special supernatural power to perform witchcraft. As in many other societies, they could turn their power toward getting spirits to do evil. Cochimí shamans sometimes boasted that they had made someone ill in another band.

The Cochimí most commonly disposed of the dead by cremation, though ground burial, in the sitting position, was also frequent. They regularly disposed of personal possessions of the deceased along with the body, and food offerings were of some importance. The disposal of personal property with the body suggests a belief in life after death. Some days after the disposal of the body songs and dances in honor of the dead were performed, and the shaman undertook a journey to the land of the dead and returned with a report of his contact with the recently deceased one.

Government and Social Order

Some would say that most Cochimí bands had a *head-man*. If a respected person with persuasion ability exists in a band, one who is especially skillful in perceiving the prevailing will, crystalizing that will, and providing leadership in carrying it out, that person may be referred to as a headman. Anthropologists seldom call such a person a *chief*, since they define chiefs as having relatively more authority than that. A headman's influence may disappear if he attempts to get people to do something they oppose or if he makes bad decisions. If no one can crystalize group will and lead the band there may be no headman for varying lengths of time and decisions of group importance are made simply by consensus among the most respected family heads. Cochimí political leadership seems to have been of this sort, since an influential man's right to lead had to be reconfirmed nearly every time he exercised it. Apparently an informal council of respected elders made many of the decisions, and the Cochimí headman, at least much of the time, was little more than a convener and activity leader under the approval of his elder colleagues. Cochimí leadership needs were greatest during trouble with other bands, extended journeys, and ceremonial assemblies involving other bands. Among the Cochimí the shamans seem to have provided most of the political leadership.

Since Euroamericans have so strongly believed that "primitives" are governed by powerful chiefs, they have often created such figures in tribal societies. The first step is to identify a "chief," then give that person special attention, privileges, and responsibilities. The culture of the Washo of Nevada and California was like Cochimí culture in several basic ways, including the weak authority of their headmen. But through contact with the Americans "captains" emerged whose newly found power derived from their success in dealing with whites. A "Captain Jim" emerged who was especially effective in winning the whites' good will, and when he died in 1875 a local newspaper referred to him as "King James I" (Downs 1966:90). One of the missionaries thought the Cochimí had monarchs, but this kind of notion is nearly always the ethnocentric projection of a cultural outsider.

Some anthropologists use the word *tribe* for a grouping of communities under a government that binds them together. Others use the word to designate a number of communities that recognize a linguistic and cultural unity and think of themselves as a distinct people. The Cochimí as a whole were not a tribe in either sense. They were only a linguistic grouping identified by outside observers. One collection of Cochimí bands came to be called the Guiricatas (sometimes Velicatas) and may have had sufficient unity to be called a tribe in the second meaning, but information is apparently too incomplete to confirm this. For the Cochimí as a whole the local community seems to have been the largest permanent sociocultural unit.

Though there may have been no Cochimí tribes, there were groupings of neighboring bands more friendly with one another than with more remote communities. These assembled from time to time for social and ceremonial activity when food and water were abundant in some favored place. Though they assembled at least annually, not all the same bands participated each time. So there was no combination of communities forming a permanent multi-band unit. A dozen or so bands could be involved, though there were times when only two got together. In the southern two-thirds of the Central Desert several bands would normally assemble in the late summer and early fall where there were large stands of organ pipe cacti. They could usually collect enough food for all within a relatively short time each day. North of the range of the organ cactus such assemblies took place when winter rains were good enough to produce a large spring seed supply. At these large ceremonies the people held mourning and thanksgiving rituals with the shamans acting as ceremonialists. The people sang, danced, played musical instruments, feasted, held races and wrestling matches, played games, watched shamans perform and listened to their speeches, and engaged in some sexual activity with members of other bands. Sometimes band membership changed at the fiestas, small struggling communities affiliating with larger bands. Cochimí band organization was somewhat flexible this way.

Two bands might meet for some purpose several times a year. One band would invite another to meet with them for a wrestling contest, arranging a marriage, or feasting on some large food bonanza such as a stranded whale. The activities were generally similar to those of the larger assemblies.

Cochimí bands feuded with one another some, but the Central Desert people were like most other gatherer-hunters in lacking full warfare. Band societies lack the strong organization and food and other resources to sustain intense, violent, prolonged military campaigns, and the reasons that constrain more complex societies to war on one another are generally absent. They feel little need for territorial acquisition or exclusive control of scarce natural resources. Full warfare would also wreak more destruction than most band societies could survive.

Violence between gatherer-hunter communities usually stems from some sort of personal conflict or imagined injury, and when a fight occurs there may be more noise than blood and death. Cochimí bands apparently fought at times to take revenge for physical damages occurring during a scuffle, a rough game or, conceivably, an insult made during an argument. Sometimes a band would attack another because they believed someone had worked witchcraft against them. Sometimes there was trouble over organ pipe cacti. Band societies have territories, but the boundaries between one and another tend to be fuzzy and overlapping. Usually, at least parts of their territories are shared. One band might attack another not so much because of territorial trespass as the fact they were strangers and enemies.

Band societies tend to exhibit a configuration of traits involving familial relationships, sharing, egalitarian attitudes and behaviors, and democratic decision-making. Individuals and groups have disagreements and worse as surely as in any society, but survival demands in marginal habitats usually put a premium on cooperative, nonviolent ways. The gatherer-hunters of earlier millennia, before they were pushed out of rich habitats by agricultural and industrial groups, were probably somewhat different on these points, but anthropologists were not around to observe them. Those we have been able to study exhibit community ownership of land with neighboring communities sharing resources. Both individuals and groups share food and other things with one another. This does not mean artifacts and food are not individually owned—there are simply many transfers of individual ownership by giving gifts. Some have used the term *generalized reciprocity* for giving not in expectation of an immediate return but in the realization that somewhere along the line either the person you gave to or someone else will give you something you want and need. This tends to be strongest if people are close kin, so it makes sense for generalized reciprocity to prevail in the strongly kinship oriented communities of gathering-hunting societies. These obligations are so strong and so taken for granted that some groups place no emphasis on thanking one another. In fact, some people consider it an insult to be thanked for something they tend to do as a matter of course. Neither is there reason for one person or group to dominate others as they do in more complex cultures. No social classes or castes have been reported for the Cochimí, and it would be a surprise to find them in such a culture.

Exchanges of food and other things are important among bands. In marginal environments the resources of one band may fail, and other bands will share with them in the knowledge that they will be provided for in return if they experience a similar resource failure. Also, one resource may be abundant in one band's territory and another elsewhere, so it makes sense to exchange. Gatherer-hunter bands do not go it alone.

Marriages facilitate interband exchanges. Some anthropologists say marriage is a political and economic institution in band societies. This was certainly true among the Cochimí, since the practice of exogamy established a network of kinship ties among their bands.

Art and Play

Tribalistic people generally lack the idea of leisure time activity for recovering from the rigors and tensions of work. The Cochimí undoubtedly enjoyed conversation and perhaps joking, good natured scuffling, and the like and probably a few games in the course of a day's activities. Observing shamanistic performances is often a major enjoyment among gatherer-hunters, as it was among the Cochimí. Cochimí fiestas, of course, were major times of relief from the isolation of life in small groups, and the ceremonial singing, dancing, and shamanistic healings were good times, as were the games and physical contests. An extended treatment of Cochimí pastimes could have been written had the information been recorded.

The Cochimí pursued aesthetically rewarding activities in the course of their daily routines and ceremonial activities. There are seldom full time artists in tribal societies, but we expect to find individuals who excel in one or another art form and specialize in it. The small decorated fiber bags made by Cochimí women can undoubtedly be considered works of art, though their first purpose was utilitarian. There were probably aesthetic skills involved in the decoration of their bodies with feathers, shells, and the like, and painting the body may have been the major Cochimí art form. Both men and women painted their entire bodies for major ceremonial occasions, using mostly red, black and white, and, occasionally, yellow and green (Aschmann 1959:111). After contact Cochimí men and boys painted their entire bodies in the pattern of a Spanish soldier's uniform—buttons, belt, and stockings included. In aboriginal times each sex had its distinctive designs.

Spectacular cave paintings have been found in a number of remote areas of the American deserts, and the Central Desert is one of them (Crosby 1984). Not many outsiders have seen these impressive polychrome murals, since they are found in deep canyons of mountainous areas. None of the descriptions of the Cochimí indicate that painting cave murals was part of their culture, but Aschmann suggests the Cochimí must have produced them (personal communication). In many parts of the world paintings and/or rock carvings were created by forebears of the people known to the explorers and the missionaries, and this may be the case in the Central Desert. If the people the missionaries knew were not producing cave paintings, perhaps they were painted by earlier generations of Cochimí.

Religious Beliefs and Practices

Supernaturalism is always important to gatherer-hunters, since they normally think the natural world is populated by personal spirits that must be dealt with if things are to go right. Much of their religion consists of maintaining the right kinds of relationships with the supernaturals. There are no religious organizations for this in most gathering-hunting societies, but religious activities are carried out as part of daily life and at special social and ceremonial gatherings. An individual may take care of many of his or her own religious needs, but there are also persons who have special power to deal with certain spirits or familiars that enable them to diagnose illnesses, divine, or effect control over disease, weather, and the like. These people are *shamans*, and shamanism was the outstanding feature of the religious system of the Cochimí.

The Cochimí shamans were mainly healers, but they also served as ceremonialists at meetings among bands and on other special occasions. In most shamanistic cultures the shamans make a display of securing the attention of the spirits and getting them to reveal a disease's cause and cure. One of the commonest explanations of what is wrong with the body of a sick person is that something alien has entered it, and it must be removed if the patient is to get well. This is often done by sucking out the intruder, and the

Cochimí probably did this. They had cylindrical pipes that they might apply to the spot where they intended to extract the intrusive item by sucking it out through the pipe. Shamans also smoked while healing and sometimes applied tobacco juice to wounds. They also used herbal preparations some.

The Cochimí pipes were made of lengths of cane, stone, or, in the northern groups, clay. All shamans used them in healing rituals, both for smoking and for sucking out intrusive causes of disease. They also used cloaks of human hair, wooden tablets, figurines, rattles, fans, and other material aids. The hair cloaks were especially important parts of the Cochimí shaman's equipment, and their possession indicated a shaman's ability and right to ask good payments. The cloak completely enclosed the head, though the shaman could see through the weave. A cloak usually fell to just below the waist, and some reached the ground. The shamans got the hair in payment for instructing boys at initiations and healings and, also, from the heads of the dead. A cloak was kept hidden when not in use, and the shaman added to it in secret as he acquired additional hair. The part resting atop the head was often decorated with hawk feathers or deer tails. A band was proud to have at least one full, hooded hair cloak in camp, and reportedly one band might raid another for a shaman's cloak or steal it.

A Cochimí shaman also used a wooden tablet, probably about an inch thick and about 15 by 30 inches. The missionaries either had difficulty understanding the meanings and functions of the tablets or their place in the cultures differed from group to group. In one area they were apparently placed in front of small idols or figurines, perhaps to serve as altars. In this area each shaman had a tablet, and each family had one in some bands. In some places the tablets had carved or painted designs on them, which may have been mnemonic markings enabling the shaman to go through a long ritual in proper sequence. These decorated tablets also had a hole in the middle through which the shaman placed his tongue during a ceremony. Aschmann suggests this may have indicated the tablet was speaking (1959:116). There is also the chance that the Cochimí thought of the shaman's familiar spirit as dwelling in the tablet or having entered it at his bidding. This could explain the statement that some groups venerated the tablets. Anthropologists often refer to objects indwelt by spirits as fetishes.

Figurines were not widespread in the Central Desert, but they acquire significance from their presence in nearby cultures. In some places the Cochimí had carved wooden figures about two feet high that they used in ritual. In some northern groups shamans and headmen had figures of grass on frameworks of twigs, with heads made of netted feathers, shells, and human hair. These were kept in a matted wrapping, and they are reported to have been closely associated with the wooden tablets. A sixteen inch cloth or net hung from the neck, which suggests that the figures may have been two or three feet high.

The Cochimí probably believed in a number of beings that could be called deities, but the missionaries' writings provide a very inadequate view. This probably reflects a greater interest in stamping out the religion than understanding and describing it. One describes with pride how he collected and burned five shaman's cloaks from three bands. There is a fair amount of description of hair cloaks, tablets, idols, sucking pipes, and other religious objects but little attention to their uses, their significance, and how they functioned in the culture.

Culture Change

Had the Cochimí survived until Euroamerican society had produced trained field anthropologists someone might have explored the memories of elderly Cochimí so as to reconstruct pre-contact Cochimí culture. Nineteenth and twentieth century Cochimí customs could have been studied and some inferences made about whether or not they were survivals of the pre-contact lifeway. But the Cochimí died out from a combination of disease epidemics and destruction of the will to live. Aschmann's studies (1959:186) show that the death rate reached 100 per 1,000 some years. The epidemics hit the children hardest, often reaching 100 percent. This has led Aschmann to suspect pandemic syphilis as the main cause of the extinction of Cochimí (personal communication). The adult population was not adequately replaced, and the population grew steadily smaller.

The peninsula of Baja California was missionized intensively by the Jesuits, who established missions in the Central Desert at points usually 40 to 65 miles apart through the three to four hundred mile long central region. They established Guadalupe in the south in 1721 and Santa María in the north in 1767. The people were generally receptive to the Jesuits, but the missionaries exercised such tight control over their lifeways that the Indians were unprepared to cope with subsequent developments. When Spain expelled the Jesuits in 1768 the Cochimí had been so weakened by epidemics and Jesuit control that they were unable to cope with the Franciscans and the Spanish military. The Jesuits had protected the Indians from exploitation by secular authorities, but the Franciscan missionaries cooperated with Spanish officials. The Spanish drive to push their control into what is now the state of California and used the missions more as advance bases than religious enterprises. Soldiers and others moved through in greater numbers than before, and the impact on the already dependent Indians was devastating. Remnants of mainland Seri and other gatherer-hunters in various parts of the world had the will and the places to escape to recover a bit, but the Cochimí culture and the will to endure had been weakened too much to escape the destructive effects of the Spanish push to the north. By 1850 there were probably only a few Cochimí families left, and by 1900 none were to be found.

Chapter 3

THE SERI OF SONORA

European and North American readers have long been fascinated by the lifeways of the so-called primitive or savage gatherers and hunters of the world's remote forests and deserts. A number of them, like the Cochimí of Baja California, were wiped out by disease or genocide before the public heard much about them. Others, such as the Seri (approx. SEH-ree) of northwestern Mexico's coastal desert, have survived to be romanticized and marveled at as societies of rude, animal-like, and even cannibalistic savages. We do not know exactly what Seri life was like before the Spanish and Anglos came, since no one has passed on to us a comprehensive description of their aboriginal lifeways. In many cases ethnologists have been able to reconstruct pre-contact cultures by talking with older people who lived the aboriginal lifeway as children or younger adults. Anthropologists sometimes refer to this as the study of *memory cultures* since the customs are no longer lived but, in a sense, survive in the memories of those who used to live them. Many of the native cultures of Canada and the United States were reconstructed this way, but no one did this for mainland Seri culture. There has been some description of Seri culture as remembered by Tiburón Island Seri who lived on the island under basically aboriginal conditions. The Seri called themselves *Kongkaak*, which, like so many other societies' names for themselves, means "the people" (E. Moser 1963:14).

The coastal desert environment of the Seri provided a relatively abundant plant and animal life, supporting at least two or three thousand Seri. Some have said there were nine to ten thousand or more Seri before their numbers were severely reduced by genocidal efforts and disease. While the Seri were adept at eluding intruders, disease, demoralization and Spanish efforts to exterminate them quickly reduced their numbers. About the turn of the century there were only about 150 left, though they have become more numerous under modern conditions.

Before the whites arrived, then, several thousand generally tall, slender, well-muscled, dark-skinned Seri wrested an adequate livelihood by collecting and hunting the diverse forms of animal and plant life on land, hunting and collecting sea life, and fishing. Much of the time many

wore little or no clothing, a kilt or skirt of skins being the basic garment for both sexes. There were probably a half dozen or more subtribes living in different areas and manifesting minor cultural differences. Each subtribe was divided into a number of nomadic bands, each band consisting of the few families that customarily camped together as they moved from place to place with the seasonal changes of food availability. Sometimes the people slept in the open around their fires, but they built houses of ocotilla poles stuck in the ground in two parallel rows, bent to meet one another and tied at the top to form a rounded framework. To this they added mats, turtle shells, and other items for whatever protection they needed. The Seri carried and stored water in thin-walled, globular clay pots, and they made excellent baskets, some of which were nearly water tight. They made their tools from stone, bone, horn, shell, and wood.

When Seri couples married they lived with the groom's family, which, when they had children, resulted in the three generation unit anthropologists know as the *patrilocal extended family*. Some writers allege that the Seri once had the common ancestor groups known as *clans*, though others have seriously disputed this claim. None of the subtribes or bands had formal governments. Instead, administrative decisions rested in the hands of informal leaders known as headmen. Shamanism was a major component of Seri religion.

History

Coronado's soldiers passed through Seri country in 1540, but they may not have made actual contact with the Kongkaak. Pearls were discovered in the Gulf of California during the middle 1500s, but Seri culture was hardly affected by the outside world until sometime in the middle 1600s. The Seri were living on Tiburón Island and, possibly, San Esteban as well as along the nearby mainland coast. They had superficial contacts with the pearl hunters, and the only significant change stemmed from the use of boards, nails, and barrel hoop iron that washed ashore after ships were wrecked in the Gulf's treacherous seas. Most of the world's lithic societies quickly abandoned their stone tools in favor of iron as the result of trading chains or finding the flotsam and jetsam of civilization well before they had much contact with the people themselves, and so did the Seri.

Father Juan Fernandez established the mission Santa María del Pópulo in 1679, but he left in 1683 because of an epidemic among the Seri (Di Peso and Matson 1965:35). The notable pioneer missionary Father Eusebio Kino obtained permission to reactivate Pópulo, and Father Adamo Gilg, newly arrived in the Americas, was assigned to the post.

The Seri story illustrates the consequences of Euroamerican stereotypes about the characteristics and abilities of tribal peoples and the best ways for them to adjust to civilization. The Spanish and German Jesuits tried to bring civilization to the Seri by persuading them to abandon their desert life and take up irrigated farming in the inland valleys (Spicer 1976:9). They combed the desert for Seri some 80 years, beginning in 1679, and managed to persuade almost a thousand to move into farming towns. Most Seri were unconvinced of the advantages of the new life, and many returned to the desert for varying periods. Another dimension of the situation developed as Spanish colonists moved into the area. The Seri treated their livestock as game and raided their settlements.

A large and fairly stable community of several hundred Seri endured for a time at Los Angeles on the San Miguel River some miles to the northeast of present-day Hermosillo. But the process was scuttled by the coming of Spanish soldiers, who, in spite of the objections of both Seri and missionaries, deported all the Seri women to some place far to the south. The embittered Seri men abandoned the settlement and, with three thousand or so remaining Seri, began a war to expel the whites. This permanently ended the Jesuit efforts to civilize and Christianize the Seri.

The people fought effectively and heroically for some 30 years, repeatedly attacking the Spanish settlements and gaining one military victory after another during the first years. Eventually, so many Spanish troops were brought in that Seri resistance crumbled. The people were starving in their mountain strongholds, and many had to surrender. This left only a few nomadic bands along the coast. The Spanish settled the surrendering Seri in a newly prepared community just to the south of Hermosillo, where they took up farming again. But the Spanish were so intolerant and hostile that the Seri families left, one by one, to live on the Sonoran coast. By 1793 all but forcibly adopted children were gone. The Spanish continued to capture Seri families and return them to the inland community, but each effort failed. One of the largest was in 1844 when 500 Seri were captured. In 1880 the final effort failed when Mexicans poisoned Seri flour and the 150 people there at the time fled again into the desert (Spicer 1976:11).

After 1880 Mexican cattle ranching expanded from inland Sonora into the hunting and gathering grounds of the few hundred surviving Seri. The livestock destroyed some of the plant life the Seri depended on and moved about in the same territory where they were accustomed to taking mule deer, mountain sheep, and other game, and the Seri continued to treat the Spanish livestock as game. Whenever an animal was killed, the ranchers sought to punish the Seri, and the Mexicans mounted one effort after another to exterminate them. By the turn of the century there were probably only a hundred or hundred-and-fifty left, but the attempts to exterminate them or change their lifeway by force had failed. The Mexicans thought the Seri remnant would die out. The whites were finally to leave them alone, which set the stage for their comeback. This they accomplished to a significant degree on their own by a series of realistic responses to economic opportunities afforded by outside contacts.

Ethnography

Father Adamo Gilg, who spent 18 years among the Seri, was a keen observer and recorded a number of data on Seri culture in his letters. In many places around the world missionaries prepared comprehensive written descriptions of aboriginal cultures, but such either was not done by Gilg or ethnohistorians have as yet failed to locate and make available more than one of his letters. It contains valuable cultural data, but not in the desired volume. As the result of their contact with the missionaries, soldiers, and ranchers the Seri were changing in various ways. So by the time a qualified observer attempted a study of their lifeway near the end of the nineteenth century significant parts of the native culture had been destroyed.

The observer was William McGee, an ethnologist working under the auspices of the Smithsonian Institution. His report has been used widely by those interested in tribal cultures, and several popular accounts of Seri life have drawn heavily from it. Unfortunately, though McGee prepared the earliest extensive view of Seri life available, his work is inadequate. He studied Seri custom for only a few days, while modern anthropologists require at least a year or 18 months to produce a relatively balanced, in-depth description of a previously unstudied culture. Some insist that years are necessary. Second, McGee was unable to associate with Seri living their everyday customs and relied on statements of missionized Seri and the views of a few Mexicans living there. So he never saw the Seri in cultural action. Finally, McGee, influenced as he was by the intellectual climate of his time, assumed that the Seri and other gatherer-hunters were crude, inferior, and animal-like and that their culture was a survival from earlier stages of human cultural evolution (Kroeber 1931:25). Later investigators have shown that some of his perceptions were questionable or clearly wrong. Yet he was a keen observer, and his data have provided a useful starting point for understanding earlier Seri culture.

Ethnologist Edward H. Davis undertook a study of the Seri in 1922 in behalf of the Museum of the American Indian, Heye Foundation. He contributed valuable information, but in spite of contacts with the Seri as late as 1940 he did not produce a balanced, comprehensive ethnography.

In 1930 the accomplished American anthropologist Alfred L. Kroeber spent about a week among the Seri. Kroeber, often referred to as the dean of American anthropologists during the decades before his death in 1960, produced a reliable general summary of Seri culture and carefully discriminated between those elements of McGee's report that were reliable and those that were unacceptable.

Anthropologists have processed Seri cultural data from McGee, E. Davis, Kroeber, and several other investigators for the Human Relations Area Files (HRAF). These files categorize data on Seri and over three hundred other cultures around the world under 88 cultural headings such as language, food quest, machines, entertainment, family, sickness, religious beliefs, and sex. These are subdivided into a total of more than 700 subheadings such as grammar, fishing, agricultural machinery, exhibitions, polygamy, bodily injuries, animism, and general sex restrictions. Accordingly, the files constitute a sample researchers can draw on to compare cultures in one or more of their features. About 13 cultures from Mexico and Central America have been processed for the files. Anthropologists and other students of human behavior have produced books and journal articles using these data. Many colleges and universities have the Files on microfilm, so they are widely available to undergraduates and scholars for cross-cultural research projects. The Seri files also include short reports by ethnologists Borys Malkin, Robert Ascher, Arturo Monzón, and Alejandro Marroquín as well as data collected by naturalist E. Yale Dawson and linguistic missionaries Edward Moser and Mary Beck Moser. The HRAF data are from the years 1894-1961.

This chapter also depends on several recent studies not processed for the Files as of 1988. Anthropologist William B. Griffen, who spent a little over a month with the Seri in 1955, published an especially valuable description of Seri culture of that time. And several anthropologists and other trained observers have produced valuable specialized studies of various aspects of Seri life for different time levels from the 1940s through the 1970s. Most of these appeared in *The Kiva*, a publication of the Arizona State Museum of the University of Arizona in Tucson. The Museum has one of the largest collections of Seri artifacts. Finally, an excellent recent source on a number of aspects of Seri culture is a volume on Seri ethnobotany by Richard S. Felger and Mary Beck Moser (1985).

This summary is designed to describe what Seri culture may have been like before the changes resulting from the intensified contacts of the twentieth century, but in many respects it is impossible to be certain what customs were practiced at what time levels. We are tempted to conclude that twentieth century Seri customs different from those of Mexican nationals and North Americans are survivals from either aboriginal or pre-twentieth century times, but it is often impossible to know. Some could have been originated relatively recently. For example, Seri dance leaders of this century have worn antenna headpieces, which consist of two knobbed sticks about a foot long held in position against the forehead by a headband. These are not found in Mexi-

can and North American cultures, and they do not appear to be survivals of early Seri custom. The Seri say they were originated only a few decades earlier by one of their own dance leaders–a man whose name they know (Bowen and E. Moser 1970:168). Perhaps some of the customs the Seri are unable to remember the origin of were invented recently, too. We can be reasonably sure that most of the description applies to old Seri culture, but we are unable to be sure which traits may have been originated since contact or, even, since McGee was there in 1895. That is why this chapter may describe a configuration of customs from different times as though they belonged to the same time level.

Seri Country

Europeans and Americans have forced many of the world's tribal societies to give up most or all of their pre-contact territories, but Seri country is so difficult for outsiders that the people remained within their aboriginal area into the latter part of the twentieth century. This has helped them maintain the integrity of their culture. They have changed their locations from time to time, but the old Seri pitched their camps at various places within a coastal strip beginning with Guaymas Bay and extending three hundred or more miles northward to Punto Peñasco. They have also occupied at one time or another the island of Tiburón and, probably San Esteban in the Gulf of California. So-called tribal territories lack precise boundaries, so it is inappropriate to try to specify them. Malkin mentions that the Seri have long been familiar with a much larger area than they have normally lived in (1962:1). They visited several of the islands of the Gulf, the Baja California coast, and inland points beyond present day Hermosillo, which lies thirty miles from the coast of Sonora. In recent times they have lived mostly on a relatively short stretch of mainland coast and, from time to time, on nearby Tiburón Island.

Seri country is so difficult for outsiders because of the climate and the wide scattering of resources (Kroeber 1931:52). Ascher (1962:4) estimates average rainfall at less than eight inches annually, and some places may receive less than two. The few streams flow beneath the sands nearly everywhere, and permanent surface water is rare. There are only a few places where the water table intersects the surface at the base of a cliff or other low place. What little rain there is comes during the months of July and August or December and January, so it is hot and dry most of the time and windy, too. It is not surprising that one of the uppermost concerns of Seri life has been getting water and that they have had to thoughtfully regulate their movements and daily activities in relation to the water situation.

In spite of surface aridity, food and fiber are relatively abundant. Succulent plant life prevails in the Sonoran Dessert, and the Seri used it effectively. There are mesquite, elephant, ironwood, and *palo verde* trees as well as creosote bushes, *ocotillo*, clumps of bamboo-like *carrizo, agave*

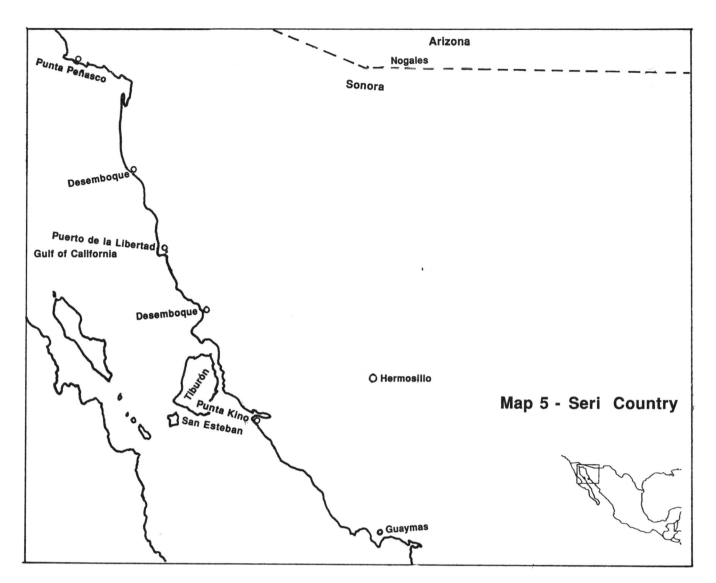

Map 5 - Seri Country

(*maguey*), and a variety of cacti including *saguaro, cardón,* organ pipe, *pitahaya agria, sena, senita,* and *viznaga.* Land animals include mule deer, jaguars, jaguarundi, bighorn, cougar, badgers, coyotes, porcupines, kit foxes, peccaries, rabbits, kangaroo rats, ring-tailed cats, lizards, snakes, toads and, since the coming of the Spanish ranchers, semi-wild burros. There are frigate birds, egrets, cormorants, ibis, ducks, turkeys, roadrunners, ravens, turkey vultures, sandpipers, willets, curlews, gulls, pelicans, gila woodpeckers, doves, and a large variety of other birds. Sea lions, gray whales, killer whales, sharks, dolphins, turtles, tuna, flying fish, octopus, and many other forms of sea life frequent the coastal waters, and along the shore are clams, limpets, cockles, and many other kinds of shellfish.

Gathering-hunting societies are often erroneously pictured as living on the verge of starvation most of the time, using literally every edible form available. But, like the Seri, many of them have plenty of food and know well how to obtain it. An exhaustive description of how the Seri have obtained and used Sonoran life forms would fill several books, even though they failed to take and consume some of the edible Sonoran forms.

The rocky coasts of Seri country are interrupted here and there by small beaches, and the rocks and sand are often colorful. There are sea caves and blow holes along the shore. The inland landscape is comprised of sands, red volcanic hills, large often colorful rocks and boulders, and mountains up to several thousand feet high. The hills and mountains are pitted with caves. The Seri frequently crossed the narrow and treacherous strait between Tiburón and the mainland known as Infiernillo (Little Hell), where the currents swirl and the waters boil as the winds and tides run. This has been one of the more impressive features of Seri habitat to outsiders. The Seri respected those dangerous waters, moving onto them only when conditions were right.

Language

Since the Seri have survived civilization's impact so well, it has been possible to study their language. The results agree with the conclusion of linguistic anthropologists that there is no such thing as an undeveloped language consisting of only a few animal-like sounds, crude grammar, and a vocabulary of only a few hundred words. All tribal languages, including Seri, are complex.

The language of the Kongkaak belongs to the Hokan or Hokaltecan phylum of languages (Voegelin and Voegelin

1977:158). This suggests that the Seri dialects ultimately stem from the same origin as the Yuman family of languages in the Baja California peninsula and parts of California, Nevada and Arizona, the Coahuiltecan languages of Texas and extreme northeastern Mexico, and the Tlapanec and Tequistlatec languages of southern Mexico.

Linguists have analyzed Seri as consisting of 19 consonant *phonemes* (units of sound) and four vowel phonemes. Still other phonemes are neither consonants nor vowels. Nasalizing and stressing vowels, for example, change the meaning of an utterance just as surely as the consonants and vowels themselves. In all languages the sounds known as phonemes may be pronounced differently in different utterances, but as long as the varying sounds do not change the meaning of the word or word element in which they are used they are considered part of the same phoneme. Or, as we could say in a nontechnical way, they are the same sound even though pronounced slightly differently. In English, for example, /k/ is pronounced in somewhat variant ways in different utterances, but we are unaware of them because any one of them can be used without changing the meaning of what we are saying. Some Seri phonemes are similar to those of English and Spanish, but others differ. The Mosers' analysis provides evidence of at least three Seri dialects (Moser and Moser 1965:50).

Because of characteristic intonation and stress patterns the sounds of some Seri dialects have sounded like sing-song chanting to many outsiders. Such characteristics indicate nothing about a group's genetic makeup, since language sounds and speech patterns are learned, socially standardized customs just as surely as housing, religion, and other cultural elements.

Personality and Behavior

It is important for users of literature on gatherer-hunters and other small-scale cultures to evaluate its quality. Anthropologists and other scholars of the nineteenth and earlier centuries often regarded tribal groups as arrested survivals of humanity's ancient evolutionary past and supposed they could examine their customs to find out what primitive cultures of our own ancestors were like. Consequently, they regarded them as crude, simple, undeveloped, stupid, pre-logical, savage primitives and tended to be blind to evidence to the contrary. McGee, for example, repeatedly stressed the alleged primitiveness of the Seri. He believed they could outrun horses and characterized them as of noble physique, animal-like symmetry, and slow to mature. He also held that they had fixed "military instincts...(like the habits of primitive men generally)." (1898:181).

Several observers were convinced the Seri were cannibals and provided hair-raising examples. It is clear that they misinterpreted the evidence or imagined it and that the Seri did not practice cannibalism. Actually, some modern anthropologists think incontrovertible evidence of true cannibalism (consuming human flesh as part of the diet) exists

for no human group. There are many examples of ceremonial cannibalism and cases of eating human flesh to avoid starving but, some maintain, nothing more. The basic point is that early scholars and even a few modern nonanthropologists have unjustifiably attributed cannibalism, stupidity, violence, animal instincts, and other objectionable or inferior traits to tribal groups. Since the Seri have so often been labeled inferior savages, it is appropriate to note that some have commented favorably about them. Father Kino described them as a gentle people (E. Davis 1945:139), which harmonizes well with the anthropological finding of a low violence level among gatherer-hunters as compared with agricultural and industrial societies. The often mentioned Seri hostility of recent generations may well be a result of their mistreatment by whites. Kroeber found them "casual, informal, and slovenly" (Kroeber 1931:8), and he also noted that their personality could have undergone changes since aboriginal times. Other observations point definitely to humanitarian concern and mutual sensitivity. McGee noted that the Seri felt ethically obligated to care for those in need (1898:272), and there is other evidence of prescriptions for considerate social interaction. Father Gilg commented that the Seri lacked both avarice and lewdness, though he thought them otherwise "half bestial." (Di Peso and Matson 1965:45). Anthropologist William Neil Smith, who has been in contact with Seri since 1946, characterizes them as tranquil, self-reliant, alert, intelligent, curious, and generally friendly (1970:4). A lot rests on one's viewpoint and prejudices, and no extensive, objective study of Seri personality is available.

Clothing and Personal Appearance

Anthropologists have found that adornment and identification are more widely found purposes of wearing objects and enveloping portions of the body in cloth or other materials than either protection or modesty. The Seri and others around the world have been relatively unconcerned about keeping the genitals covered. It was warm much of the time in Seri country, and the people seemed to feel little need to fully cover themselves. It is also clear that nudity is not always associated with sexual stimulation, and Gilg found the Seri lack of "lewdness" remarkable in view of their nudity (Di Peso and Matson 1965:45). Children, older boys, and the elderly generally went without clothing.

The breechclout has been the basic garment for many tribal groups, but not for the Seri. Instead, the women and possibly the men wore a knee-length kilt or skirt held in place by a waist cord of fiber. Apparently, the skirt was nearly always of skin, but there seems to be no way to determine whether it was usually of pelican skins or mammal hide. In 1895, McGee reported, pelican skins were standard, but Gilg does not mention them for the late 1600s. It may be that only the women wore them. Also, since all cultures are always changing somehow, there is no reason there could not have been a change in native clothing between 1692 and 1895. Gilg, in fact, mentions fox skins for men that covered their genitals and buttocks. The pelican skin skirts were made by sewing several pelts together. The waist cord was probably of woven mesquite root fibers, human hair, or skin. If extra warmth or protection was desired the Seri added a robe of pelican or other skins or of strips of rabbit skin braided or woven together. The rabbit skin robe was used in a number of groups in the southwestern United States and northern Mexico. McGee also mentions a long-sleeved shirt. The people wore rawhide sandals if needed but went barefooted much of the time. The Seri also used their kilts to sleep on, as shades, to carry things in, and so on.

Both men and women wore their hair long–sometimes loose and sometimes braided. The Seri were noted for their luxuriously long and often flowing hair, which they took time to keep well brushed. One source mentions the women brushing their husbands' hair in the evening–apparently a time of pleasant conversation and relaxation (De Grazia and Smith 1970:62).

Like many other tribal groups the Seri pierced the nasal septum for the insertion of a bone or stone skewer or hanging various objects. Some, especially females, painted lines, dots, etc. on their faces, and they might tattoo themselves around the eyes and mouth. They made necklaces of shells, colored or precious stone, seeds, or wood or bone beads. They also wore decorative waistbands of various materials as well as other ornaments that suited their inclinations. Even a person without covering was likely to be wearing some kind of ornamentation.

Houses and Other Structures

Since the Seri moved frequently and the climate was warm and dry, they had little desire for elaborate dwellings. Seri women made the house frames from the branches of the attractive *ocotillo* (*Fouquieria splendens*). The plant consists of a cluster of straight, uniformly unforked stems or wands arising from a single crown and extending upward and slightly outward from the ground surface. The women removed the thorns, placed the ends of five or six of the wands in parallel rows six feet apart, and bent them together to form half-circle bows. The tops were overlapped and either twisted or lashed together, and a horizontal member was tied to the bows a foot or so above the ground on each side, holding the bows in position. The resulting half-cylinder frame was twelve feet long and four-and-a-half feet high. The people covered the framework with turtle shells, hides, shrubbery, robes, and other available items. Occasionally, they added more than one horizontal tie so additional branches or other items could be woven into them. One end of the hut was closed, most often toward the prevailing winds. Some double-length huts have been seen, and sometimes two of them were joined at one end to form a V-shaped structure.

Various domestic and other items were lodged in the framework and in the niches behind the bows and tie sticks. Hunks of meat, bows, paint containers, awls, pots, baskets,

hair brushes, and other items were thereby protected from animals or misplacement. There were no stools, benches, or other distinctively household furnishings.

Livelihood

If they are to exploit their environment effectively, gatherer-hunters must be keen, intelligent observers of their natural habitat and its life forms. Anthropologists have noted that all known cultures, in this or other ways, place a premium on intelligence. So, we can reasonably assume that racially or biologically different categories of humans have developed societies composed of those who are likely to survive the longest and who, consequently, pass more of their genes to the next generation than less intelligent individuals. The long-survivors are mostly those who show wisdom, maturity of judgement, and ability to get along well with others (Montagu 1963:79). The Seri are no exception. They had to know intimately the weather patterns, botanical characteristics, animal behaviors, and water availability and act on that knowledge with intelligence to avoid death from thirst and starvation. This is especially important in a country where the relatively abundant resources are widely scattered and of variable availability.

This does not mean a group genetically inherits the specific knowledge and skills by which it survives. It is rather the ability to learn readily and use what is learned effectively that is inherited. Malkin noted that how well the Seri of the 1950s knew different animals depended on how important they were to them for food and fiber (Malkin 1956:88). They mastered a good deal more detail about large sea forms and large mammals than they did about insects and small fish, which reflected a correlation between knowledge and degree of interest.

The ocean was the most important source of Seri food, and the giant green sea turtle was the main single item. The Seri usually put to sea to obtain a turtle, using a type of watercraft found in widely scattered parts of the Americas. Clumps of bamboo-like cane known as carrizo are found in many of the warmer parts of the hemisphere, including Seri country. These jointed canes have many uses, not the least of which for the Seri was the construction of thirty foot long, four foot wide, cigar-shaped rafts called *balsas*. Women and children probably collected the stalks of carrizo, and the men bound them into cylindrical bundles. Then they bound three bundles together so as to form a craft with raised, somewhat pointed ends. The balsa accommodated several people and could be either paddled or, in shallow water, poled.

The Seri approached a turtle on a dark, quiet night with the balsa, harpooned it, and dispatched it with an ironwood club. Harpoons by definition have a point on a short foreshaft which, after the point has penetrated the animal, comes away from the shaft. The foreshaft has a cord attached to it, so the hunter has a line fastened directly to the animal without the interference of the long shaft. The Seri harpoon point, which may have been a sea lion tooth in aboriginal times, penetrated and caught beneath the turtle's shell. The animal could then be pulled onto the balsa or towed to shore.

After beaching a turtle the Seri sometimes turned it on its back and built a fire on the plastron. This partially cooked the adjacent tender white meat, which would be eaten immediately. The rest of the meat was removed for later consumption. The Seri often kept a large chunk of uncooked turtle meat on top of the front end of a house, using from the chunk as desired. They ate turtle and other meat within a few days, since they had no way of preserving and storing meat for extended periods. Meat often became rather odorous before they used it all.

The Seri were not whalers, but they would consume a beached animal. There is also evidence they took porpoises and sea lions at times. Large ocean fish were very important, possibly second only to the turtle. They used two kinds of fish spears at one time or another, one with a single point and the other double-pointed. The double-pointed spear seen by Kroeber in 1930 had serrated iron points about six inches long that spread to about five inches apart at the ends. Fish were caught between the points (1931:19). In 1895 McGee saw only a single-pointed spear, so what the Seri had in aboriginal times is unclear. Fish could be speared either from the balsa or from shore.

A number of smaller fish were regularly trapped in tidal pools and presumably taken by hand. Apparently the early Seri made no use of nets or hooks and lines. Occasionally, at least, they fastened a pelican by a cord to a shrub or rock so other pelicans would bring it fish. The bird stored them in his large pouch, and, reportedly, all the Seri had to do was open the beak periodically and remove the fish. The Seri also took clams, mussels, and a number of other shellfish, but gill fish were more important. The people used shells of appropriate shape to dig up clams. They also took crabs.

Birds were of intermediate importance as food, the pelican, perhaps, being most important. Apparently, the Seri took them mainly on Isla Tassne in the California Gulf. On a quiet evening during the dark of the moon a large party would leave so as to arrive after dark. The women remained near the shore with the balsas while the men and older boys went onto the island and clubbed the large number of roosting birds. It is reported that the group ate a considerable amount of flesh during the night on the spot, though the people remained several days to consume the remaining meat. During the first day the women skinned the pelicans whose pelts remained in good enough condition after the night's carnage. Ducks and other water and shore birds were taken by the Seri, too.

The people also hunted inland as well as taking sea life. In fact, hunting large land and water animals seems to have yielded a greater quantity of food and fiber than fishing and collecting small animals and plant items. Small groups stalked and ambushed deer, bighorn sheep, peccaries (javelinas), cougars, and jaguars. They used the bow and arrow, but they sometimes ran down, surrounded, and attacked by hand deer and other animals that were not too

dangerous for it. They might break the animal's neck or smash its skull with a stone. Several other groups of Mexico and the southwestern United States also pursued animals on foot until they tired enough to be caught.

No description of the aboriginal bow is available, but McGee saw a bow a little under five feet long with the inside flat, the outside convex, tapered ends, and notches to receive a cord of mesquite fiber (1898:200). No detailed description of the stone points is available. The chipped points once used were replaced rather early by iron the Seri found along the beaches. They used poison on their arrows, possibly from more than one source. Davis reported they extracted poison from the leafy shrub, *Sapium biloculare*, which was found on Tiburón (1965:138). The people feathered their wooden arrow shafts to ensure straight flight. Various societies use different postures for discharging arrows. The Seri, according to McGee (1898:201), assumed the posture only at the moment they were going to shoot, holding the bow vertically while bringing the arrow to eye level and the elbow above the head. If the shot was successful, they physically attacked the animal.

While Seri men did most of the hunting and fishing, the women gathered cactus fruit, mesquite tree beans, ocotilla poles for houses, carrizo canes, and many other plant items. They also collected small animal forms such as lizards, snakes, small fish, and shellfish. This kind of labor division—women the collectors, men the hunters—prevails in gatherer-hunter societies around the world.

The cacti bear their fruit mostly during the summer. The fruits of the giant saguaro (*Carnegiea gigantea*) begin to ripen at the ends of the trunk and branches in mid-June, and as many as two hundred lemon-sized fruits may develop on a single saguaro. The main trunk, an "accordion-pleated" cylindrical column, reaches a diameter of 12-16 inches, and up to five or six major upwardly curving branches extend from different levels along the trunk, with some secondary branches on some of the oldest specimens (Shreve 1951:139). Mature saguaro reach 30-40 feet high and are covered with stout spines, so the Seri removed the fruits with long poles having crosspieces or hooks at the ends (Felger and M. Moser 1974:260). They also used poles with spikes extending from the ends or at right angles to take the fruits of other large cacti.

The cardón or *sahueso* (*Pachysereus pringlei*) is even more massive than the saguaro. Its branches extend upward at a sharp angle rather than curving as much as those of the saguaro, and the fruits appear along the upper 12 to 16 inches of the stem. The organ pipe cactus (*Lemaireocereus thurberi*), sometimes called the *pitahaya dulce*, also produced a great deal of fruit for the Seri. The orange-sized fruits of the *pitahaya agria* (*Machaerocereus gummosus*) appear late in summer and into the fall. The plant is large and sprawling, forming a tangle of upright, arching, and leaning stems. The fruits of these columnar cacti were normally eaten on the spot. During the fruiting season the Seri would often remain in the stands of cacti, living largely off the fruits until they were gone. The senita cactus was small enough that poles were not required, and though the Seri would eat the fruits they were not harvested like those of the columnar cacti. The *nopal* or common prickly pear (*Opuntia spp.*) was also eaten occasionally.

If cactus fruit was not eaten fresh, a woman might open the skin with an awl or stone, squeeze the pulp into a basket, work the juice out of the pulp, and form it into flat, round cakes. These were then dried and stored in a clay pot. The people toasted cardón seeds and ground them into a paste (Felger and Moser 1974:265). They made wine from cardón, organ-pipe, pitahaya agria, or saguaro, and modern Seri have said that they used organ-pipe and saguaro fruit almost entirely for wine-making before the 1920s. They mixed the mashed fruit pulp with water and allowed it to ferment in a clay pot.

The people used mesquite tree pods for food in several ways, depending partly on the several stages of growth in which they might be taken. There are extensive open stands of mesquite trees here and there in Seri country, making it possible for them to take the beans wherever a well-loaded tree was available. The Seri most often used the fallen dry pods, which they pulverized on a grinding stone or with a mortar and pestle. The mortars were either depressions in bedrock or small bowl-shaped excavations in hard earth. The latter is possible because the mesquite is woody enough to form a hard wall against the bottom and sides of the hole as it is pounded. The Seri often toasted the dry pods before pounding them. They heated a spot on the earth by a wood fire and piled the pods on that spot. They also made fires on top of four piles of sand surrounding the pile of pods and, after the fires were out, sprinkled the hot sand on the pods (Felger and M. Moser 1971:56-7).

After pulverizing the pods the Seri alternately ground the material further and winnowed it by tossing it in a basket until a fairly uniform bean meal resulted. The meal was sometimes eaten raw in small amounts, but the people more often combined it with water to make a thin soup. Soups of water and meal, whether made from corn, beans, wheat, or other items, have been generally referred to as *atole* in Middle America. The Seri apparently drank the atole cold or boiled it. They also mixed meal with water and formed the dough into balls or cakes that would last for a long time when dried and stored in containers. The Seri processed mesquite beans in several additional ways not described here. They also used mesquite for firewood, to make cord, and to prepare black face paint.

The Seri habitat also provides a variety of grass seeds and small nuts as well as a few berries.

The Kongkaak made extensive use of the seed from eelgrass (*Zostera marina*). In 1977 this was the only documented case of human use of a submerged marine seed plant as a major food source. The Seri probably used the seed in aboriginal times, since Jesuit missionaries took note of its use as early as 1645 (Sheridan and Felger, 1977:91). They harvested large quantities of the seed in April and May and named one of their months accordingly. The seeds would keep for a long time in sealed clay containers. Families collected eelgrass at the stage when the top parts of the plant broke and floated to the surface. They would wade into the sea to gather the masses of vegetation. They extracted the seeds and pounded, winnowed, and ground them to make flour. The flavor was bland, so they usually combined the flour with something like sea turtle oil or honey. Sometimes they ground the seeds with cardón seeds, and they often made atole from the meal. Earlier reports that seeds of the Ruppia plant were used were in error (Felger and Moser 1971:356), and reports that the Seri took seaweed resulted from the fact that the broken sections of eelgrass were mixed with other kinds of floating vegetation when the people gathered them.

Like the Cochimí of Baja California the Seri made use of agave or maguey a great deal. There are several species in the Sonoran region, and *Agave subsimplex* is common and widely used. The Seri gathered this relatively small agave in January or February just as the plant was getting ready to send up a shoot and bloom. They prepared a cutting edge on one end of a green ironwood digging stick and used it to chisel the plant from its root by pounding the end with a stone (Felger and Moser 1970:161). They trimmed the spine-edged leaves from the whitish core, except for a strip of fibers from one leaf. They tied the leaf strips from the two hearts together to make a carrying cord. To prepare the hearts for eating they piled them on a bed of coals at the bottom of a deep pit and covered them with flat rocks, several inches of earth, and a bed of coals from a fire built on top. After an overnight baking the Seri enjoyed the juicy sweet pulp that resulted. They prepared flat cakes from the outer portion of the baked hearts, and when they were ready to consume them dissolved them in water and drank the resulting fluid. The dried cakes would last indefinitely. The Kongkaak also prepared cakes from pulp made by pounding the basal ends of the agave leaves.

Sometimes they made trips to San Esteban Island to obtain another favorite agave, *Agave dentiens*. When they ran out of water the Seri might roast slabs of dentiens leaves and pound them to a pulp to obtain a potable liquid. They also made a wine from the fermented juice of dentiens leaves.

The foregoing descriptions provide only a few glimpses of the Seri food system. Several other items were of major importance, such as desert amaranth, goosefoot, wooly plantain, desert wolfberry, and palo verde. Felger and Moser (1976:15) listed 75 species the Seri used for food, 58 for their seeds and/or fruits and 26 for roots, greens, stems or other vegetative parts. They did not always have an abundance of food, but there was enough variety available at various times and places for them to have enough most of the time. When their favorite foods were scarce they resorted to less desired items.

McGee characterized the Seri diet as of "less average nutrition than the selected and cooked foods of higher culture." But he also remarked on their exceptional stature and strength, and Gilg observed that the Seri usually reached advanced age. Actually, the diet was probably quite well-balanced and nutritious. Felger and M. Moser note that the people often mixed foodstuffs in ways that provided well-balanced foods (1976:16). Modern cross-culturally oriented nutritionists are becoming aware that the modern North American diet is probably a source of health troubles and that a number of tribal groups enjoyed rather high health levels before their diets were restricted and otherwise altered by contact with Europeans.

It became customary for Europeans and Americans to remark on the apparent improvidence of tribal peoples, since they so often gorged on food when it was abundant and might have little in times of scarcity. This often neglects the fact that the foods they gorged on are not easily preserved and stored, but it also overlooks the many examples of long term food storage–mainly plant foods. Several examples of drying and storing cakes of plant food in clay pots by the Seri were mentioned earlier. The people also might keep meat as long as they could, though it often became rather putrid. But people of many societies eat meat in various stages of decay and may prefer it that way. Even modern North Americans prefer their meat slightly aged.

The Seri shared with the Baja Californians and other groups in the region the so-called second harvest. When they ate the cactus fruits whole, the seeds of some did not digest. So the Seri retained the feces full of seeds, and when other foods were in short supply they extracted the seeds and ground them for consumption. Of course, writers have had a great time expressing incredulity and disgust about this. Gilg wrote about the practice among the Seri but indicated it should not be mentioned aloud or explicitly, only under the breath (Di Peso and Matson 1965:55).

Food sharing is common in gathering-hunting societies, and the Seri were no exception. Many of their food-taking activities were cooperative ventures such as the slaughter of pelicans and the collecting of eelgrass, and those participating took their share. But there were also mechanisms built into the culture, so to speak, that provided for people unable to take their share. A Seri man in need could wait on the beach for a returning balsa, knowing that if he helped gut and clean the catch he would be given the heads of fish or the head, blood, and intestines of a turtle (Griffen 1959:33). A latecomer, however, was expected to wait for the arrival of another balsa.

Crafts, Tools, and Techniques

Anthropologists have identified four main ways of making fire–percussion and three friction techniques. People can produce friction made fire by twirling a wooden shaft in a depression in another piece of wood, sawing a rigid or flexible strip of something across the grain of a piece of wood, or running the end of a stick back and forth in a groove running with the grain in a block of wood. The Seri used the first friction method–the *fire drill*. They twirled a shaft of cottonwood driftwood in another section of wood until the resulting fine wood dust became hot enough to form a glowing coal. Then they placed the coal in dry grass and held it into the wind.

The Seri had to spend a lot of time carrying water, since there were so few places to obtain it. McGee, in fact, stated that carrying water was the main industry. Seri women carried water on their heads in thin-walled, globular clay pots with narrow mouths and moderately conical, round bottoms. Pots of this shape are common in Mexico and Central America and are called *ollas* in Spanish. Different pottery techniques have been reported for the Seri, and it is difficult to say which prevailed in aboriginal times. McGee said they took a lump of tempered, kneaded clay and hollowed and shaped it over the hand, gradually expanding it by kneading, rubbing, and pushing (1898:184). Kroeber indicated that they formed strips of clay and laid them in coils in some receptacle. The pot's walls were finished by smoothing the coils with a stone inside and scraping them with a shell outside (1931:17). They did not fire the pots completely and seldom if ever added glazes or slips. Since the thin walls were porous the water evaporated slowly, giving a cooling effect. When Seri men carried water they suspended the ollas in nets from the ends of a balance pole resting across their shoulders. The women used woven head rings or pads to receive the pots' rounded bottoms. The people also used pots for cooking and for storing seeds, flour cakes, and other food items (Bowen 1967:119). They used marine shells, largely unmodified, for cups, dippers, and dishes.

Many of the Indians of northern Mexico and the southwestern United States made highly serviceable, attractive baskets. Baskets were so important in Seri life that a woman was considered unfit for marriage until she had learned to make good ones. Men seldom touched baskets, but every woman owned a basket that was her most important utensil. The baskets were excellently made, some of them being of such fine weave that they were nearly water tight. The Seri used their baskets to transport food, firewood, trash, dirt, sand, household possessions, and babies (E. Moser 1973:133). Baskets also served as food preparation platforms, winnowing devices, seed parchers, serving and eating dishes, mud mixing containers, wash basins, nests for coiling clay pots, baby tubs, temporary cribs, gambling stake holders, and resonators for musical instruments.

The Seri women collected basketry materials from a species of *torote* shrub (*Jatropha cuneata*). They stripped off the twigs and bark and split the shrub's branches into the strips they used in making the basket. They formed a number of the less flexible strips into long bundles, which they wrapped with more flexible members to form the coils that made up the basket's walls. One way of starting a basket was to make a knot in the bundle of foundation splints and begin the coiling at what would be the center of the bottom. The weaver wrapped the flat, flexible strips continuously around the bundle of foundation splints, and as she inserted the wrapping strips around the bundle and between the coil being worked on and the previous one, she inserted the awl carrying the strip into the adjacent coil far enough to catch it and hold the two together. The Seri made their best baskets by stitching the coils together from four to five times each centimeter. They also tried to avoid splitting the strips. As they wrapped and stitched they added new foundation splints to the bundle by poking them into the end. The slope of the basket's wall and the overall shape was controlled by the angle at which the weaver inserted the awl through the edge of the previous coil (E. Moser 1973:115). A weaver skillfully worked the end of the last coil into the previous one to form a smooth rim. Traditional Seri baskets were shaped like shallow bowls, deep bowls, trays, and ollas. The sizes varied according to the purpose. Most utilitarian baskets lacked designs, though ceremonial baskets were decorated. The designs were worked in by dyeing the wrapping strips and inserting the proper color of splint at the appropriate place.

A fiesta might be held and a giant decorated basket made for it as the result of a shaman's dream or vision. A four night fiesta was held to celebrate the completion of the large olla-shaped basket (E. Moser 1973:136). The Seri also made plaited or woven rectangular baskets, and Gilg mentioned woven mats (Di Peso and Matson 1965:55). The box-like basketry containers were of open weave and were used as strainers to separate seeds from cardón pulp.

The Seri satisfied their need for containers largely by making pots and baskets and using shells. To process materials, shape their utensils and containers, and make their clothing they prepared tools of stone, bone, horn, shell and wood. To pulverize seeds and work plant materials into desired form they used only slightly altered stones. Cobblestones were picked up along the beach and used without alteration for hammering or grinding, and large stones of suitable shape served as *metates* (bases for pounding or grinding substances). The people found shell especially useful for cutting and scraping things, for digging, and for paddling. Bones from deer and other animals made good awls, needles, necklace beads, and other items. The people found the turtle carapace served well for house covers, dog shelters, cradles, and cisterns. They also found use for bird mandibles, fish spines, thorns, and animal teeth.

All groups find cordage and rope useful for many purposes, and the Seri produced theirs mainly from the outer tissues of mesquite roots. After soaking the mesquite tissues they pounded and split them and worked them with hand and mouth until they had the slender fibers required. Then they braided them to make rope or to form the doughnut-shaped head pads for carrying water pots. The Aztecs and others of Mexico and Central America used fibers from the thick fleshy leaves or outwardly extending rays of the agave plant to make cord, paper, and woven fabric. The Seri made limited use of agave fiber. For example, they made hair brushes by bundling the fibers of *Agave dentiens* (Felger and M. Moser 1970:165). They also used fiber from the yucca plant some.

Social Organization and Relationships

Ideally, Seri couples went to live near or with the husband's parents when they married, which meant either in a separate hut or one joined to that of the bride's parents-in-law. When the couple had children, a three generation domestic unit resulted that anthropologists refer to as a patrilocal extended family. While this was the ideal, actual practice was variable. Sometimes, for example, a man served his bride's parents for a time, so the couple would be living with the woman's parents for a period and join the man's parental family when the service was completed.

There is little information about Seri family life. It is said that husband and wife treated one another kindly, and hair brushing sessions have been mentioned as times of pleasant companionship between spouses. There is at least one report of wife beating but no way of knowing how frequent it could have been in aboriginal times or even later. The Kongkaak seem not to have thought of men and women as having essentially different temperaments. As in a great proportion of other societies in all parts of the world there were tensions between in-laws. This is reflected in Seri and many other patrilocal societies in a taboo on conversation between a woman and her husband's parents. Among the Seri there were also avoidance relationships between a man and his wife's parents and between a person and his or her spouse's brothers and sisters (Bowen, personal comunication).

It seems that the Seri have usually practiced monogamy. McGee said they were polygynous (*polygyny* meaning one husband married to two or more wives), but Kroeber indicated this was a special, temporary situation, since the war of extermination against the Seri had seriously reduced the ratio of males to females (Kroeber 1931:24). Reportedly, a Seri leader might take a second wife on occasion. Gilg, however, clearly stated that the Seri of his time were monogamous (Di Peso and Matson 1965:45). There is no evidence of the *sororate* (marriage of a woman to her late sister's husband) or the *levirate* (marriage of a man to his late brother's widow).

Kinship groups larger than the family such as *clans* or *lineages* are more common in horticultural groups than among gatherer-hunters, but several scholars have suggested that the Seri had localized common ancestor groups or clans. McGee said the Seri had *matrilineal* (female descent) clans, and other investigators followed him in this. He based much of his description of their social organization on his assumption of their presence, but Kroeber insisted that there was no evidence of matrilineal clans and that McGee misinterpreted his data. His misinterpretation was probably based on the assumption, widely held in his time, that tribal peoples passed through a matrilineal and matriarchal stage in their early evolution. He apparently saw the Seri as arrested in this evolutionary stage. The declaration by several other writers that the Seri had matrilineal clans gives the impression of strong evidence, but they apparently were uncritically repeating McGee's judgement and interpreting what they knew of the Seri accordingly. If the Seri had matrilineal clans it would mean that the society was divided into common ancestor groups, each Seri belonging to one of however many groups were present. A person's mother and father would normally have been born into different clans and each person would belong to the mother's natal clan rather than the father's and trace his or her ancestry through the generations only through female links. Probably no specialist on Seri culture continues to believe they had matrilineal common ancestor groups.

During the 1950s Edward Moser probed the memories of Seri who remembered belonging to groups that he concluded were localized *patrilineal* clans. If this were true, each Seri would have belonged to one of the various patrilineal common ancestor groups, one's mother and father would have been born into different clans, and each person would trace ancestry though the father only.

More recent scholarship has brought the notion of patrilineal common ancestor groups among the Seri into serious question. In all probability we will never know for sure whether they had them or not, but several specialists now hold that the Seri were probably exclusively *bilateral*, reckoning descent through both men and women in all generations rather than being either matrilineal or patrilineal. Anthropologist Thomas Sheridan reviewed the evidence for patrilineal clans and found it too fragmentary and ambiguous to be convincing. Furthermore, using the cross-cultural comparative approach anthropologists hold to be so highly productive, he showed that the ecological opportunities and constraints of the Seri natural environment are similar to other gatherer-hunter groups lacking unilineal common ancestor groups (Sheridan 1982:185).

Both Kroeber and Griffen have noted that the Seri used quite a few more kin terms than many other societies. Their terms also tended to be reciprocals of one another. For example, a person who called his paternal aunt "my father's sister" was likely to be referred to by the father's sister as "my brother's child." Third, the Seri used different terms for older and younger siblings and the older and younger siblings of near relatives. They had *Hawaiian* terms for siblings and all cousins, which means a speaker uses the same terms or set of terms for cousins as for brothers and sisters. Accordingly, a Seri woman referred to all her older brothers and male cousins as "my older brother." She referred to a brother or male cousin younger than herself as "my younger brother," each of her sisters and female cousins younger than herself as "my younger sister," and each older sister and female cousin as "my older sister." Male Seri followed a similar pattern, although Griffen found the men used some of the age-differentiating terms only when drunk (1955:40).

Hawaiian terms are for siblings and cousins, but the question of how people refer to their parents, aunts, and uncles may also be important. Seri terms for the first ascending (parental) generation were *bifurcate collateral*, which means they used different terms for their parents than for aunts and uncles and distinguished their maternal aunts and uncles from paternal aunts and uncles. The Seri were like modern North Americans in reserving "my mother" and "my father" for the biological parents only, but unlike Americans they kept maternal and paternal aunts and uncles in separate categories and distinguished among them according to whether they were older or younger than their parents. A Seri man, for example, referred to his mother's younger brother and his father's younger brother by separate terms, and he used a still different set of terms for his mother's older brother and his father's older brother.

Examination reveals that the Seri needed ten terms to refer to their parents, aunts, and uncles while Americans require only three. Which system is best depends on one's viewpoint. The Seri system is more discriminating, since the hearer knows from the term used not just the sex of the parent's sibling but also the side of the family and whether the aunt or uncle is older or younger than the parent. Some might argue that it is overly discriminating, forcing people to know irrelevant information to refer to a relative. At least systems like that of the Seri put to rout the assumption that the vocabularies of tribal groups are inevitably less precise than those of English and other major languages.

Another feature of Seri kinship terminology is that the speaker's sex may make a difference in what term is used. For example, a boy used a different term for his father than his sister did (Di Peso and Matson 1965:49). Also, a father had separate terms for his son and daughter, but a Seri mother referred to her sons and daughters simply as "my child."

Associations are non-kinship groups formed for social interaction or the accomplishment of social purposes. They are often absent in gathering-hunting societies, though they have been important in a few, the warrior societies of the Kiowa of the American plains being one example. There is no mention of associations for the Seri.

Most information on Seri conception and pregnancy customs is for the twentieth century, and it is impossible to say how far back in time they have existed. Their belief that conception requires repeated sexual contact to fill a little pouch on the inside of the womb with semen may well be old. People of many cultures believe that more than sexual activity is necessary for conception to occur, and the Seri held that when the pouch was full of semen the baby's spirit descended as a tiny flying thing and entered the woman's body (M. Moser 1970:201).

Proscriptions against eating various kinds of foods and doing a variety of things during pregnancy are abundant in many cultures. Not many pregnancy proscriptions have been reported for the Seri, so they may have had fewer than some groups. A woman was supposed to avoid eating spotted sea bass so she would not suffer prolonged labor. Neither was she to approach a person stung by a scorpion or bitten by a snake, because it would increase the pain of childbirth. If she ate a certain fruit her sons would be born without foreskins. These and similar beliefs have been found in recent generations. However, a pregnant woman continued carrying water, collecting firewood, gathering fruit, and other normal activities (M. Moser 1970:202).

Seri women gave birth either in the house or a shelter open on one or two sides. They sat on the ground with the legs spread and the knees doubled and leaned against something. Another woman, usually a close relative, would sit before her with her hands in position to receive the baby. Sometimes these positions were maintained for many hours, though there were minor changes of position, and the parturient would stand up for a few minutes occasionally. The sitting position seems strange to North Americans, but it is far more common in the world's cultures than reclining. The husband or other helpers and observers might also be around. There were various things that could be done to promote rapid delivery or reduce pain.

When the baby was delivered, another woman cut the umbilical cord and gave the newborn a quick rinse. The mother then assumed the kneeling position for the delivery of the placenta, after which she rested. Then someone buried the placenta at the base of a cardón or saguaro cactus. The baby was given sweetened water from a certain clam shell. For four days a ritual fire was kept burning in the house. The mother avoided eating flesh of any kind for eight days, and the father abstained for four. If they ate meat during those periods the child would not be healthy. Both parents were also careful to avoid all work during the abstinence periods. The taboo on work, of course, is contrary to the stereotype that "primitive" women return to their normal labors immediately after parturition.

When a Seri baby's umbilical cord dropped off, the child was placed on a cradle frame resembling a crude snowshoe. The ends of a stick were lashed together to form the teardrop-shaped frame, and several cross sticks were tied in place. They placed the little one on a pelican robe and held it to the frame by straps and cords. Pelican down was used for diapering. Evidently, the babies could become quite fond of being carried on the cradle frame, and when older a sleepy child might try to get someone to place him or her on the board. The parents usually gave babies their first solid food when they had two or three teeth, usually some gruel at first and, later, soft foods such as bits of cooked fish. Older sisters often cared for them part of the time, and aunts or grandparents might be involved, too, especially as the children became older. Around the camp the cradle board was adequate for carrying babies, but when the Seri moved about the desert they often carried a baby in a basket held in a net suspended from one end of a balance pole across the shoulder. They suspended a pack of belongings, a pot of water, or another infant from the other end of the pole (M. Moser 1970:209).

The Seri sometimes shared their children as well as food and other things. A family that had lost a child might pay special attention to a child of the same sex in another family, and the child's parents would offer to lend their little one. The child would spend part of his time with his adoptive family, though he would sleep with his own family. The adoptive parents would help feed and clothe the child, and later in life the adoptee might contribute to the material needs of his "second" parents.

Little information on later Seri childhood is available. It is known that Seri boys had considerable freedom and spent much of their time playing with bows and arrows, spearing crustaceans with toy fish spears, persecuting small animals, and the like.

At first menstruation the Seri held a four day puberty ceremony for the girls. A sponsor was chosen from a family with whom the girl's family had a special, socially inherited relationship. The sponsor assumed certain ceremonial responsibilities at times of special supernatural danger for the sponsored one. Griffen found in 1955 that the sponsor was still called upon at puberty and at death. The sponsor took the girl to his home, gave her special clothing, and isolated her there through the ceremonial period. Members of his family painted her face, and she was allowed to eat no meat. Singing and dancing were significant aspects of the puberty celebration, and special foods were served. There were also puberty ceremonies for boys, but they have not been described. Premarital sexual activity occurred among the Seri, though its cultural significance and regulation have not been studied.

At puberty a Seri was ready for marriage. This is common in tribal cultures and contrasts with Euroamerican deferral of social adulthood until several years after puberty. Even highly individualistic North Americans often try to influence who their youngsters marry, but such influence is far stronger and quite fully standardized among the Seri and in other traditional societies. For the Seri the concerns of the group prevailed over those of the young people. For one thing, the Seri were not supposed to marry their cousins, which harmonizes with their use of Hawaiian kinship terms for their brothers, sisters, and cousins. In other words, a man was not supposed to marry anyone he referred to as a sister, and a woman was not to marry anyone she referred to as a brother. Beyond such rules the Seri had to bow to the wishes of their parents and other members of the extended family. Accordingly, marriages were arranged by the members of the patrilocal extended family rather than by the young people themselves, though the youngsters were commonly able to secure approval to marry a "sweetheart."

Once the families reached agreement that two people were to marry, the man and his relatives arranged to pay a bride price to the woman's family, or the man served his spouse's parents for a period. McGee was apparently wrong in saying there was no bride price. The Seri still paid a bride price in the twentieth century, though we cannot be sure what it consisted of in aboriginal times.

Seri married couples might divorce, but only if the difficulties were considerable (Griffen 1959:28). A man might divorce a very irritable, stubborn, lazy wife, while a woman could choose to leave a man who failed to provide for his family or was unfaithful.

Men and women of all ages were buried in four foot deep graves, though a stillborn, miscarried, or aborted fetus or infant might be put in an olla, which was placed in a tree or a cactus. Personal property was buried with the body. In earlier times a deceased man's balsa and his house were burned. The ocotillo houses were still burned as late as 1959, and the more permanent houses of wattle-and-daub were torn down and the materials used for a new house (Griffen 1959:28). The Seri appear to have tried to forget the dead as soon as possible, and their names were never to be spoken. Seri who had lived a good life went to a land situated in the sky slightly north of where the sun set. People, especially children, were careful not to look at the setting sun, since it would bring bad luck and early death. The Seri believed unmarried male thieves went to a land with no women and where they did nothing but engage in homosexual acts (Griffen 1959:21).

Government and Social Order

Seri communities were semi-nomadic *bands* made up of families who customarily camped together. This is one standard anthropological meaning for the term band, but matters are confused by many anthropologists' usage of band to refer to larger geographical subdivisions of a society. Moser follows this in his description of six Seri geographical groups. We are calling them tribelets rather than bands, since they were culturally very similar subdivisions of Seri society as a whole, and some of them seem to have been composed of more than one band community.

Griffen found that the Seri of 1955 and 1956 could remember seven territorial divisions (1959:46). Edward Moser has reported six such divisions (1963:14), which leaves out the Guayma, the southernmost Seri tribelet. The Seri had names for the people of these geographical territories, and they were aware of differences among them in behaviors and characteristic personalities. One tribelet, for example, did not use the balsa, even though they fished a lot. Another did not use the bow and arrow but wielded spears skillfully. Some were known to be more warlike than others. Several of the tribelets were composed of smaller territorial subdivisions, some of which consisted of more than one camp or nomadic band.

Since part of American and European culture is the belief that every "primitive" group has a chief, informal leaders of tribal groups have repeatedly been referred to as chiefs and, in many instances, made into chiefs by the whites. The territorial subdivisions of the tribelets had no chiefs or other formal leaders. They sometimes fought with one another, in which case the oldest capable male organized and led the effort (E. Moser 1963:22). In peacetime leadership was even more informal, with the individuals most accomplished by accepted cultural standards exercising influence according to the willingness of others to trust their judgement. Neither were there political leaders of the tribelets or the Seri as a whole.

The Spanish and the Mexicans found the Seri were good warriors. They handled their weapons well, and they effectively used rocks, shrubbery and darkness for concealment. In addition to their bows and arrows and spears they used helmets, sleeves, and shields of hide or cactus ribs for protection in battle.

Art and Play

The Seri obviously spent a goodly portion of their daily lives locating and extracting the foods and other material substances they wanted. Their technological activities, of course, were not solely individual, so much of their time was spent relating to one another in various kinds of activi-

ties. However implicit it might have been, they were concerned with enjoying one another socially, dominating and submitting to one another, and ritually dealing with the forces of their world as they conceived of them. Games or other recreational activities are found in all cultures, and the Seri were no exception. We probably know about only a fraction of all the pastimes of the aboriginal Seri, but a few glimpses are available.

Like the Tarahumara and some other tribes of this region the Seri raced while kicking wooden balls before them. The balls were of ironwood and about three inches in diameter. Teams of four men each raced along the beach in relay fashion. The women had a game in which team members sought to throw eight or ten inch hoops onto a goal with sticks carried by the players.

The people also played a game using four carrizo tubes, each open at one end. One player placed a twig in one of the cylinders, filled all four with sand, and placed them on the ground. The opposing player then emptied the sand from the tubes one by one, hoping the twig would be found in the third one emptied. If it was, the player had to give up none of his supply of shell disk counters, and he earned the right to hide the twig next. If the twig was in the first tube the player had to give up ten disks. He had to give up six if it was in the second and four if it was in the fourth (Kroeber 1931:15).

Dice of tapered splints of carrizo were also used in games. Three splints were thrown against the hand or some other object so they would scatter on the ground. The points earned depended on how many landed with the greenish-white inside of the splint up or the darker outside up. Games using various kinds of dice are found in many of the world's societies, the objects used depending on what is available and what people happen to have hit upon.

The Seri seldom produced art solely for aesthetic pleasure except, mainly, for their face painting. Their pots and baskets were usually unadorned, but they undoubtedly took some pleasure in the skill with which they produced some of them. They also lacked highly elaborated music, but music and dancing were important pastimes. They danced in connection with a girl's puberty ceremony, the taking of war trophies such as scalps, other ceremonial occasions, and simply for enjoyment. Sometimes they would dig a hole in the sand to serve as resonator and place planks across it to dance on. Davis saw Seri put sand on the planks so they could shuffle dance. They might accompany their dancing with singing and gourd, cocoon, or nut rattles. They also would dance on a turtle shell, which provided resonation, and they wore rattles on a band below the knee.

Visitors have seen the Seri place the back of a bow against a turtle shell and strike the taut bowstring with an arrow, producing a piano-like tone. According to Bowen and Edward Moser (1970b), Seri instruments have included a one-stringed fiddle, the musical bow, a mouth bow, an eleven-stringed harp, flutes, whistles, the conch shell trumpet, rasping sticks, gourd rattles, cocoon rattles, tortoise shell rattles, and the previously described foot drum. It is impossible to know whether or not this list would match closely one from aboriginal times. The Seri nearly always sang and played instruments with their dancing. No matter what its purpose, the Seri clearly enjoyed their music.

Religious Beliefs and Practices

Like all other human cultures the Seri lifeway included beliefs and practices concerning what Europeans and Americans call the supernatural. Many have declared tribal groups they observed without religion, and Adam Gilg said the Seri had no faith. But declarations like this are based on a narrow definition of religion and failure to recognize the basic similarity of tribal supernaturalistic beliefs to those of Euroamerican life. It is also difficult at times to learn about this aspect of a culture, and untrained observers have often been prone to misinterpret much of what they experienced or have been told. Systematic, sophisticated observation of aboriginal Seri religious life was not done, so we have only fragmentary and largely tentative information.

Shamanism is usually a major component of gatherer-hunter religions, and so it was among the Seri. A *shaman* is someone with special ability to utilize the power of spiritual beings with whom he or she has a special relationship, commmonly for healing diseases. Kroeber was told that aspiring Seri shamans would find a rock wall or some such place and make a sign or mark on it. It would then open to form a cave, which the person entered. If the spirit within so willed it would strike the Seri and enter his body to become a familiar spirit that would empower him to see into people's bodies to discern the cause of disease and its cure. Kroeber was told that the shaman, after learning the cause, would form his hands into a tube over the afflicted area, put his mouth to his hands, and say "cho cho." (Kroeber 1931:13). It is common around the world for shamans to suck an illness out of the body, but the Seri told Kroeber that was not what the shamans were doing.

In earlier times there may have been other ways shamans received and practiced their abilities. Judging from what the Seri told Griffen in 1955 there were probably some special vision caves one might go to for obtaining shamanistic power (1959:50). The aspirant would build a shelter and fast there for four days without leaving it. Late the fourth afternoon he would go to the cave and call the spirits with a bull roarer, which was a specially shaped ironwood piece that "roared" as it was swung in a circle at the end of a cord. He would then enter the cave and lie down on green torote shrubbery to wait for the spirits. The spirits taught him how to cure people and gave him a song he could use to call on his spiritual power. A shaman might receive a number of songs, but the first seems to have been crucial in calling the spirit on future occasions. It has also been reported that some men sought shaman power from Coyote, a mythical being in the form of a coyote who could appear as a man (Bowen and E. Moser 1970:169). Shamans also used flutes and whistles to summon spirits.

Songs were important in Seri religion. While the shaman was alive others avoided singing his songs, but after his death they would sing those they liked for enjoyment. Also, people who had not gone through the ritual necessary to become a shaman could still obtain songs for special purposes. They would build a ramada and fast there for four days, after which they would call to the sea animals with a bull roarer. The animal spirits would come and teach the songs, which the recipient could use to gain high speed in running, exceptional fish spearing skill, and other abilities. This, too, could be fitted under shamanism, although the Seri regarded the healing shamans as special people. Even so, a number of people acquired healing power over the years without going through the cave ritual, enough so that by the time they were elderly they were considered shamans. In many tribal societies it is difficult to draw the line between full-fledged shamans and ordinary people who have managed to develop special capacity to draw on the power of spirits. Most Seri old men had some shamanistic ability. As in other societies the Seri paid shamans for their services.

The shamans were important intermediaries between the Seri and the spirit world, since the Seri held that any animal, object, or natural phenomenon could communicate with a shaman through dreams (E. Moser 1973:137). The systemic nature of cultures is well illustrated in this belief and related practices, since a basket in its spiritual aspect could serve as the medium through which the supernaturals sent messages. In one instance cactus fruit chided a woman through the medium of a basket and a shaman for her reluctance to gather fruit in the severe summer heat (E. Moser 1973:137).

We noted earlier that Seri shamans said they did not suck the illness from a body, though their techniques might be so interpreted by a casual observer. The cupping of the hands over the afflicted part accompanied by a "cho cho," "zop zop," or something of the kind seems to have been standard. In addition, a shaman might tattoo or paint a cross on a part of the body in constant pain (E. Moser and White 1968:145). At least one shaman healed by painting sacred designs on a shallow bowl and dancing on the inverted bowl in the presence of the sick person while singing healing songs (Bowen 1968:111).

The Seri thought the human soul was all through the body and nearly the same as blood. The soul was lost when the blood drained from the body. The Seri also believed spirits could indwell or be associated with almost anything. Some societies are explicit in their belief that all things have souls, though it may not be appropriate to refer to the Seri indwelling spirits as souls. The senita cacus, for example, was believed to have a very powerful spirit. It hovered around the cactus like a vapor and could be called on by a Seri for certain kinds of help. Seri could place a curse on someone by cutting a small hole in the south side of a senita stem and placing some of an enemy's hair or a piece of cloth impregnated with the victim's sweat or saliva in the hole. There were also things people could do to counteract such a curse. Seri sometimes avoided the senita because it could hear conversations (Felger and M. Moser 1974:273).

Spirits were also associated with the making of baskets. According to one Seri myth, a shaman learned how to make baskets through his visions, which included a warning that making baskets was dangerous (Burckhalter 1982:40). The basketry spirit was described as a tiny, fat, large-faced old female. When someone made a large ceremonial basket, the spirit could be heard wailing in the screeching sound of the bone awl as it was pushed through the torote splints. It had to be pacified by a fiesta to remove the danger. At night it might enter sleepers and make them weak. Its contamination could be passed on to other things, too, so the Seri usually washed their hands first thing each morning. Finished baskets were not especially dangerous, but they still retained a tinge of evil that required respect. Accordingly, the Seri were careful not to mistreat or destroy baskets.

Magic is the performance of a procedure that compels the supernatural to produce a certain result. The power is primarily or exclusively in the procedure. It has been said that the Seri had no magic, but they actually had a number of magical practices. When Kroeber was among the Seri one man wore a carrizo tube of magical white powder. When he placed the powder in fresh water there would be dew, but if he placed it in salt water rain would come. Causing an enemy to die by placing a strand of his hair in a hole in a senita cactus was also a magical act. To obtain luck a Seri might paint a cross on the forehead, breast, and his or her sleeping place before going to sleep. The dreams would then reveal future happenings, though the Seri also believed that some dreams lied.

All religions include sacred accounts that people hold with varying degrees of intensity and which may or may not be manifested in their daily behavior and ritual life. McGee reported that the "Ancient of Pelicans" was the main creative deity of the Seri, but Kroeber doubted that this god was much more than a story character. Others have indicated that Coyote was an important mythological figure. McGee also referred to a "beast god," who was represented by a hunted animal and whose power had to be overcome during the hunt. This sounds like the idea, found in many cultures, that game animals have "owners" whose permission must be gained if the animal is to be hunted successfully and without bringing some kind of misfortune on the hunter.

Most societies believe in a number of mythological figures who are held to have taught the people various things and originated many of their customs. They have been called culture bringers or *culture heroes*. One Seri deity sent a fly down to show people how to make fire. He rubbed a stick between his hands to make a smoke signal and call other flies to feast on a dead thing he had found (E. Davis 1965:200). The Seri told Griffen of various beings who had lived among them and taught them much of what they needed to know. Two of these god-like beings were said to have ascended to the sun, where they remained permanently (Griffen 1959:18). The Seri also believed that giants once lived in their country and had a number of stories about them. According to one, the giants made the first of the

clay figurines the Seri once produced (E. Moser and White 1968:147). Most of the giants died in a game they played with one another, since the winners were privileged to kill the losers. But some of the survivors married Seri, and others went to Baja California. Coyote Iguana, a man known to the Seri, acquired for some a semi-mythological aura and was believed by a few to have taught the Seri various things. Griffen's information leaves the impression that the concept of supernaturalistic teachers or culture heroes has been an especially important aspect of Seri mythology.

Cultural Change

Many changes have overtaken the Seri, though they have continued into the second half of the twentieth century a lifeway that was relatively well integrated and clearly distinguishable from Mexican national culture. They adopted some Mexican and Christian protestant customs along the way, abandoned many of their aboriginal customs, and continued to believe and behave in many ways that reflected their pre-contact culture. The most complete description of recent Seri life is Griffen's account of the mid 1950s culture, but this is an uncertain base for knowing the culture of the 1980s. And with the tendency for many tribal groups to take greater pride than before in their cultural past, it is even possible that largely abandoned but remembered customs have been revived. Cultures are always changing, even in the rare instances when they are not in contact with another culture. In fact, a culture may correctly be assumed to have changed between the time an anthropologist begins his study of it and the day of his or her departure a year or more later.

When the Mexicans finally left the few surviving Seri alone, the stage was set for their comeback. During the 1930s there was a great demand for shark liver oil based on a greatly expanding world market for vitamins. So the Seri abandoned their balsas, made boats of wooden planks, fished for sharks, and sold the livers to Mexican middlemen. They took other kinds of fish, too, and in 1938 the Mexicans formed a fish cooperative to receive Seri sea products. Although this eventually failed, the main occupation of the men became fishing, and they sold their catches to the fish merchants from whom they received food and other items. The Seri continued to fish after the development of synthetic vitamins ended most of the demand for shark liver oil. They had learned valuable lessons in how to utilize economic opportunities. The Mexicans wanted the fish and provided outboard motors and other equipment to help the Seri catch more.

During the 1950s the American Friends Service Committee established a rural school in Desemboque and an agricultural mission, and a Mexican protestant evangelist arrived. A number of Seri learned to read and do arithmetic, and they became fully aware of the importance of these and other skills in dealing effectively with the outside world. The American Friends Service Committee taught both agricultural and medical knowledge, and some of the Seri responded to the evangelist's work. He persuaded a number to cut their hair, abandon the old Seri songs in favor of hymns and popular Mexican folk music, avoid the use of tobacco, alcohol, and marijuana, and stop painting their faces. Some of the Seri who initially accepted these changes returned to some of their old ways later.

During the 1940s the Seri became known to the outside world for their well-crafted baskets, and basket buyers began to appear in Seri camps. A number of women responded by producing intentionally for the outside market, and they developed a variety of new basketry shapes and designs. In the early 1970s missionary-linguist Edward Moser of the Wycliffe Bible Translators/Summer Institute of Linguistics identified seven types of newly developed kinds of coiled baskets and basketry plaques the Seri were making specifically for tourist trade (1973:121-122). Eight traditional basket styles were still being made. In 1982 Burckhalter reported that a number of Seri women were still crafting baskets, though some had stopped years before to help with the making of ironwood carvings for the tourist market.

In earlier times the Seri made oars, musical rasps, spear points, clubs, and other utilitarian items from green ironwood, and some of the shamans made wooden images of spirits. In the 1930s visitors purchased some ironwood musical rasps. Then in 1961 Seri José Astorga of Desemboque made an attractive ironwood paperweight for a Tucson resident who had been visiting the settlement for several years. He continued his carving, making bowls, spoons, hair barrettes, and other items. In 1964 he carved a turtle and, then, a porpoise. Another American encouraged him to carve all kinds of sea life, which he did. Eventually Astorga's daughters and other Seri began to carve ironwood figures of the life forms of the Seri habitat. Whole Seri families became involved in carving large numbers of items from weathered ironwood for tourists and for export. Many turned from fishing and basketry to practice the new occupation (Johnston 1968:164).

With the money from fishing, basketry, and ironwood carving the Seri were able to acquire pickups, radios, and other products they desired from industrial society. A pattern was set that enabled them to take advantage of economic opportunities, even should the carving industry decline due to the depletion of ironwood supplies.

By the 1980s the number of Seri had increased to around 500, most of them living in Desemboque and Punta Chueca. Some moved to other spots for short periods, primarily to take advantage of fishing opportunities. Some of the older people continued with customs described by Griffen for the 1950s, while many of the younger people were strongly oriented toward Mexican national culture.

Some of the men still wore their hair long, and some of the women still painted their faces on occasion. The men have long worn various combinations of clothing, including factory-made shirts and trousers. They either went barefooted or wore sandals, shoes, or western boots. Most wore the ubiquitous Mexican palm straw, cowboy style hats, and some had a cloth kilt around the waist over their trousers. Photographer David Burckhalter published a picture of a Seri man at a store counter in plaid shirt, trousers, kilt, long braided hair, a manufactured straw hat, and no footwear (1976:42). It was only one of the possible combinations. The women usually wore blouses, ankle length skirts, and shawls and either went barefooted or wore sandals. Their clothing was variously patterned and colored. Some added sweaters, and some women were wearing modern style dresses.

The shelters in which the Seri of the 1970s and 1980s slept, lounged, and worked were even more variable than their clothing. They had tar paper shacks, rectangular adobe houses with flat roofs, *ramadas* (open-sided, flat-roofed shelters) of various materials and, even, an occasional ocotillo framework house of the old type. The work and lounging areas outside their dwellings, under their ramadas, and in their houses were cluttered with pots, cans, buckets, kettles, barrels, pop bottles, saws and other tools, old auto seats, toys, carvings, clothes, dogs and cats, chickens, boxes, and the variety of other items they substituted for their aboriginal objects. All this struck outsiders as a messy jumble, but it represented what the Seri found functional in their modern lifeway.

Many of the traditional nonmaterial aspects of the culture were continuing to die out, but it is significant that the features of the social personality and basic attitudes toward life and people are often more persistent than material lifeways and sociopolitical mechanisms and structures. The Seri had to be adaptable in aboriginal times to take best advantage of the variety of types of food resources, and they remained flexible and innovative into the final quarter of the twentieth century. They were aggressive during early contacts and remained so (Johnston 1968:155), especially in dealing with strangers. The Seri also changed extensively in social and religious areas while retaining many of the attitudes that were either survivals of aboriginal times or, if not, distinctively Seri rather than borrowed from Mexicans and Americans.

Chapter 4

THE JONAZ OF NORTHEASTERN MEXICO

The Jonaz (approx. hoh-NAHS) and other gatherer-hunters of northern Mexico have often been called Chichimec (approx. CHEE-chee-mehk), but writers have used the word so many ways they have come close to rendering it useless. The Drivers (Driver and Driver 1963:4-5) have recorded its use for (1) all the hunting and gathering groups of northeast Mexico as opposed to the horticultural Mexican Indians, (2) all Mesoamerican peoples descended from or influenced by the northern gatherer-hunters, (3) Indian groups influenced or invaded by northern peoples following the fall of the Toltec empire in the thirteenth century A. D. (4) thirteenth century invaders of the Valley of Mexico (where Mexico City is now) under the leadership of the chieftain Xolotl, (5) the gatherer-hunters of northeastern Mexico that the Spanish fought during the second half of the sixteenth century and, finally, (6) the Jonaz-speaking Indians who took up a settled life at the "Misión de los Chichimecas" just outside the town of San Luis de la Paz in Guanajuato state. Here we use the term, approximately in the first sense, to refer to the gatherer-hunters of northeastern and north central Mexico and adjacent parts of the United States.

Various Chichimec (Chichimeca in Spanish) groups invaded the civilized regions of Mesoamerica from time to time, in some cases adopting the sedentary lifeway and civilization of the people they attacked or conquered. The Spanish eventually subdued others and forced them into settled lifeways that came to combine pre-Spanish with Mexican customs. We give our attention to the Jonaz Chichimec because the Drivers have written an ethnography on the San Luis de la Paz Jonaz which includes a useful review of the information available on the pre-Spanish Chichimeca of Querétaro and Guanajuato.

No one knows how many Jonaz there were in aboriginal times, since they were first identified as a distinct group in the eighteenth century. When the Drivers studied the culture of the Jonaz at the Misión de los Chichimecas in 1955 and 1956, there were about 800, but there is no way of knowing whether there were more or less than this before the Spanish came. There were probably more.

An outsider entering Jonaz territory in 1500 A.D. would have found the people living in small groups, either families or bands, and moving from place to place periodically as necessary to gain better access to the plants and small animal life they collected and the deer and other game they hunted. Most of the time they wore little or no clothing, and their only dwellings were probably caves or rock shelters supplemented by the warmth of their fires.

The Jonaz were exclusively bilateral, which means they had no common ancestor groups such as clans or lineages. They had no formal political arrangements, though occasional charismatic individuals undoubtedly exercised more informal influence than others in their families and bands. The Jonaz were effective warriors and fought groups belonging to other tribes, taking scalps and, sometimes, torturing captives and mutilating the corpses of their enemies. Certain animals and trees were of religious significance to them, and perhaps the sun was a supernatural. Shamans were undoubtedly significant religious functionaries.

Ethnohistory and Ethnography

In many cases around the world Christian missionaries have lived in nonliterate societies for extended periods and have provided excellent and sometimes voluminous descriptions of the aboriginal cultures. There is nothing like this for the Jonaz, largely because of the near impossibility of establishing fully functioning, long term mission stations among groups so hostile. The Jonaz were not only among the more hostile Chichimec, but they also occupied a mountainous area, the Sierra Gorda region of the Sierra Madre Oriental mountain system of eastern Mexico. The best available descriptions of Chichimec customs are those of missionaries and others who traveled through Chichimec country and the reports of sixteenth century scholars who received their information from the Aztecs and other educated Indian informants. The Aztecs and other Mesoamerican Indians gained knowledge of Chichimec cultures as they attempted to civilize them (Kirchoff 1966:275).

Most of the information about Chichimec tribes is found in several works of first importance to anyone interested in the pre-Conquest Indians of Mexico. The Franciscan Friar

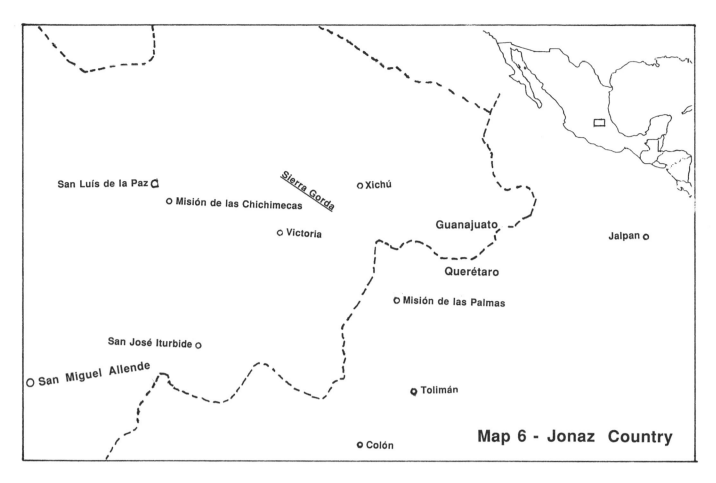

Map 6 - Jonaz Country

Toribio de Motolinía wrote of the Chichimeca in his *History of the Indians of New Spain*, written between 1536 and 1541 (Foster 1950). His observations were based in part on the reports of friars who had visited Chichimeca groups.

The famous Roman Catholic friar Bernardino de Sahagún mastered Náhuatl, the language of the Aztecs, and collected field data by methods in some respects like those of modern ethnographers. His monumental *General History of the Things of New Spain* was written between 1558 and 1569 and includes data on Chichimec cultures that he obtained from his Aztec informants. Sahagún's work is undoubtedly the major source of information on Aztec culture.

Fernando de Alva Ixtlilxóchitl was an educated descendent of Aztec royalty who produced several scholarly works, including *Historia Chichimeca*. He drew on pre-Conquest manuscripts, the traditions of his own family, and orally transmitted Aztec legends. He also interviewed a number of aged informants about how things were in their youth. Ixtlilxóchitl was born about 1577, and his work was completed by 1616 (Driver and Driver 1963:9).

Many scholars have drawn on the work of the friar Juan de Torquemada, who traveled extensively through Chichimec country and provided first hand information on them in his *Monarchia Indiana*, published in 1615.

There was open warfare between the Chichimec tribes and the Spaniards during the last several decades of the sixteenth century, and in 1574 the legal counselor Gonzalo de Las Casas wrote *The War of the Chichimecas*, which contains the most detailed available description of the Chic-

himec cultures in that part of Mexico at that time. There are several other information sources, including the work of Indian scholars Don Domingo de San Anton Muñon Chimalpahín Quauhtlehuanitzín and Diego Munóz Camargo.

The Drivers have summarized sixteenth century Chichimec traits by drawing on the work of Motolinía, Sahagún, Ixtlilxóchitl, and Las Casas as well as the recent syntheses of anthropologist Paul Kirchoff (1943) and historian Philip Powell (1952). The following summary of Jonaz culture was constructed on the basis of Driver and Driver's summary and translations with further reference works from which they tabulated their information. The summary must be understood as a constructed depiction of a lifeway that was probably very much like that of the sixteenth century Jonaz, but it is derived from descriptions of customs some of which may not have been a part of Jonaz culture. No one has left a definitive ethnography of early Jonaz culture, so we must depend on what few references to Jonaz there are plus information on cultures understood to be closely similar to the Jonaz lifeway.

Jonaz Country

During the early sixteenth century most observers seemed unaware of the Jonaz as a cultural-linguistic unit distinct from the Pame and other neighbors. But in later times they were known as a group especially difficult to conquer because they lived mainly in the rugged Sierra Gorda region of the Sierra Madre Oriental. The highest peaks of the Sierra Gorda approach 10,000 feet above sea level, and the ranges are interlaced with long, deep valleys. The area is characterized by some of the most spectacular changes of elevation within a short distance found anywhere in Middle America. A number of important rivers run through the mountains, and there are quite a number of high waterfalls. The Jonaz were far more hostile and warlike than their culturally similar neighbors, the Pame, and their hostility combined with ruggedness of their homeland in the mountains of northern Querétaro and northeastern Guanajuato enabled some bands to hold out against Spanish efforts to missionize and subdue them until the middle of the eighteenth century.

The Jonaz had both the mountains and the neighboring Chihuahuan desert country available to them. Wild plant resources included the *agave* (*maguey* or century plant), various cacti of the *opuntia* genus (e.g. prickly pear and cholla), barrel cacti, organ pipe cactus, Joshua trees, live oaks, pepper trees, amaranth, and many others. For Pame territory Basauri (vol. 3, 1940:365-66) listed, in addition to the above, acacia trees, the aloe. coconut palms, wild figs, various kinds of pines, the soap root plant, mangrove trees, sweet majorum, and wild plum.

Among the animal forms in the area were jaguars, cougars, bears, coyotes, foxes, badgers, skunks, porcupines, armadillos, rats and mice, ground squirrels, jack rabbits, cottontails, opossums, bats, ferrets, deer, and peccaries. Basauri lists about 175 different kinds of birds, including eagles, several kinds of hawks, turkey vultures, pin-tail grouse, nightingale thrushes, various kinds of ducks and geese, herons, great horned owls and other kinds of owls, cactus wrens, red-winged blackbirds, kingfishers, flickers and other kinds of woodpeckers, magnificent hummingbirds, blue-hooded euphoneas, and many more. It is apparent that the Sierra Gorda and nearby desert afforded a variety of wild plants and animals.

Language

Most of the Jonaz aboriginal culture has long been gone, for unlike the Seri they became farmers, with all the major changes entailed. But like the Seri and in contrast to the Cochimí the Jonaz survived into the latter twentieth century as a people. They were still using their native language when the Drivers were with them in the 1950s, though they knew Spanish, too.

Linguists have assigned the Jonaz language to the Otomian family of the Oto-Manguean language phylum. Oto-Manguean is the only Middle American phylum not represented outside Mexico and Central America. The other Oto-Manguean families and languages are concentrated well to the south of the Jonaz, and Pame and Jonaz are the only Chichimec groups speaking an Oto-Manguean language. Linguistically, then, the Pame and Jonaz are not allied with their Chichimec neighbors but with such major civilizations as the Zapotec and the Mixtec of southern Mexico.

These and other Oto-Manguean civilizations of Mexico were agricultural when the Spanish arrived.

Balanced descriptions of a language's characteristics would be too involved for brief cultural descriptions like this one, so it is enough to illustrate from available data how languages differ from one another as aspects of their cultures. A society's linguistic habits include the sounds they use, how they combine the sounds to form words, and the ways they build phrases and sentences. And these are learned and socially standardized as surely as technological, social, religious and other customs.

A Jonaz learned, for example, to change pitch levels within a word to change its meaning (Angulo 1932:153). Although some languages have more, Jonaz used basically two tone levels, high (´) and low (`), with a middle pitch Angulo intepreted as transitional to the other tone levels in words of more than two syllables. Whether or not one of the two tones was used and which one could determine the meanings of words that sounded identical in other respects. A male Jonaz, for example, would refer to his sister as /mánthü/ but refer to a female cousin as /mànthü/ (Angulo 1932:158, Driver and Driver 1963:150). The Jonaz also changed the meanings of utterances by nasalizing sounds, that is, by allowing the flow of air to pass through the nasal passages rather than confining it to the throat and mouth. Languages differ in some of the sounds they use as well as how they use them. Jonaz, for example, included whispered or voiceless vowels while English uses only voiced vowels. Again, the ability to use pitch, nasalization and similar modifications to change meaning is not genetically transmitted. Any normally developing child of any human group could learn these phonetic habits.

Of course, Jonaz differs grammatically from English. English has only two numbers—one or more than one. But the Jonaz use one grammatical form for one, a second for two, and a third for more than two. A Jonaz woman referring to one of her sisters would use /nàhí/; if she mentioned two sisters she would say /nàhís/; and if she was talking about more than two she would use the form /nàhín/. Also, while English uses pronouns to indicate person, Jonaz includes the information in a single noun-word (Angulo 1932:155). For example, /nàmá/ means "my hat," /úngwà/ "your hat," and /ùmá/ "his hat." There are many other grammatical differences between Jonaz and other languages, of course, and all of its characteristics must be learned by the speakers by imitating their elders and peers. Many of the Indian languages of Mexico and Central America have been modified extensively, some would say corrupted, by Spanish. But Angulo reported that as late as 1930 the Jonaz language was "pure." This was in spite of the fact that most of the Jonaz knew Spanish.

Personality and Behavior

Several pieces of research indicate that gathering-hunting societies train their children to be self-reliant, independent, assertive achievers, forming in them personalities especially qualified for success in wresting wild foods from their habitat (Barry, Child and Bacon 1956:51-63). The Chichimec tribes had a reputation for ferocity and intractability, but the Jonaz were especially independent. Their northern neighbors, the Pame, were less difficult. The legal counsel to the Spanish forces trying to pacify the Chichimec considered the Jonaz to be the very worst and most barbarous in all of New Spain (Driver and Driver 1963:44). Though the Spanish subdued the Aztecs in a few years, it took them centuries to pacify the Jonaz. Sometimes they were temporarily successful in getting a few to settle and be baptized, but other Chichimec would attack the missions, and the settled Indians would return to their old lifeway. Even in the most successful settlement efforts there were cases of Indians hanging themselves rather than enduring their new state, and over time many fled to the mountains to rejoin their nomadic colleagues. During the middle of the eighteenth century the Jonaz began to be mentioned frequently in Spanish documents. The military undertook a concentrated effort to conquer them and succeeded in destroying their main fighting forces. Even so, survivors harassed the Spanish for a while longer.

One should not conclude from this that the Jonaz were especially hostile or violent with one another. Small, isolated societies commonly suspect and despise outsiders and respond violently if pressed unmercifully. Torture and taking trophies such as scalps were part of Chichimec warfare, and their reaction to Spanish attempts to change them could be expected to be violent. But around the world many groups violent to outsiders are peaceful among themselves. Impartial outsiders have never recorded how the aboriginal Jonaz behaved toward one another.

Clothing and Personal Appearance

When the Spanish missionaries encountered people with little or no clothing, they characteristically commented on it at length. Both the missionaries and the soldiers were especially impressed that the Chichimec warriors stripped off anything they might be wearing and fought in the nude when they went into battle. Some said they did this to disconcert their opponents, which it apparently did. But it is not clear whether or not anyone learned the purpose of this from the Chichimec themselves. The custom is found in some other tribal groups, too. It seems the Chichimec men may have gone completely without clothing before 1600 unless it was too cold, and women simply covered the genitals or wore aprons in front and back. There is no way to know which of various observations about Chichimec clothing applied to the Jonaz. Also, by the time those who left written reports saw the Chichimec of the Sierra Gorda the Spanish had succeeded in getting many of them to wear more than they had before. Some also may have worn less when there were no outsiders around. This has been the case in many societies.

Both men and women wore hide clothing at one time or another for warmth and possibly other reasons. Motolinía commented that they wore items made of deer hides, rabbit furs, and snake skins during cold weather (Driver and Driver 1963:6), and Ixtlilxóchitl stated that they wore hides with the hair inside, though they turned the hair side out when it rained.

The Chichimec were probably barefooted much of the time, though some writers have mentioned sandals of hide or palm leaves. In many parts of the world people wear something on their feet only when on an especially long trek. The Chichimec may have taken to using sandals more often as the result of contact with civilized tribes and with the Spanish.

Chichimec men and women wore their hair long and either loose or braided. Some say they never cut it, but Ixtlilxóchitl mentions cutting it in front. If some groups did cut their hair it is impossible to know whether or not they did so before the Spanish came. We can safely assume the Jonaz wore their hair long, but we cannot be sure what else they did with it. Feather headdresses and "bonnets" have been mentioned, though these may have been worn only on special occasions.

Kirchoff indicated the people made some use of ornamental objects such as earrings and collars (Powell 1952:40), but the lack of information leaves the impression that the Chichimec may have been less ornamented than many groups. However, they shared with the Seri and some other northern Mexican tribes the painting of designs of various kinds on their bodies. The Guachichil dyed or painted their hair and other parts of their bodies red, probably with red ocher (Powell 1952:40), and they used other colors as well. Powell mentions a description of Chichimec being sold into slavery having designs on their faces and foreheads (1952:252). Some observers have also reported tattooing for some tribes. Although recent Jonaz informants remembered that their ancestors painted their faces, they knew little or nothing about the designs and colors. It may have been possible to identify different Chichimec groups by their distinctive painted designs and tattoos.

Houses

The Jonaz probably had little or nothing in the way of constructed shelters. Some observers said they lived only in caves and rock shelters or in the open, but it is clear that some lived in thatched huts at least part of the year. In the Sierra Gorda mountains it was easy for the Jonaz to find caves and rock shelters, so they probably used them a good deal. But they probably knew about thatched huts among their agricultural Mesoamerican neighbors and may have used them occasionally. If they never used huts they were one of the very few groups in the world to go completely without constructed shelters.

Livelihood

Like other Chichimec groups the Jonaz depended completely on wild sources for food. There is no way of knowing whether plants or animals were more important, though fishing was probably far less significant than either. Plants are more important than animals among many gatherer-hunters, including many of the desert and semi-desert peoples of the United States and northern Mexico. If investigators had been able to study Jonaz foodgetting they undoubtedly would have found them intimately familiar with Sierra Gorda life forms, just as gatherer-hunters are in all habitats.

The prickly pear and other cacti constituted a major food source. The Jonaz and other Chichimec used the fruits, known as tunas, that formed along the edges of the thick, flat, oval leaves or joints that make up the prickly pear. They ate the fruits fresh or dried them for later use, and sometimes they made wine from them. The people also ate the joints or leaves themselves, often after cooking them in an underground oven. Sometimes, probably, they chopped them into pieces and combined them with other items. The prickly pear is the only cactus mentioned specifically, but the people undoubtedly ate others, too. Driver and Driver listed nine cactus species used by the modern Jonaz (1963:58-9). However, there are no *saguaro* or *cardón,* the giant columnar cacti, in this part of Mexico. Cacti exist in greater variety and abundance in the Sonoran desert of western Mexico than here.

The mesquite tree (*Prosopis sp.*) was also of basic importance to the Jonaz and other Chichimec. The people picked the bean pods, dried them in the sun, pulverized them in a mortar (probably of wood), and used the flour to make large loaves of bread.

Like other northern Mexican indigenes the Jonaz used the agave (maguey or century plant, *Agave sp.*) extensively for its leaves and heart (the base of the center stalk) and as a beverage source. They prepared a hole a yard or so deep, built a fire in the pit to heat stones, covered the hot stones with agave leaves, put a number of hearts on them, and covered them with more agave leaves and a heap of earth. The hearts were ready after about 24 hours.

When an agave was ready to send up its tall flower shoot, the Jonaz would cut out the heart and allow the sap to fill the resulting hole. They often drank this nutritious juice in place of water during dry periods or when no unpolluted water was available. The juice would continue to collect for several months and could be removed daily. The Jonaz also drank fermented agave juice, known in modern Mexico as *pulque.* It has about the same alcoholic strength as beer.

While the Jonaz probably relied most heavily on cacti, mesquite, and agave, they also used a variety of other plant foods. They collected several kinds of roots and herbs and used the fruit of the Joshua tree (*Yucca brevifolia*) and possibly the pepper tree (*Schinus molle*). They undoubtedly used the fruit, flowers, leaves, and other parts of various wild plants not mentioned here, but no one has left a detailed description of sixteenth century Jonaz ethnobotany.

The Jonaz apparently obtained much of their food by hunting, trapping, and collecting wild animals, though there is no way of knowing whether wild game was as important as plants. Sixteenth century sources mention the hunting of deer, hare, rabbits, birds, rats, snakes, and various other small forms. Some of the Drivers' informants remembered being told a good deal about hunting by their elders, since hunting continued to be of considerable importance for at least two centuries beyond the Conquest. The twentieth century Jonaz have taken jaguar, cougars, foxes, badgers, skunks, porcupines, armadillos. opossums, ducks, turkeys, and tortoises for food.

The bow and arrow was the main hunting weapon. The Jonaz made powerful bows and were excellent archers. According to Las Casas they were adept at shooting running rabbits (Driver and Driver 1963:17). They made the bows and arrows from quince wood (*Cydonia vulgaris*). Each bow was about a meter long and was not backed with sinew or other material. The string was of plant fiber. The arrowheads were of obsidian or some other brittle stone and were bound to the arrow shaft with animal sinews or, according to Las Casas, sinews from human war victims. Sometimes the Jonaz simply pointed and hardened an arrow shaft by charring it in a fire. Some hunting groups have relied heavily on poisoned arrows to kill large game and sometimes used relatively weak bows, but not the Jonaz. Their bows were said to be powerful enough to drive arrows through several thicknesses of hide or other materials. They used the bow and arrow for small quarry, too, such as rabbits, ducks, and fish.

It may be that the aboriginal Jonaz had lances, slings, and blowguns. One sixteenth century source, Ixtlilxóchitl, reported the blow gun, and the Drivers' Jonaz informants mentioned slings and lances. Paul Kirchoff, however, found no evidence of lances for the sixteenth century. Either no one reported them for immediate post-Conquest days, or the Chichimec tribes did not use them until somewhat later. The people used traps such as snares and deadfalls to take some animals.

Apparently, the Jonaz and other Chichimec were very fond of meat, which they ate either raw or partially or fully roasted (Driver and Driver 1963:20; Powell 1952:41). They also may have eaten the flesh of certain forms to make desired characteristics of the animals their own. Apparently, they did not boil food. They probably sun dried some meat. In many hunting groups meat sharing is important, and Las Casas indicated that a Chichimec hunter distributed all of the meat among his people, keeping only the hide. Of course, he and his family received meat from other successful hunters, and the people hunted daily. Food sharing, it should be noted, does not always indicate shared ownership. This depends on how people conceptualize it, but around the world sharing is commonly a matter of transfer of individual ownership by gift rather than shared ownership.

Fishing may have been more important to the Jonaz than to some other Chichimec, since the Sierra Gorda was interlaced by rivers and smaller streams. The twentieth century Jonaz of San Luis de la Paz had no place to take fish, but fish were abundant in the mountain streams. The idea that tribal people use every edible resource available is incorrect, but Chichimec groups generally caught and ate fish where they were available.

Crafts, Tools, and Techniques

Like other societies frequently on the move the Jonaz made very few items of much size or weight. They worked hides to cover themselves in cold weather, so they must have had tools such as scrapers, fleshers, and awls. They probably had carrying bags or nets handwoven from fiber from the thick, fibrous leaves of the agave, and they also may have had coiled or twined baskets tight enough to hold water. Some desert groups have removed the flesh and one surface of the thick, oval joints of the prickly pear or *nopal*, which leaves the opposite surface as the bottom of the resulting shallow pan and the edges of the thick joint as its sides. Such a tray or pan could be used to hold food, liquids, or small objects. We do not know for sure that the Jonaz had these, but if someone had prepared a good description of their technology it undoubtedly would have taken note of a variety of useful things of this kind. Studies of the technologies of gathering-hunting societies in all parts of the world have revealed that even the simplest technologies include a number of ingenious items.

Social Organization and Relationships

Monogamy is the prevailing marital combination in nearly all societies. For *polygyny* (one husband with more than one wife) or *polyandry* (one wife with more than one husband) to prevail there either has to be a great shortage of one sex or a large proportion of one sex remaining unmarried. In highly polygynous societies, of course, the majority of men and women may be involved in multiple spouse arrangements, even while most of the combinations are monogamous. But like many other gathering-hunting groups the Jonaz were entirely monogamous or almost so. Also, the prevailing family arrangement was the independent nuclear unit of husband and wife with children.

The Jonaz seem to have obtained their spouses from either within the band or from another band. If bride and groom were from different band communities, they apparently most often resided in the woman's group. If the Jonaz were like other Chichimec, their marriages were usually negotiated by relatives. In some tribes a young man presented a deer to his bride's parents. It has been reported that adultery was rare and severely punished in Chichimec tribes and that wives divorced their husbands rather than vice versa. But it has also been said that wives were rather free sexually. There is no way to be sure about this and other Jonaz marital practices.

The Jonaz were exclusively *bilateral*, which means the people reckoned descent through both males and females, and each child was probably considered as closely related to one parent as the other. Accordingly, there were were no unilineal common ancestor groups, no lineages or clans. The usual kinship unit in bilateral societies is the *kindred*. The membership of a given kindred is usually defined as all of an individual's relatives on both sides of the family to some specified degree of remoteness. With lineages and clans the group's composition does not depend on which member one begins with first in tracing the membership, since each person belongs to only one common ancestor group of a given kind. But the composition of a kindred differs according to which person one begins with in tracing membership, and a given person belongs to several other person's kindreds as well as his or her own. The Jonaz may have had kindreds which regulated marriage, since it has been reported that a Chichimec was supposed to marry a non-relative—someone not in his or her own kindred.

The Jonaz were probably without clubs or associations, which would be based on concerns other than kinship. If so, they were like most other gatherer-hunters, since associations are more characteristic of agricultural and industrial cultures. Anthropologists have found no evidence of associations in any gathering-hunting culture of northern Mexico (Driver 1961:407).

The groups of Jonaz that moved from place to place to take advantage of the varying resources of the area were of various sizes. Probably, independent nuclear families camped by themselves much of the time, but at other times two or more might remain together to form a small band. Nomadic bands of this kind are characteristic of gathering-hunting groups. Since Chichimec marriages tended to be *matrilocal*, a band probably included men who had left their natal bands to take up residence in the nomadic community of the wife, her parents, her sisters and families, and other related females with their spouses and children.

By modern standards Jonaz women had a rough time in childbirth. Las Casas says they often had to give birth while the group was on the move, doing their best to keep up even when the placenta was still attached and there was still bleeding (Driver and Driver 1963:17). Sahagún reported that the husband assisted his wife by applying heat to her back and throwing water on her. After the birth he reportedly kicked or struck her on the back to help stop the bleeding. Las Casas indicated that a newborn infant was either bathed in water, if available, or cleaned with herbs. Sahagún claimed that Chichimec babies were carried in baskets on the back, while las Casas asserted that the people had no cradles. Since the Chichimec made fiber bags, these may be the "baskets" Sahagún referred to.

Sahagún said the Jonaz gave boys a bow at one year of age and gradually taught them its use. This would indicate that a man's archery skill resulted from constant living with the bow from early in life so that handling it would become second nature. Sahagún also mentioned that people paired female children—from different families, perhaps—at four or five years of age for them to spend their time together and care for one another (Driver and Driver 1963:9).

The death rate for infants and small children was probably high under the harsh conditions of Jonaz life, but the adults were said to be healthy because of their vigorous lives. A number lived to an old age. When we hear that people in certain societies cannot expect to live more than thirty or forty years, we may conclude erroneously that hardly anyone lives as long as in modern society. But the life expectancy in many groups is lowered by the extremely high death rate during early life, and people who survive childhood and early adulthood may well live a long time. Life expectancy is the average age to which people live, while life span refers to how long people can expect to survive if accident or disease does not take them before they expire from age alone. Life span, then, is commonly much greater than life expectancy, especially in some tribal groups.

Among the Jonaz and other Chichimec a person who remained ill for an extended time became a threat to the group's welfare and might be put to death. Sahagún said this was done by passing an arrow through the throat. The Chichimec also put to death those so enfeebled by age that they had become severe burdens. They viewed this as a compassionate act. Sahagún reported that the people honored the person killed with two or three days of feasting and dancing.

Americans and other Westerners unavoidably react *ethnocentrically* to this. They let their own culture's view of things distort what they see in other cultures. They tend to conclude that putting a sick or aged person to death is cruelty and reveals a low valuation of human life. *Cultural relativism* in its essential meaning is perceiving and understanding alien customs by relating them to the cultural contexts in which they are practiced, and it provides a more accurate knowledge and understanding of what is going on than the ethnocentric approach. Actually, there are a number of cultures in which people view putting to death the seriously ill and extremely decrepit an act of compassion, and victims themselves often favor and ask for their deaths. It is part of the culture.

We can say this without deciding whether it is a good or bad custom. We simply gain a more accurate understanding of the custom's place in the culture and its meaning to the people. We avoid the wrong conclusion that the people are unnaturally cruel, and we see how the deaths of the disabled contribute to group survival by ridding the people of the need to care for them. Whether this is the best way of coping with the problem of survival in such circumstances is a different question, and it does not follow that we must conclude the custom is good just because the people regard it as good and it does something for them. Extermination of Jews by German Nazis fulfilled some of the needs of the latter, but few would use this as a basis for saying the extermination was morally acceptable.

Observers have reported both burial and cremation for the Chichimec. Las Casas mentions that mourners cut their hair and blackened the face or body and that a feast and ceremonial bathing were held at the end of a mourning period. He asserted that they only cremated their dead, and several sources mention keeping a dead person's ashes in a small bag they carried about with them (Driver and Driver 1963:23).

Government and Social Order

The largest political unit among the aboriginal Jonaz was the band community. There was no tribal government and no specialized unit in the band or elsewhere that could be called a government. Political decisions, as in other gathering-hunting groups, were made informally by band members or independent families in the course of their daily interactions with one another. The early literature mentions Chichimec chiefs, but they probably emerged for the first time as families and bands joined under military leadership to repel the Spanish. Before that some bands undoubtedly included individuals who exercised more informal influence than others because of their abilities or charismatic personalities. If most of the people lived in family groups with the bands being temporary assemblages, informal band leaders were of minimal and transient importance. Driver suggests that northeastern Mexico lacked true political organization (1961:329).

With such rudimentary political mechanisms it would be surprising to find the Jonaz putting armies into battle. But they did fight, almost always with people from other tribes. Intergroup fighting usually has relationships to other aspects of a culture. Religious connections can be inferred from the Jonaz habit of ritually consuming the flesh of dead enemies. The Chichimec also took scalps and took them with them as they moved about. They cruelly tortured captives, even removing bones and sinews from the living, and mutilated the corpses of their enemies. They ate and drank from their enemies' skulls and tallied the number killed on a bone (Driver and Driver 1963:23). In addition to their powerful bows they may have used hafted double-edged blades or wooden clubs and javelins for fighting. Las Casas, however, says they used only the bow and arrow.

Art and Play

The Jonaz and other Chichimec had various games and other pastimes. They got drunk, since they made alcoholic beverages from the agave, prickly pear cactus, and mesquite beans. The drinking may have led to violence, since Las Casas stated that the women hid the men's weapons while they drank. They also had someone sober on guard so they would not be attacked unexpectedly while drinking. There is no indication that smoking was part of the culture.

One of their games, referred to as *batey* by las Casas, involved knocking a bouncy ball of tree resin about the ground with the hips. Las Casas also reported games in which they used mesquite beans and arm and leg bones, with the prizes being arrows or hides (Driver and Driver 1963:16). He also mentioned a target game that had ritual significance, since the red juice that flowed from the prickly pear joint pierced by an arrow was taken as a sign of success in war. The people also were said to dance, arms linked, in a circle around a fire at night, with a captive in the center of the circle. As a participant entered the circle to dance he shot an arrow into the captive.

Little is known about Chichimec graphic and plastic arts, though they made beads, ear plugs, and other jewelry of turquoise. There appears to have been little or nothing in the way of religious art.

Religious Beliefs and Practices

Many early observers have supposed that tribal groups, especially those supposed to be very primitive, had no religion, so they failed to record the religious aspects of many long-gone cultures. People inevitably react ethnocentrically to culturally alien societies. That is, their perceptions of other cultures are restricted and distorted by their own culture's way of perceiving and experiencing life. So, the highly ethnocentric early writers were blind to many elements of the tribal cultures they contacted. Actually, anthropologists have found supernaturalistic beliefs and practices in every society studied, and the Jonaz and other Chichimec are no exception.

Several sources indicate that the Chichimec had no religious images, and maybe they did not. But the Seri gatherer-hunters of the west coast of northern Mexico had religious images. The reports also indicate that praying, fasting, sacrifice, and similar modes of supplication were unusual or lacking among the Chichimec. The sun may have been a god to them, since several observers mention sun worship or addressing the sun as a deity. Certain animals and trees also had supernatural significance. There were also ritual bloodletting and ceremonial dances. The people may have believed in evil spirits, since a couple of writers mentioned surrounding a camp with stakes or spines to ward off spirits. Fear of witchcraft was also mentioned.

It is reasonable to conclude that shamanism was significant in Jonaz religion. Divining causes and cures of sickness and healing through special individual ability to draw on supernatural power is found in gathering-hunting cultures everywhere. *Shamans* are people who possess special power to cope with the supernatural, commonly with the aid of a spirit familiar or companion. In some societies almost everyone has acquired some kind of special power, with few having notably more than others. In other places only one or a few have shamanistic abilities.

If one is sick because the soul has left the body, the shaman's efforts may be directed toward recovering the soul. If something alien has gotten into the body, such as an evil spirit or a damaging object or substance sent by a sorcerer or a witch, the shaman has to extract it. In many societies this is done by sucking. The Jonaz of the 1950s believed illness was usually from the intrusion of thorns, commonly sent into the body by witches. These beliefs may be survivals from aboriginal times, but there is no way to be certain. The twentieth century Jonaz also recognized soul loss as a cause of sickness, but they could have gotten this notion from their Mesoamerican neighbors to the south since the Conquest.

Culture Change

The Drivers have reviewed the available sources to piece together a general account of what happened to the Jonaz between their first contact with the Spanish and the 1950s, when the they studied the Jonaz community near San Luis de la Paz. The Spanish pacified most of the Chichimec in the states of Guanajuato and Querétaro by the end of the sixteenth century, but it took them about two-and-one-half centuries more to completely subdue the Jonaz. The Jonaz attack on the town of Zimapán in 1585 prompted the Spanish to launch a "fiery and bloody" war of extermination against the Chichimec tribes (Powell 1952:183). Apparently, this military effort brought groups such as the Pame and Guachichil under control, but the Jonaz were difficult to run down in their Sierra Gorda strongholds. The Spanish would send in a friar or group of friars, often escorted by a military detachment, to establish a settlement. They put up a hut to serve as a church and invited the Indians to attend services. The Jonaz would often be curious enough to come, and some would be converted and settle down. But after weeks or months other Jonaz would attack and destroy the settlement, killing the friars. Many of the Sierra Gorda towns were established twice or more, and the Spanish often had to send in soldiers to make them permanent.

The Jonaz had lived mostly in small nomadic families before the Spanish began harassing them, but they grouped themselves into bands to defend themselves. By about 1748 three large bands of Jonaz were left. One had been subdued and settled at Zimapán, and two others still moved about the Sierra Gorda. In 1748 the Zimapán band revolted, but the Spanish crushed the rebellion and deported the people to Mexico City and Puebla. They used the deportation of especially obstinate Indian groups to other parts of the country in several instances to once-and-for-all remove the nuisance of people who refused to capitulate. As a result, it is hard to tell where among modern Mexican nationals the blood of Jonaz and other Indian ancestors may flow.

Also in 1748, the Spanish fought and put an end to the two remaining nomadic bands. There were a few Jonaz they missed, however, and they continued to harass the Spanish as they had opportunity. Many of those captured committed suicide or took sick and died (Driver and Driver 1963:43). A few years later several small bands of Jonaz capitulated, but the Spanish had Indian rebellions on their hands until the last quarter of the nineteenth century.

The Misión de los Chichimecas at San Luis de la Paz was established in the late 1500s. Speakers of several languages were settled there, but there is no way to be sure that Jonaz were among them. Just who were the ancestors of the 800 or so Jonaz living at the mission in the 1950s we do not know. Some may have been there since the sixteenth century, while others may have gravitated there as nomadic groups were pacified and straggler families decided to join the people at the mission. Jonaz traditions say they were forced to settle and become Christians and San Luis de la Paz was given to them on condition that they become peaceable. But as Spaniards moved into the town over time the Jonaz gradually withdrew to a hill at the east edge of town. Over the centuries they have remained sullen and aloof, and the fact that theirs is the only Chichimec language to remain in use is evidence of their independence and will to survive.

The Jonaz of the mid-twentieth century constituted what anthropologists call a *peasant society*. Peasant societies are economically and politically dependent on the nation within which they are located but remain rural, tradition-oriented, and relatively homogeneous as compared with non-peasant sectors. Some of the customs of the mid-century peasant Jonaz were survivals from aboriginal times, some were Mesoamerican Indian customs borrowed largely from Otomí the Spanish resettled in the valleys of Querétaro and Guanajuato to facilitate pacification, some were vestiges of Spanish colonial culture, and others were of modern origin.

The Jonaz of the 1950s had both domesticated plants and animals and raised corn, beans, wheat, potatoes, chickpeas, and other crops. They still gathered many of the wild plants used in aboriginal days, but about 80 percent of their livelihood came from working on nearby farms and ranches. In fact, the large majority of the people were away from the mission community, living where they worked. They were growing some of their food in small house gardens, where the women cultivated with the aboriginal type of digging stick and the post-Conquest spade. For animals they had cattle, sheep, goats, pigs, donkeys, dogs, chickens, turkeys, and bees, but no horses. The men used guns for hunting rather than the bow and arrow.

The Jonaz no longer used the wooden mortar to pulverize foodstuffs but had the three-legged grinding stones known as *metates* and a few mortars of volcanic stone. The metate's upper surface was slightly concave, and the cigar-shaped hand stone used with it was known as a *mano*. The people baked tortillas on shallow pottery disks known as *comals*, which were placed, concave side up, on three stones. The metate and mano as well as the comal are of Mesoamerican Indian origin. So were various other objects and food preparation procedures. The modern Jonaz boiled some of their foods, though they also used the aboriginal practice of roasting meat on a stick by a fire. A few metal cooking and eating containers and tools were being used.

All the 1950s clothing was post-Conquest, both in material and style. The men wore factory-made shirts and trousers of denim or tan cotton, and most of the women made and wore blouses and long full skirts of calico print cloth they purchased in stores or the market. They also used the Spanish shawl or *rebozo*, which is common throughout Mexico. Both men and women wore sandals made from old tires, though a few had shoes and socks. The women wore their hair long and still pierced their ears. The men, however, had their hair cut and no longer wore earrings.

Many of the Jonaz sleeping houses of the 1950s closely resembled the small, gabled, thatched huts used by pre-Columbian Mesoamerican Indians. The foundations and walls were of unworked stone laid without mortar and were topped by a pole-frame roof thatched with yucca or agave leaves or a mixture of the two. The smallest huts were about eight feet square and the largest about 15 feet long and 12 feet wide (Driver and Driver 1963:68). Another sleeping house was a rectangular adobe structure with a single pitch roof. The roof was of beams and cross-poles covered with earth. The sleeping houses had no windows, and the people used candles for light. The Jonaz had separate cook houses, also a Mesoamerican Indian trait. They were usually gabled, thatched buildings located near the sleeping house or, sometimes, sharing a common wall with a sleeping house. The Jonaz did not use tables, chairs, or beds in their homes.

In post-Conquest times the Jonaz began to make pottery, but by the 1950s they had stopped. Some of the Drivers' informants had seen their elders make pottery. The people processed hides by techniques learned from the Spanish, using oak bark for tanning and the steel knife for removing the hair. They tanned hides of deer, badgers, cattle, sheep, and goats and sold them in San Luis de la Paz. They made no baskets but purchased what they wanted at the San Luis market. A few men wove blankets or made rebozos.

In earlier times Jonaz men built fences in various parts of northern Guanajuato which were walls of unworked stone laid without mortar. They were four or five feet high, about three feet wide at the bottom and two feet wide at the top. These well made fences extended through the countryside for many miles, and the Drivers report they saw no other types of fences in that part of the state. The craft probably declined when most of the fences needed on the farms and ranches had been completed.

During the 1950s, Jonaz men cleared land, plowed and did other heavy agricultural work, cared for the animals, built the houses, cut fire wood, made wooden objects, produced cords and raincoats from agave fiber, and carried the heaviest loads. The women ground corn, made tortillas, carried water, collected cactus fruit, fed and groomed the small children, cooked and cleaned, traded in San Luis, and helped plant the crops. Boys and girls herded the domestic animals.

The independent nuclear family was still important, and monogamy was the marriage arrangement. There was no strict rule about residence, but most married couples lived with or near the husband's parents. This may be a shift from *matrilocal* to *patrilocal* residence since aboriginal times. If the newly married couple lived with the grooms's parents and had children the result was a *patrilocal extended family*, a three generation unit based on patrilocal residence. In earlier times Jonaz parents arranged their youngsters' marriages, but in the 1950s the young people tended to choose their own mates, and the young man would seek the girl's parents' consent. This was followed by an engagement feast and, three weeks later, a wedding in a Catholic church. There was also some elopement and wife capture. Which it was would depend on the girl's degree of willingness. Close relatives, especially first cousins, were not allowed to marry. Adultery was frequent but divorce uncommon.

The mid-century Jonaz participated in the Spanish *compadrazgo*, a system of fictive kinship nearly universal in Indian Mexico. The parents chose a godfather and godmother for each of their children, usually a married couple. The parents and godparents thereby established a special relationship with one another. They were co-parents or *compadres*. The godparents assisted when the child was baptized, took an interest in the child's welfare and development, fulfilled certain obligations at various points in the child's life, and might adopt the child if both parents died. The godchild was expected to show respect for the godparents.

The mission Jonaz used Spanish surnames and given names, but Jonaz given names were still in use. Informants sometimes gave the Drivers a person's Jonaz name when they couldn't remember the Spanish name.

The political organization of the twentieth century Jonaz apparently reflects nothing of their aboriginal ways. The mid-century government was established in 1927 by a representative from the state government of Guanajuato (Driver and Driver 1963:173). There were two commissions of ten persons each, each with its own officers. The Public Lands Commission regulated agricultural activities and handled government agricultural loans. The Council of Supervisors monitored the work of the Public Lands officers to ensure they would do a good job and not mishandle funds. Commissioners were selected by the land owners for three year terms. The land owners arrived at their selections by informal discussion and unanimous agreement rather than by voting.

The Drivers described a number of children's games, none of which they could link with pre-Spanish times. They described mid-century Jonaz music as wholly Spanish but marked by various tonal and rhythmical errors by Spanish-Mexican standards. The mission Jonaz celebrated about 15 fiestas annually, each on a saint's day as in the rest of Mexico. The more elaborate fiestas took place in neighboring Mexican towns, and some of the Jonaz undoubtedly attended some of them.

Mid-century Jonaz religion, according to the ethnographers, was a configuration of aboriginal Chichimec, Mesoamerican Indian, and Spanish elements. The Jonaz continued to hold that disease could be caused by intrusion of thorns, which local healers removed by sucking. They also continued to believe illness could be caused by soul loss, so shamans practiced recovery of the soul. The shamans still worked through familiar spirits, though the twentieth century spirits took the form of cows, bulls, or calves. The Jonaz also believed in female vampires, horse spirits, dwarfs, and the evil eye, all of which are apparently of Spanish origin.

It is impossible to know what is pre-Spanish and what is not in modern Jonaz life cycle customs. The Drivers felt the people had become far more inhibited and negative about sex than before. The Jonaz no longer killed the sick or dying and no longer practiced cremation. Roman Catholic ritual prevailed at death.

The mid-century Jonaz were like many other groups in Indian Mexico. They still spoke an Indian language and were identified as Indians by themselves, by others who thought of themselves as Indians, and by non-Indians. They did not participate fully in Mexican national life, but their pre-Spanish culture was mostly gone. Their twentieth century culture was a configuration of aboriginal, Spanish colonial, and modern elements. Though hardly aboriginal Indian, the culture was Indian as compared with Mexican national culture.

PART II   INDIAN CULTURES OF NORTHWEST MEXICO

Chapter 5

INDIAN TRIBES OF NORTHWEST MEXICO

Together, the gathering-hunting and horticultural Indians of northern Mexico and the American Southwest make up the Greater Southwest culture area. Within Mexico the gathering-hunting cultures were found in north central and northeastern Mexico as well as on the peninsula of Baja California and a portion of the mainland Mexican coast across the Gulf of California. The horticultural Indians of the Northwest Mexico region lay between these two gathering-hunting areas (see map 1).

Horticultural Northwest Mexico includes (1) the Sierra Madre Occidental highlands in the east and (2) the hot lowland coastal area of western Mexico. The Sierra Madre is high and rugged, and its western slopes are gashed by deep canyons carrying the westward-draining rivers. The northern part of the coastal lowlands is arid Sonoran Desert like that of southern Arizona and Baja California, while the southern part is subtropical. The Sierra Madre people lived in small, widely scattered agricultural settlements, relatively isolated from one another by the deep canyons and other rugged topographic features. Much of the desert lowland was uninhabited due to water scarcity, and the desert people established their agricultural villages along river valleys to take advantage of the annual floods.

The Aboriginal Cultures

The Northwest Mexico Indians spoke languages of the Uto-Aztecan phylum, which means their speech was similar to that of most of the Indians of the interior of the western United States and, also, the Aztec of the Valley of Mexico. There were three Uto-Aztecan families in Northwest Mexico. In the south the well-known Huichol, the Cora, and related groups spoke languages of the Aztecoidan family. Also, at the south end of the area the Tepehuán, Tepecan, and related societies used languages of the Piman family; and in the north the Pima, Pápago, Névome and associated groups also spoke Piman languages. The third language family, Taracahitian, included Opata, the Yaqui and Mayo dialects of Cáhita, Tarahumara, and several oth-

ers. There may have been up to 16 Taracahitian languages, and there were more speakers of Taracahitian than either Aztecoidan or Piman languages in this part of Mexico (Spicer 1969:779).

Agriculture was the basic subsistence mode of Northwest Mexico, with maize (Indian corn), beans, and squash being the most important crops. The highland people were dry farmers who used slash-and-burn cultivation. They depended on annual summer rains for water, and the yields were relatively low. So it is not surprising that the highland farmers supplemented their crop foods by a great deal of wild plant gathering and hunting. The Pápago, in fact, obtained more of their food from wild plants than anything else. But, even when most of the food came from nonagricultural sources, the people focused their concerns on growing food. Most of the lowland peoples relied on the flood waters of the several major rivers, which made it possible for them to grow more food than the highlanders. Some of the lowlanders also built dams and irrigation ditches. In spite of the abundance of crop food, the lowlanders gathered large quantities of cactus fruit, mesquite beans, and other desert foods.

The Northwest Mexico Indians engaged in a great deal of planting and rain ritual, first fruits rituals being especially important to them. In many parts of the world the women do most of the farming while the men hunt, make war, govern the society, etc. But the men did the farming in Northwest Mexico, and women assisted them. The women also did most of the wild plant collecting.

Dry-ground, parched maize, called *pinole* in Spanish, was one of the characteristic foods of Northwest Mexico. The people ground the maize on grooved and troughed milling stones. They combined much of the pinole with boiling water to make a gruel, and they also mixed maize flour with water to make a thin drink called *atole*. Their main cooking method was boiling food in pots over a fire. Tortillas were not important in Northwest Mexico, and a number of groups did not make them. Quite a few societies preserved meat by drying it. One North American tribe's word for dried meat was *charqui*, which some say is the origin of the English word, "jerky" (Driver 1961:77).

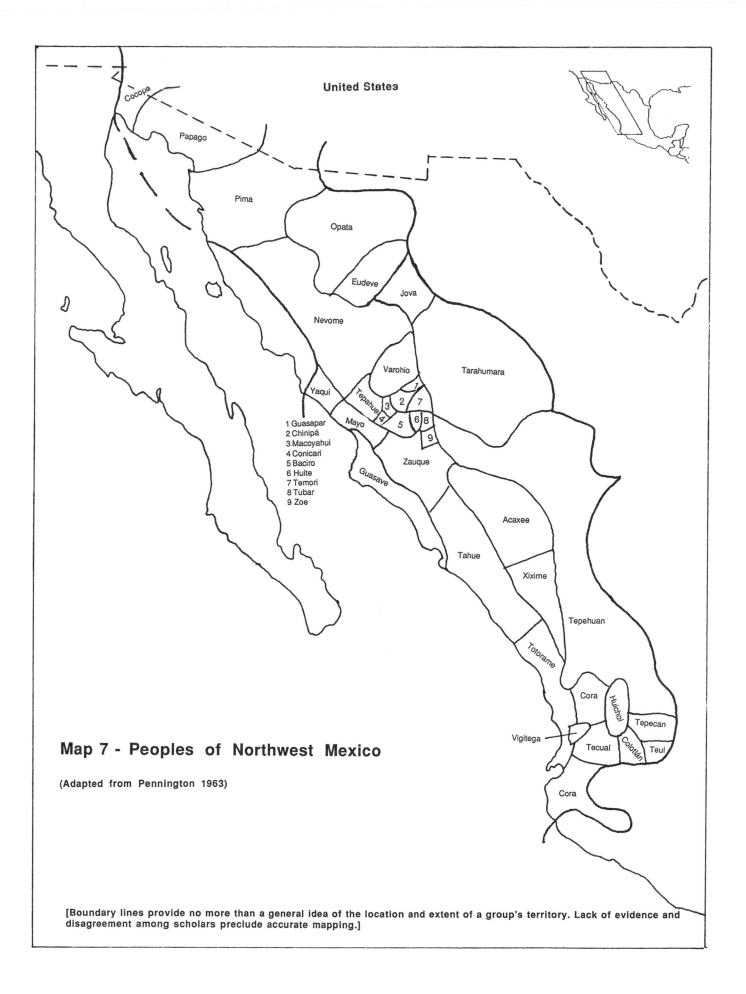

United States

Cocopa

Papago

Pima

Opata

Eudeve

Jova

Nevome

Varohio

Tarahumara

Yaqui

Tepahue

7

3 2 7

4

5 6 8

9

Mayo

1 Guasapar
2 Chinipá
3 Macoyahui
4 Conicari
5 Baciro
6 Huite
7 Temori
8 Tubar
9 Zoe

Guasave

Zauque

Acaxee

Tahue

Xixime

Tepehuan

Totorame

Cora

Huichol

Tepecan

Vigitega

Tecual

Colotlán

Teul

Cora

Map 7 - Peoples of Northwest Mexico

(Adapted from Pennington 1963)

[Boundary lines provide no more than a general idea of the location and extent of a group's territory. Lack of evidence and disagreement among scholars preclude accurate mapping.]

The people of Northwest Mexico used several kinds of alcoholic beverages. They made wine from the buds or leaves of the *agave* (century plant or *maguey*) or cactus fruit and beer from sprouted maize grains.

The men of Northwest Mexico characteristically wore the breechcloth in ordinary daily life and donned a cloak or cape in cold weather or for special events. The women wore a skirt that reached the knees. Both sexes wore plant fiber sandals. They wove some of their garments from cotton, which was grown throughout the agricultural Greater Southwest. The women let their hair grow long, while the men wore theirs in a long bob.

Different types of dwellings were used in different places, even within the same tribe. The people of the northern lowlands lived in dome-shaped, grass-covered structures. In the central and southern lowlands and the southern highlands some groups built oval houses of mud and stone with peaked, grass-thatched roofs (Spicer 1969:788). Central lowland tribes used these and other types, including a rectangular house covered with twilled cane mats. Several highland groups built rectangular structures of logs or planks and sloping roofs, and there were rectangular houses with domed roofs as well. The diversity of house types is greater in Northwest Mexico than in many other regions of the world of comparable size.

The main craft items produced in Northwest Mexico were coiled baskets, clay pots, twilled mats, and cotton textiles. The people wove cotton cloth on horizontal looms, using their fingers and a heddle but no shuttles. Specialists apparently worked only part-time. There was trade between communities and between tribes, but, unlike Mesoamerica, Northwest Mexico lacked market places. Cotton textiles, copper rattles, parrot feathers, shells, and colored stones are among the items the people of Northwest Mexico are known to have traded. Objects crafted by the Mesoamerican Indians to the south found their way through the chains of traders of Northwest Mexico into Indian groups of the United States.

Few if any of the tribes of Northwest Mexico abided by unilineal kinship principles, which would produce common ancestor groups known as *clans* and/or *lineages*. With *unilineal descent* each member of a community or tribe belongs to one of several common ancestor groups, members of each group believing they have descended from that ancestor through forebears of one sex only—the same sex in each generation for each member. But the Indians of Northwest Mexico traced descent through both sexes in each generation as modern North Americans do. This is known to anthropologists as *bilateral descent*. The group of greatest importance to a person is not a number of people descended from the same ancestor but all of the individual's *consanguineal* (putatively genetic) relatives on both sides of the family and linked to him or her through both female and male links.

The Indians of this area also used two systems of kinship terms widely found in exclusively bilateral societies. They used *Hawaiian* terms for their siblings and cousins, which means they used the same terms for all their cousins

as they did for their brothers and sisters. For the parental generation they used *bifurcate collateral* terms. This involves using one set of terms (a term for each sex) for their parents and a separate set of terms for aunts and uncles that distinguished maternal aunts from paternal aunts and maternal uncles from paternal uncles. The bifurcate collateral system is similar to the *lineal* system of modern North Americans in terminologically separating parents from aunts and uncles. But it differs by distinguishing the maternal from the paternal aunts and uncles. When an American refers to "my aunt" or "my uncle," the hearer has no way of knowing whether it is a maternal or paternal relative except, sometimes, by context or by explanation from the speaker.

Most of the Indians of Northwest Mexico lived in communities some anthropologists have called *neighborhoods*. Neighborhoods are loose clusters of homes, each located farther from others than in villages. Some of the highland homesteads were a half mile or more apart, many surrounded by fences. The highland communities usually had no more than 300 persons, but many lowland communities had more, and some had up to a thousand. The Spanish referred to the neighborhoods as *rancherías*, and so have most anthropologists. The term is of limited usefulness, however, since it is also used for other kinds of communities, including the nomadic bands of Baja California.

In peacetime the neighborhood communities were the largest politically organized units in Northwest Mexico. They were ruled by an elder or a group of elders, who met regularly with the neighborhood adult males to consider community issues. One became an elder by advancing in age and being successful in supernatural matters. Driver indicates that the Indians of Northwest Mexico were less democratic than the people of the American Southwest and that they recognized rank differences (1961:397).

A few societies put a tribal level of organization into effect during war, uniting all of the communities of the same dialect group or tribe (Spicer 1969:789). Special war leaders functioned only during that time. Many of the tribes were quite warlike, especially the Yaqui, Mayo, and other groups speaking dialects of the Cáhita language. They practiced ceremonial cannibalism and had a variety of dances connected with war.

The religions of Northwest Mexico, while different from place to place, manifested several characteristic features (Spicer 1969:789). First, they shared the notion of stages of creation, which included belief in a universal flood. They also looked at many things in terms of opposition between the supernatural beings controlling the rainy season and those controlling the dry season. They held that serpents associated with springs and other water sources gave supernatural power. Their deities included a dominant god and goddess, probably associated with heavenly bodies. Finally, they shared a strong ritual valuation of deer and flowers.

Shamanism was important in Northwest Mexico religion. A *shaman* is a person with special individual power to deal with the supernatural for diagnostic, healing, and other purposes. Shamans of Northwest Mexico obtained their power through dreams, though they did not go on a quest for them as shamans did in many other societies. Their power enabled them to determine the causes of people's diseases and prescribe appropriate curing rituals. These included the widely found shamanistic practice of sucking the disease from the body and, also, making dry ground paintings of pulverized, colored minerals, pollen, and other substances. These so-called sand paintings were also found among Pueblo groups in the United States.

The people of Northwest Mexico were strongly interested in elaborate ceremonial activity, not only in religion but in political and other areas of life. Scholars believe there were various kinds of ceremonial organizations in the region, each led by a hierarchy of officers. These societies held formal initiation ceremonies for new members, employed special forms of recruiting members, used ritual masks, may have had secret rituals, and granted membership to both men and women. Taking alcoholic beverages was an important aspect of the ceremonies. This could be magical, as when getting thoroughly soused, as a form of imitative magic, was expected to bring rain. The people seem to have prepared special representations of supernatural beings for particular ceremonies and destroyed them when the ceremony was over. The highland groups regarded the peyote as sacred. Shamans took peyote during their performances, and it was used in group ceremonies as well.

The Post-Conquest Cultures

The major work on the cultural history of Northwest Mexico since the Conquest, now a classic, is Edward Spicer's *Cycles of Conquest*. Spicer also summarized his research on cultural change in the area in other places, especially in volume 8 of the *Handbook of Middle American Indians* (Spicer 1969:782-90).

Several major types of contact modified the aboriginal cultures considerably. While a number identified as Indian still functioned during the last decades of the twentieth century, many were highly hispanicized and modified by Mesoamerican Indian traits, and many were extinct. An especially important influence was Jesuit missionary effort. The Jesuits contacted every group and eventually founded mission stations in all tribes. Under the Jesuit influence the various cultures tended to become even more alike than they had been before. The Jesuits promoted religious, agricultural, and political changes. In fact, they affected every area of the people's lives.

A second important change source was the Spanish mining program, which had great impact in areas where mining was intense. The Spanish forced the Indians to work in mines, and life conditions in the mining communities were such as to affect Indian life profoundly.

Colonization was also an important influence in places where the land was well suited for farming or grazing livestock. Where the *encomienda* system was established the impact was even greater. According to the ideology of the encomienda system it was reasonable to expect the Indians

to compensate the Spanish for the religious and other benefits they brought. The Spanish government gave a number of *conquistadores* (conquerors) responsibility over all the Indians of certain areas, charging them with protecting the Indians and looking after their religious and material welfare. In return they could collect tribute from the Indians and enjoy free use of their labor. The *encomenderos* (encomienda grantees) forced the Indians in large numbers to give up their accustomed lifeways, often separating family members and, in cases where they were made to work in mines, destroying their health and lives (Simpson 1966:39).

The encomienda system was established immediately after the Conquest and was attacked and officially dismantled within a few years. But it did its damage quickly. Moreover, many of the system's worst features continued, partly because of difficulties of enforcement. The Spanish continued to take the best land from the Indians and established great haciendas that exploited the labor of Indians who had lost their lands or who had been pushed onto unproductive land. The Northwest Mexico tribes who survived culturally were those who lived where minerals were not so abundant and the land not so desirable. Elsewhere, large numbers lived, in effect, in slavery and oppression.

A fourth Spanish program with major impact was the military effort. Most tribes resisted the Spanish and suffered their military wrath. In some instances Spanish military pressure strengthened the Indians as they united to defend themselves. In other cases the Indians were crushed and the collapse of their cultures was hastened (Spicer 1969:783).

These four sources of change were especially powerful for a couple of centuries, but new conditions emerged during the late 1700s and early 1800s. In 1767 the enemies of the Jesuit missionaries managed to get them expelled from all of New Spain, since they deeply opposed their great power and popularity among the Indians. Then, during the early 1800s, the colonists of New Spain threw off Spanish control. After a decade of wars, the new nation of Mexico was established in 1821. Since the Mexicans had their own difficulties to cope with, they did little to interfere with Indian groups for several decades. This gave the tribes opportunity to integrate Spanish introductions with Indian ways and form new cultures that were blends of Spanish and Indian traits. Those tribes most changed by the Jesuits remained the most highly hispanicized. During the last part of the nineteenth century the Mexicans began again to interfere with the Indian cultures for many of the same reasons as before. A new element in the situation was increased exploitation of Indian labor and resources in support of machine age commercial enterprises.

Following the overthrow of Mexican dictator Porfirio Díaz, who had ruled the country from 1876 until 1910, a new reform-oriented government established a Department of Indian Affairs and launched programs for improving the lot of the Indians and helping them adjust to Mexican national life. The Mexicans established the National Indian Institute (Instituto National Indigenista or INI) in 1948, which forged a many-pronged approach to Indian development that has had great impact on Mexican Indian life.

The results of these influences over the centuries varied. Many languages became extinct before they could be recorded, but others survived. Some tribes were extinguished as recognizable Indian groups. Many Indians were settled in more concentrated and larger population centers, generally laid out on the grid plan, but dislocation and depopulation were common. There may have been a half million or more Indians in Northwest Mexico when the Spanish arrived. Some tribes experienced great population reduction and others a slight or moderate reduction. Still others, after a period of decline, have grown again, in some cases to larger numbers than before the Conquest. The Mexican census of 1940 showed 542,994 people living at the "Indian-Colonial level in the Mexican states of Northwest Mexico." (Spicer 1969:785). But it is significant that only about 70,000 spoke an Indian language, this being one of the most accepted criteria of Indian identification. Large numbers who still spoke an Indian language also used Spanish, while many who spoke only Spanish still lived in ways that differentiated them from Mexican nationals.

The Indian societies that survived acquired cattle, sheep, goats, and other livestock as well as wheat and other European crops. These are among the Jesuit introductions that the Indians integrated into their lifeways during the period of relative freedom after Mexican independence. Along with this quite a few tribes hunted less and gathered fewer wild plants than before. The Spanish also introduced metal hoes and plows, yet the pre-Conquest digging stick (coa) continued to be used in widely scattered places. In some places the people accepted Spanish economic innovation and began to develop larger scale agricultural and livestock enterprises, only to lose out as subsequent events in the history of New Spain and Mexico made it impossible for them to continue. In most places Indians did not succeed in becoming well integrated into the national economic system. The Spanish and the Mexicans crowded the Indians off the best land and forced them into marginal subsistence farming (Spicer 1962:546). Some worked for wages, either part or full time, on the ranches and haciendas and in the mines. Wage work, in fact, has been the major source of income in some twentieth century Indian communities.

In practice, marriage and family arrangements continued much as they had before. Formally, the people abided by the Roman Catholic standard of permanent monogamous marriages. Actually, they often were married by Christian ritual only after a marriage had been established for some months or years. Some men took more than one woman without marriage rites. Couples often dissolved their relationships and established new ones without formal divorce and remarriage. So they conformed to the new standards outwardly and violated them in practice. Where the three generation, extended family had been strong the independent nuclear family tended to become more important.

Spanish contact changed community and tribal leadership considerably. Formerly, community headmen served as moral exemplars, admonishers, and catalysts for public decision-making, but not as autocrats or dictators. But in wartime proven warriors or shamans accomplished in war magic took over. In the face of repeated Spanish military pressure the war leaders sometimes acquired an importance and permanence they lacked before. Also, since communities joined actionally only in times of war, tribal identities and solidarity were augmented. Nevertheless, strict separation of the functions of war and peace continued in many of the twentieth century tribes. Moreover, the Indians continued to govern themselves in line with pre-Conquest ways, either alongside or in some fashion integrated with the town governments the Spanish and the Mexicans imposed. The Spanish appointed governors or judges or both, the appointees usually being Indians who cooperated with the Spanish rather than real community leaders.

Spanish and Mexican missionary efforts generally increased the diversity of religious belief and practice (Spicer 1962:504). The Indians either remained largely pagan, combined Roman Catholicism with their own beliefs without giving up much, or became full-fledged Catholics. Much of the religion of Indian Mexico became a kind of folk Catholicism that would be recognized only with difficulty by modern North American Catholics. The people of Northwest Mexico have continued to be greatly interested in ceremony and have frequently combined Catholic and pagan elements to develop whole new ceremonial systems.

When a society is so hard-pressed by a dominant culture that satisfying social and individual patterns of response are disrupted and people find life less rewarding than before, groups often respond with what anthropologist Anthony Wallace has called revitalization movements (1970:188). These are organized efforts to restructure the sociocultural situation so that life will again be satisfying. Some revitalization movements are highly nativistic. That is, they look to at least a partial return to or preservation of old ways. Others are relatively more acquisitive. Commonly, they are religious and instigated by prophets or messiahs. Within a few decades after Jesuit work began among the Tepehuán, a prophet proclaimed that a stone image had spoken to predict destruction of the Spaniards, and the Indians who followed him fought to bring that about. They gave up only after a bloody war that ended about 1618 (Spicer 1962:527). Prophets also arose from time to time among the Tarahumara, and during the last decade of the nineteenth century a Mayo prophet arose. In other cases, as among the Yaqui, revitalization movements tended to be more secular. The main point here is that the emergence of such movements points to the Indians' dissatisfaction with the new state of affairs.

Tribes of Northwest Mexico

Scholars subdivide the Piman peoples of northwestern Mexico and the southwestern United States in various ways. Frequently they have viewed one of the subdivisions, the Pápago (approx. PAH-pah-goh) as a separate tribe. Most of the Pimans (not Pima) were sedentary agriculturalists, but the Pápago, who spoke a Piman dialect, obtained most of their food from wild sources. The twentieth century Pápago, now officially known as the Tohono O'odam, lived on both sides of the border. The Mexican Pápago spoke the same dialects as the Arizona groups, and their cultures were much the same. In 1960 the Mexican Pápago were located in an area extending from the border to the Rio Concepción in an area to the west of Nogales, Sonora. There were around 300 of them at mid-century.

The Pima (approx. PEE-mah) are the other division of Pimans. They have been divided into Upper Pima (Pima Alto) and Lower Pima (Pima Bajo or Névome). The Upper Pima were found in both the United States and Mexico. The twentieth century Pima have been highly acculturated. In 1959 there were probably around 1500 of them living in several small areas in Sonora and Chihuahua along and near the border. They were living in small mountain communities and would go to the Mexican towns to trade or for religious reasons.

The Opata (approx. OH-pah-tah) lived in northeastern Sonora to the south of the border and to the east of the Pima and Pápago. In 1959 people still existed who could be identified as Opata, but none of them knew the Opata language (Hinton 1959:14), which became extinct sometime between 1930 and 1959. The lives of the mid-century Opata still reflected fragments of their Indian background, but nothing more. The Eudeve (approx. eh-oo-DEH-beh) people might be considered a separate tribe from the Opata, since there apparently was an Opata language and a Eudeve language at some point. The Jova (approx. HOH-bah) have been described as speaking languages related to Opata, and descendants of the Jova could still be identified in Sonora in 1960. Culturally, the Eudeve and Jova were probably quite like the Opata proper, and tribal maps usually show them as being within Opata territory. There may have been four thousand or so people in 1960 identifiable as being of Opata-Eudeve-Jova descent.

The Yaqui (approx. YAH-kee) spoke various dialects of the Cáhita (approx. KAH-ee-tah) language. They lived immediately to the south of the Seri of the Sonoran coast and the Pima Bajo of the interior. Two Cáhita groups, the Yaqui and the Mayo (approx. MAH-yoh) have been treated as separate tribes in the literature, though their dialects are mutually intelligible and their cultures very similar. After a long period of trouble with the Spanish and, after 1821, the Mexicans, most of the Yaqui either fled their homeland or were deported to other parts of the country. After the Mexican Revolution of 1919-20 was over, Mexican authorities followed with some consistency a policy of recolonization. Many Yaqui returned and eventually became established in several towns of their own along the Yaqui River. Estimates indicate from 11,000 to 13,000 Yaqui in Mexico during the late 1970s and some 6,000 in and near Tucson, Arizona.

The Mayo occupied areas around the lower Mayo and Fuerte Rivers to the south of Yaqui country. Though Mayo and Yaqui cultures were essentially similar in pre-Spanish times, major differences developed later from the different kinds of experiences the two groups had with the Spanish and the Mexicans. The Mayo were changed more by the Jesuits than the Yaqui, and the troubles with the Mexicans

strengthened the Yaqui while further weakening the Mayo. There were about 30,000 Mayo in 1950 (N. Crumrine 1977:143).

The Tarahumara (approx. tah-rah-oo-MAH-rah) lived in the mountainous country of western Chihuahua, and they still occupied a substantial area in the southwestern part of the state during the latter decades of the twentieth century. They also were one of the tribes least changed since pre-Spanish times. Some of the Tarahumara of the late twentieth century were still pagan, while others were fully Mexicanized. During the late 1970s there were from 40,000 to more than 50,000 Tarahumara in Mexico.

The Northern Tepehuán (approx. teh-peh-WAHN) lived in the extremely rugged, relatively untouched mountain country to the south of the Tarahumara in the southern tip of Chihuahua. There were probably from 4,000 to 5,000 Northern Tepehuán during the late 1970s.

The Southern and Northern Tepehuán may have been one people at the time of contact, but by the time their lifeways were studied and recorded there were significant linguistic and other cultural differences. The Southern Tepehuán of the twentieth century were far removed from the northern people, living mainly in the mountain country of extreme southern Durango.

The Tepecano (approx. teh-peh-KAH-noh) lived apart from the Southern Tepehuán but considered themselves a branch of them and were culturally nearly identical to them.

The Huichol (approx. WEE-chol) Indians were found in northwestern Jalisco and adjacent portions of Nayarit. Many from outside Mexico have been very intrigued by Huichol culture because of their highly developed art and because they retained peyote as an important part of their late twentieth century ceremonial life. There were some 8,000 speakers of Huichol during the late 1970s.

The Cora (approx. KOH-rah) Indians were found to the east northeast of the Huichol in the state of Nayarit. Their culture was enough like that of the Huichol that Grimes and Hinton described them in a single article (Grimes and Hinton:1969:795). The Northwest Mexico groups that failed to survive into the twentieth century include a number of large tribes, notably the 70,000 Tahue, 100,000 Totorame, and 90,000 Cáhita living in the highlands and barrancas (gorges) of the Sierra Madre Occidental (Spicer 1969:7844). They became extinct before qualified field observers could provide significant amounts of reliable data on their lifeways. Other groups became hispanicized before such observations could be made, and still other tribes whose names appear on ethnic group maps of Mexico may be subtribes of other groups, or the available data are not trustworthy. There is evidence we may gain some information on the other groups from the increasing ethnohistorical research on Mexico, a part of which involves locating documents written by early missionaries and others that have become forgotten in museum archives and private collections in various parts of the world. Archaeology may also help. Such research may provide us more information on large groups such as the Acaxee and the Xixime, as well as the cluster of small tribes shown on ethnic maps between the Tarahumara and the Cáhita.

Chapter 6

THE POTAM YAQUI OF SONORA

Yaqui aboriginal culture is long gone, but the Yaqui Indian lifeway has weathered the storms of contact with Spanish and Mexicans to become one of the more interesting cultures of Indian Mexico. In this chapter we describe the Yaqui of Pótam (approx. POH-tam) as they were during the early 1940s when Edward and Rosamond Spicer spent time among them. During this century the Yaqui have been the most widely dispersed of North American Indians, since they were scattered over various parts of Mexico and into the United States by their troubles with the Mexicans. Spicer, in fact, had studied the Yaqui of Pascua, near Tucson, Arizona, before his study of the Mexican Yaqui (1940).

The vigor and persistence of the Yaqui lifeway is evident in that wherever they have been found they have been identifiable as distinctively Yaqui and have remained aware and proud of this identity. Many societies folded under Spanish and Mexican military pressure, but, while ultimately defeated, the Yaqui fought as recently as 1927 and were maintaining military readiness when the Spicers were with them in the 1940s. Their culture has been a blend of Yaqui and European customs since shortly after the conquest, with additional modifications resulting from their forced migrations and the survival modes they created in their struggles to keep their freedom.

The village of Pótam during the 1940s was both a cluster of homes and the countryside surrounding it. The territory began about six miles from the Gulf of California and extended along both the north and south sides of the Yaqui River for about 25 miles. The width of the strip varied but averaged about eight miles. Most of the delta bottom area was covered with cactus. The settlement was in a twenty acre cleared area on the north side of the river. Wagon roads and winding trails extended from the village through the bush in all directions. Thirty-seven-hundred people lived in the village during the Spicers's time there, and some of these were scattered among several smaller settlements and in isolated homesteads here and there. The Poteños (people of Pótam) called themselves *yoemem* or "people." As with many other groups around the world, this suggested that other humans were not people in the fullest sense. The Yaqui called the Mexicans *yorim*. The yoemem were biologically indistinguishable from the 259 Mexicans living in Pótam and, like the Mexicans, varied from one another in skin color, hair form, stature, body build, and otherwise.

Most of the Yaqui of Pótam lived to the east of the village plaza and in the outlying areas of the settlement. Most of their dwellings were located in an irregular pattern, though the homes of the Mexicans and those of a few Yaqui were situated around blocks. The adobe brick church was on the south side of the plaza, which was the southern edge of town. The *guardia* or headquarters of the Yaqui military society was on the east side of the plaza, and Mexican military facilities were on the west side as well as the east some distance to the north of the guardia building. There was also a school on the plaza. There were seventeen other Yaqui settlements and a total of about 18,000 Yaqui in the eighteen places. There were probable 35,000 some Yaqui in aboriginal times and possibly as many as 60,000 in 1750 (Spicer 1980:330).

In 1940 most of the Yaqui living came from farming—corn, beans, squash, and wheat being the main crops. The people also sold products for money, and a number drew stipends from the Mexican government for serving as auxiliary troops. They continued to collect a variety of plant foods. Their clothing was hardly distinguishable from that of the Mexicans. The houses were rectangular and had *carrizo* (cane) walls, sometimes plastered with mud, and low, double-pitched roofs of carrizo covered with earth. Carrizo was used for many utilitarian objects that required little strength and mesquite and cottonwood for a variety of other items. The women made most of the variety of clay pots in use.

The Poteños defined a household as the people living within an area enclosed by a carrizo fence. Some of the households consisted of the families of a couple and some of their married children while others were composed of the families of either sisters or brothers. Usually one or more remote relatives and/or fictive kin were present. Descent was exclusively bilateral in Pótam. Parents selected godparents for their children, thereby establishing a network of fictive kin important to the Yaqui in several respects. The people were governed by five elected governors and a council of elders who presided over the all-important town meetings at which the people transacted town business. Five organizations representing realms of authority ordered much of the community life. These were a military society, a group in charge of the annual fiesta for the patron saint of the church, the managers of the church ceremonies, two organizations that administered the town during Lent, and the town administration led by the governors and elders.

The people believed in several important supernaturals, especially Our Mother, the Virgin of Guadalupe, and the Lord Jesus. They also interacted with the spirits of the dead and believed in a variety of enchanted beings who lived in the countryside and the mountains. Other supernaturals included the sun, the moon, a number of saints, and angels. Ritual activity was one of the major aspects of Pótam life. The people held and participated in a large number of complex ceremonies through the year consisting of strongly patterned rituals. Most of their recreational enjoyment and artistic activity occurred within the ceremonial context.

History

The Spanish entered Yaqui country around 1529, and the Yaqui fought and defeated the forces of the Spanish conquistador Diego de Guzmán. In 1611 the Yaqui drove the forces of Diego de Hurdaide out of their territory.

The victorious Yaquis then decided they could benefit from having the Jesuit missionaries with them, and two arrived without military protection in 1617 (Spicer 1954:25). For nearly 125 years the Jesuits and the Yaqui worked together peacefully, with the Indians accepting much of what the Jesuits offered and integrating it effectively into their lifeway without becoming culturally Spanish. The Jesuits persuaded the neighborhoods of people scattered along the river banks to concentrate themselves into eight larger communities. They built a church as the center of each, and by the time the Spanish succeeded in forcing the Jesuits out of New Spain (in 1767), the largest had about 3600 inhabitants. The Jesuits improved Yaqui agriculture by introducing hoes, plows, European crops, and livestock. Many Yaqui learned to read and write, and they developed the distinctive political, military, religious, and ceremonial configurations that were still in force when the Spicer's studied them during the 1940s. We have no details of the events of this period, but it may have been a good time for many Yaqui, quite a few of whom lived their entire lives within this period of peace.

Trouble came toward the end of the 1730s. Some of the Yaqui felt they were being mistreated by one of the Jesuits, a delegation of Indians went to Mexico City to consult with Spanish officials, and the people split into pro-Jesuit and anti-Jesuit factions. Fighting broke out and continued until the forces of a Yaqui military leader remembered as a hero by twentieth century Yaqui were defeated. The leader, known as Calixto Muni, was executed in 1741, and things seem to have been relatively quiet for a while after that. But the troubles illustrated developing tensions between Spanish civil and church officials as well as a developing factionalism within the Indian groups of northern Mexico. Here and elsewhere in Mexico these troubles culminated in the 1767 expulsion of the Jesuits, and the social system that had operated so effectively for over a century was never reestablished.

During Jesuit times the Spanish made an unsuccessful effort to survey and divide Yaqui lands. Then, four years after Mexico became independent (1821), Mexican surveyors arrived at the Yaqui villages. This provoked widespread resistance and a movement for independence from Mexico among the Indians of Sonora. A Yaqui known as Juan Bandero led the movement for an independent Indian confederacy with the cooperation of Mayo, Opata, and Lower Pima (Spicer 1954:28). But other Yaqui fought with the Mexicans against Bandera's forces, who were defeated decisively in 1832. Various kinds of trouble continued. Then, in 1874 the Mexicans made Cajeme, a literate Yaqui known to them as José María Leyva, military commander of the Yaqui towns. Cajeme, who was born in Hermosillo, Sonora and had served under Mexican commanders, wasted no time launching a campaign for Indian independence. He was an organizational and military genius, and his troops gave the Mexicans considerable difficulty. But the Spanish eventually defeated the Indians, and Cajeme was captured and executed in 1887. Some Yaqui fought on in the mountains to the north of the river, but government troops controlled the river country and occupied the Yaqui villages. Cajeme's effort brought the ongoing Spanish-Indian tensions to a climax. The people finally lived with complete defeat, military occupation, poverty, and misery, and many fled to other parts of Mexico. The Sonoran government forced hundreds of Yaqui to work on haciendas elsewhere in the state, and they sent Yaqui families captured in the mountains to other parts of Mexico. These experiences provoked an enduring and bitter resentment of the Mexicans, with significant consequences for the organization and orientation of the Yaqui lifeway. Juan Maldonado (known as Tetabiate) led continuing guerrilla warfare against the Mexicans for about ten years, but was finally defeated and executed. Even after that Yaqui bands raided the Mexicans from their mountain strongholds, and defeated river Yaqui aided them secretly or escaped to join the mountain people. The Mexicans responded by shipping thousands of Yaqui to Yucatán and other parts of southern Mexico. The twentieth century Yaqui still remembered this vividly.

With the end of the Revolution in 1920 the Mexicans decided to restore Yaqui country. They rebuilt the churches and promised to help the people restore their lands. Yaqui began to return to their homeland to take up new lives. But due to Mexican failures to fulfill all their promises, there was trouble again. Exactly what happened is unclear, but Mexican troops skirmished with Yaqui near Pótam,

Yaqui again fled to the mountains, and federal troops took prisoners. In 1927 the last Yaquis came down from the mountains, and many men were taken into the Mexican army and sent to other parts of the country. Dominga Ramírez, one of the Yaqui women Kelley wrote about, had fled to the mountains with her husband, Anselmo Romero, and when they surrendered, Anselmo chose to be deported without taking his wife and children with him (Kelley 1978:176). The Mexicans again occupied the country, maintaining military detachments in all the larger Yaqui settlements and at all the main water holes in the mountains. Dominga and her family stayed in Pótam, and she died there in 1971.

Pótam was not one of the main centers of the Jesuit work and had less than 2500 people when the Jesuits left (Spicer 1954:37). It was one of the villages where Cajeme and his family spent much of their time, but there was little distinctive about it until the late 1920s. During the 1926-27 trouble with the Mexicans the Mexican army established a military post there manned by a battalion of about three hundred former Pótam citizens who had been serving with the Mexican army. They and their descendants made up the largest group in Pótam when the Spicers were there. Later, Yaqui who had served in Yucatán were brought back and settled in Pótam, and Yaqui from other parts of Mexico took up residence there until it became the largest Yaqui community on the river. Pótam is an old village, but none of the adults living there in the early 1940s claimed to have resided there throughout their lives. A few had been there since 1910.

One of the more significant developments during this resettlement was the restoration of the eight towns that had become so important to the Yaqui during Jesuit times. Though there were more than eight Yaqui settlements the "Eight Communities" had acquired a sacred, symbolic quality for the Yaqui, and the willingness of the Mexicans to restore the communities reinforced the people's sense of identity as Yaqui.

Ethnography and Ethnohistory

Most of the information on the cultural history and twentieth century culture of the Mexican Yaqui has come from the research of Edward Spicer of the University of Arizona. Anthropologist Ralph Beals, who has provided valuable ethnographies of several Mexican Indian cultures, has reconstructed the aboriginal Cáhita culture (1943a). The result of Spicer's research during the 1940s appeared as Memoir No. 77 of the American Anthropological association in 1954, and virtually all of the material on the early history and 1940s culture has come from that publication. Insights into Yaqui life can also be found in Jane Holden Kelley's study of the lives of four Yaqui women, one of whom spent the last decades of her life in Pótam (1978). Kelley includes a valuable account of her field methods and attendant difficulties. Another important source is the book

length autobiography of the Yaqui, Rosalio Moisés (Moisés, Kelley, and Holden 1971). Finally, Thomas McGuire restudied the Yaqui in 1975 and 1976, emphasizing their political and economic situation with regard to their continuing ethnic identity (McGuire 1983, 1986).

Yaqui Country

The territory of the Yaqui is largely Sonoran Desert, though the tropical coastland of western Mexico lies not very far to the south. When the Spanish arrived the country included two strips of fertile, flood-watered land along the north and south banks of the Yaqui River extending inland from the Gulf of California at least sixty miles, a large coastal plain south of the river, and a large mountain area (the Bacatete Mountains) to the north. In the 1940s the country left to the Yaqui by Mexico was about one-fourth of their earlier territory and consisted only of a five to fifteen mile wide stretch along the north bank. Formerly the Yaqui River was usually full in the late summer and fall and during the early spring. The heavy summer rains caused the river to overflow into adjacent sloughs and the many channels of the delta. The January and February rains filled the river again but usually not to overflowing. But by the 1940s the river no longer provided adequate water for Yaqui crops, since the Mexicans were diverting ever larger quantities for the vast irrigation project south of the Yaqui.

The vegetation around Pótam varied with the distance from the river. Dense thickets of carrizo grew along the river bank, reaching a height of ten or twelve feet and a diameter of an inch-and-a-half. Beyond the carrizo was a jungle-like growth of small trees and shrubs covered with vines and, interspersed among them, large mesquite trees. This growth was broken occasionally by a seasonal stream channel that received water when the river overflowed. These channels were bordered by large cottonwood trees and, among the trees, a variety of grasses. Smaller mesquite trees and other small trees grew on the slightly rising land away from the river, and within a few miles cactus plants were dominant. There were large stands of prickly pear (Opuntia spp.), senita (Cereus schotii and Lophocereus schotii), and others.

Wild game was fairly abundant, including at least two species of deer, peccaries, bears, lynx, jaguars, ocelots, foxes, badgers, rabbits, and large gray wood rats (Basauri 1940:255) There was also a large variety of birds.

Language

The Yaqui-Mayo language belongs to the Taracahitian family, which also includes Tarahumara, Opata, and related languages. It is likely that the language is properly designated as Cáhita, since there were undoubtedly Cahitian speakers other than the Yaqui and Mayo speaking dialects

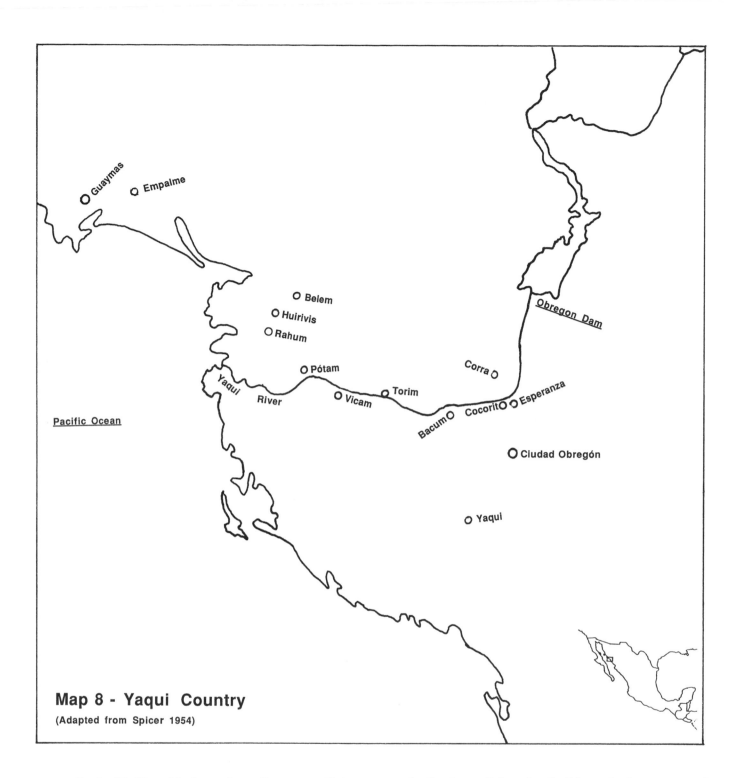

Map 8 - Yaqui Country
(Adapted from Spicer 1954)

mutually intelligible with them. According to one listing, the Tehueco-Cinaloa and Zauque were the other Cahitian dialects (Spicer 1969:779-80). The Taracahitian family of languages, along with the Piman and Aztecoidan families, belonged to the Uto-Aztecan language phylum or stock. The Aztecs of Mexico, the Hopi of the American Southwest, and the Ute of the Great Basin are among the tribes that spoke languages belonging to the far-flung Uto-Aztecan phylum.

Linguistic concepts are too technical to set forth a description of Yaqui that is both brief and balanced, but we can present enough data to illustrate cultural differences. Linguistic usages are just as surely learned and socially standardized as religion, family life, and other aspects of culture. Every language is made up of *phonemes*, which are basic units of sound that a speaker may pronounce differently in different utterances without the variation affecting meaning. So a phoneme often may be viewed as consisting of more than one *phone* (sound). Phonemes have no specific meaning; rather they may be combined with one another to form units of speech that have meanings. These units with meaning are *morphemes*. In English, for example, *in-* is a two-phoneme morpheme (a prefix) that means "not" and is used in words such as "ineffective" to mean "not effective." *Hat* is a three-phoneme morpheme that refers to a type of headwear.

An Arizona dialect of Yaqui studied by Lynne S. Crumrine consisted of 17 consonant phonemes and five vowel phonemes. Crumrine analyzed seven of the consonant phonemes and all of the vowels as consisting of more than one sound (phone), each an alternative to the others. One phoneme, for example, included sounds like the English [b] and [v] and a third sound (writteen [ƀ] like English [b] but different in that the flow of air was allowed to continue between the almost closed lips. This means that in a Yaqui word any of the three phones ([b], [ƀ], [v]) could be used without changing its meaning. The three phones (indicated in brackets) belonged to the same phoneme (indicated between slashes) (L. Crumrine 1961:3). But if any sound other than the three alternatives was used the word's meaning would be destroyed or changed. In the Yaqui dialect studied the utterances, [boʔo], [ƀoʔo] and [voʔo], meant road or path. The utterance [koʔo], however, meant something else, since [k] is not one of the alternative sounds in the b-v phoneme (/b/).

Among the vowel phonemes was one including the vowel sounds of both sin and seen in English, which means that the Yaqui could use either vowel without changing the meaning of any word in the language. Commonly, which sound is used depends on the position in the utterance. The [b] sound in the Yaqui dialect studied was used at the beginnings of utterances, while the [ƀ] and [v] were used elsewhere.

When devising an alphabet for a previously unwritten language it is best to assign a letter to each phoneme (yielding a *phonemic alphabet*) than to each sound (yielding a *phonetic alphabet*). The speakers are unable to see any point to having separate letters for sounds that only linguists distinguish from one another, and the people automatically use the alternative that comes easiest to them. Accordingly, a phonetic alphabet has more symbols than necessary. In Arizona Yaqui /b/ was used for the phoneme that included the three alternative phones described above.

Personality and Behavior

Every culture consists of the socially standardized attitudes, ideas, beliefs, percepts, concepts, or any other learned and shared personality traits characteristic of the group that lives by the culture. So when we say that the Yaqui culture of the 1940s was vigorous and persistent, we are also indicating that there was something vigorous and persistent about the Yaqui. They were proud of their cultural distinctiveness and scorned Mexican character, which they found inferior. To the Yaqui the Yorim failed to live up to the ideals they professed, they were too uninterested in ritual, they were grasping and greedy, they acknowledged no authority and, therefore, could not be trusted, they fought and were disorderly, and so on (Spicer 1954:176). The Yaqui advocated living up to their obligations, ritual and otherwise, and leading orderly lives in submission to properly constituted authority.

One of the main orientations of Yaqui life was fulfilling obligations to the supernaturals through ceremonial labor (Spicer 1954:177). They felt that their ritual, singing, dancing, participation in drama, and attendance at ceremonies was expected of them by the supernaturals. If the Yaqui fulfilled this expectation, the supernaturals would bring them health and long life. The Yaqui regarded ceremonial labor as hard work and a test of strong moral fiber. The importance of fulfilling obligations carried over to the Yaqui view of their relationships with one another.

But Yaqui life was more than just hard work to live up to obligations. The people enjoyed themselves, too, especially with regard to their interest in giving and attending fiestas. An unmistakable element of pleasure seeking was there, and much of their pleasure came from dancing, music, poetry, and other folk literature as expressed in the *pascola* arts. The Pascola dancers, the deer dancers, their musicians, story tellers, and joke makers entertained their audiences, which frequently rocked with unrestrained laughter.

The Yaqui identified themselves strongly with their territory, maintaining a consuming interest as a group in having their own land and governing themselves rather than living on someone else's land or being under outside authority. But in spite of their military ability and their willingness to defend their land and their right to live as Yaqui, the people were not especially interested in fighting and war. Spicer found nothing in their traditional lore or in their conversations that glorified military exploits, so their so-called warlikeness must be understood as willingness to fight in defense of what was important to them.

Clothing and Personal Appearance

Middle American groups have usually changed the style and/or materials of their clothing soon after first contact with Europeans. The Yaqui rather quickly accepted Spanish clothing, which consisted of cotton trousers and shirts, twilled palmetto hats, and single-thonged, leather-soled sandals for the men and ankle-length skirts and embroidered blouses for the women. Human groups almost always use special clothing for ceremonial and other special occasions, the Yaqui deer dancer costume being an example.

Housing and Other Structures

Most of the Pótam Yaqui lived in two or three room houses constructed of a frame of crotched mesquite support posts and rafters of mesquite. The walls were of carrizo (the bamboo-like cane mentioned earlier), and the low double-pitched roofs were made of layers of cane covered with earth. Some Poteños plastered the carrizo walls with a heavy coat of mud. The people slept either on floor mats of carrizo or on lengths of carrizo supported by pole frames one or two feet high. They built their cooking fires on platforms of carrizo heavily coated with mud, and they suspended food shelves of carrizo from the roof. Each homestead included at least one ramada, which consisted of a flat roof supported by forked mesquite posts. Families lounged under the ramada, and the women did much of their work there during all but the windy months. Most built plaited carrizo fences five or six feet high around their houses, though a few of the older dwellings lacked the fence. Normally there was more than one house within the fenced area.

The Yaqui felt it was of great importance for every homestead to have a wooden cross, which they usually made of mesquite. It was at the cross that the family members said their prayers, and when church groups or ceremonial societies came to the house, they went to the cross before doing anything else. The families also had their death ceremonies and all other rituals by the cross.

Livelihood

The aboriginal Yaqui farmed, gathered wild plants, and hunted. By the 1940's hunting had become relatively unimportant, while farming and collecting wild plants remained significant. There was plenty of land for cultivation, since some of it was not being farmed. But many of the farmers had difficulty producing more than enough to just get by. If the river became full enough from the summer and winter rains, there was water for virtually everyone, but when the water was low, fields too far from the river or along one of the smaller side channels might go without water. Almost all the Yaqui blamed the Mexicans for their lack of water, since they were diverting water upstream from Pótam for the irrigation farming of the coastal plain south of the Yaqui River. The Mexican government was working to remedy the situation, but most of the people doubted it would be corrected.

Corn, beans, squash, pumpkins, and wheat were the main Yaqui crops. Nearly all the families also raised onions, chick-peas, watermelons, chile and other garden vegetables. A number of housholds also had herds of cattle or goats. Nearly all had a few chickens and some owned several pigs. A minority had from one to four horses or mules for plowing, riding, or pulling wagons. The people commuted daily from the village to their fields, though those whose fields were distant had shelters where they stayed while working their crops. Some lived by their fields only part of the time, while others stayed there all or nearly all the time.

Selling products for money and drawing stipends from the Mexican government were second only to farming in making a living. About 300 households had men serving as auxiliary troops in the Mexican army for pay, though many did little or nothing to earn it. Selling surplus farming products to Mexican storekeepers in Pótam or to outsiders also brought in some money. A little money was brought in by wage work and the sale of mats and baskets. The Yaqui used this money to buy knives, hoes, metal cooking utensils, and other items they regarded as necessary. Many valued money, in short supply in Pótam, because nearly all had lived in other places where it was important. They therefore considered themselves poor.

Traditionally, the Yaqui and others of Northwest Mexico collected quite a variety of wild plant foods, and the Poteños still used them extensively in the 1940s. Many families sold or traded wild plant foods to Mexicans and other Yaqui. A few actually obtained all their clothing, coffee, sugar and other items this way. Virtually all relied on wild plants when the crops failed or other emergencies overtook them. They took a variety of wild greens and fruits from trees and several cacti. They used mainly the fruit of the organ cactus, the senita, the cardón, and the prickly pear. Traditionally the people made considerable use of the pods and beans of the mesquite and similar trees as well as seeds such as those of the amaranth plant, but only a few collected them in the 1940's.

Fishing was not important for all the Yaqui, but some went onto the waters of the Gulf, close to shore, in wooden plank boats to net fish. The swordfish was the most important. Small parties sometimes gathered oysters.

Yaqui men hunted deer, but only on the rare occasions when they could get ammunition. The boys hunted rabbits and large gray wood rats for fun and food, but few of the people were interested in eating them. The interest in hunting was generally low in spite of the abundance of game.

The Yaqui diet of the 1940s consisted basically of corn and wheat tortillas and beans supplemented as available by squash, beef or goat meat, green corn, watermelons, wild fruits, wild greens, and oysters. They also took coffee and sugar with one meal a day (Spicer 1954:52). Some of the Poteños were well-fed, and most of them felt they had enough. A small percentage struggled constantly to find enough food to get by.

Crafts, Tools and Techniques

The Yaqui used carrizo for the great variety of things that required little strength. Bird cages, corn bins, eating spoons, and many other items were made from the canes, and people usually had several bundles leaning against the house, some to dry in the sun and others ready for use. For items requiring stronger wood, such as benches, they chose mesquite wood. They used cottonwood, which carves easily, for pig troughs, mixing bowls and other containers.

Each family had a few clay serving bowls and a large *olla* for storing their water supply. Ollas are globe-shaped pots, sometimes slightly elongated vertically. The people also used pottery bowls for storing food and carrying it to fiestas. Most of the pottery, which is made by the women from local clays, was half-inch thick brown ware. Most of the people, presumably, had porcelain and metal containers before settling in Pótam, so the extensive use of pottery was probably a major change. Five gallon cans were nearly always used for carrying water from the wells to the houses, which seems to be the case in most of Indian Mexico.

Social Organization and Relationships

Most Pótam men had only one wife, but Spicer found thirty households in which two or three women were economically attached to the same man (1954:58). He was unable to determine whether or not the relationships included sexual activity. Some Yaqui shifted mates from time to time without ceremony. Their concern apparently was that each adult should have gone through a marriage ceremony at some time. Beyond that they felt that what happened was the business only of the people involved.

The marital combination of one man with more than one woman is a form of *polygamy* (multiple spouse marriage) known as *polygyny*. Some anthropologists would say that under polygyny the man is a member of more than one nuclear family at the same time, one for each wife and children. But there is no indication that Yaqui thought of it that way.

The Poteños regarded their households as fundamental groups. They had a term for households, each of which was the group living in an area enclosed by a carrizo fence. A few households may have been composed of a single nuclear family, but most were combinations of two or more monogamous or polygynous families plus one or more other persons. Spicer could find no standard arrangement, the component units being linked according to various criteria. In many cases married sons and/or daughters with their spouses and children were living with their elderly parents—a three generation arrangement many anthropologists have called the *extended family*. When the families of both sons and daughters were living with the elderly parents the result would be an *ambilocal extended family*. At their wedding ceremonies the Poteño couples went to the home of the groom's parents for the concluding ritual. If they took up residence with his parents *patrilocal* residence would be the appropriate term, but during the 1940s about as many married couples lived with the bride's parental family (*matrilocal* residence) as with the groom's.

Frequently the Yaqui lived in two kinds of *joint family* relationships. Sometimes the families of two married sisters resided in the same enclosure (a house for each sister's family) and functioned together as a household. And in about an equal number of cases the families of married brothers did the same. In addition to the related families the Yaqui household often included more remote relatives and fictive kin such as one's godparent's children or *compadres* (the godparents of one's own children). During the 1940s the Yaqui regarded households as changing in their composition through the years, which probably reflected in part the continuing arrival in Pótam of individuals and families returning from the places to which they had been deported or to which they had migrated during the times of trouble. The Poteños looked to the oldest mentally and physically

competent couple in the household as the household leaders, and either the woman or the man could dominate.

Most of the Yaqui of the 1940s had forgotten all or most of the traditional kinship terms and regarded the terminology as too complex to bother with. Only a few of the old people knew and used the traditional system, which was *birfurcate collateral* for one's parents' generation and *Hawaiian* for one's siblings and cousins (see page 30). Most viewed using the traditional terms as a mark of being out-of-date.

In spite of the changing family and terminological systems, the Yaqui regarded blood relationships as fundamentally important. Any such relationships involved social bonds and obligations of mutual help. The people thought of these relationships bilaterally rather than lineally. In *lineal* systems people reckon relationships with forebears and descendants through only one person in each generation, but *bilateral* reckoning includes all relatives in each generation. Accordingly, the bilateral Yaqui were concerned about their relationships with all putatively genetic relatives linked to them through both sexes and on both sides of the family. Of course, those a person actually interacted with formed the functioning unit. Each Poteño thought of all the individuals in town to whom he or she was related as the *wawaira*. Each person took a special interest in his or her wawaira and was especially concerned about what each member thought of him and how they behaved toward her. This actually functioning unit, which varies in membership from person to person (except for siblings) has been called the *restricted kindred* by some anthropologists. American and other bilateral societies have basically similar kindreds.

The Pótam Yaqui lived out their daily lives within the household, but they also had a fictive or ritual kinship arrangement that was almost as important. The Yaqui felt that each set of parents needed nonrelatives to help them get their children through life and, if a child died, properly ready for the afterlife (Spicer 1954:60). They borrowed and modified the European godparent system, which is found in most of contemporary Indian Mexico as well as among Mexican nationals. The Yaqui also seem to have continued elements of their traditional system of ceremonial sponsorship, but little is known about it.

Yaqui parents established fictive kinship relationships by selecting nonrelatives as godparents to their children, thereby establishing lifelong linkages between their children and the godparents and between themselves and their children's godparents. These exhibited the qualities of actual kinship relationships. In Spanish a parent and godparent refer to one another as *compadres* (coparents). The term (*kompai* in Yaqui) referred to either godparent, though *comadre* was ordinarily used if only the female was meant. A godchild referred to godparents as *padrinos* or *padrino* and *padrina* (or *madrina*) while the godparents referred to their godchildren as *ahihjados* (*ahihado* and *ahijada*).

If a godchild died the godparents had to take over for the devastated parents. They prepared the burial clothes, dressed the body, and did the other tasks that required close contact with the body. A child had more than one set of god-parents, since there were godparents for baptism, confirmation, entry into a ceremonial society, marriage, and other special times in the life cycle. The godparents selected had special responsibilities for those occasions, but all of them were expected to help if a child died.

The Yaqui thought of their fictive kin as a unit and designated the group by the Spanish term *compañía* (company). Within the company the Yaqui required godparents and godchildren to behave respectfully toward one another, and members of the company were to help one another at any time ceremonial, financial, or other needs arose. They frequently borrowed money and other things from one another. Each member found that the constant demands of the other members made it difficult to develop and maintain a surplus of money and goods, so the fictive kinship system served as an economic *leveling mechanism*. But the company also helped a person get through the various crises of life over and over again. Spicer cites one Poteño's experience to illustrate how the company may operate. A man had obligated himself to give a fiesta during Lent. He would have to feed over 150 people for two nights and two days, so he obtained the help of his own household, three households of blood relatives, and eight compadre households. The eight households were those of five pairs of compadres and three adult godchildren.

Newborn Yaqui children were bathed and clothed right after birth. But for about six days a woman other than the mother nursed the infant, since the Yaqui felt the milk was not good during that time. At about six months of age mothers would begin to wean the child by feeding it ground tortillas. The Yaqui allowed small boys to go naked during warm weather, though they kept the girls clothed. Basauri says that parents treated their children with considerable affection (1940, v. 1:280). The Pótam Yaqui of the 1940s had special ceremonies for their children at baptism, confirmation, and on other occasions, with the godparents assisting.

The Yaqui arranged their offspring's marriages, with the mothers of the young people being especially deeply involved. The traditional marriage ceremonies were elaborate. One set of ceremonies was held at the home of the bride's parents and the other at the groom's parents' house. They confirmed the husband-wife relationship at the end of the latter ceremony. After that, the Yaqui felt, the spouses were established as married people and could change partners without additional rituals.

The Yaqui buried their dead in their ordinary clothing. The night before the burial day was a feast time, and ceremonialists conducted rites at the dead person's household. The body was buried the next morning. They held a second ceremony, called the *novena*, nine days later, which was another night of feasting and ritual. Then, on the first anniversary of the death, the Yaqui held a ceremony that freed the relatives from their mourning. When a child or anyone else who had never been married died, they omitted the novena and the anniversary ceremony. They also had at least one pascola dancer at the funeral.

Government and Social Order

Associations or *sodalities* were traditionally important in the tribes of Northwest Mexico, and they remained important in the lives of the Pótam Yaqui of the 1940s. The important associations included a military society; an organization responsible for managing the annual fiesta of the Holy Trinity; a society of people who managed the ceremonial activities of the church; separate organizations responsible for honoring Our Mother, the Lord, Loreta, Guadalupe, and the Christ Child; a society of church dancers (*matachines*; the Horseman Society, which was one of the two organizations that took over the administration of the town from Ash Wednesday through Holy week: and the Judas Society, which governed the community with the Horsemen during that time. These and other groups were involved in the organization and operation of Yaqui society as a whole in a variety of ways and will be referred to again when we summarize Spicer's description of the organization and working of Pótam life.

The community of Pótam was part of the Mexican nation and subject to Mexican governance and laws. But much more important to the people was their own community government, operated by principles and procedures derived from aboriginal times, their association with the Jesuits, and the history of experiences with Spain and Mexico. They regarded their government as quite separate from those of Mexico and Sonora and operated it independently. According to them, their system was mandated by the supernaturals, and if they proceeded properly their governmental decisions were actually God's (Spicer 1954:95).

The Pótam Yaqui transacted town business through the leadership of five governors, five assistant governors, and a group of elders headed by a *pueblo mayor*. Each year the church officials, after careful consideration of many opinions, proposed five people to become governors. The incumbents would call a town meeting toward the end of the year, where the five could address the townspeople, and ordinary citizens could speak for or against them. When confirmed, the governors-elect selected five assistants, and the ten officials were installed on January fifth.

Each governor carried a two foot long cane with a silver cap at one end and an iron point at the other. They carried the canes to all meetings, where at the beginning of each the fifth governor stuck them in the ground in the order of the governors' rank and took them up when the meeting ended. This ritual was rigidly prescribed. The people of Pótam held town meetings every Sunday and, often, more frequently, with the first governor presiding.

Though the governors were ranked, any one of them could become dominant during the year. The fifth governor served as a kind of constable or sheriff. The five assistant governors were messengers and errand men for the governors and did various odd jobs of town business.

The other branch of government, the village elders, acted largely as advisers to the governors and spokesmen for the townspeople. The pueblo mayor, their head, served for life unless the people became dissatisfied with him. The mayor serving during the 1940s had been selected several years before by the highest ranking church officials, and there was a move to depose him. He also had to be confirmed at a town meeting. He selected up to four other men as his special assistants. He was usually invited to speak at all town meetings, and when he did he was expected to express the people's will. He also signed all the official town letters.

Anthropologists have confirmed that cultures function in ways the people who live it are not aware of. The Pótam Yaqui, for example, did not think of their government as having two branches, but outside observers agree that it functioned that way. The elders were primarily advisers and spokesmen, while the governors presided over meetings and saw that decisions were executed (Spicer 1954:63).

Much of the business was transacted at the weekly town meetings, which were announced by the military society drums. When the people had assembled and the first governor had opened with a formal ritual speech, he or someone else would set forth the issue to be considered. The governors ran the meetings according to definite procedures, which included giving ordinary citizens opportunity to express their ideas. The people expected the first, second, third, and fourth governors to see that relevant matters of Yaqui law were considered, either by bringing them up themselves or asking others to comment. They continued the discussion until a governor felt that people were in general agreement. He then indicated the nature of the agreement, and if no one objected, either he or the first governor closed the meeting with another ritual speech.

The townspeople never voted, nor did any official have the authority to make a final decision. Instead, continuing expressions of opinion led to a general recognition that a certain viewpoint had become dominant, and all present accepted it as God's decision. Some of the town meetings were trials of people accused of having broken the law. The people determined both guilt and innocence and the kind of punishment and treated the decisions as unanimous. One such trial lasted three days, partly because the man accused of having sexual relations with women other than his wife was a high church official. During the trial the people learned that the wife had also been having sex with other men, and they required both spouses to endure five hours of condemnation and admonition by various officials, made them declare publicly that they would live together properly, and threatened them with whipping—the usual punishment for this transgression—if they did not reform.

Every human culture is and always has been more than a collection of customs. Actually, every group's lifeway is a unit, an indivisible whole. Yet it is impossible to conceive of an entire lifeway without distinguishing among elements that both those who live the culture and outsiders experience as different from one another. In the process, however, we encounter difficulties in knowing where one custom leaves off and another begins. Do we properly speak of wearing pajama-like trousers held up by a sash wound about one's middle as a single custom, or do we say that wearing pajama-like trousers is one custom and using a sash to hold them up is another. Ethnographers do not worry about such matters in writing their descriptions of cultures, but the example illustrates that the customs we say cultures are composed of are somewhat arbitrarily distinguished. Since we unavoidably view cultures as made up of such segments, it becomes important to think of these elements as interdependent with one another. Doing this is a way of "seeing" the culture which reminds us that it is a whole.

Functionalism is an anthropological and social science doctrine that emphasizes the wholeness of cultures and the interdependence of the parts we say make up a cultural system—that of the Pótam Yaqui, for example. Those who emphasize the functional nature of cultures are apt to stress that the customs of a particular lifeway are related to other customs in the culture and that each contributes to the existence and operation of the whole lifeway.

One way of portraying the Yaqui cultural system—its family life, societies, the town, the government, the religion, and its recreational and aesthetic customs—recognizes five realms of sacred authority that tie together much of the social life. Not all of the Poteños viewed their culture this way, but a number of the village officials were among those who did. In their language they referred to each realm of authority as a *ya'ura* (plural *ya'uram*). First, there was a *civil ya'ura*, the jurisdiction of the town governors having to do with disputes, crimes, and land use. The second realm of authority was that of the *military society officers*, who handled military matters during both peace and war. The *church officials* constituted the third realm of authority, which had to do with relationships between people and the supernaturals. The fourth ya'ura, the fiesta realm, dealt with matters of the patron saint, town and church, and burials. The fifth, the customs authority, operated only during Lent and consisted of the two men's ceremonial societies charged with that realm.

Each ya'ura consisted of a set of officials arranged in a hierarchy of authority, but one realm did not have authority over another. In matters that concerned more than one realm officials from the ya'uram concerned met to discuss things and, of course, the villagers made many decisions affecting all aspects of life in the weekly town meetings. The civil government was described earlier, but it seems appropriate to note that the Poteños thought of the governors as having authority over households rather than individuals. Households, then, were the basic units within the civil ya'ura. The civil authorities stood ready to enforce what the people called "Yaqui law." Since households were the governed units, the household heads had a special stake in the legal process. This relates to how family and household affairs were interdependent with the customary modes of town government. The previously mentioned Yaqui view that town meeting decisions were God's illustrates interdependence between political and religious customs. Under functionalist doctrine customs in different aspects of culture (technology, political life, religion, art, education, etc.) may be just as tightly interlocked as customs within the same aspect. Accordingly, customs in different ya'ura were often tightly linked to one another.

The military society maintained its headquarters at a building called the *guàrdia*, which was also the office and meeting place of the town governors. The governors wrote their letters in the same room where the soldiers kept their bows, arrow quivers, rifles, swords, batons of office, and war drums. The town meetings took place on benches under a ramada outside the guardia. The commander of the twenty or so soldiers was the First Captain, though two other captains served with him. The flag-bearer was the highest ranked official, since he bore the symbol of the group. Below the captains were the drummer, lieutenants, sergeants, corporals, and soldiers. In peacetime the military society guarded the civil authorities and their office, drummed out announcements of town meetings, punished violators of the law, and performed certain rituals at village ceremonies, including the Coyote Dance. In wartime the military society would organize the village, since the Yaqui believed every adult male was a potential soldier. Some young men who did not belong to the society accepted short periods of military instruction. The Yaqui military group was entirely separate from the Mexican detachment stationed across the plaza, though several men served in both units. The Yaqui thought of the civil ya'ura and the military ya'ura as working in close harmony with each other.

The church organization was more complex in its official hierarchy than the rest. The church building was nearly two hundred feet long and made of adobe brick walls and a concrete floor. Three bells hung in the church tower. Many of the major and minor religious ceremonies took place at the church. There the people kept the images of the major supernaturals and some of the minor ones. It took five groups of people to take care of the images and the church ceremonies. The *maestros* led the altar devotions with prayers, chants, and ritual speeches. Five of them served during the 1940s fieldwork period. The second group consisted of the female singers, one or two of whom appeared with the maestros to provide vocal accompaniment in the singing of hymns and chants. The sacristans were twelve men who cared for the male images, took them to and from ceremonies, rang the church bells and the altar bell, cared for the building, and assisted the maestros in ceremonies. A fourth group consisted of women who attended to the female images and who had several other responsibilities as well. The direction of unmarried girls who waved the flags was one of them. The final church group was the *matachin* dancers, who performed a special devotion to the Virgin. There were 25 to 30 matachines in Pótam and five or six musicians with them.

Three persons presided over the church groups—the head maestro, the head sacristan, and the head female image tender. The head maestro took more responsibility than others, and the woman was less involved than the two men. One other official, the church governor, was viewed as the head of the church, but he was appointed by the three chief officials and carried out their wishes. His highest responsibility was to coordinate the activities of the component groups during the course of a ceremony. The Poteños also had a matachin governor and a position, unfilled during the 1940s, for a person who trained children in prayer, crossing themselves, etc.

The fiesta ya'ura was composed of eight men and women who organized and managed the annual fiesta of the Holy Trinity (*tiniran*) who was the church patron saint. They were called fiesteros. There were four blue *fiesteros* and four red fiesteros, and each group of four had assistants. The management of the Holy Trinity fiesta was a giant task, and actually the entire village was involved. The pascola dancers served at many ceremonies, but they gave a secular look to the fiesta organization, since they were secular or even pagan dancers. The eight or so pascolas had no obligation to the Christian supernaturals, but the eight first assistants of the fiesteros dealt mostly with them, including the deer dancer. The pascolas hosted the crowd at tiniran and passed out cigarettes, water, and food to all in the name of the fiesteros.

Tiniran took place in the village plaza and lasted three days. The main event, on the morning of the last day, was the ritual of the Moors and the Christians, or the battle of the reds and blues. The Moors' castle was a rough pole frame in the center of the plaza. The red-capped Moors (the red fiesteros) and their supporters sought to defend their castle from the attacks of the blue fiesteros or Christians. The blue fiesteros and their company would grab the reds, tear down their castle, and, with much struggling, hustle them into the church and baptize them. For an hour or so the church was full of laughing, shoving people, many drunk and many with their clothes in tatters from the "battle." The people regarded the Holy Trinity fiesta as a time to feast, drink, play, and enjoy fireworks, dancing, and good fellowship.

The customs authority consisted of the Horseman Society and the Judas Society. During the forty days of Lent the governors theoretically turned all town authority over to the two ceremonial societies, though they retained some of their authority until Maundy Thursday of Holy Week. The purpose of the societies' temporary dominance was to enforce the remembrance of the Lord Jesus. They held many ceremonies, including private household fiestas, five large processions, and a series of dramatizations of the last days of Jesus' life. It was all in memory of the hardships the Lord Jesus suffered. The climactic event was an attack on the church by the Judas Society, including the masked *chapayekam*, who played the parts of the evil beings who pursued, captured, and crucified Jesus. The church groups, the military society, the governors, the elders, the Horseman Society, the pascolas, and boys and girls representing little angels defended the church against the Judases. After three tries the Judases were taken into the church and re-baptized. More people attended this event than any other Pótam ceremony, and they talked of it for months before and after.

Spicer reviews several types of functional integration of Yaqui life. First, *formal linkage* involves the use of common elements in various parts of Yaqui culture. For example, the Poteños used the family terms mother, father, son, and daughter for family members, fictive kin, and supernaturals. They used the terms for parents and grandparents in the ritual speeches made by the church leaders, governors, and elders. This is just one way in which church, governmental, fictive kinship, and family aspects of the Yaqui lifeway were formally tied together. The sign of the cross was another element occurring in many areas of Yaqui life.

Secondly, *functional linkage* refers to activities in various areas of life occurring in relation to one another. For example, the military and political areas were linked by the protection the soldiers provided as they escorted the governors from place to place. It is interesting that Spicer could find very few formal and functional linkages between agriculture and other aspects of the culture. Their practice of erecting crosses by the fields is one of the few examples, and agriculture seemed far more separated from the rest of life than in many societies. Planting ritual, harvest festivals, and similar complexes so important in other agricultural groups were not a part of Yaqui culture.

Consistency is the third form of cultural integration used by Spicer. This involves agreement or compatibility between or among customs. Fiesta-giving, for example, was certainly consistent with the pascola arts, since one reinforced the other rather than contradicting it. Curing tuberculosis with an infusion from the creosote bush and by vowing to dance as a matachin were also consistent, since the Yaqui accepted both natural and supernatural explanations for disease.

The fourth form of integration, *compendence*, refers to the dominance of some components of the culture over others, some elements being dependent on more basic elements. Among the Yaqui, for example, ceremonial labor embraced a complex of elements so important throughout the lifeway that other complexes were adjusted to ceremonial labor rather than vice versa. Two features of the ceremonial labor complex were the sacred sermons and the sign of the cross. These were injected into pascola ritual, but pascola rituals were not injected into church ceremonialism. The pascola arts were subordinate to the ceremonial labor complex. Examples of formal and functional linkage, consistency, and compendence abound in every culture. They are different ways we can view the parts of a culture as linked to one another.

Art and Play

The Pótam Yaqui spent their time largely in either techno-economic activity or ceremonial participation. Most were little interested in games and sports as pastimes, since they thoroughly enjoyed the drinking, dancing and music, story telling, joking and clowning, speechmaking, ritual

movements, and other activities that were integral elements of their ceremonially complex lives. They did little to make their everyday utensils and containers aesthetically pleasing. The pots, for example, were plain and undecorated. Nor did they wear colorful clothing or decorate and mutilate their bodies. Instead, they directed their artistic skills toward the masks, costumes, musical devices, and the like that were used in their ceremonies. From this viewpoint their art objects included the brazil wood canes carried by the governors, the flags borne in military and other ceremonies, the well-crafted crosses in the houseyards and elsewhere, the images of the Virgin Mary and other supernaturals, the stuffed deer head and other parts of the deer dancer's costume, the long-nosed wooden masks (representing Judas Iscariot) worn by the chapayeka performers during the Easter season, and many more. Yaqui aesthetic activities would include their flag waving, drumming and flute playing, story telling, the dances of the matachines or church dancers, the elaborate dramas of the Horsemen and Judas societies, the harp, drum, and whistle music of the pascola dancers, and so on.

In most tribal societies art is not a profession. Instead the people express aesthetic values in various other contexts—in ceremonial life in the Yaqui case. Art as a category of custom illustrates what anthropologists sometimes refer to as an *etic* concept. Etic concepts are devised by generalizing scientists in order to compare cultures with one another. They can define art, as some have, as the exercise of skill in the expression or communication of sentiment or value (Honigmann 1963:219) and look into the customs of many cultures to learn how people in many places are similar to and different from one another in the exercise of skill for such purposes. This makes possible comparisons useful in developing a better understanding and appreciation of the human capacity for behaving in ways we call art. But a particular society may not experience art as a category or aspect of life distinct from others, either consciously or subconsciously. Anthropologists refer to categories and distinctions that people are aware of or that are actually functional in their culture as *emic* concepts.

Though most of their recreational enjoyment took place in ceremonial contexts, the Poteños did have some informal pastimes. Within their households they lounged and conversed under the ramadas. The young men, especially, might listen to radio music, ride horseback while becoming intoxicated, sing informally to the accompaniment of a guitar, and so on. Many of the people enjoyed trips to Guaymas, Ciudad Obregón, and other places to visit friends, take in some entertainment, or see the sights. In such ways, perhaps, they were not so unique from other societies in their recreational and aesthetic activities.

Religious Beliefs and Practices

In spite of over a century with the Jesuits, the Yaqui of Pótam and other places lived by a distinctive set of religious beliefs and practices. One of the strongest and most pervasive Yaqui concepts was the notion of a common mother, known as *Our Mother*. Though the people definitely regarded Our Mother as a supernatural, her personality was not sharply focused. Rather, they referred to a variety of things as Our Mother. Our Mother had always existed and preceded everything else. She was the land of Pótam as a unit, the church building and the land where the church sat, all the female images in the church, the crosses used in ceremonies, the cemetery where Yaquis were buried, and most specifically, a small blue-robed image known as *Rosario*, which sat atop the altar in most ceremonies. The best place to actually be with Our Mother was on the church site and, perhaps, in the presence of Rosario. *Jesus* was Our Mother's son, and when he was to be crucified she had herself made into the tree from which the cross was made. The people of Pótam brought flower offerings to Our Mother and dressed the female images in bright colors as a devotion to her. Another devotion was the matachin dancing. Our Mother was associated with color, flowers, dancing, and happiness, and the brightly colored headdresses of the dancers were referred to as flowers. She worked for the general welfare of household and village and cured people of their diseases.

In some of their sacred speeches Pótam ceremonialists referred to *Guadalupana* or the Virgin of Guadalupe as "second in command in our church." The people thought of her as the patroness or commander of the military society. She had a more defined personality than Our Mother and was associated with war and the color blue. Her image was that of a woman in a long blue robe decorated with stars and having a crown on her head.

A third major supernatural was the *Lord Jesus*, often called The Lord (*El Señor* in Spanish). Basically, he was a healer associated with health and medicine. But he was also associated with death, harsh discipline, taboo, and ritual prohibitions. The Poteños thought of him as living in the west and believed he entered Yaqui country from the salt flats and desert beyond the town of Belém. He traveled from village to village, healing people as he went. Evil men and spirits living in the countryside, which were called Jews and Judases and were lead by Pilate, pursued him. In spite of many good people who helped him they caught him at Gethsemane and nailed him to a cross. Because Our Mother (Mary, his mother) was the cross, he went straight to Heaven. The evil Jews attacked the church but were destroyed in a great battle. Annual penance under the leadership of the Horsemen and Judas ceremonial societies would influence the Lord Jesus to help people who asked for healing.

The Pótam Yaqui were much concerned about their relationships with their ancestors, the spirits of the dead. Each family kept lists of the names of all the ancestors they could remember in a little notebook. Whenever feasible some family member would take the notebook to a ceremony for a ceremonialist or singer to sing and chant over while the book lay on the altar. This evidence of remembrance and respect would please the ancestors, who would

then help their descendants. The people also went to the cemetery to be with the dead for a few minutes or hours. Most would go on the first Monday night of each month to put a lighted candle on the grave, though some went more frequently. The spirits of the dead would also come to the village to see what was going on, and on All Saints and All Souls Days in early November the spirits of a family's dead came to the household to partake of food and drink that had been put out on tables for them. The spirits consumed the essence of the food and drink rather than the substance itself, an idea found in many societies around the world who make food offerings to supernaturals.

The Poteños also believed in enchanted invisible beings who lived in the mountains and the countryside around the towns. Many knew the story of the *Talking Stick*, a bare mesquite pole that made sounds by vibrating. A girl with power to translate the vibrations explained that the Stick said anyone who was baptized would die. Some accepted the message, but others still wanted to be baptized. The two groups fought, and those against baptism burned the stick. After that they became enchanted and lived forever in all parts of Yaqui country. They were called People of the Monte and the Yaqui often spoke of them as the source of pascola dance music. Some said they had encountered the invisible people, who taught them to play the pascola music on harps or drums and whistles. The People of the Monte might also teach the dance steps. Sometimes people heard pascola music out in the bush. The Poteños assumed that especially good pascola performers had contact with the enchanted people.

The people believed there were people near the ocean who had never wished to be baptized, who were called Moors. During the annual fiesta of the Holy Trinity the Poteños dramatized a battle between the reds and the blues, which was also referred to as a fight between the Moors and the Christians. So both the Moors and the People of the Monte had not been baptized.

The Yaqui regarded the sun and moon as supernaturals. In many ceremonies the military society led a ritual salute to the sun, and the soldiers used sun symbols in their headdresses. They called the moon Mother Moon. She would struggle with the sun during an eclipse.

The people also held that there were saints, beings who served as patrons of various groups and events. Holy Trinity, patron of the church and honored by one of the largest fiestas of the year, was one of them. Others were the *Virgin Loreta*, patroness of the matachin dancers, and *John the Baptist*, who brought the first summer rains and was patron of the harvest, melons, and wild foods. Most also believed in guardian angels.

Some anthropologists have distinguished two basic kinds of religious belief—belief in spiritual supernatural persons (mainly souls, spirits, and gods) and belief in sheer supernatural power that can become concentrated in people or things. Anthropologists often refer to this power as *mana*, and belief in mana has sometimes been called *animatism*. Belief in personal supernaturals usually is called animism.

Our Mother, the Lord Jesus, the Virgin of Guadalupe, the spirits of the dead, the People of the Monte, the Sun and the Moon, and the saints and angels seem to fit reasonably well the category of supernatural spiritual beings and, therefore, illustrate animism in Pótam religion.

The ritual activities making up their ceremonies were very important to the Pótam Yaqui. Pótam and other Yaqui villages along the river followed an annual ceremonial calendar conforming to the Catholic Church calendar. The first fiesta was on January 5, when the town officials, with church officers in charge, were installed. The time of greatest ceremonial activity came from February through April, when special ceremonies were performed on Ash Wednesday, each Friday of Lent, Palm Sunday, Holy Wednesday, Maundy Thursday, Good Friday, Holy Saturday, and Easter Sunday. The people also held major celebrations on the Day of the Finding of the Holy Cross (May)), the Day of the Holy Trinity (late May and early June), the Day of Saint John the Baptist (June), All Saints and All Souls Days (November), the Day of the Virgin of Guadalupe (December), and Christmas.

There was an important ceremony called the *Surrounding* every Sunday, and families gathered each first Monday of the month to conduct rituals at the graves of their dead relatives. The people held ceremonies at baptisms, confirmations, marriages, deaths, and other events in the life cycle of the individual. Spicer recorded ceremonies for all but four days of February 1942 (Spicer 1954:137).

Not only did the 1940s Yaqui hold and participate in many ceremonies, the rituals were strongly patterned. The people knew a repertoire of fixed and sacred phrases they used in various ritual contexts. Examples are, "honorable fathers and honorable mothers," "our leader God Jesus Christ," "this weeping land," "our great fathers of the law," "a few truths," "long ago in the beginning," and many others. Public officials had to be able to speak clearly and in the proper rhythm, but most important was the ability to remember sacred words and phrases and combine them in approved ways. There were designated times for the ritual speeches in all the ceremonies, and a ceremony could not continue until the speech was given.

The same repetition of sacred elements applied to ritual acts, positions, and the sequence of events. The Poteños rigidly prescribed the positions and participants in relation to up-river and down-river directions and also in relation to the location of the church and the altar. Each official and group of participants performed its ritual in proper order.

One of the most important and most often recurring ritual acts was the *muhti*, an individual devotion for the images on an altar in the home, church, or elsewhere. There were three kinds of muhti. For the simplest a Yaqui would genuflect, which sometimes involved only a backward swing of the left foot, and rapidly make a rather elaborate sign of the cross and nod the head toward or kiss or touch an image.

The Yaqui ritually waved flags to salute the supernaturals or symbols of them. All crosses, for example, had to be saluted by flag-waving. They saluted the sacred images with flags at prescribed times. Household groups saluted the sun with flag-waving as it rose, and flag-bearers waved flags over people doing the muhti. There were many other occasions for flag-waving.

To announce important phases of a ceremony the people set off skyrockets (*cohetes*). Dozens were need for each ceremony. Some said they were messages to tell the Lord what was happening, while others said the skyrockets drove away evil.

Every Yaqui dance was a ritual. Dances had a social side, but they were never done for purely social reasons. Even in the ceremonies involving drunkenness and where nonprofessionals danced it was not just a pleasurable activity. The matachines were the sacred church dancers, who performed as an act of devotion on many occasions. A major ritual duty of the military society was to dance the Coyote Dance at certain ceremonies. The pascolas and the deer dancer performed both as part of larger church and household ceremonies and in the streets. On some occasions the young men would dance, and amateurs sometimes danced at fiestas where the pascolas were performing. Nevertheless, all dancing took place in a ceremonial context.

People in all societies find lengthy, tightly regulated ceremonies a source of boredom and tension. A cultural consequence of this may be the incorporation of comic relief associated with or part of the ritual itself. Some Pótam ceremonies were uniformly serious, but the Yaqui laughed a lot during others. This often happened as pascola performers told wild stories, made plays on words, or acted in undignified and stupid ways. The hilarity was an essential aspect of household ceremonies such as those for a child's death or a death anniversary. The pascolas satirized and burlesqued virtually every aspect of Yaqui culture, and during the forty days of Lent and Holy Week the masked performers known as chapayekam satirized Yaqui ceremony and relationships with the supernaturals. The chapayekam lampooned the ceremonial officials themselves, aping ridiculously their ritual acts even as they performed them. In such ways they delighted people and relieved them of much of the tension of observing and participating in long, difficult ritual. Yet, as Spicer noted, even these reactions against ritual were ritualized (1954:174).

Cultural Change

Many changes occurred after the Spicers' fieldwork during the 1940s. The people of Pótam have had more contacts with outsiders than many other Indian groups, since so many have lived in other parts of Mexico and in the United States. Also, Mexicans by the hundreds lived in the Yaqui communities of the 1940s, and Yaqui were living in Mexican places. The yoerem (Yaqui) and yoris (Mexicans) interacted in a variety of contexts. The yoerem read newspapers, periodicals, and books and liked to hear about the places they had lived before. They also liked to visit Mexican towns and cities. Young men and women worked in oyster canneries or on fishing boats based at Guaymas. In fact, most of the Poteños had regular contacts with Mexicans in several ways.

Yaqui and Mexican young men frequently drank together. Half a dozen or so would meet in the countryside and drink and sing to guitars and converse around small fires. A few close friendships emerged and cultural borrowing occurred—primarily in music, stories, and language (Spicer 1954:108). In the 1940s at least a dozen Pótam families were linked with Mexican families through the godparent system. Some Mexican parents asked Yaqui leaders to be godparents of their children. The Mexicans of Pótam had no church, and some of their women took to attending Yaqui church services regularly. Mexicans also might ask the head maestro to officiate at their funerals, though he used Mexican liturgy rather than Yaqui. Many Mexicans regarded the Yaqui as religious fanatics.

The Mexican municipal government system was part of the Sonora state government and consisted of a justice of the peace and a police commissioner appointed by the presidente of Guaymas. The Mexicans appointed a Yaqui as constable, but the Pótam governors ignored him. The Yaqui did not think they needed Mexican government, and the Mexicans did not interfere at that time. Most Yaqui regarded the Mexican military battalion posted in Pótam as an unlawful imposition of outside authority. They accepted Mexican military authority only to the degree they were forced to and continued to maintain their own military society and perform its operations within sight of the Mexican headquarters.

The Poteños still remembered how they suffered at the hands of the Mexicans, and in spite of the many amicable contacts with them as individuals they carried a freight of hostility toward yoris as a group. They condemned the Mexicans for not either coming to the Yaqui church or building their own, their failure to mourn their dead properly, their lack of appreciation of ritual in life, their alleged grasping, greedy behavior, their failure to submit to proper authority, and the impossibility of trusting them. The Yaqui repeatedly told stories of how Mexicans failed to live up to agreements and how they could not understand that the ultimate authority in a community is not a military commander. They would also mention the fighting and disorder in Mexican towns as evidence of Mexican lack of respect for authority.

In turn many of the Mexicans were uneasy about the Yaqui and stereotyped them as strange and inferior people. They remarked on their fanatical religious activity, their alleged improvidence and wastefulness, their supposed management incompetence, their expenditure of wealth on fiestas, and the lack of acceptance of Mexican political authority. They took the Yaqui failure to recognize the Mexican and Sonoran governments as evidence of their stupidity and said their ways of making decisions showed the lack of leadership among them.

In the decades following the Spicers' time in Pótam, Yaqui values and customs changed in some respects and persisted in other ways. The Mexicans continued to dam the Yaqui river above Pótam and other towns until in 1948 the flow of water was completely stopped. There was plenty of water for the vast irrigation project where Mexicans farmed to the south of the Yaqui River, but many of the yoerem survived only by abandoning their subsistence farming and taking wage work in other communities or with the Mexican irrigation projects (Spicer 1980:278). The Mexicans had promised years before to bring water as far as Pótam by a canal system, but the water did not arrive until 1956. Then the Yaqui had to pay for the water they had so long regarded as rightly theirs. In some cases individual farmers paid rent, but through the Banco Ejidal the Mexican government encouraged the organization of credit societies. Those Yaqui belonging to a credit society contributed to it, and the bank assessed the society for the water. This meant, of course, that the Yaqui had lost some more of their control over their own lives, with the government calling the tune on many things through its control of the all-important irrigation water.

The Mexicans also built a paved highway to the north of the lower stretch of the Yaqui River, directly through the heart of Yaqui territory, which became the main truck route between Mexico City and cities along the United States border. Cars carrying Mexicans and Americans passed within a few miles of Pótam, although most remained unaware of the history and nature of the people who had lived there since long before the Spanish arrived.

The Mexican government continued to recognize the Eight Town organization that resulted from Jesuit work and became sacred to the Yaqui. In 1958 the Mexicans tried to get the Yaqui to abandon their traditional governmental system in favor of Mexican municipal government. They asked the people to vote on whether they wanted to continue the old ways or change. A large majority in five towns voted for the traditional system, while three towns voted for municipal government. In 1966 the Mexicans tried again, and seven towns voted to keep the traditional organization. The Yaqui were continuing to emphasize their identity as Yaqui and chose to deal with the Mexicans through their own forms of political organization.

New forms of organization have affected the yoerem, however, especially since 1960. We have already mentioned the credit societies. The federal government has also introduced cooperatives, the most important of which may have been the tribal cattle cooperative (Spicer 1980:273). For various reasons many Yaqui opposed it, one being that fencing was proposed and another that the federal managers made insufficient accounting of their operations to the Yaqui towns. But more than a third of the Yaqui farmers were said to be members of credit societies by 1958. In 1964 1600 family heads belonged to 77 farm credit societies, and 75 percent of the family heads in Pótam were enrolled in 32 credit societies. The Mexicans also set up a successful fishing cooperative that was joined by several hundred Yaqui from Empalme and Guaymas. Mexican officials continued to plan such programs with minimal consultation with the

Yaqui, and the Yaqui response was to protest what they were concerned about and accept programs they came to perceive as being to their advantage. Younger Yaqui were especially supportive of the new government programs.

The Mexicans also aggressively developed the federal rural school system in Yaqui country, again without consulting the Yaqui. The general attitude of educational and other Mexican officials was that the Yaqui were backward and had to be told what they needed.

Another interesting contact area is Yaqui music and dancing, for the Yaqui have made their greatest impact on Mexican culture through the pascola and deer dances. The Mexicans first brought Mayo pascolas into their celebrations during the 1920s. They objected to their shirtlessness, however, and required the Mayo to cover their upper bodies during the dances. When the Yaqui began to perform in the 1930s they refused to don shirts. During the 1940s there were at least 30 professional Yaqui pascola dancers among the Mexican Yaqui.

Also, during the 1940s the Mexicans were becoming more interested in accurate information. The Mexican Department of Indian Affairs had a monograph on Yaqui culture published in an inexpensive popular edition, and they painted murals depicting Yaqui life in the Agricultural Training School. The Sonoran government adopted an official seal with the Yaqui deer dancer as the central figure. In 1950 the Sonorans used a figure resembling the deer dancer on the cover of a hotel directory for the state. But the figure was female, in spite of the fact that no Yaqui woman could be a deer dancer (Spicer 1980:275). A leading hotel in Hermosillo also depicted women as deer dancers in the murals they had painted on the hotel walls. The deer dance figure appeared as a trademark in comic books and other examples of commercial and popular art.

Then during the 1950s the world famous *Ballet Folklorico* of Mexico City incorporated the deer and pascola dances into their repertoire, but they altered both extremely to fit the romantic orientation of Mexican theater arts. The program notes distributed to audiences in Mexico, the United States, and Europe promoted distorted views of Yaqui culture and art. Not only did the Ballet Folklorico make the dances themselves more colorful and acrobatic than they actually were, the program notes depicted the Yaqui as racially and culturally primitive and untouched by the outside world.

During the 1960s and 1970s more of the people turned to Mexican ways, while a number of traditional elements remained strong in the lives of many. When Dominga Ramírez of Pótam died in 1971 she was a devoted member of the fiestero organization. As a younger woman who had lived in Yucatán and Mexico City she thought the Yaqui religion was "dumb," but during the last couple of decades of her life she became highly committed to it and participated deeply. She was distressed that her son, Anselmo, an official with the Yaqui Cattle Cooperative, had turned away from the Yaqui religion. But turning again to the old ways

later in life is a significant part of cultural persistence around the world, and it has continued to play a conservative role in the rate of change in Pótam.

During the middle 1970s McGuire found the Poteños tightly bound to the outsider-dominated system of export agriculture, wheat and cártamo being the main cash crops. Yet they strongly maintained their ritual traditions in the face of their market involvement and economic subordination (McGuire 1986:114-161). The people continued to govern themselves through the traditional governors and elders arrangement, but by this time a strong difference of opinion had developed, some of the people insisting on traditional methods of selecting the town leaders and others demanding general elections.

Some of the people participated fully in the traditional ceremonies, and most still participated in some measure. A number did no more than attend religious performances and political meetings. The Mexicans of Pótam and neighboring communities attended the local fiestas in good numbers. The public ritual of Pótam had become the standard against which that of other Yaqui communities was measured. Many of the fiestas continued through the night, and nearly all the Mexicans would be gone during the hours just before dawn, when the Yaqui took advantage of the opportunity to conduct non-public ceremonies they did not like for the Mexicans to be present for.

By the middle 1970s Pótam had electricity, street lights, a clinic, a physician, Mexican police, a federal agricultural school, many stores, and a restaurant. Teen-age girls could be seen in blue jeans and tight blouses, and older Poteños complained about lack of interest in the Yaqui dialect and Yaqui traditions as well as failures to respect elders. The great majority of Poteños could both speak and understand both Yaqui and Spanish well.

Land continued to be a source of tension during the middle 1970s. When President Lázaro Cárdenas issued the decree of October 27, 1937 founding the Yaqui reserve, the southern boundary was left poorly defined. Both Mexicans and Yaqui claimed to own some of the same territory, and there was trouble after the Mexicans turned it into prime irrigated farm land. Wealthy landed elite, Mexican peasants, and Yaqui Indians wanted the land. The Yaqui demanded the territory during the 1970s, but they were unsuccessful. They lacked effective skills in public advertising, lobbying public officials, getting Yaqui to turn out for public meetings in large numbers, and similar affairs. By comparison the peasants were well organized, strongly led, and government financed. In this as in so many other areas the Yaqui remained at the mercy of outsiders (McGuire 1986:104-105).

A small percentage of Yaqui, only about two percent, had become shrimpers by the middle 1970s, which reduced somewhat their participation in traditional Yaqui life. They used shallow draft boats to fish in the estuaries found in that area and sold their catches through the shrimp cooperatives, which were relatively free of outside control.

Chapter 7

THE PAGAN TARAHUMARA OF INAPUCHI, CHIHUAHUA

Modern North Americans have been fascinated by the long distance running abilities of the Tarahumara (approx. tah-rah-oo-MAH-rah) people of northern Mexico. They have also been intrigued by their attire, since the men tied their shoulder-length hair in place with a scarf and wore a loin cloth that looked something like a diaper to outsiders. Popular magazines have often featured the especially scenic railroad trip through the rugged mountain country where the Tarahumara live. In the early 1950s the Tarahumara came to public attention when large numbers were in danger of starvation because of the severe winter, and Americans collected and shipped large quantities of food to help them weather the famine. Anthropologists have found their personalities especially interesting, since they were unusually shy with one another when sober and had frequent beer parties that enabled them to interrelate in ways otherwise impossible for them. Many of the some 50,000 Tarahumara were Christianized and some lived much like Mexican nationals, but a few communities had resolutely withstood efforts to turn them into Christians or Mexicans. They maintained their traditional culture by retreating to the remotest country of northern Mexico, where, on small plateaus and shelves separated by deep gorges, they had their homes, grew their crops, and raised livestock (Kennedy 1978:v) I describe one of their communities as it was when anthropologist John G. Kennedy lived there in 1960.

Inápuchi (approx. ee-NAH-poo-chee) was a collection of small settlements of pagan Tarahumara living in the canyon country of northwestern Mexico. There they made their livelihood primarily by a combination of farming and livestock herding. Corn was the main crop, though they also grew beans, greens, and squash. The main food was made from flour produced by toasting and grinding corn kernels. The women dressed in skirts and blouses, while the men wore loincloths and blouses. They lived in almost square houses made of heavy planks and having double-pitched plank roofs. The men were highly skilled with the axe and made especially fine storage bins of planks. Neither crafts nor art were highly developed, however, though the people exhibited skill where needed to produce good equipment. They sewed clothing, wove blankets and sashes, fashioned clay pots and baskets, and made violins, guitars and other wooden musical instruments. Nearly every family had a violin, and most men knew how to play.

The nuclear family of parents and children was basic, but three generation families and units bringing siblings and their families under one roof existed, too. Nuclear families combined and broke apart frequently, even within the course of a year as economic and other circumstances changed. The people were extremely shy and individualistic, and many of the most important affairs of their lives were carried out while they were intoxicated from drinking corn beer at cooperative work sessions that brought together a number of families. When drunk they lost the reserve that prevented them from doing so many things necessary to maintaining the culture. There were no clans, lineages, or other kinds of groups larger than families and settlements. The settlement of Inápuchi had a headman who exercised his weak authority rather informally with the aid of several assistants.

The main deity was the Great Father, greatly feared by the people, who tried to keep him appeased by making the sacrifices and conducting the ceremonies he demanded. Another important deity was the Devil. The people believed in a variety of spirits and were afraid of them and the ghosts of the dead. The main religious specialist combined the functions of shaman and priest and conducted the preventive-therapeutic ceremonies that were so important in their religion. The people also believed in witches.

Prehistory

Archaeologists know little of the prehistoric backgrounds of the Tarahumara, but their ancestors may well have lived to the east of their present location. This would put them in the desert country of northeastern Mexico (W. Taylor 1966:94). There they probably participated in the gathering-hunting Desert Culture, a major tradition that flourished in the Great Basin, the American Southwest, and Northeast Mexico from about 8500 B.C. into historic times. The Desert people used baskets to collect, carry and store seeds, and hunted mainly small game. Wedges of agricultural influence spread northward from Mesoamerica and into the southwestern United States as early as 2500 B.C., and agricultural traditions established themselves in what is now Arizona, New Mexico and Northern Mexico by 1000 B.C. While many tribes continued the gathering-hunting lifeway, somewhere along the way the ancestors of the Tarahumara joined those who were turning to crop production. When the Spanish reached them in the late sixteenth century they were producing corn, beans, and squash but continued to rely heavily on hunting and gathering. They lived in neighborhoods of homesteads scattered along river valleys or on hillsides rather than in villages.

History

The Spanish established their first regular contact with the Tarahumara when Father Juan Fonte entered their country between 1607-1611 (Kennedy 1978:13). He established his mission in the Valle San Pablo de Balleza, where he persuaded several hundred members of both Tarahumara and Tepehuán Indians to settle. During the course of the century the Jesuits established a number of missions along the eastern edge of the Sierra Madre and, later, in the valleys that penetrated the mountain country. By the time the Jesuits were forced to withdraw from the area in 1767 they had nineteen missions there and had established many towns and churches. They introduced both domestic animals and the plow and generally made a heavy economic impact on the Indian cultures. The Spanish established a number of mines in and near Tarahumara country, and Spanish farmers and ranchers operated along its margins. Many Tarahumara worked for wages on the farms and ranches and in the mines, though a number were forced laborers or slaves. The Spanish followed their usual practice of trying to get the Indians to settle in compact communities, but the Tarahumara resisted with considerable success.

The Tarahumara were friendly at first but soon became disillusioned and began a general westerly withdrawal. The Tepehuán of the valley of Balleza at San Pablo revolted in 1816, and hundreds of Spaniards and Indians lost their lives before Spanish forces put a stop to the trouble two years later. Tarahumara also rebelled at various times through the century as epidemics of European diseases, kidnappings, forced labor, and attempts to force people to collect in towns provoked more intense hostility.

Though the Tarahumara continued their withdrawal into areas not easily reached by the Spanish, their culture was profoundly changed by European introductions. They integrated sheep, goats, cattle and a few horses into their economic system, improving the food system and providing wool for clothes and blankets. They also accepted plow farming and other European cultivation methods and grew peaches, oranges, apples and quince, and they made the steel axe the most important tool in their forested mountain habitat. The missionaries baptized large numbers of Tarahumara, creating a major cleavage between Christians and pagans. Yet, Christian Tarahumara continued many of their aboriginal beliefs and practices, and the pagans incorporated Christian elements into their religious systems.

After the Jesuits left in 1767 and the Tarahumara had mostly withdrawn into territory of little interest to the Spanish, they enjoyed around 150 years of relative freedom to develop a new culture, integrating the European introductions to suit themselves. Unfortunately, no observer left a written record of their cultural development during this period.

The Tarahumara were little troubled by outsiders until after Mexican Independence in 1821 and the establishment of the Mexican state of Chihuahua. The Mexicans passed land laws the Tarahumara did not understand, and non-Indians took advantage of them to drive many from their best lands. During the early twentieth century the Mexican government initiated programs to change the Indians, most of which had little enduring impact. They sent cultural missions into the area from time to time and established several boarding schools.

From the 1950s on outside influences intensified, in considerable part from the work of the Instituto Nacional Indigenista, a government agency operated mostly by anthropologists to bring the Indians the land, educational, and medical benefits of the Mexican Revolution. In many instances the Instituto has been able to represent the Indians in struggles with exploitive Mexican nationals. The Mexicans have also put a major road into Tarahumara country and extended branch roads to several towns. Lumbering and mining have been developed with this new accessibility; radios, ballpoint pens and a variety of other factory-made items became available; and the use of money increased considerably. The potential for change was magnified as Indians met non-Indians in work situations, stores, trading situations, schools, and other occasions. In spite of these kinds of developments Tarahumara culture remained relatively intact into the last decades of the twentieth century as compared with many other Indian cultures of Mexico.

Ethnography

Carl Lumholtz, an explorer and natural scientist, made the first scientific investigation of Tarahumara culture in 1892 and 1893 under the auspices of the American Museum of Natural History and the American Geographical Society (Lumholtz 1903, vol. 1:viii). He spent the better portion of two years in that part of Mexico, collecting vocabularies, making anthropometric measurements, taking samples, collecting artifacts, and making observations. While his observations are valuable, he did not produce a systematic ethnography. In 1925 and 1926 Mexican ethnographer Carlos Basauri conducted three brief field studies among the Tarahumara and published a short summary of the culture in 1929. Then, in 1930 and 1931, anthropologists Wen-

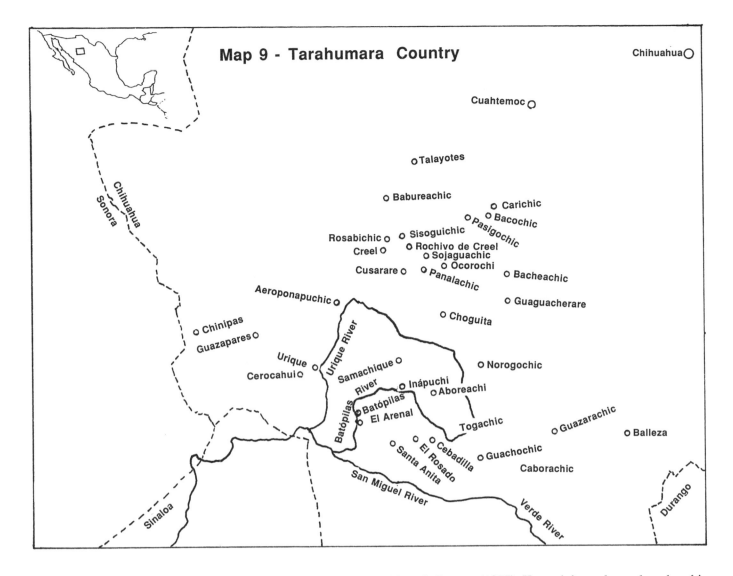

Map 9 - Tarahumara Country

Chihuahua

Cuahtemoc

Talayotes

Babureachic

Carichic
Bacochic
Pasigochic
Rosabichic
Sisoguichic
Creel
Rochivo de Creel
Sojaguachic
Cusarare
Ocorochi
Bacheachic
Panalachic

Chihuahua / Sonora

Aeroponapuchic

Guaguacherare

Choguita

Chinipas
Guazapares

Urique River

Norogochic

Urique
Cerocahui
Samachique
Inápuchi
Aboreachic

Batópilas River

Batópilas
El Arenal

Togachic

Guazarachic

Balleza

San Miguel River

Santa Anita
El Rosado
Cebadilla
Guachochic
Caborachic

Verde River

Durango

Sinaloa

dell C. Bennett and Robert M. Zingg resided for nine months in the highland community of Samachique, producing the first comprehensive ethnographic account of the Tarahumara (Bennett and Zingg 1935:vii). Anthropologists working in the area later have discovered a number of factual errors in their work, but it remains one of the major sources on the Tarahumara.

Herbert Passin worked among the Tarahumara in 1938, concentrating on social organization and personality (Passin 1942a, 1942b, 1943). Jacob Fried also investigated these aspects of Tarahumara life in 1950 and 1951, with special emphasis on social control (Fried 1952, 1953, 1961). Fried also prepared the summary of Tarahumara culture in the *Handbook of Middle American Indians* (Fried 1969). Anthropologist Jean Rene Champion's work among the Tarahumara in 1953 and 1954 served as the basis for a doctoral dissertation on Tarahumara cultural conservatism (Champion 1963). In 1955 geographer Campbell W. Pennington studied Tarahumara utilization of the natural habitat, producing a useful description of Tarahumara material culture (Pennington 1963).

Anthropologists who have studied among the Tarahumara in the 1960s and 1970s include John G. Kennedy (1963, 1969, 1970), William L. Merrill (1978, 1981), and Allen G. Pastron (1977). Kennedy's works are based on his residence among pagan Tarahumara in 1959 and 1960, and his 1978 ethnography is the most up-to-date full ethnography readily available and the only comprehensive description of a pagan community. Merrill studied the religion and world view of Rejogochi, a community near the Mexican town of Creel, and Pastron concentrated on witchcraft and shamanism in the well-known missionized community of Samachique.

Tarahumara Country

In 1960 most of the Tarahumara lived in the pine forests along the ridge of the western Sierra Madre mountains and the valleys and *barrancas* (gorges) to the west. When the Spanish arrived the people occupied a much larger area and a greater variety of habitats. They lived not only in the high mountains and rugged canyon country but in the eastern foothills and the plains and basin and range country even farther east (Pennington 1963:25). Inápuchi, the pagan Tarahumara community Kennedy studied, is a neighborhood of homesteads and small settlements situated mostly on a small plateau between two gorges, but a few lie on high shelves across the barrancas that flank the central area. The elevation is about 5,000 feet. Mountains rise to the north, east, and south, and thousand foot deep gorges descend to the west. Precipitous canyon walls drop away at the very doorways of some of the houses, making it necessary to watch small children carefully.

The climate of Tarahumara country is not as severe as some have indicated. The temperature descends below freezing during the winter months, and there is often a biting wind, but there is very little snow. Inápuchi country is warmer than the Tarahumara mountain region, so the people enjoy a longer growing season and worry little about early autumn freezes destroying their crops. Most of the rainfall, which ranges between 24 and 30 inches annually, falls either in the summer months or the late fall and early winter in Tarahumara country. But the Inápuchi area gets appreciably less than the mountain zone, and the people suffer from a limited water supply and worry about drought. Each day of the dry season people have to descend into the thousand foot barrancas to obtain water, and they often have to take their goats into the barrancas to forage. The climate in the bottoms of the gorges is similar to that of the subtropical Pacific coast.

Relatively open stands of several kinds of pines grow here and there on plateau areas of the canyon country, and there are various kinds of oaks, especially where the Indians have cut down the pines. Mixed stands of pine and oak occur on higher canyon slopes, and grass is fairly abundant under the oaks and in other places where the environment is favorable. There is a variety of other trees and shrubs, the kinds depending on the various microenvironments present there. Quaking aspens, for example, grow on protected arroyo slopes, and thickets of mainly acacia occur in places (Pennington 1963:31). The vegetation at the bottoms of the gorges is, of course, entirely different.

Basauri lists a number of wildlife forms for the Tarahumara area, including deer, coyotes, antelope, foxes, several kinds of rats, mice and related rodents, ground and tree squirrels, chipmunks, bears, bats, quails, swallows, warblers, towhees, vireos, rattlesnakes, several kinds of toads, and freshwater shellfish (Basauri 1940(1):303). His list is incomplete, and it is impossible to determine which are encountered by the people of the canyon country. Kennedy mentions that wildlife was scarce at Inápuchi in 1960 and that the occasional squirrels, birds and deer taken by the Inápuchi Tarahumara were rare delicacies (Kennedy 1978:48). There are fish in the streams in the barrancas.

Kennedy used the term Inápuchi to refer to a settlement of seven households that the people themselves called Inápuchi, plus nine nearby settlements ranging from one to five households each. The seven homesteads making up Inápuchi proper were scattered about a small peninsula-shaped plateau flanked on two sides by deep gorges, which merged with one another just beyond the settlement. This relatively flat area was about a mile-and-a-half long and varied from a quarter to a half mile in width. Thirty-nine people lived there. Other settlements were on shelves on the opposite sides of the gorges. Together they formed a collection of homesteads whose 142 residents interacted with one another more than they did other Tarahumara. It is interesting to outsiders that settlements only a few hundred yards from one another were sometimes an hour or two apart, since a fatiguing hike to the bottom of a canyon and up again was required to go from one to the other (Kennedy 1978:92).

Language

The Tarahumara spoke a language belonging to the Taracahitian subfamily, which includes those of the Yaqui, Mayo and other Cáhita to the west and southwest of Tarahumara country. Longacre lists a total of 41 Taracahitian languages for northwestern Mexico. Taracahitian languages and two other subfamilies, Piman and Aztecoidan, make up the Mexican group of Uto-Aztecan languages. The Tepehuán groups to the south, who live in somewhat similar country and are culturally similar to the Tarahumara in a number of significant ways, speak languages of the Piman subfamily. The Nahua, commonly known as Aztec, speak Aztecoidan dialects, and several other groups scattered through northern, central, and southern Mexico as well as Central American countries, speak Aztecoidan languages.

Personality and Behavior

When the Tarahumara of Inápuchi were sober they exhibited a complex of characteristics which might be subsumed under the term reserve. They seem to have shared some of this with other Indian groups throughout the Western Hemisphere, since so many observers have taken note of the emotional and verbal restraint and dignified bearing of various Indian groups. But the Inápuchi people and other Tarahumara groups took this reserve to an extreme. They were intensely shy and withdrawn, some avoiding conversations with all but those they were closest to. Their standard technique for dealing with an unwanted or threatening social contact was to withdraw. Lumholtz is only one of the many who commented on Tarahumara social reluctance, noting that they were shy and bashful and that the women turned their backs whenever he came along (Lumholtz 1903:147). Kennedy commented on the frequency with which elderly Tarahumara women would break into a run if approached by a stranger.

Kennedy credits the intensity of Tarahumara withdrawnness partly to their experiences with the Spanish and Mexicans and partly to their extreme physical isolation (Kennedy 1978:228). During the first years of contact the Tarahumara rebelled violently, but they were always crushed. Unlike some other Indian groups, they lived near areas the non-Indians were little interested in, so they withdrew into these remote territories, separating themselves from their tormenters and, in the extremely rugged environment where they took refuge, separating themselves from one another as well. All this also may have helped ingrain within them the deep suspicion and, sometimes, fear of others that characterizes them. Kennedy found it difficult to develop and maintain relationships of trust with some of the people, and even toward the end of his field term he would be surprised by expressions of distrust and hostility (Kennedy 1978:5). He also noted how distrust and fear entered into religious attitudes and behaviors. The people feared the ghosts of the dead, and when things went wrong they were quick to suspect their neighbors of working witchcraft against them (Kennedy 1978:156).

While reserve and withdrawal were strong in the Tarahumara makeup, there was another side to their personality. Fried noted that the Tarahumara were also ego-centered, proud people— independent-minded and individualistic (Fried 1969:869). The notion that all should have the right to make their own decisions without others interfering was a pervading *cultural theme*. Morris Opler noted the presence of such themes in human cultures, defining them as postulates or positions, either implicit or explicit, which control behavior and stimulate activity (1945:198). Cultural themes may be viewed as helping to integrate the various elements of life where they manifest themselves. The Tarahumara of Inápuchi taught their children how to behave, but rarely forced them to do things against their will. From the age of five or six they allowed their children to wander great distances alone. After about age six they would leave their children alone at home to look after the fields and the animals while they went to distant beer parties, and by seven or eight the children spent many hours herding livestock. By ten or so the parents required their children to sleep outside the house, and by a year or two later they sometimes stayed away from the homestead overnight. Kennedy notes that such training seemed to foster both individualism and independence on one hand and shyness and restraint on the other (Kennedy 1978:195).

An aspect of the individualism theme was the people's strong respect for others' needs and wishes. It was manifested in their lack of use of corporal punishment for children, the custom of visitors to sit some distance from a house and wait until someone extended them a greeting and an invitation to approach, the freedom of young people to choose their own spouses, the ease with which either spouse could terminate the marriage, the near equality of the sexes, the lack of powerful leaders, the failure to prosecute witches, and many other elements of their lifeway. Their individualism clearly tied together many elements of their culture.

Tarahumara individualism and social reserve seemed to connect with the frequency of their beer parties and the marked release of inhibitions that characterized them. The people threw beer parties for the purpose of securing the help of their friends and neighbors for tasks such as weeding fields or harvesting. However important this was, anthropologists have concluded that the beer parties served as much or more to enable them to engage in wanted and needed social interaction they were otherwise too reserved

for. For days or weeks the people worked alone or in small groups, going to bed early each night because of fatigue and lack of light. But at the beer parties they laughed and joked, heard sermons, found spouses, made economic deals with one another, arranged races and ceremonies, engaged in religious ritual, had sexual experiences, resolved disagreements and, sometimes, fought. When under the influence of alcohol they did the things they found difficult or impossible when sober, a number of which were of considerable importance to their social functioning.

Kennedy cites several other aspects of Tarahumara personality. He found them generally nonviolent, noting they seldom attacked one another or outsiders, even during their parties. They were also materialistic and practical, giving little attention to history, philosophy, theology, and art. They were generally present-time oriented and "this worldly" (Kennedy 1978:197). In addition to these orientations, which a Tarahumara might be only weakly aware of, the people were explicit about their high valuation of wisdom, industriousness, wealth, organizing initiative, self control, physical skill, and oratorical ability (Kennedy 1978:198).

Clothing and Personal Appearance

The people of Inápuchi made their clothing mainly of white muslin, though they also used bright red material and colored prints some. A woman wore several long, full skirts and a blouse having a collar and long puffed sleeves. To this she added either a kerchief or headband and sandals cut from old automobile tires lashed to her feet with thongs. The women also added bead necklaces to this costume. A man wore a loin cloth and a triangular piece of muslin held in place over the hips by a woven sash, as well as a blouse similar to those of the women. He completed his outfit with a cloth headband, a blanket, and sandals like those of the women. Both women and men wore their hair down to below shoulder level, leaving it loose except when they wore the headband or kerchief. Men from different areas wore slightly differently cut loincloths and wrapped their headbands in distinctive ways, making it possible for Tarahumara to tell where they were from. So, those familiar with the area could identify people from Inápuchi by their costumes.

Houses and Other Structures

The non-Christian Tarahumara of Inápuchi lived in single-roomed wooden structures with double-pitched roofs. The houses were often rather crudely fashioned, since the climate in the canyon country was not severe. The best made dwellings were about 10 or 15 feet square with walls of thick planks prepared by Tarahumara axemen. The builders sank a post at each corner, stacked the heavy planks on edge inside the posts, and held them in place with lighter uprights on the inside (Bennett and Zingg 1935:51). This formed walls about four feet high. Posts extending about seven feet above ground were planted midway between the corner posts on two sides to support a ridge pole. Along the top of each wall that was to receive the roof boards they placed a beam that was V-shaped in cross section, with the open side up. This formed a trough along the top of the wall to receive the lower ends of the roof planks and served as a rain gutter. The roof boards were also V-shaped and laid so they overlapped, one with the open side up and the next with the open side of the V down, like tiles, so that the water would run into the gutters. On one side the roof boards extended from gutter to ridge pole, while on the other side the boards were longer and extended well beyond the ridge pole. This kept water from dripping into the house at the ridge. A framed door opened through one of the walls. The people of Inápuchi often added a kind of temporary room to their dwellings by leaning planks against one side of the house. Children or guests could sleep there in good weather, it served as a shade on hot days, and child-curing ceremonies were sometimes held there (Kennedy 1978:45). Some of the people left the planks out of their house walls, using loosely piled stones instead.

The people of Inápuchi furnished their houses sparsely. They might have crude wooden benches along one wall and small stumps or blocks to sit on scattered about the room. A grinding stone was kept near one wall, and other objects included items such as gourd halves, clay bowls, a wooden bowl, baskets of corn kernels or corn flour, enamel cups and plates, galvanized buckets and, possibly, a violin or guitar, a blanket or two, and pieces of cloth hanging from the eaves. The people might keep cow or goat skins to sleep on near the open fireplace on one side of the room. There was usually one nuclear family (parents with children) in each dwelling. When the cold weather of late November arrived, the people moved to the bottoms of the nearby gorges, where they lived in caves and structures of brush and stone.

The Tarahumara of this area built their storage structures with greater care than their houses. The walls of horizontal planks were carefully notched at the corners and fitted tightly together so that neither rodents nor light could enter. The plank floors were raised about 18 inches above ground on boulders beneath each corner. There was also a tightly fitted plank ceiling, topped by a roof of slanting, V-shaped planks. The only opening into the approximately eight foot square box was a framed, two-foot square door opening inward on one side. Here the people stored dried corn on the cob, beans, animal hides, cloth, balls of yarn, and other valued items. Between the ceiling and the roof they stored baskets, horsehair ropes, and other equipment, and a few things might be kept on the ground beneath the structure. Most families had at least two and, sometimes, three or four storage buildings.

Inápuchi homesteads included wooden structures other than the houses and storage buildings, such as chicken coops and corn drying racks. They always kept a number of logs lying near the house for building movable livestock corrals.

Livelihood

In 1960 the Tarahumara of Inápuchi got most of their foods from their fields, where they cultivated mainly maize (Indian corn) beans, mustard greens, and squash. They also raised a little wheat and potatoes and grew a few peaches, oranges and sweet potatoes. Livestock herding was tightly linked to farming, since they used the manure of goats and cattle on their fields and cattle to pull their plows. Livestock also symbolized wealth and prestige for the Tarahumara, constituted a form of savings, and protected them from starvation when the crops failed. The people seldom used milk or meat, but they would be unable to maintain their lifeway and their independence of the Mexicans if they lost either their animals or their crops (Kennedy 1978:54). There were also a few sheep, pigs, burros and chickens at Inápuchi. The people also took wild forms through hunting, fishing, and gathering. They killed all wild animals on sight if they could, but they were scarce and provided little food or fiber. They caught the larger fish in the river in the barranca and collected the hearts of a species of century plant (*agave*) and the fruit of the *nopal* (prickly pear) cactus.

To prepare the fields the men of Inápuchi had to clear them of brush and trees and fertilize and plow them. So much of the vegetation had been destroyed over the centuries that it usually took little effort to clear a field. But fertilization was a major project, and Inápuchi farmers manured their maize fields by confining 15 to 50 goats at night in 20 foot square corrals, moving the pens every four days until a field was done. It took them about 45 days to fertilize an acre, and it was necessary to repeat the process every four to six years. They also might pen five to fifteen cattle in 25 foot square corrals, but this took twice as long as using goats and lasted only two or three years. During the winters the herders confined the livestock in the barrancas in caves or corrals and, later, carried the accumulated manure up to their fields in blankets or burlap bags.

It was impossible to keep all the land well fertilized, and people with few animals had to borrow from others. A family inevitably had some fields that yielded less than others and left about a quarter of the fields unplanted. Generally, they could not leave a plot unused longer than six years, since someone else might claim it. The Tarahumara held to the concept of *usufruct,* which provides that land ultimately belongs to the whole community, and, to maintain their right to land and the privilege of passing it on to their heirs, people must use it. The Tarahumara understood that any of them had the right to clear and fence a parcel of land that had not been used for a long time, but they got into disputes over land rather frequently.

If grown in the corn fields, beans were fertilized in the same way as corn, but it was commoner to use another approach. The people grew fewer beans than maize, and the yield was higher. So they often prepared narrow strips on slopes, along streams and in other small areas, where they plowed the ashes of dried leaves and branches into the soil.

The soil at Inápuchi was shallow and stony and had to be plowed several times a year. Hard ground was plowed first in the late fall, following harvest, and again before spring planting and during the planting process. To make their heavy wooden plow, the Tarahumara selected a log with a branch in the right position to serve as a handle. They skillfully shaped a hardwood log so that it either had a notched point to receive a share of stone, metal, or harder wood; or the point of the log itself broke the earth. Near the base of the handle they prepared a socket to receive the butt of the pinewood tongue, which they fixed in place with wedges (Bennett and Zingg 1935:20). They carved the yoke from a long piece of hardwood and lashed it to the oxen's horns with leather thongs. The front end of the tongue was attached to the yoke between the two oxen by means of a rawhide cord secured around a peg through the tongue. A plowman walked beside the implement, guiding it with one hand while wielding a long, switchlike pole with the other to control the oxen.

To plant corn, men driving one or two yokes of oxen plowed a furrow. Planters followed, withdrawing four kernels from a cloth sack suspended from the waist, poking four to six inch deep holes with oak digging sticks, dropping the kernels in the holes, and covering the seed with earth with the foot. The planters spaced the hills about four feet apart. Most of the men planted their corn in early May.

The people were anxious between planting and about the end of July about whether the rains would come when needed or would come at all. The older people remembered years of drought and hunger. Also, in some years large numbers of worms demolished much of the corn, but the people did nothing to harm them for fear they would become angry and ruin the whole crop. Also, the food supply was low just before the rains came, and people were weak from hunger and thirst. Moreover, they believed that God would at some future time destroy the world in anger over failure to dance and make the required sacrifices, and they feared this might be the year. Accordingly, they sacrificed more animals to the Great Father at this time than others, which added more protein to the diet when they needed it (Kennedy 1978:61). During this period of intense anxiety, shamans dreamed that they were being ordered to conduct the annual "curing" ceremonies, which were performed to protect the livestock against sickness and accident for the coming year, protect the people from lightning and sickness, and ensure that the fields would yield their crops. They also "called" the rain and petitioned the worms to stop destroying the crops.

This illustrates *functionalism*, the social science view that the elements of a culture are interdependent with one another and with noncultural phenomena. In this case it is clear that Inápuchi maize technology is linked to religious belief and practice. Such examples remind us that the cultural categories with which we divide our lifeways are artificial. In fact, customs in different aspects of culture can be just as tightly interdependent as customs in the same aspect. Policy-makers and administrators often forget this,

treating economic and political problems as though they were unencumbered by religious, aesthetic, kinship, or other cultural concerns. The example also illustrates the linkage of cultural beliefs and practices to noncultural elements, in this instance to the uncertainty of rainfall in Tarahumara country.

As the maize plants grew, the people protected them from animals and weeds by material means. They fenced most of the fields against animals with log fences or stone walls, and family members scattered to watch their fields for several days at a time. They were not idle as they watched but repaired tools and other equipment, wove baskets, mended clothing, ground corn, cut firewood, repaired fences, played guitars or violins, and so on.

When the rains came the weeds began to grow, and the fields had to be hoed the last two weeks of July. The people usually cooperated to weed the fields, so weeding was one of the occasions for a beer party. The host made beer and invited people from the surrounding settlements to the party. They drank and worked. Though it rained most afternoons, they did not care and laughed drunkenly as they hoed. With the corn coming well and grass growing the adults often joined in a round of weeding parties, leaving the children to care for the fields and livestock. About six weeks later the fields had to be weeded again. This time they carefully made a small hill around each stalk, which took from three to five hoe strokes for each plant.

Around the first of August, normally between the two maize field weedings, the people planted the bean patches by plowing furrows, dropping the beans in the bottom, and covering them with the foot. About when the bean patches had to be weeded, they planted their spinach-like greens in some of the newly fertilized soil under preparation for the next year.

In late September or early October the men cut off the tops of the corn stalks above the ears and stored them in the lower branches of nearby trees or other safe places. This was the animals' winter feed. In late October and early November they harvested both maize and beans and picked the squash. The family usually picked about half the crop themselves, preparing beer on the side. Then they threw a beer party to finish the job, since they needed help to carry all the heavy sacks of ripe ears, the bundles of beans, and the squash to the storage bins.

Herding put more unrelenting demands on Inápuchi life than any other techno-economic factor. The livestock destroyed peoples' crops when unattended and had to be taken to forage daily. Herding was easiest for a short time after the rains began, since there was plenty of grass near the settlement. Even small children tended the herds at such times, leaving the adults free for other things. But as the nearby pastures gave out during the course of the dry season, trips to adequate pasture required as long as two or more days, and these excursions were ideally the responsibility of the women and children. Wives did some of their work while watching a herd, but many of their tasks required them to stay home, and an older boy or girl often tended a herd in some remote location alone. But many men had no alternative but to do the herding themselves much of the time. Sometimes the women demanded release after several days of exhausting herding or the need to do other things. Sometimes a family reached the place where they either had to persuade a neighbor or relative to take over the herds or take the animals with them on some imperative errand. Families with herds got an occasional break when those without livestock or insufficient numbers of goats or cattle wanted to borrow them to fertilize their fields. The borrowers paid by herding the animals for the owner during the daylight hours.

During the winter in the bottoms of the canyons, a thousand feet below their settlements, the people cared for their animals; fished; collected agave for beer; collected materials for baskets, cordage and medicines; made violins and guitars; sewed and made baskets; and grew a little chile and tobacco. Occasionally, they climbed to the plateau to get corn or other supplies, a trip of an hour or two. Winter was a more restful, leisurely time than the rest of the year, though herding and a few other economic tasks still required regular attention.

The people made *pinole*, a characteristic food in Northwest Mexico, the basis for several food dishes. They prepared it by roasting dried corn kernels in a special small clay pot and grinding them two or three times on a grinding stone. This produced a flour that could be used in a variety of ways. For a refreshing drink a Tarahumara sprinkled a handful or two of pinole into a gourd or enamel cup of water and stirred it for several seconds. This was especially good for renewing oneself along the trail. *Esquiáte* was an important food made by adding water while the parched corn was being ground and mixing the resulting soupy stock with ground herbs or corn flowers. The Tarahumara kept the esquiáte in an *olla*, a round clay pot somewhat elongated vertically, and dipped it out at meals to be consumed with beans, greens and other foods. Tarahumara families had a jar of esquiáte on hand most of the time.

The people of Inápuchi also made tortillas, tamales, and *atole* from corn, but they were much less important than pinole and esquiáte. Like other Indian groups, they cooked dried corn for several hours in lime water to soften it, ground it into dough, and shaped the dough into round thin cakes, which they cooked on a flat clay disc to make tortillas. The tamales, made either from tortilla dough or green corn, lacked meat or other filling and were wrapped in corn leaves and baked in a pit. Inápuchi atole was a cooked corn gruel mixed with sugar and/or ground seeds or fruits. It was made from boiled corn rather than from pinole.

Beans were the second most important food in the Inápuchi diet and their main source of protein. The Tarahumara of Inápuchi roasted dried beans in a small pot with sand, ground them twice on the *metate* (grinding stone), and boiled the flour in water to make a hot soup to drink. When it thickened or congealed they ate it cold. Sometimes they boiled beans in a pot and used them in tortillas.

Mustard greens were the third important food in the Inápuchi diet and were commonly taken cold and with pinole or esquiáte. The people of Inápuchi grew the greens in large patches during the rainy season, dried them, and kept them for year around use. They also enjoyed squash, which they baked in a pit or cooked in water and ate either hot or cold. They also boiled squash flowers in water with salt. Squash was less important than corn, beans and greens, because they ate it only in season.

Wheat and potatoes contributed little to the Inápuchi diet, but they were important because they became available during the season of scarcity before the rains. Wheat was prepared much like corn, and wheat flower was sometimes added to tortillas, pinole, or atole. Bennett and Zingg reported that the Tarahumara boiled or roasted potatoes, mashed them with squash seed, and ate them with chile sauce (Bennett and Zingg 1935:147).

Most of the settlements had gardens of nopal cactus, or prickly pear, some of the plants growing seven or eight feet tall. They enjoyed the fruit when it matured, and they also removed the spines from the large, thick, oval links or leaves and cooked them. Most Inápuchi families had several peach trees in 1960, and they picked and ate the peaches when they were green. They also went to gather oranges in the nearby canyon of the Batopilas River. Generally, fruit was minor in their diet, providing mainly a change from their regular foods.

The Inápuchi diet differed significantly from that of the Mexicans. The Tarahumara ate meat only on ceremonial occasions or when an animal died, and they did not use baked wheat bread and sweet pastries. Those Indians who survived childhood were in generally good health, so their diet appears to have been quite adequate nutritionally.

Crafts, Tools, and Techniques

The basic tool of Inápuchi culture, as well as other Tarahumara cultures, was the axe. All of the men became skilled axemen early in life, and the evidence of their proficiency was to be seen in their houses made of planks hewn from logs, the V-shaped logs of their house roofs, their well fitted storage bins, their doors, and their plows. The women were not so skilled with the axe, but they were quite proficient wood splitters in their husbands' absences.

Other Inápuchi crafts included weaving blankets and sashes; making crude clay pots; basketmaking; sewing clothing; and manufacturing violins, guitars and rattles. Some of these activities were highly skilled, but, in general, Inápuchi crafts were not greatly developed. Most of the blankets were of fairly simple design, requiring relatively little skill. The women did most of the weaving, but a number of the men knew how, also. The Tarahumara loom was basically two parallel logs resting on boulders (Pennington 1963:207). Apparently, sashes required greater skill to weave than the blankets, and it might take a person several years to become an expert sash maker. The sashes incorporated fairly complex geometric designs in three or four colors, and Kennedy found them quite beautiful (Kennedy 1978:197).

The Inápuchi Tarahumara fashioned various sizes of rounded pots with flared rims, the smallest being three or four inch high vessels for cooking greens and the largest beer pots two or three feet high. They also made an elongated, pouch-shaped container they leaned over a fire to toast maize or bean kernels before grinding them. The potters, nearly always women, used local clay, sometimes mixed with old, crushed pottery; and they formed the pots by coiling strips of clay or modeling them with the hands (Kennedy 1978:76). *Coiling*, *modeling*, and *molding* the clay to a basket or other container are the three basic pot-forming techniques humans use, but molding isn't mentioned for Inápuchi. When a woman had formed the container, she smoothed it with a stone or gourd, dried it in the sun, and fired it under a pile of dry branches. Sometimes a potter applied a slip of red ochre before firing. Red ochre is abundant in the mountains, and potters might keep a supply in the storage bin until they wanted it. They made a paste of ochre powder and water and applied it with a feather, sometimes both inside and out (Bennett and Zingg 1935:86).

The Tarahumara made and used fairly simple twilled baskets with square bases and rounded tops (Pennington 1963:200). The baskets were of various sizes, and the sides were commonly of a height about half the width of the container's square base.

Many Tarahumara men made violins and guitars, most often the former. Most of them were on the crude side by Euroamerican standards, but they were entirely hand-crafted and required considerable skill. Well-crafted instruments of this kind are unusual for societies at the level of technological sophistication of the Tarahumara. Curers produced well-made rattles of wood or gourds for one of their most important sacred dances.

The Tarahumara exhibited considerable skill in a number of their crafts, but their craft development was rather limited as compared with many other nonliterate groups around the world. Kennedy stresses that their relative lack of attention to arts, crafts, and architecture is consistent with the strongly utilitarian emphasis that pervaded their culture. They exercised skill where necessary to produce artifacts that served their purposes well, but elaboration beyond that point was unusual.

Social Organization and Relationships

Independent nuclear families of parents and children occupied most Inápuchi dwellings, but related nuclear families tended to live near one another. In some cases this tendency was manifested in the presence of two nuclear families in the same house, and in others the related families lived in separate houses in the same compound or homestead or, failing that, in nearby settlements. Many anthropologists refer to combinations composed of the nuclear families of close relatives of the same generation as *joint*

families, and there have been examples at Inápuchi of brothers with their wives and children living in the same house and functioning as a single family unit. This unit is a *fraternal* joint family (Kennedy 1978:376). The Tarahumara also formed *extended families* of various kinds. Probably most anthropologists think of the extended family as a three generation unit resulting when an older couple's married offspring live with them and bear children, creating the third generation. When a woman and her husband and children live with her parents, the result is a *matrilocal* extended family. When a man and his wife and children reside with his parents, a *patrilocal* extended family results. And if the unit consists of both sons and daughters and their families living with their parents, it may be called an *ambilocal* (or *bilocal*) extended family.

Significantly, all of these units—independent nuclear families, joint families, matrilocal extended families, patrilocal extended families, and ambilocal extended families occurred among the Tarahumara of Inápuchi. Moreover, a major reason they occurred was that family composition changed rather frequently. Commonly, in fact, people would live in one arrangement at one time of year and a different one another. While Kennedy was in Inápuchi two brothers and their families lived in the same house in the plateau settlement, but when they moved to the bottom of the barranca for the winter, they lived in separate nearby caves. Then, during the season of food scarcity, one of the brothers moved out with his spouse and children to live with his wife's parents for awhile. The composition of Inápuchi families changed, then, as people moved about for economic and other reasons. In addition, they changed as people were born and died and as they married and divorced. An extended family could become a joint family due to the deaths of an old couple. If the siblings established separate households, the consequence was independent nuclear families. And if the children married and bore their own children while still with the parents, the unit became extended again.

There were other kinds of households at Inápuchi, often because members of the same family lived separately but near one another. One Inápuchi man and his wife and stepson lived in one house, while his mother and younger unmarried brother occupied a house about fifty yards away. His two other unmarried brothers lived in a third house about half a mile away. Each of these three living units, united by kinship, worked their land and stored their food separately, but they cooperated to make beer and throw beer parties, herded their separately owned livestock together, and occasionally ate together. The old mother made most of the blankets for all (Kennedy 1978:177).

Land tenure standards influenced residence and family composition to a significant degree. Inheritance was strictly *bilateral* at Inápuchi, which means the people divided land equally among all the children of both sexes when parents died. This had the important consequence of making it impossible for a small percentage of the society to gain control of large portions of the land. Actually, the Tarahumara often allowed children to receive all or part of their land when they married, since they felt that a married couple should be economically independent. Here their emphasis on individualism and independence came into play again. Sometimes the land was gone by the time a much younger sibling reached marriageable age, and, to gain access to some, one would have to marry someone who had inherited land. Also, since Tarahumara relatives tended to live close to one another, many could find a sufficiently unrelated person to marry only in some distant settlement. If each spouse had land the family plots became widely dispersed, and the people were faced with the question of where to reside with relationship their fields.

Among the Tarahumara, kinship, convenience, economic advantage, and inclination seemed to operate together to produced a variety of changing family arrangements. In contrast, many other societies have adhered fairly closely to well-standardized residence rules. Though there is some variation in modern U. S. society, independent nuclear family households are standard.

The Tarahumara of Inápuchi were bilateral with respect to both inheritance and descent. In societies with *unilineal descent* each person belongs to a common ancestor kinship group whose members trace their descent from ancestors through forebears of one sex only. This is especially pertinent when the kinship groups are *exogamous*, that is, when the members are expected to marry someone from a different group. The result is that husbands and wives belong to different kinship groups and all their children belong to only one parent's group. In societies with *matrilineal descent* all the children belong to their mother's matrilineal group, while the father belongs to a different matrilineal group. They also trace their ancestry through just one woman in each generation, through a line of mothers. In societies with *patrilineal descent* all the children belong to their father's patrilineal group, while the mother belongs to a different patrilineal group—her father's. They also trace their ancestry through just one man in each generation—through a line of father's. But the Tarahumara had none of this. Being bilateral, they considered themselves equally related to both the father and mother and traced their relationships through both sexes in all directions. No discrete kinship groups result from bilateral descent, so the Tarahumara had no clans or lineages. Both the inheritance and descent concepts were consonant with the Tarahumara emphasis on equality and individual rights, since men counted as much as women.

Different societies refer to their near relatives by different kinds of terms, observing some criteria of distinction and not others. Many societies use different reference terms for siblings (brothers and sisters) and cousins, but the Tarahumara of Inápuchi included all cousins under their sibling terms. Anthropologists call such reference terms *Hawaiian*. Some reference terms distinguish between relatives according to their sex and others do not. Inápuchi terms did. They had one set of sibling-cousin terms for their brothers and male cousins and a different set of terms for their sisters and female cousins. In quite a few societies males use different terms than females for the same kind of relative. For example, a Tarahumara male used one set of terms for his younger sisters while a female used a different set of terms for them. Finally, it is fairly common for people to use different terms for their older siblings and/or cousins than for their younger ones, and this was true at Inápuchi.

Following all of these criteria, a Tarahumara woman referred to all her sisters and female cousins who were older than she as *kochí* and all those younger than she as *biní*. For each of her older brothers and cousins she used the term *bachí*, and she called those younger than she *boní*. A male used the same term for his older sisters and female cousins as the females, calling them *kochí*. But he used a different term, *wayé*, for his younger sisters and female cousins. He referred to his older brothers and male cousins as *bachí* and his younger brothers and male cousins *boní*, just as the females did. To generalize on these points, males and females of Inápuchi used different terms for the younger siblings and cousins but the same set of terms for their older siblings and cousins.

Some societies separate their aunts and uncles terminologically from their parents, while others do not. For an individual's parental generation of close relatives (parents, aunts, and uncles) the Tarahumara lumped different kinds of relatives together, just as they did on their own generation, referring to their aunts and uncles by the terms they used for their biological parents. Anthropologists call this *generation* terminology. This system, then, does somewhat the same kind of lumping for the parental generation as the Hawaiian system does for a person's own generation. Tarahumara, whether male or female, referred to their mother, the mother's sisters, and the father's sisters by one term, *chichi*. They referred to their father, their father's brothers, and the mother's brothers by a second term, *tata*. Obviously, they did not distinguish older from younger aunts and uncles, and both sexes used the same terms. So they brought fewer criteria of distinction into play for the parental generation than for their own.

Anthropologists have found that people usually behave in similar ways to different kinds of relatives for which they use the same term. Tarahumara behavior confirms this, since people tended to relate to their aunts and uncles in ways similar to their interaction with their biological parents, though less intensely. The same applied to a person's own generation. People tended to relate to cousins in ways similar to relations with actual brothers and sisters. Correspondence between terms and social behavior is the main reason anthropologists study kinship terms. Undeniably, a few enjoy learning about and charting the various categories of kin, but many are primarily interested in the clues to how relatives behave toward one another yielded by such studies.

The Tarahumara of Inápuchi did not constitute a society of stable social groups in 1960. The most stable group was the nuclear family, though that stability was frequently broken by death or divorce. Nuclear families and parts of them were combined to form the composite joint and extended families, but these changed from generation to generation at least and, commonly, within the year. The people had no kinship groups such as lineages and clans, no religious organizations such as cult groups or churches, no secret societies, no dance societies, no military societies, and no recreational groups. It was a society completely without formal organizations (Kennedy 1978:1220). Partly for this reason, and partly because of the physical isolation and the concomitant shyness and individualism, a social network for getting drunk on beer assumed major proportions in the life of the pagan Tarahumara. Functions which other societies exercised in more conventional contexts were carried on by the Tarahumara within the context of their beer parties. Kennedy calls the social units involved *networks* rather than groups, since they were quite unstable. Only when the Tarahumara were drunk were they sufficiently relaxed to do many things of cultural importance to them. The beer party was a major occasion for work, play, resolution of legal matters, sexual interaction, marriage arrangement, religious ceremonies, and so on.

The occasion for a beer party was cooperative labor. A Tarahumara worked alone or with close family a good deal of the time, but there were some economic activities that could be accomplished more readily and more agreeably by a group of some size. When a family faced weeding, harvesting, cutting fodder, spreading fertilizer, cutting roof timbers, building fences, erecting a house, and similar major techno-economic jobs, they made a large amount of corn beer called *tesgüino* and invited men from nearby settlements to attend the cooperative work event known as a *tesgüinada*. The hosts provided the tesgüino as remuneration for the work, but the various reciprocal obligations and privileges among men of the vicinity prompted the men to participate more than the work and their enjoyment of the drinking warranted (Kennedy 1978:71).

Kennedy stresses the freedom and flexibility of the tesgüinada pattern. Some of the wealthier men would give a party two or three times in a few days to get some major task completed, and a number threw more beer parties than needed for economic reasons. Other men nearly always got their work done alone or in the family context, avoiding contact with their neighbors and only rarely giving a tesgüinada. The networks also changed from time to time and with which household was hosting their neighbors. The result was a netlike arrangement of overlapping, household-centered systems of interaction extending across the region (Kennedy 1978:120).

One of the most influential residents of Inápuchi invited to his parties all the people of Inápuchi proper, those of two other settlements, one household from each of three other settlements and, sometimes, a family from another place. The others reciprocated by inviting this man and his family to their tesgüinadas, but not all of them. Some invited him more than others and they hosted still others that he did not. An observer shifting his attention across the region would note that the overlapping was a regular feature over a large area, none of the networks having discrete boundaries. They were not groups. In addition, their stability was undermined by the movement of the Inápuchi Tarahumara into the gorges in the winter.

Since the pagan Tarahumara of this area lacked the institutions that carry out important social functions in many other societies, the tesgüinada institution carried a staggering functional load. It was the occasion for important economic, religious, entertainment, social control, and other basic functions. The people insisted that all drink and get as drunk as they could, and while in a state of inebriation they settled disputes, punished offenders, arranged marriages, concluded economic exchanges, preached sermons, demonstrated leadership abilities, arranged kickball races, had sexual experiences within and outside marriage, engaged in standardized sexual jokes and horseplay, played music, conducted curing ceremonies, had wrestling matches, and, to a minor degree, got into fights that sometimes resulted in injury or, rarely, death. Since the people were drunk on these occasions, important social functions were prosecuted with somewhat different consequences than if they were sober. It was clear that they sometimes failed to work out matters of major importance as well as other groups did in more formal and sober situations and that some minor matters acquired inflated importance and took up an inordinate amount of time. Yet, important matters did get taken care of that would not have otherwise. The personalities of most pagan Tarahumara of 1960 simply were not well adapted to accomplishing so much while sober.

It is important for outside observers to avoid the easy assumption that Tarahumara tesgüinadas were just irresponsible drunken orgies. Some may find the assumption easy because they are viewing the institution in terms of their own culture's perspectives. Anthropologists call this *ethnocentrism*, and ethnocentrism distorts one's view of alien lifeways. A vastly superior approach to understanding other customs is *cultural relativism*, which is discovering how customs function within the total cultural and ecological context within which they exist. This approach clearly reveals that the beer party is of fundamental significance for the effective functioning the Tarahumara lifeway.

Some might be tempted to conclude that the tesgüinada is a "good" institution, but most anthropologists through the generations have insisted that there is no way to evaluate customs and cultures—that any attempt to do so is ethnocentric. They point out that evaluating some customs as better than others requires us to suppose that there is some ultimate standard of right and wrong—good and bad—and that science cannot verify the existence of such absolutes. Nor is it possible for science to verify the existence of a supernatural person or other absolute entity that can define good and bad for us.

The consistent implication of this position is that scientific cultural evaluations are impossible. Time and again, assertions that one custom is superior to another are silenced with the question, "Who is to say?" One society finds good what another society finds bad, and there is no absolute standard for determining which society is correct.

But most anthropologists are troubled by the implication that their position prevents them from condemning Nazi extermination of Jews, torture of political prisoners, and other customs that injure or kill humans or make them psychologically miserable. Some are troubled and unsure what to do about it and leave the issue unresolved in their minds while choosing as persons to condemn violations of human rights and to work for their elimination. A few stick to their assertions that one custom or culture is as good as another but maintain that we can rightly condemn practices detrimental to human welfare, apparently unaware of the inconsistency of their position. Still other anthropologists hold that there are certain practices that satisfy inclinations characteristic of all human groups better than their alternatives. They are willing to evaluate carefully and, often, tentatively.

In applying this approach to complexes of customs such as the Tarahumara tesgüinada they may find some elements good and some bad. Kennedy strongly indicated the positive features of the Tarahumara beer parties and explained how they satisfied Tarahumara needs. At the same time he rejected the idea that all practices are equally beneficial to humankind simply because they exist and, indeed, insisted that "we must develop some kind of supercultural measuring stick which will enable us legitimately to transcend the bog of total cultural relativism." (Kennedy 1978:221). He spoke of *costs*, by which he meant practical losses and threats to life and health, and *dysfunctions*, which he designated as social losses such as built-in conflict-generating customs and institutions that throw things "out of phase" because they change at different rates. For the Tarahumara beer parties he mentioned an intoxicated mother accidentally dropping her baby in the fire or rolling over and crushing it, a man falling off a cliff and killing himself on the way home, the spread of disease by drinking from a common gourd, depending on corn beer to heal diseases, getting sick from overexposure on the way home from a party, the curtailment of creativity that would help solve economic deprivation, the use of corn for beer when it was needed for food, and the time and effort spent on tesgüinadas that might be expended to great advantage on more helpful activities. He notes that many of the Tarahumara were aware of some or all of these costs and expressed regret about them. He also notes that Tarahumara intoxication caused them to violate their own standards of what was good and bad, especially their strong proscriptions against fighting and adultery, and they also recognized this. He found the insecurities, resentments, and frustrations that resulted from such failures easy to detect. Kennedy's conclusion was that, in spite of the important functions of the tesgüinada, it is in order to consider the possibility that the losses outweigh the gains when all factors are considered (Kennedy 1978:224).

One alternative, then, is to hold that there is no way to evaluate customs and deal with questions of human rights and misery as best one can on a personal, nonscientific level. The other alternative is to assume that, given the freedom to choose, humans everywhere would prefer customs that maximize their feelings of well-being and that this is a valid basis for cultural evaluation. Anthropologists do not agree on which alternative is correct.

A Tarahumara woman often bore her child in some secluded spot, though a female relative or her husband sometimes went with her. She prepared a bed of grass to receive the baby and gave birth in a crouching position while hanging onto a branch. After the umbilical cord was cut and the afterbirth buried, the newborn infant was washed and wrapped in a cotton cloth. Unwanted babies might be killed. On the third day after a boy's birth, the shaman conducted a "curing ceremony" designed to protect the boy and his parents from sickness, and the ceremony was repeated every two or three weeks for three more times. A similar ceremony was performed for a girl four days after birth and repeated four times (Fried 1969:868).

Inápuchi mothers kept their children close to their bodies for the first two and a half or three years, carrying them on the back, front, or side while continuing their work. They usually gave babies the breast whenever they wanted or were at all disturbed. After this early period, they left their children on the ground more, and older children began to help care for their younger siblings. Kennedy often saw seven or eight year old children carrying a child on the back, sometimes while herding goats (Kennedy 1978:163). Though Inápuchi parents usually cared for their small children carefully and gently, life for children was rough. Adult responsibilities sometimes kept the parents from caring for their children as well as they would like to, and sometimes they were neglected at tesgüinada times. Many were injured or killed by falling from steep trails or being bitten by rattlesnakes. Diseases such as measles, smallpox, and tuberculosis, as well as malnutrition, also troubled and killed many children. The infant mortality rate was high.

The Tarahumara felt they should be gentle with their children and relied on reasoning more than corporal punishment. Weaning was gradual and gentle, largely involving the introduction of pinole, esquiáte, and atole. The people toilet trained their infants primarily by taking them outside if they were seen quickly enough, and they explained to them what was expected and praised them for success. Most children knew where they should go to relieve themselves by the time they were two or three years old. Parents worried that a child might become frightened and die if struck (Kennedy 1978:164). The most common punishment was a lecture following the standard sermon-giving pattern used for adults. From about seven or eight years of age on a child that was beaten or unhappy might run away and stay with a relative at another place. Both the parents and the relatives accepted this, and it illustrates how the Tarahumara extended the ideal of individualism and independence to include their youngsters. This high valuation of children as persons in their own right helps account for the concern of many Tarahumara about the dangers and difficulties to children from the beer parties.

Gradual development also prevailed during later childhood, and both boys and girls enjoyed considerable freedom. Boys began to imitate their fathers fairly early, and the fathers encouraged and rewarded them and gave them greater responsibilities as they progressed. But the boys also had to spend great amounts of time herding goats in the mountains or forests, either alone or with siblings. They were not permitted to sleep in the house at night and often slept in small lean-tos near the corrals. This time of aloneness continued until the boy married, sometime between fourteen and twenty-five, and some of the young men were not well prepared to assume adult roles. It was different for the girls, since they spent more time with their mothers. They were usually married shortly after puberty and were well skilled in doing women's work.

The strongest family ties among the Inápuchi Tarahumara developed among siblings, especially those of the same sex. As boys, brothers often herded the animals, watched the fields, and slept together separate from everyone else. Sets of brothers often participated in kickball races together or played other games as teams of brothers (Kennedy 1978:169). When grown the brothers often brought their families together in the same household (the joint family), and even if they did not, they supported one another in disputes. Brothers took things from one another's storage bins or appropriated one anothers stray animals without permission. They were not to complain about such things, but some resented such behavior. Sisters also grew up together and developed strong relationships, though they were not so isolated from other family members as the boys. Tarahumara extended sibling relationships to their cousins, whom they referred to as their brothers and sisters (Hawaiian terminology), but the relationships were much weaker than those of nephews and nieces to some of their aunts and uncles. The strength of the relationships between cousins might depend on whether or not they had lived together. If so, they probably had worked together as children just as siblings had.

Adult sons usually consulted with their fathers on important questions throughout their lives, and father and son generally trusted and helped one another. The way they expressed that relationship provided an occasion for ethnocentric misunderstanding by outsiders, since fathers and sons spoke of ordering one another to do one thing or another. To U.S. citizens and other outsiders this implies authority, but the key element to the Tarahumara was mutual obligation rather than authority. Both knew, for example, that a son was obligated to run in a kickball race if the father asked him to, and a father had the right to make this request in the form of an order and expect the son to comply. Sons also had the right to call on their fathers to meet mutually understood obligations, such as making beer for them. The people did not view these things as a matter of authority of one person over another.

Tarahumara parents and adult children manifested respect and affection for one another, and the children were expected to care for their parents when they became too decrepit to care for themselves. Old people worked until then or until they died, since they had no concept of a retirement period.

Consonant with their custom of referring to their aunts and uncles by the same terms they used for their actual parents (generation terms), Tarahumara behaved toward their parents' brothers and sisters in ways similar to their behaviors toward their parents. The relationships were weaker however, and their intensity depended considerably on how much the respective parties had associated with one another. Nephews and nieces who had lived in joint or extended families including brothers and/or sisters of their parents would become involved in parent-child type relationships with them much more than they would with aunts and uncles they had never lived with.

Inápuchi Tarahumara women usually married soon after puberty, while men usually did not marry until fifteen or so and sometimes several years later. They were allowed considerable freedom of choice, and personal qualities counted heavily. Men valued youthfulness, plumpness, regular features, skill in women's work, and industriousness. Women generally favored a husband who was youthful, slim, vigorous, not pugnacious, wealthy, and well skilled in men's work. Women often initiated a courtship, normally at a tesgüinada. Many of the world's cultures provide for *cross cousin marriage*, cross cousins being those related to one another through the father's sister or the mother's brother, but not the Tarahumara. People with any traceable biological relationship on either side of the family (bilaterally, that is) were expected to avoid marrying each other. Consequently, people sometimes had trouble finding a spouse and had to wait several years to get married or marry someone who lived a great distance away. It was also fairly common for one spouse to be considerably older than the other. The Tarahumara permitted *polygyny*, which is marriage between a man and more than one woman, but Kennedy knew of only two cases (personal communication).

Inápuchi married couples seldom showed affection toward one another in public, but they did have such feelings. At their homes many wives combed their husbands' hair or deloused them, and Kennedy frequently saw husband and wife lying side by side in the morning sun by their house before beginning their daily work (Kennedy 1978:170). Many of the people had been married several times, mostly because of the death of one of the spouses. Many marriages also ended in divorce, which was accomplished simply by one partner's departure. This often happened at a beer party, which was the time that tensions and jealousies otherwise kept under cover manifested themselves. At tesgüinadas husbands often asked a respected man to admonish his errant wife through the standard sermon-giving pattern, and wives sometimes did the same to a wayward husband.

Many cultures include a highly standardized kind of social relationship that anthropologists have long called *joking relationships*. These commonly exist between persons in some kind of tension with one another, and the teasing and horseplay involved seem to be ritual ways of dealing with the tension. Among the Inápuchi Tarahumara there were joking relationships between people and their male and female in-laws of the same generation and, also, between grandparents and grandchildren. A man referred to all of his female in-laws of his own generation as his wives, and the women referred to the males as their husbands. The joking included taunts and insults combined with sexual horseplay, often rough. It took place at tesgüinadas, could be initiated by either a woman or a man, and was greatly enjoyed by those who witnessed it. A woman, for example, might lift a man's loincloth while making suggestive comments or even try to wrestle him to the ground or rip off his clothing, with both insulting one another loudly and lewdly. Such behavior never occurred when people were sober.

Joking relatives of the same sex often pretended homosexual interest in one another, all the while making a big joke out of it. No homosexual intercourse actually occurred, the people denied that it ever did, and Kennedy was unable to find any evidence for it. Men often wrestled at a tesgüinada, and the wrestling matches sometimes took on a homosexual flavor. Grandparents and grandchildren, either of the same sex or different sexes, often engaged in sexually suggestive horse play with one another. The kinship terms and the relationships were not limited to actual grandparents and grandchildren, but were extended to include others. People in their fifties and older involved themselves in the joking.

Inápuchi Tarahumara older people continued to work and participate in other cultural activities as long as they were able. They did not retire, but when they needed help and care, their children, their own or others they referred to as sons an daughters, provided it. At death joking relatives (in-laws of the same generation as the deceased) relieved the close biological relatives of the task of carrying out the burial arrangements. They wrapped the person in a blanket and laid the body in the house. They tied the person's hands folded on the breast with a crucifix or small wooden cross, built a small fire by the head, and stuck a foot high cross into the dirt floor nearby. They then stacked the person's most important possessions near the cross and placed symbolic offerings of food there in a bowl or pouch. The next day a number of other rituals were conducted in the presence of the family, immediate neighbors, and others who had learned of the death, and the body was wrapped in the blanket, lashed to a pole, and taken to a burial cave in the barranca. There they placed the body with the head to the east, left offerings, and conducted more ritual. When the pall bearers returned to the settlement, there were still more rituals.

There were death fiestas held at intervals after the funeral, three for a man and four for a woman. The first took place three days later for a man and four for a women. The second was supposed to occur three months later for a man and four months afterward for a woman. The last fiesta for a man was to take place three months later, and the two last fiestas for women were to be held in the fourth and eighth months. These were the ideal ritual times, but the people often altered the schedule to suit their convenience, and some might not attend. They performed many specific ritual acts, but it is interesting to outsiders that at the first fiesta the joking relatives danced up to the deceased person's belongings, kicked at them, and made obscene jokes.

One of the most common elements of death observances around the world is ritual designed to send the soul on its way and prevent it from returning to worry or bother the living. During the first death fiesta the joking relatives of a pagan Tarahumara deceased person engaged in mock combat with machetes or knives in the belief that the clashing of the blades would prevent the ghost from returning (Kennedy 1978:153).

Government and Social Order

In every culture there are discrepancies between ideals as perceived and stated by the people and the actual situations. A number of communities around the world have strong ideals of social equality, but there are always some individuals of greater wealth and prestige than others. This was true of the pagan Tarahumara of Inápuchi, who, when asked about status always declared that everyone was equal (Kennedy 1978:83). Though status differences were not apparent in areas such as housing or clothing, some people had more animals, land, and maize than others because of their greater aggressiveness, competence, or both. Having enough land to produce a large amount of maize affected status mainly by making it possible for a person to give more beer parties, which brought prestige to the host. But the most important form of wealth was animals. Cattle were of highest value, since they were so important in farming and required such a large investment in training time. They also were scarce, since the canyon environment is a difficult place to care for them and keep them alive. Though an ox was of greater value than a goat, goats were more important to status, since their manure made it possible for a man to produce larger quantities of food. Men with oxen to pull the plow, goats to fertilize their fields, and enough land to produce a good supply of maize found themselves more influential than others, since poorer people had to borrow their animals and depend on them to host the beer parties that were so important to all.

According to Inápuchi ideals, none of the people had the formal power to coerce others. Still, they looked up to some more than others and allowed them to organize group activities and, sometimes, accepted their influence in matters of wide concern in the pagan area (Kennedy 1978:185). In addition to their competence in acquiring land and building herds and their hosting of many tesgüinadas, these men exhibited admired personal qualities that brought them prestige and influence. A man that exhibited competence and showed signs of wanting to provide leadership would be given minor responsibilities such as organizing kickball races, keeping small children away from the tesgüinada activity, or carrying messages for the local headman. If he discharged these responsibilities well the people would come to see him as a potential leader. He then would be asked to give sermonic orations at tesgüinadas. Curing ability was another way of gaining prestige, though it was not indispensable. A man of influence or who wanted to maintain or increase his position commonly tried to demonstrate his leadership by leading several other men into the tesgüinada festivities when he arrived in a settlement to participate in them. He would dramatically lead a single file of men to the ceremonial table, cross himself, make a counterclockwise turn near each of the table's four sides, greet the host, and receive from him three gourds of beer. Then, one by one, each of his followers did the same. Those observing this ritual were expected to be properly impressed by the man's evident support. Ritual, the affirmation of important values through culturally standardized utterances and/or actions, both expresses and stimulates people's commitment to those values. All societies incorporate rituals which function to maintain the influence or power of its leaders, and this is an excellent example.

The Tarahumara people are divided into territories commonly called *pueblos* (*municipios*), which are a product of Spanish and Mexican attempts to bring about some kind of organization compatible with their views of proper and exploitable social arrangements. Like municipios in other parts of Mexico, the Tarahumara pueblos are territories including a number of towns and settlements, one of which serves as the seat of government for the municipio and gives it its name. In 1960 the people of Inápuchi proper belonged to the municipio of Aboreachi, a larger settlement lying out of sight over a ridge to the east of Inápuchi. Some of the settlements of "greater Inápuchi," however, belonged to the municipio of Samachique, and the people of the area Kennedy studied were more concerned with one another than with their municipio head towns. Anthropologists and other social scientists have found in all parts of the world numerous instances of the failure of official community boundaries to coincide with real boundaries. They have found that this failure results in a great many miscarriages of administrative projects and, sometimes, miscarriages of justice, but decision-makers are seldom aware of the problem or willing to do anything about it. At Inápuchi and the surrounding settlements people continued to relate to one another according to criteria other than where municipio boundaries lay. Actually, they had no special sense of being pagan Tarahumara as opposed to the Christian Indians, though the distinction had functional significance in that there was almost no intermarriage between pagans and Christians.

The pagan Tarahumara were linked to the municipios through the headman or governor at Inápuchi, who had a seat on the municipio council in Aboreachi. But they handled most administrative matters rather informally without the involvement of the municipio authorities, and municipio officials seldom advised the headman of their meetings unless something was coming up that involved the pagans. Also, some of the more remote pagans did not recognize the authority of the Inápuchi governor and took care of their own affairs. The governor had the official responsibilities of representing the pagans in Aboreachi and handling internal administrative matters, the second being by far the most important. He called meetings on matters of group concern, acted as judge in trials of criminals, gave orations on expected behavior and penalties for violations, and dealt with minor disputes and interpersonal tensions. He had a small number of assistants charged variously with apprehending and punishing criminals, carrying messages, and policing tesgüinadas. The local officials had little power and operated quite informally most of the time. Commonly, the adult males considered major issues and came to a consensus on them, with the governor going along with their decisions. A recognized position outside the set of officials was the race organizer, who made the necessary arrangements for kick ball races.

Though quite unusual, murder was the most serious crime in Inápuchi and the only one in which Mexican authorities were involved. But both the Indians and the Mexicans were rather casual in their handling of the crime. The local officials would deliver the offender to the authorities for jailing, but the murderer sometimes escaped or bribed the Mexicans for his freedom, in which case little more might be done. One murderer the people delivered to the Mexicans escaped before they got him jailed, but the Mexicans did not come after him, nor did the people apprehend him again. He kept largely to himself and his family for a while, but people tended to minimize his crime on the grounds that he was drunk at a tesgüinada when he committed the crime. Even the son of the man he killed got along with him (Kennedy 1978:200).

Serious injury due to aggression was also rare, and the people sometimes took informal action without involving Mexican authorities in such cases. The headman severely lectured one offender at a beer party and fined him a goat, and he was no longer invited to tesgüinadas outside his own settlement. Those who stole anything could be taken to Aboreachi, but this had not been done yet when Kennedy was there in 1960. Theft was also uncommon, but people worried about it considerably. The Tarahumara of Inápuchi used difficult-to-open wooden locks on their storage bins and sometimes put seals of white clay on the locks so they could easily tell whether or not they had been opened.

All fiestas and large beer parties began with a sermon by the headman, who lectured the people to behave properly while drinking and, especially, to avoid fighting and adultery, the two most common Tarahumara offenses. The people permitted most fights to progress until blood flowed or someone reached for a weapon. They considered roughness to be expected when men wrestled at tesgüinadas and allowed for considerable boisterousness in the joking relationships that existed among some relatives. Their reluctance to interfere also expressed their individualism and independence. They would finally intervene when serious injury or death threatened, breaking up the fight and taking the combatants away from the area or having a good sermon-maker lecture them according to the traditional pattern. After things had cooled off, the drinking would resume its earlier amiability.

The Tarahumara held rather inconsistent or ambivalent attitudes about adultery and fornication. They prohibited both but engaged in both, frequently in the tesgüinada context, without inhibition and without apparent contrition when they became sober. Spouses worried about the possibility of unfaithfulness at a beer party but might anticipate participating in sexual activity themselves. They sometimes became jealous and fought because of the sexual activity. But they blamed the beer for both the fights and adultery and seldom punished people. This enabled them to continue to think of themselves as gentle people, which they were outside the tesgüinada context.

The Tarahumara were also concerned about damage to their crops and fields by other people's animals, and if it was clear whose animals were involved, the owner usually compensated for the damage in kind. Sometimes someone would claim unused land before the possessor was ready to give it up, which might result in persisting tensions between disputants. In both instances victims had the right to bring in the authorities, but seldom did.

Art and Play

Consonant with their strong pragmatic orientation, aesthetic components of pagan Tarahumara life were weakly developed in comparison with those of many other cultures. The people manifested skill in fashioning their storage bins, pots, baskets, sashes and other utilitarian artifacts, and exhibited aesthetic feelings by incorporating elements not necessary to their usefulness in some cases. The sashes, with their varicolored geometric designs, especially illustrate this. The Tarahumara achieved their greatest aesthetic heights in music, however, especially in the manufacture of violins and the playing of violin music. Kennedy calls the Tarahumara a society of violinists. Most families had a violin and nearly all the men could play. They were entirely hand-made, and many of the men knew how to make them. A few instrument makers were especially skilled, and a person wanting a top-notch instrument would have it made for him. The Tarahumara also made and played guitars, rattles, drums, and flutes. Music was an important part of all ceremonials and beer parties, and people also made music in their homes and in the countryside. A man sometimes played his violin at home before going to sleep, and a herd boy sometimes carried a violin, playing it while out watching the goats. The Inápuchi Tarahumara also danced, but dancing was hard ceremonial labor more than a pastime.

The tesgüinada was the main Tarahumara pastime, but the people also enjoyed several sports and games. The major sport was the kickball racing the Tarahumara are so famous for. The men carved the small kickballs from oak roots. They laid out a race course, divided into teams, and made bets on the outcome. One race witnessed by Kennedy was organized after a mild tesgüindada when the men were a little high but not drunk (Kennedy 1978:106). The course was made up of about six three-and-a-half mile circuits, seven men were on each team, and the race organizers took bets of money and various other objects. Runners dropped out along the way until only one man on one team was left. His team won the race without finishing the entire course. The last survivor ran about twenty miles of the total twenty-one mile circuit. The Tarahumara also had larger, longer, and better organized races, sometimes between different communities.

The players did not actually kick the ball but lifted it into the air with the toe in a motion so swift that it appeared that they kicked it. The runners were not supposed to use their hands, unless it was necessary to retrieve a ball lost in grass, caught in a rock crevice, or something of the sort (Pennington 1963:170). There was a ball for each team, the one getting theirs across the finish line first being the winners. The spectators cheered their team along, sometimes running alongside the course themselves, and they would help recover a ball that had gotten off the course. Kennedy observed women with small babies on their backs running for five or six miles alongside the teams.

Religious Beliefs and Practices

Most of the Inápuchi Tarahumara showed little interest in theologizing about their religion or ordering their beliefs into a standardized system of concepts transmitted by oral or written traditions (Kennedy 1978:127). A number of the people professed to know nothing about the details of their religion, and those willing to express themselves were vague and contradicted one another in a variety of specifics. Still, a number of elements were commonly held and pervaded their religious beliefs and practices. The salient factor was fear.

The people believed in two major deities, Great Father (*Onorúame* or *Tata Diósi*), and his enemy, the Devil (*Diablo*). Both gods were assisted by a large number of soldiers or angels. The people usually thought of the Great Father as an old white-bearded fellow living in the sky. He was a dangerous god, the major supernatural threat in their lives and, therefore, much feared. He got hungry every so often and demanded offerings by sending an angel or other messenger to tell people that he wanted a white goat, chicken, or a deer sacrificed at a prolonged dance. If the people failed to comply they expected the Great Father to make the mountains fall, send showers of blood, cause gigantic floods, cause the sun to die, bring total drought, or send a wasting sickness to all the people (Kennedy 1978:128). Some of the men said the Great Father created the earth, people, and animals, but others indicated that they did not know about this. Creation mythology was weakly developed. Some said the Great Father took most people to the sky when they died, but the Tarahumara showed little fear of what happened after death. They were present oriented and concerned mostly about the troubles and disasters of this life.

The Devil was much less dangerous than the Great Father, though he made people aggressive and caused fights at tesgüinadas. He lived underground in a place with a lot of fire or under the river and might appear as a snake or a fox. He was said to take murderers or habitual thieves with him into his underworld when they died.

Anthropologists have noted that Tarahumara religion is a syncretism of Christian and pre-Columbian elements (Fried 1969:862). While the Great Father is hardly the Christian god, it is easy to detect Christian influences in beliefs about both the Great Father and the Devil.

The Inápuchi Tarahumara also worried about trouble from a variety of evil nature spirits and the ghosts of the dead. They held that spirits lived in whirlpools, whirlwinds, and rivers and other bodies of water. They also believed that certain animals, plants, and people had supernatural powers that could bring evil. They felt that toads and horned toads could cause sickness if one touched them, and they regarded peyote as having a powerful spirit that could trouble people.

Two major specialists served in the religious arena, the most important being the shaman-priest (*owerúame*). The oweruame was a *shaman* in the sense that he had personal power to deal with the supernatural as he divined the causes of illness, healed people, and provided protection against disease and disaster. Shaman is the term anthropologists most often use for religious specialists who have such power in themselves. Shamans differ from *priests* in this respect, since anthropologists define priests as specialists who conduct religious ritual in behalf of a group or cult. The power lies not in the priest but in the ritual he or she knows and performs. The Tarahumara specialists worked both as shamans and priests, though they would not make a point of the difference between the two roles as anthropologists do.

The shaman-priest's most important power was being able to see what was happening to people's souls and sending his own soul out to correct the situation. He obtained this power through dreams and exercised it in dreams. He dreamed of patients' souls being in some kind of danger and cured them by rescuing their souls. That was his shamanistic function. But he also conducted ceremonies for the people, and this function rested heavily on knowledge of "medicines" and how they should be ritually utilized.

A shaman-priest's career began when he dreamed a great deal and imagined himself to have curative abilities, usually when he was a boy. When that developed, the young person was encouraged and another shaman-priest might give him minor ritual responsibilities and begin to teach him. After a time he would begin to perform some shamanistic and priestly acts alone, and someone might call on him to heal a sick person. If he was successful on such occasions he would gradually be called on more and more until he became a recognized shaman-priest.

There was a still higher level of achievement, however, when the practitioner was able to carry out the most diffi-

cult functions and had achieved a good enough reputation over a large area to be called upon to conduct major ceremonies. At this point he might become virtually full-time. In 1960, however, there was only one full-time shaman-priest in all of the municipio of Aboreachi (Kennedy 1978:74).

Another important religious specialist was the chanter or dance leader. He was less significant than the shaman-priest, but he remained important because properly performed dancing was an indispensable part of community preventive-therapeutic ceremonies. The dancing was necessary for ceremonies of protection from hail, worms, and drought, and it was important at funerals and before important kick-ball races.

There were also witches in Tarahumara society. *Witchcraft* is doing evil through one's personal supernatural power or extraordinary ability to manipulate or influence the supernatural. Often it involves working through a familiar spirit or utilizing some kind of specific power to accomplish the evil. Commonly, the power comes to one without any effort to acquire it. Often a witch is able to do evil simply by willing it—as a kind of psychic act. In culture after culture, too, the witch has the ability to turn himself or herself into an animal or other form representing his familiar in order to do evil. People called witches may also use black magic or sorcery. The concept in all kinds of magic is that the power lies in the procedure, the formula or the medicine rather than in the person performing the act. When sorcery is combined with witchcraft there is power in the procedure, but it may be reinforced by the personal power of the witch. Tarahumara witches in 1960 performed evil primarily by thinking it or by using a "medicine. Peyote, for example, was a medicine which could travel in some mystical way to find and harm the victim. The witch might also eat the victim's soul, another notion widely found in societies believing in witchcraft. Some Tarahumara witches had familiars in the form of invisible birds they could direct at night to attack someone's soul. One shaman-priest at Inápuchi claimed the ability to see and ward off such birds (Kennedy 1978:136). He also agreed with other Tarahumara that there was a wife of a great shaman-priest of another settlement who was especially powerful and had harmed many, including killing four of her husbands. She did these things simply by thinking evil of the victims. For example, she killed one of her husbands by sending a knife into him simply by her thoughts. He awoke in the night with an excruciating pain in his abdomen and, after two days of suffering, died.

The people of Inápuchi held that some witches were born that way but that most of them were unsuccessful shamans. Both shamans and witches have special power to deal with the supernatural, and both can turn that power to either evil or good. A frustrated shaman, then, might turn to witchcraft, and witches sometimes doubled as shamans. The powerful witch believed to have killed her four previous husbands assisted her fifth husband, a powerful shaman-priest, with his curing ceremonies. The Inápuchi Tarahumara, however, held that there were no witches in Inápuchi, though most said they had been attacked at one time or another by witches from other Tarahumara places.

The curing rituals were the major ceremonies at Inápuchi. Curing or healing may be said to be an *etic* category anthropologists use to describe and compare cultures. While observing a particular group's customs anthropologists recognize customary beliefs and practices pertinent to restoring people who suffer some disorder. They use the label *curing* to designate them, describe what they consist of, and compare the curing beliefs of one culture with those of others. Anthropologists have to use etic categories if they are to compare cultures and make generalizations about humanity on the basis of those comparisons. Witchcraft, sorcery, clan, matrilocal residence, ritual, and shaman are examples of other etic categories widely used by anthropologists.

But given etic categories may or may not be recognized by the people as part of their experience and thought, so even when anthropologists recognize customs they call curing, the people may have no such category. The Tarahumara of Inápuchi had a term that included what anthropologists call curing, but its meaning was much broader than that of the English word. This category, an *emic* category (recognized by the people in question or functional in their culture) included rituals that strengthened and prevented as well as restored. So what, in translation, the anthropologist calls a curing ceremony was a complex of rituals designed to prevent harm and alleviate trouble that had already developed (Kennedy 1978:140). This concept of prevention-alleviation ritual was the central element of pagan Tarahumara ceremonial life. Each year everything important, including crops, animals, and people had to be cured in the broader sense to prevent harm and restore the diseased.

The ceremonies usually took place on a specially cleared area near a house. It was a sacred area for the duration of the ceremonies. The people set up a wooden table or altar on the eastern side so that it faced westward. Three crosses about three feet high and draped in muslin rose from the eastern side of the altar. Baskets and bowls of pinole, tortillas, tamales, and boiled meat were placed on the altar and used for several hours as offerings to the Great Father, who partook of the essence or smell of the food before the people feasted on it. Jars of tesgüino were placed behind the table. Minor offerings to the Devil were placed under the table to keep him from interfering with the offerings to the Great Father.

The first major aspect of the ceremony was the *yúmari* dance performed by the chanters. Usually two or three danced for many hours, chanting with rattles in hand. Later they speeded up the dance tempo and young men and women joined the chanters in the *tutubúri* dance. All the elements of the ceremony were ordained by the Great Father. When the chanters stopped the dancing, the food was distributed for a feast. Other rounds of dancing and feasting followed, and the people began to drink beer. The Great Father and the spirits required this, and the ceremonies were dedicated by tossing small ladles of beer in the four directions. The beer was a ritual medicine in this context, and other medicines were the blood of animals, cedar smoke, corncob smoke, the smoke of a native incense, red clay, certain parts of maguey and other plants, esquiáte, and several other substances. Not all were used in every ceremony, but all those used were supposed to work together to prevent illness and crop damage. The shaman-priest performed a number of ritual movements, such as gestures to the four directions, counterclockwise circuits by the men, and marking crosses in the air with smoke, beer, or other substances.

The cross permeated Tarahumara ritual, since they used many wooden crosses of various sizes and made gestures in the form of a cross. The people also had curing ceremonies at their fields and their corrals as well as ceremonies for children. While Kennedy was among them in 1960, the people held separate curing ceremonies for every field and corral at the Inápuchi settlement. They also had rituals for the prevention of diseases in their children.

Cultural Change

In 1960 the people of Inápuchi had no place to go to withdraw from advancing civilization as they had during previous generations. There is no readily available account of the cultural changes that took place at Inápuchi after 1960, but their future looked bleak at the time. Kennedy noted that the traditional pattern of withdrawing into mountainous regions would no longer serve and that even the pagans living in their remote canyons were soon to be forced to confront the onward rush of civilization (1978:229).

Chapter 8

THE HUICHOL INDIANS OF JALISCO AND NAYARIT

For a long time outsiders learned little about the Huichol (approx. WEE-chohl) of the mountains and canyons of the Sierra Madre Occidental of west central Mexico. But things changed as North Americans became interested in Huichol use of peyote and became more familiar with their religious art. During the 1960s many American young people took to using drugs, and some became interested in other societies that used them. This interest also stimulated more study of drugs in culture by anthropologists, and it was inevitable that they should turn their attention to one of the few Mexican groups still using a hallucinogen as a basic feature of their lifeway. As outsiders learned more about the Huichol they became increasingly intrigued by their colorful religious art, which was intricately interlaced with their religion and drug use. In addition the Mexicans have continued their efforts to bring Indian groups in the remotest regions into Mexican national life. Researchers, developers, art collectors, journalists, and others put out a continuing stream of reports on Huichol art and culture for a fascinated public, and major exhibits of Huichol art appeared in American, Mexican, and European museums. The Huichol are also interesting because of their resistance to acculturation. Like some other groups they have been aided in their resistance by their homeland's inaccessibility. But some think their culture had a special vitality that strengthened their opposition to Spanish and Mexican culture. Huichol is the term for these people most widely used by outsiders, but its origins are unclear, and the Huichol usually call themselves Wixarika (Myerhoff 1974:53).

As with so many other things about the Huichol it is difficult to say how many there were during the second half of the twentieth century. There were at least 8,000 during the late 1970s, and Weigand's opinion was that there were between 14,000 and 15,000 (1978:102). Not more than 1500 of these lived on the Nayarit coast, among the Cora, and in nearby Mexican towns and cities.

The Huichol of the 1960s and 1970s were farmers using the slash and burn technique on the steep mountainsides and living in widely scattered farmsteads or small clusters of them. Such scattered neighborhood communities, often called *rancherías*, have been characteristic of the Northwest Mexico tribes since before the Conquest. Each Huichol neighborhood was made up of a number of farmsteads, some of which were occupied by independent nuclear families and others of which consisted of several related nuclear families.

One or more neighborhoods centered around administrative-religious centers, called *pueblos*, that the Spanish established at already existing ceremonial sites. Only a few people lived in the pueblo centers, however, since most preferred to be near their fields. There were five major pueblos and several minor ones. The five main ones were grouped into *communidades*, which were land grants chartered by the Spanish. Each communidad had a *presidente* and other elected and appointed officials.

The people believed in a large number of deities, each of them having different powers the people sought to benefit from. A fire deity, a sun god, a trickster-intermediary, and many deities of maize, deer, and peyote were among the most important. Shaman-priests were important for drawing on the power of the supernaturals for healing and other purposes. Like other Northwest Mexico Indians the Huichol had an elaborate religious ritual system. The peyote pilgrimage was one of the major ceremonial events of Huichol life, and the Huichol are renowned for their religious art.

Prehistory

Scholars have not been able to settle the question of the origins of the Huichol. Some think they came from other parts of Mexico and had not been where the Spanish found them for very long. Others think they had been there for many hundreds of years at least. Anthropologist Phil Weigand, who has done both archaeological and ethnographic research in the area, points to archaeological evidence suggesting that the Huichol were well established in their present country by A.D. 200. The twentieth century Huichol had large, round ceremonial buildings, sometimes called temples, and carbon 14 testing indicates similar structures by A.D. 200. As the Spanish troubled the surrounding tribes, which Weigand sees as being strongly Mesoamerican, a number joined the ancestors of today's Huichol, contributing some of their customs to the culture now known as Huichol (Weigand 1978:101).

In 1974 Barbara Myerhoff felt that the Huichol most likely came from the northeast, perhaps due to disturbances from the Spanish conquest effort. The Huichol themselves have a tradition that they came from the east or northeast and settled for a time near present-day Guadalajara before moving into their present territory (Myerhoff 1974:55). She also noted that the twentieth century Huichol seemed to have a peyote ceremony similar in important ways to those of some of the Chichimec gatherer-hunters of north central and northeastern Mexico. But more significant is the annual pilgrimage of Huichol to the Chihuahuan Desert of San Luís Potosí to obtain a year's supply of peyote, especially the fact that along the pilgrimage route they are intricately familiar with the mountains, caves, groves of trees, water holes, springs, rivers, and rocks and have names for them in the Huichol language. Myerhoff notes they could obtain peyote more easily than by going to San Luís Potosí and that it doesn't seem reasonable that they would return there, know the route so well, and have the whole pilgrimage complex so tightly integrated into their lives unless they had acutally migrated from the Chihuahuan Desert. She felt they came to their twentieth century country as Chichimec hunter-gatherers and that, at an even earlier time, their ancestors may have resided in the southwestern U.S.A.

While Weigand emphasized the Mesoamerican character of Huichol culture, Peter Furst has stressed the even stronger similarities between the Huichol and the Indians of the American Southwest (Furst 1972a), and Grimes concurs with his view. The disagreement over Huichol origins reflects a long standing question as to the cultural position of the tribe and whether the Huichol belong in the culture area of Northwest Mexico, which is part of the Greater Southwest, or in Mesoamerica.

A *culture area* is a geographic territory within which the cultures are more like one another than they are those of neighboring regions. Early twentieth century anthropologists explored the possible theoretical significance of culture areas but obtained rather insignificant results. Today the concept is used mainly to classify cultural diversity. Yet, it is difficult to know where to draw the line between one area and another, since cultures often vary only slightly from adjacent cultures. Ethnologists have found it useful to distinguish a Northwest Mexico type of culture from a Mesoamerican type, but they have continued to disagree over whether the Huichol and Cora and some of their neighbors are Northwest Mexican or Mesoamerican. The question of the origins of the Huichol reflects that disagreement and remains unsettled. We have included them in Northwest Mexico because of Grimes' and Hinton's feelings that Huichol and Cora cultures are more like those of Northwest Mexico than those of central Mexico (Grimes and Hinton 1969:79) and because of Myerhoff's and Furst's view that the Huichol came from the North.

History

Francisco Cortés de San Buenaventura entered Jalisco and Nayarit in 1524, but Nuño de Guzmán made the first definite impact on the area in 1530-31. While the Indians probably borrowed a few Spanish traits during subsequent years, the Spanish did not establish a sustained presence until 1722. The Franciscan missionaries set up mission stations in three Huichol centers, but they made little impact. The Spanish subdued the nearby Cora Indians, and the Jesuits gathered them into concentrated communities. Undoubtedly, a number of Spanish traits found their way to the Huichol via the changing Cora. During the centuries after contact the Huichol acquired metal artifacts, livestock, elements of Catholicism, *matachin* dancing (a kind of church dance), and so on, but in general they resisted extensive acculturation. They participated in various raids and revolts against Spanish and maintained a degree of independence because of the remoteness of their mountain homeland.

Ethnography

For the first four decades of the twentieth century the report of Carl Lumholtz was the only major source of information on Huichol culture. He published the results of his 1895 expedition through this part of Mexico at the beginning of the century (1900, 1903, 1904), and the next major work did not appear until the publication of Robert Zingg's study in 1939. Grimes and Hinton regard Lumholtz' work as reliable for technology but not for social organization and religion (1969:795). They regard Zingg's report as fairly accurate descriptively but poorly integrated and full of unacceptable interpretations. One of these is that primitives think prelogically, an idea extensively developed by the French anthropologist Lucien Levy-Bruhl (1923). Zingg declared that the Huichol belief that rock-crystals, hail-stones, clouds, and the like are somehow associated with souls and the attributes of gods is "prime evidence of the illogicality of the primitive mind in mystic participation" (Zingg 1938:165-166). But anthropological studies have shown that so-called primitives think by the same processes as Europeans and Americans and no less logically. They often arrive at different conclusions because they start with different presuppositions, not because their minds work differently. In the face of the accumulating evidence Levy-Bruhl abandoned his original position later in his career.

In 1934 the social psychologist Otto Klineberg made a very limited study of Huichol personality. More in-depth and accurate portrayals of Huichol life came only in the 1960s and 1970s. The missionary linguists Joseph and Barbara Grimes worked among the Huichol and published descriptions on kinship terminology, economic organization, and language (J. Grimes 1955, 1959, 1960, 1961 and 1964; J. and B. Grimes 1962). Joseph Grimes worked among the Huichol for almost fifteen years and is one of the few

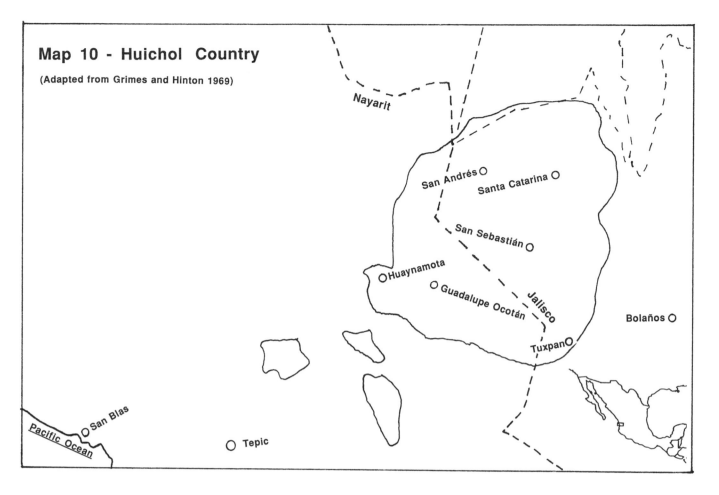

Map 10 - Huichol Country

(Adapted from Grimes and Hinton 1969)

Nayarit

San Andrés ○

Santa Catarina ○

San Sebastián ○

○ Huaynamota

○ Guadalupe Ocotán

Jalisco

Bolaños ○

Tuxpan ○

○ San Blas

Pacific Ocean

○ Tepic

outsiders to speak the Huichol language. He also collaborated with Thomas Hinton to write a summary of Huichol and Cora cultures for the *Handbook of Middle American Indians* (1969:792-813).

During the late 1960s anthropologists Peter Furst and Barbara Myerhoff, who were interested in religious symbolism and related matters, became acquainted with a Huichol shaman-priest, Ramón Medina Silva, and his wife, Lupe, who were living on the outskirts of Guadalajara. Furst and Meyerhoff did not live with the Huichol but worked for the most part at the Medinas' Guadalajara home. The Medinas had tried to eke out a living by farming in San Sebastián Teponahuastlán, but they decided they could do better by selling Huichol art and craft objects to non-Huichol. In 1966 they built a small hut and a *ramada* (a flat-roofed, open-sided shelter) on vacant land just outside Guadalajara, where they cultivated maize and beans and became folk artists for a government institute that was promoting Indian arts and crafts. Their homestead was on a road used by many Huichol on their way to and from the mountains, and it soon became a meeting and resting place for traveling Huichol. There it was the Fursts and Myerhoff learned about Huichol religion from one Huichol shaman's point of view. When Myerhoff met Ramón he was about 38 years old and had made three of the five peyote pilgrimages required to become a full-fledged shaman. By 1971 he was dead, a victim of a shooting that took place during a quarrel at a celebration at his homestead in the mountains of Nayarit near the Lerma River. He had become a full shaman by

then and had provided a great volume of information.

Both Furst and Myerhoff were aware that Medina only gave them one man's version of Huichol culture, and a shaman's version at that. In addition Medina may have modified a few of his ideas as the result of his interaction with Furst and Myerhoff. In fact, even the informants of anthropologists living in the field clarify and modify their views of their own culture under questioning by anthropologists. This is one of several reasons ethnographers use several informants, test their statements against one another, and carefully check people's behavior to see how it squares with their words.

Both Furst and Myerhoff studied Ramón's religious knowledge, and both accompanied parties of Huichol under Ramón's leadership to the sacred peyote country. Furst has published several articles on Huichol mythology and religion (1966 [with Myerhoff], 1967, 1972a, 1972b, 1976 [with Myerhoff], 1976 [with Anguiano], 1977, 1978) as well as making an outstanding film of one of the peyote pilgrimages (1979). Myerhoff also published articles on the Huichol (1966 [with Furst], 1970, 1975a, 1975b, 1976, 1976 [with Furst], 1977, 1978) and a major book-length study of the peyote religion of the Huichol (1974).

Archaeologist and ethnographer Phil C. Weigand has done at least two years of field research among the Huichol and the Tepecano since 1960, including a period in San Sebastián Teponahuastlán, the same area in which Ramón Medina grew up. In addition to his archaeological studies Weigand has given special attention to Huichol social, political, and economic organization (1969, 1972, 1976, 1977a, l977b, 1978). During the early 1980s anthropologist Jay Courtney Fikes studied the relationship between Huichol identity and adaptation to change (1984). Several nonanthropologists have made valuable contributions to Huichol ethnography, one of the most noteworthy being the work of the prominent Mexican writer, Fernando Benítez (1975).

Huichol Country

The mountains and canyons of Huichol territory begin some sixty miles to the east and somewhat north of the coastal Mexican town of San Blas. Tepíc, Nayarit, on the main north-south highway of western Mexico, lies thirty some miles southeast of the main Huichol area. Cora country is north of Tepíc, to the west and slightly north of the Huichol area. The territory is something like that of the Tarahumara and Tepehuán, since the mountains approach 10,000 feet and the country is gashed with barrancas and steep-walled canyons. Of course, this makes movement about the area difficult.

The vegetation varies with altitude and other factors. Oaks and various kinds of pine trees are common in the mountain areas, and cacti and other typical desert plants prevail in low elevations. Wildlife includes jaguars, cougars, deer, peccaries, coyotes, rabbits, rats, foxes, squirrels, and other animals common in the mountains of Mexico. Birds are present in considerable variety, including Cooper's and other hawks, vultures, various kinds of owls, ravens, crows, magpies, *chachalacas*, parrots, turtle doves, canyon wrens, and many more. There are iguanas, chameleons, salamanders, scorpions, several kinds of rattlesnakes, and other kinds of snakes, lizards amphibians, arachnids, and insects.

Language

Huichol and Cora belong to the Aztecoidan family of languages, which, along with the Taracahitian and Piman families, belongs to the Uto-Aztecan phylum or stock. Cora and Huichol are similar but somewhat more distantly related to each other than Italian and Spanish. They do not differ greatly from the Náhuatl language spoken by the Aztec (Grimes and Hinton 1969:795).

Grimes has analyzed Huichol as consisting of 22 *phonemes*. Phonemes are sounds or classes of sounds that affect the meaning of utterances in that, if a sound (*phone*) not in the phoneme is used, the meaning of the utterance is different or is destroyed. Linguists find that many phonemes consist of alternative sounds, and the speaker may use any of the alternative phones (sounds) within the phoneme without changing or destroying the utterance's meaning. One of the consonant phonemes of Huichol, for example, includes voiced and voiceless alternatives. It is as though in

English we could use either *z* (voiced) or *s* (voiceless) without changing the meaning of any English utterance. Actually, the *z* and *s* belong to different English phonemes, since the difference between them makes a difference in meaning—as in *zip* and *sip*. But there are no such cases in Huichol. The two sounds belong to the same phoneme. They are alternatives in Huichol speech. Grimes has analyzed several other phonemes in Huichol as consisting of more than one alternative.

Phonemes in all languages are grouped in combinations that have specific meanings, the combination and the meaning together being known as a *morpheme*. Phonemes have no meanings; they simply operate to differentiate meaning-bearing elements of speech from one another. The morpheme is the smallest linguistic unit with a specific meaning. Grimes has studied Huichol to find out what morphemes exist and how they are related to and combined with one another to form words. He has also studied Huichol syntax, which has to do with how words are arranged to from phrases and sentences. But one of the reasons Grimes received advanced training in both anthropology and linguistics and studied nonlinguistic aspects of Huichol culture is that language, the major vehicle of culture, can be adequately understood and analyzed only by learning about its relationships with the rest of the lifeway.

Personality and Behavior

Many urban-industrial moderns think of so-called primitives as dull and unresponsive to life, either because primitives are less human than civilized people or because they have been demoralized by European domination and exploitation. It is true that European influences have often produced personality constriction, but not in all cases by any means. The Huichol of the late twentieth century illustrate the vitality that characterizes many tribal societies. When interacting with non-Huichol in Mexican towns and cities the Huichol were aloof, but often they have been seen to frolic and laugh as they related to one another (Myerhoff 1974:29). Many of the Huichol manifested no feelings of inferiority or demoralization. They believed their culture was beautiful because it was right and willingly said so. Many Huichol were confident and self-assured. They had a strong sense of purpose manifested in a kind of urgency and intensity that made observers feel they always had something of value and significance to do (Eger 1978:36). Coupled with this was their high level of motivation and energy along with exuberance and laughter. Underlying these was their keen awareness of a supernatural world and their confidence in meeting that realm's requirements. Many of the Huichol had what so many civilized people feel they lack, a rewarding sense of meaning and purpose in life.

The shaman-priest who served as informant for Myerhoff and Furst manifested these traits with unusual strength. The shamans can be expected to manifest the best of Huichol character, and Myerhoff described Medina as a man of great courage, poise, and balance (1974:46). In his dealings with Mexicans and Americans he was confident and effective. He knew how to cope with Mexican bureaucrats, how to handle money and keep records, how to adapt to the time and schedule requirements of urban society, and how to use Spanish expertly and elegantly. Nevertheless, he considered these things foolish and wasteful and would comment readily on the superiority of Huichol ways. His competence in dealing with outsiders led him to help his fellow Huichol in their contacts with Mexican officials, and many of the Mexicans of Guadalajara recognized his expertise and asked him to describe his culture and demonstrate in public his artistic skills. Ramón was unique among Huichol, but his very uniqueness highlights the typical orientations of Huichol culture.

Clothing and Personal Appearance

The Huichol were one of a number of Mexican tribes noted for their rather colorful dress, the more so since they were engaged in ceremonial a good deal of the time, dressed in their colorful ceremonial garments. For daily wear the men wore white cotton shirts and trousers like those of so many other Indian groups, a wide-brimmed, low-crowned palm hat, and sandals. They wound sashes around the waist and hung small embroidered bags below the sash. They also might wear one or two shoulder bags. The women did the embroidering of the shirts, sashes, and bags. The men also wore capes at times and frequently added bead earrings and hat decorations. Sometimes they wore denim jeans. On ordinary occasions the men often dressed plainly, perhaps with only a few hat decorations and some embroidered symbols on the shirt. At special times they often dressed elaborately. They might add large bead necklaces, mirrors, Catholic medals, beadwork rings, wrist bands, macaw and hawk feathers to the hat, and so on.

The women wore skirts that hung to midcalf or ankle and high-necked, three-quarter-length sleeved blouses. They usually wore a cotton garment that served either as a head scarf or a cape. It consisted of two squares of cloth stitched to one another on two adjoining edges but with the corner and the other two edges left unstitched.

Both sexes might paint their faces with red and yellow pigment mixed with lard or honey. Not infrequently Huichol appeared in full ceremonial garb on the streets of a Mexican city, their shirts, blouses, and capes embroidered with stars, butterflies, flowers, squirrels, mice, deer, and various whimsical animal and bird figures. Myerhoff describes them as alive with color (1974:30). Their hats might be decorated with red felt crosses and have deer hoofs, beads, or felt ball danglers hanging all around the hat brim.

Houses and Other Structures

Most of the Huichol built rectangular homes, though a few were round or hexagonal. They used various materials, depending on availability and climate. They made some of the walls of stone, some of adobe, some of poles, and some of wattle (interlaced canes daubed with mud). They thatched the steep, four-pitched roofs with grass or palm leaves. They built a table of rock and mud to prepare food on, either solid from the ground or applied to a pole frame. They slept mostly on beds of *carrizo* (bamboo-like cane) laid on the floor or on supports. Some slept on the floor on mats or hides. People had a stool or two in the house but usually no chairs. A few of the elders and shaman-priests owned ceremonial chairs. Some of the houses had two rooms, each eight or more meters square. One was for sleeping and the other for cooking. Most of the people preferred to be outside. They kept the yard swept and did most of the cooking under a ramada. They were likely to eat, sleep, and grind food inside.

In addition to the house and ramada they usually had a separate cook house, maize granary, animal corral, and *oratory*. An oratory, which resembled an ordinary house but was smaller, was the place where the Huichol kept the souls of dead relatives who had returned in the form of rock crystals.

Livelihood

The Huichol produced maize (Indian corn), beans, squash, and other crops by slash-and-burn agriculture on their steep hillside fields. They also grew chile, tobacco, gourds, tomatoes, sugarcane, sweet potatoes, watermelons, bananas, and mangos. They brought peyote plants in from the desert for planting, though they would not reproduce in Huichol country. The whole family worked together to plant the fields, using the *dibble* (digging stick). They made holes about a pace apart and dropped in two or three kernels of maize and one or two beans. Every third or fourth hole they added a squash seed (Weigand 1978:109). In a few places the Huichol had plots level enough for them to use the colonial type of plow without moldboard. Clearing the plot for planting was difficult and time consuming and sometimes took a family up to six weeks. When they burned the piles of brush the adjacent mountainsides often caught fire.

The Huichol of the 1960s and 1970s raised cattle for cash, kept cows for milk and cheese, and had various kinds of barnyard livestock. Some had a few sheep for wool and kept animals for packing or pulling plows.

The Huichol hunted deer and peccaries and caught iguana, crustaceans, and fish. Many of the men of San Andrés used .22 rifles, which were introduced during the 1940s and 1950s. In spite of the high cost and limited availability of cartridges, the Huichol almost completely wiped out the deer population.

Some Americans have thought tribal peoples to be perfect conservationists, but this is incorrect. Many tribal societies around the world have had conservationist ideologies and have often maintained a stable relationship with their environment. But time after time the same people have participated in the destruction of certain aspects of their habitat when they acquired the means. Traditionally, the Huichol took deer with nets and asked forgiveness before killing them. But they also believed they saw deer because the supernaturals sent them and that they could not kill one unless it wanted to die. When they obtained rifles this ideology permitted them to kill deer in large numbers, including the does, without regard to the limited population.

Americans and urban-industrial peoples are so much more destructive to the habitat than others primarily because they have the instruments to do it rather than because of any basic ideological flaw. Actually, American ideology, in addition to that of mastering or conquering the environment, includes the concept that humans are stewards and conservators of the resources their God has entrusted to them (Schaeffer 1971). People everywhere seem to have difficulty perceiving the many relationships between their behaviors and the total ecosystem and tend to damage the habitat if they have the means.

The Huichol also used wild plant products such as *agave* hearts, the joints or pads and fruit of the *nopal* or prickly pear, fruit from the organ pipe cactus, seed pods from the mesquite tree, grain amaranth, and various tubers and wild greens. They used collecting baskets for wild products and cotton hand nets, hook and line, and poisons for taking fish.

The basic food item was the tortilla, supplemented by whatever else was available such as beans, squash, chile, tomatoes, meat, fish, fruit, or wild greens. Some drank some coffee or cinnamon tea or took corn gruel.

Like others in Northwest Mexico the Huichol made and used maize beer, which was a ceremonial beverage. But by the 1960s and 1970s they more often bought *mezcal* or *tequila* from outsiders for their ceremonies. They seldom got intoxicated outside the ceremonial context. Other fiesta foods were tamales, parched corn balls, and soups of deer meat, fish, beef, or beans. (Grimes and Hinton 1969:797).

Aboriginally the Indians of Northwest Mexico typically used *pinole* (parched corn flour) as a base for their food dishes. But the Huichol softened corn kernels by boiling them in lime water—a Mesoamerican trait. During the 1970s Huichol women were grinding the softened maize in metal corn grinders and regrinding it on a stone *metate* (grinding stone). They then patted a ball of the resulting dough into a very thin, round cake and baked it on a clay griddle. This was the tortilla.

The Huichol neighborhood or pueblo commonly held ultimate ownership of the fields, though as long as people continued to use a certain plot they treated it as though it were their own and passed it on to their heirs, and no one asked them to give it up. However, if an applicant could show that he needed a piece of land and could demonstrate to the pueblo authorities that it had not been planted for a long time, the officials would award it to him. This kind of arrangement has often been called holding land in *usufruct*. There were also some agricultural communities organized as *ejidos*, which are groups of family heads (usually) plus land they were granted under agrarian laws stemming from the 1910 Mexican revolution.

Crafts, Tools, and Techniques

The Huichol used machetes and axes for a variety of cutting tasks. They had two kinds of machetes, a short curved one and a long heavy one. Dibbles, or digging sticks, were important for planting, and a few digging sticks had steel points. They also used a tool of steel or bone to detach the maize ears from the stalks, and they had baskets for collecting maize and other produce and wild plant items such as fruits and seeds. They also had sacks made of *ixtle*, which is the fiber prepared from the long, thick leaves of the agave, or century plant. The people tied together about fifty disks cut from corn cobs to make a scraper for stripping kernels from the ears of maize. They dug holes with steel bars, sharpened tools on special stones, tied roof thatching in place with strips of material threaded through the eye of a large carrizo needle, dipped and carried water with gourds, carried mud for mortar or adobe bricks in cord nets, and shaped adobe bricks in a special wooden frame.

The Huichol used galvanized buckets for cooking the mixture of lime water and maize, though they rarely used clay pots. The metate, used for grinding the softened maize, was the rectangular, sloping, slightly concave, three-legged type conventional in Mesoamerica. The *mano* (hand stone) was somewhat cigar-shaped and was held by grasping each end. The women also had hand-operated metal grinders for the preliminary grinding of the softened maize kernels. The tortilla griddles were flat or slightly concave clay disks about 18 inches in diameter, placed with the concave side up on three stones, with the fire built among the stones. The Huichol had a variety of other small utensils of metal, clay, or wood for preparing food, cooking, and eating. Their kit of tools was actually quite like those of thousands of other Mexican and Indian villages.

The belt (or backstrap) loom is found in many parts of the Americas, including Huichol country. The Huichol women were expert weavers, seamstresses, and embroiderers. They wove the material for the shoulder bags and sashes from cotton and wool, and they used agave fiber (ixtle) for sacks and utilitarian shoulder bags. They made string and rope by hand twisting, spinning on a spindle with a wooden whorl, or using a whirler. They also had a variety of small tools for crafting ceremonial objects from carrizo, gourds, cotton, wool, muslin, cardboard, feathers, beeswax, beads, and other materials.

Social Organization and Relationships

A Huichol household might consist of just one nuclear family, but it usually included the families of the elderly parents' married children. A newly married couple lived with the bride's family, a practice known as *matrilocal* residence. Under this arrangement the husband was to gather firewood and plant for his mother-in-law for several years. This produced a *matrilocal extended family*, extended families being the units formed by the residence of married children with their parents. As soon as the couple could build their own house, they established a separate household on the same farmstead, but the young man planted his own fields, and the couple with their children functioned as a nuclear family household. Sometimes the family moved to a different farmstead after a few years.

A few men would take additional wives, a form of *polygamy* (multiple spouse marriage) known as *polygyny*. Usually the second wife was the first wife's sister, a practice known as *sororal polygyny*. Societies that practice sororal polygyny seem to feel that sisters make good co-wives because they have grown up together and have already established ways of relating to one another. The Huichol would seem to fit this, since *siblings* (brothers, sisters, or brother and sister) generally had good relationships with one another. About five per cent of Huichol men had more than one wife, and some had up to five. Men could divorce a wife for sterility, and either spouse could terminate a marriage because of cruelty.

Families living on the same farmstead were usually related to one another, so the farmstead, too, was a unit of kin. If there was more than one family on the farmstead, the dominant household head acted as the elder and represented the group in relationships with other units within the Huichol neighborhoods and larger political units. The bilateral *kindred* was also an important Huichol kinship unit. Under *bilateral reckoning* individuals consider themselves related to others through both parents, their children of both sexes, and so on. A Huichol's kindred (since kindreds are individually defined) would simply be all those he or she recognized as blood relatives. This, of course, would include all on one's farmstead except those related to the person by marriage only, but it also included relatives on other farmsteads and in other neighborhoods and pueblos. A Huichol was expected to find a spouse within his or her kindred, and first cousin marriages were frequent. When people moved from one farmstead to another they normally chose one that included some members of their own kindred.

One of the kinds of kinship terminology frequently found in exclusively bilateral societies is *Hawaiian* terminology. This means referring to one's siblings and cousins by the same term or set of terms. A Huichol referred to brothers, sisters, and cousins by using one of five terms: a term for (1) any sibling or cousin of either sex, (2) any younger brother or male cousin, (3) an older brother or male cousin, (4) a younger sister or female cousin, or (5) an older sister or female cousin (Grimes and Grimes 1962:109). Only the use of the same terms for both siblings and cousins makes this a Hawaiian system. Some cultures with Hawaiian terms do not make the age distinctions.

Anthropologists study kinship terminology not just because it is there but because how people classify their kin provides clues to their behavior toward one another and reflects various social arrangements. Joseph and Barbara Grimes pointed out that most Huichol children grew up on a farmstead consisting of two or more related families.

Accordingly, they played daily with cousins as well as brothers and sisters. And when a household moved to another farmstead the children became close to even more cousins. Families from different farmsteads visited one another, sometimes for extended periods, so the children grew up having contacts with cousins on several farmsteads (Grimes and Grimes 1962:105). They were almost as close to cousins as to brothers and sisters, which harmonizes with the Hawaiian mode of referring to cousins as brothers and sisters.

The Huichol used *lineal* terms for their parents, aunts and uncles, lineal terms also being common in exclusively bilateral societies. Like North Americans, Huichol separated parents from the parents' brothers and sisters (the aunts and uncles), but did not separate maternal from paternal aunts and uncles. In one way the lineal terms differed from those of modern North America, since the sex of the Huichol speaker affected what terms were used. For example, a male referred to his father by one term, while a female used a different term for her father. The sex of the speaker affects what kinship terms are used in a fairly high percentage of the world's cultures.

Anthropologists generally like to stress that different aspects of life are interlaced with one another. Aspects of cultures such as religion, family, art, education, and so on, as well as the various customs by which we describe people's lifeways, are rather arbitrarily distinguished from one another. It is somewhat more accurate to view a culture as an indivisible whole, but to talk or write about a lifeway requires us to segment or analyze it. Since this is unavoidable, it becomes important to view the elements or segments of culture as interdependent. Spicer has referred to one form of interdependence as *formal linkage*, which is the occurrence of similar cultural forms in different aspects of the lifeway. Huichol kinship terms occurred not just in family and kindred contexts, but in religion, since the people used some of the kinship terms for groups of deities. "Our Aunts," for example, were the rain deities, and the Huichol referred to the gods of the maize-deer-peyote complex as "Our Elder Brothers."

The Huichol participated in the ritual or fictive kinship arrangement known as the *compadrazgo*. This system, introduced by the Spanish, is nearly universal in Mexico, though it was not as important to the Huichol as to some other tribes. Huichol parents might select godparents for a child at baptism, confirmation, a cattle sale, or for the rare Catholic marriage ceremony. This established a lifelong set of obligations between the godparents and godchildren and between the parents and godparents. Basically the godparents were supposed to assist the parents with their children, especially in life crisis situations. The institution probably lost some of its force among the Huichol because they preferred to have close relatives as their children's godparents. In other societies the practice has been to extend kinship-like relationships by selecting nonrelatives.

As noted before, the Huichol farmsteads were scattered throughout a territory or district to form neighborhood-type communities. It is easy to be confused by the usages prevailing in the literature, since some have referred to homesteads as rancherías, while others have used ranchería for the neighborhood community. The Huichol themselves called their homesteads *ranchos* in Spanish. The homesteads within a neighborhood were sometimes several miles apart, and some of the neighborhoods had names and some had none.

Before the Mexican Revolution displaced numbers of Huichol the farmsteads composing a neighborhood were strongly bound to one another by kinship. The related farmsteads combined for certain economic enterprises and ceremonial activities under the leadership of the farmstead elders. In earlier years each neighborhood shared a religious compound containing a temple, a round ceremonial structure thirty or forty feet in diameter. A temple's relatively low stone walls were topped by a steep, cone-shaped, thatched roof, which did not come to a point but curved upward so the roof as a whole formed a severely truncated cone. A number of the temples were in ruins in the 1960s and 1970s due to the weakening of neighborhoods. Myerhoff reported that Ramón Medina expected to build a new temple when he had completed his fifth journey to the sacred land of the peyote (1974:179).

A Huichol mother usually gave birth while clinging to a rope hung in the corner of the house. Usually her husband was there and, sometimes, a woman to help her. Others might watch. Five days after the birth the Huichol named the baby, perhaps using a name dreamed by an elder or a shaman-priest. They also took the infant out of the house for the first time on that day. Sometimes they took the child to the caves of the gods, sprinkled it with sacred water, and presented it to the deities.

They usually weaned a child after about two years, though some were nursed longer. The mothers carried their babies on their hips. Training in urination control was begun before they were eight months old and bowel elimination training when they began to walk. When children needed punishment, parents either withdrew expression of affection or spanked or beat them, but most did not punish their little ones severely for their failures.

A boy's father arranged his son's marriage when the young people were from 13 to 15 years old. He made up to five formal requests to the girl's family before getting an answer. Some Huichol young people did not know they were going to be married until the ceremony began. After the ceremony, which included admonitions and the breaking and eating of a tortilla by the couple, they were put to bed. Sometimes the people took their clothes away to keep them from escaping. Since residence was initially matrilocal the boy might try to run away even several weeks later.

The Huichol buried their dead either on the farmstead or in a neighborhood cemetery. After five days they conducted ritual to send the soul on its way. People around the world seem concerned that the souls of the dead leave the community for wherever they go so they do not trouble the living. The Huichol placed a carrizo cross, with a diamond-shaped yarn winding where the carrizos intersect, at all entrances to a farmstead but one, and the shaman-priest chanted to bring the soul from the spirit dancing ground to the ceremony. The shaman then made offerings to the soul and announced the disposal of the dead person's property. On the way to the dancing ground souls had to pass through five pools of successively hotter water for cleansing and suffer for their misdeeds by eating rotten fruit and drinking stagnant water. When the shaman-priest dismissed a soul he gave it the choice of returning to the dancing ground or going with the sun. Supposedly, it would follow the sun rather than endure the hot pools, rotten fruit, and stagnant water (Grimes and Hinton 1969:812).

Sometimes a dead relative's soul could return to the Huichol in the form of a rock crystal. Occasionally a shaman-priest would conclude that a patient was ill because a deceased relative was lonesome for the person and was calling him or her to die. The shaman-priest would counter by performing a ritual to bring the deceased person's soul to the sick person in the form of a rock crystal (Lumholtz 1903:198). Soul crystals were kept carefully wrapped in the family's oratory, and there they received offerings from the living (Myerhoff 1974:109).

Government and Social Order

In aboriginal times the largest peacetime political units were the neighborhood communities. The Spanish tried to concentrate the Indians in towns, but in some tribes the dispersed settlement patterns continued or were resumed after periods of centralization. This left the administrative-religious centers built by the Spanish as focal points to which the people might go for various purposes. This is what happened in Huichol country, and during the late twentieth century and well before, a Huichol neighborhood or group of neighborhoods would have a named town center where people went for fiestas, cattle sales, school, legal business, or other matters. The pueblo, then, was composed of the town center plus the neighborhood or neighborhoods that surrounded it. The only town center residents were the main town officials and, perhaps, some storekeepers. A few Huichol had houses in the center, but it was considered a convenience rather than a necessity (Weigand 1978:104).

Not all the Huichol towns had exactly the same officials, but there was usually a governor at the top of a small hierarchy of officers. Each incumbent had to find his own successor when the officers changed every one to five years (Grimes and Hinton 1969:805). In addition to the governor and other officials, each town also had a *mayordomo*, who headed a hierarchy of religious officers, who were responsible for various ceremonies. This resembles the civil-religious hierarchy characteristic of so many other Mexican communities.

The Spanish imposed the town or pueblo, and it eventually became the traditional (not aboriginal) Indian government. Still another entity imposed by the Spanish was the *comunidad*. The comunidades were chartered land grants from the Spanish crown. There were three of them among the Huichol which, in the twentieth century, incorporated five Huichol towns originally chartered to be part of the comunidades. But a number of Huichol towns were not taken into a comunidad. Two chartered towns made up the comunidad of San Sebastián Teponahuastlán, where Ramón Medina's home was. A third town was added while Weigand was living among the Huichol during the 1960s. The second comunidad was Santa Catarina Cuexcomatitlán, but Santa Catarina was the only town chartered to be a part of this comunidad. The third communidad was San Andrés Cohamiata, which included the chartered towns of Guadalupe Ocotán and San Andrés. Most of the rest of the Huichol neighborhoods were not associated with a comunidad.

The town governments were fairly well under the control of the Huichol elders, but the comunidades were controlled by the Mexican government. The Mexicans assigned a *comisario* from each neighborhood to serve as a delegate responsible to the comunidad government. The top official in each comunidad was the *presidente*, and other officials were a security chief in charge of a police troop, a secretary, and a treasurer. These officials were elected rather than chosen by incumbents. They had taken over some of the functions the town governments had not done well and legally had considerable power. But the Huichol did not respect the comunidad officials nearly so much as the more traditional officials of the towns.

Art and Play

The Huichol of the 1960s and 1970s were at least as productive in art as they were when Lumholtz observed them just before the turn of the century. Since religion permeated Huichol life, their violin and guitar music, their songs and chants, and their art objects were integral elements of their religious life. Books have been written on Huichol art, but a survey of some of their main religious productions will serve here to give an idea of their aesthetic accomplishments.

The most common offering was the ceremonial arrow. Arrows were prayer messages asking for some material benefit, health, or rain (Muller 1978:93). The people made nine to twelve inch long arrows from cane shafts into which they inserted lengths of hardwood. They decorated the shafts with colored bands representing different supernaturals and attached feathers associated with the god to be contacted and pieces of cloth embroidered with appropriate religious symbols.

The people made votive bowls (*xukuri*) from the bottom sections of gourds. They coated the inside of the bowl with beeswax and pressed maize kernels, beads, coins, tufts of cotton, yarn, and the like into the wax to symbolize deer or other entities. The bowls held offerings made during various rituals.

The Huichol prepared offerings of canes and yarn they referred to as *tsikiri*, which are popularly but erroneously termed gods' eyes. They tied two sticks or canes together to form a cross and wound colored yarn from stick to stick where they intersected, forming a diamond-shaped unit of yarn. This offering constituted a request for protection from harm. Students of Huichol art have popularized Lumholtz's interpretation that these have something to do with the eyes of a god and are requests for a god to "keep an eye out," for the supplicant's welfare, but this is not the way the Huichol viewed them.

Sometimes Huichol tied shorter sticks across the arms of the cross so additional diamonds could be made. For a certain children's ceremony they made such yarn-wound objects of from one to five diamond-shaped windings, depending on the child's age. For five-year-olds, for example, the objects consisted of five diamonds

The people also made yarn plaques on flat, round or polygonal pieces of wood as requests to various gods. To either the wooden plaque or, sometimes, crossed sticks they attached a large number of thin splints radiating from the center to the edge and wound the yarn around the splints. Some of these were only a few inches in diameter, and others were at least 15 to 20 inches across. The plaques and other objects were often called *nieríka*, which means likeness, face, or picture. Each represented a specific deity.

The Huichol made stools and chairs to which they attached prayer arrows and other offerings. They inscribed round disks of solidified volcanic material with designs symbolizing their gods and kept them in their temples. The embroidered and beadwork designs on their shirts, blouses, skirts, trousers, sashes, shoulder bags, and other items of attire might also be religious symbols. The people depicted flowers in much of their beadwork and embroidery. Flowers played a part in some Huichol ceremonies, but they were used mainly because of their beauty. The most common animal design on clothing was probably the deer. The colors in their art were the peyote colors seen in the visions they had while they were taking peyote. They were the colors of reality.

Tribal groups who acquire more efficient tools and techniques and new materials from Western civilization often elaborate some aspect of their art or technology far beyond its pre-contact state. The large, intricately carved totem poles of the Northwest Coast of Washington and British Columbia apparently developed only after the people acquired metal tools. Not only did they begin carving larger, more elaborate poles than before, they produced spectacular wooden masks with moving jaws and eyes manipulated with cords by the wearer. The Indians of the Plains used glass beads in place of porcupine quills, producing a profusion of beaded items. The Huichol also used beads extensively.

An additional spur to such efflorescence comes from the demands of urban-industrial collectors of art objects. The demand for the carved ironwood figures produced by the Seri of the Sonoran coast is one example, and the yarn windings of the Huichol are found in homes and museums in many parts of the world.

The twentieth century Huichol participated marginally in a money economy and modified their art and increased its production for sale to outsiders. Some of the objects were hastily and carelessly prepared and of inferior quality. Some Huichol also produced items based on but not typical of the objects they used in their ceremonies. Moreover, outsiders have tried to duplicate Huichol art objects and passed them off as genuine. Outsiders have produced yarn windings far larger than any made by the Huichol and with more than their limit of five windings. Calling them god's eyes has also contributed to their popularity.

One of the more impressive forms of new art was the "yarn painting." Traditionally the Huichol made small designs by pressing yarn into beeswax. More recently, at the suggestion of anthropologist Peter Furst, they have produced large, intricate, rectangular yarn paintings on fiberboard or plywood panels. The shaman-priest Ramón Medina apparently was the first to produce these pictures, each of which depicted figures important in Huichol myth and religion. The production of these yarn pictures soon became a cottage industry for the Huichol.

Religious Beliefs and Practices

European and American scholars set religion apart from the rest of life, and anthropologists usually include a chapter on religion in their ethnographies. But many societies make no distinction between religion and other aspects of their lifeway, and Huichol culture illustrates this very nicely. Myerhoff points out that Huichol religion was far more intricate and elaborate than their technology and social organization and could not be separated from them. Everything was sacred to the Huichol, including all the ideas, behaviors, and objects that made up their culture.

Each twentieth century Huichol believed in some 120 deities. Slightly more than a hundred were common to virtually all Huichol, while others varied some from person to person. A Huichol might pray to any god for any purpose, but some of them had special powers and a special place in the pantheon. One of the main gods was a fire deity, Tatewarí, "Our Grandfather Fire." He was shaman to the rest of the gods. He led the gods on the first peyote hunt and formulated the myths and ceremonies associated with it. Tatewarí also built the first community temple and taught the Huichol how to behave correctly and make offerings (Myerhoff 1974:77). He protected people and gave the Huichol shamans their knowledge and power to cure and recover lost souls. He sent deer and, as fire, provided warmth, made it possible to cook, and burned off the fields for planting. The Huichol were openly affectionate toward the fire god, addressing him by diminutive terms normally used with children.

In parts of Huichol country the sun god, Tayáu, "Our Father Sun," was as important as Tatewarí. The sun deity was dangerously powerful, and the people lacked the companionship with him they had with Tatewarí. The sun god regularly sent misfortunes, either as warnings or punishment, though any neglected deity would send sickness or agricultural disaster. The shamans obtained some of their powers from the sun god, but they had to be careful not to be burned by him, especially on their flights to the sky to recover someone's lost soul. Various kinds of dangerous animals, such as poisonous snakes, were sacred to Tayáu. Much of the Huichol belief and mythology about the sun god was similar to that of the Aztec, indicating a possible Mesoamerican influence.

A group of deities called "Elder Brothers" included gods of maize, deer, and peyote. One of them, a very influential supernatural, was Sacred Deer Person (Káuyúmari) Sometimes he was equated with a being known as Deer Tail, but he was commonly regarded as a separate being. He was also a companion of the sun deity in some contexts. Sacred Deer Person illustrates a widespread type of deity, the *trickster*. Tricksters are sometimes clever, sometimes stupid, getting themselves into and out of all kinds of scrapes. They are also often culture heroes. Sacred Deer Person was both courageous and frail. He possessed magical powers, and he taught the people about sexual relationships and engaged in extravagant and amusing sexual adventures himself. The Huichol greatly enjoyed the stories about Sacred Deer Person, but they often rationalized that he engaged in his questionable behavior before he became sacred. Sacred Deer Person was the shamans' tutelary, and one of his most important jobs was to be an intermediary between the shaman-priest and other deities in all ceremonies. His symbol was deer horns, and deer horns and tails were often displayed together in the neighborhood temples (Myerhoff 1974:86).

Another figure of some importance was Our Elder Brother Deer Tail (Máxá Kwaxí). Though not so important as the fire and sun gods or Sacred Deer Person, he had special significance for the peyote hunt and was associated mainly with hunting, especially deer hunting. He was a culture hero, a type of supernatural found in most of the world's polytheistic religions. A culture hero is one who originates many basic things in people's lifeways, such as fire, sexual reproduction, healing knowledge, and others. Deer Tail helped the Huichol obtain deer and peyote in the beginning of things. He also protected them against sorcerers and other enemies. The deer tail was his symbol, and many kept deer tails in their family oratories.

The Huichol had many other male deities besides the four mentioned so far. They were not as important, but they were involved significantly in the deer-maize-peyote complex and were often represented in the peyote pilgrimage. The Snarer of the Deer was the patron god of the deer hunt. Clearer of the Fields replenished the land and its people. Our Great Grandfather was one of the main assistants to the fire god Tatewarí during peyote hunts.

The female gods of the Huichol were responsible for rain, earth, growth, and maize. The people referred to them as Tátéetéima (Our Mothers or Our Aunts). The main female deity was Nakawé, who remade the world after the great flood and recreated the plants and animals it had destroyed. The Huichol portrayed her as a very old, long-haired woman who walked alone in the barrancas, leaning on a staff. People visited her in a sacred cave near Santa Catarina to ask for long life, health for their children, or good crops. The people associated both Nakawé and Maize Mother with the earth and maize. They believed in a large number of female rain and water goddesses. Many of them dwelt in a cluster of permanent water holes in the desert of Zacatecas, which contained the sacred water that had to be obtained during the peyote pilgrimage. The Pacific Ocean was also a female deity. There were a few moon and star deities, but they were much less significant than those connected with fire, the sun, maize, deer, peyote, water, earth, and growth.

Shaman-priests, known as márá'aakáte, (singular márá'akáme) were the only important religious specialists among the Huichol. *Shamans* are people with special individual power to heal or perform other beneficial acts, which they accomplish by drawing on the power of supernaturals. The Huichol shaman-priests divined the causes of sickness with the help of Sacred Deer Person, making it possible for them to cure people. They could make magical flights to the world of the gods and follow the souls of the dead to the afterworld, a place near the Nayarit coast where the souls danced. They also transformed themselves into various kinds of animals. During the healing rites the shamans would spit, suck, massage, blow smoke, and so on to remove the sickness or restore the soul to the body.

Huichol shamans were also *priests*, a priest being one who conducts ritual on behalf of the group. The Huichol márá'akáme officiated in ceremonies involving making offerings, presided over life crisis ceremonies and temple services, officiated at the fiestas of the annual ceremonial cycle, and chanted each morning to bring the sun up.

There may have been as many as five-hundred shaman-priests among the Huichol of the 1960s and 1970s. A person (nearly always a man) was usually called to shamanism through a vision or dream while still a child but often did not become a full shaman until middle age. One had to master an enormous body of knowledge and skills in singing, playing the violin, telling stories, making ritual offerings, and producing religious objects to become a shaman-priest. A márá'akáme had to be highly intelligent, wise in making judgments, self-controlled, and well respected. To become a full-fledged márá'akáme one had to participate in the peyote pilgrimage five times and visit the places where the gods lived. Myerhoff stressed that the shaman-priests were crucial in maintaining the integrity of Huichol culture. As they officiated at the group ceremonies, they admonished, taught, modeled, explained, and advocated all that it meant to be Huichol (Myerhoff 1974:95).

In many societies there is a fine line between being a shaman and a witch. A witch is a person with special supernatural power to do evil, and in many societies shamans may turn their supernatural talents toward evil. This sometimes happened among the Huichol, too. Other shamans, however, might identify the evil-doer and neutralize his work or take revenge against him.

Like other Northwest Mexico Indians the Huichol were strongly interested in elaborate ritual. They had almost no games or sports but found their enjoyment of life in their techno-economic, ceremonial, and aesthetic activities. Myerhoff summarized the types of rituals common in the peyote-deer-maize aspect of Huichol religion. One is the circling of the fire. The shaman-priest led a group counterclockwise in single file around a fire. This expressed gratitude, affection, and respect toward the fire god. Another fire ritual was passing one's clothing over a fire so the fire god could cleanse and purify the owner. The shaman-priest would brush the clothing with sacred plumes and motion the filth into the fire, where it was consumed. A third fire ritual was collecting small portions of food and drink used on a deer hunt, peyote pilgrimage, or other sacred mission, as well as twigs, and feeding the fire god by putting them in the fire. A certain offering ceremony involved sharing everything eaten and drunk with the four cardinal directions and the center, with the fire god, and each person present. During their feasts the Huichol performed this ritual informally and with gladness. On more sacred occasions they were more formal and sober about it.

The Wixarika made many kinds of sacrifices and offerings. For sacred missions they had to give up salt, bathing, large meals, and sexual activity. They offered foods and beverages to the gods in the oratories, notably deer soup, deer tamales, peyote, chocolate, candles, decorated coins, votive gourd bowls, tobacco, maize, sacred arrows, feathers, sacred water, and wool yarn pictures. They commonly acknowledged the directions by waving ceremonial plumes or by spraying or scattering liquids and food in each of the five directions. The number five was sacred, and the center was the fifth direction. The Huichol sang, chanted, and danced during their ceremonies, sometimes led by a shaman-priest. The circling of the fire and the acknowledging of the directions were among the most commonly performed Huichol rituals.

The peyote pilgrimage was one of the major ceremonial events of Huichol life. Some tribes of Northwest Mexico feared the peyote, but not the Huichol. They might use one to four heads from the peyote cactus to inhibit hunger, thirst, fatigue, or sexual desire. Five or more heads produced hallucinations and communication with the gods. The shaman-priests took either peyote or alcoholic drink to be able to chant for extended periods, and they chewed peyote to divine the causes of illness and the needed cure (Muller 1978:92). The Huichol made annual pilgrimages to the desert in San Luís Potosí near Real de Catorce some 350 miles away to obtain a year's supply of peyote. The shaman-priests had to participate in five of these to become full-fledged shamans. Others made the pilgrimage when a shaman-priest judged it might be good medicine, and some went in fulfillment of a vow to the supernaturals. Some went to find out whether or not they should become shamans.

The peyote must be understood as an element of the deer-maize-peyote complex. The people associated the deer with their hunting past and maize with the beautiful, but mundane, difficult, and demanding present. Peyote was equivalent ritually to both deer and maize and, in a sense, mediated between deer and maize and between past and present. It provided the people with a sense of belonging to one another.

The pilgrimage traditionally lasted several weeks, taking about 21 days each way, though the pilgrims traveled by bus most of the way by the 1960s and 1970s. They retraced the route of the Ancient Ones, performing at point after point along the way the same actions as the deities who first made the journey. They also experienced the same attitudes and feelings as the gods. They rejoiced, celebrated, grieved, and mourned as appropriate. They pledged their complete loyalty to one another and to the shaman-priest, since total agreement and harmony were necessary for the peyote hunt's success. They also considered the journey dangerous. They could lose their souls if they failed to give the shaman-priest and the other pilgrims their whole trust and affection. Before leaving for Wirikuta, the sacred peyote land, they held a ritual in which each person made a knot or knots in a cord, which the shaman priest kept during the trip. A knot was made for each of the pilgrim's illicit sexual experiences, which purified them for the pilgrimage. After the pilgrimage the knots were untied, ending the special unity so indispensable to the pilgrimage's success and releasing the participants from the proscriptions they had observed.

During the trip they reduced or eliminated sleep, eating and drinking, excretion, and sex. They became gods and were therefore relieved of mortal needs. They engaged in reversal rituals along the way, old men becoming children, the sad and ugly being spoken of as beautiful and joyful, and so on. This reflected the belief that when the world ended everything would be the opposite of what it was on earth. The concept that the other world is the reverse of the present world is found in a number of the world's cultures.

The Huichol put blindfolds on those making their first trip when they first arrived at Wirikuta because they were in danger of being blinded by the glory of that sacred place. After a special ritual, including a baptism with sacred water, the blindfolds were removed. After making camp the Huichol hunted for peyote by finding the deer tracks it left behind. The shaman-priest stalked the peyote-deer and, when he found it, quietly approached and killed it by shooting two arrows, one on either side of it. The people grieved at having killed their brother peyote and cut away his bones—the plant's roots—and buried them so he could be reborn.

They also rejoiced at the hunt's success. They placed offerings around the hole left from digging out the plant. Then the márá'akáme sliced the cactus and gave a piece to each person, and his assistant gave him a piece. At this point perfect unity was achieved. The people were gods, the deer and the peyote were one, the past and present were merged, all differences were obliterated. The people spent the rest of the day collecting more peyote and in the evening sat around the fire and took large enough doses to have visions. They saw beautiful lights, brilliant colors outlining familiar shapes, little animals, and other strange shapes and creatures. Each vision was a private, highly rewarding experience, usually with no special significance beyond the experience itself. Only a shaman-priest received messages from the gods through his visions, and the people did not share with one another what they saw. But the colors were those of reality and were manifested in Huichol art.

After their visions the party left Wirikuta as quickly as possible, for lingering was dangerous. They also left the remnants of everything they had used there, and when they had returned to the ordinary world they felt both exhausted and grief stricken.

In earlier times the people walked to Wirikuta, but in the 1960s and 1970s they rode on busses or whatever was available, and some walked the most essential parts of the route. They tried to stop at all the sacred spots, but the busses might not take the traditional route. When they did go by a sacred spot the bus might not stop, and they had to throw the offerings out the window. If a private car or truck was available they had no trouble getting to all the sacred places, and that was the most desirable way to make the pilgrimage.

When the pilgrims got home they planted the peyote in their household gardens for use during the year, but the peyote would not reproduce in the mountains. The peyote sold in the Mexican markets could not be used, since it had not been hunted properly and was not sacred. It was bad peyote, and if they ate any of it they would go mad—seeing scorpions, serpents, and dangerous animals.

The people ate the good peyote casually and at any time for energy, endurance, and courage as well as to relieve pain and other physical difficulties. Peyote was also applied to wounds. The people took either peyote or alcoholic drinks ritually to bring them into communion with the gods, but they ordinarily took too little peyote to bring on visions. Peyote was an important motif in Huichol art, being manifested in many ways in their embroidery and weaving.

The Huichol also had a Jimson weed (*Datura*) cult. Taking Jimson weed is far more dangerous than taking peyote, and its ingestion was under heavy ritual control. In spite of this control, the taking of Jimson weed sometimes made a participant "go crazy," which is one of the reasons the people favored peyote.

Anthropological studies of drug use in various cultures indicate that abuse (bad trips, personal disintegration, etc.) is reduced and relatively well controlled when people take hallucinogens in a ritual context where all aspects of the experience are carefully defined by the common cultural background. Hallucinogens taken outside of such a context often trouble people considerably. But in the cultural context all participants know why they are doing each act and what is expected, and these cultural controls make a great difference. The result is that some societies find that the use of drugs may enhance the group's goals, bind the people together, strengthen their beliefs, and so on (De Rios and Smith 1977:16). This does not mean that taking drugs is not genetically or otherwise physically damaging or that drug use is compatible with a lifeway involving automobiles, surgery, and other complex machinery or techniques affecting people's lives and health. Those are different questions. The point here is that drugs affect people differently in a culturally defined and regulated context than when taken experimentally or recreationally.

It is important to understand that the foregoing picture of Huichol religion is extremely fragmentary. We have drawn mostly on data concerning the deer-peyote-maize aspects, with very little reference to other major facets. The Roman Catholics have had an impact on Huichol religion, but not nearly so much as in some tribes. Many tribes combined Christian teaching with pagan religion to emerge with a syncretic system different from both Indian and conventional Catholic belief and practice. Grimes and Hinton indicate that some Huichol equate saints with Indian deities, a common kind of syncretistic response to Christianity in many Indian societies. The Christian saint often functions as the pagan deity did. Saint Peter in the Zapotec town of Teotitlán del Valle, for example, was the god of rain (R. Taylor 1980:283). Most Huichol, however, regarded the saints as additional deities, and many paid little attention to them. Essentially they isolated the Catholic features they accepted from their own religious system, so the two coexisted rather than blended.

Cultural Change

The Huichol of the 1980s were very much like those of the 1960s and 1970s, and Joseph Grimes has stressed that

most of the customs described in this chapter were still in force during the 1980s. Still, a few things have changed. In fact, no culture stops changing. Even during the seventies investigators disagreed or were uncertain about how much change had taken place among the Huichol. One scholar indicated that the people of San Andrés Cohamiata had preserved their aboriginal culture to a remarkable degree (Muller 1978:84), while another felt that those of San Sebastián and other Huichol, too, had changed greatly (Weigand 1978:104). Part of the problem may be in the investigators' areas of interest, since Huichol communities have changed far more in some aspects than in others. An observer looking at the social and economic life is apt to see more change than one considering the ideology and religion. Another problem is that some communities are much more acculturated than others.

All recent investigators agree that the pressures and opportunities for change accelerated greatly during the last half of the century, especially since 1970. The government comunidad structure, put in place shortly after the Conquest, needed only to be used to become a powerful force in the mountain country. In the early 1970s, for example, banks penetrated the comunidades and, directly and indirectly, controlled comunidad finances through government agencies (Weigand 1978:103). Several federal programs for economic development were activated, and schools, clinics, stores, airstrips, veterinary services, and radio communications were introduced or more fully developed. Some of the Huichol, finding it difficult to continue the traditional agriculture, moved to the cities, and others took advantage of government credit to remain in their home territory. Weigand holds that the Huichol have responded to the new challenges realistically and creatively (1978:115).

PART III CULTURES OF MESOAMERICA

Chapter 9

PRE-COLUMBIAN CULTURES OF MESOAMERICA

Mesoamerica embraces the territory to the south of the gathering and hunting areas of Baja California and Northeast Mexico and the horticultural Northwest Mexico that lies between them. It is by far the best known of the Mexican and Central American culture areas because of the several major civilizations that developed there and the events of the Spanish conquest of the Aztec and the Maya.

Generally, the Mesoamerican peoples are found in the southern half of Mexico and in Guatemala. Some anthropologists have included all of Mexico in Mesoamerica, but most have excluded the peoples of northern Mexico, as we are doing here. But even those who exclude the northern peoples disagree on which tribes belong in horticultural Northwest Mexico and which in Mesoamerica. This illustrates the common difficulty of drawing precise boundaries between culture areas, since it is impossible to describe a line along which the cultures on each side differ significantly from one another. So, in this book I somewhat arbitrarily follow the boundary as delineated in the *Handbook of Middle American Indians*. For the western portion I follow the late Edward H. Spicer of the University of Arizona, who placed the Huichol and Cora in the geographically and culturally diverse Northwest Mexico (1969:779), thereby excluding them from Mesoamerica. Paul Kirchoff (1968:23) and some others, however, include both tribes in Mesoamerica. The map of Middle American culture areas (see map 12), following Spicer, shows the western boundary beginning on the Pacific Coast west of the city of Colima in the southern part of the state of Jalisco. From there it follows an irregular course along the borders of Cora and Huichol country, extends eastward to Lake Chapala, and follows the Lerma River along the northern boundary of the state of Michoacán. East of Michoacán, and northeast of Mexico City, the line dips southward around Jonaz territory and, then, sharply northward and, eventually, eastward along the lower Pánuco River to a point just north of the present city of Tampico. Accordingly, the northernmost tribes of Mesoamerica, from west to east, are a cluster of poorly known groups on the coast, the Purépecha or Tarascans, the Otomí, the Nahua, and the Huastec Maya.

The southern boundary of Mesoamerica, which runs north and south, extends from a point on the Pacific coast near the city of San Salvador north through San Salvador and Honduras to a point on the Caribbean east of the Gulf of Honduras. A few Mesoamerican tribes migrated to the south of this boundary into what is now Costa Rica and Nicaragua several hundred years before the Spanish came. They adopted the Circum-Caribbean type of culture for the most part (Steward v. 5, 1948:33), and I exclude them from Mesoamerica for this treatment. Accordingly, the southernmost Mesoamerican tribes, from south to north, are the Pipil, the Achí, and the Chortí.

Mesoamerican territory includes a great variety of natural habitats. There are both desert and tropical ocean coasts, high and low mountains, valleys, and plateaus. The Sierra Madre Occidental that runs through Northwest Mexico parallel with the Pacific coast continues into Mesoamerica, where it merges with the Sierra Madre Oriental that extends southward from the northeastern section of Mexico. Central, west central, and southern Mexico north of the Isthmus of Tehuantepec is an extended region of mountains and high valleys and plateaus, one of the valleys being the Valley of Mexico, where the city of Mexico is. Forests of pine, fir and other trees are common on the mountain slopes, and scrubby vegetation prevails in many of the relatively arid lower plateaus and valleys. Active and inactive volcanoes are scattered about the area, including the magnificent snow-capped mountains Popocatépetl and Ixtaccíhautl. Mountains approach the shore along much of the Pacific coast, but on the Gulf of Mexico side there is a fairly wide strip of hot, moist lowland country.

To the south and east of this part of Mexico lie the tropical lowlands of the Isthmus of Tehuantepec, the lowlands of the Yucatán Peninsula of Mexico and northern Guatemala, and the mountain highlands of the state of Chiapas and neighboring southern Guatemala. Most of the Yucatán Peninsula is a great rolling limestone plain, though there are a few mountains in the southern part. The mountains of Chiapas and Guatemala range up to more than 10,000 feet above sea level, and numerous valleys, large and small, interrupt them. The average elevation is 4,000 feet (Vogt v.

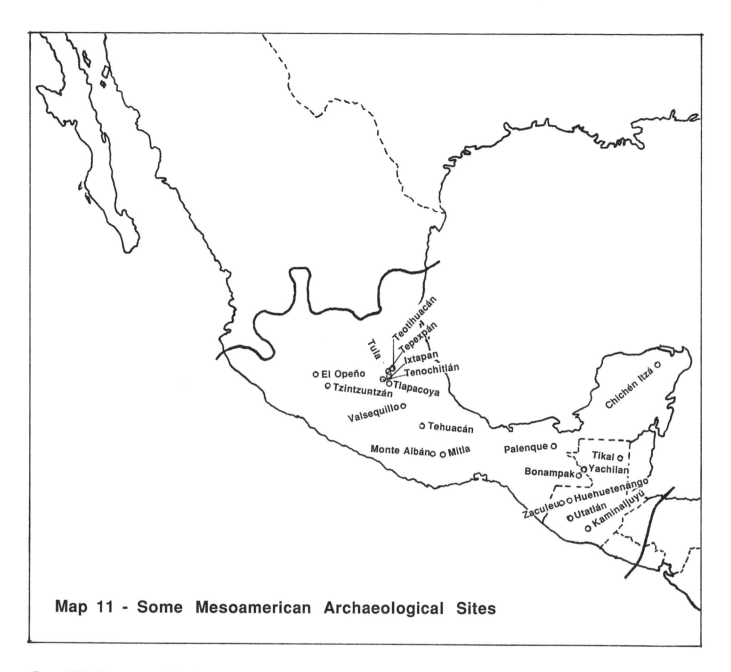

Map 11 - Some Mesoamerican Archaeological Sites

7, pt. 1:21). There are relatively narrow strips of hot country along some of the coastal stretches.

The Spanish found Mesoamerican Indians living in hamlets, villages, small towns, large towns, and cities in the various kinds of environments described above, though the bulk of them lived in the mountain valleys, the lower slopes of the mountain country, or on the plains of Yucatán. Most of the people were peasants who grew corn, beans, squash and a variety of other crops by the slash-and-burn technique. Their agricultural techniques were productive enough to allow the building of architecturally elaborate ceremonial centers and cities and to support large numbers of religious and administrative specialists. The Nahua (Aztec) and Maya civilizations were developed there, the former in the valleys of central Mexico and the latter in the mountains and lowlands of southern Mexico and Guatemala. But many who know about the Aztec and Maya are unaware that there were a number of other major civilizations in

Mesoamerica. Those civilizations are gone, but the descendants of their creators are still there, speaking many of the Indian languages and living ways of life that combine Spanish, pre-Columbian, and modern customs.

The Aboriginal Languages

The Mesoamerican Indians spoke languages of the Uto-Aztecan, Macromayan, and Oto-Manguean phyla, each of which is represented by one or more language families, as well as two language families not assigned to a phylum at the time Longacre wrote his account of Middle American linguistics (1967:120). The Uto-Aztecan family found in Mesoamerica was Aztecoidan, which was spoken by the Aztec, the Pipil of Guatemala, and some of the groups of Mesoamerican origin in Central America. As noted in the chapters on Northwest Mexico, the people of that area speak languages of all three Uto-aztecan families—Piman, Taracahitian, and Aztecoidan. There are nearly forty extinct Middle American languages that linguists know too little about to decide what language family they belong in (Longacre 1967:map facing 120).

There are seven Oto-Manguean families of languages in Mesoamerica and three Macromayan families. Each family is represented by several languages, and 33 of the 40 Macromayan languages listed belong to the Mayan family.

When the Spanish arrived most of the Mesoamericans spoke either a dialect of Nahua (the Aztec language) or one of the 33 Mayan languages. Researchers have found it impossible to estimate accurately the population of pre-Columbian Mesoamerica, but there were may have been between ten and twenty million people. Two or three million may have spoken one of the Mayan languages about A.D. 800 (Thompson 1966:29), and possibly about the same number spoke the language of the Aztec about the time the Spanish arrived (Gibson 1964:5)

Archaeology of Mesoamerica

Some archaeologists think there were people in Mesoamerica by about twenty thousand years before Christ walked the roads of Palestine. In the Valsequillo Gravels of the Valsequillo Reservoir area in the Mexican state of Puebla (see Figure 11) archaeologists have excavated several sites containing hearths, stone tools, and debris from human chipping of stone objects, and they found them in the same levels as the bones of mammoths, mastodons, camels, and horses. The archaeologists are especially confident that they have the correct age at one of the sites, where they used the carbon 14 method to obtain a date of about 21,850 years ago for the fossil mollusks occurring there. In that same stratum they found one stone flake tool of obviously human origin (Stark 1981:347). But they wish there were more artifacts, since it would strengthen their case considerably. Other sites at Valsequillo provide more abundant evidence of human activity during the times that now extinct Pleistocene animals flourished, but some archaeologists question the notion that the artifacts were originally deposited in the strata they were found in and doubt that the dating is correct. In addition to the difficulty of knowing whether or not the artifacts are really so old as 20,000 or more years archaeologists are troubled by the lack of similar data from a sufficient number of other Middle American places. If, over the years, archaeologists find several additional sites with good evidence for humans and 20,000 year old animals in the same strata, most will accept the date.

At a site called Tlapacoya in the Valley of Mexico archaeologists found additional possible evidence for the presence of humans before 20,000 years ago. One of the hearths found at Tlapacoya was dated at 24,000 years before the present (B.P.) by the carbon 14 method, and another

yielded a date of nearly 22,000 B.P. There were thousands of human tools in strata below the hearths, but none of them were clearly associated with the remains of the Pleistocene animals found there. Archaeologists who favor an early date for humans in Middle America would like very much to find an arrowhead or spear point or two between the ribs of a mammoth or some other extinct animals as evidence people hunted them.

Archaeologists are much more satisfied for the evidence of American humans by about 12,000 years ago. They know of several places in Mexico that have yielded evidence for the association of human tools with remains of extinct mammals 10,000 B.C. or shortly thereafter. The most famous is Tepexpán near Mexico City, where an investigator reported a human skeleton in the same stratum as a mammoth. Archaeologists found the evidence weak, however, and they might have dismissed the find completely had it not been for sounder evidence from other sites. At another place in the Valley of Mexico, Ixtapan, researchers made two finds of human tools clearly associated with mammoth bones. In the highlands of Guatemala investigators excavated campsites they estimate as nearly 11,000 years old (Gruhn, Bryan & Nance 1977:241), and MacNeish and his associates have found campsites in the archaeologically famous Tehuacán Valley in the Mexican State of Puebla that are 10,000 years old or older and contain bones of extinct horses and other animals (1978:136). Archaeologists have turned up preliminary evidence of this kind in Belize (MacNeish, Wilkerson, and Nelken-Turner 1981). Accordingly, it looks like a continuing series of finds will confirm the already existing evidence that humans were in Middle America by at least 10,000 B.C.

In addition, archaeologists find the evidence more acceptable at this time level than for 20,000 plus years ago because they have evidence for human hunting of extinct game animals in widely scattered places in the United States. Many lay people in the United States know about the Folsom and Clovis people of New Mexico. At Folsom archaeologists found their first fully authenticated evidence of human tools undeniably associated with bones of an extinct type of bison. The hunters killed and butchered 23 bison, and archaeologists found 19 of the projectile points that came to be known as Folsom points (Jennings 1974:58). The Clovis people, generally older than the Folsom hunters, hunted mastodons and mammoths.

Archaeologists recognize a period of North and Middle American prehistory, based on finds such as the foregoing, called *Paleo-Indian*. The Paleo-Indian people hunted bison, elephant-like animals, and other now extinct forms and collected plant and small animal life. We have seen that scholars do not yet know the date of the first Paleo-Indians, but it is clear that they prevailed in many places until eight or ten thousand years ago. Scholars frequently refer to their cultures as *lithic*, since what we know of them is based largely on the stone tools they left behind. Archaeologists also frequently refer to lithic cultures as *pre-ceramic*, since the people were without pottery.

Cultures that many archaeologists have called *Archaic* appeared at various times and places in North and Middle America, replacing the Paleo-Indian lifeways. Their earliest appearance in Middle America appears to be about 9,000 years ago (7,000 B.C.). The Archaic peoples were largely collectors of wild plant foods, though they also hunted some and collected small animal forms—insects and rodents, for example.

In a number of places these Archaic hunters and gatherers began a couple of activities of great consequence for later development. Some of them began to make containers and other objects of fired clay, and some began to cultivate plants. From cultivating plants, a few began to domesticate them. That is, they altered the plant populations genetically by selecting the most desirable specimens or, inadvertently, simply by saving seeds for the next season (Stark 1981:352). Even in those places where people domesticated plants, largely in the highland valleys of Mesoamerica, the people got most of their food by hunting and gathering, so agriculture remained "incipient" during Archaic times.

This is not a balanced review of the archaeology of Mesoamerica, but the finds in one place are worth special mention because they are especially well-known and have had a notably powerful impact on archaeological thinking about cultural development in Mesoamerica. For several decades Richard MacNeish and his associates have excavated in the Tehuacán Valley, which lies in the mountainous area of southeastern Puebla, roughly 150 miles southeast of Mexico City. They found evidence of Paleo-Indian life there as well as Archaic and later sites. They learned that a wide variety of plants was collected or cultivated in the Valley at one time or another and that some of them were domesticated. The archaeologists recognize nine cultural phases in the Valley, lasting from sometime before 9,000 B.C (11,000 years ago) until 900 B.C.—a period that saw the cultures change from hunting and gathering lifeways to fully developed agriculture. The people of the Tehuacán Valley domesticated chili peppers, amaranth, and squash by 5,000 B.C, and between then and 3400 B.C. they began using domesticated beans and maize (Indian corn). Interpreters differ about whether the maize in use at certain times was wild or domesticated, but it appears that a form of domesticated corn was being raised in the Tehuacán Valley by 5,000 to 4,500 years before Christ, nearly 7,000 years ago. The Tehuacán Valley is apparently one of several centers of plant domestication in Middle America, and what happened there seems to harmonize well with findings in other places.

As domesticated plants came into use, archaeologists assume, people ceased moving so often. But, agriculture was still incipient in many groups for some time after its beginnings, and the people of Tehuacán Valley still got 70 percent of their diet from wild foods as late as 2300 B.C. (Culbert 1983:34).

But by that time sedentary village life and pottery were found in most parts of Mesoamerica, marking for archaeologists the beginning of the next period, which they refer to as either the *Formative* or the *Preclassic*. Both labels reflect the archaeological view that the great civilizations of Mesoamerica were developing during that time. The villages increased in size, and the people began to build the earthen platforms that preceded the coming of pyramidal ceremonial structures. They built civic-religious centers; developed complex pottery, stone working, and other arts; divided into social strata; established states; developed intersocietal trade patterns; established religious cults; and built cities.

Archaeologists came to refer to the Mesoamerican culture from 250 or 300 years after Christ's birth until about A.D. 900 as the *Classic Period*. They pictured the Mesoamerican civilizations as having reached their greatest levels of achievement in many areas of life. Some scholars also pictured the Classic as a time of religiously oriented civilizations having highly developed priesthoods and religious organizations, theocratic governments, complex ritual, ceremonial buildings, and religious art in harmony with that orientation.

During the latter part of the Formative, or Preclassic, Period the great city of Teotihuacán was developing in the Valley of Mexico 25 or 30 miles northeast of where Mexico City is now. This city, with its population of between 125,000 and 200,000, dominated most of Mesoamerican life until roughly A.D. 600. The partially restored ruins of Teotihuacán with its great Pyramid of the Sun, the Pyramid of the Moon, and many other religious-ceremonial structures is one of the most outstanding archaeological attractions of Mexico. Important Classic civilizations also developed in the Valley of Oaxaca (approx. wah-HAH-kah) some 350 miles southeast of Mexico City and among the Maya-speaking peoples of both the highlands and lowlands of Guatemala and southern Mexico.

During the last centuries of the Classic many civilizations went into decline, and the way was prepared for a different type of culture, the *Postclassic* civilizations. Mesoamerican archaeologists have portrayed the Postclassic civilizations as much more secular and militaristic than the Classic cultures. Conquest was a major theme, and new cities emerged as centers of power. Early in the Postclassic the Toltec people of Tula, some seventy miles north of today's Mexico City, established control over a great portion of Mesoamerica, and the remains of Tula remain a major archaeological attraction of modern Mexico. Later in the Valley of Mexico the Toltecs went into decline, and the Valley country entered a period of great turmoil.

One of the weakest peoples during this time were the Mexica (approx. meh-SHEE-kah), an uncivilized tribe that had migrated from the north around A.D. 1300. They served as mercenaries and allies of the more powerful tribes and turned their newly acquired abilities to their own advantage to become the dominant group in the Valley and establish what came to be known as the Aztec Empire. Their capitol city, Tenochtitlán, stood where Mexico City is now, and, as all students of New World history know, Cortés conquered the city and razed its pyramids early in the sixteenth century. Mayan civilizations also continued to flourish during the Postclassic, especially in the northern part of Mayan country.

The Aztec and Mayan civilizations are well-known to the American public, but not many know about the Zapotec, Totonac, Tlaxcalans and other groups that participated in and contributed to the development of Mesoamerican civilization. There were other politically and religiously complex groups that had the calendar, writing, highly developed art, and the like that did not build large cities and ceremonial centers or build monumental pyramidal structures.

Recently a number of archaeologists have concluded on the basis of new research that the five period scheme outlined above fails to portray as accurately as it should what happened in pre-Columbian Mesoamerica. For example, it is apparent that the Classic civilizations need not be regarded as more highly developed than Postclassic cultures, and they seem to have been a lot more warlike than some archaeologists had believed. And the Postclassic peoples were still quite religious and theocratic. Moreover, rather different kinds of things took place in various parts of Mesoamerica. At this writing a number of scholars retain the more traditional sequence—Paleo-Indian, Archaic, Formative (or Preclassic), Classic, and Postclassic (Culbert 1983:29), while others are experimenting with different schemes. It remains to be seen whether or not the older one is eventually superceded.

Archaeology and Ethnohistory

The foregoing is only a sketchy view of pre-Columbian cultural development in Mesoamerica, and we turn now to a summary of the area's cultural features around A.D. 1500. Archaeology depends fully on a *comparative method*, also referred to as *ethnographic analogy*. That is, none of the artifacts and other evidences of human presence can be understood without relating them to something that we know about groups whose cultural behavior someone has been able to observe and keep a record of. A projectile point (arrow point or spear head) cannot be identified as such without comparing it with similar objects from living societies and assuming that objects of that kind had the same functions in the extinct cultures whose bearers we have never been able to observe as it does in the cultures of people we have observed. If no one had ever seen such an object made and used and talked about in a living society, we would be completely unable to say what it could be. It has to be compared with things whose uses and functions we know and, by analogy, we assume the prehistoric objects had similar uses and functions.

But for the Mesoamerican cultures since 1500 we have more than this. We have the records of people who saw Aztec, Maya, Zapotec, Quiché, and others living their cultures and who left for our perusal records of what they saw. The soldiers, administrators, and religious functionaries who came with Cortés in 1520 and others that arrived shortly thereafter included some who recorded Indian custom. In addition, there were a few Indians who were educated by some of these men and who recorded the customs of their people as they were in the decades just before the Spanish arrived to begin the relentless destruction of Indian lifeways.

Ethnography, strictly speaking, is describing in writing some society's customs. Many anthropologists have also used the term more broadly to refer to the field work undertaken to observe and learn about a group's culture. Anthropology as a discipline did not exist in the sixteenth century, so there was no one to study the Indian cultures with the accuracy, comprehensiveness, and depth of interpretation that a modern ethnographer would. The relatively untrained observers of the time, then, overlooked a few things and misinterpreted some of what they saw and heard about. Nevertheless, some of them were very good observers indeed, and that is why we know as much as we do about the Aztec and some of the other Middle American Indians. Scholars refer to the study and interpretation of these documents for cultural information as *ethnohistory*, and the combination of ethnohistorical and archaeological data provides us with what we know of the early sixteenth century Mesoamerican cultures.

Pre-Columbian Subsistence Technology

The main subsistence mode of pre-Columbian Mesoamerica was agriculture, with maize, beans, and squash being the main crops. But the Americans also cultivated nearly a hundred other plants, nearly all of which were present in Mesoamerica when the Spanish arrived (Palerm 1967:40). All the Mesoamerican tribes raised the three main crops and chile, too, and many groups grew tomatoes and amaranth. Palerm lists these six as the staples of pre-Columbian Mesoamerica. Modern North Americans are generally unfamiliar with amaranth, since it is so much less important than in pre-Hispanic times. The plants consist of a single stalk several feet tall, topped by massive heads loaded with tiny seeds. The Indians made amaranth bread and used the seeds in their rituals. Some of the other pre-Columbian plant items were pineapples, the *epazote* plant, lime-leaved sage (for its seeds), sweet potatoes, manioc roots, *jícama* roots, the chayote plant (for its fruit, leaves, shoots and roots), vanilla, *maguey*, the *nopal* cactus (for its fruit), and mesquite. Fruit trees comprised a third of the known cultivated plants, most of them unfamiliar to modern North Americans. The Mesoamericans may have used alligator pears almost as much as squash, chiles, and tomatoes. The many fruits they used included the papaya, cacao (for chocolate), the cherry-like fruit from the *capulín* tree, the *zapote*, avocados, and the plum-like spondia. Nearly all Mesoamerican agriculturalists grew the staples corn, beans, squash, and chile, but the other food plants were not grown in every region.

In most parts of the preindustrial world the women cultivated the crops, but Mesoamerica is similar to much of the horticultural Greater Southwest in that the men did the farming and gardening. The Mesoamericans used the slash-and-burn cultivation system more than any other. They burned an area of forest or other growth and planted several kinds of crops in holes made with a digging stick. Often they placed more than one kind of seed in the same hill. They hardened the pointed sticks with fire, and many had metal points. The implement they most frequently used for working the soil, both before and after planting, was the *coa*. Instead of a sharp tip it had a wide, flat, thin, wooden blade, sometimes edged with copper. Under the slash-and-burn system the soil lost its fertility within a very few years, and the people would have to clear another garden.

Highland groups made the greatest use of the slash-and-burn system, but a few lived where they could cultivate in other ways. The *chinampa* system of the Valley of Mexico is an example. The people living in the vicinity of the lakes and marshes of that area would prepare a rectangular garden island by dragging several masses of floating vegetation into place one atop another and fixing it in position by cypress stakes that rooted and grew into trees. They excavated canals around the island and piled the mud on top of the vegetation. To maintain the island, they added mud from time to time and applied human waste, much of which they collected in the Aztec city of Tenochtitlán. The islands were usually about 330 feet long and 30 feet wide and laid out in a grid pattern, so the water from the canals dividing the islands percolated through the soil. The island gardens did not float, so it is not accurate to call chinampas floating gardens, but the gardeners did prepare floating seed nurseries made from water plants and towed these small nurseries to the gardens when they were ready to transplant the seedlings. Each family farmed several of the chinampas, or garden islands, and grew enough corn and other vegetables to feed themselves and others, too. Investigators have estimated that in 1519 one 25,000 acre zone of chinampas would produce enough for 100,000 to 180,000 people (Armillas 1971:9). Researchers have also found evidence for chinampas in Puebla and elsewhere, though they may have originated in the Valley of Mexico.

Slash-and-burn and chinampa systems are opposites in the sense that one is a form of nonpermanent dry farming and the other involves gardens permanently sitting in water, so to speak. But there were both dry farmers and irrigation farmers in Mesoamerica who used neither approach (Sanders 1981:190). A number prepared fields by rooting out all the vegetation and maintaining the plot in one place over the years by intensive working of the soil, interplanting different types of crops, rotating crops, letting the land lie fallow for a season, or adding materials to maintain and restore fertility. In some places the people terraced slopes and preserved the terraces by building retaining walls of stone or adobe or planting hedges along the edges. This, of course, retains rainfall much better than a slope and reduces erosion. In other places Mesoamericans apparently prepared their fields where they would receive flood water occasionally, and a number dammed streams and diverted water into their fields through systems of canals. Slash-and-burn agriculture prevailed in Mesoamerica as it did in many other parts of the world, but the several other systems just described were used where resources permitted.

The protohistoric Mesoamericans also hunted some and collected wild plants and small animals, and fishing was of some importance along the coasts and other places where fish were available. In Mesoamerica as a whole, however, fishing provided only a small fraction of the food gotten from gardening and farming. By protohistoric times the population of deer was greatly reduced in much of Mesoamerica, and there were few other large animals of much value for food. In addition to deer, hunters took *javelinas* (peccaries), rabbits and hares, and various birds with bows and arrows, pellet bows, blowguns, slings, and clubs. Much of the hunting among the Aztec was apparently for sport more than for food. The Aztec also caught iguanas and other lizards, snakes, worms, newts, frogs, tadpoles, grasshoppers, and a variety of similar forms on occasion. Where fish were available Mesoamericans took them with spears, nets, basketry ladles, or by poisoning them.

The habitat provided a large variety of edible wild plants such as nuts, berries, mesquite beans, wild onions, fungi, and greens of various kinds, but the people relied on them heavily only in times of scarcity.

Although the prehistoric Americans cultivated and domesticated a large number of food plants, they had far fewer kinds of domesticated animal forms than Old World groups. In one place or another Mesoamerican groups raised turkeys, ducks, geese, hairless dogs, quail, bees, and maguey slugs. But there were no large forms such as sheep, cattle, or horses. Of course there were wild horses there in Paleo-Indian times, but they became extinct long before the agriculturally based cultures arose. The Mesoamericans obtained only a small fraction of their food from the animals they kept.

Like many of the farmers of Northeast Mexico the Mesoamericans coupled their agriculture with a great deal of ritual, much of which was complicated and highly formalized. They had elaborate rain rituals and ceremonies for both planting and harvesting. Tlaloc, the Aztec god of rain, was one of the most important Valley of Mexico deities, and the Mayan groups had important rain gods known as *chacs*. Some of the Maya offered fermented honey to the chacs and sometimes sacrificed birds or even children as part of their rain ceremonies.

The men did the farming in protohistoric Mesoamerica, and they accordingly conducted the rain ceremonies. The women did most of the collecting of plants and characteristically held first-fruits ceremonies when the first plant food of the season was taken.

Tortillas were the major food item in the Mesoamerican diet. Mesoamerican women first soaked the kernels of corn in pots of hot lime water, then ground them into a dough with the *metate* and *mano*, The metate, still used in

Mexico, was a rectangular or oval grinding stone with a flat to slightly concave upper surface. A woman would place the lime-softened corn on the grinding stone, kneel at the higher end of the metate, and reduce the material to dough by application of the somewhat cigar-shaped hand stone (mano) she held by each end. It took a long time to produce dough fine enough for tortillas, and a woman might spend several hours a day at the arduous task of grinding the corn for the large number of tortillas each Mesoamerican family consumed daily. When she had the dough right she made a ball from some of it and patted it between her hands into a very thin, floppy disk, apparently 10 or 12 inches in diameter. She then baked it on a clay griddle that rested on the tops of three stones positioned on the ground or floor to form approximately an equilateral triangle. She would have the griddle hot from a fire made among the stones. The griddle itself was a disk-shaped, very shallow clay pan. The convex side rested on the stones and the concave side served as the cooking surface.

The people might eat tortillas alone if they wished, but they usually combined them with one or more other foods. They might place some beans boiled in a clay pot on a tortilla or fold them inside, and they might add some chile sauce, greens and salt. They also made drinks or soups of various consistencies from the maize dough. The simplest was *pozole*, which was made simply by mixing tortilla dough with water. *Atole* is another maize drink, common in modern Mesoamerica but possibly less used in protohistoric Mexico. The Mesoamericans made atole by cooking the mixture of tortilla dough and water a bit and adding chocolate or some other flavoring. Many Mesoamericans probably varied their diet from the foregoing only in minor ways as other things became available to them. The wealthy elite had a host of other foods prepared for them, and hundreds of the dishes known to have been prepared in prehispanic Mesoamerica were mainly or exclusively fiesta and ceremonial foods.

Drug Technology

Like the Northwest Mexican Indians the Mesoamericans used alcoholic beverages. They made the wine drink now known as *pulque* from the fresh juice of the *agave*, or century plant. They cut the heart out, which left a basin into which the juice flowed. They baked the agave heart in an earthen oven and ate it. They removed the juice from the basin for several days, and each batch was ready to drink after it stood for a few days. By then it was three to four percent alcohol, but it had to be consumed within a day or it would decompose beyond use. This wine is 88 per cent water, and it probably induces the formation of flora that tend to check dysenteries (Driver 1961:95). The Mesoamericans also made maize beer, mainly from juice squeezed from green cornstalks. Cornstalk beer prevailed among the Mesoamericans, while beer made from sprouted maize grains was important in Northwest Mexico. Beer made from chewed corn kernels was widely used in the rest of Central

America and the Caribbean islands. The Mesoamericans also boiled the cornstalk juice to obtain syrup from which they made a wine. They may have had as many as forty other kinds of alcoholic drinks made from a variety of items, such as wild plums, pineapples, the sarsaparilla root, the palm, the *sotol* plant, the *mamey* fruit, and honey. A fermented honey drink (*balché*) was especially important in some Mayan groups.

The Mesoamericans used alcoholic beverages in both recreational and ceremonial ways, but drinking and the offering of alcoholic drinks were especially important as religious rituals. The Maya of the Yucatán peninsula, for example, made offerings of fermented honey to their rain gods, and ceremonialists and healers got drunk as an essential part of the ritual they performed for individual and community welfare. The people of Mesoamerica also used other drugs. The Aztec were using peyote some when the Spanish arrived as well as Jimson Weed and narcotic mushrooms. These narcotics were sacred to the Aztec, and though little is known about it, they were also important in other Mesoamerican tribes.

Mesoamerican Clothing and Ornamentation

Mesoamerican groups differed from one another in their clothing styles more than the Northwest Mexican tribes, and within a given Mesoamerican tribe there was often more color and variability. Nevertheless, several basic items were typical. The basic dress of ancient Mixtec, for example, consisted of a wrapped skirt and *huipil* (sleeveless blouse) for the women and the breechcloth, shoulder cape, and mantle of cotton or *ixtle* (agave fiber) for the men (Spores 1967:8). Rulers, priests, and nobles wore more elaborate clothing and, especially on ceremonial occasions, various other items. The Mixtec elite used all kinds of feather work and brightly colored embroidery and tapestries on their ceremonial garments and wore rings, earrings, and lip and nose ornaments of gold and precious stones.

Common Tarascan women wore short skirts only (Foster 1948:15) except, presumably, as added garments were needed for warmth. The male Tarascans wore leather loin cloths, and both sexes used deerhide sandals secured by ties around the ankles. The elite Tarascans added feather and robe capes as well as obsidian lip plugs inlaid with turquoise, and necklaces, earrings, and bracelets of turquoise, gilded copper, silver, and gold. To make their capes the Tarascans applied colored feathers in various patterns to material made from the fiber of agave leaves, and the Spanish were astonished at their technical perfection and beauty. The Tarascans and other Mesoamerican tribes grew cotton, and the women spun, dyed, and wove the fibers for clothing, offerings to elite friends, and tribute.

Ancient Mayan women also wore wrapped skirts and huipil-type blouses that could vary considerably in length, sometimes being long like a dress. The men had the breechcloth, a square shoulder cloth, and deerhide sandals. The elite costume differed from that of the commoners during Classic times, at least, by the wearing of an elaborate headdress. Its main structure, of wickerwork basketry or wood, was shaped to represent a god, jaguar, bird, or serpent. This structure was covered with skin, a mosaic of feathers, carved jades, and a high crest of feathers. In addition to cotton and agave fiber some Mayan tribes used aloe fiber and the inner bark of the wild fig or other trees (King 1977:465).

These fragments of description for Mixtec, Tarascan, and Mayan dress illustrate how the basic clothing styles could differ from tribe to tribe and that the clothing and adornment of the elite was more colorful and elaborate than that of the commoners. The two most common materials were ixtle (cloth made from agave fiber) and cotton, with a tendency for cotton to be used more by the elite than by commoners. Bark cloth was important in some of the southern Mesoamerican groups.

People of different tribes also wore their hair differently. Ancient Mayan men and women had long hair. Mayan men also burned a spot bare on top of their heads and braided and wrapped most of their hair around the head, leaving a queue hanging behind. But most of the Aztec men wore their hair cut short across the forehead and long otherwise. The Aztec priests shaved the front and side of the head and left the top hair long. And young warriors wore a long lock of hair, which they removed after their first military exploit (Soustelle 1961[1955]:130).   Mayan men painted their bodies in various colors, and both men and women had themselves tattooed extensively. The Maya and the Tarascans are among the Mesoamerican tribes that intentionally deformed the head. The Maya tied boards on the front and back of an infant's head so the forehead would slope and the back of the head would flatten. This ensured the child's social acceptability.

Dwellings and Other Structures

We find housing differences among and within tribes in Mesoamerica, but three major types prevailed. In the western and central highlands of Mexico and among many of the Tarascans rectangular, flat-roofed structures of stone and adobe and poles or just adobe were common. These were usually one-storied. Many groups in southern Mesoamerica lived in rectangular, gabled dwellings with walls of upright poles and grass-thatched roofs. A third major type was a rectangular house with a steeply-sloped, pyramid-shaped roof. The walls were variable, being made of different combinations of poles, reed canes, adobe bricks, puddled adobe, or, sometimes, stone. The men of Mesoamerica built their houses, though the women usually participated by gathering material for the thatched roofs.

The houses of the city elite were commonly more substantial than these. As one came closer to the center of the Aztec city of Tenochtitlán the simpler structures like those just described were replaced increasingly by more luxurious dwellings. Most of them were adobe one-storied structures forming a solid, windowless wall along the street, with a separate kitchen building in the courtyard. In addition to the kitchen and a sleeping room there was usually a small shrine and a sweat bath (the temazcal). Most of the courtyards had a canal on at least one side and a landing-place for small watercraft. Wealthy people would have more rooms in their houses and perhaps two stories. But no matter how large their houses might be, the furnishings were similar, consisting of mats on low earthen or wooden platforms, low chairs, wickerwork chests for valuables, and a fireplace. The houses of the most important people might have low tables, decorated wooden screens for isolating parts of a room, and probably frescoes and wall hangings.

Several Mesoamerican groups have become known for their monumental structures—their public buildings, temples, palaces, pyramids, ball courts, dance platforms, monasteries, and astronomical observatories. The Spanish systematically destroyed the pyramids and temples of Aztec Tenochtitlán, but the remains of many remain intact in other places and have become major tourist attractions. We know the monumental structures of the Aztec and the Maya best, but the Zapotec, the Tarascans, and the Totonac are among the other groups that built pyramids and temples. Some other tribes, such as the Mixtec, had writing, the calendar, exquisitely wrought jewelry, and highly crafted pottery, though they did not build large structures and cities.

Mesoamerican Arts and Crafts

Consistent with the complexity of other parts of their lives, the Mesoamericans developed their arts and crafts extensively. They produced nicely done objects of stone, including polished obsidian and pyrite mirrors. Their use of copper tubes to drill holes in stone illustrates the sophistication of their tools and techniques. Both men and women produced a great variety of decorative and utilitarian objects of fired clay, such as cooking pots, dishes, water jars, food storage containers, incense burners, spindle whorls decorated with stamped and incised designs, burial urns, and religious figurines. Male specialists, virtually full time, made floor coverings, raincoats, sleeping mats, and containers of all shapes by means of a variety of basketry techniques. The women, and sometimes men, wove cotton textiles using the belt or backstrap loom. One of two bars was fastened to a post or tree several feet above ground, and the other bar was attached to a belt around the weaver's waist or hips, making it possible to maintain tension on the warp threads running from bar to bar simply by leaning against the belt.

The Mesoamericans knew how to produce gold-copper, copper-lead, and silver-copper alloys, and they gilded copper and made bells, axes, picks, blow pipes, chisels, helmets, needles and other items of copper (Driver 1969:179). They cast copper and gold with the lost wax method. This involved making a clay model, coating it with wax, and encasing the wax with another layer of clay. They heated the mold until the wax ran out a hole in the bottom. Then they plugged the hole and poured the molten metal into the mold. When the metal cooled they broke off the mold.

The Mesoamericans traded extensively, and, unlike Northwest Mexico societies, one of the most impressive aspects of their communities was the market places. There was marked ecological variation in much of Mesoamerica, some areas producing one thing, others another. In a local Zapotec market a buyer would find metal objects, hides, fish, feathers, fruits, precious stones, herbs, tobacco, and a great variety of other items. Some of them came from their neighbors in Oaxaca and Guerrero, the Mixtec, who provided, among other things, agave fiber, chili, beans, dyes, and, possibly, paper and pottery (Spores 1967:6). In Tarascan towns some craftspeople specialized in clay pots, and others made clay plates and casseroles. Others received turquoise and fashioned it into lip plugs, earrings, and the like, while woodworkers used copper tools to make canoes, trays, benches, and other items. The major Tarascan towns held markets periodically for the exchange of the great variety of items produced by different specialists there and by those in other towns. These included evening markets, brightly lit by large torches of agave stalks or resinous stakes of pine (ocote) (Foster 1948:11). The people transported these goods mainly on their backs in baskets or other packs supported by the tumpline—a strap across the forehead, chest, or across the front of one shoulder. Those living on lakes or along the coasts, of course, could use dugout canoes or balsas (cigar-shaped bundles of buoyant reeds).

Apparently the Indians of Mesoamerica had complex music intricately integrated with their religion. Since the Spanish did so much to destroy their religion, their music was destroyed. Undoubtedly, certain qualities of the pre-Conquest music continue, but musicologists are unable to reconstruct the full texture. Ethnomusicologists believe Aztec music was characterized by rather doleful melodies, though none of them remain. Musical instruments included a pottery kettle drum, a tube-type drum with a skin head at one end and the other end open, a log drum with an H-shaped slit, turtle shells, gourd rattles, copper bells, animal hoof rattles, musical rasps, various sorts of whistles and flutes, and conch shell trumpets.

Family, Marriage, and Kinship in Mesoamerica

The Mesoamericans tended to live in patrilocal extended family households. This means that a newly married couple would take up residence in the home of the boy's parents, and when the couple had children the household would consist of three generations. The parents normally decided who their young people should marry and made the arrangements. They often used go-betweens, and the negotiations were frequently extended, with the woman's parents expected to exhibit much reluctance, perhaps including a considerable expression of anger. The ceremonies were often complex, and there were several exchanges of gifts during the course of the negotiations and the ceremonies.

The Spanish explorers, priests, and administrators who saw something of the functioning Mesoamerican societies knew little of what modern anthropologists have learned about the variety of kinship arrangements humans have invented, and failed to adequately report them. Apparently, many of the Mesoamerican tribes lacked unilineal common ancestor groups, but a few had them. Most of the Maya of Guatemala and the Yucatán Peninsula and other parts of southern Mexico had exogamous, patrilineal common ancestor groups. Each was a group of relatives who actually or putatively had descended from a common ancestor several generations back through father's only. If they were exogamous, each person had to find his or her spouse in a common ancestor group other than his or her own, with the consequence that husband and wife belonged to different groups. And since they were patrilineal all children became members of the father's group. Foster believes that the Tarascans probably had such groups, too (1948:11), and common ancestor groups have survived in Nahua Tlaxcala into the twentieth century. Most of the remaining Mesoamerican tribes were bilateral only, that is, people regarded themselves as descended from ancestors on both sides of the family and through both fathers and mothers in each generation. Bilateral descent does not result in common ancestor groups. The United States and other modern urban-industrial nations are exclusively bilateral in descent and therefore do not have the common ancestor groups known as clans or lineages.

Different Mesoamerican groups had variant systems of kinship terminology, depending on whether they had unilineal (patrilineal in Mesoamerica) common ancestor groups or were exclusively bilateral. The Mayan and other tribes with patrilineal common ancestor groups normally used bifurcate merging terms for the parental generation. This means that people addressed a parent and the parent's brother or sister of the same sex as the parent by the same term. That is, the father and father's brother were called the same term, possibly "my father," and the mother and mother's sister were addressed the same way, possibly as "my mother." With patrilineal descent one's father and father's brother belong to one's own common ancestor group, and the mother and her sister belong to the person's mother's patrilineal group.

Societies with the foregoing terminology system (bifurcate merging) tend to use Iroquois terms for siblings and cousins. Accordingly, they call the children of their father's brother by the same term they use for their siblings (brothers and sisters), and the same for the children of the mother's sister. Anthropologists call these individuals parallel cousins. Accordingly, a Mesoamerican using this system might address a parallel cousin as "my brother," or "my sister." Notice that in a patrilineal society parallel cousins that are children of a man and his brother belong to the same kinship group. In societies that consistently use bifurcate merging and Iroquois terms of address the father's sister, mother's brother, and the other cousins (*cross cousins*) are addressed by terms other than those just indicated.

Mesoamerican Communities

The prevailing kind of community in Mesoamerica was a sedentary cluster of homes—a hamlet, village, town, or city. The dispersed neighborhood communities of Northwest Mexico were generally small, but Mesoamerican communities varied from clusters of a very few homes up to cities of two or three-hundred thousand souls.

Many Mesoamericans lived in towns and cities. Driver estimated that there must have been at least a hundred cities in Mesoamerica. They were less compact than modern urban-industrial cities, since the people maintained courtyards and gardens among the houses. They also used various internal settlement patterns, often determined largely by the local geographical features. Many of the towns and cities, in fact, were quite irregularly laid out. The Yucatec Mayan city of Mayapán, a city of perhaps 12,000 people living in about 2,100 dwellings, was a maze of alleys running among the haphazardly scattered house lots bordered by stone walls (Adams 1977:263).

Whatever the street or road arrangement, the center of a Mesoamerican city was the plaza containing the temples, pyramids, palaces, ball courts, and similar structures. In many cases there were few dwellings by the ceremonial centers, perhaps only those of the priests and other dignitaries who remained at the plaza, and most of the people who used the ceremonial center for religious, economic, and other purposes lived in villages and hamlets scattered about the surrounding area.

Mesoamerican communities also tended to differ from those of modern urban industrial societies by their organization around kinship principles. A Mayan village, for example, might be occupied by the members of a *localized patrilineal clan* or *lineage*. The core of the village consisted of men and women patrilineally related to one another, tracing descent from a common ancestor through fathers only—one male ancestor in each generation for each member. The other village members consisted of women who, following the *patrilocal residence rule*, moved there when they married.

In still other cases a village would be composed of people related to one another because the village was *endogamous*, that is, people were expected to find a spouse within the village rather than marrying someone elsewhere. This type of community was common in those parts of Mesoamerica that were exclusively bilateral and therefore lacked common ancestor groups. Large villages, towns, and cities tended to consist of a number of such units, each in its own territory or *barrio*. The organization of the Aztec city of Tenochtitlán, which may have had nearly 300,000

citizens, reflects this. The city was divided into twenty districts or *barrios*, each occupied by a large number of patrilocal extended families that were supposed to be related to one another. In the many smaller communities, the towns and villages of Mesoamerica, each barrio would be occupied by relatively fewer related extended families.

Social Order in Mesoamerica

In many parts of the world the cultural-linguistic territorial units known as tribes are not organized as political units. The Hopi of Arizona and the Cherokee of the American Southeast had no tribal governments but were politically organized only at the village level. The Yaqui and other tribes of Northwest Mexico had no tribal level government in peacetime, though some organized tribally for war. But several of the Mesoamerican tribes had governments for the tribe as a whole.

The Aztec city of Tenochtitlán was a true state, which means that it had a government with officially recognized power to compel submission to its rule. In each of the twenty *calpulli* (approx. kahl-POOL-yee) as the city's subgroups were known, the heads of the extended families and other elder males comprised a council. The *calpul* (singular in Aztec speech) council selected its government officials. The three main officials were an economic affairs officer, a military-police official, and a speaker, who was the calpul representative on the national-city council. Other accomplished men served as market officials, judges, teachers, record-keepers, and the like.

The national council of 20 calpul speakers selected four of its members to handle military and judicial matters among the calpulli. The four officers chose two of their number for the two top national positions. One handled foreign affairs, both military and diplomatic, and the other was in charge of internal affairs. The foreign affairs officer was known as "the chief of men," and Moctezuma held that position when Cortés arrived.

In population size the Aztec city-state was the largest political unit of pre-Conquest North America. It established and dominated an alliance with two neighboring city states and dominated many of the other tribes of Mesoamerica by military force and diplomatic wile. But the Aztec never welded these tribes into a single nation or political empire. Nor was the "chief of men" a dictator. He had to share power with others, and Aztec officials could be impeached.

The Tarascans probably had the largest political unit in Mesoamerica in terms of territory, and it may have been militarily superior to all other Mesoamerican states. The Tarascan ruler was a dictator, unlike the Aztec "chief of men," sharing his power with no one. The Tarascan army used bows and arrows as well as slings rather than depending so heavily on swords as the Aztec did (Brand 1971:646). Ethnohistorical evidence indicates that, when Aztec and Tarascans confronted one another, the Aztec normally were bested. Had the Spanish not intervened it is possible that the Aztec might have lost to the Tarascans a good deal of the territory they dominated (Brand 1971:634). The Aztec gods demanded ever larger numbers of war captives for offerings of human hearts and blood, which was not so true of Tarascan religion. So it is understandable that small groups near the boundary between the Tarascan nation and Aztec-dominated country willingly accepted Tarascan affiliation.

Brand's research indicates that the Tarascan nation extended north to south from southern Querétaro into the Sierra Madre del Sur in Guerrero near the highest peak in that chain. From east to west it extended from the Aztec dominated territory almost to Colima. Unlike the Aztec the Tarascans colonized the areas they took, making them effectively a part of their empire.

The Tarascans apparently lacked large cities. Their capital was Tzintzuntzán, but there is a possibility that it was little more than a ceremonial-governmental center with the only people living there being the religious and political leaders and various lesser functionaries and retainers. Some believe there were only a few hundred there, but others hold there were over 30,000.

In other parts of western Mexico the largest political units were villages or, sometimes, small territories consisting of a few villages within a valley or other small region. The Totonac tribe of eastern Mexico was organized politically as a tribe, but the Zapotec and Mixtec were not. The latter two groups tended to have local government only, though it is clear that in the Valley of Oaxaca several towns were sometimes allied with one another, with one of them being dominant (Spores 1965:966).

The Mayan area is one of dozens of small states. There were sixteen on the northern plains of the Yucatán peninsula when Córdoba got there in 1517 (Adams 1977:263). Each nation had a ruler, and each town had its own administrator. The nation of Chikinchel, however, was governed by a council rather than a single official, and perhaps others were, too. A few Mayan states, especially in the Guatemalan high country, became larger than most. About a century before the Spanish arrived the Quiché Maya of Guatemala, under the leadership of an aggressive ruler, expanded their territory considerably. But none of the Mayan units became as large in either population or territory as the largest in non-Mayan Mexico.

Many Mesoamerican societies were strongly egalitarian, but the larger, wealthier tribes tended to be socially stratified. The basic division was between a ruler-noble-priest stratum and the common people. The Tarascans may have come by their social distinctions through a conquering people setting themselves over their subjects (Foster 1948:11). The lowest ranked Tarascans were tenant farmers, servants and slaves who worked on the lands and in the households of the elite classes.

The Mixtec kingdoms, according to Spores, were divided into four classes (1967:9). At the top was a privileged kin group including the king and his family, constituting a caste. Next, a relatively small, supporting contingent of hereditary nobles served as administrators, assistants and advisers to the ruling family. Most of the people belonged to the commoner class. They were farmers, merchants, artisans, and priests, though there appear to have been some priests in the noble class as well. Finally, there was a relatively small category of tenant farmers, servants, and slaves.

The Aztec were even more highly stratified. Soustelle divided them into rulers, tradesmen, craftsmen, commoners, and slaves (1961[1955]: 37-73).

Whitecotton notes that the Zapotec were differentiated into three primary divisions, the nobility, the commoners, and the priests (1977:142). There were also serfs or tenants and slaves. Morley divides ancient Maya society into four general classes—nobles, priests, commoners, and slaves (1947:168). Bishop Landa said there were four general classes among the ancient Maya—nobles, priests, commoners, and slaves (Morley and Brainerd 1983:214).

Probably, all Mesoamerican groups had *associations*, that is, societies or organizations not based on kinship. Organizations of priests were especially important. Roys mentions the possibility of organizations that owned land among the lowland Maya (1965:668). We have the fullest information for the Aztec, who had youth houses for training boys, schools for priests, military societies, a large number of religious cults centered on the worship of a single deity, and organizations of priests (Vaillant 1944:182ff.).

Religion in Mesoamerica

People tend to think of some societies has having especially simple religions, but it is less misleading to regard all religions as complex, some being more complex than others. The Mesoamericans developed some of the most elaborate religions known. A given group had a host of gods and goddesses of varying functions, personalities, and ranks. They had deities of pulque, rain, fire, planets, death, and many other elements of nature. The priests conducted group worship ritual, and the people built temples for their worship.

To the outsider one of the most impressive features of Mesoamerican culture was the pyramid, which served as the base for one or more temples. The famous great pyramid of Aztec Tenochtitlán was the base for two important temples, the temple of the war god Huitzilopochtli and the temple of Tlaloc, the god of rain (Soustelle 1961[1955]:18-19). Its stairway had 114 steps, and it was probably about a hundred feet high. There were many other pyramids in the city, too, supporting temples dedicated to other deities.

The Aztec gods demanded ever increasing quantities of human hearts and blood, and some estimate that, during a period of four days and nights in 1487, the priests sacrificed more than 80,000 victims on the pyramid's summit (Padden 1967:74). This was highly unusual in Mesoamerica, even for the Aztec. Some human sacrifice seems to have been a part of Mesoamerican religion in general, though not always like the Aztec did it. The Mixtec apparently did not build pyramids to support temples, but they did practice human sacrifice (Spores 1967:26). Scholars once thought the Maya of Classic times were less bloody than the Post-Classic Aztec, but they now know that they sacrificed humans in large numbers. Maya of Yucatán sometimes sacrificed young women by casting them into *cenotes*, the large, deep sinks in the limestone plains, in which water collected. The Aztec themselves practiced other forms of human sacrifice. They sacrificed children to Tlaloc by drowning them, decapitated women dedicated to earth goddesses while they were dancing, and threw victims into a fire to sacrifice them to the fire-god (Soustelle, 1961[1955]:98). We should not leave the impression that they offered only humans to the gods.

They also presented the gods with animals, birds (notably quail) flowers, incense, and other things they desired. All these matters were normally handled by the priests.

In other ways the Mesoamericans held beliefs and practiced rituals a little less unique. They believed in a variety of nature spirits—which they located in springs, hills, trees and other natural objects. Various kinds of spirits also helped individuals and families and other groups.

Mesoamericans believed that the dead lived on and might return under certain circumstances as ghosts. In the Mayan region, especially, the people were much concerned with maintaining satisfactory relationships with their ancestors, since their daily well-being depended on it.

Chapter 10

POST-COLUMBIAN INDIANS OF MESOAMERICA

Many of the same kinds of influences that affected Northwest Mexico changed the cultures of Mesoamerica. The missionaries, the miners, colonists, and military forces exerted varying degrees of change influence, some affecting certain tribes a good deal more than others. In 1940 anthropologist Oliver LaFarge tentatively suggested a post-Conquest change sequence for the Mayan region that other Mesoamerican scholars have accepted as basically applicable to all parts of Mesoamerica (LaFarge 1977:290). The five periods LaFarge recognized are Conquest (1524-ca. 1600), Colonial Indian (ca. 1600-1720), First Transition (ca. 1720-1800), Recent Indian I (ca. 1800-1880), and Recent Indian II (ca. 1880-present). The dates for such periods are necessarily approximate, since things happened in different places at various times and the change from one situation to another was often gradual.

The Conquest period lasted from about 1524 until the latter part of the century. During those few decades some of the Indians suffered considerable violence, while many did not. The Valley of Mexico, where Mexico City is today, was a scene of a great deal of activity, whereas some other places were relatively quiet. We hear mostly about the Valley of Mexico, but Cortés and others conducted military campaigns against important Indian groups in many places. The Spanish and Indians might live in peace for a few years, and then incidents of Spanish oppression or Indian rebellion would break into military violence and further oppression.

Missionaries from different Catholic orders went into tribal areas with the military, soon followed them, or, sometimes, went ahead of the army. Some missionaries used harsh means; others were devoted to Indian welfare and used gentle, rather enlightened approaches. Much of the missionaries' massive and effective educational effort was directed at the younger members of the ruling class.

During early Conquest times the Spanish impressed large numbers of Indians into slave labor, largely by means of the *encomienda*. Through this arrangement both Spanish conquerors and cooperative Indians of prominence received grants of land from the Spanish crown, with the responsibility for the material and spiritual welfare of all the Indians on that land as well as the right to their labor

without pay and the collection of tribute from them. They often moved the Indians from place to place, broke up families, and destroyed health and lives. While the Spanish Crown tried to eliminate abuses connected with the encomiendas, they continued. They are the kinds of experiences that change cultures rapidly.

In addition, the Spanish soon added the *repartimiento*, which provided that citizens could be forced to work for wages on government projects necessary for the commonwealth's existence. Under this system the Spanish took Indians from their homes and lands to work in mines, on churches and public buildings, on roads, and on other projects, with destructive impact on many aspects of Indian welfare and culture.

In many of the rural areas the Spanish were able to do little to change the lives of the common people, who lived on much as they had before. Much depended on how greatly Spanish wanted a given area, so many places where the land was poor and there was little mineral wealth escaped heavy Spanish activity for extended periods.

For Mesoamerica as a whole the Spanish had quite firmly established control by 1600 or, in many places, earlier. During the Colonial Indian period, from roughly 1600 until around 1720, according to LaFarge, the Spanish maintained that control vigorously. Apparently, there were two rather contrasting aspects to the Indian situation during colonial times. The Indians in most of Middle America remained thoroughly subjugated to the Spanish, but some were prospering and pleased with their new lives, and others were not. Many were practically slaves or were destructively exploited in a variety of other ways. The church consistently suppressed expressions of pagan religion through persecution.

By this time all who remembered the pre-Spanish lifeways were gone, and still surviving pagan customs were practiced underground. Under such pressures the Indian cultures were undergoing various modifications. The Indians seemed meek, but underneath, many were hostile and resentful. LaFarge suggests that it was a time of much destruction and modification of the pre-Spanish culture.

Many of the Indians of Colonial Indian times were interested in adopting Spanish ways. In the upper class levels

Indians and Spanish were intermarrying, and some of the Indians were enjoying the economic prosperity that came with mining and other enterprises. Beals has suggested, in fact, that many of the common Indians were no more oppressed during the Colonial Indian period than they had been under the Aztec (Beals 1968[1952]:228). It seems that the situation differed from place to place and for different individuals.

This also was a time when the Spanish were adopting many Indian ways, thereby forging the Mestizo culture which was to be so different from the lifeways of Spain.

In 1720 the Spanish abolished the encomienda and repartimiento, and several changes took place in their relationships with the Indians that brought about what LaFarge calls the First Transition. The Spanish slowly relaxed their control in several ways. They were relaxing their firm administrative control because continued exploitation was requiring greater efforts for diminishing yields. They no longer provided effective military support for the missionaries and priests or the colonists in the more remote places. With the encomienda and repartimiento completely gone, the Spanish exploitation of the land became more difficult and costly. The Indians, therefore, had more opportunities to live on their own and work out their own destinies. They began practicing suppressed customs openly and integrated the new ways they had gotten from the Spanish with those old ways that had survived the Conquest and Colonial Indian days. Of course, there was no possibility of returning to the pre-Conquest life. Many things were completely forgotten, and the Indians wanted many things they had received from the Spanish and more. During these 80 years from 1720 to 1800 the Spanish continued to relax their grip on the Indians, who continued to build their new lifeways.

By 1800, LaFarge judged, the Indians had integrated their lives into the stable blends that manifest the individuality and roundness that characterize generally undisrupted cultural systems. Some twentieth century anthropologists would say that the new Indian cultures of this time manifested equilibrium, with the various parts in harmony with one another and with the culture's integrating themes. The new cultures of this time (Recent Indian I) continued to evolve until about 1880. Then things changed again.

By 1880 the industrial age was on the march and the stability of the new Indian cultures was destroyed by renewed intervention from outside and the conflict and acculturation that resulted. During Recent Indian II times, then, the American Spanish and Indian cultures came into conflict again, since the governments of the industrializing nations as participants in an international economy launched programs that disrupted the well-tuned new Indian cultures. The coffee industry was the first of this kind and was especially important in Guatemala and parts of southern Mexico. The new industrialists and governmental officials wanted Indian land for plantations and the Indians as laborers. In 1877 the president of Guatemala abolished

communal land ownership and instituted the *mandamiento*, by which the government contracted to supply plantation labor and forced the Indians to work on the plantations. These and subsequent developments continued to change the Indian cultures radically. Events in Mexico took a somewhat different turn in 1910, since a part of the revolutionary ideology that was set in place at that time idealizes the Indian heritage. While the Mexicans have considered Indian interests and rights under this ideology, it has not altered the fact that their cultures have continued to change under various pressures to integrate Indian cultures into the national lifeway. In Guatemala the Indians have found the strength to begin to break out of the oppression that the plantation system brought upon them, and the conflict has escalated to the level of destructive military violence, with Indians on both sides of the issue. The conflict and acculturation that mark LaFarge's Recent Indian II continue.

All cultures are always changing to some degree, however fast or slow. The Indians of Mesoamerica, those that can still be identified as Indians, remain in constant change, and any description of the typical Mesoamerican lifeway is to some extent out-of-date as soon as it is attempted. But in 1952 Robert Redfield and Sol Tax, two of the leading students of twentieth century Mesoamericans, presented a now classic characterization of contemporary Mesoamerican cultures (Redfield and Tax 1968[1952]). Enough of the cultures fit their portrayal sufficiently that it remains a useful foundation for our summary.

It is important to remember that some Indian communities retain much less of pre-Columbian origin than others. Also, pre-Columbian Indian traits are now part of the non-Indian national cultures of Mexico and Central America. The result is that, in some places, there is little or no cultural difference between rural Mestizo communities and Indian communities. In many cases the community's pre-Columbian origin and limited use of an Indian language are basically the only elements distinguishing it from some nonIndian places.

Mesoamerican Languages and Tribes

The population figures in this section, derived largely from survey work by the Summer Institute of Linguistics (B. Grimes 1984), indicate that there may have been over nine million Mesoamerican people still speaking Indian languages in 1980. Large portions of some tribes were able to use Spanish, with only a handful of older individuals speaking only the Indian language; and other groups remained mostly monolingual. Some Indian societies had become either mostly bilingual or Spanish-speaking so recently that they were still identified by themselves and others as Indians.

Estimates indicate that about five and three-quarter million of the Mesoamericans resided in Mexico in 1982, the total population of the country being nearly 72 million at the time (B. Grimes 1984:15). Another three million speakers of native American languages lived in Guatemala and nearly 28,000 in Belize. The Indian tribes of Guatemala, Belize, and most of southern Mexico spoke one of the thirty some surviving Mayan languages, while most of those of the rest of Mexico used languages of the Oto-Manguean or Uto-Aztecan stocks.

By far the most important phylum in terms of the number of tribes whose languages belonged to it is Oto-Manguean. Oto-Manguean is further subdivided into five language families. The Otomian family of languages included nearly 200,000 Otomí (approx. oh-toh-MEE), most of whom lived in the state of Mexico to the northeast of the Distrito Federal (Mexico City) and in eastern Hidalgo. The approximately 250,000 to 400,000 Mazahua (approximately mah-TSAH-wah) Indians of the western part of the state of México and a few villages in neighboring Michoacán also spoke an Otomian language. To the southwest of Mexico City, in the states of México and Morelos, about 1500 Ocuiltec (approx. oh-kweel-TEHK; Ocuilteco in Spanish) Indians spoke a language belonging to the Otomian family. (The combination *eh* in pronunciation guides indicates a Spanish sound that begins like the long *a* in English but stops short of gliding into a short *i* or long *e*.) Also, from 2,000 to 2,500 Matlazinca (approx. maht-lah-TSEEN-kah) Indians, living in Mexico State just to the south of the Otomí and Mazahua, used an Otomian language. These four tribes, then, Otomí, Mazahua, Matlazinca, and Ocuiltec, concentrated in the state of Mexico and located not far from Mexico City, spoke languages of the Otomian family.

Other Oto-Manguean languages are those of the Zapotecan family. In 1980 there may have been more than 475,000 Zapotec (approximately SAH-poh-tehk; Zapotecos in Spanish) tribespeople widely distributed in the mountains and valleys of Oaxaca (approx. wah-HAH-kah) as well as on the coast and the Isthmus of Tehuantepec. Some talk of a Zapotec language, but there were mutually unintelligible Zapotec languages as different from one another as Spanish, Italian, and French. A second language of the Zapotecan family is Chatino (approx. chah-TEE-noh). The some 75,000 Chatino lived in a mountainous area near the coast and to the southwest of the Zapotec.

A third Oto-Manguean family is Mixtecan, represented by three linguistic groups. The well over 200,000 Mixtec (approximately MEES-tehk; Mixtecos in Spanish) were concentrated mostly in northern and western Oaxaca to the west and slightly north of Zapotec country. Both they and the Zapotec have been major tribes of Mexico since ancient times. Most of the Mixtec were living in rather rugged country. The Trique (approximately TREE-keh) Indians also spoke a Mixtecan language. The some 16,000 Trique lived in a small mountain area of Oaxaca, entirely surrounded by Mixtec. The third linguistically Mixtecan group was the about 18,000 to 20,000 Cuicatec (approximately KWEE-kah-tehk; Cuicatecos in Spanish) living in a relatively small highland area to the west of a northwestern branch of Mixtec territory and to the north of the Zapotec in the state of Oaxaca.

A fourth Oto-Manguean language family of Mexico is Popolocan, represented in 1980 by four tribes. The over 25,000 Popoloca (approx. poh-poh-LOH-kah) lived in the semi-desert country of the southern part of Puebla. There was one community of Ichcatec (approximately EECH-kah-tehk; Ixcatecos in Spanish) in the high country of northern Oaxaca whose language was of the Popolocan family, but the language may have been extinct by the 1980s. The approximately 2,500 Chocho (approximately CHOH-choh), who were found in a number of small towns in the mountains of northern Oaxaca, also spoke a Popolocan language. A larger group, the well over 100,000 Mazatec (approximately MAH-tsah-tek; Mazateca in Spanish), also used a Popolocan language and lived in a region of mountains and small valleys in northern Oaxaca.

On the northern slopes of the mountains of northern Oaxaca lived around 60,000 Chinantec (approximately chee-nahn-TEHK; Chinantecos in Spanish) whose language was the only member of the Chinantecan family of Oto-Manguean.

To the south of the Mixtec people, near the coast, lived 30,000 or more Amuzgo (approximately ah-MOOS-goh; Amuzgos in Spanish) Indians. Their language was the only representative of the Amuzgo family of Oto-Manguean languages.

A second major phylum represented in Mesoamerica is Uto-Aztecan. The Aztec spoke a Uto-Aztecan language, which allies them linguistically with northwestern Mexico and the American southwest. The family is Aztecoidan, and the language of the people commonly called Nahua (approx. NAH-wah) is Náhuatl. There were nearly a million Náhuatl-speaking people in 1980 concentrated mainly in several states in Central Mexico, though small enclaves of Nahua were found in southern Mexico and Central America. There are five major dialects of Náhuatl, one being the classical Náhuatl of the Aztec, and another being Nahuat, which omits the terminal *l* sound (Madsen 1969:602).

The Tarascan (approx. tah-RAHSK-ahn; Tarasco in Spanish) people of west central Mexico are among the major Mesoamerican tribes, and they are linguistically unique. While linguists have suggested linkages to other phyla, evidence is too weak to do more than regard their language as the only example of its phylum. There were approximately 60,000 Tarascans in 1980.

The Huave (approx. WAH-beh) Indians of the southern coast of the Isthmus of Tehuantepec were linguistically unique in the same way as the Tarascans. The Huave numbered some 13,000 persons.

Two tribes spoke languages thought to belong to the Hokan or Hokaltecan phylum. The approximately 40,000 Tlapanec (approx. TLAH-pah-nehk; Tlapanecos in Spanish) were found in southern Mexico not too far to the north and east of Acapulco. The Tequistlatec (approx. Teh-keest-lah-TEHK; Tequistlatecos in Spanish), also known sometimes as Oaxaca Chontal, numbered 9,000 to 10,000 and lived in a small mountainous area near the south central coast of the state of Oaxaca.

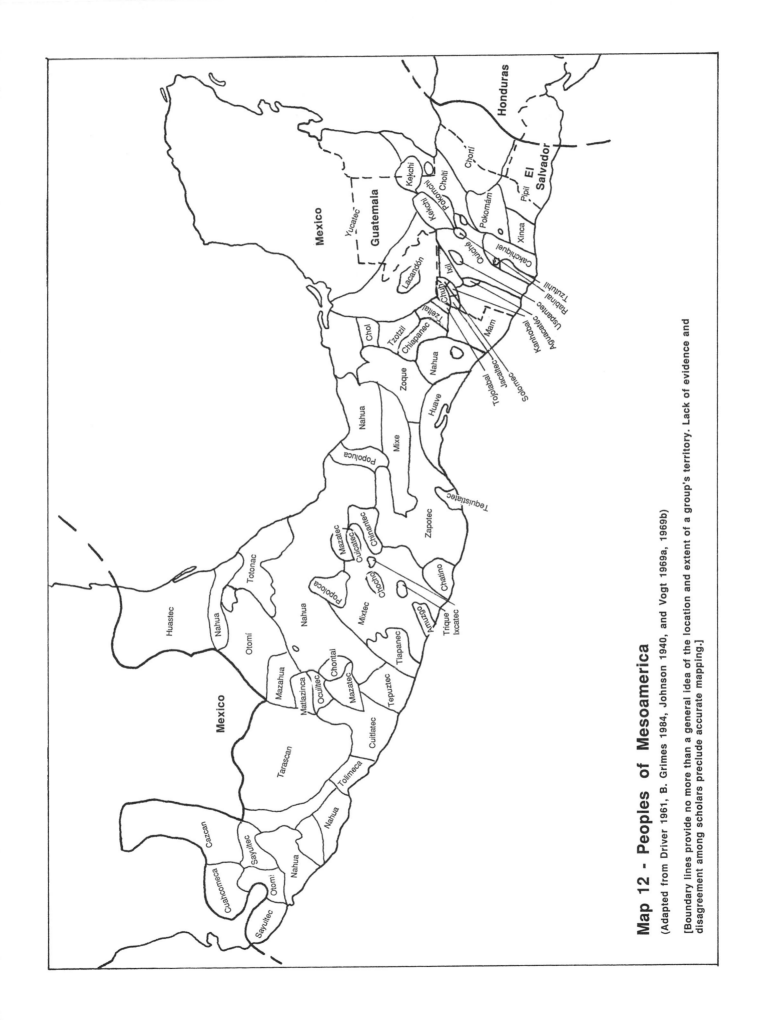

Map 12 - Peoples of Mesoamerica

(Adapted from Driver 1961, B. Grimes 1984, Johnson 1940, and Vogt 1969a, 1969b)

[Boundary lines provide no more than a general idea of the location and extent of a group's territory. Lack of evidence and disagreement among scholars preclude accurate mapping.]

A third major phylum of Mesoamerica is Macromayan, which includes the languages of the various Maya tribes as well as those of several others. One of the Macromayan families is Totonacan. The between 255,000 and 267,000 Totonac (approximately TOH-toh-nahk; Totonacos in Spanish), who still lived mostly on either side of the boundary between Veracruz and Puebla in 1980, spoke a language of the Totoncacan family. So, also, did the nearly 9,500 Tepehua (approx. teh-PEH-wah) who lived in four towns in Veracruz and Hidalgo.

Three twentieth century groups in southern Mexico spoke languages belonging to the Zoquean family of Macromayan. The 35,000 to 38,000 Mixe (approx. MEE-heh) of the mountains of northeastern Oaxaca and an adjacent section of Vera Cruz used a Zoquean language. The Zoque (approx. SOH-keh) lived in the moderately mountainous country of northwestern Chiapas, where there were probably more than 17,000 of them. The Popoluca (approx. poh-poh-LOO-kah), not to be confused with the Popoloco, also spoke a Zoquean language. There were in the neighborhood of 33,000 Popoluca in 1980 living in Veracruz, to the north of the Mixe.

The other Macromayan family of languages is Mayan, spoken by several tribes in Mexico, all of the surviving tribes of Guatemala, and a few groups in Belize, Honduras, and El Salvador. The Huastec (approx. wah-STEHK; Huastecos in Spanish) were outlier Mayans, since they lived in the states of Veracruz, San Luis Potosí, and Tamaulipas in eastern Mexico. They numbered a little under 75,000.

Three tribes in the highlands of Chiapas in southeastern Mexico spoke Mayan languages. These were some 105,000 Tzotzil (approx. TSOH-tseel) and approximately 45,000 Tzeltal (approx. TSEHL-tahl), living to the northeast of the Tzotzil, and twelve to fourteen thousand Tojolabal (approx. toh-hoh-LAH-bahl), found just to the east of the southernmost Tzotzil.

Cholan Mayan tribes were found both in Mexico and Guatemala. Just to the north of the Tzeltal is a small area of Chol (approx. chohl) Maya and, north of the Chol and extending to the Gulf of Mexico coast, the Chontal (approx. chohn-TAHL) Maya. There were more than 85,000 Chol and thirty to forty thousand Chontal in Mexico, though Chontal territory was larger than that of the Chol. There was a small town of Chol in Guatemala, just across the border where the Chixoy River divides Mexico and Guatemala. Another Cholan group, the Kekchí (approx. kehk-CHEE) were found to the north and east of the Guatemalan Chol as well to the south of the Chol and extending past the eastern border of Guatemala into Belize. There were about 250,000 Kekchí in Guatemala and another ten to twenty thousand in Belize. Two other Cholan groups in Guatemala were the 28,000 Pocomchí (approx. poh-kohm-CHEE) who occupied a relatively small area of central Guatemala south of the Kekchí, and the 25,000 some Chortí (approx. chohr-TEE), who were found mostly on the Guatemalan side of the border between Guatemala and Honduras in 1980.

Another major Mayan language is that of the the nearly 540,000 Yucatec (approx. YOO-cah-tek; Yucatecos in Spanish) Maya of the Yucatan Peninsula of Mexico. The closely related Lacandón (approx. lah-kahn-DOHN) Maya are also found in Mexico, where there were only about 550 in 1980.

There is a group of Mayan-speaking tribes in western Guatemala known as the Mamean peoples. The largest of these in 1980 were the Mam (approx. mahm) themselves, who occupied a large section of southwestern Guatemala and numbered over 265,000. Just to the north of the Mam, in the northwestern highlands of Guatemala, was a cluster of four Mamean groups occupying only small areas. The Chuh (approx. choo), who were just across the border from the Tojolabal of Mexico, numbered about 14,500. Adjoining the Chuh on the southwest were around 15,000 Jacaltec (approx. hah-kahl-TEHK; Jacalteca in Spanish) Maya and 41,000 or so Kanhobal (approx kahn-hoh-BAHL; Kanjobal in Spanish). Two more Mamean groups were located at the northeastern corner of Mam territory. The Ixil (approx. ee-SHEEL) numbered about 55,000, and, just south of the Ixil lived approximately 20,000 Aguacatec (approx. ah-wah-kah-TEHK; Aguacateca in Spanish)

The south central section of Guatemala, to the east of the Mam and the other Mamean tribes, is commonly referred to as the midwest highlands and is occupied by tribes known as Quichean people. The largest in 1980, both in population and territory occupied, were the more than 900,000 Quiché (approx. kee-CHEH), whose territory lay immediately to the east of the Mam. The 412,000 some Cakchiquel (approx. kahk-chee-KEHL) were found immediately to the east of the Quiché, and the approximately 50,000 Tzutuhil (approx. tsoo-too-EEL) occupied a small area between the Quiché and Cakchiquel. The Uspantec (approx. oos-pahn-TEHK; Uspanteca in Spanish), who numbered about a thousand, and the some 21,000 Rabinal (approx. rah-bee-NAHL), or Achí (approx. ah-CHEE), lived in small areas near the northernmost parts of Quiché country. The Uspantec lived near the Ixil, while the Rabinal were near the Pokomchí.

Finally, the approximately 28,000 Pokomam (approx. poh-koh-MAHM) lived in central Guatemala not far from Guatemala City. They have been allied linguistically both with the Quichean and the Cholan tribes.

Some of the numbers indicated above may have increased some since the early 1980s, while others have declined, so it has seemed appropriate to write in the past tense when describing specific groups. But the generalizations about twentieth century Indian culture that follow are written in the present tense largely because, even though individual communities and tribes may have changed in given ways since a qualified observer last reported on them, we can count on the fact that some groups in Mesoamerica are practicing the customs described at this writing.

Mesoamerican Personality and Behavior

The personalities and behavioral tendencies of twentieth century Mesoamericans are the result of pre-Spanish personality orientations as well as replacement and modification due to Hispanic influence. It is quite difficult to determine which of the two cultural traditions contributed how much to certain characteristics. Scholars have noted a certain pessimistic fatalism in many of the pre-Spanish cultures, which continues in modern times. But some things could also be due to the way so many were crushed by the heavy European hand. This seems to apply for example, among the Pokomam of Chinautla in Guatemala, who often feigned perplexity in their dealing with Ladinos who pressed them about something (Reina 1966:26). Whatever their origin, a number of traits are widespread among the Indians of Mesoamerica.

Several anthropological studies of Indian groups indicate a constellation of personality traits that appear to be based on the feeling that the natural, social, and supernatural worlds are basically hostile, threatening, and dangerous. Under this assumption Indian feelings about themselves, others, and life in general and the behavior that results are often rather negative. Accordingly, they tend to be pessimistic; they generally lack much hope that things will turn out well in life, nor are they optimistic that specific endeavors can be carried forward without mishap and with good result. They do not see themselves as able to manipulate circumstances successfully but emphasize adjusting and submitting so as to minimize trouble. They are afraid the gods and spirits may punish them. They distrust other people and suspect their motives. If people attain a high level of material-well being, they suspect they have done so at someone else's expense or have entered into a pact with the devil or some other evil being. They are concerned about the possibility of witchcraft or sorcery.

With such a set of concerns, it seems best to many Mesoamericans to hide their feelings from others, mind their own business, and conduct themselves with great circumspection so as to avoid attracting the attention or provoking the anger or jealousy of whomever might damage them. Some scholars believe the emphasis on work reflects this attitude. A person who works faithfully and competently, meeting his or her obligations satisfactorily, is less likely to be bothered by angry others, supernatural or human.

Many are strongly practical and present-oriented. Their concern is to make the best of the present situation rather than plan or save for the future or improve themselves. Such behavior would only attract the envy of others. They also are much more concerned with this life than with achieving a rewarding afterlife.

Mesoamericans tend to be extremely formal with one another, especially those outside the family, since they feel insecure and distrustful. The extensive ritual of etiquette helps them cover their own feelings and enables them to interact with others with minimum danger of destructive emotional outburst. Their extensive use of intermediaries in marriage negotiations and other situations can also be seen as reflecting this concern. Much of their formal interaction involves showing proper respect for one another, especially those older than themselves. In many contexts they also avoid unnecessary interaction outside the family, because it might involve them in threatening situations. Accordingly, it may be said that they manifest a kind of self-protective individualism. So they are careful to avoid quarrels, fights and other confrontational behavior and to conduct their interactions in a manner that covers their true feelings and reduces the possibility of confrontation.

One apparent consequence of these things is that people may release their suppressed hostility through alternative channels. They may gossip maliciously and deprecate others through indirect or veiled criticisms. In addition, people may take aggressive action that does not involve direct confrontation. They may perform sorcery (black magic), steal, destroy property secretly, or attack or murder someone by surprise. When intoxicated they may resort to the aggression that is normally so carefully avoided when they are sober.

While a number of anthropologists have been impressed with this set of traits, it would be a mistake to leave the impression that Mesoamericans feel no security and cannot live contentedly and enjoy life. Much of their self-defensive behavior effectively provides them with the sense of security humans desire and permits them to avoid the disruptions that plague many societies that allow greater expression of the emotions. While Kearney concentrated on the negative components of Ixtepeji Zapotec life, since they were the salient features, he granted that there were more amicable sides of their lives (Kearney 1972:134). And Colby, writing of the Zinacantán Tzotzil, noted that they showed relaxed behavior most of the time. He found them as a society, witty and especially adept at puns (Colby 1967:419). From some ethnographies, Colby notes, one would get the impression that some Mesoamerican societies live in a state of sustained high tension, which is not the case. The traits described are significant in many places, and life may have a rather somber, quiet tone. But there are differences from community to community, and those in which this configuration are strongest have their pleasant, harmonious side.

Twentieth Century Mesoamerican Clothing

Many Mesoamerican women still wear skirts and blouses, though a number have taken to wearing dresses. In many places they use a wrap-around skirt held in place by a long sash and may don a second dressier, long-sleeved blouse over the basic short-sleeved, square-necked, everyday garment when they leave the house or attend special events. They usually go without shoes or sandals, except when they leave the community. The Spanish introduced the shawl or *rebozo*, which most Indian women now wear on their heads or across the shoulders and use to carry babies and other items. The hair is usually long and tied or braided. Except in a few places, the men no longer use the breechcloth. The traditional costume now is the Spanish colonial shirt and relatively short trousers of white cotton cloth, a usually rather broad-brimmed hat of felt or straw, a blanket, and sandals. In many places the men hold their trousers in places with a sash. In many Indian communities the men now wear manufactured shirts and trousers of suntan or denim most of the time. Many don the traditional white shirt and trousers only when working at a craft or in the field. Clothing is an area of continuing change in Mesoamerica. In some places the men's clothing is hardly distinguishable from that of the Mestizos, while it is possible for the knowledgeable observer to determine a woman's home community by her distinctive and sometimes colorful traditional costume. The men seldom wear ornaments, though women wear earrings and rings.

Twentieth Century Dwellings

There continues to be a variety of dwellings in use among Mesoamericans, sometimes within the same community, and it is impossible to more than begin to describe it. The colonial Spanish rectangular houses with thick adobe brick walls and shed-type roofs of clay tiles are used in many places. In many communities some still use rectangular huts with thatched gabled roofs and walls of cane or poles, and round houses with cone-shaped roofs have not disappeared. The Amuzgo of Guerrero and Oaxaca, for example, were still using them recently (Ravicz and Romney 1969:421, 425). In the Valley of Oaxaca, which is Zapotec and Mixtec country, the adobe brick with tile roof structures dominate in certain towns, with some of the poorer families living in ramshackle buildings with cane walls and either tiled or thatched roofs. Only a few miles away, however, one finds small hamlets composed solely of thatched dwellings.

Commonly, the people sleep in the main building, whatever its structure, and maintain the family altar there, but they cook and do other work elsewhere. The kitchen is often a separate place, either adjoining the main structure or standing alone. The kitchen's structure is often less durable than that of the main house.

Related nuclear families, which may function as components of a larger *extended* (three generation) *patrilocal family* or a *joint family* (a composite of siblings' families or other related families) often reside in the same compound, each with their own main dwelling. Whether or not there is more than one family, the people customarily maintain a fence or wall around the yard. They commonly have other structures in the yard, too, such as a sweat bath (*temazcal*) storage structures, or animal and fowl pens.

Livelihood in Twentieth Century Mesoamerica

Mesoamericans still make the production and consumption of maize (Indian corn) the center of their lives. *Milpa* is a central term in their vocabularies. The corn plant is milpa, the corn field is the milpa, and the complex of activities involving the production of maize is making milpa. Maize is special, even sacred, to Mesoamericans, and it still has an important place in their ritual.

Mesoamerican men use plows in many places if the slope and the depth of soil permit, and sometimes they are modern moldboard plows drawn by tractor. But, even yet, most use the Spanish colonial type, pulled by oxen, which plows a V through the soil but does little to turn it. Yet, many of the milpas are on steep hills and mountainsides where even the Spanish colonial plow cannot go. So they use the slash-and burn technique, cutting the vegetation back with the machete, burning it, and poking holes in the ground to receive the kernels of maize and beans. Some are growing hybrid corn in modern ways, but many have yet to see an ear of hybrid corn. They still find beans and squash and chile important, though they have added chickpeas, wheat, and other European crops where feasible. The men still do nearly all the agricultural work.

The people still consume more maize than anything else, mainly in the form of tortillas. Today, though, after soaking a pot or bucket of maize in lime water overnight, the women take the softened kernels to a motor-powered mill where, for a small charge, they have it ground. Then they return to their kitchens, kneel before their three-legged stone *metates* and, with the *mano* (hand stone), grind the mass until it is fine enough to be shaped into tortillas. So, for virtually all of the women the long hours each day at the metate are gone.

When they have the dough fine enough they shape it into a ball, pat it into a thin, round, floppy disk, and flop it onto the griddle. This remains, in many instances, the large fired-clay, disk-shaped griddle, concave on one side and convex on the other, which sits on three stones on the ground with a fire going among the stones. There is an undetermined number of women, still speaking an Indian tongue, using various more modern arrangements. Some, for example, have their fireplaces on raised platforms, and some bake their tortillas on iron griddles or stove tops.

Mesoamericans also prepare *atole,* the corn drink made by mixing the dough with warm water and something sweet or chocolaty, as well as *pozole*, the mixture of cold water with the maize dough. When they eat tortillas, they may add a few beans or a piece of fat or meat or chile. They may include some tomatoes or greens, too, and they always add some salt to their food. Many drink coffee sweetened with cane sugar. For special occasions they may prepare tamales, meat, or sweet rolls, and take some honey. They still maintain a distinction between everyday foods and ceremonial-fiesta foods.

Twentieth Century Arts and Crafts

Community craft specialization remains important in Mesoamerica. A high percentage of people in a given place specialize in making certain kinds of pots, baskets, hats, mats, rope, woolen blankets (*sarapes*), or a variety of other items; or they may concentrate on producing salt, building houses, raising sheep for their wool, or other technological activities. Whatever they produce, then, is exchanged for items they want from other places, usually in market places. Weekly and daily markets are still important in Mesoamerican life as places where people from several communities and/or tribes come to display their products. Most transactions involve money, though some may barter. There is less bargaining than in earlier times, and, when there is, both parties often have a fairly accurate idea of the price they will settle on in advance.

Twentieth Century Social Life in Mesoamerica

Mesoamerican married couples tend to reside in the compound of the boy's parents and function as a unit within the resulting *patrilocal extended family*, though many, sooner or later, live independently or with a sibling's family. The older male members dominate the younger. They stress the relationship between father and son more than that of mother to daughter and transmit names through males rather than females. But most Mesoamerican societies remain *bilateral*—that is, all regard themselves as descendants of both males and females. Accordingly, most tribes have no *unilineal descent groups* such as *clans* or *lineages*, in which each person belongs to the common ancestor group of one parent rather than the other.

Unilineal groups were more common in ancient Mesoamerica than now, but Tzeltal, Toztzil and, perhaps, Lacandón Maya still have them, and they still exist among some Nahua. Guiteras-Holmes has expressed the opinion that the Tarascans, Otomí, and Totonac, which are non-Mayan tribes, formerly had patrilineal lineages or clans. The clans and lineages of Mesoamerica have been dying out as the communities have continued to undergo change from outside contact.

Mesoamerican lineages are patrilineal, since each person belongs to the father's lineage rather than the mother's. One's father and mother belong to different lineages because the groups are *exogamous*—that is, members of the same lineage do not marry. These descent groups are regarded by anthropologists as lineages because the common ancestor and how people are related to him are known. Accordingly, genealogical depth is shallow, that is, the group consists of only a few generations. Mesoamerican lineages own land, their dead are buried on the land, and the male members usually live close to one another and cooperate. Women do not change lineage membership, even when they move away

from their fathers and brothers at marriage (Guiteras Holmes 1968:103).

Clans, which are structurally like lineages except for having greater genealogical depth, have survived into the twentieth century in several places. In the 1940s and fifties Villa Rojas reported that the Tzeltal community of Oxchuc had six patrilineal, exogamous clans, each made up of a number of lineages. The largest consisted of 39, and the two smallest, which were dying out, had only one or two (Villa Rojas 1969:213).

The elders of the Tzeltal clans used witchcraft to maintain conformity to the mores. By means of a supernatural familiar, usually thought of as animal in form, the elders were able to learn of the misdeeds of the clan members and, also through the agency of the familiar, punish the offenders by bringing illness or misfortune upon them (Villa Rojas 1947:585). Each Tzeltal and Tzotzil lineage had its own land, but the clan retained ultimate ownership. The clans were not associated with insignia, a tutelary supernatural or special ceremonies (Guiteras Holmes 1968:103).

The Mesoamericans retaining patriclans and/or patrilineages tend to refer to parents and aunts and uncles with *bifurcate merging* terms. That is, people refer to a father's brother by the same term used for one's own father and refer to the mother's sister by the same term as that for the mother. Accordingly, the terminological system separates aunts and uncles who are not of the same sex as ones parent from those that are of the same sex as the parent. There is a strong tendency around the world for bifurcate merging terms to exist with unilineal (patrilineal or matrilineal) kinship groups.

Also, people who use bifurcate merging terms for parents, aunts, and uncles tend to use Iroquois terms for siblings and cousins. *Iroquois* terms lump brothers and sisters with *parallel cousins* (the offspring of father's brothers and mother's sisters), and *cross cousins* (offspring of father's sisters and mother's brothers) are referred to by different terms. But some Mesoamerican societies that retain patrilineal kinship groups and bifurcate merging do not use Iroquois terms. (Guiteras Holmes 1968:98).

It would use too much space to go into kinship terminology further at this point, but it should be remembered that there is a relationship between the terms kin use to refer to one another and how they behave toward one another.

Most Mesoamerican tribes have neither patrilineal clans or lineages nor bifurcate merging kinship terms. They are bilateral in that people think of themselves as descendants of both sides of the family. Many of these groups use *lineal* terms for their parents, aunts, and uncles, which is the system used in the United States. The lineal system separates the parents from aunts and uncles, lumps matrilateral and patrilateral aunts under one term, and includes uncles from both sides of the family under the same term. Some bilateral groups using lineal terms have separate terms for siblings and cousins, while others lump them together under the same terms.

A few bilateral groups, especially some of the Mayan tribes, make some use of *bifurcate collateral* terms. That is, they use one term to refer to a parent, another for that parent's sibling of the parent's sex (e.g. father's brother), and a third for the parent's sibling of the opposite sex (e.g. father's sister). Occasionally, *generation* terms occur, which lump aunts and uncles under the same terms as those used for the parents without regard to whether or not they are the same sex as the parent. Accordingly, the term for a mother would also be applied to one's mother's sister and father's sister, while the term for the father would include the father's brother and mother's brother. Bifurcate collateral and generation terms have often been used in the same groups that have bifurcate merging terms, which is thought to reflect change from unilineal clans and lineages to purely bilateral social arrangements. For example, the Huastec Maya of Northern Veracruz and adjacent San Luis Potosí use or have used at the same time bifurcate merging and bifurcate collateral terms (Driver 1961, Map 35). This and other evidence suggests that they once had patrilineal clans (Laughlin 1969:305).

Anthropologists have found that societies around the world establish relationships and groups involving nonkin but exhibiting the same interdependence and intimacy characteristic of kinship ties. Some call this fictive kinship, others ritual or ceremonial kinship. The *compadrazgo* system, or *compadrinazgo*, of Latin America, derived from Europe and adopted and elaborated by Indian groups throughout Mesoamerica, is a major example. Parents establish these relationships at some time of ritual importance in the lives of their children. In Mesoamerica as a whole Christian baptism is a practically universal occasion for this. At that time the parents ask another couple or person to become godparents to the child to be baptized. The godparents assume certain obligations in connection with the baptism, such as buying appropriate clothing for the infant. From that point on the godparents maintain special relationships with their godchild and the parents. They usually take a special interest in the godchild's welfare and participate in events of importance in his or her life. They are, in a sense, backup parents, and will probably see that the godchild is cared for if the parents die. The godchild is taught to respect the godparents and to show that respect by rituals, such as kissing the godparent's hand in greeting.

In Spanish the parents and the godparents refer to one another as *compadres* (coparents), and they, too, commonly maintain friendship and ritual respect and provide mutual aid, too. This relationship between the parents and godparents is usually more significant than that between godparents and godchild. Sometimes the term compadre is extended to other members of the family and biological kin of the participants, thus forming a network of people who regard themselves as ritually related to one another.

People may establish ritual relationships on other occasions, too, marriage and confirmation being common ones. Sometimes parents select new godparents at marriage; at other times the baptism godparents function as marriage godparents also. Regions and communities differ more from one another with regard to other occasions for establishing ritual relationships. One of the best known and rather unique occasions is the *hetzmek* of the Yucatec Maya. This occurs when a mother stops carrying the infant across her arm and places it astride the left hip, where she holds it in place with her left arm as she moves about. At this time the parents select a second set of godparents and conduct a special ceremony (Redfield and Villa 1962:188-9). Other occasions for selecting godparents found in one place or another include a child's first participation in communion and a variety of occasions relating to the prevention or healing of childhood disease—for example, burning a candle in church for a sick child.

Pregnant women in Mesoamerican tribes continue with most normal activity, but they may also avoid certain kinds of foods or situations because of various deleterious consequences. The people are concerned about ensuring successful delivery, and there may be special prayers and other rituals for the mother-to-be during her pregnancy. When delivery time comes nearly all Mesoamerican women are attended by either another woman or a professional midwife. In fact, women of some groups are visited by a midwife during the pregnancy. In many groups a woman kneels for childbirth while grasping a rope, post, bench or other object. The sitting position, either on a bench or a floor mat, has been reported for some groups.

Newborn are bathed, and the mother may bathe as well, perhaps in the temazcal or steam bath. The umbilical cord is often disposed of in some manner indicative of the people's desire for the infant's future. The Tzutuhil of San Pedro La Laguna in Guatemala hid a girl's umbilical cord in the roof thatch or buried it near the hearth so she would be an obedient wife (Wagley 1969:98). The afterbirth may be disposed of without special observance or, in many groups, with care. In many communities mothers who have just given birth observe a prolonged period of restricted activity. In some they remain out of circulation for about a week, but the time is longer in a number of places. The Nahua of Tepoztlán expected a mother to remain in bed from thirty to forty days after birth (Lewis 1951:63). Specific rituals and treatment modes applied to both mother and baby vary considerably from tribe to tribe.

Mothers nurse their babies for a prolonged period—for a year in some instances and commonly for from two to four years. The baby remains in close contact with the mother, who is attentive to its needs. If another baby arrives, however, there may be a sudden change in the child's treatment. Little ones are often expected to keep out of the mother's way and submit to care by older children after they are weaned.

Mesoamericans generally regard baptism of major importance for a child's welfare, and it usually takes place within the first weeks or months of life. At this time, in most groups, the parents obtain godparents for their child, initiating ritual kinship ties of lifetime importance. There are other ritual observances at various points in the child's development in some groups, such as the previously mentioned hetzmek ceremony of some Mayan communities.

Mesoamerican parents normally do not discipline their children much. They encourage them to learn adult activities early in life, and there is little in the way of organized games or play. Parents are generally reluctant to have their children in school, since it prevents them from helping with livestock and performing other chores. In a number of places Mesoamericans have come to appreciate the advantages conferred by knowing Spanish and ways of getting along in the national society, but attitudes vary considerably from group to group.

Mesoamerican Indians do not subject their young people to puberty rites. In a number of communities, however, teenagers go through a period of service to the community or the church.

Marriage is the important transition point in a young person's life, and it commonly takes place in the early or middle teens for girls and the late teens or early twenties for males. The Mesoamericans ordinarily establish their families through monogamous unions negotiated by the couple's families. The couple may conduct a highly furtive courtship, with the young man contriving brief meetings by waiting along a trail as the woman fetches water, sending notes by friends, and similar measures. Or the couple may accept the will of the parents. Usually, the man's parents employ an intermediary to conduct prolonged negotiations with the family of the woman chosen by the son or by themselves. The petitioner may have to make repeated visits, as the parents usually show reluctance.

When they have completed the arrangements, the man's family takes most of the responsibility and stands most of the expense. Gift exchanges are a major part of the procedures. In a number of communities some couples elope, and after tempers cool the appropriate ceremonies are conducted. When a boy's family is too poor to provide the necessary gifts for the negotiations and wedding ceremonies, he may serve for his wife by working for her parents for a time, a custom known as *bride service*. Local *endogamy* is very strong in Mesoamerica, which means that a person marries someone in his or her own community. Marriage ceremonies are elaborate in many places.

Family responsibility, community service, and age are important factors in a Mesoamerican's cycle of life. Early marriage is an unstable period in many communities, and divorces often occur. The arrival of the first child normally stabilizes the marriage tie considerably, and it may be at this time or not too much later that a couple living with the husband's father, according to the *patrilocal* rule, sets up an independent household. Under what is sometimes called the *cargo* system young men also hold various lower level community and church positions, and as they become older advance to more responsible offices. Eventually, the most successful become respected and influential elders, holding high office and, even when not in office, exerting considerable influence.

The Indians of Mesoamerica become sick mainly from emotional disturbances such as a fright, entrance of evil air or wind into the body, the evil eye and other forms of contamination, or eating or experiencing too many hot or cold things. They view hot and cold in terms of effects upon the body rather than temperature. In some places, for example, ice cream is hot. To avoid sickness people try to maintain the right internal equilibrium between hot and cold and avoid too much contact with just one of the two.

Mesoamericans use a variety of curing techniques, sometimes employing a *shaman*. Healers often remove winds or other elements foreign to the body through an opening or an extremity by making a pulling movement along the body with the hands. They also may pass an egg or other object over the body so that the object can attract the sickness into itself. Sometimes curers chew tobacco or another plant substance and spray the stuff over the body. Incensing the body, magical strengthening, prayer, charms, candle burning, herbal infusions, massaging, and other techniques are also used.

When someone dies Mesoamericans lay out the body in the house and hold an overnight vigil accompanied by prayers, candle burning, and other ritual acts. They bury the body the next day, usually in a cemetery, and place a cross on the grave. They commonly perform additional rituals at the first anniversary of the death and perhaps at other times, too. In many places the funerals for children are outwardly cheerful, since baptized infants who die are thought to become little angels. Godchildren, godparents, or compadres, depending on the circumstances, take charge of the funeral and burial.

Community, Government, and Social Order in Mesoamerica

Mesoamericans greatly value the local community, which is most often a village but may be a set of hamlets or a neighborhood of scattered dwellings. Their high valuation of their communities is reflected in the civil-religious center that binds the people together and the image of the patron saint that is kept there. It is also reflected in local endogamy (the practice of marrying within the community) and by differences in speech, dress, or other customs. Anthropologists have found that the people of one Mesoamerican community strongly distrust those of other communities, often characterizing themselves as peaceful and trustworthy while they view those of neighboring communities as hostile and treacherous.

Many Mesoamerican communities are divided into smaller territorial units called *barrios*, and it is common for the people of a barrio to feel considerable solidarity and a degree of distrust and hostility toward those of other barrios. Sometimes each of the two or more barrios making up an Indian community will have its own chapel, ceremonies, and social events distinct from those of the other barrio or barrios and the general community. There may also be a strong tendency for people to find their spouses within their own barrio. Some of the Indian communities of Mesoamerica are barrios within largely non-Indian towns or cities.

The next step above a community is a *municipio*, which may consist of a single community or a small region of two or more communities, one of them being political center, or *cabecera*, of the municipio. The municipio as a whole takes its name from the cabecera. The Pokomam municipio of Chinautla in Guatemala, for example, consisted of the town of Chinautla and seven hamlets or villages from three to six miles away. The town was over 98 percent Indian, while two of the hamlets were composed of mainly Spanish-speaking Ladinos (Reina 1966:8). There are 17 municipios in the Departamento of Guatemala, which is one of the 22 Departamentos, or administrative divisions, that make up the nation. The municipio and its head town, then, are part of the national structure of Guatemala, and the situation is similar in Mexico.

The physical center of an Indian town's government is a municipio building in the town center, where the church, market, school, and other community institutions are located. The chief official is often the *presidente*, an elected official roughly comparable to the mayor of an town or city in the United States. The office is highly respected. A presidente characteristically manifests considerable interest in the welfare of the entire community and outsiders, and he is another symbol of community. Outsiders do well not to ignore him if they contemplate extended or major activity in that place. He enjoys considerable executive power in the making of policy and the settlement of disputes. He is assisted by a council of elected officials, one of which is the *síndico*, who may be almost as important as the presidente because one of his major responsibilities is dealing with other municipios and with the state and national government. He is often better educated than many of the other officials. The council members, often known as *regidores*, may represent different subdivisions of the municipio and may specialize in various governmental responsibilities. The council members may also have assistants who carry out various police, custodial, communication and other community activities and responsibilities.

An outstanding characteristic of this system of officials is its hierarchical nature. Younger men prove themselves first in minor positions and, over the years, serve from time to time in places of increasingly greater responsibility until, if they are competent enough, they occupy the highest positions. The division of labor among the positions in the heirarchy and the patterns of superordination and subordination among those occupying them are well-defined. Age differences are fundamental, so much so that there are clearly differentiated, community-wide elder and junior age fraternities in some Mesoamerican communities.

Politics and religion go together for Mesoamericans. In most places the political hierarchy is tightly integrated with a similar hierarchy of religious positions. Each political and/or religious obligation assumed by a man is known in Spanish as a cargo, an important kind of Mesoamerican institution. Where the religious and political cargo systems are strongly interrelated a man serves terms in both church and governmental positions as he climbs the ladder of increasing prestige and responsibility. Actually, it is more accurate to view this as a single system of hierarchically arranged cargos rather than two interrelated systems. Outside observers see it in the latter way because of their habit of distinguishing government from religion, but the Indians are normally unconcerned with differences of this sort. The result is that, from the outside scholar's perspective, all governmental and political activity is undergirded by and functions within the context of religious beliefs and concerns.

Many Mesoamerican groups, especially in the Mayan region, have religious brotherhoods, *cofradías* in Spanish, that exercise most of the political power. A cofradía's main responsibility is caring for one or more saints and carrying out fiestas in their honor, and men hold offices in cofradías as part of their advancement through the cargo system. The cofradías' top officials work together to bring their favorites into political power and work their will on the political process through those they have brought into governmental positions. The *mayordomía* institution provides for the care and honor of a saint in places that lack cofradías. A man serves as *mayordomo* for a particular saint for one year, expending his time and wealth on his responsibility. This, also, is part of a man's advancement through the politico-religious cargo system. Mesoamerican women may hold certain religious offices and may help their husbands with their ceremonial responsibilities, but they do not participate in the cargo system.

The Mesoamericans of today tend to lack social classes, that is, their communities cannot be divided into groups of families occupying differently ranked social strata. Instead, rank and prestige are mainly individual matters, depending largely on a person's age and success in participating in the cargo system. Many Mexican and Guatemalan communities include both Indians and Mestizos or Ladinos, and the Indians may constitute one class while the non-Indians form a higher social stratum.

Twentieth Century Mesoamerican Religion

Anthropologists often refer to many of the religions of twentieth century Mesoamerica as Christo-paganism, since they resulted from syncretism of pre-Conquest and Catholic elements (Madsen 1957). Some aspects of Mesoamerican religious systems are highly syncretic. In many Mesoamerican tribes the people are concerned mainly with a set of deities known by Christian saint names, but they are not just like the Christian saints. Some of their characteristics and functions may derive from Christian tradition, but many of the most important are of non-Christian origin. So it is, for example, that Saint Peter in some places is the god of rain, functionally somewhat like the pre-Columbian rain god. Mesoamericans definitely deify saints, so they remain polytheistic in this respect, just as they were in ancient times. They almost seem to have a pre-Columbian religion in Christian dress, but more accurately, it is largely a combination of Christian appearances with both Christian and pagan meanings and functions. Other elements of Mesoamerican religious systems are almost entirely Christian or totally pagan rather than syncretic.

Communities and individuals differ from one another in which saints are most important and which are associated with what functions. People also think of the saints as patrons of communities, groups, and individuals. Each community has its patron saint, that community's special god, so to speak, who resides in the church, looks after the community welfare, and is honored annually by an important fiesta. The physical image of the saint is the deity in question, and many Mesoamericans worship the image itself.

In many, but not all, Mesoamerican communities, each family has a household altar—a table or masonry bank against a wall of the main room of the house where the family saint or saints reside. Some of the family saints are three dimensional images, others are pictures. The family burns candles and places offerings before them on the table. Visitors may be expected to pay their respects to the family saints before taking up whatever interaction with the family they have come for. Everyone knows of many saints, but given individuals, families, or communities are actually concerned with only a few. This may also change through time.

In addition to deified saints, God, derived from Christian teaching, is to many Mesoamericans the supreme deity. But he is a kind of vague, general being to whom some pray but with whom many do not concern themselves. Some, undoubtedly, still have little concept of such a supreme being. They seem to regard God as just another deity, no more important than the saints and, perhaps, much less significant. For everyday living most Mesoamericans deal with saints and other supernaturals, who some think of as carrying out what God wants done.

Christ and the Virgin are often no more than additional deities, and they are variously regarded in different places. Christ is often identified with God, or he may, in one aspect or another, be one of the saints, perhaps a community's patron saint. The Virgin, often not identified with Mary, takes various forms in different places and commonly is regarded as little more than another saint.

Crosses, usually made of wood, are also important to many of the Indians. They have different meanings in different places and to different people. Most groups seem to grant them protective and curative significance. Each one seems to be somewhat distinct from all others, and in a number of places the people treat a cross as a deity, much in the same way they relate to a saint. The Mesoamericans erect crosses on homes, at important intersections, on high places such as hills and mountains, in church yards and house yards, and in a variety of other places. They often decorate them and may make offerings to them and use them in their rituals and ceremonies. For some groups, especially Mayan tribes, the cross seems to be a point of access to the ancestors. In many communities the Day of the Cross, May 3, is a fairly important fiesta.

Many elements of Mesoamerican religious systems are either almost entirely Christian or totally pagan rather than syncretic. A number of Mesoamerican communities maintain their beliefs or relationships to one or more pagan deities. These include gods and goddesses that the people think of as in charge of some aspect of nature or type of activity. Some of them are deified elements of nature or life. The people have gods of rain, rivers, the winds, agriculture, maize, childbirth, and other things. And some regard the sun, moon, the earth, and the directions as deities. They feel that the activities of these and other deities are responsible for lightning, earthquakes, plant growth, floods, rain, knowledge, and so on. In some places the Christian saints are associated with these functions.

The Mesoamericans regard many of the pagan deities, as well as Christian saints in some communities, as guardians and preservers of aspects of nature. They believe in owner-protectors of mountains, forests, milpas, deer, cattle, certain kinds of medicinal plants, and a variety of other items. The people respect this guardianship role and conduct their hunting and other activities in accordance with the requirements of the guardian deity.

Religion students are unable to define sharply a difference between gods and spirits. Gods are usually more powerful than spirits and preeminent in some aspect of life or the universe such as a crop, rain, war, agriculture, wind, and so on. Mesoamericans believe in a large number of minor supernatural spirits, such as spirits of springs, high points on trails, caves, strangely-shaped stones, and similar entities. They are concerned to maintain satisfactory relationships with the spirits so they will not be troubled by them or may enjoy some advantage the spirit might confer.

Among the lower order of supernaturals are a variety of forms that are often malevolent or, simply, frightening. The devil is an important being of this kind in some places. Many people believe in various kinds of dwarf spirits, dog-like apparitions, or a beautiful woman who lures men to lonely places and injures or kills them.

Many Mesoamericans are quite interested in the spirits of the dead and maintain various kinds of relationships with them. In some communities people honor a spirit on the anniversary of the person's death, sometimes for several years. In addition, they invite all the spirits to return to the family altar on the Day of the Dead in early November, where they offer them food and speak to them. They feel a need to express their affection for them, but they also are afraid of them and want to forestall any trouble from them.

It is sometimes difficult to know whether people are actually deifying spirits or are simply interacting with them as they would other humans. Most summaries of Mesoamerican religion fail to mention ancestor worship, but some anthropologists refer to the concern with the spirits of the dead, especially in some Mayan areas, as ancestor worship. Certainly, some form of ancestor religion is of primary importance in some places. Vogt identified the ancestral gods of the Tzotzil Maya of Zinacantán, Chiapas in Mexico as their most important deities (Vogt 1969b:298).

The Zinacantecos believed that they were elders who, in mythological times, went to live in the sacred mountains surrounding the community. In other places, too, there are cases of humans, such as shamans, becoming supernatural beings when they die, so that Mendelson speaks of the divinization of ancestors (Mendelson 1967:409). The Zinacantecos and some other Maya regard the ancestors as being in control of the entire community and its customs. They communicate with the ancestors at shrines and conduct rituals to maintain proper relationships with them, since they can both reward people for living right and punish them for misbehavior.

Mesoamericans of Mexico and the Guatemalan highlands believe each individual has a counterpart or companion animal spirit, known as a *tonal* in Spanish, that becomes associated with a person at birth and serves as protector until death. When a tonal suffers misfortune or death, the same thing happens to the person associated with it. The *nagual* is a somewhat similar supernatural entity that some, including Indians, often fail to distinguish from the tonal. The nagual is an animal familiar associated with a witch, who can transform himself or herself into the animal in the course of performing witchcraft.

The Indians of Mesoamerica spend a great part of their time in ritual and ceremonial activity. They have a large number of calendrical ceremonies, making up an annual ceremonial cycle of fiestas in honor of the Roman Catholic saints or other deities and concerned with agriculture, weather, and various natural phenomena. The Nahua town of Tepoztlán, near Cuernavaca, celebrated 27 town-wide festivals annually when Lewis studied there in the 1940s (Lewis 1960:13). One of the main Mesoamerican festivals honors the community's patron saint and normally lasts several days. The Mesoamericans also hold unscheduled ceremonies at times they think they are needed, such as ceremonies propitiating wind gods and animal owner-protectors. *Priests*, who are essentially specialists in conducting rituals, and *shamans*, who possess individual supernatural power for divining and curing, lead the ceremonies. Anthropologists usually associate shamanism with divination, curing, and similar activities, so shamans who also conduct ceremonies can be called shaman-priests.

There are quite a few shaman-priests in Mesoamerican society, but there are also many ceremonialists who are not shamans. For household fiestas the people can burn candles, make the cross motion, and conduct other simple rituals themselves; or they may enlist the services of a ceremonialist for important family rituals such as weddings, ritual kinship, and funerals. The rituals variously consist of prayers, offerings, sacrifices, burning candles and incense, consuming alcoholic beverages, processionals, decorating sacred objects and places, assuming various positions of ritual significance, making ritually standardized motions, feasting, fireworks, speeches, music, dancing, fasting or avoiding specific foods, avoiding or engaging in sexual intercourse, and a number of other activities.

Magical attitudes and behaviors occur in a variety of contexts, though *magic* (performing a spell or procedure to compel supernatural action) is not nearly as important in Mesoamerica as in some other parts of the world. Mesoamericans use magical divination some, such as scattering kernels of corn on the ground to divine the cause of an illness or determine who has stolen something. Witches may use black magic (*sorcery*) to bring illness upon someone, such as sticking pins in a figurine or working magic on someone's possession and placing it in the owners house.

Witchcraft is a major supernaturalistic activity in Mesoamerica. A witch can change into the nagual or familiar animal spirit in order to work evil and commonly sends it to eat the soul, Sending winds or foreign objects into the victim is one of several other ways witches may damage people. *Brujo* is the Spanish word for witch.

Shamans are also important in this area. Shamans, like witches, use their personal ability to draw on supernatural powers to divine and cure disease. A shaman also may have a nagual or may have special power to enlist the aid of other spirits or Christian or pagan deities. Shamans may also behave as witches, and some of them are thought to combine both activities extensively. A Mesoamerican shaman is frequently referred to as a *curandero* in Spanish.

Chapter 11

THE CHERAN TARASCANS OF WESTERN MEXICO

Both anthropologists and tourists are familiar with the impressive Tarascans (approx. tah-RAHSK-uns) of Western Mexico, who live in several communities around the shores of colorful Lake Pátzcuaro in Michoacán, on the high volcanic plateau to the west of the lake region, and in a large mountain valley to the northwest. Anthropologists have found it interesting that the culture is rather distinctive within Mesoamerica and that the Tarascans were defeating the Aztecs in battle before the Spanish arrived. Tourists have found the lake communities colorful and accessible. Tarascans who fish the lake still use the ancient butterfly nets, since they know the unusual and picturesque practice attracts tourists and their money. Cherán (approx. cheh-RAHN) is a mountain community lying almost due west of Lake Pátzcuaro.

When Ralph Beals and his associates lived in Cherán in 1940-41, the town followed a Spanish settlement pattern, with a central plaza at the center of a rectangular grid of streets modified only where required by rough topography. The church and the school were across the street from the plaza on one side and the town hall on one of the adjacent sides. A number of stores, a couple of restaurants, and other facilities were nearby. Travelers along the highway between Carapan and Uruapan passed between the plaza on one side of the street and the church and school on the other.

At that time Cherán was a community of about 5,000 Tarascans, who supported themselves mainly by growing maize, since they had no other major occupation. Their main foods were tortillas, a meat and cabbage stew, and corn soup, though they had a variety of other food dishes. Domesticated animals were fairly important to them, including sheep, cattle, pigs, and chickens. Hunting and gathering were least important. They supplemented their agriculture with a fair variety of other occupations, only one or a few individuals specializing part-time in each. Most of them stored their possessions and maintained the family altar in almost square houses with walls of thick planks on edge and four-sided, steeply pitched roofs covered with wooden shakes. They cooked, ate, and slept in smaller, usually simpler structures elsewhere on the same lot as the

larger building. Some of the women wore dresses, while others wore the more traditional costume of a blouse and a voluminous tubular skirt held in place by a long wrapped belt. Most of the men wore trousers, shirts, straw hats, and huaraches.

Newly married couples of Cherán became members of the groom's parental household for at least a year, after which a number established their own homes. Each person had mutual obligations with relatives on both the mother's and father's sides of the family. There were no common ancestor groups such as clans and lineages. The godparent-godchild and co-parent relationships were very important to the people, especially those established at baptism. The people elected five men for two year terms to serve as the town council, one of whom served as *presidente* and the other as *síndico*.

The people of Cherán were strongly Roman Catholic, though they concerned themselves mostly with several saints rather than God. They had long had a resident priest. The main aspect of their religion outside standard Christianity was witchcraft. Their most important aesthetic and recreational activities were the dances, music, and other activities that occurred within the context of the town fiestas and the celebrations honoring one or another saint.

Prehistory

Archaeologists have given us much less data about this part of Mexico than some other regions. They have evidence for Paleo-Indian big game hunting in the Valley of Mexico and other parts of Mexico and Guatemala, but nothing from Michoacán. Neither do they provide us with information on Archaic times, which replaced the Paleo-Indian hunting cultures in other places around 7,000 B.C. (Stark 1981:345). During this period people in some parts of Mesoamerica began to plant and cultivate crops, though agriculture remained a minor activity for thousands of years. In several areas agriculture and ceramic (fired clay) work came into their own around 2300 B.C., marking the beginning of what archaeologists often call the Formative or Preclassic Period. But many continued an essentially Archaic way of life well beyond this time.

Archaeologists have evidence for these times that places in Michoacán may have been participating in the development of more complex cultures. Excavations of tombs at El Opeño, Michoacán yielded sophisticated figurines and other ceramic finds and a carbon 14 date of about 1280 B.C. (Oliveros 1974:197). During late Preclassic times, the several centuries just before the time of Christ and two or three centuries afterward, a number of Mesoamerican groups were developing complex cultures based on fully developed agriculture.

During what many archaeologists call the Classic Period, from around A. D. 300 until about A.D. 900, the civilizations reached a level of complexity that continued in some places until the Spanish arrived. Even so, there is no evidence that the Tarascans themselves participated in Classic civilization. Wherever they came from, they mingled with Chichimec groups, the Chichimec being uncivilized peoples of parts of northern Mexico. Wherever they originated, they had begun to participate in Postclassic Mesoamerican civilization by the 1300s, which means they were coming into power about the same time as the Aztec and that both groups were latecomers to Mesoamerican civilization.

The Tarascans established their capital at Tzintzuntzan on the eastern shore of Lake Pátzcuaro not too far from the lake's northern end. There they excavated a giant platform from the mountain slope and erected on it a row of five temple-pyramids known as *yácatas*. The five pyramids were tied together by a bottom tier that formed a common base. Each yácata was approximately T-shaped, portions of the structure being rectangular and others rounded

Though some have suggested Tzntzuntzan was a ceremonial center with few residents, it may be that as many as 35,000 people lived there. (Gorenstein and Pollard 1983:63). It was the dominant political, economic and religious center of the Lake Pátzcuaro basin and regions beyond, it's leaders presiding over an empire far more tightly integrated than that of the Aztec. Though Tzintzuntzan was the chief center, many other Tarascan places were important, several of them having populations in the thousands. Tzintzuntzan collected tribute regularly from regional tribute centers, each of which was responsible for receiving tribute within its area. Administrators in Tzintzuntzan received the tribute and distributed it to the royal family, administrative bureaucrats, religious functionaries and, in emergencies, to the population (Gorenstein and Pollard 1983:101). Unlike the Aztec emperor, the Tarascan king was a despot, and Tzintzuntzan under his governance exercised full power over the other Tarascan communities.

History

The Aztec sought Tarascan help when they were being troubled by the Spanish, and the Tarascans sacrificed the Aztec emissaries. But when the Spanish entered Tarascan territory in 1522 under Olid, the Tarascan king capitulated with little resistance.

The single most powerful influence on Tarascan culture during the sixteenth century was the leadership of the first bishop of Michoacán, Vasco de Quiroga, a Christian humanist who worked to reconstruct the virtues of primitive Christianity among the Tarascans, closely following the ideas of Sir Thomas More's *Utopia* (Beals 1969:727). His program produced a great deal of acculturation, and twentieth century Tarascan culture was probably less like that of pre-Spanish times than that of almost any other Indian groups in Mexico. Yet, it was not just a variety of Mestizo culture, since the Tarascans were quite selective, accepting what fit their interests and rejecting other things if they could. They managed to build a culture that was Tarascan rather than Mexican in spite of its great divergence from pre-Conquest Tarascan culture.

As in other parts of the New World the Spanish established *encomiendas* in Michoacán. The encomienda was a grant of land and the Indians living on it to a private party, usually one of the conquerors, who was to see that the Indians were Christianized and their welfare provided for. Cortés laid claim to Tzintzuntzan and neighboring communities as one of his encomiendas. The system does not seem to have been so widely spread or to have had so heavy an impact as in other parts of Mexico. Later there were haciendas in the area, though little is known about their impact.

The Tarascans must have been affected considerably by the War of Independence during the early 1800s, since major routes crossed their territory from north to south and east to west. In the latter part of the same century the Mexicans developed a major lumber industry in the area and extended railroads into some of the mountain regions, which resulted in a major influx of non-Indians.

During the revolution of 1910-20 and, also, during the agrarian ferment that continued during the thirties, Tarascan country was a center of intense and destructive conflict. Many Tarascans starved, towns were burned (Cherán twice burned to the ground), and thousands of Tarascans fled to the United States. Some never came back, but many returned after the great depression set in. In the 1940s, Beals reports, a considerable number had been born in the United States, had lived there for many years, or still had relatives there (Beals 1969:728).

From the middle 1930s on the Mexican government, UNESCO, and other agencies carried out a number of cultural change programs designed to improve sanitation, health, agricultural production, educational levels, and so on, but the Tarascans of the late twentieth century continued their traditional selectiveness in the face of change pressures, and their culture remained identifiable by long-established themes and values.

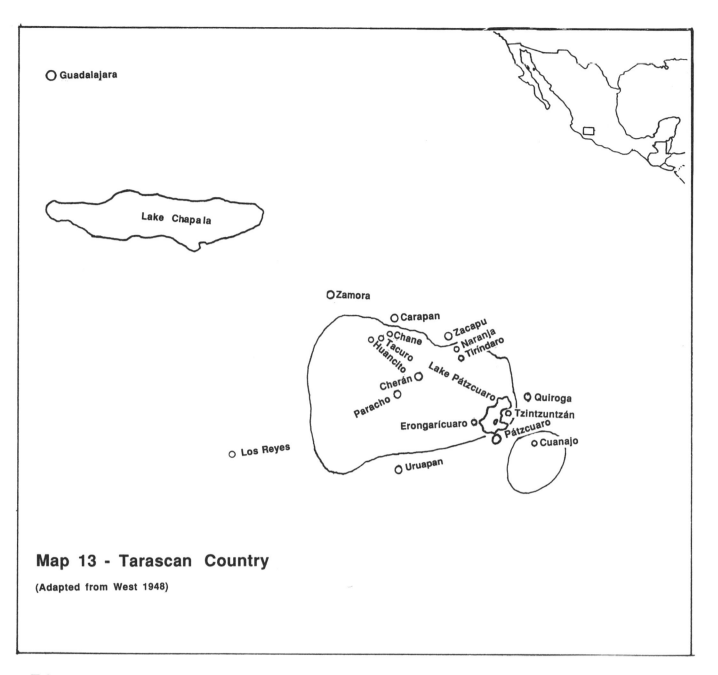

Map 13 - Tarascan Country

(Adapted from West 1948)

Ethnography

Very little is known of Tarascan culture between the sixteenth and twentieth centuries. At various times during the decades preceding 1940 explorers, folklorists, geographers, and others studied selected features of Tarascan life, but the first modern ethnographic study began in 1940 when prominent Mesoamerican specialist Ralph Beals and several assistants collected cultural data in the large mountain town of Cherán. Beals' study was one component of the Tarascan Project, a cooperative effort of the National Polytechnic Institute, the University of California, the Mexican Bureau of Indian Affairs, and later, the Institute of Social Anthropology of the Smithsonian Institution (Beals 1969:732). Beals' ethnography of Cherán culture was published in 1946.

At one time or another during the years since 1945 anthropologists have published important studies of a num-

ber of other Tarascan villages and towns. Thirty years after Beals' pioneer research there, anthropologist George Castile studied Cherán, giving special attention to the changes that had occurred since Beals original fieldwork (Castile 1972, 1974).

Cherán Country

While the center of the Tarascan empire was the Lake Pátzcuaro Basin, it extended over much of Michoacán and, in places, beyond. But by the twentieth century the Tarascan area covered only a fraction of what it had before the Spanish came. The basin of Lake Pátzcuaro remained Tarascan in 1940, though Tzintzuntzán was no longer a Tarascan-speaking place. There was an island of Tarascan speakers to the southeast of the Lake where Cuanajo, studied by James Acheson, lies, but the largest area of Tarascan speakers lies to the west of Lake Pátzcuaro, extending roughly two-thirds of the way to Lake Chapala at its northwestern corner. In 1985 highway 15 between Mexico City and Guadalajara ran just inside the northern boundary of twentieth century Tarascan country in some places, and in others just outside. Huáncito, Tacuro, Chane, Carapan, Naranja, Tiríndaro, and Comanjaare were some of the Tarascan towns on or near highway 15. At the northeastern end of Lake Pátzcuaro lies Quiroga, where a highway runs southeastward to Tzintzuntzan and southward from there to Pátzcuaro. So, most of the twentieth century Tarascan settlements lay to the west of Lake Pátzcuaro, south of highway 15, and north of a line from Pátzcuaro to Uruapan to Los Reyes.

Cherán sits on a sloping bench in the mountain country to the west of Lake Pátzcuaro, on a paved highway running from Carapan on highway 15 to Uruapan. La Sierra, as the mountain area is known, is a temperate area with many steep, forested slopes and lava flows intermingled with numerous extensively cultivated valleys and depressions of various sizes. The typical Tarascan skyline, in fact, is a chain of old volcanic cones, often enclosing valleys or long depressions; and many of these contain newer, lower cinder cones (Beals 1946:4). One of these long depressions, dotted with villages and interrupted here and there by volcanic cinder cones rising up to a thousand feet above the surface, lies to the west of Cherán. The western boundary of the depression is a series of peaks running north and south, two of which reach 10,000 feet above sea level. To the east of Cherán is another, smaller basin, also interrupted by cinder cones. One of them, El Pilón, also rises to more than 10,000 feet. Most of the mountain villages lie between 6,000 and 9,000 feet, and Cherán itself is 8,500 feet above sea level. In spite of the heavy rainfall there are no permanent streams there, and springs are seldom found. Most Tarascan towns are troubled by a shortage of drinking water.

The forests of Cherán and the surrounding region contained little wildlife in 1940. Beals found there were a few deer, peccary, and badgers in the area, and squirrels, rabbits, wild pigeons and quail were of some economic importance to the people. The Indians knew of no jaguars in the area. They could remember only one mountain lion being killed, and smaller cats also seemed to be rare. Rattlesnakes and other reptiles were present but uncommon. There were many coyotes in the area, however.

Language

Approximately 25 percent of the some 50,000 Tarascan-speakers during the 1960s were still monolingual (M. Foster 1969:1). Foster studied the language of the lake villages of Ichupio and Tarerio during the 1960s, and I draw on her analysis here, since Tarascan dialects do not vary from one another greatly. Tarascan is closely related to no other language and constitutes the only representative of its

phylum or stock (Longacre 1967:120 facing). This seems to be a part of the distinctiveness of Tarascan culture as a whole within Mesoamerica. The Tarascans themselves call their language and themselves Purépecha, but the Tarascan name has become so well established that most writers continue to use it.

Linguistic anthropologists believe that nearly any message can be communicated in any language, but languages, like the total cultural configurations in which they are embedded, differ notably from one another phonologically and grammatically. *Phonology* has to do with the speech sounds groups use and how they consciously and unconsciously classify those sounds into categories that affect meaning. Since linguists are outsiders, linguistically inexperienced as far as a language they intend to study is concerned, they have no way of knowing what sounds and classes of similar sounds are significant to the speakers of that language. As a necessary step toward finding out, they begin their investigation of an unstudied language by listening for and recording all of the sounds their ears distinguish as being repeatedly used in the people's daily speech. They use an alphabet of phonetic symbols to record these repeatedly heard sounds and take pains to understand just how the people employ their breath, vocal cords, tongue, teeth, and other features of the speech anatomy and physiology to produce them. They call these sounds *phones,* and they are studying the language's phonetic characteristics.

A trained linguist remains fully aware that the people themselves will not recognize all of the sounds she has recorded as being distinct from one another. The speakers of all languages treat some of the different sounds a linguist hears as the same sound, and the reason is that those sound differences have no relevance to the meaning of any of their utterances. Using their highly trained ears and their scientific knowledge of how humans produce speech sounds, field linguists produce a list of phones. But to get an inside view of the language they must investigate how the people group those phones into categories of alternative phones, categories linguists term *phonemes.* Two languages may have many of the same phones but group them differently because they find different sound distinctions to be relevant to meaning.

A given phoneme may consist of only one phone, which means that, if the speaker were to use any other phone in an utterance it would change or destroy its meaning. Other phonemes consist of two or more alternative phones, any one of which can be substituted for the other in any utterance without changing its meaning. It should be apparent that the linguist will have a longer list of phones than phonemes. Under the rubric of phonology, then, linguists study what they hear to be the phones of the group's speech and then proceed to identify how those phones are grouped into phonemes.

Foster found that the sounds she was able to hear in Lake Pátzcuaro Tarascan could be classified into 31 phonemes (M. Foster 1969:14). A couple of comparisons of

Tarascan phonemes with English will illustrate how cultures can differ in their phonological customs. English includes the *t* pronounced with little air, [t] (brackets indicate a phone), and one accompanied by a considerable puff of air, [t'], in the same phoneme. English-speakers do not think of a phoneme as including those two sounds, but as they talk they treat them as the same sound. In words like *steam*, *star*, and *stall* they use very little air with the *t*, but in *teem*, *tar*, and *tall* they emit a considerable amount. Linguists say the [t] in the first set of words is *unaspirated* while that in the second set is *aspirated*. The two sounds belong to the same phoneme because the difference never makes a difference in meaning. If someone says steam with a puff of air instead of the way it is usually pronounced, hearers will find it strange, but the utterance will still communicate to them the concept of hot water vapor.

By contrast the Tarascans keep the two sounds in separate phonemes, because using one instead of the other changes meaning. For example, a Tarascan who says *patani* means, in English, "to extinguish the fire," but if she says *pat'ani*, she means, "to carry it" (M. Foster 1969:24).

Foster also heard the Tarascans pronouncing vowels both with voice and without voice, so she had to find out whether or not using one type instead of the other would alter the meaning of any of their utterances. She discovered they could switch from one to the other without affecting meaning and that they used the voiceless vowels in some sound environments and the voiced in others. Foster notes that the Tarascans typically speak in bursts of staccato, rapidly delivered, rather short phrases, each phrase being accompanied by a characteristic sequence of stresses and pitches that trails off into voicelessness with the final vowel (M. Foster 1969:15).

As a part of grammatical analysis linguists must discover the *morphemes* of a language and how they are used to form words and, also, how words combine into phrases and sentences. A morpheme consists of one or a combination of phonemes that has a specific meaning. In Tarascan, *eca* is a morpheme of three phonemes plus the meaning "plural." It is a suffix attached to nouns and pronouns to form plural words (M. Foster 1969:69). Tarascan, like English, uses a variety of kinds of suffixes, whereas some other languages make little use of suffix morphemes.

Syntax has to do with sentence construction, including word order. Languages differ in how they order the words and other components of sentences, so it is impossible to transliterate when attempting to translate a passage. For example, the Tarascan sequence for the sentence, "On the fourteenth there is always a big fiesta in honor of Christ the Lord." transliterated from Tarascan would read, "A at-day fourteen it-always-makes-itself big fiesta in-order to-go-there to-celebrate-fiesta Lord of-Christ concerning." (M. Foster 1969:188,190).

Personality and Behavior

It is difficult from the information available to make direct comparisons between the personalities of the Tarascans and other Mesoamerican tribes, but they clearly exhibited some typically Mesoamerican characteristics. One of these is their distrust of others and the associated defensive behavior. The people of Cherán in 1940 retreated to their yards behind walls and fences and were reluctant to admit strangers and casual visitors. One did not walk into a Cherán yard but waited at the gate until invited in. As in other places this would seem to have some connection with a concern that others might harm them, and the people of Cherán, in fact, exhibited a deep concern over the possibility of bewitchment.

Like other Mesoamerican as well as peasant communities elsewhere the people had a negative attitude toward wealth. According to George Foster's concept of *limited good* they felt that anyone who became very wealthy had done so at the expense of others, since wealth and other good things were part of a nonexpandable supply. While the people of Cherán decried wealth and exalted poverty, there was an unresolved contradiction in the way some men displayed their wealth on certain occasions. Generally, wealthy Mesoamericans hide their wealth or at least avoid making a point of it. Not all anthropologists agree that the notion of the limited good is especially strong in peasant communities

Mesoamericans in general have tended to avoid open confrontation, hiding their feelings of distrust and hostility under a relatively pleasant exterior. The people of Cherán may have been a little more open than some, since they seemed more openly aggressive than some other Mesoamerican societies, and being brave enough to fight was sometimes expressed as an ideal. The Nahua (Aztec) of Milpa Alta near Mexico City are another group in which people seem readier to confront their enemies than in some other Mesoamerican places (Madsen 1960:224).

The people of Cherán emphasized the contrast between good and evil rather strongly. The Devil was the source of a good deal of evil and trouble, including witches and witchcraft. Drunkenness, fighting, violation of the sex mores, anti-family behavior such as desertion of ones spouse, failure to meet godparent obligations, money, land-grabbing, unwillingness to accept ceremonial obligations, failure to obey the priest, and failure to accept the blessings of the church were major evils in Cherán and other conservative Tarascan communities (Carrasco 1957:46). Several of these reflect Cherán's general alignment with the *sinarquista* faction, comprised of those who opposed the anti-clerical agrarian reformers known as *agraristas*.

In spite of a tendency to distrust others the Cherán Tarascans were a sociable people and loved to meet and talk. The women gossiped at length at the water fountain and the corn mill; men met and talked in street, plaza, store, saloon, and billiard parlor; and young unmarried men spent their evenings in small groups in the streets or in pool halls, talking and joking.

The people of Cherán also loved music, which they enjoyed on phonographs, radios, at fiestas, and in small groups. Tarascan bandmasters have composed tunes that have been included in Mexican *mariachi* repertories (Beals 1969:773).

Clothing and Personal Appearance

In 1940 the majority of the women wore cotton print dresses or blouses and skirts for everyday wear, though nearly all owned the traditional Tarascan costume. Many of the women still wore the traditional garments daily, while others donned them only on special occasions. The print dresses were of old-fashioned cut rather than like the manufactured dresses of Mexican women, and longer, too. They were often pleated at the waist, and many had flounces or ruffles on the bottom of the skirt or at the back of the waist. In these ways they resembled the more traditional garments.

The complete traditional costume consisted of two skirts, a blouse, an apron, a shawl (*rebozo*) and several woven belts. The blouse was usually made of unbleached muslin or, sometimes, flour sack material, though the people sometimes made better ones of good cotton, rayon, or silk. The neck openings were square and, usually, bordered by a cross-stitch design. The short sleeves were tied around the arm with a drawstring, giving them a puffed-sleeve look, and bordered with a one inch wide crocheted band of a different color than the blouse fabric.

The basic skirt, the only one worn on ordinary occasions, was usually of ordinary cotton or unbleached muslin. It extended almost to the ground, and the lower edge was decorated with a nearly two inch wide band of cross-stitched designs in blue, pink, or red. It was tubular and at least six yards in circumference, so when they donned it, the women pleated it in back, with the top coming several inches above the waist. Then they bound it in place with a brilliantly-colored woven belt a couple of yards long and almost two inches wide. They added the outer skirt for formal occasions. This was of very dark blue or black woolen fabric, manufactured or loom woven in another Tarascan town. It also was tubular and commonly ranged in circumference from 15 to 30 yards. The women pleated it at the back like they did the basic skirt and secured it around the waist with several narrow, woven, brightly-colored belts, one on top of the other until it made a kind of shelf around the waist up to two inches wide. When they put on both skirts it created a hump of cloth across the middle of the back large enough for a small child to sit on, carried in the mother's shawl (Beals 1946:41). The outer skirt hung almost to the ground and got wet and muddy in rainy weather.

The apron was also part of the formal costume. It was also of white cotton or muslin and hung almost to the bottom of the skirt.

The shawl or rebozo was of hand-loomed cotton, dark blue with fine light blue or white longitudinal stripes. Women commonly wore it from side to side over the head, and they also slung it across the back to carry a child or some small object. Often the shawl covered their arms, and an embarrassed woman would hide the lower face behind part of the shawl.

The women carefully combed and brushed one another's hair, often applying oil or lemon juice to give it a sheen. They parted it in the middle and made two braids that hung down the back. Women went barefooted and hatless most of the time, though one might don a straw hat over the rebozo when traveling in the hot sun, and some were wearing shoes in 1940.

Both women and girls wore earrings and a number of strings of red glass beads around their necks.

Many Cherán men wore a working costume of trousers, blouse, a straw hat, and sandals; and they sometimes added a muslin coat or a *sarape*. For many, it was their only costume. The trousers of cotton or unbleached muslin were cut full at the waist and in the seat, but tight in the legs. A man lapped the two wide sides of the fly over one another and secured the top of the trousers with a long, six inch wide sash. On the bottom of the trouser leg was a cloth tape with which he tied the bottom tightly around the ankle.

The blouse had a rolled collar, no buttons, and was open part way down the front. It had either no tail or a very short one. The coat, which was for formal occasions, was open all the way down the front and was made of heavier material than the blouse.

Most of the hats, which were sewn from palm straw braid, had low crowns and broad brims. The men kept their hats on at all times, and they often wore bright colored string or flowers on them. They wore their hair cut short. The open-toed sandals or huaraches worn by the men were mainly of woven leather fastened to heavy leather soles.

None of the men were wearing fully Mexican clothing in 1940, but they were using a few Mestizo items. Many had coats, sweaters and jackets, for example, and some wore modern cotton trousers. Town leaders had taken to wearing blue denim jeans and overalls, though they wore Mexican clothing for important civic events or visits to the cities of Uruapan or Morelia. Both girls and boys wore adult clothing.

Houses and Other Structures

The people of Cherán built their houses along the streets on building lots varying from 10 or 12 feet wide to almost a whole block wide, and most lots were from around 20 feet to a half block deep (Beals, Carrasco and McCorkle 1944:7). The house normally sat along the street, with a gate at one side and a separate kitchen, an oven, and other structures situated at various places around the lot. The door to the house faced the yard rather than the street. The street side of the lot was usually fenced with a dry rock wall or a wall of stone or combined stone and adobe brick masonry. The fences on the other sides were often of poles arranged in one way or another.

Nearly all Cherán families had wooden cabins characteristic of the mountain Tarascan towns. They were rectangular, almost square, structures with four-pitched roofs, the door in the center of one of the long sides, and a front veranda. The Indians usually built the floor on nine stones, one for each corner and the middle of each side and one in the center. They laid floor timbers from 8 to 10 inches square across the stones and floored the house with planks. They made most of the walls of heavy planks set on edge, though some people used logs. In either case they notched them at the corners so they would interlock. Wooden pillars supported the roof over the veranda. The builders laid a plank ceiling across the tops of the walls before constructing the roof, thereby forming an attic or loft.

The rafters of the steeply pitched roofs extended from the corners and the tops of the walls to the ends of a relatively short ridge pole. The result was a visible roof ridge shorter than the house length when one looked at the roof from the building's long side. But it appeared only as a peak when one viewed it from the short side. With the rafters in place, the builders fastened horizonal stringers to them and completed the roof with two layers of wooden shakes held in place with nails or small wooden pins.

These houses lasted between 50 and 100 years, though the shakes had to be replaced every few years. They could also be dismantled, moved, and reassembled in a day or day-and-a-half.

A few people built houses of combined stone and adobe masonry, though they usually made only the front and side walls of masonry and the back wall of upright planks. Some of these houses had double-pitched wooden roofs while others had roofs similar to those of the wooden cabins.

The Cherán Tarascans used the main building primarily as a storage place and to house the family altar, since they ate and slept in a separate kitchen-bedroom building. The altar usually consisted of a table against the wall opposite the door, with either an image of a saint on it or pictures of saints on the wall behind it. Candles and a pottery incense burner usually sat on the table, along with various objects temporarily there for safekeeping. Sometimes the people decorated the ceiling over the altar with colored tissue paper and strings of miniature household objects. They kept several wooden chairs in the room for reception of visitors, as well as tin trunks or wooden chests for clothing storage. Many had a sewing machine in the house, and rarely there would be a bed for guests. There was a ladder in each house for climbing into the storage attic.

The kitchen-bedrooms were usually smaller and often quite simple and had only a two pitched roof, though a few closely resembled a house. Each kitchen had a hearth on the ground, usually of six stones, one in the middle and five forming a rough circle around it. Two of the outer stones were relatively close to the center stone, providing three points on which cooking pots could be placed and a place for a fire under them. The other three stones were positioned on the opposite side of the center stone, so that the four stones (center and three outer), enclosed a fire area where the round, flat clay griddle for cooking tortillas could rest, elevated over the fire. To provide light at night the Tarascans drove a branched stake into the ground, placed a plate of some sort on the ends of the branches, and burned splinters of pitch-pine there.

The people put shelves at the back of the kitchen for their pottery jars, pots, plates, and other utensils. *Metates* (grinding bases of stone) and other larger or heavier items sat on the ground below the shelves. Various other items kept in the kitchen included brooms, fire fans, various kinds of baskets, and gourds. The women placed the metate on a plank near the hearth when they used it and removed it at night so straw mats could be placed on the ground around the fire for sleeping.

During waking hours in the kitchen the women knelt on the ground, while the men sat on their heels or on low wooden benches. In good weather they sometimes sat outside or on the veranda of the house.

Sheds ordinarily consisted only of a sloping roof leaning against a wall, but some built small structures with double-pitched roofs on four posts to serve as elevated hen houses, fodder storehouses, and the like. A lot might also include a dome-shaped oven, watering troughs, a chopping block, a pig pen, a stable, and so on.

Livelihood

The men of Cherán spent most of their work time producing several kinds of maize, with wheat production being a distant second. They also grew a variety of other items in relatively small amounts, including beans, squash, pumpkins, broadbeans, amaranth, potatoes, barley, oats, cabbage, mint, fennel, silantro, pears, plums, cherries, apples, peaches, quinces, agave, chayote, crab apples, and zapote blanco (Beals 1946:20). They made some of their fields in valleys, depressions among lava flows, the craters of cinder cones, within the town itself, or in other places that were level or gently sloping. They found a few low-lying areas, where soil and manure from higher ground were washed in, fertile enough to be planted annually. Some of their permanently cultivated lands were more sloping than these, and people cleared temporary fields on the steep mountain slopes.

Like many other Mesoamerican farmers, the people of Cherán plowed maize fields twice before planting, once in the late summer or fall and again in late winter. They ran the furrows of the second plowing at right angles to those of the first. When they planted, which was in March in the lower areas and later elsewhere, they used two ox-drawn plows. One plow opened a furrow, and a planter followed, dropping the kernels in the bottom of the furrow a step apart, covering them, and firming the soil with his foot. The second plowman made a furrow between the rows, covering the seed with about four inches of soil.

Pocket gophers did much damage to maize, and the people usually exploded gunpowder in their burrows before plowing and planting to kill as many as possible. When the plants were small, they drove stakes here and there in the fields as perches for hawks. Badgers did a lot of damage in a few places.

The farmers cultivated the maize for the first time when it was about a foot high, running a plow between the rows to throw the dirt against the plants. This was repeated when the plants reached 18 inches. Beyond that size, plowing would cut many of the roots. Later, when the tassels appeared, they weeded by hand with a short machete having a sharp curve at the point, and they piled dirt around those plants that had been insufficiently covered by the plow. Sometimes they had to hand weed a second time.

When the first soft corn was ready they had to post guards against animals and theft. Sometimes entire families would live in temporary field shelters until harvest time. For lower areas they trimmed and set 20 foot pine trees for watchers to climb and stand in. Sometimes they hired watchers.

They roasted some of the first ears for food and left the rest for further ripening. After the ears were well formed, but while the stalks and leaves remained green, they prepared fodder for their livestock. They removed the stalks above the ears and cut down those from which the ears had already been removed, dried them, and stored them in sheds at their houses. The men harvested the ripe corn two rows at a time, picking, husking, and throwing the ears in large harvest baskets held on the back by a *tumpline* across the forehead. They emptied the full baskets onto piles made in convenient places and, later, stuffed them into nets and hauled them on burros to their storehouses at their homes in town. The women brought food to the workers during the harvest and, with the help of the children, gleaned the fields of the ears that had missed the baskets.

Beals reports that digging sticks were never used in the fields except for replanting crops destroyed by worms, but digging sticks or hoes were probably used on some of the steep temporary fields because of the impossibility of using plows and oxen there.

The plow was a Spanish colonial type, since the pre-Spanish Mesoamericans had no plows. The curved handle and the beam, which was pointed at the front end, were made from a single piece of wood. A pointed metal share was fastened atop the point of the beam. The end of the tongue was fitted into a socket in the top of the beam just in front of the handle and, farther forward in the beam, a stake running through the tongue and into the beam held the tongue in position. The other end of the tongue was pegged into an opening through the center of the yoke, each curved end of which was lashed to the head of one of the two oxen. The types of plows and yokes differed some from one part of Mesoamerica to another. In 1930 the municipio of Cherán had 30 steel moldboard plows, which were donated by the Government and which farmers borrowed. While they were in full use, they were not enough to take care of more than a small fraction of the plowing.

The people of Cherán grew most of their wheat on sloping land where corn did poorly, and they seldom obtained good crops. They also grew some in town lots, where it yielded better. Sometimes they fertilized their wheat lands by paying someone for a flock of sheep to bed down there at night. They plowed just once before planting and then broadcast the wheat seed. They then plowed again, making the furrows at right angles to the first, and drug thorny brush under weights across the seeded ground to break up clods and cover the seed further. They harvested the wheat with a hand sickle, tied it in bundles, and took it to town for threshing. They flailed the wheat either on hard, cleanly swept ground or on a stone threshing floor they could use for a small donation of grain to the owner. The flail was a slender pole about eight feet long with two or three heavy 10 to 12 foot long wires attached to the end. Both men and women winnowed on windy days by tossing double handfuls of the threshed material into the air, letting the chaff and straw blow away and the kernels fall onto the straw mat below. They then stored the grain in sacks. Wheat was probably the main cash export crop in 1940, though they used some of it themselves (Beals 1946:26).

These techniques of handling wheat were not necessarily typically Mesoamerican. The Zapotec of Teotitlán del Valle in Oaxaca, for example, drove a string of burros around a circular threshing floor to thresh their wheat and tossed the material into the air with huge wooden paddles to winnow it (R. Taylor 1960:71). The plows and yokes were also different in Teotitlán.

None of the other field crops were of much importance in Cherán. Beans, so important in some other Mesoamerican places, apparently grew poorly in Cherán's soils or climate. The people grew most other items around the house or in yard gardens. They planted a few pumpkins, *chilacayote* squash, and *chayote* in their gardens as well as cabbages, a few other vegetables, and herbs. The chayotes were usually planted near the house, where the vines spread over kitchen and shed roofs and along fences. They dug up the chayote tubers every third year and boiled or fried them for eating.

The people planted *agave* along the boundaries of their fields to help keep animals out, and they collected its juice, drank some of it, and shipped most of it to Uruapan for making alcoholic beverages. Sometimes they roasted the hearts of wild agave plants. The agave plant consists of wide, shallowly V-shaped, fleshy leaves of stringy fiber radiating upward and outward in all directions from ground level. On large plants the leaves, which terminate in hard sharp points at the ends, rise several feet into the air. The people of Cherán cut a pit in the heart of the plant and let juice collect there, gathering it twice daily by means of a small pottery vessel.

They cooked agave buds for three days in earth ovens. They filled a hole with stones, heated them by building a fire atop them, threw the buds on the hot stones, and covered them with leaves and earth. About 20 men did this in season, avoiding sexual intercourse during the three days of cooking and eating sugar so the buds would come out sweet.

Agave was important to the ancient Aztec and remains important in many Mesoamerican communities.

The Cherán Tarascans produced a fair quantity of pears, which were carried by traders as far as the state of Guerrero to the south. They used a special picker to avoid bruising the fruit. They made it by cutting three narrow pieces of shake to a near point at one end and leaving them wide at the other so, when the three were tied together, a triangular funnel resulted. Finally, they tied the pointed ends of the shakes in position around the end of a long light pole to complete the implement. The several other kinds of fruit grown in Cherán were much less important than pears.

The domesticated animals kept in Cherán included cattle, horses, mules, burros, sheep, goats, pigs, dogs, cats, chickens, and bees. The people raised no turkeys, ducks, or geese in 1940, though other Tarascan towns had them. Many of the men raised cattle, which were used for meat, milk, ox teams, and for sale. Only a few kept milk cows, however. Most cattle were pastured in the mountains, away from the town.

Pigs were probably of second importance, and it was the most commonly seen animal in town, almost every family having at least one sow. The people raised them for their meat and for lard.

Not many families had sheep, but those that did had fairly large flocks. Some families specialized in herding sheep, but boys and old men and women herded most of them. They trained dogs to assist by keeping them on a leash with the sheep during the day and tying them near them at night. They also trained them to bark when coyotes approached and to attack them. The sheep were kept in the fields between harvest and planting and in the mountains the rest of the time. Though the people ate some mutton, they raised sheep mainly for wool. They kept a small number of goats with the sheep, most frequently selling them outside the town for food.

Many people had burros in Cherán, commonly kept in a shed by the house and used to carry firewood, harvested corn, trade goods, and other burdens. Only a few had horses, which seemed to do poorly in Cherán. Wealthy, prestigious men valued them highly for riding. The few who could afford mules used them mainly as pack animals.

In addition to sheep herding, dogs served for hunting, guarding the house, and as pets. There were only a few cats, but the people valued them highly as enemies of the many rats that ate the stored corn. They also enjoyed them as pets, giving them affectionate names. They gave them tortillas to eat as well as a little of whatever the family was having at mealtime.

A few people had chickens, which they sometimes ate on special occasions. They sold most of the eggs to traveling merchants.

A few of the men practiced apiculture, having from 20 to 30 wooden box hives, and a fair number of other families kept a few hives. They used the honey mainly to sweeten *atole* (one kind of corn drink) and as a treat for children, and the wax served primarily for candles.

Gathering and hunting were rather unimportant in Cherán. The people collected no wild plants regularly, though they took edible greens if short of food or for the sake of dietary variety. They collected the hearts of a small wild agave that grew in the mountains, roasted the hearts in pit ovens, and sold them. They also gathered certain roots they used for soap, and they collected some wild honey. They sometimes ate wild bee larvae as well as the larvae of another insect.

Some of the men hunted for enjoyment or, sometimes, to augment their food supply or income. They took deer, peccaries, squirrels, rabbits, quail, pigeons and, less often, armadillos. Sometimes they trapped deer in pitfalls, and they used snares for squirrels, quail, and pigeons. They sold a good deal of the meat from wild forms rather than eating much of it. Apparently they did not care much for venison.

The Cherán Tarascans stored maize, wheat, beans, and broadbeans in the house, generally in the loft. They kept sugar, coffee, fruits, herbs, meat. bread, and similar items in covered pots or baskets in the kitchen (Beals 1946:48). Tortillas and other corn foods made up most of their diet, supplemented extensively with meat, fish or cheese, and green plant foods.

To prepare tortillas they used a method common to all Mesoamerica. They boiled the maize kernels in lime water to soften and partially dissolve the outer shell, washed it in a basket, and ground it into dough. The women of poor families used the *metate* (grinding stone) and *mano* (muller or handstone) exclusively, but others had the *nixtamal* (lime-soften corn kernels) ground at one of the power mills in town and finished it at home on the metate. All over twentieth century Mesoamerica the coming of mechanical and power corn mills relieved women of many hours of work each day at the metate.

To make a tortilla a woman scooped a ball of dough from the metate and patted it into a disk about an eighth of an inch thick and six or seven inches in diameter. She then baked it on a round, flat griddle of clay, the *comal*, which was supported above the fire by three stones.

Sometimes the women made *gordos* from the corn dough, though they most often made them from wheat dough. Gordos were smaller and thicker than tortillas and were fried in deep pork fat.

To make a fiesta drink known as *pozole* the people boiled the maize with oak wood ashes instead of lime, which removed the shells completely. They washed the grain thoroughly and boiled it with pork, chile, and chopped onions.

They made several kinds of tamales from corn, the main one being *kurunda*. They mixed the dough with bicarbonate of soda, molded a portion into a flattened ball, and wound it tightly with several thicknesses of corn leaves so that it was triangular in shape. Then they boiled it in a covered pot. For various special occasions they modified the kurunda in a number of ways. For example, they sometimes added layers of cooked and ground beans in the dough, filled it with meat and chile sauce, or mixed it with lard and salt. Another kind of tamale was made from dough prepared from amaranth seed, with brown sugar mixed in. They commonly ate the tamales with sauces, stew, or other concoctions.

The people also made several kinds of *atole* from maize dough by mixing it with water and cooking the thick broth with various flavorings. The most common form was flavored with an herb called *nurite*. For another kind of atole they added ground, toasted corn husks and brown sugar to the mixture. Unfermented agave juice, green cornstalk juice, chile peppers, anis, amaranth seed, rice, tamarind, blackberries, and milk are among the other substances used to make one or another kind of atole. The people of Cherán drank atole mixtures with many of their meals and in combination with a number of other foods.

The Tarascans of Cherán made a few tortillas from wheat flour and, at harvest time, toasted wheat kernels on the clay griddle. They also made round wheat breads, wheat gordos, and a wheat drink cooked with an herb called *epazote*.

The people often cooked and ate cabbage, and they used several other plant items as available, such as boiled chayote roots, peanuts, boiled squash, boiled and fried squares made from the leaves of the prickly pear cactus, boiled squash greens cooked with lard, boiled dried beans, and fruit.

The townspeople used meat far more than many other Mesoamericans. All who could afford it had a meat stew daily, eaten in combination with tamales or, when available, boiled chayote tubers. The meat was usually combined with cabbage, chickpeas and, frequently, a small amount of carrots, and seasoned well with salt and ground dried chile. The people also made *mole* for special occasions, using turkey if they could get it, but chicken, pork, or beef, if they couldn't. They made a gravy-like mole sauce from ingredients such as cloves, ginger, chocolate, cinnamon, ground toasted bread or tortillas, pumpkin seeds, garlic, onions, and *pasiya* chiles. They fried the chiles or dipped them in hot water, ground them with the other items, and boiled them in the broth of the meat. There were also at least a couple of fish dishes.

Most people in Cherán ate three meals a day, though the very poor might have only two. The most common morning meal consisted of tortillas and either meat or greens, but people included some kind of atole every few days. The midday and evening meals nearly always consisted of tortillas and beef stew with cabbage, though a few poor people could afford only some kind of vegetable dish. These basic meals were modified some from time to time as other foods were available and people were so inclined.

Crafts, Tools and Techniques

Cherán had a better water supply than most mountain Tarascan towns, since water often flowed through a ravine that passed through town and there were some small springs in the ravine walls. The people built concrete tanks to collect the water, but the supply was still too limited. About 1930 they laid a two inch pipe to bring water from springs near the base of the mountain, El Pilón, to the edge of town, a distance of nine miles. They also built an aqueduct of wooden troughs made from logs resting on forked posts to bring the water to tanks in the center of town, and they piped some of the water to a fountain in the plaza.

Much of the timber of the heavily forested *municipio* of Cherán was on communal land, where any citizen could cut for a small fee to get lumber for buildings, posts, firewood, charcoal and other purposes. All Cherán males were fairly good with the ax, and some were skilled woodsmen and woodworkers. After cutting down a tree they cut it into sections with a two man saw and squared the sections by splitting off slabs with wedges of oak driven by a maul or the butt of an axe. They also used the wedges to split the squared timbers into smaller beams and thick planks. When they needed thinner planks they elevated a timber on a pole scaffold or on poles across a pit and sawed them lengthwise. The sawyer stood on top of the timber and sawed along a charcoal line about two-thirds of the timber's length, after which he turned around and cut from the other end to meet the first cut. This technique of making boards, which many outsiders find picturesque, is used by a number of other Mesoamerican groups.

Another important woodworking tool in Cherán was the *adze*, which had the blade running perpendicular to the handle rather than in line with it like the ax. The people used the adze for dressing planks and for various other kinds of woodworking. They used a machete and oaken clubs to cut timbers to the thickness of roof shakes, and they split them off with a special implement made of oak.

Many Mesoamerican communities specialize heavily in some craft or other technological activity besides farming. Commonly, all or nearly all the men farm and spend the rest of their time on whatever the town specializes in. In the Mexican state of Oaxaca, for example, the Zapotec town of Teotitlán del Valle specializes in weaving the woolen blankets known as sarapes, while other towns specialize in activities such as building houses, making certain kinds of pots, manufacturing hats, transporting goods, and so on (R. Taylor 1966:117).

Here and there, however, a Mesoamerican community has no such specialization, and Cherán was one of them. The people of Cherán were primarily maize producers, and different families obtained cash by producing and selling different things. People sold roasted agave hearts, agave juice, deer meat, pears, pigs, wool, and a variety of other items. In 1940 from one to a small number of persons made sleeping mats, straw hats, woolen blankets, women's belts (using the *backstrap loom*), blouse and skirt borders, houses, wooden chocolate beaters, candles, paper flowers, sweetened breads, fireworks, doorsills and post and pillar bases of stone, grinding stones, lacquer work, rope, hair brushes, shoes, and other items. There also were people who butchered cattle and pigs, operated corn mills, built masonry houses, cut hair, carried water, painted and plastered, and threshed wheat with a machine. Normally these activities supplemented agriculture and housework rather than being full-time specialties.

A number of Cherán men were traders, some of whom made fairly regular short trips and others who went on one to three long trips annually. Most of them transported goods on burros, though a few carried items on their backs. For a major trip they assembled items from Cherán and other Tarascan towns, such as pottery, spices, dolls, or pears. They returned with fish, dried beef, coconuts, cheese, and other products, most of which they disposed of in the market of another Tarascan town. There were also several stores in Cherán, and markets were held twice weekly and during fiestas. The largest weekly market was on Saturday afternoon and evening in the plaza, and there was a smaller market Monday morning. Neither of them was very important in terms of the amount of goods moved. The large Tarascan market in the town of Paracho on Sundays, the only large regular market in the mountain Tarascan area, was far more significant to the Cherán Indians.

Social Organization and Relationships

There were at least three types of households in Cherán, *patrilocal extended family* households, *joint family* households, and *independent nuclear family* households. Newly married Cherán Tarascan couples observed the patrilocal residence rule, taking up residence initially with the groom's family. When children arrived this resulted in a three generation family commonly known to anthropologists as the patrilocal extended family. Patrilocal extended family life has long been widespread in Mesoamerica, though some communities have a number of cases of *matrilocal* residence, where the couple lives with the wife's parents. In Cherán a newly married couple normally slept in the main house for their first year of marriage. Joint families developed when sons or both sons and daughters with their spouses and children lived together on a lot inherited from their deceased parents (Beals, Carrasco and McCorkle 1944:29). This has happened in other Mesoamerican places, too.

After a year or so of marriage or following the birth of the first child the couple's status in relation to the parents and their living situation changed. In any case, they stopped sleeping in the main house and either established their own household on another lot or moved into a separate kitchen-bedroom. One household situation was for two or more sons with their families to have their own kitchen-bedroom structures and share a main house. The patrilocal extended family, then, continued, while the sleeping and eating arrangements changed. Those parents who could afford it gave the son either a lot or both a lot and a house, and he with his wife and children established an independent nuclear family household. In fact, this was common, so there were many such households in Cherán.

In 1940 the kinship system of Cherán was entirely *bilateral*, that is, all reckoned themselves relatives of both the father's and mother's people through both male and female links. The same kind of kinship arrangement prevails in modern North American and European nations. The Cherán Tarascans had no common ancestor groups whose members traced their ancestry through only one person in each generation. Kinship, in fact, was not of great interest to them, though they recognized their kinship to aunts, uncles, cousins and more remote relatives on both sides of the family and maintained reciprocal obligations with them.

Anthropologists commonly refer to any individual's relatives on both sides of the family through both male and female links as his or her *kindred*. The society is not divided into kindreds, each person belonging to only one kindred. Instead, each person normally belongs to the kindreds of several of his or her relatives. A parent and child, of course, belong to one another's kindreds, but each has some people in his or her kindred that the other one does not. The same is true of cousins. Only full siblings have exactly the same people in their kindreds. In Cherán the remotest members of the kindred seemed to be people one referred to as *primo* or *prima*. A person sometimes referred to first cousins as primo (for a male cousin) and prima (for a female cousin) but these terms were also used for relatives as remote as the children of the cousins of one's aunts and uncles. For such distant relatives the people used the terms if there was some friendship basis for it, such as their parents having been close friends. Otherwise, they did not use the terms or maintain the mutual obligations associated with the relationship.

This was the situation that defined kinship relationships in Cherán in 1940. Each person in Cherán normally maintained relationships with his parents, children, aunts, uncles, cousins, grandparents, grandchildren, nieces, nephews, and more remote relatives on both sides of the family. Parents provided material care for their children, saw that they were properly educated, obtained godparents for them, and helped them get married. The children were to respect their parents throughout their lives and help them when they became old. Siblings (sisters, brothers, or brother and sister) understood that they were to be close friends and help one another, though many actually had poor relationships and many quarreled, usually over property. Boys apparently had especially close relationships with one or more of their uncles. In fact, young men seemed to turn to their uncles in crises instead of their fathers. In some instances aunts and uncles cared for nephews and nieces from poor families, and some of them, in turn, aided elderly aunts and uncles.

Any person had the right to expect that his or her relatives (members of ones kindred) would take part in special occasions such as weddings, house movings, deaths, and fiesta obligations. A family wanted to have as many people as possible at such affairs, and failure of a relative to attend without making an acceptable excuse and sending a gift aroused bad feelings and provoked retaliation by refusal to attend future affairs of the kind in the life of the absentee.

The strength with which the people of Cherán felt these obligations was manifested in their reference to them as work. The obligations extended to all one referred to and addressed as primo or prima, however remote the relationship and whether or not the two could trace it. The refusal to reciprocate if someone in the circle of kin failed to meet his or her obligations illustrates the universally found operation of *reciprocity* as a means of social control. If people do not conform to what is expected of them they find that others withhold aid from them and refuse to participate in affairs of importance in their lives.

Fictive or ritual kinship systems often take up the slack where kinship institutions fail to meet human welfare desires and needs. Adoption is one of the most widespread non-kinship institutions that partake of the quality of kinship relationships, and ritual friendships are widespread, too. Many societies provide for some kind of sponsorship by a nonrelative, which meets desires that might otherwise be taken care of by relatives. The system known as *compadrazgo*, which came to Latin America in part from Europe and which is so strong in so many twentieth century Indian communities, is an example of the latter type. Under this system parents select an individual or couple to serve as godparents to their children when they are baptized, confirmed, married, and, perhaps, on other occasions. This establishes a relationship, usually for life, between the godchild and the godparents, but the tie between the parents and the godparents is often even more important. Many Mesoamericans, in fact, have godparents for special occasions, such as house dedications or basketball games, which establish fictive kinship ties between the godparents and those who select them. The compadrazgo is probably weakest in those communities that have especially strong kinship institutions. The Nahua people of San Bernardino Contla illustrate this, since they had a strong clan and lineage system that took care of many of the matters handled by the compadrazgo group in other places.

In spite of their insistence on maintaining reciprocal obligations among kin, the people of Cherán were more interested in the relationships between *compadres* and the other ties that stemmed from those relationships. The compadrazgo system was strong there, and they made as much of the relationships between parents and godparents as they did those between godparents and godchildren (Beals 1946:102). The parents and godparents referred to one another as compadres (co-parents), and most people had at least 20 or 25. The strongest compadre relationships formed at baptism. The godparents carried the child to the church and paid the small baptismal fee. From then on they treated the child as nearly like their own as their resources permitted. They gave the child clothing from time to time if they could afford it, and they made sure the child was well trained and educated. If the godchild died before age ten the godparents provided the burial clothing. The compadres visited one another when one of them was sick or faced

some other kind of trouble, helping out whenever possible. They were also expected to help when a compadre had some obligation such as a wedding, funeral, fiesta, house roofing, or house moving, even if it required days.

Mature godchildren and their godparents had similar obligations toward one another. When a godson kidnapped a girl he intended to marry, his father was expected to go to his compadre's house and tell him so they could go to the bride's house together to deal with the matter. Compadres addressed one another as such when they greeted each other on the street, especially baptismal compadres. They were to show mutual respect and appreciation throughout their lives. The godchildren were also supposed to treat their godparents respectfully, including the special greeting.

The most important occasions in Cherán for establishing godparent relationships were baptism, confirmation, circumcision, and marriage. They also used the compadrazgo on special church occasions, as when they blessed a new image. There may have been other compadrazgo occasions as well, though they were not reported.

Usually, people tried to select compadres of their own social and economic level. A number looked for people who could read, since they felt the child would be more likely to be intelligent and learn to read. Some tried to select someone who was brave and bold to fight if necessary, hoping that their child would grow up to be the same. They selected people who had done them favors in the past or whom, for some other reason, they desired favors of in the future (Beals 1946:103).

There were two types of marriage compadres, the parents and godparents of the bride and groom and the parents and the aunts and uncles of the bride and groom. They established the relationships with these relatives at a special ritual near the end of the wedding ceremonies, held in the main house or the kitchen-bedroom of, usually, the groom. For this reason a Cherán Tarascan acquired most of his or her compadres through marriages. Marriage compadres were expected to greet one another properly and respect and appreciate one another throughout their lives, but their mutual obligations were not as strong as those between baptismal, confirmation, and circumcision compadres.

Cherán parents wanted children, and most valued large families. Women concluded they were pregnant when their menstrual periods failed to occur, though they also recognized lassitude, heaviness, and loss of appetite as common symptoms. Most gave themselves over to a midwife's care early in their pregnancy, and she visited the mother-to-be frequently and massaged her to make sure the fetus was properly positioned. A pregnant woman was supposed to be careful not to lift heavy things or work too hard, and she was expected to take frequent cold water baths in the house. She observed several avoidance practices, such as not tying animals so the child wouldn't be strangled by the umbilical cord during birth. Fathers avoided several similar things, and it was thought that they should avoid work on the day of the birth.

A midwife, of which there were several in Cherán, was assisted by the woman's mother or mother-in-law. Most women gave birth in a kneeling position, while others reclined. While kneeling the woman might hold onto a metate or hang onto two loops of rope suspended from a house beam. Her husband was usually absent. The newborn infant was received on a mat and clean cloth on the floor. When the afterbirth was delivered the umbilical cord was tied with thread and cut. The child was then wiped with a clean cloth, oiled, and wrapped in clean rags.

The mother remained in bed from eight to fifteen days after parturition, then got up and bathed. During the next five days she rested in a reclining position much of the time and observed several food taboos. Then she bathed again and was free to leave the house. Until then the midwife visited her daily and gave her a massage. After leaving the house the mother did only small tasks until about 40 days after the birth. As in other Mesoamerican communities the practice here illustrates how erroneous is the popular idea that peasant and primitive women go back to work immediately after their babies are born. A long period of recovery after birth is general for Mesoamerican Indians.

Cherán parents had their babies baptized within a couple of months and sometimes within a few days. They kept them in cloth diapers until they were able to walk, at which time they clothed them, usually with a shirt-like garment and a straw hat. They toilet trained their children by various gentle and indirect measures, such as being slow to change their clothes when they wet or soiled themselves.

Cherán parents treated their children affectionately and played with them and fondled them considerably. About the time the next baby arrived, the child might be given over to older brothers and sisters for part of its care, and this seems to have begun a period of difficult adjustment. In spite of crying and tantrums the parents apparently continued to be relatively gentle with their children. At five or six years of age boys might be sent on errands and girls began to play at adult activities. In 1940 about a quarter of the boys of six or eight years of age began school, but none of the people sent their girls. Boys began to do some adult work when they were about eight, helping their fathers carry firewood back from the forest, caring for the livestock, guarding the fields, guiding a plow, and so on. By fifteen years of age a boy might be working for wages. Girls began to care for younger children at about six or seven and learn how to grind corn on the metate. They also received a small water jar and helped their mothers carry water. An eight year old girl might be going alone to the mill to have maize ground. Children were usually confirmed between the ages of six and ten after going through several weeks of instruction at church.

The young men of Cherán were usually either earning much of their own living by wage work or working full time on the family farm. From about sixteen to eighteen they spent little time in the household, tending to hang around the streets in their spare time. Gangs of young men, in fact, are rather significant in a number of Mesoamerican communities. Girl-watching while hanging around a street corner in the evenings is a major pastime in many places, and in Cherán the gangs often worked out plans for one of their members to kidnap or elope with a girl. Some of the older unmarried men sometimes went to one of the several houses of prostitution in town operated by older women.

When a girl's first menstruation occurred the mother informed her husband, and he urged her more than ever to watch over her. Careful mothers from that time on kept their daughters from walking about the streets alone and from going for water or to church by themselves. A small number of young women engaged in prostitution, in some cases the meetings being arranged by their mothers, who had also been prostitutes. The young men knew of these girls, and it was difficult for them to find husbands. The people claimed there was almost no premarital intercourse, especially on the part of young women. This was the ideal, but anthropologists have found that performance commonly differs from ideals to some degree. The people of Cherán were especially insistent that young women were sexually innocent. Beals and his associates found that their informants seemed embarrassed by inquiries into sexual matters, and it was difficult to obtain information in this area. Certainly, young people were not ignorant of the sexual aspect of life, since they grew up observing the many animals they kept. Also, the young men discussed sexual matters in some detail among themselves.

The people of Cherán and other Mesoamerican communities did not allow their young people to court freely. Boys had to take what few opportunities came along to communicate with girls they were interested in. Sometimes they could have a few words with a girl at the gate to her lot or while she was going with her mother to obtain water. The most satisfactory interchanges occurred when a girl was sent on an errand or a visit by herself, though this was fairly unusual for most. Another good opportunity came when the girl was allowed to go out with several other girls, usually on a Sunday afternoon. After a boy indicated which girl he wanted to talk to she would drop behind the group if she was willing to see him, and the others walked on slowly.

A young couple who wanted to marry arranged for the young man to kidnap or steal her. Though it was actually an elopement, everyone considered it proper for the girl to struggle and her family to pursue them. The boy obtained the help of some of his age mates, who assisted him to carry her away and blocked pursuit. They usually kidnapped her when she came out of the church building after Rosary on a Sunday with only female relatives. The women always screamed and fussed, and someone immediately called the men, who gave chase. The young men tried to block the streets and might push or trip the pursuers, but they avoided hanging on to them or striking them. The groom's object was to get the girl to the home of one of his relatives, but if he was caught he did not resist. The girl's parents always gave their consent to the marriage, because it was difficult for a girl who had been stolen and did not marry her kidnapper to find a husband. Moreover, the municipal authorities were supposed to force a young man to marry a young woman he had kidnapped.

In Mesoamerican communities marriage arrangements and wedding ceremonies are characteristically prolonged and complex, and most ethnographies devote many pages to describing them. Beals suggested that this was perhaps the most complex aspect of Cherán culture (Beals 1946:180). There were petitions, respect rituals, gift-giving, admonitions, getting drunk, civil registration, vespers, dancing, ceremonial dressing of the bride and groom, band music, money payments, a Mass, special meals, candles and flowers, prayers, serenading, distribution of bread, clothing gifts, processions, displays of clothing and bread, compadre ritual, and other elements. Some of the weddings were elaborate and lasted up to three days, while a few were relatively simple. A marriage manager usually presided over the events from beginning to end, since most people were unfamiliar with the proper elements and their sequencing. From the time of the wedding on the relatives of the bride and groom regularly participated together in all kinds of ceremonial events.

Another way Cherán was like other Mesoamerican communities was the practice of "free union," by which couples lived together without having had a ceremony. Usually one or both parties had been married before. The people treated the households established in this way as fully legitimate.

At marriage a Cherán Tarascan became fully adult for the first time, since unmarried young people were not consulted in family matters. The first year of marriage was often difficult for the bride, who was under her mother-in-law's authority. Outwardly, however, many of the relationships between mother and daughter-in-law seemed friendly, and it seems there was less difficulty in this relationship than in some other Mesoamerican societies. Both the father and mother expected the newly married couple to make it easier for them by taking on much of the harder work.

The ideal in Cherán was harmonious cooperation between husband and wife, and many couples seemed to achieve it. There were some who did not, of course, and some couples divorced. In those cases drunkenness, wife beating, failure to support the family, or infidelity were important reasons. In spite of the high value placed on having children the people did not seem to consider childlessness an adequate reason to get a divorce. The town officials investigated all divorce cases and either forced the couple to remain together or supervised the disposition of children. They usually kept small children with the mother and placed those over six or seven years of age with the parent who could rear them best.

In some societies, including Mesoamerican groups, people are considered old when their children have married and moved out of the household. This was not the case in Cherán, and the level of vitality seemed more significant. The ethnographers knew of one man, apparently in his eighties, who supported himself by his own farm work and was a tireless dancer at fiestas, and they noted that women far past

child-bearing age were often the most active fiesta workers and dancers. The happiest people of advanced age seemed to be those who were still involved in a successful marriage relationship and who possessed adequate economic resources. The unhappiest were a few elderly women with no children or husbands, who had to carry their own wood and who lived in hovels or lean-tos. Only a few elderly in Cherán were so helpless.

Cherán responses to disease were similar in many respects to those in other Mesoamerican communities. The people recognized a variety of ailments caused by conditions vaguely thought of as natural as well as several having a supernatural component. They believed witches caused a great deal of illness, and people could also become ill from a fright (espanto in Spanish), air or wind (aire or viento), the evil eye (mal de ojo), or getting too hot or too cold. People were also sometimes "taken by the wind," as some put it. Some also referred to air getting in the stomach or a pain in the side being caused by air, and air could be hot or cold. Witches used black magic or afflicted people with various damaging substances, sometimes delivering them while changed into an animal. Some of the people reported that drunkards or people out at night might be frightened by ghosts or other supernatural things, possibly imaginary.

The evil eye afflicted mainly small children. People with the power of the evil eye might not realize they had it and were apt to damage someone they especially liked or found attractive, such as pretty or clean children with nicely combed hair. Lovers who wanted to see one another but were prevented might also damage one another. Children suffering from evil eye became weak and cried a lot, and their complexion became pale or yellowish. Adults suffered depression, sleeplessness, pain and other symptoms. Both adults and children died of fever and vomiting if not cured. Anyone could cure the disease by drawing a piece of clothing belonging to the one who caused it along the patient's body, a process called "cleaning." Parents who did not know who had caused their child's illness would go into the street and ask all who passed by to "clean" the child, hoping that one would be the causer.

The hot-cold concept, which originated in Europe, was rather vague to the people of Cherán. The basic idea is that certain experiences and foods or other substances can overheat or overcool the body, making one ill. People in Cherán, for example, reported that a person who became very agitated and drank something cold might suffer from heart pains.

A number of people thought that the strength of the blood located just below the nape of the neck, which was where a person's life resided, was important to health. Persons with much blood there were healthy, while those with too little blood to nourish their lives became seriously ill and died. Presumably the evil eye and other causes of illness affected the blood supply. Most of the people thought the blood of animals was dangerous, and many would not use meat until several days after butchering.

In 1941 all the curers of Cherán were women, usually middle-aged or old, though a medical student practiced there for part of the time the ethnographers were there. In Mexico medical students had to spend eight months in a town without a doctor and write a report on the community's medical and health conditions before they could receive their degree. In the anthropologically well-known Zapotec town of Mitla, near Oaxaca City, the medical student continued to practice there after he received his degree, providing a series of interesting confrontations between modern and traditional medicine. Though there was a physician in the nearby town of Paracho, most of the people of Cherán used the curers.

Most of the curers specialized in dealing with from one to three illnesses, using for the most part herbs, unguents, and drugs. They had no special abilities, only greater knowledge than most. Many of the people treated themselves or other members of the household at home, going to a healer only when they felt their own resources were inadequate. A different kind of specialist handled broken bones, though some of the bone-setters were also curers. They simply worked the bones into their proper positions and bound them in place with splints. When people found an illness so stubborn that it must be due to witchcraft they might go to a "good witch" to have the witchcraft counteracted. By one account the good witch would enter an empty house, strike the walls with a stick, and call the bad witch. When she came, they would fight, and the fate of the patient depended on who won (Beals 1946:158).

The Cherán Tarascans regarded death as a normal occurrence and mourned with restraint and, mostly, in private. They were much less concerned with the dead and spirits of the dead than some other Mesoamerican societies, since they feared them little and did not interact with them much. Occasionally, someone would dream often about a dead relative, which meant that the person had returned for a member of the family and that someone in the household would die.

The people believed that small children who died went directly to heaven, while adults had to spend some time in purgatory. A small child's godparents placed special clothing, including a crown, on the body and placed it on a table surrounded by appropriate items. The people held an all night wake, the parents provided a meal for the relatives the next morning, and they took the body to the graveyard in the afternoon. At the cemetery they placed the body in a coffin, lowered it into the grave without ceremony, and filled the grave with earth.

There was also a wake for an adult, though more people came, and atole was served at midnight. They dressed the body in black clothing and placed nothing on the head. In the morning the people ate beans and tortillas and at noon, broth, stew, and tamales. In the afternoon they put the body in a coffin and carried it to the cemetery. Some families hired a prayer-maker to come to the house and pray for nine days after burial. In preparation for the Day of the Dead on November 2 men from each *barrio* (division of the town) cleaned the cemetery. The night of November 1 the people attended Mass at the church, and the next day they went as individuals and in small groups at different times to the cemetery. There they more thoroughly cleaned the graves, decorated those of the recent dead with flowers, and placed pine bows and baskets of food at the foot of the graves or, sometimes, on the grave. Afterward, they sat around and talked.

Government and Social Order

The *municipios* of Mexico are small, politically unified territories consisting of a head town (*cabecera*), smaller settlements and/or rural neighborhoods, and the fields and other open country belonging to the municipio. Cherán differed from most municipios in that nearly everyone lived in the cabecera, which was also known as Cherán. A few people lived in one small hamlet. Most of the cultivated lands lay in the southern half of the municipio, largely to the south of the town, though there were a few cultivated areas in the northern portion. The transition between the town and the country around it was abrupt.

Like many other Mexican towns Cherán was divided into barrios, four in this case. Barrios vary in importance from place to place. In many communities there is rivalry among the barrios, they may have their own chapel and barrio ceremonies, and the people may prefer to marry within their own barrio. When Beals and his associates were there in 1940 and 1941, however, the Cherán barrios were little more than residence units with a few administrative functions. They had no chapels and had nothing to do with regulating marriage or other social relationships.

Cherán had a governmental system basically similar to those of other Mexican towns. The governing council consisted of five elected persons, one from each barrio, and a fifth whose selection mechanism Beals could not learn. One of the five men served as *presidente*, or mayor, and another as *síndico*, the positions being rotated among the barrios on an annual basis. In addition to this governing council there were five alternates who stood ready to substitute if one of the five council members died or had to be away. The five councilmen and their alternates were elected for two year terms, two being elected one year and three the next. Together they made up the *ayuntamiento*, or elected municipal government. The elected leaders appointed a number of other officials, especially the secretary and the treasurer. There was also an elected judge and his alternate, a secretary of the court, a chief of each barrio, 45 block chiefs, a representative of the people, police officers, a military unit, and various other minor officials.

The presidente, as chief officer, initiated most governmental acts, while the síndico was responsible for carrying them out. The presidente presided at town meetings and meetings of the council, settled minor disputes, levied small fines or ordered offenders imprisoned temporarily, supervised expenditures, appointed most nonelected officials, and initiated most public works. Either he or his alternate were supposed to be present at the city building each day.

The síndico supervised most of the public works projects and initiated minor work. These had mostly to do with street maintenance and construction and repair of bridges. He also maintained surveillance of the water supply, the slaughter house, and similar matters, and he dealt with questions of inheritance of property.

The secretary was charged with making documents and maintaining the municipal archives, and the treasurer received funds, paid bills, and kept financial records. The judge heard cases sent to him by the síndico and could fine or imprison people.

The barrio chiefs were responsible for the block chiefs and for the night patrol. They transmitted instructions from the council to the block chiefs of their barrio, who were called on to notify the residents of calls for communal labor and saw that each person took a turn. This probably amounted to two or three days a year for each eligible man.

Each night a group of eight to twelve men patrolled the town, with all but the older, most prominent men taking a turn of a week at a time. The military reserve was armed by either the State or Federal Government (Beals was unable to find out which) to defend the town from outside disturbance. No one knew how the members were selected, and it was commanded by a man known to be the real political boss of the town.

The representative of the people was named at a town meeting along with two other people to form an administrative committee that had certain responsibilities to the State Government. The committee members seemed to have little more to do than sign a few papers.

Each barrio cared for the water aqueduct passing through its part of town, maintained bridges, cleaned the graveyard before the Day of the Dead, and repaired roads, all under the ultimate direction of the síndico.

Art and Play

Humans in all communities engage in a range of activities that provide alternatives to workaday responsibilities. Many of them are diversions requiring little skill, while others involve varying degrees of skill exercised to express and communicate culturally standardized sentiments. The latter may be called *art*. Much of the artistic expression of Cherán occurs within the context of the fiestas and *mayordomías* (complexes of ceremonies honoring a saint), and the enjoyment of those expressive activities has to be considered the major kind of pastime in Cherán.

Dancing was one of these arts, there being several kinds of dancers in Cherán. The *moros*, also found in other Mesoamerican communities, danced during the fiesta of the patron saint. They wore special costumes made mostly of velvet and richly decorated with gold braid and ornaments. The headdress was an elaborate crown of upright pieces of split *carrizo* (cane) a foot or more high, decorated with brightly colored papers, feathers, little mirrors, and other bright ornaments. The moros wore a bright kerchief across

the face, shoes, and a pair of spurs with bright metal disks in place of the rowels. The dancers paraded around on their horses and dismounted to dance in various places, usually singly or in pairs. They clashed their spurs together as much as they could as they danced, their movements apparently reflecting European country dances. When they danced at stores and saloons they received gifts of cookies, cigarettes, money or drinks.

For the mayordomía of the Christ Child on December 25 the brothers and relatives of the *mayordomo* (sponsor for the mayordomía) invited 30 to 35 unmarried men or boys and four little girls to do the *negrito* dance. Each participant selected a godmother, who dressed the dancer and took care of the costume. The men and boys wore dark-colored trousers, woolen sack coats, shoes, and a black wooden mask with European features. Up to two dozen silk ribbons, about two inches wide and of many colors, hung from the top of the mask down over the head and nearly to the ground behind the dancers. Two files of dancers walked through various fairly simple figures, with a little girl at the end of each file, while they delivered a long recitation in praise of the Holy Child and sang several songs. A specialist was hired to train the young people for this dance.

Another dance performed at Christmas time was the *pastorela*, or Dance of the Shepherds. Four or perhaps six girls who had served the church during the year led the dance. They invited a total of twelve girls and three adults to participate in the event. One adult played the part of the devil and another a hermit, and the third taught the dancers and actors their parts. A recitation and songs were part of this dance also. The pastorela dancers performed between the church and the municipal building first. Then they danced at the houses of the members of the *cabildo* (a group of males who organized mayordomías) and those of various mayordomos. They usually performed for three or four days beginning the evening of December 24.

The dance of the *viejos* or *Europeos* (old people or Europeans), has long been traditional in many Mesoamerican communities. In Cherán it was performed in connection with the Fiesta of the Three Kings on January 6. About thirty dancers, mostly young men, appeared in special clothing and various kinds of wooden masks with European features. The dance involved a recitation as well as marching and dancing in various figures, including some rather spirited dancing by pairs of men holding hands. Dancers who performed well and with verve provoked the others to cry out in falsetto voice.

Three dance groups not connected with any organization or mayordomía were performed at Christmas time. One group, representing blacks, performed steps resembling the Mexican *jarabe tapatío* (sometimes called the hat dance), accompanied by guitar and drum music. Another group, each person dressed like an old man, danced to the music of five or six stringed instruments. The third group, known as Apaches or black savages, painted their faces, stuck feathers in their hair, and leaped about considerably while shouting and brandishing bows and arrows. They also danced to guitar and drum music. People said the dancing of the three groups signified the following of the star of Bethlehem by various persons.

Several other dances were performed in connection with various fiestas and mayordomías.

Instrumental music was a big part of Cherán life, even as it was in other Tarascan and Mesoamerican communities. The bands played for fiesta mayordomías, dances, weddings, house roofing celebrations, and civic events. Smaller string groups played the violin, cello, bass, and guitar, with a clarinet sometimes added. Members of musical groups gathered at one anothers houses and played for their own enjoyment, but they were also hired for mayordomías or other fiestas sometimes. Some Tarascan groups have become very good and have achieved fame beyond Tarascan country. Another musical group consisted of a drummer and several men playing *chirimías*, which are short, double-reed wind instruments with several finger stops. The ethnographers heard them play at the fiesta of the patron saint, and, after listening to the shrill, spirited music for a time, they finally recognized it as the Beer Barrel Polka. Combination guitar and drum music has already been mentioned.

A major pastime at the fiesta of the patron saint was the bull riding. The men built a corral or bull ring for the spectacle. During the several hours of bull riding they teased the bulls to get them agitated, and if they charged someone the crowd was delighted. They helped a rider onto a bull and turned the animal loose in the corral to see if he could dislodge his tormenter. Clowns distracted the bull from thrown riders.

Another major event at many fiestas was the fireworks tower at night, known as the *castillo*. A specialist was hired to build a tall framework, sometimes 20 feet or so high, covered with rockets, pinwheels, and other kinds of fireworks. These were assembled so many of them would go off at once but sequenced so the display would last for a long time. This made an especially spectacular show at night, and everyone much enjoyed it. The feeling about having successful castillos was so strong that fireworks specialists who failed in any major way to produce a good display were jailed and fined and sometimes got mauled by the angry crowd. Castillos were major elements in the fiestas of many Mesoamerican communities.

These are only some of the events that people enjoyed performing or watching at fiestas and mayordomías. They involved the exercise of varying degrees of artistic skill. The people appreciated them both for the skill of the performers and their aesthetic value, and they provided many opportunities for a change of pace. As such events do in all cultures many occasions combined dancing, drama, music, and verbal exercises in a single event.

Games were relatively unimportant to the adults of Cherán. Some played basketball, but most people seemed more interested in watching other kinds of activities. Children played various tag games, a hockey-like game using a rag ball, and marbles. They also spun tops, walked on stilts, flew kites, and played on swings. Both adults and children played a ring and pin game. If it was like the widespread ring or cup and pin game elsewhere, they threw the ring into the air and tried to catch it on the pin.

Gossip and other conversation were among the most enjoyable pastimes for Cherán people of all ages. The women chatted when getting water or having their corn ground, mature men talked in the street and elsewhere, and young men talked and joked with one another in the streets in the evening. People also enjoyed listening to music outside the fiesta context, either when groups got together to play for the pleasure of it or on phonographs or radios. The people also enjoyed collecting miniatures. They also had a corpus of folk tales.

Religious Beliefs and Practices

The religious systems of the Mesoamerican Indians have been described as *Christo-paganism* as opposed to more conventional Roman Catholic Christianity. This means that many of the beliefs and rituals are essentially pagan customs in Christian dress. By 1940, however, the religious systems of Cherán and many other Tarascan places had become strongly Roman Catholic and no longer fit well under the rubric of Christo-paganism. Most Tarascan communities had come to center their religious life on the saints (Carrasco 1957:23) and held beliefs and engaged in rituals largely devoid of pagan survivals. Undoubtedly, their greater concern with several saints instead of God reflected pre-Spanish polytheism, but generally their version of Roman Catholicism was hardly distinguishable from that of many other Mexican towns.

There were four types of church rituals. The central rituals followed Mexican Catholic patterns reasonably well and were entirely under the priest's direction. These were the Mass, Rosary, confession, baptism, confirmation and similar ceremonies. The members of several religious societies were involved in these aspects of church life, such as the Sacred Heart Society, the Daughters of Mary, the Apostles of Saint Joseph, and the Third Order of Saint Francis. A group of men known as the cabildo was also partially linked with the church organization.

A second area, the fiestas, might as well be treated under social and recreational life, since they were basically secular celebrations centered around religious objects, mostly images of saints. The political leaders organized and supervised them, though the Mass and other church rituals were part of them. Third, there were religious ceremonies known as mayordomías, which were maintained and organized by the cabildo group but conducted mostly by lay people. Finally, there were mayordomías and dances controlled neither by the priest nor the cabildo.

The priest, appointed by the Bishop in Zamora, said the regular Masses and conducted special Masses occurring with the fiestas, mayordomías, and weddings. The religious societies were rather secret, and the ethnographers were able to learn little about them. They were important, however, and the majority of the townspeople belonged to one or another of them. Membership was by invitation only, issued by the society's board of directors. They held all their meetings in the church or at the priest's home. The societies of St. Joseph and St. Mary were for boys and girls, respectively.

Perhaps the saints' days were basically excuses for holding the major fiestas, which were essentially secular occasions with religious overtones. They were times for making the major purchases of the year, showing hospitality, getting drunk, enjoying the large crowds, and taking a break from ordinary life. The fiesta of the patron saint, San Francisco, was a four day fiesta beginning the first Sunday after October 4. It consisted of band music, fireworks displays, bull-teasing and riding, processions, dances by men called moros, a basketball game, and buying and selling at vendors' stands. The events varied some from fiesta to fiesta, but they usually included dance or dance-drama performances, music, processions, the eating of special foods, fireworks, a Mass, special ceremonies of one kind or another, and one or more other events unique to the particular fiesta.

The Fiesta of La Octava, held on Saturday and Sunday the week following Easter, was mainly a commercial fair much like the fiesta of the patron saint but lacking the fireworks display, bull riding, and dancers.

Carnival was observed the Tuesday before Lent began. The people fasted until noon, and in the afternoon the young men went about the streets and bought elaborately painted eggshells filled with confetti from girls sitting at the doors of their houses, after which they broke them over the girls' heads.

Lent and Holy Week involved many events unique to that time. There was a Mass in church each day during Holy Week. An image of Christ was placed in a cage on Thursday, Christ carried the cross and was crucified on Friday, and boys washed one another's feet on Saturday. There were also several minor church fiestas.

The people also attended fiestas in other Tarascan towns. The Cherán band played at fiestas in many other places, and others went to buy, sell, and enjoy.

The people of Cherán held mayordomías for 13 saints, six of them under the control of the group known as the cabildo. There were waiting lists of people wanting to be a mayordomo, since it was an important act of religious devotion. Usually the mayordomo had made a promise. For example, a man with no sons would promise to seek the office if he could be favored with a son, or someone might promise to serve if released from a sickness. Sometimes a man who had become wealthy would want to be a mayordomo to express his gratitude. A person selected as a mayordomo, or carguero, for a certain saint for a year kept and cared for the saint's image in his home, removing all else from the room and preparing a special altar. He also kept it ready for anyone who wanted to honor it by burning candles, praying before it, or leaving alms. Meanwhile he accumulated food and property for the ceremonies, which might involve dances, candle burning, taking the image to the

church to visit Christ, a Mass, gift exchange, and other events.

The most expensive mayordomía was in honor of the Holy Child, and it was celebrated on December 25. Other cabildo mayordomías honored the Virgin of the Snows, the Virgin of Guadalupe, San Isidro, San José, and Santa Inez. The Virgin of Guadalupe was the patron saint of Mexico, San Isidro was the patron of cultivators, San José the patron of shake and plank makers, and Santa Inez the patron of cattle and pigs.

Other mayordomías were controlled by other individuals and organizations. The mayordomía of San Rafael, patron of merchants, for example, was apparently administered by an official selected by the town merchants. Other mayordomías not controlled by the cabildo honored San Antonio, patron of muleteers; San Anselmo, patron of honey gatherers; the Three Kings; Santa Cecilia, patroness of musicians; and the Miraculous Holy Child. There were probably others not discovered by the ethnographers, since no one in town seemed to know about all the mayordomías (Beals 1946:142).

Though pagan supernaturalism was unimportant in Cherán, the people held a variety of beliefs outside the standard Christian system, the main one being the belief in witchcraft. In 1940 Cherán had the reputation for miles around as being the outstanding center of witchcraft, and Beals and his associates found evidence in harmony with that notion. All the witches were women, though the people often spoke of them in male terms. The most powerful witches got their power from the Devil. To obtain this power they visited the summit of a certain volcanic cone a mile or two southeast of town, where they called for the Devil. The seeker felt or heard a strong wind, followed by the Devil's appearance. She would then make a contract to last 20 years, after which she was to die. Other women became witches by taking instruction from another one.

The witches of Cherán were sorcerers to a significant degree, that is, they used black magic. *Magic* is a procedure for compelling the supernatural and, since the power lies in the procedure rather than the person, is usable by one who is not a witch. Some witches use magic and some do not, but the witches of Cherán used both magic and their specially-acquired supernatural powers. The most common magical act was to take a victim's comb, hair, piece of clothing, sweat from a coin, or other very personal item; use it in the preparation of a doll resembling the person; and stick pins in the doll. This involved two of the fundamental notions of magic around the world, contagion and imitation. The sorcerer used something that had been in contact with the intended victim (contagion) and performed acts in imitation of what she wanted the victim to suffer. Witches often delivered damaging items to the person's house at night, such as the bones of dead people, candles (associated with the dead), or earth from the jail floor.

As an aid to this sort of activity the witches called upon a special power common to their kind around the world-- they changed into an animal. The witches of Cherán could transform themselves into cats, owls, dogs, roosters, or burros. If a strange cat came into the kitchen it might well be a witch come to deliver harmful medicine or to obtain something for magic against a member of the household. Witches could also afflict people by talking softly to them at night. They would sit in trees outside a house and speak to people, though they could be heard from a distance, too. People said a large cherry tree south of town was a popular roosting place for owl-witches in action.

The Cherán Tarascans had a few supernaturalistic beliefs beyond Christianity and witchcraft. Probably, the most common was a belief in a malevolent spirit that lived in one of the barrios. At night, in town or countryside, people would think they were going one way, since they recognized certain places, but suddenly discover they were in an entirely different place. In more serious cases people were carried away by this spirit. By some accounts the spirit might try to strangle the victim and sometimes succeeded. In other cases people frightened by the spirit and fleeing from it might injure or kill themselves by falling from a bridge or suffering some other accident resulting from the encounter.

Additional supernaturalistic ideas included the belief that coyotes had magical power over other animals. They could shake themselves, causing chickens to walk over to them and let themselves be eaten. The people also believed in a lizard that lived in the walls or pillars of houses and suckled at the breasts of nursing mothers while they slept. If anyone cut it in pieces the parts would only fly back together again. It could be killed only by burning it with coals. Outsiders often refer to beliefs of this sort as superstitions, but anthropologists are rather shy of using the term. It indicates for many users the notion that a group other than their own is ridden by erroneous, irrational beliefs, and anthropologists are aware that such beliefs exist in "civilized" cultures just as surely as in others. Members of other societies regard many American and European beliefs as superstitions.

Cultural Change

A number of the societies studied by anthropologists have been restudied either by the same anthropologist or by another. The results are always different. A major reason for the differences is that cultures never stop changing. We expect them to be different at various points in time. Also, many differences between original studies and restudies are due to varying circumstances of field research, contrasting personal styles and abilities of the ethnographers, and different fieldwork objectives. For Cherán, which was restudied about thirty years after the original fieldwork, we stress change.

Anthropologist George Castile noted that Cherán had long maintained an strongly defensive stance toward the outside world. The highway through town brought pressures and opportunities that undermined that stance. At the same time many important cultural features persisted through the three decades.

Cherán was not a major stopping place. The highway bypassed the central plaza, and the people did little to attract tourist trade (Castile 1972:91). Nevertheless, it brought new people into the area and stimulated various automotive service enterprises. In 1970 there was a service station, a tire repair shop for trucks passing through, an electrical and mechanical repair business, and five businesses along the western edge of the plaza, all depending on highway traffic. Busses passed through the town frequently, stopping to pick up and discharge passengers. Eight or ten taxis were based in Cherán, serving villages the busses did not reach. Burros, however, remained an important kind of transportation, and there were a few horses and wagons.

Outsiders had established certain activities in or near Cherán. The National Indian Institute of the Mexican government (Instituto National Indigenista) had a center there, and the Summer Institute of Linguistics missionaries maintained a center as a base for their linguistic missionary work in the area. The INI had trucks and jeeps, and the priest, doctor, school principal, and the missionaries used cars. The municipal government of Cherán also had an International Carryall in constant use. There were two other passenger cars that Castile never saw used while he was there.

Castile found there were more houses of either brick or plastered adobe than there had been before, but the plank houses still prevailed. There had been a major change from houses built of the heavy, horizontally-laid planks to those with lighter, vertically-placed wall planks. A number of the houses had TV antennas on them. Many homes also had electricity, but the only telephone to be found was on the central plaza.

Most of the women were wearing the same kind of clothing they had in 1940, but a few sophisticated young women were to be seen in slacks or mini-skirts. The men were wearing denim jeans or slacks, sports shirts, and wind breakers.

Only a few of the older people of Cherán were monolingual in 1970, and Spanish was the language of the streets. The civil-religious hierarchy described by Beals was no longer viable, having been replaced by the standard Mexican municipal government. The cabildo was also gone, though several mayordomías remained. Castile found that only about a hundred people were involved in the mayordomía system (Castile 1972:203).

The fundamental change between 1940 and 1970 was the transition from a *closed corporate community* to an *open community* (Castile 1981:185). Before the Spanish came the town had been an integral part of the Tarascan empire, but its connections with the Tarascan nation had been severed by the Spanish, and Cherán became one of hundreds of Indian communities in Mexico forced to adapt to the new situation by turning inward and holding most of the outside world at bay. This they did to a significant extent through their system of ranked civil and religious offices. They became what Wolf called closed corporate communities (Wolf 1957), and this is what was largely destroyed in Cherán during the thirty years after 1940.

Chapter 12

THE CONTLA NAHUA OF TLAXCALA

Just to the east of Mexico City and ancient Aztec country lies the small state of Tlaxcala (approx. tlash-KAH-lah). The Tlaxcalan Indians are noteworthy as unconquered enemies of the Aztec who helped Cortés raise an Indian army and besiege the Aztec capital of Tenochtitlán. Twentieth century guidebooks send tourists to the city of Tlaxcala and, especially, to nearby Santa Ana Chiautempan to purchase *sarapes* (serapes). San Bernardino de Contla is one of the communities of the western slopes of La Malintzi volcano, where the communities have been characterized as Indian and traditionally oriented (Nutini and Bell 1980:xiii). The Contecos (people of Contla) and other Tlaxcalans speak the Náhuatl language, as do the Aztec, and they are sometimes referred to as Aztec. Their twentieth century culture is similar to that of modern Aztec in many basic ways.

The Contla Nahua (approx. NAH-wah) of 1962 lived in a municipio of 10,699 people, 6,863 of whom lived in the *cabecera* (head town) of San Bernardino Contla. The rest lived in small towns and dispersed settlements. Only a little over 2,000 spoke Spanish only, so it was predominantly an Indian municipio. Virtually all families grew corn and other crops, but only one-third farmed full time. Weaving was the main full-time occupation by far.

For the early part of their married lives the people commonly lived in *extended families* consisting of the parents, their sons, and unmarried children, and the sons' wives and children. Later, most separated from the larger family to establish independent nuclear family households. The people were also grouped into common ancestor descent units of relatively shallow genealogical depth, called *lineages*, the founders of each being known to the members. Lineage members had to find their spouses in a different lineage from their own, and the children belonged to the father's lineage. A woman changed lineage membership at marriage from that of her parents to that of her husband. The lineages were grouped into larger common ancestor groups called *clans*. Most clan members also married out. The men remained in the natal clan for life, and the women changed membership at marriage. Each clan lived in a territorial division known as a *barrio,* most of which were equivalent to the clan. Four of the ten barrios were

divided into two clans each, making a total of 14 clans. The municipio was governed officially governed by a set of officials required by the state of Tlaxcala, but the people largely ignored it and handled problems of social order within the context of their kinship and religious organizations.

Four saints were especially important in the religious system, and these and many other saints were propitiated in an annual round of elaborate ceremonies. Several classes of pagan supernaturals and related beliefs remained important in their daily religious life.

Prehistory

Archaeologists agree that humans were in central Mexico by 10,000 B.C., since they have found evidence in several sites for the association of human tools with remains of extinct mammals about that time. The most famous is at Tepexpán near Mexico City, where an investigator reported a human skeleton in the same stratum as a mammoth. Though the evidence was rather weak at Tepexpán, it was confirmed at Ixtapan, another Valley of Mexico site, where archaeologists found human tools clearly associated with mammoth bones in two places. The valley of Mexico is just to the east of Tlaxcala. Some archaeologists claim to have evidence of human presence in Mexico 20,000 years ago, but the finds are controversial and still under discussion.

For Tlaxcala, archaeologist García Cook (1974) has offered a sequence of seven cultural phases. Four of them fall within the period archaeologists of Mesoamerica have called Formative or Preclassic (Snow 1976:9). For the centuries immediately preceding 1200 B.C. there is evidence of communities of less than a hundred people who may have farmed part-time and most of whom located their villages or hamlets on the tops or eastern slopes of large hills. There is no evidence of ceremonial structures, but the people were terracing hillsides some. Between 1200 B.C. and 800 B.C. subsistence was a mixture of farming with hunting and gathering, but some of the settlements were notably larger than before, and the people were building larger terraces with canals along their outer walls to control erosion and flooding on the steep slopes. By the end of the period they were building some low platforms which might have been the sites of small temples.

Between 800 B.C. and 300 B.C. the people lived in still larger communities, had a well-developed system of irrigation agriculture, and built temple platforms of adobe and stone. During the last phase of the Preclassic, from 300 B.C. to A.D. 100, the patterns characteristic of the previous phase became even more elaborate, and Tlaxcala reached a peak of development. The largest places had well-developed ceremonial centers with streets, plazas, drains, ball courts, stuccoed buildings, and stepped temple bases using what is known as *talud-tablero* construction (Weaver 1981: 106, 193). In addition to highly developed irrigation agriculture, the people began to dig trenches in level areas having a high water table to drain away the water, and they piled the earth between the trenches to make raised beds for their crops.

The Classic Period in Mesoamerica was a time of highly developed agriculture, large pyramids in a number of places with temples atop them, large towns and cities, and complex religious, political, and aesthetic features.

But Tlaxcala did not participate in these developments. During this phase, A.D. 100 until A.D. 650, settlements actually became smaller, the population seems to have decreased, and there were no new architectural and other developments. Apparently, as urban centers grew rapidly during Classic times, several nearby areas were partially depopulated, and this may have been what happened in the Tlaxcalan region (Snow 1976:11). It was during this time that the great city of Teotihuacán, which lay about 28 miles north of Mexico City and some 55 or 60 miles to the northwest of San Bernardino Contla, reached its zenith. Some scholars believe that craftsmen from Tlaxcala may have gone to Teotihuacán and participated in its construction, demonstrating there the talud-tablero style that became a hallmark of that large city (Weaver 1981:106).

During Postclassic times, from A. D. 650 to 1500, the situation reversed dramatically in the Tlaxcalan area. The population increased notably as new groups came in, and there was a new surge of cultural development. Tlaxcala became an area of settlements ranging from isolated farmsteads through villages of several hundred to towns of several thousand people. These new communities were no longer located around the earlier ceremonial centers with their temples atop low, stepped pyramids, which archaeologists interpret as a secular trend (Snow 1976:11). Also, the people seem to have resumed the development of raised fields surrounded by trenches of water, bringing new areas, including much of central Tlaxcala, under intensive cultivation. These raised fields in water are called *chinampas*, and they are basically like the so-called floating gardens of Xochimilco to the south of Mexico City, where cultivators created small rectangular islands in the lake on which to grow their crops.

The changes in Tlaxcala during Postclassic times were part of a larger phenomenon involving the arrival of various Nahua-speaking groups from northwestern portions of

what is now Mexico. Apparently, they came in two waves, one about 800 and the second around 1200 (Wolf 1959:11). The earlier people spoke a dialect known as Nahuat (approx. NAH-waht), while the later immigrants spoke Náhuatl. The names of these dialects reflect the lack of the *tl* sound combination in the Nahuat dialect. Probably the Nahua-speakers moved into both the Valley of Mexico and Tlaxcala during Postclassic times, which would help account for the increased population of Tlaxcala at that time (Snow 1976:11).

The Aztec arrived in the Valley of Mexico as part of the second wave of Nahua-speaking groups. They are supposed to have migrated from a place called Aztlán, which accounts for their best-known tribal name, Aztec, meaning "people of Aztlán." Aztlán may have been in or near the southern part of the state of Nayarit, which lies along Mexico's Pacific coast to the northwest of Guadalajara (Horcacitas 1979:17). When the Aztec got to the Valley around 1250, they found other and far more powerful Náhuatl groups already established there, and there was hardly a place for them. They were abused and enslaved by their neighbors, but they learned from them and became stronger.

At one point, possibly about 1325, they fled into a marshy area. There, their tormentors left them to shift for themselves for a couple of generations, though they made them pay tribute. The Aztec drove stakes into the marsh and filled the spaces between with stone and rock to gain dry land on which to build. They also built elongated platforms bordered with stakes, and they scooped rich soil from the lake bottom onto the platforms to make chinampa gardens like those of Tlaxcala and other places. They were building on the site of the future Mexico City, but they called the place Tenochtitlán, "the place of the prickly-pear cactus." They called it that because, according to legend, they found an eagle sitting on a cactus with a serpent in his beak when they first arrived there (Horcacitas 1979:22).

The Aztec were also known as Tenochca (approx. teh-NOHCH-kah) and Mexica (approx. meh-SHEE-kah). The Tenochca name was connected with their location, though there also was an Aztec patriarch by the name of Tenoch (Wolf 1959:130). Mexica may have derived from the name of one of their great tribal leaders during their time of wandering, namely Mecitli (Padden 1967:2). At any rate, the people were Aztec, Tenochca and Mexica, and it avoids confusion to remember that, when archaeologists, ethnohistorians, and other Mesoamerican scholars refer to Mexicans, they mean the Aztec.

The Mexica soon became strong at Tenochtitlán. Their new home lay in territory claimed by two other groups, the Tepanecas (often Tepanec in English) and the Culhua. The Mexica paid tribute to the Tepanecas, the most powerful people in the area at the time. But they had managed to secure a daughter of the Culhua king as one of their wives, and, allegedly, the king's grandson was a Mexican citizen. In 1376, with the permission of the Culhua, the Aztec made the grandson their first formal ruler. This annoyed the Tepanecas, and they were further upset by the Aztec decision to call themselves the Culhua-Mexica. But the Mexica continued to pay tribute to the Tepanecas and, in fact, were at their mercy because their only adequate source of potable water lay in their territory. Peace continued until, in 1427, under a new and tyrannical ruler, the Tepanecas announced plans to exterminate the Mexica. The people of Tenochtitlán reacted immediately by attacking the Tepanecas and destroying their city in one day (Horcacitas 1979:25). The Aztec-Tenochca-Mexica were off to a good start because they not only destroyed the most powerful city-state in the valley, they now received tribute from all those states that had been under the thumb of the Tepanecas. They shared this tribute with two other states, forming a triple alliance, but Tenochtitlán soon dominated the alliance. As the years went by the canny Mexica added one state after another to the area they dominated, until by the appearance of the Spanish almost a century later, their influence extended from coast to coast and southeastward into Guatemala.

History

The Aztec were not invincible. The Tarascans to the west of them repeatedly and soundly thrashed them when the Mexica bothered them, and the Mexica were probably lucky the Tarascans had no interest in conquering them. Moreover, they had never managed to subdue Tlaxcala, though it was only a few miles from Tenochtitlán. They fought repeatedly, and the Aztec took Tlaxcalan captives for their sacrifices, but the Tlaxcalans survived to join forces with Cortés to bring the Aztec to their knees. After a series of battles with the Tlaxcalans, Cortés and his men prevailed, and the Tlaxcalans seized on an alliance with the Spanish as a way of finally getting rid of the Aztec threat (Gibson 1952:22). After a time Cortés accepted Tlaxcalan help, and some scholars think it may have been indispensable to his defeat of Tenochtitlán.

The Spanish supposedly awarded the Tlaxcalans special privileges in return for their help, but they hardly kept their promises. But the sixteenth century Tlaxcalans worked hard to secure those privileges, and, because of their effort, they thrived and prospered (Nutini 1968:97). They maintained a tradition of greatness through the centuries that was first manifested in their resistance to the domination and exploitation of the colonists. The Spanish reacted by isolating Tlaxcala both economically and socially, and neither the *encomienda* system (see page 49) nor the hacienda system became strong there.

Tlaxcalan remembrance of former accomplishment and renown abetted the maintenance of certain customs and orientations as well was the generation of others that differentiated them from other twentieth century Indians. Nutini's view is that the Tlaxcala of the 1960s and 1970s was probably more homogeneous culturally than any other area of Mexico of comparable size and that this was rooted in the pre-Spanish situation and augmented through the 450 years since then. During the late twentieth century the Tlaxcalans still maintained a pride in their Indian status of greater importance to them than their identification as citizens of Mexico. Actually, this was so strong that Tlaxcalans were generally proud to be thought of as Indians, which contrasted strikingly with the embarrassment at being known as *indios* that has long prevailed in some other parts of Mexico. While the state of Tlaxcala may have been less than 25 percent Indian during the 1960s, the majority of the citizens, including some of the urbanites, identified themselves as *indios tlaxcaltecas* and would not be insulted if anyone so identified them (Nutini 1968:100).

Ethnography

Manuel Gamio did the first intensive ethnographic study of Nahua culture, publishing three volumes on the people of the Valley of Teotihuacán in 1922. The American anthropologist Robert Redfield spent eight months in the Nahua town of Tepoztlán in 1926 and 1927, his being the first of a series of community ethnographies produced by Mesoamerican specialists (Redfield 1930). Oscar Lewis made a more comprehensive study of Tepoztlán during the 1940s (Lewis 1951), his work and Redfield's making the community anthropologically famous. Zantwijk studied Aztec survivals in Milpa Alta (1960), and William Madsen lived in San Francisco Tecospa, not far from Milpa Alta, in the early 1950s and published the results of his work in 1960. Mexican scholars Carlos Basauri (1940) and A. Fabila (1949), respectively, studied the cultures of Ocotepec in Morelos and the Náhuatl-speakers of northern Puebla. French anthropologist G. Soustelle (1958) did field work in a Náhuatl village in Veracruz. These were the only Nahuan ethnographies available when William Madsen wrote the summary of Nahua culture published in the *Handbook of Middle American* in 1969.

From 1960-1962 and for short periods later on Hugo and Jean Nutini collected cultural data in the Tlaxcalan village of San Bernardino Contla, emphasizing social organization (1968). Between 1968 and 1972, Hugo and Jean Nutini did field work in another Tlaxcalan town, Santa María Belén Azitzimititlán, where they devoted special attention to the ritual kinship system (Nutini and Bell 1980). This summary is based primarily on Nutini's study of San Bernardino Contla.

Contla Country

The municipio of San Bernardino Contla is situated between the highway from Tlaxcala to Apizaco and the middle slopes of La Malintzi volcano. It lies on a gently sloping plain to the west of La Malintzi. The area is generally flat, though it is interrupted by a few low hills never more than 200 feet high. In the town itself several of these hills are unexcavated pyramids. Many ravines (*barrancas* in Spanish) cross this area, usually from east to west, from the volcano toward the Zahuapan River on the west side of

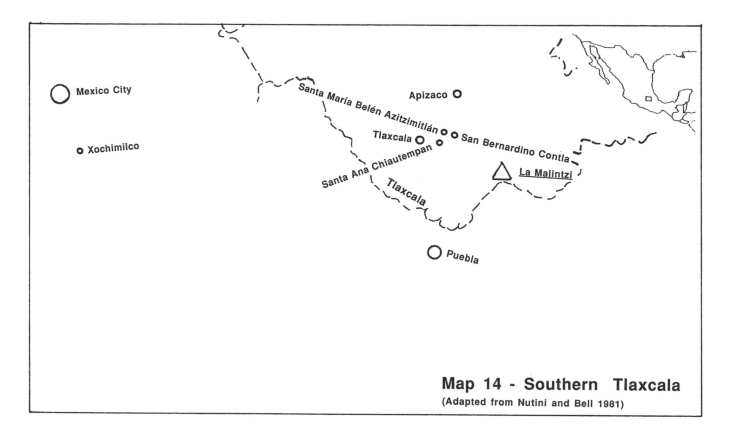

Map 14 - Southern Tlaxcala
(Adapted from Nutini and Bell 1981)

the Tlaxcala-Apizaco highway. Some of them are small and some large. Some die out before reaching the town. In some places they become two or three hundred yards wide and erode large areas of cultivatable land. One of the ravines contains a creek, while the rest are dry, containing no water unless heavy rains fall, which can turn them into temporary rivers. (Nutini 1968:25).

Like other Mexican municipalities, San Bernardino Contla is a territory consisting of the town of that name, which is the head settlement, (*cabecera* in Spanish), smaller settlements in other parts of the territory, and the countryside. The town itself lies 8,200 feet above sea level, and other parts of the municipio range from 7,875 to over 10,000 feet. Besides the head town there are two other pueblos and three pueblitos (little towns). The central area of the cabecera is highly nucleated, that is, the houses cluster along the blocks formed by the intersecting streets, while in the outlying portions of town and in the other towns and hamlets they are more dispersed. Often, in fact, a house is situated in a *milpa* (cultivated plot).

The town square, or *zócalo*, occupies the center of the cabecera, surrounded by the church, municipal building, school, marketplace, and other important buildings. Some of the other settlements also have a school and a chapel.

Language

The people of San Bernardino Contla, at the time Nutini studied them in 1961, spoke a Náhuatl dialect of the Náhua language. The people referred to their language as Mexicano, and four percent of them (419) spoke only Mexicano at that time. Seventy-seven percent, however, could speak both Spanish and Mexicano (Nutini 1968:24).

According to Longacre's synthesis the Nahua dialects belong to the Aztecoidan family of languages, spoken over a large area of north central and western Mexico (Longacre 1967:facing 120). Aztecoidan languages, in turn, belong to the Uto-Aztecan stock, which includes the Taracahitian and Piman families of northwestern Mexico and the languages of many tribes in the interior of the Western United States. Most of the Mesoamerican tribes speak languages other than Nahua, but the Nahua dialects are widely scattered there because of the extensive movements of the Aztec and other Nahua peoples into parts of the area. Nahua dialects extend from central Mexico through Veracruz and into the northern coast of the Isthmus of Tehuantepec, and enclaves can be found in Guatemala, El Salvador, Nicaragua, and Costa Rica.

The structure of Contla Náhuatl is generally similar to that of other Nahua places, so, to give an idea of some of the characteristics of Náhuatl speech I draw on a linguistic analysis of the language of the Náhuatl of the far northern sector of the state of Pueblo, thirty or more miles to the north of Contla.

Linguists use the term *phonology* to designate a language's sound system. The *phones* are the sounds the linguist hears the people utter repeatedly, but they may not be the same sounds the speakers are aware of. After getting a list of the sounds they hear, linguists then determine which of them belong to the same *phoneme* because the differences between or among them do not affect an utterance's meaning. In north Pueblo Náhuatl, for example, the linguist heard the people repeatedly using a sound made by raising the back of the tongue against the velum to stop the flow of air and sound, then releasing that flow. The sound was without voice and approximately like the English *k*. He also found that the people produced a sound very similar to *k*, the difference being that they did not raise the tongue against the velum tightly enough to fully stop the air flow. Instead they allowed it to continue with friction. Linguists usually write the first sound phonetically as [k] and the second, often, as [x]. If the field linguist could have found any two utterances having different meanings and phonetically exactly alike except for the difference between [k] and [x], he would have to place the two in different phonemes. It would mean the difference between them made a difference in meaning, just as the difference between [k] and, say, [g] affects meaning in English words such as *kill* and *gill*. But the analysis showed no such functions for [k] and [x], which means that the Nahua treated them as the same sound; they belonged to the same phoneme. The linguist found that the people used [x] when it occurred before another velar stop, and they used the stop [k], in all other sound contexts (Brockway 1963:14). The two phones [k] and [x] were alternative sounds within a phoneme for which Brockway used the symbol /k/. (Phonetic symbols are enclosed in brackets, phonemic symbols between slashes.)

Other phonemes, some of which also included alternative sounds, or *allophones*, include /p/, /t/, /tl/, /c/, /kw/, /ʔ/, /s/, /l/, /m/. /n/, /w/, /y/, /i/, /e/, /a/, and /o/. The sound represented by /i/ includes two English sounds, the vowels of the words *seen* and *sin*, written phonetically as [i] and [I]. The Nahua of northern Puebla use either sound next to stops, since, unlike in English, the difference between them makes no difference in meaning in any of their utterances. The /tl/ is voiceless, a Náhuatl phonetic feature that is reflected in the way many non-Indians of central Mexico pronounce Spanish words of Nahua origin. In the Mexico City area, for example, one can hear the name of the volcano Popocatépetl pronounced with a voiceless *l*.

The customs by which people order the meaningful elements of their speech to communicate with one another also differ notably among the world's cultures. Space is inadequate to even make a good beginning in describing Náhuatl grammar, so one example of word construction in northern Pueblo Náhuatl will suffice. Linguists say that a society builds its words from *morphemes*, a morpheme being the smallest unit of a language with a specific meaning. As far as phonology is concerned, a morpheme may consist of either one phoneme or a combination of phonemes. In northern Pueblo Náhuatl, for example, /a/ is a one phoneme morpheme indicating present tense. A morpheme consists then of two basic elements, the phoneme or phonemes and the associated meaning. /Ki/ in this dialect of Náhuatl is a morpheme of two phonemes plus the meaning "it." Salt is designated by the morpheme /ista/, and the morpheme /wi/ indicates that the unit is a verb. The word kistawia means "He salts it," or, transliterated, "it-salt-verb-present" (Brockway 1979:155). This example also illustrates how morphemes may be phonologically modified when combined with one another, since the /i/ (ee) sound of /ki/ is omitted, so to speak because the next morpheme, /ista/ (eestah) begins with the same sound.

Another grammatical custom of possible interest to some is the way the northern Pueblo Náhuatl handle questions. Questions for which the appropriate answer is negative or positive begin with a unit that so indicates. One of these is /tla/, which the speaker uses for polite requests. It is the equivalent of the English, "Will you please?" Other yes-or-no questions begin with /tlen/, which means "what" or "what then." So, said the rabbit to the coyote, /tlen tineckwas/ ("Are you going to eat me?") /Tlen/ indicates that the utterance is a question, while the rest of it literally says "you-me-eat-future" (Brockway 1979:152, 196).

Linguists have analyzed Náhuatl extensively, and anyone wanting to learn the language can use their descriptions to help. During the 1980s Náhuatl could still be heard occasionally on the streets of communities within sight of Mexico City and, without difficulty, in the streets of San Bernardino Contla.

Personality and Behavior

The Contla Nahua exhibited many of the same basic attitudes toward life as the Aztec and other Mesoamericans, though no comprehensive description of their personality is available. The people have long maintained considerable pride in their Indian heritage and a degree of conservatism, since they remember that they helped Cortés vanquish their neighbors and enemies, the ancient Aztec Nahua. In 1961 even people who knew no Náhuatl and had left behind Indian ways were ready to accept the Indian label with pride.

While many Mesoamericans were rather strict with women in the sexual area, the Contecos were rather liberal. Most young people had sexual experience before they were married, and marital infidelity was a way of life during marriage for both spouses. In neighboring communities female adultery might be severely punished, even by death. There was also an unusually large number of *polygynous* (involving more than one wife) marriages in Contla.

The Contecos devoted considerable time to maintaining the proper ritual relationships with the supernaturals, emphasizing correct procedures rather than correct belief. In this way they shared with other Mesoamerican groups the emphasis on form and appearance as opposed to inner piety and conviction. Perhaps this Mesoamerican trait was especially strong in Contla.

Livelihood

In 1961 agriculture was relatively unimportant in Contla. Nearly all the people had land, but it was poor and yielded too little for most to be self-sufficient. Each family head worked at least one *milpa* (field), but less than 15 percent of the working people were full-time farmers (Nutini 1968:37). Around 70 percent of the people had to purchase some of their corn and beans, which were their main crops and dietary staples. In addition to corn and beans, lima beans, peas, wheat, and potatoes were relatively important. The Contecos earned the cash for purchasing these foodstuffs mainly by weaving blankets and other items and selling them to the middlemen of a nearby town or through other channels.

The agricultural year began sometime between the middle of November and the middle of January, when the Contecos gave their fields their first plowing. They plowed them a second time before planting them in March or early April and cultivated twice during the summer before harvesting in September or October. Most used donkeys and mules to pull their plows, though some had oxen. In many other Nahua communities plows were pulled mostly by oxen. Other agricultural tools were spades, shovels, hoes, crowbars, mattocks, axes, pitchforks, sickles, rakes, and machetes (Nutini 1968:38). The men did most of the agricultural work, though women sometimes helped them.

In spite of the reduced importance of agriculture in Contla, the people still loved and wanted to own land just as surely as in other Mesoamerican places. A little over 40 percent of the land was privately owned, while the rest was communal. All the privately owned lands lay below the uppermost part of the settlement of Cuauhtenco, and these were more productive than most of the communal fields.

Contla had two main kinds of communal lands, the lands located above Cuauhtenco and the barrio lands, some of which were above Cuauhtenco and some below. Each year the barrios awarded, for that year only, plots of their communal land to members who held important religious assignments This helped them meet the heavy financial obligations that went with those positions. The lands were available to those Contecos who needed more. They petitioned the officials, who granted a request as long as a satisfactory plot was available.

In addition to communal and private lands, there was also land owned by several saints. The people responsible for a particular saint's fiesta in a given year farmed the land for that year, using the money made to pay for candles, masses, flowers, and other items needed for the occasion. Many Contecos pawned their fields to pay for the costs of fiestas, marriages, baptisms and other special occasions (Nutini 1968:42).

The Contecos of 1961 ate mostly corn tortillas and beans, supplemented by lima beans, string beans, chile peppers, tomatoes, onions, potatoes, squash, various greens, and eggs. They either fried beans or used them in soup. They often dipped their tortillas in *mole,* a sauce made of chili peppers and tomatoes. Most of the people in the town of Contla ate pork, beef, or poultry at least once a week, while others had it less often. Wealthy families ate meat several times weekly. In general, meat has not been an important part of Nahua diets, and it appears to have been more important in Contla than many other places. The women did the cooking and other household tasks.

The most important fiesta food in Contla was a dark, soup-like mole of ground corn, eight varieties of chiles, and sesame. The Contecos served this on nearly all religious and social occasions of importance, though they also prepared several other kinds of mole for festive occasions. The moles were often served with barbecued or steamed meats. Bread was also a festive food.

The Contecos consumed large quantities of *pulque,* an alcoholic beverage made from the *agave* plant. It was especially important in the mountain sections, where children drank it with their meals. They also enjoyed various kinds of tea and infusions of boiled orange, lemon, or camomile leaves sweetened with sugar. The thick corn meal and water drink known as *atole* was also used in several forms, and some atole was made from wheat and barley in Contla. The people also consumed large amounts of soft drinks, as well as some beer.

Clothing and Personal Appearance

Nearly all the men and women of Contla bought store clothing similar to that of most rural Mexicans. In the early 1960s less than two percent of the men wore the traditional tightly-fitted trousers of white cotton, while about four percent of the women wore the wrap-around skirt of wool held in place by a waist sash (Nutini 1968:42). No one wore the traditional *huipil,* a sleeveless blouse, manufactured dresses being the conventional costume. About half of the people went barefooted, while about a quarter wore the woven leather sandals known as huaraches. The rest wore shoes. Most of those wearing shoes were men, and in many families the children had shoes while their parents were barefooted. In remote parts of Nahua country the people continued to wear the more traditional costume, but Contla was one of the many Nahua places where they had largely abandoned it, even though many continued to use the Náhautl tongue.

Housing and Other Structures

Twentieth century Nahua lived in two basic types of houses, thatched huts of bamboo-like reeds (*carrizo*) with floor of earth, and adobe brick structures with flat roofs or tiled, shed-type roofs. Both were rectangular. Most of the houses of Contla were of the second type, though some had shingled roofs or petroleum-covered cardboard on their roofs. Most of the floors were of packed earth, though a few had brick or tile floors. Some of the people in the mountain area built stone houses.

The houses in the central area of the cabecera opened into walled yards, while those elsewhere lacked the walls. The homesteads away from the central area often consisted of a house, sometimes with two rooms, and a separate kitchen adjoining it. Poorer families built their kitchens of branches and dried grass and roofed them with shingles. Most homesteads had a separate kitchen for each nuclear family living there. Each main sleeping room in a household, which also served as a receiving room, had a relatively large altar holding statues of saints, pictures of saints, candles, and flowers.

Most of the Contecos slept in the main house on the woven straw or palm mats called *petates*. They placed these on the floor for sleeping and rolled them up in the daytime if they needed them out of the way. People also sat on petates while working. Less than a fifth of the people, mostly those living in the central area of Contla, had beds. About half of the households had chairs, and 90 percent of the people used tortillas or their fingers to eat with rather than forks and spoons (Nutini 1968:44).

Almost all households had a corn bin (*cuezcomate*) situated in the middle of the lot in the walled yards or three or four yards in front of the house at other homesteads. Most of them were of a kind commonly seen in Nahua communities. This type of cuezcomate was an egg-cup-shaped or cylindrical structure of adobe or of mud applied to a framework of sticks or branches. It rested on a mortared stone foundation and was six to nine feet high and up to six feet across. The top was covered with a shingled or tiled, cone-shaped roof. A different type of corn bin was most often found in the more heavily forested elevations of the municipio. It was a square or rectangular wooden structure no more than six feet across and raised two or three feet above the ground on poles, which sat on a stone foundation. The roof was shingled. In 1961 the square cuezcomate seemed to be disappearing.

Most households also had a *temazcal*, or steam bath, of the type typical of Nahua cultures. In Contla this was a dome-shaped structure of stone or concrete and adobe, four or five feet high and six to eight feet across. The entry was cylindrically shaped, and on the opposite side was a fireplace for heating the stones. The floor was of smooth concrete or brick, slightly inclined so the water would drain away. When bathers entered the bath, they poured water on the hot stones to form steam. A temazcal was located either against the yard wall or a few yards from the house.

In the central area of the town of Contla each yard had its own well, and other settlements had one or two communal wells each. In the lower places some of the wells were only 20 to 120 feet deep, but some wells in the higher elevations were over 500 feet deep.

Crafts, Tools, and Techniques

Nahua communities and Mesoamerica in general are characterized by a strong tendency for occupational specialization by region, community, and even parts of communities. The most important occupation in the municipio of Contla was the weaving of sarapes, the blankets and other articles of cotton or wool that are so much in demand by tourists and others. There were 2,438 looms in Contla in 1961, most of them in two sections of the cabecera. Some of the smaller settlements had no looms. Weaving was far more important than agriculture, half of all the full-time workers being involved in sarape production. Only 15 percent were full-time farmers.

The Contecos used the pre-Spanish *backstrap*, or *tension-type, loom* to weave the relatively narrow woolen belt and the European frame loom to fashion blankets and most other items. When they used the backstrap loom they prepared warp threads so that two sets of alternating threads crossed in two places, inserted sticks where needed to hold them apart, and stretched them between two horizontal sticks or beams. One beam was attached to a cord around the weaver's waist and the other to a post, tree, or other convenient upright. Loops from a cross stick passed around every other thread so the weaver could alternate the two sets of threads by pulling one set between the other. This separation made it possible to pass the weft thread across the warp between the two sets of threads. Then the raised threads were allowed to lower again in preparation for insertion of the next woof thread.

On the *frame loom* the warp threads were stretched between rollers, and the weaver used pedals attached to heddles through ropes and pulleys to alternate the two sets of threads. Local carpenters made these looms, which varied in size.

At one time the people made only woolen articles, but by 1961 most items were a mixture of wool and cotton. They made several kinds of woolen blankets of various weights and designs, rugs of different sizes and designs, sleeveless jackets, belts, poncho-like garments, various kinds of cloth, woolen capes, ponchos, and sweaters. Different parts of the town tended to specialize in different kinds of articles (Nutini 1968:46).

If a household had less than five looms the operation was normally handled by the family, but most households with more than five had to hire help. Several households had over twenty looms, and some over thirty. The weavers themselves were the only full-time craftspersons, while the spool-makers, carders, skein-makers, and dyers—mostly women and children or, sometimes, old men—were part-time.

The Contecos delivered around 12,000 sarapes a week to the warehouses of Santa Ana Chiautempan, where the guidebooks commonly sent tourists for sarapes, and retailed another 3,000 in Contla itself or outside the through itinerant traders.

Santa Ana Chiautempan had a strangle-hold on the Contla weavers in 1961. The industry had become so large that the weavers had to depend on outside sources for their raw materials, and Chiautempan was the only place they were available. The Chiautempan middlemen paid the Contecos enough for their products to give them a small profit and wholesaled them for slightly less than they paid the Contecos. But they made their money by charging the Contecos 30 percent more than the open market cost for wool, cotton, dyes and the other raw materials needed to manufacture sarapes. Moreover, the middlemen of Chiautempan paid with a combination of cash and raw materials rather than cash alone, preventing the weavers from going elsewhere for what they needed. In this way they made the Contecos little more than their employees (Nutini 1968:49).

Though the Contecos complained bitterly and tried to secure other arrangements, the middlemen of Chiautempan defeated their efforts through a powerful lobby in the Tlaxcala state government and an ongoing campaign of defamation against the Contecos.

Social Organization and Relationships

The majority of Conteco families in 1961 were independent nuclear families, that is, the two generation family of a couple and their children. Still, a large portion were *patrilocal extended* units, consisting of a man and his wife, unmarried daughters, and married sons with their wives and children (Nutini 1968:176). About 56 percent of the households were occupied by independent nuclear families, while some 36 percent were occupied by extended families. Under patrilocal residence rules a couple lives with or near the groom's family, and when the couple have children the family extends to include three generations. Patrilocal residence and the resulting patrilocal extended families have long been characteristic of Mesoamerican Indian cultures.

There were also a few polygynous families in Contla and some other Mesoamerican communities, *polygyny* being the marriage of a man to more than one woman at the same time. *Polyandry*, the marriage of a woman to more than one man at the same time, is another form of *polygamy* (multiple spouses), but polyandrous families were not reported for Contla. Polygynous families may or may not be extended to a third generation.

Families and households do not always have the same membership, since members of the same family unit may occupy different households and some dwellings may be occupied by individuals or unrelated people. In 1961 some polygynous families in Contla formed a single household, while others were divided among two or more houses. Some men with two wives, for example, established two households, one for each wife. Nutini found that 160 of the 1,685 households were of this kind. Still other households were occupied only by a widow, widower, bachelor, or other single person.

Within a few years after an extended family came into existence each nuclear family had its own cooking facilities or kitchen and its own sleeping room. Frequently, each also had its own cuezcomate, or corn bin. Though the best room, occupied by the household head, contained the household family altar, the sleeping quarters for the constituent nuclear families usually had their own altars as well.

The Contecos observed a hierarchical principle in arranging extended family households, that is, the best quarters belonged to the household head, and the quality of the living quarters decreased in relation to the position of each nuclear family head within the extended family. The most recently arrived couple, of course, had the poorest facilities. Observance of this accepted principle did much to reduce the tension level within Contla extended families, which is quite in contrast with societies where several nuclear families sleep in the same quarters and there is no mechanism for reducing the interpersonal stress inherent in such situations. We find that people's performances in all societies fail to conform to all their ideals, and some Conteco household heads precipitated trouble by playing favorites and failing to adhere to the hierarchical principle.

It should also be apparent that maintaining a separate household for each wife in polygynous families helped reduce tension. In fact, this device has been used in other parts of the world, too.

Though the majority of Conteco households were occupied by independent nuclear families, it is also true that no Conteco went through life without having been a member of an extended family household (Nutini 1968:210). About a quarter of the Contecos spent their lives in extended families, and another 25 percent became members of extended families for the first time when their older brothers married and had children, turning what was an independent nuclear family into a three generation extended family. The other half of the people were born and raised in extended family households but separated from them a few years after marriage as nuclear components of extended families became independent households. So the extended family experience was virtually universal in Contla in spite of the prevalence of independent nuclear families.

Most of the young men marrying and bringing their wives into their parents' family looked forward to developing the economic independence to establish their own households. The main exception to this was the youngest son's expectation of remaining with his parents permanently and eventually inheriting the household and his father's remaining lands. Expectations of separating from the parents were reinforced by the wife's desire to escape domination by her in-laws and the tensions that went with it. A daughter-in-law resented the husband's mother and often quarreled with her. The household head, while sharing the expectation that his older sons would leave the family, tried to keep them with him as long as possible. When they finally separated, however, he assisted them economically and in other ways. The new independent nuclear family usually set up housekeeping adjacent to the father's compound, or at least not too far away, and the two continued to maintain relationships.

Other kinds of families developed as situations changed. For example, when the older pair was taken by death, if the sons and their families remained together, a *fraternal joint family* was formed. If or when the brothers had grandchildren the household was occupied by a family that was both extended and joint. In fact, some families could be extended, joint, and polygynous families at the same time.

Scholars have often characterized Mesoamerica as largely *bilateral* with regard to descent. By that they mean that most Mesoamerican cultures reckon people to be related to both parents and trace descent through both males and females. Modern American society is bilateral, each person regarding himself or herself as equally related to both the mother and father, and to trace ones ancestry a person counts both parents, all four grandparents, the eight great grandparents, and so on. *Unilineal descent* differs from bilateral reckoning in that only one person in each generation is counted in tracing ancestry, and that person is of the same sex in each generation.

Scholars recognize that some Mesoamerican tribes are unilineal, tracing descent *patrilineally* (through males only). Patrilineal descent produces common ancestor groups, known as either *lineages* or *clans*, in which members actually or putatively descended from the group's founder through males only, one in each generation for each person. Specialists have described patrilineal descent groups in a number of Mayan tribes and think a few non-Mayan groups, for example, some of the Tarascans or Totonac, have had them. Most have concluded that the ancient Aztec lacked unilineal groups, and they characterize the Nahua in general as bilateral. But the people of San Bernardino Contla were still reckoning group membership patrilineally in 1961, so there might be reason to consider the possibility that the same has been true of other Nahua groups. After all, the conquerors, missionaries, and colonists were from bilateral societies and unfamiliar with the concept of unilineal descent groups and might not have noticed them. Moreover, there have been few careful studies of the social organization of Nahua communities by modern anthropologists, and evidence for unilineal groups might have been overlooked in some.

When Nutini was there in 1961 patrilineal descent ordered Contla social life more than anything else (Nutini 1968:126). The Contecos had common ancestor descent groups usually referred to by anthropologists as clans and lineages. The clans were the genealogically deepest groups, the lineages being subdivisions of the clans. In observance of the patrilineal descent rule, all children, both boys and girls, became members of the father's lineage and clan at their birth, the boys for life and the girls until they married.

The clans and lineages of Contla were not purely *consanguineal*. That is, they were not limited to people who were supposedly genetically related to one another. This was because husband and wife were not so related, though they belonged to the same descent group.

Some societies, but not Contla, have purely consanguineal common ancestor groups. All remain in the group into which they were born for life, no matter who they marry or where they take up residence. The members of these purely consanguineal groups are inevitably scattered residentially rather than residing together. The clans and lineages of Contla resulted from a compromise between the descent rule and the residence rule, both of them coming into play in determining the group membership of the women. In fact, Murdock, a leading specialist in kinship studies, referred to this type of group as the *compromise kin group* (Murdock 1949:66).

To focus on the composition of the Contla descent group, each consisted of a core of males and unmarried females who belonged together because they were supposed to have descended from the same ancestor through males only and, in addition, women who had joined the group by marrying one of its male members. It was both a descent group and a residential unit, since both patrilineal and patrilocal rules defined its membership.

The lineages were consistently exogamous common ancestor groups, *exogamy* meaning that each person had to marry someone from a different group. Accordingly, future Conteco spouses belonged to different lineages before they married, at which time the woman took her husband's lineage name and thereby changed lineages. The people defined lineage membership by surname (family name or, in Spanish, *apellido*) and barrio membership, which means that all the people with the same surname who lived in the same barrio were members of the same lineage. There were lineages in different barrios which had the same surname, but they were unrelated because they belonged to different barrios.

Conteco lineages varied in size from seven people up to two or three hundred. Those in a small lineage had no difficulty tracing their relationships to one another and back to the common ancestor that founded it, the founder having lived no more than four or five generations earlier (Nutini 1968:134). Those in the largest lineages had more difficulty tracing their genealogies, since the lineage founder had lived at least eight generations earlier and, in some cases, more than ten. Some of the members were unable to trace their ancestry to the founder, but there were several knowledgeable older men in each large lineage who were familiar with the crucial genealogical links. In some societies the people are intensely interested in the details of their ancestry, but this was relatively unimportant to the Contecos.

Most of the small Conteco lineages were completely localized in the sense that the members lived together in a small territory known as a paraje. A *paraje* was a small area, variable in size, known by a surname or name referring to its topographical or other physical characteristics. Most of the members of some the larger lineages lived in the same paraje, while a minority of them, say 25 to 35 percent, lived in up to three other parajes found in other parts of the settlement. In still other lineages less than half the members lived in the same paraje, the rest being dispersed among several others. Even when the majority of a lineage's members were scattered through other parajes, the paraje containing the largest single block of the lineage's members, in all but a few cases, was identified with the lineage and carried its name.

Anthropologists have found that the two most widespread functions of unilineal descent groups are the regulation of marriage through exogamy and mutual aid. Contla lineages conformed well with this generalization. Economically, members of the same lineage helped one another in cases of financial crisis. This included a custom called *ayuda*, a donation of cash or something else to an individual or family to help them meet economic, religious or other obligations, with no expectation of direct return. Ayuda was volunteered rather than given in response to a request. Lineage members also exchanged labor and participated and helped in various ways at marriage, sickness, death, and other life crisis situations. They also cooperated on religious occasions such as processions, ceremonial banquets, and special masses, and members who held religious office were always supported by their lineage mates.

When Nutini scrutinized the functioning of Contla lineages he found that the larger ones did not function as units. He could discern subdivisions of these large lineages that carried out the functions just mentioned, though the people seemed unaware of them and thought of the lineage as a whole as the group that took care of its members needs.

One step below the lineage, Nutini found, were *lineage segments*, and *minimal lineages* functioned at an even more specific level. The minimal lineage was a group of closely related, patrilineally linked families, the founder living or having lived two to five generations earlier. The minimal lineage was like an extended or joint family, though the component families lived in separate households. One of the constituent households would be either a single extended family or an extended family plus nuclear family households. Purely economic functions such as labor exchange, borrowing economically important items, and asking for help in building a new house were taken care of largely within the minimal lineages. It was also within the minimal lineage that people usually aided one another and participated together in matters having to do with birth, baptism, confirmation, first communion, banquets for inaugurating a new house, holding relatively minor religious offices, and other occasions not requiring large outlays of money or materials or the participation of large numbers of people (Nutini 1968:151). The minimal lineage was the group that initiated lineage undertakings, even if they were carried out at a higher level.

The larger subdivision of the lineage, which Nutini calls the lineage segment, extended from three to eight generations back and exercised social, religious, ritual, and economic functions not easily handled by some minimal lineages. A large minimal lineage in some cases was the equivalent of a lineage segment, but a number of lineage segments were made up of several minimal lineages--as many as nine, in fact. The households, which ranged from three to seventeen in number, lived close to one another--never more than a hundred yards apart (Nutini 1968:153). The lineage segment functioned especially in connection with marriage and death.

So the Contecos held the lineage name and membership in mind and thought of their mutual aid and cooperation as lineage doings even when the lineage segment or the minimal lineage actually carried them out. Their ideals about this did not correspond with their performance, a situation that exists to a significant degree in all cultures.

Since the anthropologist constructed the concepts of minimal lineages and lineage segments, it might be tempting to say he had imposed something that had no cultural reality. But all cultures include realities the people neither have labels for nor think about in the normal course of

events, and anthropologists or other qualified observers often detect and describe them. These unrecognized constructs are indispensable to adequately understand any culture, and, to the extent that the anthropologist has accurately grasped the realities, they can be communicated to members of the society and be recognized as valid. Nutini comments that the lineage segments and minimal lineages were not any less real or concrete than the lineage simply because the Contecos had no words for them (Nutini 1968:161n).

Anthropologists commonly think of lineages as unilineal common ancestor groups that span few enough generations for the living members to be able to remember the founder and trace their ancestry. The largest Contla lineages did not quite fit that definition, in spite of the fact that a few knowledgeable oldsters knew the genealogical links.

Anthropologists usually define clans as having such great genealogical depth, that is, going back so many generations, that the people are unable to trace their ancestry to the common ancestor but simply think of themselves as having a common ancestry. Like lineages, these groups of great genealogical depth tend to be exogamous, and a unilineal rule determines each newborn's membership. The commonest term for this type of unilineal group is clan. Some societies have lineages without clans, some have clans without lineages, and some have clans subdivided into lineages. The last, as noted earlier was the case in San Bernardino Contla.

In 1961 the people of Contla were divided into ten districts known as barrios. Four of the ten were divided into halves, each half functioning like an undivided barrio, so there were 14 of them functionally speaking.

Many Mesoamerican communities have barrios or territorial subdivisions, some only two and others several. They often tend to feel some degree of rivalry or hostility toward one another, they are often endogamous (preferring or requiring marriage within the barrio), and they often have their own chapel, fiestas, and other functions.

The barrios of Contla were different from those of most Mesoamerican places, because they were exogamous and patrilineal. They were clans. The people thought of themselves as related, but they could not trace their relationships to a common ancestor and, in fact, did not think of the barrio as a common ancestor group. Some societies have clans that are purely consanguineal (everybody supposedly being genetically related to everyone else in the clan), which means that both men and women normally remain members of the clan into which they were born for life, regardless of who they marry or where they come to reside. But the clans of Contla, like the lineages, were based on a compromise between descent and residence, so, as noted before, women changed clan membership to that of the husband when they married.

Until about 1920 the Contla clan-barrios were strictly exogamous, and several remained entirely or largely exogamous in 1961. But members of a few barrios had begun intermarrying in between 1920 and Nutini's time there, some of them rather extensively (Nutini 1968:112). As far as the municipio as a whole was concerned, and especially in the cabecera, this had not yet greatly affected the general clan structure.

The members of some of the barrios lived very much within the same territory, whereas the members of other barrios were scattered through several sections of the community. The people identified themselves as belonging to a particular clan-barrio by their lineage names, their surnames, since each clan had a fixed number of lineage names. Children, under the patrilineal rule, took the father's name, which defined both their lineage and barrio membership. A woman, under the patrilocal rule, took up residence with her husband's family when she married and took his lineage name. This cut her ties with her natal clan and made her a member of her husband's clan. By composition, then, the barrios or clans of Contla consisted of a large core of patrilineally related males, the unmarried offspring of those males, and the wives and children of the married clansmen.

In Contla the clan dealt with religious fiestas honoring saints, administration of communal lands, appointment of religious officials, disputes with other clans, settlement of internal disputes and litigations, organizations and arrangements having to do with Holy Week, and various related matters. The clans were the largest socio-religious units in Contla and the highest level at which the people dealt with social and religious matters. The component lineages handled matters that did not require the resources and authority of the clan.

Each clan was lead by the oldest male in the barrio, who automatically inherited the headmanship when the preceding headman died. From time to time the wealthiest, most influential members of the lineages in the clan-barrio met to discuss whatever economic and religious matters required attention. At least until about 1920 the clan headmen were the undisputed political leaders of the community, but they had lost that control to the political parties by 1961. Nevertheless, the Contecos handled the social, ceremonial, economic, and religious matters of most concern to them within the context of their clan, lineage, and family.

Many of the world's cultures include ritually established relationships between people considered unrelated to one another genetically which exhibit the closeness characteristic of many family and kinship relationships. Ritually established special friendships are a widespread type, as are relationships by adoption. These have been referred to as fictive or ritual kinship relations.

Indian and other communities of Mexico and Central and South America have long had a ritual kinship system known as the *compadrazgo*. Its essential feature is someone's ritual assumption of a godparent relationship to a person, object, or event, which establishes a social relationship between the godparent and someone else. The rites and ceremonies attending the establishment of the relationships and those that occur later symbolize and communicate a number of sentiments of culturally defined importance. The most frequently described compadrazgo relationships are established at a child's baptism, when the parents find someone to serve as their child's godparents. This sets up a set of relationships comprising those between godparents and children and parents and godparents. Nearly all Indian groups of Latin America also select godparents at marriage as well, though the baptismal godparents sometimes function at marriage instead of newly selected persons.

There are many other occasions for the appointment of godparents, some widespread and others of very limited distribution. Some are unique to a particular community or tribe. During the late 1960s and early 1970s, Hugo and Jean Nutini researched the compadrazgo institution in the Tlaxcalan Nahua community of Santa María Belén Azitzimititlán as it functioned within the rural areas of Tlaxcala (Nutini and Bell 1980:3). They found 31 kinds of *compadrazgo* (godparent-coparent relationships) in Belén, 12 of which were present in Contla and the rest of the Tlaxcalan area they studied. In addition, Contla shared with Belén 12 more kinds of compadrazgo which were not universal in the area studied (Nutini and White 1977:372). All of the rural Tlaxcalans established compadrazgo relationships at baptism, marriage, confirmation, first communion, death, blessing an icon on a household altar, ritual cleansing, protection against temptation and mortal sin, new house blessing, protective cross blessing, house construction blessing, and twin fruit or vegetable finding. The other occasions at Contla included the return of an image of the child Jesus to its permanent household altar after certain ceremonies, school graduations, a girl's fifteenth birthday, taking a mother to a Mass 40 days after she gave birth to a child, presenting a child in church at age three, blessing a church repair or improvement project, first use of a newly purchased car or truck, establishment of a special friendship, silver wedding anniversary, first pair of earrings for a baby girl, acquisition of a new possession, and acquisition of a new pitcher or friends drinking pulque out of a new gourd cup.

Space allows only a few remarks about these. It may be obvious that some were very important occasions, while others were far less significant. A number of them were rather new, whereas some were rooted in colonial or preConquest times. Both points illustrate that the people fairly readily applied the compadrazgo concept to situations thought to have special significance.

It may also be apparent that a given individual might accumulate a large number of compadres of various kinds. Some of the relationships were vital until death, while others were limited to a few years or tended to grow cold.

Baptism ceremonies were expensive in Contla, so few parents had their infants baptized before six months from birth. Usually, it was not done until after one year of age (Nutini 1968:90). Members of the minimal lineage assisted the parents at this time. In Belén the father contacted a couple and arranged for them to sponsor his child at its baptism. The sponsors then became the child's *padrino* (godfather) and *padrina* (godmother), and the child their *ahijado* (godson) or *ahijada* (goddaughter). The parents and godparents would address one another as *compadre* (cofather) and *comadre* (comother). These terms and the triadic relationship indicated applied even when houses or other objects were involved. For example, when godparents of a house to be blessed were selected, the house was the godchild.

By agreeing to sponsor a child padrinos assumed a series of obligations. In Belén the first economic exchange occurred when the parents ceremonially requested the padrinos to serve. For the baptism they had to buy baptismal clothing for the godchild; pay the priest; and give some money to children present in the church atrium, to each adult guest and household member, and to the child's mother (Nutini and Bell 1980:63-4). The parents gave a banquet after the baptism and presented their coparents with a basket of food and either a large turkey or some chickens. After these and other immediate obligations were met, the parents and godparents maintained other economic obligations that endured until death. It was the continuing obligation of the godparents to clothe and feed the godchild if the parents were unable to, pay the godchild's medical expenses, provide a meal for a godson and his bride the day before the wedding, take care of several matters should the child die before reaching twelve years of age, and take the godchild into their home should the parents die during his or her childhood. The godchildren had no clearly stated economic obligations, but they performed various services at marriage banquets and other occasions in their godparents' life cycle and ceremonial observances.

The parents and godparents ceremonially agreed to trust one another at all times, which implied a set of economic obligations and behavior patterns. In Belén this meant that they were free to ask each other for a variety of favors, such as help in finding day laborers, substituting for them in meeting the obligation to serve as communal laborers, giving economic help at the marriage of one's children or in case of sickness or death, and labor and other kinds of exchanges.

When a Belén family decided to build a new house they petitioned someone to be padrino for the occasion of laying the first foundation stones. There was a sequence of rites and ceremonies involving the exchange and consumption of food and liquor, the firing of rockets, circuits around the traced house foundations, laying of the first stones, a rosary, and exchange of speeches (Nutini and Bell 1980:180). After the group left, either a weatherman-rainmaker or a sorcerer arrived and conducted pagan rites petitioning the supernatural owners of the hill of Cuatlapanga and La Malintzi volcano to protect the house, see that it was successfully completed, and provide its occupants with a pleasant life there.

The people of Belén might have protective crosses set up for a variety of structures or objects, such as a cultivated field, an orchard, a first haystack, a new well, and a number of others. For some things they had a cross put up at least every three years, and in these cases the compadrazgo relationship lasted for only three years rather than for a lifetime. The ethnographers have provided descriptions of these and other compadrazgo complexes at Belén amounting to

some 130 pages, and even they are incomplete. These sketchy references may be enough to convey the extent and complexity of the institution in some Mesoamerican communities.

The Contecos made much less of the compadrazgo than Belén and many other Mesoamerican societies. The reason was that their patrilineal lineages took care of many of the needs provided by the compadrazgo in other places. Though they had 24 of the 31 compadrazgo types found in rural Tlaxcala, they remained less important. The people went through the ceremonies establishing the relationships, and the relationships continued, but they served basically to express and reinforce the sacred ideology and world view of the people rather than providing economic, social, and religious support for individuals and families confronting life situations. In the absence of kinship groups or other institutions providing such support, the people of Belén relied more on the compadrazgo arrangements. Contecos involved in compadrazgo relationships continued to address one another by the appropriate terms and to respect and trust one another, but little more in most instances.

A pregnant Contla Nahua women went about her affairs as usual until about a month or so before childbirth, when she began to avoid heavy work that required stooping. She continued sexual relations with her husband, however. The husband, by contrast, had difficulty during his wife's pregnancy. He was restless, belligerent, and got sick easily for about the first six months of her first pregnancy. Later pregnancies became easier, and his trouble lasted only a month or month and a half when he had his fourth child (Nutini 1968:89). This kind of thing has been found in other Mesoamerican communities and seems to reflect a tendency in many societies for husbands to be affected by the wife's pregnancies. In parts of South America this reaches its fullest development in the form of the *couvade*, which involves the husband going to bed, experiencing birth pains, and having to recover from childbirth.

Most women of Contla arranged for a traditional midwife to attend them at birth time, though well under a third of the births were attended by one of the two certified midwives. A traditional midwife would give the mother a preparation of boiled *zoapatl* leaves and forcefully massage her stomach. The mother usually clung to a rope or embraced a ladder during birth, with her body at about a 60 degree angle. After the baby had been born she cut the umbilical cord and gave the placenta to the husband so it could be burned under the ashes of the temazcal (steam bath) hearth or buried by the husband and members of his extended family and lineage. The mother remained in bed for three days, and then two women, ordinarily her husband's mother and another woman in the household, carried her each day for eight days for a sweat bath in the temazcal. They anointed her with sweet pulque to make the bath "take hold" and, as the steam poured in, rubbed her vigorously with *capulin* (a tree) branches to drive away evil spirits. After the eight days of baths she was up and around again, avoiding only making tortillas and washing clothes for another month or more. Contla spouses were said to resume sexual relations five or six months after the birth. The popular notion that women in small-scale societies normally return to their work immediately after childbirth is false, and the length of the recovery period varies considerably from culture to culture.

The Contecos had their children baptized when they were ready to undertake the heavy expenses required, which was frequently not until the child was over a year old. Two weeks after baptism the baptismal godfather took the child to church for a blessing by the priest. Children took their first communion between nine and twelve and were confirmed a year or two later. All these occasions required the participation of godparents, which resulted in new compadrazgo relationships.

During the first three years of life the mother and other women of her extended family watched over the children carefully but intentionally taught them nothing and gave them no work. They were considered babies. A mother usually nursed her child for at least 16 to 18 months, though the time could extend to two or three years if she did not have another baby. The Contecos did almost nothing to train small children and disciplined them little, and the father seldom involved himself during this time.

Beginning about age five the adults would send boys on various errands and had girls helping with small tasks around the house. Girls could not go out alone until they reached seven or eight. Before 1945 there were only 150 children in school in all of Contla, but after that all started to school at age seven. In 1961 the people of the cabecera and the town of Xaltipac sent their children to school willingly, while those in the Monte, the more remote, higher areas of the municipio, tended to be opposed to schooling. In 1961 less than five percent of the students finished the sixth grade.

Around eight the boys began to help with the farming and the girls with household tasks, and both helped their mothers make spools and skeins of yarn. Their parents gave them allowances for this work but carefully controlled what the children did with the money. By thirteen or fourteen boys began to operate looms full-time, and girls of fourteen often ran the household in the absence of the mother. In the Monte (outside of the cabecera and the town of Xaltipac) the boys worked in the fields, gathered agave juice, and herded goats and sheep.

The adults gave the boys considerable freedom of movement, but they exercised considerable control over the young women. The families watched the girls so closely not so much to maintain their virginity as to keep them with them as long as possible. Under patrilocal residence practice girls were lost to their families when they married, visits in their former homes every couple weeks or so being all the contact they had with their natal families.

The young people courted one anothers attentions aggressively, while their elders tried to prevent them from seeing one another. There was a fair amount of premarital sexual activity, especially on the part of the young men, but both unmarried men and women were open about their de-

sire to marry for sexual reasons (Nutini 1968:250). Men usually married when they were 23 or 24 years old, and by that time most of them had experienced many sexual encounters, mainly with married women but also with unmarried young women. Mesoamerican Indians have generally been strict about premarital sex, and the large amount of recognized extramarital sexual activity among members of the same community that characterized Contla is not typical of the Mesoamerican culture area.

A man also thought about the need to establish a family and prepare to participate in religious and ceremonial life, and a woman was commonly impatient to escape the authority of her family. Most young women married between the ages of sixteen and twenty-two.

In 1961 romantic interests in marriage were becoming more important and parents were having less to say than before about who their children married. Occasionally, a young man who felt a girl had spurned him or whose engaged or betrothed sweetheart got involved with another man would retaliate by abducting her. The Contla Nahua both condemned such abductors and their families and felt sympathy for them. An abductor's purpose was to dishonor the woman by cohabiting with her for two or three days, and he usually had no intention of marrying her. He would have two or three close friends help him kidnap her and take her to the open country, after which she and her abductor remained alone. After sexual intercourse they usually spent two or three days together in a nearby town, or, if the man had enough money, even in Puebla or Mexico City. After a few days the man sent the woman to Contla, and he stayed away for a time for things to cool off. The parties almost never agreed to live together, and the young man's family usually had to pay the girl's family a stiff fine. Usually the *presidente municipal* (the governmental head of the municipio) arbitrated such cases.

Couples wishing to marry had to take many kinds of secretive and deceptive measures to see one another. A young man often first approached a woman that interested him through one of her sisters-in-law or an unmarried female cousin. Once she accepted him as a sweetheart, they could cooperate with one another and enlist the cooperation of siblings and friends in getting together. They usually saw one another at night, commonly in the milpa (corn field) behind the woman's house. When parents, usually the mother, discovered their meetings, they urged the young man to tell his parents so the ceremonies leading to marriage could begin.

The first event was engagement, which the girl's and boy's households were supposed to arrange at the instigation of the young man's father and lineage mates. The man's kin took gifts of liquor, bread, a candle, and flowers to the woman's household, where a series of speeches on both sides, eating, and other ritual events eventuated in agreement that the sweethearts were engaged. After that the young women's parents relaxed their vigilance, the young man often ate with her family, and the two almost invariably had sexual relations.

Two or more months after the engagement, when the families had accumulated enough money for the wedding expenses. The couple became formally betrothed. Many people attended the betrothal ceremonies, which involved a great deal of food exchange, speeches, a blessing on the couple, a banquet, and drunkenness. Even to outline the specific, well-defined rites and procedures of betrothal and marriage ceremonies requires several pages of print. They involved the families and lineages of both parties over a period of weeks. The selection and petitioning of the marriage godparents was a major component of the proceedings in itself, involving the usual candles, liquor, food, flowers, speeches, gift-exchange, and other elements. There were ceremonies connected with weekly announcements of the marriage by the priest, the registration of the marriage with the municipal government, a ceremony involving the godparents of baptism and confirmation, and ritual connected with the preparations that began in both households a couple of days before the wedding itself. The two wedding days included a wedding banquet, orchestras playing, long speeches, drinking, dancing, predictable jokes, a breakfast, the drinking of mole, fireworks, the putting on of garlands, conventionalized exhortations, and, sometimes, Catholic rites. All was concluded with a ceremonial handing over of the bride—her delivery to the boy's household by the girl's family.

The course to marriage was not always so smooth and conventional, though probably over half of the marriages were of this standard type. Sometimes antagonism between the families complicated things, and other times one or both families were unable to afford to pay for the wedding. Enmity between families was common, and couples sometimes eloped under such circumstances. Couples also eloped with the approval of their families when they were unable to pay for a traditional wedding. In such cases the couple began their marriage and had children without a formal betrothal and wedding, though they tried to marry formally as soon as possible, which was sometimes several years later.

Married couples often developed genuinely satisfying partnerships, but not without difficulty. The Contla Nahua put considerable emphasis on a man's right to sexual experience, and this manifested itself in the husband's right to have extramarital sexual encounters. The wife was supposed to remain faithful, and admonitions to this effect were part of the wedding ceremonies. Moreover, a young woman who had chafed under the heavy hand of her parents soon realized fully what she had already known inside, that the hand of her mother-in-law was heavier than her mother's. A young wife quickly became disillusioned and found the expectation of sexual faithfulness while her husband philandered an unbearable burden. Most eventually yielded to the idea that they should have the same prerogatives as their husbands and had sexual affairs outside the marriage tie. Women commonly had their first affair shortly after the first child was born, though some committed adultery before that. Their first extramarital relations were usually with young members of the lineage segment, both married and unmarried. A husband was upset by his wife's adultery when he learned about it, and most husbands beat their wives and asked them not to do it again or, at least, to be more careful so that no one would learn about it. Eventually, most husbands and wives accommodated themselves to a lifelong pattern of marital infidelity on the part of both. Contla wives gave three reasons for committing adultery--enjoyment, making money, and dissatisfaction with their husbands.

The divorce rate was high in Contla, not specifically because of unfaithfulness but because of the difficulty a woman had living with her mother-in-law and the household head. The Contecos held that a couple would stay together permanently if they could get through the first seven or eight years, and nearly all divorces took place during those years (Nutini 1968:292).

A Contla Nahua man began to participate in the community political and religious life as soon as he married, usually as a messenger of the local police or as a junior member of a religious committee. Three or four years later he might serve in one of several relatively unimportant religious positions. The Contecos considered men to be young people until they reached thirty. By this time most of them had acquired lifetime occupational involvements and were relatively secure economically, and most were ready to hold more important offices. The women were classified as young people until about age twenty-five.

From the beginning of their maturity until about age fifty-five, Contecos considered both men and women mature persons. It was the period of a man's deepest involvement in religious, social and political matters, since he had the necessary experience and wealth. The women helped their husbands and other male family and lineage members by preparing banquets, refreshments, and religious meetings as well as serving as incense bearers, candle bearers, and the like in religious processions.

Contecos became ill mainly because of bad air or evil wind, a fright, the evil eye, and damaging proportions of hot and cold foods and conditions. They associated evil air (*mal aire*) with death, humors released by dead bodies, and certain animals such as coyotes or snakes. They were most apt to get sick when they thought about the dead too much, and weak-spirited people were most susceptible. Speaking of another Nahua region, Madsen indicated that bad air could come from rain dwarf spirits living in caves and other damp or wet places, the ghosts of people who died violently, loose women and whores, and violation of the hot-cold principle (Madsen 1969:630).

People became ill from becoming too hot or too cold when they ate too much hot food without compensating proportions of cold food to neutralize it and vice versa, or, for example, when their bodies were overheated, and they took hot foods or medicines instead of cold to counteract it. Mesoamerican and many other Latin American communities classified various foods and substances as hot, cold, or temperate, and they were categorized in terms of their effects on the body more than their actual temperature. The

Nahua of San Francisco Tecospa, not far from Mexico City, considered ice, frost, snow, and sherbet to be hot (Madsen 1960:162). People tried to avoid illness by maintaining a temperate state and, if they got too hot or too cold, taking whatever would restore the balance.

A fright was a psychological disturbance characterized by a sudden nightmare lasting 10 or 20 minutes. It could cause unconsciousness, and after one came to, it took an hour or two to get back to normal. A more severe type of fright left a person unconscious for several hours, and attacks might recur for several days.

The Contecos held that some people had very sharp eyes and could destroy or disturb objects and people they especially admired just by looking at them. They thought children were especially susceptible to evil eye (mal ojo). When afflicted their eyes drooped, their cheeks became red, and they cried all the time.

The Contecos suffered from a number of other diseases as well, many of them at least partly supernatural in origin, and they also recognized illnesses known to Western medicine and might consult physicians about them. In 1961, however, most continued to be concerned about the traditional diseases and consulted herbalists, bone setters, or sorcerers for healing. The herbalists, known as curanderos, used mostly herbs and flowers. The bone setters treated broken bones, bone deformations, and unnatural protuberances through massage, applying pressure at certain points, herbal applications, and compresses (Nutini 1968:92). They appeared to be especially successful, and the people trusted and respected them. Neither the herbalists nor the bone setters possessed any special supernatural abilities, but the sorcerers did. They could both cure and cause sickness, and the people feared them so much they went to them for healing only when the case was serious and they had tried every other kind of practitioner. People also retained the services of sorcerers to make their enemies sick or to kill them. In 1961 Contla had ten herbalists, three bone setters, and eleven known sorcerers. All of these practitioners charged for their services.

When peoples' children had grown up and married, usually when the parents were sixty to sixty-five years of age, the Contla Nahua considered them old. Their involvement in public life declined, though they exercised new influence in baptisms, betrothals, burials, and similar social functions. Most were supported during these years by their children and grandchildren, though a few were economically independent, and some without family joined a lineage mate's household.

The Contla Nahua dressed the dead in their best clothes and buried them within 48 hours. They placed the body in a coffin on a table in the house and held either a one or two night wake, depending on the hour of death. They had a plate at the foot of the coffin where guests, mostly lineage and barrio members and friends and neighbors, left contributions. A band or orchestra played for several hours during the wake, using funeral music for adults and festive music for children. Children's funerals were supposed to be joyous occasions, since the Contecos and other Mesoameri-

cans held that they became little angels and went directly to heaven. After the burial the mourners returned to the house for a banquet. The oldest member of the lineage spread a bucketful of earth from the yard under the table that had held the coffin and placed five stones on it in a cross-like arrangement, and the women placed candle holders and flower pots around it. For eight days they performed a rosary there, with the lineage mates of the deceased and neighbors in attendance. On the fifth day they selected a godfather for the setting up of the cross, and on the eighth day the godfather brought a wooden cross to the house, placed it on the five stones, and conducted a rosary in the presence of the usual guests. They then took the cross and the earth and stones in a bucket to the cemetery, with a band playing during the procession. At the cemetery they placed the earth and the stones on the grave and set up the cross at the foot. Finally, they returned to the house for another banquet, and the godfather received a basket of food for his services. The Contecos were outwardly calm and accepting during funeral observances, though the closest relatives might cry out and lament while the body was lowered into the grave.

Government and Social Order

There are 42 municipios in the Mexican state of Tlaxcala, divided among districts. San Bernardino Contla belongs to the district of Hidalgo, which has its seat in the city of Apizaco some 15 miles away. The name of the municipio was changed to Juan Cuamatzi in 1936, but it continued to be known to most by its former name. There were six settlements in the municipio, with the administrative seat and two thirds of the population being in San Bernardino Contla. For administrative purposes the municipio was divided into nine sections, with each having a representative (regidor) on the municipal council. Five of the sections were in the town of Contla. Three of the sections lay in the higher elevations of the municipio, closer to the volcano than the rest, and were occupied by the poorer and generally more conservative people. Nutini refers to them as the people of the Monte and the rest, who live in the cabecera and one other town, as the people of the Centro (Nutini 1968:33).

The government followed the standard Mexican pattern. The municipal head was the presidente, and the other officials included nine councilmen (regidores), and secretary (secretario), a treasurer (tesorero) a municipal judge (juez menor), and an attorney general (agente del ministerio publico). Also, each locality outside the cabecera had two officials responsible to the presidente--a municipal agent and a judge. All except the secretary and the treasurer, which were appointed by the presidente with the concurrence of the other elected officials, were elected to three year terms by popular vote. The presidente coordinated the municipal government, and each regidor had his special responsibilities, such as road upkeep, sanitation, the schools, and so on.

The attorney general represented the Mexican government and was directly responsible to his counterpart in the city of Tlaxcala. Projects such as road construction, bridge repairs, and the like were taken care of by communal labor, an institution known as the *faena*. The faena was usually arranged by one of the councilmen having that responsibility, though the municipal representatives selected the workers and made sure that the work was fairly shared among the men of their settlements. There was also a police force, including a chief, subchief and four policeman. They were supposed to patrol the streets at night, help people who asked for it, and generally keep order.

In many other Mesoamerican communities the municipal government is controlled by prominent old men, known as *principales*, who have gained their positions of influence by occupying a series of increasingly important positions in the hierarchy of community political and religious offices. But the principales of Contla, who were the clan headmen, lost control over the municipal government well before 1961. They were displaced in large part by the Obreros, a political party composed of textile factory workers employed in the cities of Tlaxcala and Puebla. Between 1955 and 1960 another party known as the Campesinos was challenging the Obreros for power. These were primarily the loom owners and loom operators of Contla. The Campesinos outnumbered the Obreros and were more conservative.

Actually, however, the municipal government had little to do with the average Conteco's life in 1961 or for decades before. It was no longer directly articulated with the family, lineage, and clan system, and the major political functions of the community of significance to the Contla Nahua were handled within the descent group and family context. Every three years the people went through the motions of electing municipal government candidates selected by outsiders, but aside from that conformity to state law, they did not participate. They considered the government a largely useless imposition by outside authorities and mostly ignored it. They had to obtain death and marriage certificates from the municipal officials and had to register their marriages with them if they wanted them to be state approved. The municipal officials also handled various other matters of state or national concern. Beyond these and a few other minor activities the government was not involved in anything the people cared about much.

There was very little crime in Contla, and people solved most of their disputes within their clan barrios, lineages, and families. Thefts, fights, and drunkenness were especially rare, but rape and spouse desertion were common. The Contecos considered rape and desertion minor crimes, however, and the two families involved tried to settle such cases on their own. If they failed they asked the clan headman to arbitrate. Only rarely did such cases reach the judge or the presidente. The police were not needed in Contla, and they only ran errands for the municipal officials.

Art and Play

The designs worked into the loom woven textiles were undoubtedly the most highly developed Conteco art, but no full account of these has been published. Speechmaking, which was so important in Contla religious ceremonies, was also an important art. Pastimes consisted in large part of participation in the extensive round of ceremonies.

Religious Beliefs and Practices

Like the religions of Mesoamerica in general, Contla Nahua religion in 1961 was a syncretism of pagan and Roman Catholic elements. The people regarded San Bernardino, Contla's patron saint, as the most important supernatural being. According to their legends, San Bernardino gave them their lands in ancient times. They conceived of him as alive, sometimes appearing as a tall, light-haired boy. He protected them, guarded their communal lands, and cared for them in trouble. The many legends about him depicted him as fighting side by side with the Contecos in their clashes with nearby municipios and defending particular individuals against exploitation and injustice inflicted by people of Tlaxcala and Chiautempan. He was a kind of overseer of the world and life, looking after the community welfare and alert to individual needs and requests. Apparently his name in pre-Conquest Tlaxcala was Camaxtli, a tribal and tutelary god to whom a great temple in Contla was dedicated. This illustrates the common syncretic phenomenon by which pre-Catholic deities assumed the names of the Roman Catholic saints, often with the encouragement and approval of the missionaries of early colonial times (Nutini 1968:78n).

The Contecos venerated several other saints as well. The saints, Jesus Christ, and the Virgin were deities who protected the people and granted favors in times of trouble if propitiated in the proper ways. This was the justification for the elaborate system of religious fiestas occupying so much of the Contecos' concern and time. There were four important religious officials known as *mayordomos*, each in charge of seeing that one of the four most venerated saints, including San Bernardino, was honored by a fiesta and that an elaborate complex of administrative, economic and ceremonial functions connected with the saint's stewardship was organized and properly carried into effect. In Contla these mayordomos made up the cofradía, a term which is reserved in other Mesoamerican places for the religious brotherhoods that assume responsibility for stewardship of a saint. The four cofradía mayordomos were responsible to a group of *fiscales*, the first fiscal being the highest religious authority in Contla. Each week the fiscales collected alms throughout the municipio, had charge of and led all religious processions, made sure the local priest did his work properly, and handled many other religious matters as well. The fiscales were the most powerful body in Contla's folk religious life. Most of the fiscales were over fifty-five years of age, and they were highly respected.

There were many other religious occasions to be taken care of besides those of the four main supernaturals. Some of the responsibilities were rotated among the ten barrios, each of which had its own mayordomos and other religious officials to sponsor the observances. Still others were sponsored by individuals in any part of the municipio, regardless of their clan-barrio membership, and the people of a given settlement, section, or paraje worked with a mayordomo to carry out the observances. In 1961 there were 186 saints for which fiesta organizations of one kind or another had to carry out a set of rites and ceremonies.

The Contecos had little interest in the Roman Catholic religion. They seldom attended Mass or other church functions, going in large numbers only during Holy Week, at Christmas, on All Saints Day and similar special functions they were interested in. Neither did they join the three Catholic associations sponsored by the priest, the less than 40 involved being people who had lived somewhere else for a long time or who had traveled a lot. To ensure that the priest would not interfere with their religious affairs the Indians made sure he was well taken care of economically through fees for marriages, funerals, baptisms, Holy Week celebrations, and other functions he was involved in, and they provided him with ornaments, candles, wine, wood, and all the other things he needed in the church. In 1961 the priest at Contla owned a station wagon and a jeep, unusual possessions for priests in village Mexico. On four occasions the religious council of Contla managed to get uncooperative and meddlesome priests dismissed.

In addition to their folk Catholicism the Contecos maintained a number of pagan religious beliefs. La Malintzi, the owner of the volcano of that name, was a fairly important supernatural. She was a woman who lived in a luxurious house inside the mountain. She, like San Bernardino, was a protector of Contla. She helped people financially, corrected them when they had gone astray, and helped them when they had been treated unjustly. They did not pray to her as they did to San Bernardino. Rather, she simply helped people as she wished. She damaged people only if they provoked her. The Contecos talked about her often.

El Cuatlapanga was the master of a big hill on the volcano's western slopes. He was easily provoked and did nothing good for the people unless he was properly propitiated. He could send rain, hail, or wind storms and destroy people's crops, and the Contecos were afraid of him. Functionaries called weathermen got most of their power to make rain and influence the weather in other ways from El Cuatlapanga, and most of their rituals were for the purpose of keeping him happy.

A number of Contecos possessed supernatural power, the weathermen being among them. The sorcerers and female witches were others. Contla Nahua culture included a complex system of rituals and ceremonies built around the activities of such persons. The Contecos also shared in the belief in *naguales,* people able to transform themselves into an animal, such as a donkey, turkey, or coyote, and play tricks on people. They were also concerned with the spirits of the dead, who returned to visit their families on All Saints' Day and who, if the person had died violently or in other undesired ways, might bother the living. In addition, they recognized a number of other kinds of spirits and apparitions, some of which made people ill by frightening them.

The Contecos believed in a variety of kinds of enchanted or sacred places where one might meet with an apparition or suffer a physical disturbance by going too near them. There were many such places in the municipio. The people had many kinds of sacred objects, such as stone images, red stones, and herbs that had special powers. They could use some of them to cure certain diseases or to cause someone to sicken or die, and some were effective for driving away the Devil and evil spirits. In their fields the Contecos performed various rituals to propitiate weather spirits.

Cultural Change

While the Contecos adopted many of the material items of Mexican national culture, more than in many other Mesoamerican places, they remained among the most conservative in the social, political, and religious aspects of their lives. Nutini and Isaac (1974) have characterized the 200 communities in the 42 municipios of Tlaxcala as Indian-traditional, Indian-transitional, Transitional-Mestizo, and Mestizo-secularized. Twelve percent were Indian traditional and 35 percent Indian-transitional, and Contla fell in the first category in some aspects of their lives and the second in others.

The Nahua of rural Tlaxcala were modernizing rapidly by 1980, that is, they were rather quickly adopting the material culture and economic life of the modern world. At the same time many communities throughout Tlaxcala maintained their traditional ideological and socio-poltical commitments and the associated institutions, such as the mayordomía system, politico-religous governmental mechanisms, the compadrazgo system, and kinship as a significant element in social control and other aspects of life (Nutini and Bell 1980:368).

Researchers have taken note of this phenomenon in cultures in all parts of the world. When we see people living in modern homes, driving cars, farming with modern equipment, and taking advantage of a wide range of other modern economic and material opportunities, we are apt to assume the old culture is gone. Commonly, as in many communities of rural Tlaxcala, the basic structure of the group's personalities and their social and ideological commitments are much as they have been for long periods of time.

Chapter 13

THE IXTEPEJI ZAPOTEC OF OAXACA

When someone mentions ancient civilizations of Mexico and Central America, most think of the Aztec and the Maya, but the Aztec were not around to help develop the civilization and did not arrive in the Valley of Mexico until sometime during Post-Classic times, perhaps around the twelfth century A.D. The Maya, of course, go back to ancient times, but so do a number of other major Mesoamerican groups, including the Zapotec (approx. SAH-poh-tehk; Zapotecos in Spanish) people now found in much of the state of Oaxaca (approx. wah-HAH-kah). The Aztec gained power rapidly in Mesoamerica and, by the time the Spanish arrived, dominated the Zapotec and many other major groups. The Zapotec were not part of the Aztec empire, but the Aztec defeated them militarily at times, collected tribute from them, and had to put down occasional Zapotec rebellions.

The Zapotec are scattered over a wide area and may number over 475,000. They occupy a variety of habitats, including coastal and Tehuantepec Isthmus lowlands, tropical valleys, and high mountain regions. People commonly refer to Valley, Isthmus, and Mountain Zapotec. But they are more linguistically and culturally diverse than this three fold division indicates, and scholars have yet to study that diversity comprehensively. The Zapotec are bound together mainly by the occupation of contiguous geographical areas, the similarities among the various Oto-Manguean languages and dialects they speak, and the common name Zapotec. This unity clearly indicates a common origin, but in the interest of accuracy we must remember the diversity.

The valley habitat of the Zapotec is found in the center of the state of Oaxaca where three large valleys merge with one another in the area where the capitol city of Oaxaca is located. The city of Oaxaca Juárez lies approximately 350 miles to the east and south of Mexico City. One of the three arms of the Oaxaca Valley extends northwestward, another to the south, and the third to the southeast. This valley region is surrounded by mountains, most notably a massive portion of the Sierra Madre Oriental to the north. It is in this region, not too far from the valley, that the town of Ixtepeji (approx. eeks-teh-PEH-hee) is found. A third area is an extensive flat region on the Pacific side of the Isthmus of Tehauntepec. The fourth region is mountain country lying to the south of the valley portion.

There is considerable dialectical variation among Zapotec groups, but beyond that there are several mutually unintelligible language divisions. Anthropologists and linguists have yet to get a full reading of the linguistic situation, but Laura Nader and Robert Weitlaner held in 1969 that there were at least nine different Zapotec languages (Nader 1969:331).

Anthropologists often have difficulty drawing the boundaries between one culture area and another, and they often find that one or more subgroups belonging to the same labeled cultural category may resemble a group from a different category more than some groups in the category to which they belong. The people of the northern Zapotec town of Choapan, for example, seem to resemble their Chinantec neighbors more than they do the Sierra Zapotec (Nader 1969:331).

In view of the cultural diversity of the Zapotec and the lack of comprehensive knowledge about it, it would be unwise to try to say much about what distinguishes the Zapotec as a whole from other Mesoamerican societies. But it is worth noting that outsiders subjectively regard them as different from other Indian groups. Many of them have impressed outsiders as being "intelligent, industrious, acquisitive, and progressive." (Starr 1901:50). Many of them have also impressed outsiders with their interest in business and trade, though, as Nader indicates, most Zapotec are basically subsistence farmers. These impressions, however, result from comparisons of Zapotec with various non-Zapotec groups experienced as being less industrious and progressive, and such experienced differences are most reasonably accounted for in this instance by assuming that they reflect actual variability, in spite of the problem of confirming or measuring it.

In 1970 and 1971 the Zapotec of the mountain town of Ixtepeji made their living primarily by growing corn and beans in mostly steep, badly eroded fields. A few other items were locally available to them, but the variety was limited and the diet rather poor. Many Zapotec communities enjoyed a significantly higher level of material well-being than the Ixtepejanos.

An Ixtepeji woman wore a long dress, an apron, and a shawl around her head or over her shoulders and went barefooted most of the time, while the men's costume differed little from that of other rural Mexican places. Most of the houses were rectangular structures of adobe blocks with single-pitched, clay-tiled roofs. About half the families built separate structures of lighter materials for their kitchens, usually against one wall of the house.

Kinship groups were unimportant to the Ixtepejanos, since they found it difficult to trust one another sufficiently for groups of relatives to interact productively with one another. The godparent-godchild system (*compadrazgo*) was quite important to them, apparently, in part, because the people felt most secure cooperating with people that knew them, but not intimately.

The *cargo* system of political and religious offices was important in Ixtepeji for the men, who began by accepting a minor office or cargo and working their way through more prestigious cargos during their lives. The *presidente* was the chief town official. Men were selected for office at town meetings, which were quite significant in community life.

The Ixtepejanos believed in God, Christ, saints, and a variety of kinds of spirits, especially spirits of the dead. Witchcraft and magic were also important parts of their religion. The people regarded the world of supernaturals and humans as threats to their personal well-being, saw themselves as being extensively afflicted by diseases caused by supernatural beings and hostile or envious relatives and acquaintances, and held that things were generally becoming worse all the time and would continue that way.

Prehistory

Archaeologists believe the Zapotec and a neighboring tribe important in Mesoamerica's history—the Mixtec—were once one people. They have found the question of when the groups diverged from one another and from other tribes troublesome, and they have turned for help to *glottochronology*, a technique developed by historical linguists. Glottochronology is a way of trying to determine when two related languages separated from one another. It is based on the assumption that vocabularies made up of certain kinds of words change at a constant rate and, more specifically, that vocabularies of words for certain very basic concepts, such as body parts and pronouns, change at the rate of 19 percent every thousand years (Gudschinsky 1964:613). By comparing the percentage of difference between two vocabularies the linguists attempt to calculate how long ago the two languages from which the vocabularies are drawn diverged from one other. Continued research has shown that these assumptions may not always hold true, and some reject glottochronology. Others feel it can be helpful when

used with caution and in conjunction with other evidence, and it has been applied to the question of linguistic evolution in Mesoamerica.

On the basis of both glottochronological and archaeological evidence, archaeologist Kent Flannery has concluded that groups sharing a language from which Zapotec and Mixtec were to evolve separated from one another some time between 4100 and 3700 B.C. At this time these were gathering-hunting groups without pottery but with incipient agriculture (see page 188). Finally, between 400 B.C. and A.D. 100, the Zapotec and Chinantec languages, until then indistinguishable, separated. Since then further divergence has occurred within Zapotec (Flannery 1983:7).

About 500 B.C. the people of the Valley of Oaxaca built what is now one of the most famous, most studied archaeological sites in Mesoamerica. On top of a mountain rising some 1,300 feet above the valley floor and situated in the large area where the three branches of the valley converged, so that the inhabitants could look into all three, a number of Zapotec groups apparently combined forces to build a ceremonial-political center. The site is known as Monte Albán (approx. MOHN-teh ahl-BAHN), and it dominated the valley of Oaxaca for over a thousand years (Flannery and Marcus 1983:74). From its beginning Monte Albán was the Valley of Oaxaca's largest community, and over the centuries it grew larger, with defensive walls, irrigation dams, agricultural terraces, courtyards, public buildings, tombs for the elite, ball courts, pyramidal structures, temples, residences, and various kinds of monuments. At some point before it began to decline around 600 A.D. the city may have had more than 30,000 inhabitants.

The people who eventually became Chatino may have participated in the first phases of Monte Albán's development, but after that the ancestors of the modern Zapotec were its developers. The evidence for Zapotec hieroglyphic writing extends back to a time just before Monte Albán was founded, but full texts of written material do not appear until the early days of Monte Albán. In 1983 these inscriptions were the oldest known writing in Mesoamerica (Marcus 1983:95). Evidence for a 260 day ritual calendar also precedes Monte Albán times in the Valley of Oaxaca, with full development of the calendar apparently taking place during the early days of Monte Albán. Monte Albán continued after A.D. 600, but it had lost its dominance.

The language of the Sierra Zapotec seems to have separated from Valley Zapotec sometime between A.D. 500 and 1000, and other linguistic divergences are thought to have taken place during this period, too (Flannery and Marcus 1983:185). A number of other Zapotec centers became more important than before. This fragmentation of the Zapotec world continued until the Spanish arrived, centuries before then Mixtec were moving into the Valley, largely dominating it, according to some scholars. The Spanish found both Zapotec and Mixtec in the Valley of Oaxaca and Zapotec only in the Sierra regions and the Isthmus.

It is impossible to know how long Ixtepeji, a Sierra community, has been occupied, but there are prehistoric remains near the community's edge. According to a Spanish magistrate's report the original settlers of Ixtepeji came from Chinantec country to the northeast between A.D. 650 and 700. This and other groups from the Chinanteca formed temporary military alliances with both mountain and valley Zapotec groups. During the centuries before the Spanish arrived the Mixtec of Oaxaca and the Aztec from time to time made the Zapotec of this area pay them tribute of gold, bird plumes, corn, and other items, and the Aztec sometimes forced individuals to work for them in Oaxaca.

History of Ixtepeji

The history of Ixtepeji differs in significant ways from that of other Zapotec places, affecting their world and life view and how they have responded to their total social and physical environment.

A fighting force of 200 from Ixtepeji joined Cortés in his siege of Tenochtitlán, the Aztec capital on the site of today's Mexico City, most of them losing their lives in the campaign. Within two years the Spanish took over the Valley of Oaxaca, and the Ixtepejanos joined other Zapotec towns in an attempt to oust them. The ultimate result was that the Spanish made Ixtepeji part of an *encomienda*, a grant of both land and the Indians on it to a private party of prominence. Serious epidemics reduced the population to around 160 during subsequent decades. In 1565 the Spanish built up the population at the town's present location so as to better extract tribute and convert them (Kearney 1972:29). Many responded by trying to move into more remote mountain country, and the Ixtepejanos themselves look on this period as the beginning of the hard times that have dogged them into the latter twentieth century.

In 1660 the town was a major center of a widespread but unsuccessful Indian uprising in Oaxaca. The town also fought with other towns in the area at one time or another, a continuation of a pre-Spanish pattern. Actually, there is little specific information about Ixtepeji for the centuries until the Revolution of the early twentieth century.

While the people of the Oaxaca Valley were largely revolutionists, the leaders of the Sierra Juárez as a whole supported the dictatorship of Porfirio Díaz. But the leaders of Ixtepeji threw in with the revolutionaries, putting them at odds with the surrounding Indian communities. Subsequent events took many a complex turn, and, beginning with their armed revolt in 1910 against the owners of a large textile mile operated by workers from Ixtepeji, the people experienced an extended time of terror and tragedy. Eventually the Ixtepejanos found themselves branded enemies of the new revolutionary government of Mexico, and government forces attacked and destroyed the town. Many of the men were impressed into the army and sent to other parts of Mexico, and others scattered to Oaxaca City or towns to the east, where they had friends. People returned to resettle in Ixtepeji as opportunities developed, and this continued with the arrival of relative peace by 1924.

The town was never the same after its destruction and depopulation in 1912. The land was less productive than before, the main route into the Sierra no longer passed through Ixtepeji, and the people were less prosperous and seemed to have lost a pride and security they once had. They evinced a strong desire for internal solidarity and a fear of both internal and external conflicts.

Some 1,200 to 1,300 people lived in Ixtepeji at the time anthropologist Michael Kearney was there in 1969 and 1970. The Zapotec name for the original community means "field by the lagoon," and though the location had shifted slightly since earlier times, the term was still used some. Ixtepeji is a corruption of the Aztec name for the town, Ixtliptepji, which means "the precipice where there is obsidian" (Kearney 1972:3). Physically, the town was a rough grid of unpaved streets, five running from north to south up and down the mountain slope and ten across them. Toward the edge of town, however, the streets and trails meandered. The usually one-room adobe houses were located on lots of usually a little over an acre, with corn, beans, fruit trees, alfalfa and other items growing here and there.

The midtwentieth century Ixtepejanos had never recovered from the social and economic disruption of the Mexican Revolution. They were keenly aware of their difficult lot, and closed mines, the ruins of grain mills, a foundry, and threshing floors in the fields and woods reminded them of a more abundant past. They noticed the increasing deforestation and aridity of their country. They saw that other towns and villages were more progressive than they. They were poor peasant farmers with meager cash income. The water supply was limited. Since the town was small, everyone knew everyone else, and since they seldom married out, many were related to one another.

Kearney presents a threefold characterization of the town's reputation in that area. First they were known as muleteers, since many of the men moved trade goods by pack animal between the capital city of Oaxaca and a number of the mountain towns to the east. Second, their neighbors saw them as the "rebels of the Sierra," since, until the community's destruction and the dispersal of its population during the Revolution, the Ixtepejanos were more than willing to take up arms to defend the cause of the moment. Finally, they were known as good musicians, since they liked to sing a variety of songs they learned during their years of exile to many parts of the nation.

Ethnography

Anthropologists have studied the cultures of a fairly large number of Zapotec places. A classic study was done in a valley town not too far from Ixtepeji by Elsie Clews Parsons. Anthropological studies of Mesoamerican communities were scarce during the first decades of the twentieth century, but several pioneer studies had been completed by the early 1940s. These included Parsons' study of the now anthropologically famous Zapotec town of Mitla, where she

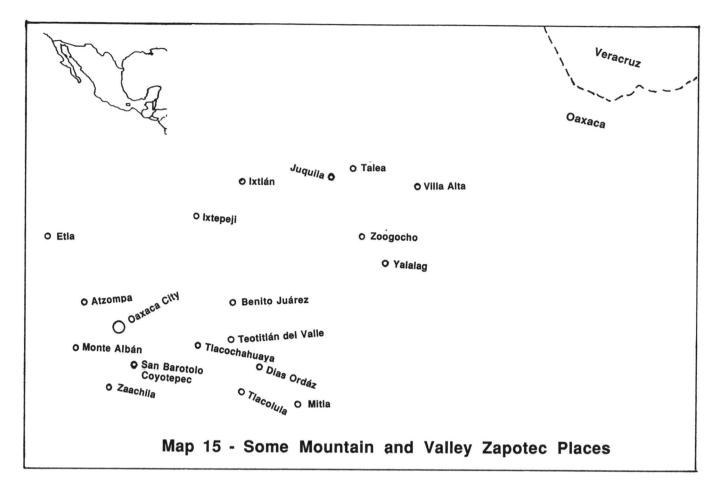

Map 15 - Some Mountain and Valley Zapotec Places

spent three periods of time between 1929 and 1933 (Parsons 1936:x). The only published data on the town of Ixtepeji are those provided by Michael Kearney, who spent time there between 1965 and 1972 (Kearney 1969, 1972).

The Country

Ixtepeji lies just to the east of the continental divide in the mountain region known as the Sierra Juárez, which lies to the northeast of the city of Oaxaca. The road to the Sierra leaves the Pan-American highway about three miles from Oaxaca. The climb into the mountain forests is steep, since there are almost no foothills. On the other side of the divide the road crosses a number of deep canyons. Ixtepeji lies on a mountain slope around three miles from the road, which continues through the mountains to the important town of Ixtlán and, eventually, Tuxtepec near the border of Veracruz (Kearney 1972:2). Around 23 miles from the Pan-American Highway, a steep dirt road descends the mountainside to this town of 1,200 to 1,300 mountain Zapotec.

The terrain is rough, the canyons deep, and the soil generally poor, partly because of the erosion that occurs due to many years of deforestation. The countryside around Ixtepeji is best described as semi-arid and brushy rather than forested, and one of the most serious problems is the great amount of soil slippage and the frequency of earth slides due to the lack of vegetation to hold the soil in place on the steep slopes. The town itself sits at an elevation of

6,500-7,000 feet, and the surrounding mountains rise to more than 8,000 feet.

Language

The Ixtepejanos of 1970 spoke less Zapotec than those of other mountain communities, except for the larger, more progressive town of Ixtlán. The people explained that during their time of exile from 1912 to the 1920s they became accustomed to using Spanish, and those born out of town during this period learned little Zapotec as children. Accordingly, Spanish was the main daily language, though older adults continued to use a dialect of Mountain Zapotec in the homes and fields. Most of the people, of course, were bilingual, some speaking Spanish better than others. Also, many of the men that traded in other parts of the mountains were able to use other Zapotec dialects (Kearney 1972:5) Zapotec is one of the Oto-Manguean languages.

Personality and Behavior

The Ixtepeji Zapotec manifested a number of psychological and behavioral traits rather widely found in Mesoamerica, which is one of the reasons it seemed useful for one cultural description to draw largely on Michael Kearney's study of world view and society in Ixtepeji. A society's world view consists of those elements of its outlook on life and the universe that govern how people react to and cope with the experiences of living. World view elements are thematic in nature. That is, they appear in many contexts of living—they tend to permeate the culture, affecting people's behaviors in family, economic, religious, aesthetic, political, and other aspects of daily life. Morris Opler, who expounded the concept of *cultural themes*, noted that they control behavior and stimulate activity in various areas of life (Opler 1945:198). They also may be either explicit or implicit. If they are explicit the people are conscious that they hold the beliefs and attitudes concerned, and they can talk about them. If they are implicit, the attitudes and feelings involved operate largely or entirely below the level of consciousness, but they are part of people's socially learned personalities and affect their behavior.

Kearney suggested that the world view of the Ixtepejanos involved five basic propositions. First, the world was a dangerous place full of hostile natural and supernatural beings that could not be relied on. These included natural phenomena, spirits, strangers, friends, and relatives.

Second, hostile people and supernatural beings attacked their victims by deceiving them. They appeared as someone or something the person should be able to trust, so the people had to be suspicious of appearances and constantly test them.

Third, people were easily frustrated and subject to becoming envious, which made them want to harm others. Accordingly, one had to be careful to behave in ways that did not provoke discontent or envy in other people or the supernaturals. Generally, Ixtepejanos limited their involvement with others to avoid such an eventuality. Of course, they had to cooperate with others, but they kept it to a minimum.

Fourth, changes were likely to be for the worse, and things were generally getting worse. Thus, the Ixtepejanos avoided strange and new things and emphasized exploitation of the present and whatever they had, since the future was likely to be worse.

Finally, hard work and suffering were inevitable parts of life. Personal effort could not change this, and the people emphasized enduring the inevitable struggle.

Undoubtedly, a major reason for the strength of these traits in Ixtepeji is the tough times the people went through since the Spanish came. It is easy to understand how their sufferings at the hands of the Spanish, Mexicans, and other Indians would reinforce the feeling that the world was a dangerous, hostile place.

Anyone becoming acquainted with a number of Mesoamerican Indian communities in sufficient depth will recognize these characteristics, since all of them have been fairly strong in other communities and ethnic groups. But it would be a mistake to stereotype all Mesoamerican Indians as having these traits to the degree they were found among the Ixtepejanos. In a number of Mesoamerican groups, in fact, these world view characteristics have been weak or nonexistent. The appropriate way to use these concepts is to be aware of their presence in Mesoamerica and apply them as they prove relevant in specific individuals and groups.

Such world view characteristics also appear in the personalities of some Mexican and Guatemalan nationals. The modern cultures of Mexico and Central America are products of Indian and Spanish cultures and the formative historical events that have occurred since the arrival of the Spanish. So, with care not to misapply it, we can use knowledge of Indian world views to help us better understand the culture and behavior of twentieth century nationals in Mexico and the Central American countries.

Clothing and Personal Appearance

Clothing has been more distinctive and colorful in some Zapotec and other Mesoamerican communities than in Ixtepeji. The women, apparently, no longer wore the wrapped skirts and blouses traditional in many places. Commonly, they garbed themselves in relatively long dresses with sleeves coming part of the way down the upper arm. They were what most North Americans would term "house dress" in their quality. Over the dress, especially when they were at work, they wore an apron, often full with a loop around the neck to hold the upper part in place. Most of them were barefooted except when they had to go some distance from home, when they wore sandals. They also used the *rebozo*, the long, dark colored shawl introduced in colonial times by the Spanish. They wore it around their shoulders or over their heads and to carry things in. The men of Ixtepeji wore trousers and shirts gotten in stores, as well as straw work hats.

Housing and other Structures

The Zapotec lived in two main kinds of structures. The more traditional type was a rectangular hut with walls of *carrizo* (bamboo-like reeds) lashed vertically to a pole framework and a thatched, gabled roof. But the Zapotec of many towns used almost entirely the single-roomed structure of adobe blocks with a single-pitch roof covered with clay tiles.

To make the blocks they first prepared a large pile of mud, well mixed with whatever was lying about on the ground's surface and, usually, dry mule or donkey manure. They placed a wooden frame of the appropriate size on the ground, poured the mud into it, smoothed the top surface, and lifted off the frame. They left the approximately four inch thick by fifteen by twenty-two inch blocks in place until dry enough to move and, then, propped them against one another to finish drying.

In the house walls the blocks rested crosswise on a stone foundation. The people used mud for mortar in the walls and, sometimes, in the foundations. Some used stone and other rubble in walls. The highest of the two long walls contained the door, and there might be two or three shuttered windows without glass. Log rafters ran from the top of one long wall to the other, and thin boards were fastened across them to support the curved tiles that usually topped the roof. Some people used corrugated tar paper or metal instead of tiles. Some applied lime plaster to the surfaces of the adobe walls. Most of the houses had beams set horizontally into the walls, to which the builders lashed cane stalks to make a platform on which the family stored the year's supply of corn.

Against one wall the family maintained an altar, which they decorated with a crepe paper canopy, flowers, colored tinsel, ribbons, and moss (Kearney 1972:13). The hearth was on the dirt floor in one corner against the wall opposite the altar or, sometimes, on an adobe brick platform. Most people slept on *petates* (plaited palm mats) on the floor or on planks elevated above the ground, though a few families had beds.

A sloping roof with open sides extended from the front wall outside to provide more storage and work space. About half the families built a separate kitchen, usually against the outside of one of the adobe house walls. They usually used lighter materials for this structure, such as carrizo, shingles, or unmortared bricks.

Ixtepeji dwellings provided no protection against the entry of mice, rats, and other pests, and the main room where the people slept was cold, drafty, and damp during the winters. The Ixtepejanos built no privies, but relieved themselves outside near the house. The household water, already contaminated, was stored in large round-bottomed clay pots (*ollas*), and the utensils with which they dipped the water lay on the contaminated dirt floor.

Livelihood

Many societies around the world hold land by *usufruct*. This means that the land is, in an ultimate sense, regarded as belonging to the whole community rather than to the individual. Normally, however, families and individuals treat house lots, fields, etc. as their private property, holding it as long as they use it and use it properly. If no one is using a tract of land, anyone may lay claim to it or receive it from the community for their personal use. In Ixtepeji the system came down from pre-Columbian days. The area around Ixtepeji was municipal land administered by the town authorities. All adult members of the community had the right to hunt there, cut wood for firewood and for charcoal, and pursue other legitimate activities. But they were not free to sell, trade or bequeath the land to others; it remained community property. The house lots and houses, however, were private property and could be sold and inherited.

The officials and citizens of Ixtepeji, like those of other Mesoamerican communities, zealously defended their municipal land and maintained its boundaries against encroachments by neighboring communities. There had been bitter, violent land disputes between Zapotec towns over the years, as well as between Mesoamerican towns in other tribes.

The people of Ixtepeji were careful to keep the municipal boundary well marked and maintained a swath free of all vegetation.

The Zapotec of Ixtepeji relied on corn more than anything else, though they found it difficult to get satisfactory yields on the steep, eroded soil. The best fields were in and around the town, since they were relatively level, easy to get to, and could be plowed easily and irrigated. Most of the land, however, lay on the surrounding mountain slopes, suitable only for slash-and-burn cultivation. When a mountain field no longer produced, the people cleared another area and let the vegetation grow back on the old one.

They prepared the fields with a plow drawn by a pair of oxen. The plow was a home-made implement of wood with a narrow metal share attached to the beveled front and top of the beam. It broke the ground and plowed a V-shaped furrow but did not turn the soil over as a moldboard plow would. If the people had planted by poking holes in the ground with a digging stick the fields would not have eroded so badly. But, since the seasons were short at the higher elevations and the rains unreliable, the people were anxious to get the crops planted quickly. With the furrows plowed all they had to do was drop the kernels in the furrow and cover them by kicking soil over them with their feet. After the harvest they sometimes tethered livestock in the fields to eat some of the cornstalks and deposit manure, but most of the manure washed away with the first rains. The Ixtepejanos had to abandon exhausted mountain fields for several years, but they only had to rest fields in and around town for a year or two.

The Ixtepejanos also grew several varieties of beans, and corn tortillas and beans made up a large portion of their diet and often comprised the only solid food they had for several days at a time. They kept a small number of fruit trees, which, in season, yielded small amounts of peaches, apples, pears, quince, plums, oranges, lemons and limes, pomegranates, and cherries. They also bought some fruit in nearby markets. From time to time they had eggs; turkey, chicken, or pig meat; and, even less often, fish, beef, or horse meat. They also might obtain a variety of other items not grown at Ixtepeji, such as squash, chiles, onions, tomatoes, potatoes, and blackberries. They either grew or purchased various leaf and seed items such as mint, coriander, and parsley. Both the men and women watched for edible wild plants while in the fields or forests. Corn and beans, however, were the only regularly used items. The people were increasing their use of white bread (unenriched and usually stale), white sugar, and bottled beverages.

For beverages the people used coffee, chocolate, *mezcal*, *tepache*, and beer. Mezcal was a distilled alcoholic beverage made from the fermented juice of a special variety of agave. Mezcal producers removed the heart of the agave and collected the juice that ran from the leaves into the basin formed by the heart's removal. Tepache was made by allowing, agave, sugarcane, or pineapple juice to ferment.

The social ritual of sharing food and drink illustrates several elements of the Ixtepeji world view. *Ritual* may be defined as the symbolic affirmation of values through culturally standardized utterances and actions. Whatever else they are, values are things people are concerned about, and Ixtepeji behavior concerning food expressed the concerns that made up their life and world view. A highly standardized Ixtepeji ritual was for them to offer food to anyone who came along while they were eating and, also, to offer alcoholic beverages to all present or who came along while they were drinking. In fact, it went farther than that. The people insisted that others eat or drink with them. Ixtepejanos responded by first declining the food, but eventually they would give in. Kearney reported that he got a sore arm several times from the vise-like grip of Ixtepejanos who forcibly insisted that he accept their invitation to eat and drink with them, and he collected accounts of men being shot for refusing to accept a drink (Kearney 1972:75).

According to Kearney's analysis, Ixtepejanos offered food and drink to guests partly because it was dangerous not to. They felt that visitors might be hostile in some respect, and if they were not treated well, they might become dangerous to the host. Offering food and drink accomplished two things. First it reduced the possibility that visitors would become envious of the hosts enjoyment of food when they did not have any. Recall that the Ixtepejanos believed people were easily made envious of those more fortunate than they. The second accomplishment of sharing was that it gave the hosts a chance to watch the visitor's speech and behavior so that they could ascertain whether or not there was any dangerous hostility or envy. The sharing was part of the Ixtepejanos ever-present concern with defending themselves against possibly hostile or envious persons. If visitors refused to share, it was a matter of considerable concern, since it could indicate that they harbored hostility and envy and intended to cause the host trouble or take advantage of any opportunity to do so. When offering food and drink, hosts often emphasized that they were poor or had very little food, another measure for avoiding envy.

The ritual of food sharing is not limited to Ixtepeji. It is common throughout Mesoamerica and rural Mexico and Guatemala. Moreover, it is one of the most noticeable characteristics of peasant societies in general. Scholars have advanced a variety of theories to account for this feature of peasant cultures and all of them may have merit. Kearney's explanation seems applicable to Ixtepeji and rural Mexico and Central America and, perhaps, peasant groups in other parts of the world as well. Accounting for insistent food sharing is one of many interesting and significant problem areas in anthropology.

If insistent food sharing was stronger in Ixtepeji than many other places, it makes sense in terms of their food situation. There was little variety of food available to them. Corn was the all-important staple, and corn tortillas were a near-essential part of every meal. But the land was poor, poorer than ever before and getting poorer, and the Ixtepejanos lived under the threat of not being able to produce enough to keep them from going hungry. In some years, in fact, erosion from unusually heavy rains destroyed much of the crop, and many people had to buy corn elsewhere at high prices. This forced some people into debt or required them to leave the municipio temporarily to take wage work. Hunger was not unknown to a number of the Ixtepejanos. Living with this might have intensified their concern over food.

A world view, as noted before, includes feelings that are implicit—feelings that affect people's behaviors but which they are hardly aware of. This may be the case with one factor Kearney brought out. He inferred from Ixtepejano behavior that pressing a drink on an unwilling person was a hostile act, because it inconvenienced the recipient. He noted that there was a good deal of suppressed hostility in the Ixtepejanos and that it was expressed in disguised form, often in the form of kindness. The Ixtepejanos felt that inviting a person to drink was an act of kindness and might not realize fully that it masked feelings of hostility. But the Ixtepejanos had no difficulty being explicit about another reason for insisting that someone drink with them. They said that if one person remained sober he would be in position to take advantage of those who were intoxicated. The possible connection with their concern that others might be dangerous to them is apparent.

Kearney also confronted the question of why the Ixtepejanos drank so much and connected this with their view that life was a difficult struggle with little or no hope of controlling one's fate. Drunkenness was more than an escape from this negative reality, it enabled people to intensify life's few enjoyable elements. He saw this exhibited in general Mexican culture by affinity for loud noise, bright colors, colorful fiestas, and emotionally stirring experiences in general (Kearney 1972:102). The Ixtepejanos drank so much as a way of making the most of the present. The future was uncertain. The present was in hand. There was little anyone could do to make it better, but one could transcend its sadness by intensifying its enjoyable dimensions, and drinking was the main avenue to this transcendence.

The Ixtepejanos were basically producers of corn and beans, with the men doing most of the agricultural labor. In this way they were similar to other Mesoamericans. Also, like other Mesoamericans, they specialized part time in one or more other economic activities. Mesoamerican towns variously specialize in making hats, mining salt, weaving woolen sarapes, making certain types of clay pots, building houses, and so on. Many of the men of Ixtepeji, as noted before, were *arrieros* (muleteers), who obtained items in Oaxaca City and elsewhere that people in the mountain villages needed or desired. They transported these items by pack animal to the various villages.

Another outstanding characteristic of Mesoamerica, linked to economic specialization, is the market system. Many towns have regular market days, often weekly and, in some, daily. People from different villages and towns set up displays of what they have produced—salt, hats, cloth, black water pots, chiles, tomatoes, etc.—in the market area, usually in or near the town square. With a market it is easier for people to obtain foods and other items not produced locally, which enriches their diets and provides them with a variety of products on a more regular basis than if there were no market. But Ixtepeji had no market, and that is one of the reasons their diet exhibited less variety than that of many other towns.

In addition, the Ixtepejanos were not as wealthy as some other Zapotec groups. Their land produced poorly, and they had never fully recovered from the exile and destruction visited upon them during the Mexican revolution. Some Ixtepejanos, of course, enjoyed a higher level of material well-being than others, but the differences were relatively small.

It was characteristic of the Ixtepejanos to feature their poverty and related liabilities in their relationships with one another. This was another of the defensive strategies they used to cope with the perceived hostility and potential envy of others. Many spoke often of their poverty, backwardness, weakness, and the like. They wanted to avoid the appearance of having more than others, and they tried to avoid this appearance by talking about their poverty and inadequacy. When conversing with visitors from wealthier places, including foreigners like anthropologists and tourists, they compared themselves and their possessions unfavorably with the knowledge, wealth, and beauty of the visitor's world. They mentioned repeatedly their illiteracy, their humble houses, their simple meals, and the town's general backwardness.

Anthropologist George Foster, one of the leading students of Mesoamerican cultures, especially Tarascan culture, has proposed a widely debated theory that purports to account for this and related kinds of behavior among peasants. He calls this explanatory model, which he worked out using data from his studies of the Tarascan town of Tzintzuntzán, the *image of limited good*. According to this model peasants believe the good things of life, such as land, wealth, health, friendship, love, power, respect, and security, exist in finite quantity and are always relatively scarce. Since there is a limited and unexpandable supply of these things, people who acquire larger amounts of such good things than others can do so only by getting more than their share, that is, part of other people's shares (G. Foster 1965:296-7). This provokes envy and resentment toward anyone who is notably better off than others, and to avoid envy and resentment, people stress their poverty and inadequacy. Groups with a view like this can hardly be expected to organize their lives to produce wealth, for they have no conception that the total supply of wealth and good can be enlarged. They are without hope that they might progress in material and other forms of well-being. Hopelessness in this respect is a salient feature of the Ixtepejano personality.

Many anthropologists have dissented from Foster's theory, in some instances by citing cases where peasants have taken advantage of opportunities to augment their level of well-being. Acheson, for example, has described how individuals in one Tarascan town markedly increased their wealth as compared with others by establishing furniture-making enterprises when electricity was brought into the town and credit and other economic mechanisms made it possible for them to purchase the necessary equipment (Acheson 1972;1152-1159). However, such criticisms may not invalidate the theory. Perhaps they simply show that other forces can undermine the influence of the image of limited good or that the model is more powerful in some communities than others.

Kearney has suggested that the Ixtepejanos lived by an image of diminishing good (Kearney 1969:889). He also indicated there was one good the people felt they could augment through personal effort, the emotionally moving experience. This the Ixtepejanos accomplished through their fiestas and the drinking of the mezcal and beer that accompanied them.

Social Organization and Relationships

The *patrilocal extended family*, the three generation unit consisting of the parents and their married sons, and their sons' wives and children, is strong in Mesoamerica as a whole and in many Zapotec towns. But it seems to have been relatively weak in Ixtepeji. Newlyweds normally went to live with the groom's family, but they were anxious to establish their own household. Within a year or two, then, frequently about the time they had their first child, they formed an independent nuclear family household by moving into their own home. This appeared to reflect the Ixtepeji view that other people were hostile and, therefore, dangerous to them. In fact, their closest relatives were among the most dangerous. Since they knew the most about them, they were most likely to become envious of them and were in the best position to damage them (Kearney 1972:79). Living apart from them constituted a defensive strategy against being envied and, possibly, made the object of aggression. Perhaps this is why most Ixtepeji houses were occupied by nuclear families.

Kearney saw the preference for independent nuclear family households as part of a defensive strategy he called *individualism*. The Ixtepejanos in general, he found, avoided unnecessary social involvements, depending on their own resources instead of joining one another in communal activities. In this way they reduced troublesome and dangerous obligations to relatives and friends and, in general, avoided many possibly dangerous entanglements with other people.

In some Mesoamerican communities *joint families* are fairly common. Siblings remain together in the same homestead, managing their affairs together, though the nuclear families of each sibling usually occupy separate sleeping houses and might even eat separately. But the Ixtepejanos felt it was best for the siblings to divide the property they inherited and manage the units separately. They felt that, if they stayed together, one brother would surely succeed in taking advantage of the other. The people of Ixtepeji, then, generally preferred to avoid any combination family arrangement if they could.

The Ixtepejanos were like the great majority of Mesoamericans in being exclusively *bilateral* and, therefore, without *unilineal* common ancestor groups such as *clans* and *lineages*. With unilineal groups husband and wife normally belong to different kinship groups and all the children are assigned automatically to the clan or lineage of the parent of one sex only. In a society using a *matrilineal* rule, for example, all the children automatically become a member of the mother's common ancestor group. But the Ixtepejanos and other bilateral peoples, including modern North Americans, think of children as related to the relatives of both parents.

In some bilateral societies an individually defined social unit called the *kindred* is quite important. A kindred is simply any individual's genetic relatives on both sides of the family—the people related to the person through both male and female links rather than through only male links or female links.

In groups where kindreds are important a person's relatives assume certain social responsibilities toward him or her, constituting a source of support in meeting culturally defined obligations and coping with life's troubles. In Ixtepeji, however, kindreds were so weak as to be almost nonfunctional, simply because the people defensively avoided this kind of involvement.

Yet the Ixtepeji Zapotec participated in the fictive kinship arrangement known as *compadrazgo* (ritual coparenthood). Fictive kinship relationships among people exhibit the features frequently characteristic of relationships among kin. The fictive kinship relationships of the compadrazgo are established when, at baptism, confirmation, marriage, or other special occasions in their children's lives, the parents choose unrelated adults to serve as godparents to their children. This establishes a lifetime relationship between the parents and the child's godparents, who call one another *compadres* (coparents) and, of course, between the godchild (*ahijado* or *ahijada* in Spanish) and the godparents (*padrino* and *padrina* in Spanish). The compadrazgo system was introduced by the Spanish and is virtually universal among both Indians and non-Indians in Mexico and Central America. The Zapotec and, perhaps other Mesoamerican tribes, may have had some type of godparent system before the Spanish came.

The people of Ixtepeji were relatively secure in their relationships with their compadres and with their godparents and godchildren. They tended to feel less threatened by a compadre than a close relative because the compadrazgo relationship was less intimate. The individuals involved could carry out their ritual obligations to help one another without having to get so deeply involved with or knowledgeable about one another that they would envy and hurt one another. In addition, they knew one another just well enough to judge whether or not the other parties were envious or hostile toward them, which gave them a special confidence and security. But they felt less secure with strangers, simply because they did not know enough about them to judge whether or not they were a threat. Accordingly, the Ixtepejanos felt most secure with people who knew them but did not know them too intimately and with whom their relationships were defined by well-standardized rules—in this case, the ritual obligations and privileges of coparenthood and godparenthood.

Since Kearney concentrated on those aspects of Ixtepeji culture that most strongly reflected their world view, he mentioned little on conception, pregnancy, and birth. The Zapotec in general wanted children and used prayer and other means to promote conception. They also imposed a number of food prohibitions during pregnancy. At birth, mothers were usually helped by a midwife or friend or relative, and husbands were often present. The kneeling position was common during childbirth. Like many other communities around the world, the Ixtepejanos gave special attention to the disposal of the afterbirth. The Zapotec bathed mother and baby and kept the mother in bed for around 20 days.

Zapotec mothers nursed their children for a year or two, the time depending on how many other children she had (Nader 1969:356). They usually weaned their little ones by placing bitter herbs or other unpalatable substances on the nipples. Sometimes, as in the valley town of Teotitlán del Valle, the child was sent to stay with grandparents for a time (R. Taylor 1960:193). Kearney emphasizes that Ixtepejano weaning was abrupt, as it is in other Zapotec places, and he fits this into a larger pattern of abrupt changes, from harshness to gentleness and back, in the way parents in Ixtepeji treated their children.

The adults had to suppress the hostility they felt toward others, since giving way to open aggression might provoke witchcraft or other counter measures. This load of unreleased aggression, Kearney surmised, might be released in the privacy of the home against safe objects such as animals and children. Parents were relatively patient with their children most of the time, but the annoyance with childish behavior often became so strong that they exploded with harshness and rejection. This happened especially when parents were drunk, as they often were. A mother who had been responding patiently to her little girl's endless chatter would suddenly shout at her and slap her or hit her with a stick of wood. A father might give his child a loving kiss when he left in the morning and return the same evening to treat the same one intolerantly and abusively. This inability to predict such changes seems certain to have had an impact on the developing personality.

Kearney characterizes Ixtepeji Zapotec childhood as a time of insecurity. The parents thought it important to discipline children early in life so they would be obedient as they grew older, and some beat their children with firewood and other things. Others felt this sort of thing was too harsh and preferred to punish children by shaming them. So they laughed at them and made them the butt of jokes. They also used stories of good versus bad daughters and sons. When milder measures failed they might scare the children or spank them.

Though Ixtepeji parents used shame extensively, Kearney found the use of deception more common. Sometimes they promised some favor they had no intention of delivering. In other instances they frightened their children with the threat that a specially feared animal, such as the coyote, the dog, or the owl, would get them. For example, they sometimes tried to frighten children into going to sleep by telling them the Cat was coming to eat them if they did not. Sometimes this backfired because of the fright it produced. In one instance the mother alternated between harsh shouting and threats and gentle cooing and murmuring to her sleepless little son. The extensive use of deception in raising children seems consistent with the Ixtepejano adults' expectations and fear of being victims of deception.

In Ixtepeji parents handled their children in such a way as to promote ill feeling among siblings. In fact, one of the commonest diseases of children was *chípil*. The child suffering from chípil was envious and directed his or her feelings of frustration inward. This was believed to poison the blood, which then caused the heart to swell. Children with chípil turned red, their heads felt hot, and they lost their appetites. They got chípil because they were envious of the next youngest child, both while the mother was still carrying it and after birth. A child became envious because the mother was diverting much of the attention and affection he or she formerly enjoyed to the newcomer. The parents ridiculed, scolded, or punished children who cried or misbehaved because they were envious (*chipiloso*), and the children typically reacted by withdrawing and brooding and, if opportunity afforded, attacking a helpless animal, destroying something, or abusing a sibling (brother or sister). The latter is illustrated by one parent's dramatic telling of how one of his daughters, trying to make it look like an accident, shoved a hot flatiron against her younger sister's leg.

In 1953 John W. M. Whiting and Irwin L. Child published a study relating types of child training to cultural characteristics. Their statistically tested, cross-cultural evidence suggested that high socialization anxiety produced by harsh weaning practices, severe punishment by parents, and the like, produces adults that are afraid of other people and spirits. Kearney notes that the evidence from Ixtepeji supports the hypothesis (Kearney 1972:57).

Kearney provides little information on older childhood, adolescence, and young adulthood. Both boys and girls were put to work on the tasks appropriate to their sex as soon as they were old enough, and even their play times largely imitated adult responsibilities. Apparently, the Ixtepejanos, like other Zapotec, were without puberty ceremonies for either boys or girls.

The Zapotec considered girls ready for marriage at puberty, and girls tended to marry younger than boys. Some did not marry until around twenty, but all were expected to. Boys usually married between twelve and twenty-two years of age (Nader 1969:357). They courted their sweethearts furtively rather than openly, and when they were ready to marry, the boy's family formally petitioned the family of the girl, sometimes enlisting the help of a go-between; or the couple eloped. In many places the families postponed marriage ceremonies until the first child arrived. In Ixtepeji the couple usually lived with the husband's parents during this time, after which most tried to establish an independent nuclear family household. Marriages were nearly always monogamous, though mountain Zapotec monogamy manifested some tendency to be serial (Nader 1969:347).

Adult Ixtepejanos, including spouses, did not relate to one another so intimately and comfortably as people in some societies. Yet, this is not to say that they could not and did not enjoy interacting with one another. Kearney admits to having emphasized the negative side of interpersonal relationships, but he stresses that his description of that aspect of the Ixtepejano personality is as the people themselves told it and that these were the salient features of their personality and behavior (Kearney 1972:x, 134).

Verbal interaction among Ixtepejanos reflected elements of their world view. The people engaged in a good deal of lively conversation that conveyed openness and contentment, but not too much. They talked to convey the impression that they were not envious of anyone, since they assumed that a sullen, silent person was suffering from the adult disease of envy called *muina*. Such a person, of course, was a danger to others, and all, including those who were feeling envious, tried to appear free of it through their verbal behavior. On the other hand, they were in a bit of a bind, because if they appeared too happy they might cause someone to envy them, so, they were moderate in their verbal exuberance and, as we have noted already, introduced enough statements of self-disparagement and plead limitations enough to avoid stimulating dangerous envy.

Another aspect of their verbal behavior seems to reflect their time orientation. Modern North Americans are concerned when someone interrupts them when they are talking, but the Ixtepejanos permitted such interruptions without annoyance or verbal complaint. They did not allow anyone's interruption to deflect the flow of conversation. When it was over the interrupted speaker simply continued with no comment of any kind. This was even true when a child interrupted. The adults would shift their full attention to the child, and, when the matter was resolved, pick up where they left off. This was connected with Ixtepejano present-time orientation. The people did not think of a conversation as something existing through time, so they were unconcerned about breaks in a nonexistent continuity (Kearney 1972:87). They experienced interruptions as present events, and the present was their concern, not the unknowable, uncertain future, including future conversation.

All societies have manifested concern about diseases, and Ixtepejano concern was magnified by their realization that illness could be caused by hostile humans or supernaturals. The basic concept of disease in Ixtepeji seems to have been the notion of *aigre* (air). Anthropologists have noted two widespread ideas as to what is wrong with the body of a sick person, one being soul loss and the other intrusion of something alien. Ixtepeji Zapotec believed that the intrusion of aigre was a major cause of illness. The aigre was placed in the body by someone's sorcery (evil magic), or by witches; or malevolent air simply got into the body on its own somehow. In fact, the natural aigre all around them got into their bodies. Sometimes it was sent by God. The most common symptom was a sharp ache in the back of the neck, and the people treated it with herbs, patent medicines, and other household remedies. Evil spirits also might enter the body. Spirits were air-like, and the air was thought to be permeated with these invisible, unpredictable, dangerous beings.

One of the commonest preventive and curative measures used by the Ixtepejanos was the burning of copal incense. They burned it in large quantities on all religious occasions in the church, homes, religious precessions, and elsewhere. They used copal because it produced such large billows of strong smoke that they felt it was especially effective. It drove aigre and aigre-like entities away so they did not get in the body, or it drove them from the body of a sick person. People who had to go out at night carried a burning ember or censer or smoked a cigarette for protection against aigre.

The Ixtepejano illness called *susto* (fright) illustrates both soul loss and intrusion as disease states. Susto resulted from a sudden scare by humans, animals, inanimate objects, or supernaturals. This might either dislodge the soul or make the body vulnerable to the entrance of bad air.

Susto, muina, and chípil were similar to one another in that each involved a disturbing emotional condition. Both muina and chípil resulted from envy or anger. Both susto and muina poisoned the blood, which then poisoned the whole body and caused the heart to swell (Kearney 1972:70). But the effects of susto soon dissipated, while the symptoms of muina would build and might eventually cause permanent physical deformities or, even, paralysis. A person attacked by susto blanched, while the victim of muina turned red, felt hot in the head, and lost appetite. The childhood disease chípil was like muina but was much milder and usually of short duration. Ixtepejanos were quite concerned about muina, because the victim might attack others through witchcraft or other means. People who became aware of this threat took steps to defend themselves.

Those experiencing muina tried to conceal their condition. Eating and drinking during a muina attack could poison the blood further, but, knowing the danger, people with muina would eat and drink anyway so others would not know they were experiencing the attack. Some are said to have died from doing this.

Evil-eye (*mal ojo*) was another cause of illness in Ixtepeji as well as in Mesoamerica in general. People with "strong vision" for example, could make children sick just by glancing at them. Such strong vision could afflict people who were envious. Parents in Mesoamerica commonly kept their children secluded from strangers and others that might have an evil-eye.

The Ixtepejanos conceived of a God-given life force that energized the body but was gradually expended or might be reclaimed by God at any time. As this life force declined or was taken away people aged, died, or experienced natural sickness. The people believed the life force could be lost or drained away faster than it should by sickness and overwork. Accordingly, they felt it necessary to rest at least one day a week, and those who held political office had to be allowed a period of rest between jobs.

In line with the Ixtepejano view that everything got worse through time, death did not lead to a superior state. Life was hard, but the next stage would be worse. At death one became a shadow-like spirit inhabiting the air, and there was no escape. It may be that this explains why Ixtepejanos did not commit suicide (Kearney 1972:85). As deaths increased the population of malevolent spirits in the atmosphere the environment, in that sense, was becoming gradually more dangerous.

The people strongly desired that they and their friends and relatives have a "good death," that is, a comfortable death in one's own house with the relatives providing care and good food to eat. That way the spirit of the deceased would be relatively well-off and contented. But if a person had a "bad death," dying from an accident, murder, or other sudden, unanticipated event, the spirit would be unhappy and, therefore, strongly malevolent. The troubled spirit made buzzing noises in the house at night, turned objects over, and otherwise disturbed the survivors, and the living relatives had to try to appease it. A bad death was always accompanied by a great fright (gran susto).

The Ixtepejano's concern with the spirits of the dead peaked on All Souls Day at the beginning of November. On that day the souls returned to the families they had lived with and feasted with them. The families prepared special food offerings and placed them on the altar, and the spirits consumed the aromas and vapors that emanated from the food.

It is important to keep in mind that the attitudes and behaviors we have reviewed were more intense in Ixtepeji than in some other Mesoamerican communities. We can use our knowledge of these things in Ixtepeji life as clues to what we might find elsewhere, but it is always important to remember that they are much weaker or virtually absent in some other places.

On the other hand, remembering that the personalities of Mexicans, Guatemalans and other nationals have been derived in part from Indian sources, it is worth noting that both Mexican and foreign scholars have seen some of these things in the personalities of the general public. Tannenbaum suggests (1950:16-17) that all of Mexican life is burdened by an expectancy of sudden injury, violence, and death, which is tied to a kind of fatalism and indifference to life.

Government and Social Order

The Mexican state of Oaxaca is divided into *distritos* (districts, somewhat parallel to U.S. counties), and the distritos are divided into political units known as *municipios* (municipalities). A municipio can consist of one community or several, but it includes the surrounding land rather than just the cluster of homes and businesses. Accordingly, a municipio adjoins other municipios on all sides so that all the area within a distrito is taken up by municipios. Ixtepeji was one of 28 municipios making up the distrito of Ixtlán. When, as is nearly always the case, there are several towns and other settlements within a municipio, one of them is the capitol or *cabecera*. The town of Ixtepeji was the cabecera of the municipio of Ixtepeji, which included 15 settlements in addition to the cabecera. Four of these were larger settlements known as *agencias*, and eleven were hamlets known as *rancherías*. The elected officials of the municipio governed the entire unit, not just the town of Ixtepeji.

Many Mesoamerican communities are subdivided into *barrios*. There were five barrios in the town of Ixtepeji, and legend had it that they originated when the Spanish congregated people from five settlements in order to administer and convert them more efficiently. The barrios remained well-defined until the town was destroyed in 1912. When the people returned in the early 1920s, they built their houses where they could, and the members of the five barrios became scattered around the town. In 1970 the people remembered the original boundaries, however, and knew which barrio they were affiliated with (Kearney 1972:22). Each barrio had its own patron saint and an annual fiesta in his honor.

The so-called *cargo* system is an important complex in Mesoamerican communities. The cargos are the community's formal governmental and religious offices, and people make no practical distinction between the two. The complex of offices is hierarchical, and a young man begins by accepting a minor office and moves to increasingly important cargos as he ages and gains experience. Every competent Ixtepejano male had to participate in the cargo system, or he would not be allowed to live in the municipio. A few avoided cargo service at certain times by leaving town for a period including election time or paying another to take their cargo. Ixtepejanos criticized such behavior, and the administration fined anyone who was absent from a cargo duty without excuse. Generally, men were allowed two or more years rest between cargos. Most of the cargos were filled at town meetings, though some of the minor appointments were made by the barrios. At age sixty a man became a *principal*, free of cargo obligation, attendance at town meetings, and making financial contributions.

The *presidente* was the formal municipio head, comparable to a mayor in modern North American communities, the person of greatest prestige and authority in the local administration. He represented the municipio in most outside contacts and presided over local civic events. He heard and settled disputes and punished people by fining them, jailing them, or making them do public work.

The second most important official was the *síndico*, somewhat comparable to an attorney general in his formal responsibility to his counterpart in the district government. The district held him responsible for investigating crimes, seeing that violators were punished, and adjusting claims in minor cases. While the formal responsibility was his, he and the presidente worked together on these matters. He made frequent trips to Ixtlán, the seat of district government, and Oaxaca City, the state capitol. The síndico also organized and directed the *tequio*, which was a work party of municipio men. All men were supposed to participate in tequios, which are also important in other Mesoamerican communities. By this means the town constructed and maintained its streets, public buildings, bridges, and other public facilities.

There were ten officials who made up a kind of advisory council for the presidente and the síndico and who often worked closely with them. Another officer was responsible for the municipio's communal lands, granted requests for use rights on those lands, and settled land disputes. Several subsidiary officers worked under this major town official. Other town officials included an *alcalde*, who handled minor ceremonial functions, and a treasurer. A group of police officials included a police chief, five other police officers, and twenty young policemen known as *topiles*. They handled violent disputes, apprehended anyone accused of a crime, and subdued drunks. At other times those on duty lounged around the town hall, where they were available for service to the higher town officials. Five groups, a police official and four topiles each, took turns on duty.

A group of church officials, one of whom was the head officer, maintained the church, handled day to day church activities, and managed several church plots where crops were grown to help pay church expenses. There were various other cargo positions, including maintainers of the water canal, checkers of municipio boundary markers and violations of municipio land, agencia representatives, representatives to the Mexican Party of Revolutionary Institutions (PRI), and educational officers.

The higher municipio officials carried their cargos, officially, for three years, but in practice they served only half their terms and turned their cargos over to elected substitutes known as *suplentes*. Minor officials served for a year and might also split their terms with substitutes. The men of Ixtepeji made many of the important decisions of community concern, including the election of cargo holders, at assemblies of all the town's adult males. They selected the town officials at regular meetings scheduled for that purpose and met at other times as needed. The Ixtepejanos were known in the area for the importance they gave to their town meetings. The municipio governmental officers, the church committee, and an education committee met monthly to handle ordinary minor matters.

Virtually all Ixtepejanos were genuinely reluctant to accept cargos. In fact, they thought of cargos as part of the inevitable burden of living. This fit into their view that hard work and suffering were an inevitable part of living, and they repeatedly commented about what a struggle and burden life was. As in other rural Mexican communities cargo holders in Ixtepeji were not paid, so they suffered financially from holding office. In some places the people, nevertheless, accepted cargos in good spirits, but not in Ixtepeji. They could complain bitterly about the troublesomeness of holding cargo, and when someone was nominated at a town meeting, he would decline, insisting that he had not had enough rest. The men discussed these points and, usually, elected the person by a show of hands. Seldom did anyone express readiness to accept a nomination, and some who did were applauded and cheered at a town meeting Kearney attended (Kearney 1972:21).

The Ixtepejanos defended themselves in a hostile world in several ways. We have already mentioned self-disparagement and avoiding social involvement. They also ritually emphasized conditions that they valued, especially at fiestas. They were quite concerned about their history of factionalism and its persistence, so they lost few opportunities to affirm the ideal of community solidarity. In addition to including such affirmations in their fiesta ritual they sought solidarity in the way they conducted their town meetings. They took their hand or voice votes only after it became apparent that a decision would be unanimous, so that the vote ritually expressed solidarity. As they voted, some might cry out, "Todo el pueblo" ("the whole town"). Kearney emphasized that community solidarity was a strong ideal in Ixtepeji.

Anthropologists working in Mexico regularly hear from the people they work with how terrible the people of neighboring villages and towns are in contrast with those the anthropologist is with. This tendency to describe those of other communities and other regions as violent and untrustworthy is found in many places around the world and was especially strong in Ixtepeji in spite of their fairly regular and successful interaction with people of other communities economically, at fiestas, and in other ways. The truth, of course, is that there is seldom much difference in violence levels among communities.

As we have already seen, the people of Ixtepeji distrusted one another in spite of the ideal of solidarity. Their feeling that humans and supernaturals performed aggressive acts through deception and trickery was one of the strongest themes of their world and life view, and they worried a good deal about this possibility. They almost never stole from one another or broke into one another's houses, but they were quite concerned about the possibilities and took precautions against them that seemed quite unnecessary to an outsider. They were careful to conceal their affairs from others so that adversaries could not take advantage of them. They therefore intentionally tried to deceive others about the circumstances of their lives.

Art and Play

The themes that permeate a culture find some of their most intense manifestations in the aesthetic and other expressive aspects. Undoubtedly, the Ixtepejanos expressed many of these in the songs they sang, but Kearney's ethnography does not expound this part of the culture. He generalizes that aesthetic standards in Ixtepeji reflected primarily material and functional considerations rather than abstract standards of beauty and that they were like some other Zapotec groups in this. The Ixtepejanos were interested in material things and how well they worked. This seems to be largely because, in line with the idea that deception was standard and things were not as they seemed, people should always test appearances. It is easier, of course, to test physical objects than ideas and ideals, so the people trusted material things more than anything else (Kearney 1972:66). They seemed less illusory.

Fiesta drunkenness, as noted earlier, was a major way for an Ixtepejano to transcend life's burdens and sufferings. The fiestas, as a major recreational time in Ixtepeji life, also reflected world view themes.

Folklore, especially the stories people tell, reflect world view themes profoundly, and Kearney examined this in some depth. The folktales of the Ixtepejanos strongly indicated their concern with deception and trickery as standard forms of aggression and defense against aggression. Both jokes and stories often focused on an ironic double-cross. Their version of Androcles and the Lion, for example, told how, when Androcles was thrown into the arena with the lions, the lion from whose paw Androcles had earlier removed a thorn tells the other lions not to bother him because, since he already knows him, he will eat him himself (Kearney 1972:60).

Many Ixtepeji Zapotec stories also reflected their fatalistic acceptance of suffering and struggle, coupled with the idea that there was no choice but to resign oneself to it all. There were a large number of treasure stories that incorporated an ironic "so near, yet so far" aspect. According to one a man organized thirty people to dig for treasure in an enchanted cave, and after six months of hard work the cave suddenly filled with water. They were not destined to have the treasure. By another account, Benito Juárez was said to have gone to Spain to bring back Moctezuma's royal crown. After accepting proof that the crown belonged to the Indians of Mexico and assuring Juárez that he could have it, they poisoned him and sent him home dead. Here again is the element of deceit and, also, the fatalistic concept that the crown's return was not destined to occur.

The *Matlaziwa* tale also mirrored the Ixtepeji world view. It was a variant of the *La Llorona* (Weeping Woman) tales widespread in Mexico and other parts of Indian Latin American. La Llorona could be heard at night crying for her children, whom she had killed in her grief over being abandoned by her husband. She also seduced men, luring them into remote places and injuring or killing them. In this way she punished men who, like her own husband, neglected their wives and children. The people viewed Matlaziwa as a spirit-being in some way connected with aigre (air or wind) that brought illness. Matlaziwa might deceive a man by appearing as a friend or other person the man should be able to trust, such as a sweetheart or a wife. His usual fate was to be shoved into a canyon or river. Usually,

Matlaziwa attacked men who were drunk or out at night, since they were undoubtedly neglecting their families.

Religious Beliefs and Practices

If, as many do, we define religions as given cultures' complexes of beliefs and practices relating to the supernatural, it is safe to say every known human society has a religion. Commonly, however, people in peasant and tribal cultures make no distinction between the natural and the supernatural, and what we as outside observers see as being supernaturalistic beliefs and practices pervade the people's cultures.

Twentieth century Ixtepeji Zapotec religion was, in terms of its origins, a blend of elements from Spanish and Indian sources. The Ixtepejanos believed in God, Christ, and the saints. They did not have a great deal to do with God. They had no material image of him, and they were uncertain where he might be. Some of the older people spoke of him maintaining their lives or their strength, and they assumed that God could take their strength and their lives from them at any time. In their daily living, however, the people were more concerned with spirits and the saints than with God. They had many images of Christ, but he was exclusively a suffering Christ, reflecting the Ixtepejano preoccupation with trouble. The realistic images portrayed Christ's suffering in gory detail. There was nothing of the triumphant, risen, and glorified Christ.

The Ixtepejanos exhibited their high valuation of the material in their belief that the saints were the images themselves. While they did not know where God might be, they knew that the saints were in the church and on the altars in their homes. The people prayed largely to the saints for food, health, money, protection, and other benefits having to do with their material well-being. They made their offerings and prayed to the saints mostly before the family altar, the most striking thing in the family sleeping house. In Mesoamerican communities a family altar is commonly either a table or a high masonry bench located against one inside wall. In many Mesoamerican communities, and perhaps Ixtepeji, this single room is known as the saints' room. Pictures and statuettes of religious personages reside on the altar, which is decorated with paper flowers, ribbons, colored tinsel, and moss and covered with a crepe paper canopy

Animism, defined as belief in personal supernatural beings, is a significant element of every religion. If God is conceived as person and spirit, this is an animistic belief. Anthropologists sometimes contrast animism with *animatism*, which is belief in sheer supernatural power that is sometimes thought of as impersonal and other times entertained without thought of whether it is personal or impersonal.

The religion of Ixtepeji was strongly animistic in the sense that the people believed in a large number of spirits and manifested considerable interest in and concern about them. Spirits of the dead were especially important to the Ixtepejanos, as they have been to many other Mesoamerican Indian groups. The Ixtepejanos found spirits air-like in their invisibility. They were mysterious, unpredictable, uncontrollable, threatening, and malevolent. They most commonly attacked and made people ill by placing bad aigre (air) in them. Since the spirits were persons, they had to be dealt with accordingly, so the people prayed to them and offered them gifts, hoping to keep them from becoming annoyed and attacking them. All of this fit well the Ixtepeji belief in a hostile, dangerous universe.

Anthropologists often define *witchcraft* as doing evil through one's personal supernatural power or through one's ability to influence the spiritual world to perform such evil. Ixtepejanos and other Mesoamericans entertained several such beliefs. Fire witches, so called because they flew through the sky at night as balls of fire, were dangerous at night and, at some times of year, during daylight hours, too. Some of the people said they were living townspeople with the ability to change themselves into spiritual beings, while others indicated they were lost spirits of the dead. They agreed that they were able to make people ill by causing a kind of bad air called *aigre de hora* to enter the person (Kearney 1972:50).

The fire witches also had a protective function, because those they afflicted were mainly people going around at night to steal, carouse, and engage in other illicit activities. Still, they might also attack innocent people out on a night errand. The people believed the fire witches were organized, with a leader and a hierarchy of officials roughly like Ixtepeji's governmental hierarchy. Each evening they met with their chief, who sent them to various posts from which they watchfully prevented evil winds and diseases from blowing in from other towns. So, they both protected the people from outsiders and, sometimes, attacked townspeople.

Like other Mesoamericans, the people of Ixtepeji also believed in witches with the power to turn themselves into supernatural animals called *naguales*. They did not use the word witch (*brujo*, in Spanish) for such people or for the animal they could become, but the notion fits the concept of witchcraft in that individuals had supernatural power to harm others. The naguales were usually coyotes, snakes, bats, or foxes, though cougars and jaguars were sometimes naguales. People transformed themselves into naguales in order to do evil, mainly because they were envious of others. So, it was wise for an Ixtepejano to avoid any appearance or behavior that might stimulate envy in another person. That person might be a witch, one with the power to become a nagual. These beings attacked most often by killing people's counterpart animals, their *tonales*. Naguales were also air-like, and they were so deceptive and cunning that there was no effective defense. The best defense was to avoid occasion for attack.

Magic differs from things like witchcraft and prayer in that the supernatural power rests in a procedure rather than in a person. In *imitative magic* a person goes through some procedure that resembles the desired result, while in *conta-*

gious magic the perpetrator does something to an object or substance that has been, is, or will be in contact with the object of the magic. Ixtepejanos might engage in evil imitative magic by making a material image of someone they wanted to harm and sticking pins in the image or forcing mud into its stomach or head. This caused a bad air to penetrate the same part of the victim, giving him pain and, maybe, bringing death.

Cultural Change

For most of their history the Ixtepeji Zapotec's contacts with the outside world seem to have been fairly similar to the patterns general to Mesoamerica. Eventually, however, they became known as the "rebels of the Sierra," willing to fight for any cause that seemed worthy. This seems to have contributed to trouble with neighboring communities and Mexican political-military factions of various persuasions. This, combined with the swirl of events connected with the Mexican revolution of the early twentieth century, probably reinforced the negative elements so strong in Ixtepejano personality. The town, recall, was destroyed, and Ixtepejanos were scattered about the country, lived as guerrilla bands in the mountains, or lived in other mountain communities where they had friends or relatives

The Ixtepejanos, then, were pessimistic about change. Their experience was that change made things worse, and they entertained few thoughts of a better future. They did not plan for the future because they were preoccupied with doing the best they could with the present and because they could not know the future. They would have to cooperate to make the future better, and their need to defend themselves from a hostile social environment limited cooperation. They also felt their destinies were largely out of their hands, determined by the destiny with which each person was born and which one could do little if anything to modify. If other people had things better, it was because of destiny.

Other towns in the Sierra have adjusted to the shortage of good land and other economic problems by building up indigenous crafts, but Ixtepeji had no major craft specialty. The Ixtepejanos had to depend on farming, and the land was becoming poorer. Ixtepejanos had learned from the work of a North American in Ixtlán and from experimental introductions by the Papaloapan Commission that fruit trees would grow on their land and that they would damage the soil much less than corn. But the people lacked capital to establish orchards and had to wait several years for them to produce. Credit facilities were almost entirely inadequate. So the people were left with improvement of corn produc-

tion as the only possibility. But for historical and cultural reasons, they did not practice crop rotation, composting, seed selection, and other improved agricultural techniques. Apparently, the farmers did not respond to opportunities to learn about and apply more intensive techniques because of their deeply ingrained pessimism, fatalism, and general negativism.

In spite of all this, Kearney witnessed evidence that the people could respond favorably to improvement opportunities. If their conservative attitudes were the consequence of historical events and environmental circumstances, new events and changed circumstances might change those attitudes. In 1970 Kearney talked at length with several Ixtepejanos about the experimental *milpas* (corn fields) planted by a botanist in Ixtlán, and two of the men accompanied him to visit the plots and received instruction in the use of artificial and natural fertilizers. The two men obtained good enough results on their own land that they continued the experiment. This demonstrates that, though pessimism reigned in Ixtepeji, the capacity for hope was not completely gone.

A major question is whether or not the people might develop the willingness and the expertise to cooperate on the larger scale that would be necessary for significant change in their level of material well-being. On the basis of several developments, Kearney's answer is that the potential was there. For example, there had been a change in sponsorship of the annual fiesta in honor of the town's patron saint. Whereas forty or fifty people once financed the fiesta, they changed to asking every adult male to contribute a small amount. This was forced by a breakdown in the older system, but is nevertheless an example of community-wide participation.

Another example was the acquisition of a town truck. Four men formed an association to buy a truck, which they used for hauling passengers and cargo. The men fell out with one another and the project eventually folded, but men continued to buy trucks and to prosper until the town itself acquired a truck. The use of the several trucks provided the potential for increased production of fruit, chickens, eggs, flowers, and other items that might be sold in the city for cash. Kearney's conclusion in 1972 was that another decade would be likely to reveal whether or not Ixtepeji could change enough to remain a viable farming community. The alternative, he indicated, would be increased decline and emigration of large numbers of Ixtepejanos into the slums of Mexican cities (Kearney 1972:133). Subsequent events have revealed that this is exactly what has happened to multitudes of Indian and other Mexican rural communities throughout the land.

Chapter 14

THE HUAVE INDIANS OF THE ISTHMUS OF TEHUANTEPEC

In some geographical regions most of the cultures are similar to one another, and anthropologists call such regions of cultural similarity *culture areas*. Inevitably, the cultures within an area vary, one of the greatest sources of difference being the presence of large rivers, lakes, or a sea teeming with water life. The Huave (roughly WAH-beh) of southern Mexico lie within the Mesoamerican culture area and exhibit characteristics common in that region, but their culture is also in large measure a set of standardized responses to the ocean, the salt water lagoons of their territory, and the beaches. Their culture was not prominent in ancient Mesoamerica and has not caught the imagination of the outside world like those of the Seri, Lacandón, Kuna, and other Middle American tribes. They are fairly well known anthropologically, however, and their rather distinctive lifeway adds to the picture of Mesoamerican cultural variety.

The some 6,000 San Mateo Huave of the 1960s and 1970s grew sweet potatoes, maize, and other crops, fished in their lagoons, herded large flocks of sheep and goats, and hunted and collected in their forests. They made clay pots and griddles and a number of wooden items but purchased or traded for many of their tools and utensils. They were noted for the artistry of the multipurpose cloths (tablecloths or napkins mostly) woven by the women. They traded in their own markets, often with Zapotec merchants who lived in their communities, but they also took items to markets in other places.

In 1970 the people of San Mateo occupied a village laid out on the grid plan, about seven or eight sandy streets running parallel with the shore of the lagoon and ten or so running across them. There was a market area at the center of the village, with the school buildings and the teachers' quarters nearby (Cheney 1976:6). Somewhat to the southeast of the market and school was a block containing the Catholic Church, the rectory, the clinic operated by the Catholics, and the men's house, where the people kept their sacred bells. In the block to the east of the church was the town hall, jail, another school building, and a reliquary chapel. The Baptist Church lay several blocks away in another direction, and there were bars, corn mills, still another school building, and a couple of graveyards.

In San Mateo del Mar most households were occupied by a three generation *extended family*, which was commonly *patrilocal*. San Mateo's households were grouped into a small number of *barrios*, each of which had political and religious functions. The *municipio* of San Mateo consisted of the town itself, a number of outlying hamlets and homesteads, and the communal and privately held municipio lands. Each Huave male was expected to participate in a graded system of civil and religious offices called *cargos*, at least at the lower levels. The most successful climbed to higher levels of responsibility and held major offices such as *presidente*, chief of police, or first or second *alcalde*. There were seven governmental levels and four church levels, and the first and second alcaldes exercised authority over both the government and the church. Men could also gain prestige by serving as a *mayordomo*, that is, sponsoring a saint for a year and standing the expense for the maintenance of the image and the annual fiesta in its honor.

The Huave believed in a variety of deities, some of them of Christian origin and others survivals of pre-Christian times. A creator god, the Devil, several saints, the cross, the sun, the moon, and several other powerful sky beings were among them. They also assumed the dead remained in contact with them, and they believed in witchcraft and sorcery. Each person had a counterpart animal in the wild, and those who knew what it was could transform themselves into that animal to do witchcraft. *Shamans*, whom the people called knowers, divined the causes of illness and healed people, though there were other kinds of healers as well. The people held that there was an afterlife and that their state there depended on how they lived in this world.

Prehistory

Many origins theories lack definitive supporting evidence. If a reputable scholar propounds a reasonable origins theory and little or no contrary evidence is forthcoming over many years, the notion tends to receive more general acceptance than it deserves. This appears to be so with the theory that the Huave immigrated into the Isthmus of Tehuantepec from Central or South America about two hundred years before the Spanish arrived. In his widely used 1674 work, *Geográfica Descripción*, Francisco de Burgoa reported a Huave legend that their ancestors came to Central America from some remote southern place (Cheney 1976:7). They supposedly remained in their new location for a relatively short time, since they were in conflict with their neighbors there. They allegedly took to their canoes and moved northward along the Pacific coast until they reached the southern coast of Oaxaca, where the Mixe Indians allowed them to settle in the hot lowlands. Some popular sources repeat Burgoa's account as fact, but investigators have failed to produce archaeological or other independent evidence of Huave origins.

History

The Huave once occupied a larger area than now. They apparently retreated from parts of the Isthmus of Tehuantepec due to the late fifteenth century troubles between Aztec armies and Mixtec and Zapotec forces. Zapotec farmers periodically encroached further on their territory after the Spanish arrived between 1521 and 1523, until the Huave were left only with the area immediately around the salt water lagoons on the southern side of the Isthmus.

The Spanish were rather uninterested in Huave country and did not establish *encomiendas* and haciendas there, but the Dominican missionaries installed themselves among the Huave during the early 1600s and remained there into the eighteenth century. They built large stone churches in three of the largest Huave communities and imposed much of the Spanish vocabulary, religious and governmental institutions; and customs concerning health, medicine, and witchcraft. This constituted the first major force for Huave acculturation to non-Indian ways. The second was the incorporation of the Huave into the highly developed Zapotec and Spanish market system, making them greatly dependent economically (Diebold 1969:481). The Spanish and the Zapotec wanted Huave marine products and forced them to accept agricultural produce and other items in return. Disputes between Huave and Zapotec over land and other matters have consistently been settled in the courts and otherwise in favor of the latter.

Like other Mesoamerican tribes the Huave were left more or less free of Spanish dominance during a hundred years or more before Mexico became independent in 1821. As anthropologist Oliver LaFarge pointed out (LaFarge 1977[1940]:290), there was a slow relaxation of Spanish control from about 1720 throughout New Spain. For the Huave this included the departure and reduced influence of the Dominicans. Like other Middle American tribes, they resumed customs that had been suppressed and integrated Spanish-Christian elements with surviving Indian ways to form a new pattern of life they could be relatively comfortable with. By the time of Mexico's independence they were living a blend of pre-Spanish Huave, Zapotec, and Spanish customs that could be called Indian in the sense that the people spoke the Huave language and were otherwise culturally distinct from Mexican nationals. By then the town of San Mateo del Mar, like hundreds of other Mesoamerican places, had become what has been called a *closed corporate peasant community* (Wolf 1957:1). Anthropologists define peasant communities as traditionally oriented places politically and economically dependent on a larger society of which they are part. For the Huave, of course, this larger society would be the nation of Mexico. At the same time, the town was relatively closed to the outside world. In spite of participating in the regional market system Mareños (people of San Mateo) married within the community almost entirely, a practice anthropologists call *endogamy*. There was hardly any travel outside the community, very few emigrated, and new members were not welcome. All of the community land was owned corporately by the town and was available for use only to those who had been born in San Mateo and who met their obligations to community life.

San Mateo's way of life would also fit anthropologist Ralph Linton's well-known concept of a folk culture. Linton characterized a *folk culture* as a well-integrated, slowly changing lifeway borne by a small, closely integrated social unit (Linton 1936:283).

The prominent American anthropologist Robert Redfield built on this concept of folk culture to formulate his notion of a *folk-urban continuum*. He pictured a folk community as isolated, well adjusted to the local habitat, and culturally homogeneous. It was also characterized by strongly personal as opposed to impersonal relationships, the importance of family, an emphasis on the sacred as compared with the secular, a strong development of ritual, and a tendency of individual behavior to take place in group contexts (Redfield 1941:343). Redfield saw the urban pole of the continuum as manifesting the opposite of these features and viewed communities as existing at some point between the extremes of the continuum and changing at various rates from the folk toward the urban cultural type. He compared four communities of Mexico's Yucatán Peninsula to illustrate the continuum, a village of tribal Maya, a Mayan peasant village, a town, and a city. He found the peasant and tribal villages relatively closer to the folk end of the cultural continuum than the town and city. If we were to try to fit San Mateo into this continuum, it would lie relatively closer to the Mayan peasant village than the tribal village.

Anthropologists debated Redfield's scheme for years. Many pointed out how few communities fit very neatly into the continuum, since so many places seem to be a mixture of folk and urban characteristics. Few continue to use Redfield's formulation, though many note how cultures vary from one another with regard to the characteristics Redfield specified. His conceptions, in fact, were derived from the work of earlier scholars, and they retain their essential validity.

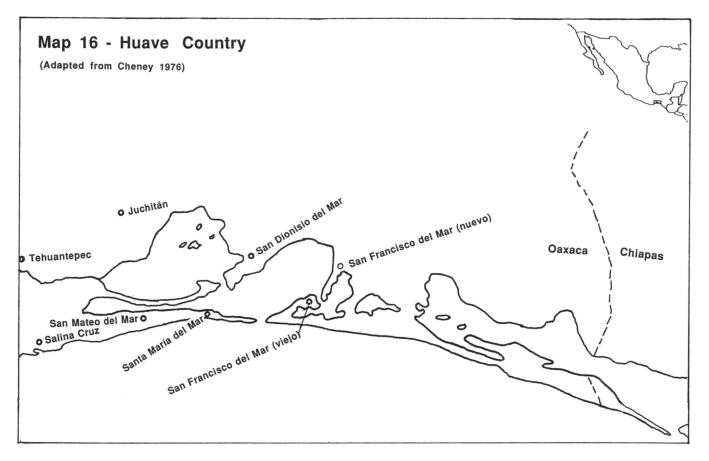

Map 16 - Huave Country

(Adapted from Cheney 1976)

Juchitán

Tehuantepec

San Dionisio del Mar

San Francisco del Mar (nuevo)

Oaxaca   Chiapas

San Francisco del Mar (viejo)

San Mateo del Mar

Salina Cruz

Santa María del Mar

San Mateo continued to change slowly over the years while maintaining it's relative isolation and continuing to be dependent on regional and national systems. Outside forces began to undermine this stability just before the middle of the twentieth century. By around 1940 the fighting that had troubled southern Mexico during and for some time after the Mexican Revolution had subsided, and during the 1940s and 1950s the Mexican government greatly reduced the incidence of malaria. Missionaries brought in modern medicine, resulting in rapid population growth (Cheney 1976:10). Zapotec merchants began to settle in San Mateo during the 1940s, and about forty lived semi-permanently in the town center, dominating the town market and strongly challenging the traditional culture. During the same period missionary linguists have resided for various periods in San Mateo, developing a writing system for the Huave language, translating the Bible, and converting a hundred or so to Christianity. The presence of so many Huave Christians tended to undermine the town's traditional civil religious hierarchy.

During the 1960s a Catholic priest took up residence in San Mateo, converting around a hundred people to orthodox Catholicism, opening a road, constructing an apartment and a clinic, and bringing in religious teachers, physicians, and nurses. This also undermined the civil-religious hierarchy and challenged the town's traditional Christo-paganism.

From the early 1960s and even earlier the Mexicans have exercised increasing political supervision over the Huave, pressing upon them national standards concerning separation of church and state, private property, law en-forcement, legal procedure, elections, political parties, and education. They established public schools, staffed with outsiders, thus introducing both Huave children and their parents to alien ways. In 1971 the Mexican government launched the "Huave Plan," a program for improving Huave living conditions through economic development. Federal and local officials, research teams, and journalists visited the town, and by the time anthropologist Charles Cheney studied among the Mareños during the early seventies, potable water had been brought in and gravel-surfaced roads built into San Mateo and two other Huave towns (Cheney 1976:12). The ongoing changes prompted Cheney to call for intensified anthropological work among the Huave to document both the disappearing culture and the circumstances of change.

Ethnography

Relatively little has been published on Huave culture. None of the Spanish wrote of Huave customs, and explorer-ethnographer Frederick Starr's observations made about the end of the nineteenth century provide the first useful information (Starr 1899, 1900-02). Writer-explorer Ludwig Rohrsheim visited the Huave briefly in the 1920s and published an article giving his impressions of them (Rohrsheim 1928). Prominent North American anthropologist Paul Radin worked among the Huave early in the century and published an article on Huave linguistic relationships (Radin 1916) but little or nothing on the culture. Mexican anthropologist Arturo Monzón studied among them some decades later and has published a popular article on their religion (1943). A. Richard Diebold, Jr. collected cultural data in San Mateo during two visits between 1958 and 1960, published an article on Mareño kinship, and wrote the summary of Huave culture for the *Handbook of Middle American Indians* (Diebold 1966, 1969). In 1967 Charles C. Cheney began a study of cultural change among the Huave of San Mateo with special attention to their community organization and their religion (Cheney 1976, 1979). Several Italian anthropologists have also looked at various aspects of Huave life, including their agricultural practices (Bamonte 1977), population anthropology (Marzotto 1977), godparent-godchild system (Signorini 1977), cultural change (Pelliccione 1979), and cosmology (Lupo, 1981). This description relies heavily on Cheney's and Diebold's reports.

Huave Country

In 1970 there were five Huave villages and a number of nearby hamlets situated on or near the salt-water lagoons along the Pacific coast of the Isthmus of Tehuantepec. San Mateo, the largest village, lies about one-third of the way out on a 35 mile long sand peninsula extending eastward from the mouth of the Tehuantepec River. The town sits on the inland shore of a long narrow lagoon separating it from the ocean beach—near enough that townspeople heard the waves crashing on quiet nights. The peninsula averages a mile-and-a-half in width. Larger lagoons lie inland from San Mateo as well as to the east of the end of the peninsula. Another Huave village lies 14 miles east of San Mateo on the same peninsula, and the other three villages are to the north and east around two of the other lagoons. Tehuantepec, one of the main towns of the Isthmus, is 26 miles to the northwest of San Mateo, and the coastal town of Salina Cruz lies 21 miles west.

The Huave live in rather difficult territory. It is an arid area afflicted by cold northern winds during the late fall and winter, scorching droughts during the summer, and frequent storms and floods (Covarrubias 1946:58). The territory closest to the lagoons is marked by the presence of mangrove swamps, salt flats, and enclosed or nearly enclosed bodies of brackish water (Diebold 1969:482). Away from the lagoons a bit lies an area of grassy zones alternating with drier sections of sand dunes and palm trees. Beyond this is a region of low hills where intermittent thorn tree forests grow. In 1970 the people fished in the lagoons, pastured their animals in the grassy zones, planted their crops there and in the thorn forest, and hunted deer, iguanas, and rabbits in the forest.

Language

Linguists have experienced some difficulty determining the relationships of Huave speech. They agree that the language shows similarities to other Middle American languages, but they are so equivocal as to make it difficult to place Huave in any larger linguistic category. According to some analyses, it is most closely allied with the Oto-Manguean group of languages, sometimes called Macro-Mixtecan, while others think it is directly related to Mayan or some other family. Because of the continuing disagreement, Longacre listed Huave as the only representative of its group and, accordingly, as distinctive as Oto-Manguean, Uto-Aztecan, Tarascan, Macro-Mayan and other Middle American stocks (Longacre 1967:77).

All languages are too complex and the necessary description too technical to present balanced treatments in summaries of this kind. Linguists treat the speech of all groups as consisting of a number of *phonemes*. Some phonemes consist of only one sound, while others are made up of a set of closely similar alternative sounds. In the latter case, a speaker can use any of the alternative sounds of a given phoneme without changing or destroying the meaning of an utterance. In Huave, for example, *mbol* means "to fear" (Stairs and Hollenbach 1969:45). This utterance consists of four phonemes, and data are not at hand to tell us whether any of the four consist of more than one sound.

Linguists have analyzed the Huave sound system into 30 phonemes, several of which are not found in English (Stairs and Hollenbach 1969:38). They include both long and short vowels, which means, for example, that saying *mbool* instead of *mbol* would change or destroy the meaning associated with that utterance. This is because *oo* belongs to a different phoneme from *o*.

Linguists use the term *morpheme* for the smallest unit of language that has a specific meaning. A morpheme is made up of either one or a combination of phonemes plus the meaning. *Mbol* is a morpheme of four phonemes and the meaning "to fear. Morphemes are the elements from which words are built. A morpheme can be a word by itself, or it can be combined with one or more other morphemes to make a word. *Ermbol*, for instance, means "you fear" and *imbol* means "he fears" (Stairs and Hollenbach 1969:45). Words, of course, are combined to form phrases and sentences. Note that the Huave are able to use one word for utterances that would require more than one English word.

The first thing linguistic anthropologists or other linguists do in studying a language is to record all the sound differences they can distinguish consistently in the people's speech. Then they discover which sound differences make a difference in meaning and place similar sounds that can be used as alternatives without making a difference in meaning in a single phoneme. After they have decided what the phonemes are, they find out how the phonemes are used to form the units with meaning called morphemes and the processes by which the people use morphemes to build words. Finally, they investigate the customary ways they use words to make phrases and sentences. This provides them with the data necessary to describe the sound system (phonology) and the grammatical system (morphology and syntax) of the language.

Personality and Behavior

The Huave have long been known as timid and distrustful as compared with their neighbors. The Zapotec have seemed much more aggressive and have successfully taken advantage of the Huave in many of their encounters. On the other hand, the Huave have not been totally without recourse. Covarrubias reported that, while the people liked to wear fine clothing at home, they wore their worst rags to the market in Tehuantepec so the people they dealt with would pity them (Covarrubias 1946:60). The nonaggressiveness of the Huave seems to accord well with their propensity for isolating themselves from the outside world as much as possible.

Fatalism has been strong in the outlook of some Mesoamerican groups, and the Huave were among them. They regarded the universe as morally indifferent, saw fate as capricious, and regarded themselves as relatively powerless to control or change things (Cheney 1979:59). Their way of avoiding unwanted change has long been withdrawal, and when Mexicans, missionaries, and others have sought to interfere in their lives, they have been reluctant to resist openly and actively. Accordingly, they have from time to time undergone considerable acculturation in spite of their tendency to withdraw. They have always been conservative while, at the same time, hardly very effective in resisting change. They have become less Indian than many tribes.

Clothing and Personal Appearance

The Huave women wore clothing similar to that of the *tehuanas* (Zapotec women of Tehuantepec), a skirt of cotton cloth wrapped about the hips, and a *huipil* (blouse). During the 1940s, according to Covarrubias, the skirts were indigo or red with white or yellow stripes, and the blouses were of black or blue cotton cloth with a border of yellow and red stitching (Covarrubias 1946:63) They went without the blouses in the home or while working, apparently as late as Diebold's time there in 1960. A number of the women had taken to wearing dresses by the 1960s. The women braided their hair with ribbons entwined and, outside the house lot, wore the shawl-like *rebozo* by crossing it over the front of the head and tucking it in on the sides to resemble a turban. Most of them also wore bead necklaces. Covarrubias says that, during the 1940s, Huave women could be distinguished from Zapotec women by their beads and by the white cloth or towel they wore tied over the head.

The men wore long serge trousers, cotton shirts, and high-crowned, straw hats. When fishing they replaced their trousers with shorts, or, rarely by the 1960s, a G-string. Both men and women wore leather sandals some, but they preferred to go barefooted. Children dressed just like their elders, though boys wore little until about six years of age. They made their clothing, except for fishing jackets, festive clothing, and shawls, from manufactured cloth.

Houses and Other Structures

The people's home lots lined the streets, containing, typically, a rectangular, gabled house of thatch, a ramada (covered work area), fish drying racks, an outside kitchen, net-drying racks, a ground oven, a well, animal pens, a garden, and benches. The lot was surrounded by a tightly-spaced fence of the bamboo-like reeds known as *carrizo*. and a gate opened onto the street. Some plots included more than one main living structure.

The members of a barrio, a subdivision of the town, cooperated to build the large, rectangular, one-roomed house. They planted corner posts, ran horizontal beams from post to post, and fixed tall end posts in place to receive the ridge pole. Then they ran widely spaced rafters from the ridge to the beams atop the side walls, placed a cross member over them at ridge and wall beam, and lashed them in place. Then, they prepared a grid of lighter members for both walls and roof and attached palm leaf thatching to the grid. The door was in a side wall, and there were no windows. The houses might remind some of house-shaped stacks of hay. Typically there would be several shade trees on a lot. There was little furniture—mainly hammocks, sleeping mats, and benches.

Livelihood

Most economic systems combine two or more modes—hunting-gathering, horticulture, fishing, and/or herding. Often one or more of them is very weak, but they were relatively balanced in Huave culture. Like other Middle American tribes the Huave produced maize and other crops by slash-and-burn agriculture, but they also hunted and collected in their hilly thorn forests, fished in their lagoons, herded large flocks of sheep and goats on their grassland pastures, and kept horses, cattle, and burros.

Fishing was important in Huave life, but some have conveyed the erroneous idea that it provided most of the livelihood and agriculture was unimportant. Fishing may have been the single most productive subsistence system among the Huave, but the combination of horticulture, animal husbandry, and minor artisanry combined outstripped it (Diebold 1969:483.) Its relatively great importance may well have developed from Huave confinement by outside pressure to the lagoon country of the southern part of the Isthmus, where agriculture is difficult and the fish readily available. Diebold points out that the Huave lacked the hook, gig, traps, and other simple devices and techniques that would greatly increase their catches and that they were less skilled fisherman than many other fishing societies. In addition, many of their words for species of fish and related cultural items have been borrowed from Spanish. If fishing had long dominated their economic lives, one would expect a variety of techniques, high skill, and a better developed fishing terminology.

The Huave of San Mateo used two devices for taking sea perch, mullet, shrimp and other fish—the dragnet with poled canoes and the throw net, which individual fisherman cast from shore (Diebold 1969:483). They imported their canoes, which were square-nosed, trough-shaped dugouts between 15 and 20 feet long, over a yard wide, and about two feet from bottom to stern level (Cerda Silva 1941:98).

Several canoes of men had to work together to operate a dragnet, so a number of canoe crews made up a voluntary association with a leader selected to coordinate the fishing and divide the catch. Gatherer-hunters usually lack *associations* (clubs or other organizations), but they are more common among horticultural peoples like those of Mesoamerica. The Huave fishing clubs illustrate *instrumental* associations, those formed to accomplish some specific purpose of importance to the people. Some societies have purely *expressive* associations, such as sewing or singing clubs, whose main purpose is pursuit of some activity the members enjoy in common.

The Huave preserve fish by drying them in the sun, either split or whole. The fish are important to them both in their diet and for trade.

The Huave pastured their large herds of sheep and goats and their horses, cattle, and burros on the community-owned grasslands. They also kept pigs, chickens, and turkeys in their house lots. They took much of their wool, meat, and eggs to markets in nearby Zapotec towns and sold some to visiting or resident merchants from the outside world.

The main Huave crop was sweet potatoes, but they also produced maize (Indian corn), beans, peanuts, and cotton. They planted them in small plots in the thorn forests, some being permanent fields worked with ox-drawn plows and others slash-and-burn *milpas* (corn fields). They cleared the temporary fields with machetes and worked the ground with hoes. As with all *swidden* (slash-and-burn) agriculture the fields were abandoned as soon as the soil was exhausted, and the farmers cleared new plots. The people also grew chili peppers and a few other items in their house lot gardens, and some had fruit trees, coconut palms, and calabash trees. The Huave were unable to produce enough in their fields to meet all their needs and traded the products of the sea, their animals, and their crafts for additional maize and other foods.

The people also took deer, rabbits, and ignuanas in the thorn forests.

There was a variety of foods available to the Mareños, but like other Mesoamericans, they made maize their staple, using it mainly for the round thin corn cakes known as tortillas and the corn drink *atole*. Sometimes they made tamales and other corn foods. They also made fish an important part of the regular diet, eating them either dried or in a stew. They added chili peppers to all their foods. Though they produced more sweet potatoes than corn, they ate relatively few, and beans were also of secondary importance. They also traded most of their meat and eggs, though they used them in fiesta dishes. They ate fruit whenever the trees were producing.

Crafts, Tools, and Techniques

The Huave of San Mateo were not outstanding artisans, and though they made a number of their tools and utensils, they also purchased various things. They obtained metal items such as machetes, hoes, and spades from outside, as well as the *metates* or grinding stones. The women made clay pots and the round clay griddles for baking tortillas but also bought a few (Diebold 1969:484). The Mareños used calabashes to make many of their containers and fashioned a number of wooden items, such as their three-legged benches. The fishermen made and repaired their own nets, using cotton thread gotten mostly from the outside world.

The people bought manufactured cloth for most of their clothing, but women wove material for fishing jackets, festive blouses, shawls (*rebozos*), nicely done multipurpose cloths of cotton, and a few other items on the *backstrap loom* (Diebold 1969:84). The backstrap loom was general in Mesoamerica and was found in other parts of the Americas and in the Old World as well. One of the crossbars holding the warp threads was attached by a cord to a post or tree, while the crossbar holding the other end was attached to a cord or belt around the weaver's waist. In this way she could control the tension of the threads, alternate the position of the two sets of warp threads, and pass the shuttle containing the woof threads (crossthreads) between them.

A few Mareño men wove baskets full-time, mainly the large carrying and storage basket with *tumpline* attached, and enough others wove part-time to make it an important craft. Men also made a good deal of rope of palm fiber. In addition, certain part-time craftsmen specialized in making religious equipment, musical instruments, featherwork, and leather items.

The Mareños might travel for trading purposes in their dugout canoes, and they transported various things in wooden carts, which, like canoes, they obtained from outside the community. They also carried things with the tumpline, the strap across the forehead, which was attached by cords to whatever they were carrying on the back—commonly a large basket of something.

The full-time activities of men were fishing, farming, or a craft, and their part-time work included building houses, making the tools they used, doing communal labor of various kinds, and trading. A few men sometimes worked elsewhere for wages for short times. The women made pots, wove, and traded in the market-place. Of course, they spent much of their time at house work and caring for their children.

Though there was a small market in San Mateo, the Huave went to the markets in larger places for most manufactured items and much of their maize, either selling or bartering fish, eggs, sweet potatoes, and other items for what they needed. Economically, then, they were tightly linked to the outside world. They also obtained items from merchants who entered San Mateo and who actually dominated the local market (Diebold 1966:39).

Social Organization and Relationships

During the 1960s the standard Mareño household was either an extended family or a *joint family*. Extended families are very common around the world and consist of basically three generations, the oldest set of parents, their married offspring and their spouses, and their unmarried children. Most of the extended families were patrilocal when Diebold studied in San Mateo during the 1960s, which means that a man remained in his parents' household after marriage, bringing his wife into that household with him. There were also *matrilocal* extended families, consisting of the oldest couple, their married daughters and their husbands, and their grandchildren. Finally, there were some *ambilocal* family households, composed of the oldest couple, both married daughters and sons with their spouses, and their grandchildren. There were 376 households in San Mateo when Diebold was there. He found that each was the fundamental unit of production and consumption and the focus of family life.

Anthropologists have found that extended families seem to provide for their members' needs better than smaller families, and this may be one of the reasons for their high frequency around the world. There are simply more people around in an extended family to help in case a parent is ill or otherwise unable to function effectively. At the same time the anthropologically well-known Six Cultures study of child-rearing and personality found that children reared in extended family households were more authoritarian and aggressive in their behavior toward one another than those in independent nuclear families. This may reflect some of the tensions and conflicts associated with so many people having to interact so closely and constantly with one another (Whiting and Whiting 1963:00).

Each extended family household in San Mateo occupied a house lot. Some of these extended families were *stem families*. That is, there was only one offspring with his or her spouse and children living with the older couple. In such households the three generations nearly always lived in a single house (Diebold 1966:43). Moreover, extended families of the stem type among the Huave tended to be bilingual, and their members referred to one another and their other relatives by less traditional kinship terms than other kinds of extended families.

There were also extended families of the *lineal* type among the Mareños, which means that there was more than one married offspring with spouse and children. In this type of family, Diebold found, many of the younger families lived in separate dwellings. One of the junior families lived with the senior couple, making a three generation unit, while the other junior family usually lived in a separate structure. This revealed that the monogamous nuclear family was a dependent unit within the household context, sometimes within a dwelling and, in some contexts, within the house lot group. Diebold's study also showed that the lineal extended families of San Mateo tended to be monolingual—speaking only Huave—and used more traditional kinship terms to refer to one another (Diebold 1966:66).

Anthropologists emphasize the *functional* or *systemic* nature of cultures, that is, that the elements they are made up of are interdependent with one another. Anthropologists and other social scientists divide cultures into aspects such as language, social organization, religion, art, and the like in order to describe them, but customs in different aspects are linked to one another. The foregoing is an example of two features of social organization—family type and kinship terms—that are interdependent with language.

Anthropologists use the term *kindred* to designate any individual's relatives, their relationships to that person being traced through both males and females. This collection of relatives is a *bilateral* social unit. In *unilineal* societies a person traces descent through only one person in each generation, males if it is a *patrilineal* society and females if it is *matrilineal*. Societies which include both males and females in each generation when reckoning relationships are said to be bilateral, so kindreds are by definition bilateral. Kindreds are not groups, however, since they are defined by people's relationships to individuals. Full siblings (brothers, sisters, or a brother and sister) have the same people for their kindred. It is different for parents and children, cousins, and other close relatives. They have many of the same people in their respective kindreds, but not all.

This overlapping is one of the ways kindreds differ from *clans* and *lineages*. Crow Indian society, for example, was divided into 13 clans, each person belonging to one clan only, but there were as many kindreds in San Mateo as there were people, each individual belonging to several other Mareño's kindreds. Things are simpler in one way in societies with clans than in those with kindreds. If two people from different clans quarrel or fight, each one's clan members lend their support. But if two people of different kindreds quarrel, people belonging to both kindreds may be caught between a rock and a hard place as both disputants demand their loyalty on the basis of kindred affiliation (Murdock 1949:61).

The Mareño kindred was what might be called an *affinally augmented* kindred, which means that it included relatives by marriage (*affinal* relatives) as well as *consanguineal* ("blood") relatives. This does not mean a Huave interacted in the same manner and with the same intensity with all members of his kindred, since in all human groups proximity, personality compatibility, and other factors affect behavior among relatives. In fact, some of the members of a Huave kindred might not even know one another (Diebold 1966:45).

The members of both a Mareño household and a kindred were tied to one another by consanguineal and affinal ties. But households are residential units, while a kindred is little more than a category of people related to a certain person, and its members are scattered among many residential units rather than living together like the members of a family.

Many Mesoamerican communities, though not all, are subdivided into territorial units known as barrios, and there were four barrios in San Mateo during the 1950s and early 1960s. Of course, the smallest residential unit was the family household, and these were grouped into barrios. The next higher territorial unit was the cluster of residences known as the town or *pueblo*, but the barrios extended beyond the boundaries of the town to include the outlying hamlets within the municipio (township) of San Mateo. Diebold found that one of the barrios within the town itself was a good deal larger than the others. The largest consisted of 151 households and 1,080 people; a second had 527 people and 65 households; the third 783 people in 92 households; and the fourth consisted of 544 people in 68 households (Diebold 1966:45).

Barrio membership was related to religion, government and marriage. Each of the four barrios carried out certain religious activities in from two to five small, thatch-roofed chapels located on the larger streets. In addition, each barrio was politically organized in ways patterned after the municipio government, and the people saw that each barrio was represented among the municipio officials. Finally, the large majority of Mareños married within their own barrio.

Fictive kinship refers to relationships between nonkin which exhibit qualities characteristic of ties between consanguineal relatives. Adoption and institutionalized friendship ties such as blood brotherhood are especially common examples of fictive kinship around the world. The Spanish brought to the Indian cultures of the New World a fictive kinship institution known as the *compadrazgo*, which involves the establishment of special relationships between godparents and godchildren and between the godparents and the children's parents. Only a few of the Mesoamerican tribes, such as the Lacandón Maya of southeastern Mexico, failed to accept this social institution, and it became quite important in the lives of a number of societies. San Mateo Huave parents selected godparents to sponsor each of their children, either when the child was born or when it was baptized. Also, best practice dictated that they select an additional set of godparents when the young person became betrothed. Usually the father asked a married male to become a godparent to his child, and, if he accepted, the man and his wife became the child's sponsors and the two married couples became *compadres* (coparents). The compadres were either entirely unrelated or only remotely related to one another, they had to belong to different households, and they were virtually without exception residents of San Mateo. A father chose someone he trusted and was friendly with, someone he was associated with in political, religious, fishing, agricultural activities, or some combination of them. He also chose someone of about the same age, but, commonly, slightly older.

The godparents were expected to act as the ritual sponsors of the couple's child for whatever occasion, baptism or otherwise. From the time of their selection they took a special interest in their godchild. If a parent died, they might accept partial responsibility for parenthood or become the child's full foster parents. The sponsoring couple referred to their godchildren as such, and the child referred to his or her sponsors as "godfather" and "godmother." As in so many other Mesoamerican groups the relationship between the two couples was more important than between godchild and godparents. The compadres were expected to help one another with goods and labor during sickness and other troubles.

Anthropologists devote considerable attention to the terms relatives use for one another, mainly because it provides valuable clues to how people behave toward one another. They concern themselves most with *reference* terms, the terms people use when talking about one another, partly because reference terms are simpler and more stable than terms people use to address one another.

Diebold has described both the terms of address and the terms of reference for the Mareños of the 1960s. A Mareño used one term to address all male relatives of older generations, a second term for all female relatives of older generations, a third term for all older relatives of his or her own generation, a fourth term for all younger relatives of his or her own generation, and a fifth term for all relatives in younger generations. It is apparent that the Mareños used address terms that distinguished the sexes only in older generations, that they distinguished persons of their own generation who were older than they from those who were younger, and that they used different terms for people of different generations rather than lumping people of different generations together. An exception to the last point is that one addressed his or her spouse by the same term used for relatives of older generations. All of the people of this address system were members of one's affinally augmented kindred, though the people experienced considerable uncertainty about how to address the most remote members.

The San Mateo Huave also used these kinship address terms for other people, such as godparents and godchildren, stepkin, political associates, and even supernatural beings. Godchildren addressed their godparents by the terms for relatives of older generations, and younger officials in the political system addressed the older officials, who directed their activities, by the terms for older generation kin. The people also addressed the moon, a supernatural being in their religion, by a name derived from their term for older generation females. There are many other examples of these kinds of extensions of address terms for relatives.

Huave terms for referring to relatives differed from those for addressing them, and they were not extended outside the kindred. Moreover, bilingual Mareños living in stem type extended families used one system of reference terms for their relatives while those living in lineal type families used different kinds of terms. The Mareños living in lineal family households tended to speak Huave only and used what anthropologists call *generation* terms for their parents, aunts, and uncles, which means they included aunts and uncles under the same terms they used for their parents. Accordingly, they referred to the mother, mother's sister, and father's sister by just one term and the father, father's brother, and mother's brother by a second term.

On a person's own generation the monolingual Mareños used what anthropologists call *Hawaiian* terminology, lumping cousins under the same terms they used for their brothers and sisters. Within the Hawaiian terminology they made no distinction between the sexes, using the same term for brothers as for sisters and for male cousins as for female cousins.

One generalization, then, is that the monolingual Huave distinguished the sexes terminologically within the parental generation but not in their own generation. However, they distinguished siblings and cousins that were older from themselves from those that were younger, so there was one term for older siblings and cousins and a different term for younger siblings and cousins. They extended the term for father and uncle to include the husbands of aunts and the term for mother and aunt to include the wives of uncles, since these people were affinal relatives within one's kindred. They also referred to their nephews and nieces by the same terms they used for their own children.

Again, these were the kinship terms that members of lineal type extended families tended to use. The members of stem type extended families, who were generally bilingual, tended not to use them.

As in other Mesoamerican groups, a midwife attended a woman giving birth. The people believed each person acquired a *tonal* at birth, a wild animal counterpart born at the same moment in the immediate vicinity of the newborn's home (Cheney 1979:61). Some of the Mareños of the 1970s alleged that a shallow bowl of sand or ashes was placed under a pregnant woman's bed and examined immediately after birth for the spoor of the baby's tonal, but many denied this was done. Cheney found that very few knew which animal was their tonal and that they often guessed from the person's physical characteristics. They might assume, for example, that a person with prominent canine teeth was associated with a shark. Newborn apparently were bathed in warm water, and the umbilical cord was buried beneath the kitchen hearth (Cerda Silva 1941:102).

The parents selected godparents for their children either at birth or at baptism and again, preferably, when the young person was betrothed. The rituals accompanying these transition points in the life cycle appear to have been limited as compared with those of many other Mesoamerican groups. Cerda indicates that the parents arranged the marriage when their sons were between 13 and 16 years of age (Cerda Silva 1941:101). The boy's father gave food gifts to the girl's family, and their acceptance confirmed the arrangements. The couple went through both civil and religious ceremonies and, apparently, no special celebrations followed. The bride and groom carried burning candles during the wedding to symbolize their union (Cheney 1979:63).

All societies include a set of standardized responses to the illnesses that afflict people at various times during their lives. According to the Mareños the way to remain healthy was to maintain equilibrium within oneself, with other people, with the dead, and with nature (Cheney 1979:65). According to a system of belief derived from the Spanish, sickness came when certain hot and cold bodily characteristics became unbalanced, and healing involved bringing

them back into equilibrium. This hot-cold syndrome did not depend on actual temperature, but food, drink, and other things were classified as hot, cold, or neutral according to how they performed in relation to other items. A person could catch a cold by exposure to cold weather or eating too much cold food and should be given hot food and kept warm. The Mareños regarded intestinal disorders as hot diseases, which required that they should be given cold foods in moderation to bring things back into balance. The moderation was important, because the sudden change could make people sicker. An overheated person should not be doused with cold water, nor should a cold person be given especially hot food like beef.

The Mareños recognized diseases from natural sources, which included those caused by imbalances of hot and cold, wounds and broken bones, colds, malaria, smallpox, and common childhood diseases. Second, they recognized diseases resulting from strong emotional experiences of seven kinds—public shaming, suppressed anger, a fright, sexual intercourse when one was too hot, grief from death or loss of a lover, being thought about by a dead person, and encounters with a malignant spirit (Cheney 1979:667). The idea that people get sick from disturbed emotional states, especially a scare, intense anger, shame, and the like is especially strong in Mesoamerican cultures. During such overcharged emotional states the person is especially vulnerable to attack from malevolent forces or entities. The Mareños of the 1970s believed emotionally-induced diseases were apt to be lasting and included cancer, tuberculosis, chronic amoebic dysentery, blindness, epilepsy, asthma, and mental disorders among them.

A third type of sickness was caused by the injury or death of one's tonal, the wild animal counterpart born at one's birth. These were diseases with a sudden onset. If the person died it indicated that the tonal probably died of injuries inflicted by a human hunter, and if he or she survived it indicated the tonal had recovered.

Evil eye, also common in Mesoamerica, was an important cause of illness among San Mateo children. A person with a strong look might make children sick, in which case the child was taken by a sudden high fever, cried inconsolably, and, sometimes, suffered convulsions. Parents might hang a small palm cross or dried cocoon around the child's neck to absorb the power of strong glances. If they could locate the person who caused the illness, the parents could obtain a cure by having the person come to the home, touch the child's head, and wrap a length of thread soaked in his spittle around the victim's arm or leg.

The Mareños also believed that witchcraft and demon possession caused much disease. Witches were thought to send foreign elements and animals into a person's body.

There were four types of traditional healers in San Mateo—*knowers*, *incensers*, *midwives*, and *massagers* (Cheney 1979:67). The knowers were shamans, which means they had special power to use supernatural entities and powers in their diagnosis and healing. They could be of any age or either sex and had obtained their knowledge and power through dreams. There were between 30 and 35 knowers in San Mateo when Cheney was there. The knowers diagnosed illness by taking a sick person's pulse, taking the body temperature, touching the patient's body at certain points, examining the face, and gathering information from the person and the family. Knowers then recommended either a home treatment or referred the sick person to a specialist. Special foods, drinks, and herbs might be recommended, or prayer at the family altar. If they concluded the illness was from something sent into the body, they tried to remove it by cupping or sucking. They charged several hundred pesos for their work.

Though there were only eight incensers in San Mateo when Cheney was there, they enjoyed greater prestige than the knowers. All of them were old men who had acquired their abilities through many years of apprenticeship. They relied heavily on sixteenth century Spanish Catholic traditions, making extensive use of confession, prayer, exorcism, rituals incorporating the crucifix and multiples of the number three, and, especially, the burning of copal incense (Cheney 1979:68). Along with three incense burnings they offered flowers and prayed to sacred crosses, repeating the patient's description of his or her illness in detail. During the third session an incenser blew mouthfuls of alcohol on the part of the body needing treatment. Incensors knew and used several other treatments, too, depending on the nature of the illness. They received only food and liquor and a few small gifts for their services.

The midwives were all middle-aged and elderly women, and the massagers were men or women who gave alcohol massages for aches and pains, treated certain illnesses with herbal teas, and attempted to remove illnesses from the body by passing eggs from black hens over the afflicted areas.

The Mareños shared the widespread rural Latin American belief that those who die before puberty are sexually sinless and go directly to heaven as little angels, so their funeral ceremonies were joyful. A deceased adult's body was placed on a *petate* (mat of flexible basketry) in the middle of the dwelling, where a candle was burned, and a wake was held. The following day the body was carried to the cemetery and buried wrapped in the petate (Cerda Silva 1941:102).

Government and Social Order

In Mexico and other Middle American countries the fundamental unit of government is the municipio, which is a territory incorporating a town or towns, perhaps several hamlets and/or isolated homesteads, and the agricultural and other land belonging to the unit. If there is more than one town, one of them is the seat of the municipio government. The municipio of San Mateo consisted of the town, a number of outlying hamlets and homesteads, and the municipio lands. Many Mexican municipios are divided into several districts or barrios, and San Mateo consisted of four in the early 1960s. The town itself was divided into four barrios, each extending to include people living elsewhere

in the municipio. Since the 1940s, however, Mareños had been moving in increasingly larger numbers from the town into the outlying areas of the municipio. Accordingly, during the 1960s the town was reorganized to accommodate the new distribution of population. By the 1970s there were three barrios in the central town and two outlying hamlets.

During the 1970s the municipio (the three central districts, and the two outlying hamlets) functioned around a graded system of civil and religious offices that all adult males were expected to participate in, at least to the extent of holding some of the minor positions. It was basically the same kind of organizational system that has prevailed for so long in many other Mexican communities. Each male climbed the prestige ladder by holding positions of increasing responsibility and prestige in the governmental system and, for some, in the church organization. And while the church offices were limited to religious responsibilities, many of the civil positions combined secular with sacred functions (Cheney 1976:13). This system of increasingly prestigious positions has been known to anthropologists as the cargo system, since the people refer to the holding of the various offices as cargos. They were burdens they had to bear if they were to be responsible community members and advance to higher levels of prestige and responsibility, and all males were expected to participate in at least the lower levels.

There were seven levels in the governmental ladder, the lowest consisting of six town criers and twelve daytime policemen (*topiles* in Spanish). The criers moved about the community before dawn each day to the music of the flute and drum, announcing the day's religious and civil activities, notifying the people of required communal participation, and making known the names of any new officials.

The topiles slightly outranked the criers. They were divided into two six-man squads that alternated week-long shifts. They were expected to maintain order and apprehend offenders. If necessary, they brought into play a *macana*, a foot-long wooden club with a length of rope attached to one end. It was used to strike offenders who resisted and to lash their wrists together while taking them to jail (Cheney 1976:15).

The second level on the civil ladder consisted of 24 night police positions and the offices of first and second night police commander (*comandante*). Two groups of twelve night police, one under the first commander and the other under the second, alternated week-long shifts.

The third level contained the offices of *síndico*, alderman (*regidor*), treasurer, and scribe. The scribe maintained a list of men obligated to do communal labor, the treasurer collected taxes from the merchants in the market place, and the six aldermen served as an advisory council for higher community officials. The síndico was the chief executive officer and legal investigator. The scribe was elected for one year, while the treasurer, aldermen, and síndico served for three years. Any man who had held a level three office was known as a *principal*, even if he achieved no higher office, and was granted the right to be present at community meetings and voice his opinions.

At the fourth level were the positions of senior and junior *alcalde*, municipio vice president, and three substitutes (one for each of the foregoing positions). The alcaldes, along with the presidente, sat in judgement on civil cases and minor criminal trials. The substitutes prepared themselves for the positions they might have to step into.

Level five included the positions of *juez de mando* (judge) and first and second chiefs of police. The judge presided over the town criers and selected people for minor roles in religious ceremonies, while the chiefs of police supervised the daytime police and kept the jailhouse keys. The police chiefs also selected couriers and certain other religious participants and officers.

The only office at the sixth level was that of *presidente municipal*, recognized as the highest town office by the Mexican government. Accordingly, he represented the community to outside authorities, and he also had certain religious functions of community importance. The most important was a series of prayer vigils for abundant rainfall, crops, and marine life (Cheney 1976:16).

At the highest level of the governmental ladder were the first and second alcaldes, who, with the presidente, formed a triumvirate that made the most important community decisions, prayed for rain during the spring rituals, and oversaw the church officials and church property. As the top officials these men tied the church and governmental systems into a single complex.

There were four levels to the ecclesiastical ladder, the church police at the lowest level, the sacristans or ritualists at the second, the *fiscal* (assistant to the chapel master) at the third level, and the chapel master himself in the highest position. The chapel master was the chief church officer and equivalent in rank to the presidente at level six. He was directly responsible to the alcaldes and conducted baptisms and gave extreme unction in the absence of the priest, guarded the sacred objects, kept the almanacs of saint's days and other religious events, and selected and instructed the lower church officials and other religious participants.

Men especially interested in religious cargos could also gain prestige by serving as mayordomos. The *cofradías* (religious brotherhoods) were responsible for caring for saints and other sacred entities and holding the associated ceremonies. A mayordomo accepted the stewardship for the saint for a year, visiting the saint's image in the church, placing candles and flowers before it, and sponsoring and standing the expenses for the annual saint's day celebration.

Cheney indicated that Huave community order was based on three principles (Cheney 1976:20). It was important, first, that all the sections be represented equally. The people rotated the highest offices among the sections, although each nominated a candidate each time the position was to be filled.

Second, all men had to participate at the two lowest levels. If one refused he was fined and imprisoned for a short time. He was not nominated for another position, people did not ask his opinion about community issues, and he was made to feel unwelcome at group activities, including informal drinking sessions. In fact, his position in Huave society might become insecure in a variety of ways. He might find others questioning his right to the lands he held in usufruct from the community, and municipal officers would tend to rule against him in legal disputes with other community members.

The third principle is that only a few of the older men participated at the higher levels of the hierarchy. They advanced through the lower three levels in order, but above that they might skip one or more levels either temporarily or permanently. It was considered best by most not to depart too far from the usual sequence, since one should not be overly ambitious. Men were respected most for neither striving for nor rejecting cargos. Those who modestly accepted the nominations of their fellows as they came and gradually climbed the prestige ladder over the years thereby manifested both piety and community-mindedness.

In every society there are many discrepancies between ideality and performance, that is, differences between what people say and believe they do and what they actually do. The Mareños held that anyone could attain positions at several prestige levels and that wealth and power remained relatively equally diffused among the different segments of the community or, at least, did not become concentrated in the hands of any particular individuals or groups for a long period of time. This seems parallel to the beliefs of some modern North Americans that any boy can become president or that anyone can become rich. In San Mateo there were just too few positions and too many steps for more than a few men to advance all the way to the top. Also, by the 1970s a number of people converted to Protestant Christianity by American missionary efforts were refusing to participate in the system, thus retaining their wealth rather than dissipating and redistributing it by standing the great expenses associated with holding important offices.

Art and Play

A number of Mesoamerican communities have manifested greater aesthetic elaboration than the Huave of the late twentieth century, though an examination of their craftsmanship in the areas of pottery, woodworking, and weaving reveals some creativity and skill. Perhaps the cotton napkins and table cloths woven by the women exhibited the greatest artistic effort, since the geometric designs and figures were arranged in various patterns aesthetically appealing to Mexicans and other outsiders (Cerda Silva 1941:106).

The Huave also exhibited creativity in the areas of music, dance, and story telling, some of the elements being obviously similar to those of other Indian cultures and others unique to the Huave. *The Danza de los Malinches*, for example, was similar to the same dance in other Indian tribes. They also had a *Danza de los Negros*, which is also found in other groups. Among the Huave it was a burlesque of their Zapotec exploiters. This helped them drain off some of their frustration over how the Zapotec treated them.

Other tribes, however, had nothing comparable to the Huave swordfish dance, snake dance, and turtle dance. These dances expressed Huave concern with various forces and events that affected their lives and, in some measure, constituted efforts to control them. The snake dance signified the prosecution and death of a snake that was killing their livestock and involved the shepherd's use of a bow and arrow against the snake. Various elements of their dancing also helped control the winds and storms that afflicted fishermen (Warman 1974:n.p.).

The music that accompanied the dances was rather distinctive. The people played on flutes made from the bamboo-like carrizo stalk, beat on turtle shells with deer antler drumsticks, blew on sea shells and whistles, played on cow bells, and beat double-headed drums made from hollowed tree trunks. They kept these instruments in a special building near the church along with sacred bells and certain other items.

The common discrepancy between ideals and performance in human culture is illustrated by the people's generalization that the instruments were constantly guarded, each member of the community taking a turn, but observers noted that they were frequently unguarded. According to Huave legend the bells were made by the patron of the town of Juchitán, San Vicente, who threw them into the ocean. The Mareños recovered them, and the story was that the gods and people of Juchitán, as well as the ocean itself, had tried several times to take back the bells. That is why they were to be constantly guarded.

Anthropologists and others who have studied the world's folklore have found that many stories are widely diffused within large regions or, even, over much of the world. But as they become part of the lore of a given society, the people modify them to fit their own concerns and ways of looking at life. Many Latin American Indian groups have incorporated the tale of a beautiful woman who lures men into the bush to frighten or harm them. But the stories vary from place to place. According to the Huave there was a woman so beautiful that every man desired to meet her in some remote place and become her lover. But when they met she would change into a snake and frighten him into flight. The story continued that the dullest, poorest, no account man in the community arranged to meet her, and when she turned into a snake, he put his hat on his back and changed into an armadillo. Then he flipped up his tail, almost undoing the snake, and then he did it again. Upon this, the snake turned back into a woman, and she acknowledged defeat. So the armadillo changed back into a man and the two became sweethearts. Later, at a dance, the men began to annoy this man, who became angry, turned into an armadillo, and began to strike his tormentors with his tail. Then all the people respected him because they saw that he was a *nagual* (the animal the man could become).

Another story collected in San Mateo illustrates the explanatory function of folk tales. A boy killed his little brother and began to eat him. His mother then ran for a stick to slug him with, but he climbed a tree. The mother obtained increasingly longer sticks in order to reach him, and when he reached the top he jumped to the moon and stayed there, hiding from his mother. From then on he would eat on the moon whenever he became hungry, causing the blood to run and producing an eclipse. When this happened, the people would ring a bell to scare and stop him, and the moon would recover.

Religious Beliefs and Practices

Anthropologists regularly emphasize interdependence among the various elements they identify as making up any group's culture. In fact, it is often difficult for people, whether considering their own culture or another, to decide where one custom leaves off and others begin. This is because customs are artificial units of socially learned activity—necessarily artificial because it is impossible to think of or talk about a society's entire culture at once. Observers and discussants also classify a society's customs into artificial aspects such as economic life, religion, technology, government, art, and social organization. They view each aspect as a complex of customs related to one another because they have to do with some central purpose or concern of human existence. Technology, for example, may be seen to be concerned with how humans relate to material objects and substances. But customs in one aspect of a culture may be as firmly linked to customs in another aspect as those within the same aspect. This is reflected in the fact that we have already described elements of Huave religion, notably in connection with sickness and healing and community order. These connections are practically important for change agents, since any modification a cultural element will affect linked elements in other parts of the lifeway.

Like other Mesoamerican religions, the Mareño religious system was a blend of pre-Columbian beliefs and practices with sixteenth century Spanish Catholic features (Cheney 1979:60). Some refer to this kind of religion as *folk Catholicism*, and a number of Roman Catholics have sought to reform Indian systems of this type so they conform more closely with standard Catholic belief and practice.

Another feature the Huave share with other Indian groups, including the Aztec, Maya and other pre-Columbian civilizations, is a set of dualistic concepts, such as living and dead, hot and cold, and north and south (Cheney 1979:60).

Third, Huave religion was strongly fatalistic, based on the notions that fate is capricious and the universe morally indifferent. Some Mesoamerican groups have been a good deal more fatalistic than others. Most at least seek to heal their diseases with a fair measure of hope for good results, but the Pokomam of Chinautla, Guatemala did little to restore ill people to health on the grounds that it might be against God's will for them to get well (Reina 1966:254).

A fourth strong feature was the belief that the dead continued to interact with the living. In some instances in

Mesoamerica, this has even approached ancestor worship, with dead persons being almost deified and venerated.

Finally, there was a variety of religious beliefs and practices based on the assumption of intimate interdependence between humans and the natural world. The belief in a tonal, the wild animal counterpart of every person, is an outstanding example.

The Huave held that there was an all-powerful creator deity, but, like the supreme beings of many other cultures around the world, he was remote and uninterested in the affairs of this life. The Mareños did not pray to him for help, forgiveness, or anything else. He sent other powerful beings, known as *monteok*, to care for the Huave, but had no contact with them himself until the hereafter. Another remote being was the Devil, who dealt directly only with the dead, but the Mareños were troubled in life by his assistants.

A number of the saints of Catholic origin were important to the Huave, especially San Mateo, the community's patron saint, and the Virgen de la Candelaria. San Mateo's spirit resided in an image hanging above the church altar. Though his spirit might go wherever it chose, the church image was never removed from its place. The people kept another image of him in a chapel near the town hall, which they used in ceremonial processions and thought of as an intercessor with the real San Mateo. Some Huave thought it possible to see San Mateo's spirit leave the church and move about if they sat quietly at night in the church yard and watched carefully. Still others contended that San Mateo no longer lived in his image, since he had left in anger because the people permitted the American priest to touch his image and take over the church (Cheney 1979:62). The image of the Virgen de la Candelaria also hung above the altar, and her intercessor image was kept in the same chapel with that of San Mateo.

One of several other deities, a goddess, was said by the Mareños to be the chief deity of the Huave before the Spanish came. The Huave regarded several other gods and goddesses as representations of the Virgin Mary and Christ. This, too, seems to correspond with pre-Columbian belief, since pre-Spanish Mesoamericans assumed that some of their deities could exist in several versions. Similarly, the Mareños referred to Santa Cruz and large crosses in chapels and special places in the town as gods and venerated them. Crosses protected them from evil, and they could communicate with the dead through them.

The Huave held that both the sun and the moon were deities active in their lives. They thought the stars were remote gods of people in other places. They believed in a number of other deities, powerful and active, called monteok (fathers). These beings appeared and disappeared rapidly as thunderstorms. They protected the people but would kill with their lightning swords anyone who defied them or showed them disrespect. Tata Rayo, or father thunderbolt, was another powerful god of the heavens, but the Mareños disagreed as to whether he was the chief monteok or a post-Conquest arrival.

Everything that sustained life was sacred to the people of San Mateo. These included especially the earth, rain, fire, sea, and salt.

The people also felt close to the animal world, especially dogs, since the people were supposed to be descendants of dogs. Cognitive anthropological studies have shown that societies differ in how they classify phenomena linguistically. What one society puts in separate categories, another may place in the same category. The linguistic domains of meaning, or *semantic domains*, are the categories actually functioning as part of the people's cultures. In modern North America killing humans comes under homicide, while animal killing belongs in a different category. But the Huave included both the killing of humans and the killing of dogs under the same linguistic term (Cheney 1979:61). This linguistic custom was linked to their legend that they had descended from dogs.

The Huave believed the earth to be a disk supported by a giant, and earthquakes came when he had to shift the weight from one shoulder to the other. The Huave were little troubled by earthquakes and found it amusing when they knocked chickens and turkeys from their roosts.

They thought of the earth as divided into two parts, north and south, a reflection of their dualistic orientation. They regarded north winds as masculine and south winds as feminine. There was no danger from complaining against or cursing the uncomfortable sand-bearing north winds of the late fall and winter, but to speak against the sea breezes, storms, hurricanes, and tornadoes from the south was to risk the south wind's anger.

According to the Huave the spirits of the dead returned at night and moved about the town streets. They were breathing and getting their exercise, and the people were afraid to go out at night unless they had to. They did not bother either those with necessary reasons for being out or those that were drunk, but those out on mischief were liable to come across them. The dead sometimes liked to scare people for fun, but the ghosts of those who had died young were under the Devil's control and entered people to injure their souls or cause large pustules or subcutaneous tumors to develop in them (Cheney 1979:64). The spirits of people who died violently wished to communicate with the living, but they appeared in such frightening forms, such as skeletons or beings with balls of fire for heads, that they terrified people. At one time these beliefs kept people in at night most of the time, but the 1960s young people were out at night, frequenting the soft-drink stands under the new street lights; and the municipio found it necessary to create a night police force.

Most of the Huave did not know which animal was their tonal or counterpart animal. Those who did could change into the animal to become a witch. *Witchcraft* involves the exercise of supernatural power, often with the aid of a supernatural familiar, to do evil. Like witches elsewhere around the world, Huave witches had the power to transform themselves into a nagual, which was either their animal counterpart or some other wild or domesticated animal, to do evil. The Huave believed there was once a fair number of both male and female witches among them, but when Cheney was there they held that there was only one person with witch power left, who no longer practiced witchcraft. The witches made people ill by sending foreign items into their victims.

Many anthropologists have distinguished *sorcery*, or black magic, from witchcraft, since magical power lies in the procedure, medicine, or formula used, while in witchcraft the power rests in the person. The commonest type of *sorcery* among the Mareños was to inflict damage on a victim by leaving a burnt offering in his or her path. This consisted of candle stubs, copal incense, and flowers which had been cursed and dedicated to the earth. The magician had to prepare the offering properly, however, since it's effectiveness lay in doing things right. If mistakes were made, the earth would either not respond or the damage would be inflicted on the perpetrator. They considered it best to pay a knower, who was expert in such things, to do the magic.

Culture Contact and Change

Cheney characterized the San Mateo of 1979 as a conservative society that emphasized maintaining equilibrium and a balanced dualism in all aspects of their world. But they were quite disturbed by the obvious disruption of this ideal by the changes being forced upon them. Plan Huave, initiated earlier in the 1970s, continued to have its impact upon them. The people were clinging to many of their old ways, and many felt the supernaturals were displeased with them and were punishing them for yielding to outside pressure. At the same time they were continuing to accept new elements into their lives, and fairly readily if they had obvious advantages and were not too incompatible with their existing lifeway. It was clear that they would continue to undergo acculturation as they had in the past, but, unless especially disruptive forces descended on them, not precipitously. The community was gradually coming to resemble the non-Indian towns of the Isthmus of Tehuantepec.

Chapter 15

THE NORTHERN LACANDON OF SOUTHERN MEXICO

Like a number of other nonliterate societies, the Lacandón (approx. lah-kahn-DOHN) have captured the interest of people in many nations. Explorers, journalists, tourists, and anthropologists have found themselves drawn to their jungle home, and there are more books and articles on them than there are Lacandón. Their long white tunics, their long black hair, and physical features which appeal to many Westerners confer a unique appearance that excites the interest of outsiders. Those fascinated with the ancient Mayan ruins of that region are intrigued with the idea that the Lacandón are descendants of the civilized Maya, and the thought that their ceremonies are survivals of ancient Mayan observances excites them. Many also admire the Lacandón for their tenacious resistance to the encroachments of civilization and are incensed at the now virtually complete destruction of their mahogany forests and the threatened disruption of the unique lifeway that depended on the existence of those forests. The late 1970s and early 1980s constituted a critical period of change for the Lacandón. They were showing themselves conservative and resilient as they were pushed ever closer to the what some observers viewed as the limits of their ability to either retreat or resist. This treatment views the Northern Lacandón, the most conservative branch of Lacandón, as they were between 1970 and the middle 1980s.

During the late 1980s the Northern Lacandón were still living around Lake Najá (approx. nah-HAH) in the tropical rain forests of Chiapas in southeastern Mexico, not far southeast of where the great Usumacinta River forms the border between Mexico and Guatemala. Both men and women wore full white cotton tunics, though the women wore a red skirt beneath the tunic that hung several inches below it. The men wore their black hair long and loose, while the women braided theirs into a single tress down the back. Most of their houses were elongated, thatch-roofed structures with rounded ends and walls of upright mahogany slats or boards. They were located in small clusters in forest clearings, each normally containing a man and his wife or wives. The families of sons and/or daughters commonly lived in the same clearing as one of the spouse's parents. Each settlement, at least, and sometimes each house, had its god-house or temple, where the men burned incense and made offerings to the gods. The people were efficient slash-and-burn agriculturalists, excellent hunters with the bow and arrow, and also gatherers of jungle products. Maize or Indian corn was their main food crop, and tortillas, corn drinks, beans, and meat were their main foods. Their crafts included weaving on the backstrap loom, woodworking, pottery-making, basketry, and the making of bark cloth.

Polygynous marriages were the ideal, and married couples took up residence near either the groom's or the bride's parents. The people also were divided into animal name groups, the name being patrilineally transmitted. Earlier these groups may have been clans. There was no formal government, though a civil-religious headman in his eighties exercised leadership at Najá in the 1970s and early 1980s. The religion reflected much of the ancient Mayan system, including belief in some thirty major gods as well as a number of minor supernaturals. The major ceremonies were held in the temple, where the men assembled to drink a ceremonial alcoholic beverage and burn copal incense in clay pots, each of which had the face of the god it embodied molded onto one side.

The twentieth century Lacandón were descendants of the ancient Maya of the Yucatán peninsula, their language being only slightly different from those that prevail in the peninsula. Other Mayan-speaking groups gave the Lacandón their now widely used name, and its meaning is uncertain, but the Lacandón called themselves Hach Winik, or "true people." As late as 1987 the *Hach Winik* were still living, largely intact, the lifeway described in these pages.

Prehistory

Humans were living in the Mayan area by at least eleven or twelve thousand years ago, but archaeologists have been unable to establish how much earlier. Most scholars remain untroubled by the notion that people inhabited the New World by 20,000 years ago, and some would extend the time of human entry to as long ago as 100,000 B.P. Archaeologists refer to the earliest inhabitants of North America as Palco-Indian peoples. They hunted big-game animals such as mammoths, mastodons, bison, and camels, which became extinct because the climate became too warm for them at the end of the Pleistocene period. Archaeologists have found remnants of the weapons used by the Paleo-Indian hunters in the Valley of Mexico, where Mexico City lies, and in Guatemala, so people both to the west and east of Lacandón country were hunting large game during Paleo-Indian times (Lowe 1978:345).

Other ancient Indian groups exhibited a lifeway known to anthropologists as the Desert Tradition, which may date back to 10,000 B. C. in places. This cultural tradition was one of several types many archaeologists include in the Archaic period. Desert people lived in extended family groups of 25-30 people, hunted forms smaller than those taken by the big game hunters, and collected much wild plant food, leaving many remains of baskets and grinding stones as evidence of their predominantly collecting lifeway. Such evidence is abundant in the Tehuacán Valley of Oaxaca, which lies around 300 miles west of Lacandón country, and people of the Desert tradition occupied an area of Chiapas some 125 miles to the East of Lacandonia between 9000 and 6700 B.C. (Johnson and MacNeish 1972:40).

During later phases of the Archaic certain groups began to make containers of fired clay and cultivate plants on a limited scale. Wild plant foods remained the major part of their subsistence, so agriculture was only "incipient" during the Archaic. Evidence for domesticated plants was found in the Tehuacán Valley of Oaxaca by 7,000 B.C. and maize appeared there between 5500 and 4500 B.C. Agriculture remained incipient, but the people of Tehuacán between 3500 and 5000 years before Christ obtained around 14 percent of their diet from cultivated plants (MacNeish 1967:299). Near Mitla, in Oaxaca, archaeologists have found additional evidence of incipient agriculture by nearly 7,000 B.C., but as of about 1980 they had found no indications of domesticated plants in or near Lacandón country for such early levels.

The basic patterns of Mesoamerican civilization developed during the two-and-a-half centuries immediately preceding Christ's birth, a time archaeologists know as either the Preclassic or Formative Period. In many places people got most of their food from agriculture. The people of northern Belize, 225-250 miles east of the Lacandón area, were cultivating maize and root crops at least by 1000 B.C.

Scholars disagree about where the Lacandón came from, some holding they are survivors of the ancient Mayan civilizations that prevailed in the area they now inhabit, while others say the ancestors of today's Lacandón immigrated from the Yucatán peninsula only a few hundred years ago. During 1980s Northern Lacandón still made pilgrimages to the Mayan ruins at Yachilán and visited the impressive Palenque ruins. Bruce and Perera contend they felt their gods once lived at Palenque, but R. Jon McGee notes the lack of evidence that the Lacandón ever worshipped at

Palenque and that Yachilán is the site of greatest religious significance to them (Perera and Bruce 1982:13, 244; McGee 1987:12).

Archaeologists have ceramic (fired clay) evidence that people were living at or near Palenque before Preclassic times, that is, before 2500 B.C. No especially noteworthy cultural developments took place there during Preclassic times or during the first several centuries of the Classic period of Mesoamerican prehistory. But shortly after A.D. 600 Palenque experienced spectacularly rapid development, apparently due to the aggressive and imaginative leadership of a line of quite unusual rulers. Within 150 years it became one of the four leading Mayan centers (Weaver 1981:315). By 790, however, it was in decline, and the site was abandoned as a ceremonial-political center by around 810. Other major Mayan centers fell soon after Palenque's demise, possibly from a combination of ecological abuse, mismanagement, overpopulation, famines, epidemics, bad weather, and military attack from Valley of Mexico states (Adams 1977:224).

Palenque's outstanding architecture has attracted both archaeologists and tourists over the years, and it is famous along with Tikal for the practice of burying a ruler in a tomb constructed within a pyramid. It is possible that some of today's Lacandón carry genes derived from the rulers of Palenque, though it is impossible to be sure. The supposition that they are descendants of ancient Maya from various places, rather than just Palenque, is reasonable in the light of our knowledge of how often individuals and groups move about. It is interesting that late twentieth-century Lacandón hold that their gods once made their homes at Palenque and Yachilán, but this belief could have arisen for reasons other than biological descent from the people who built those places.

Anthropologist Didier Boremanse concurs with linguistic anthropologist Robert Bruce's conclusion that Palenque was the home of the ancestors of the twentieth century Lacandón (Boremanse 1982a:90). But Ian Graham, archaeologist with Harvard University's Peabody Museum, has indicated archaeological evidence for Yachilán as a more likely ancestral home (Perera and Bruce 1982:246). R. Jon McGee, who was visiting the Lacandón regularly during the 1980s and who by 1987 had spent 16 months among them, cited a number of weaknesses in Bruce's arguments. He stressed the likelihood that the present twentieth century Lacandón were immigrant Yucatán Maya (R. McGee 1987:15). He concluded that this immigration occurred since the sixteenth century, which brings us into historical times. If so, we should look for the prehistory of the twentieth century Lacandón in Yucatán rather than in Lacandonia. Another anthropologist, James Nations, states that the Spanish used the term Lacandón for both the western Chol Maya (Polencano) and the Cholti or eastern Chol, both of whom occupied the Chiapas jungle when the Spaniards began to pacify the region in the mid-sixteenth century (Nations 1979a:39). Maya who came later from Yucatán also became known as Lacandón.

History

Lacandón country was too poor and difficult for Europeans to survive in or the Spanish and Mexicans to spend much time there. Rivers and marshes, impenetrable jungle, and rough rock outcroppings characterize the area, making it difficult for both animals and humans as compared with most other parts of Mexico (Perera and Bruce 1982:10). Elsewhere Mayan civilization was destroyed, but the Lacandón clung to their ideology and religion and fragments of their writing, mathematics, astronomy, and calendrical lore. The rulers, astronomers, priests, and warriors became maize farmers and hunters, but it is impossible to know whether most of their calendar, mathematics, and writing disappeared within a few decades or whether significant amounts of that knowledge persisted into the nineteenth or twentieth centuries (Perera and Bruce (1982:11).

The early evangelistic efforts of the Spanish priests to convert the Lacandón to Christianity yielded no enduring results, unless some of the Catholic Mexican nationals of that area are of Lacandón ancestry. The missionaries gave up their attempts about 1790, and the Lacandón were left to live their own lives for some 150 years. Then, during the second half of the nineteenth century, lumbermen found mahogany and cedar in the Lacandón forest and moved in. The Lacandón along the larger rivers shared their knowledge of their forests and streams in return for machetes and axes. Tribal groups everywhere have found metal tools more efficient than their stone tools, and the Lacandón stopped making and using their stone axes. In spite of this and other material changes, they maintained their ideology and religion. An exception occurred when a visiting Catholic priest told one group suffering from the diseases brought by the lumbermen that their gods were responsible for the many deaths, so they renounced their religion. At the same time a Lacandón priest there died, taking much of the group's religious knowledge with him. In such ways disease can bring about cultural change (Duby and Blom 1969:278). Toward the end of the nineteenth century several explorers contacted the Lacandón.

Change accelerated during World War II when *chicleros* entered the country to search the jungle for *chicozapote* trees. The *chicle* gatherers made contact with the many Lacandón living away from the rivers, trading knives, guns, ammunition, flashlights, rice, sugar, steel needles, manufactured cloth, corn mills, and other items for corn, fruits, and help in locating the chicozapote trees. One of the results was a new wave of epidemics, and the Lacandón began to use modern medicine for the new foreign diseases (R. McGee 1987). Still the people used traditional treatments for traditional illness, held to their native religion, lived in the same kinds of houses, wore the same kinds of clothing, and farmed their *milpas* (corn fields).

At midcentury Protestant missionaries entered the area, and Wycliffe Bible Translators and Seventh Day Adventists converted some of the Lacandón. The conservative Northern Lacandón remained in the vicinity of Lake Najá,

the vast majority of them rejecting Christianity and western ideology. They accepted rifles, radios, phonographs and other alien elements but coined native terms for them. The Southern Lacandón, particularly the younger people, were so open to western custom that many began to wear western clothing and hair styles (Baer and Merrifield 1971:x). Tension developed between the conservative community and the Southern Lacandón and, also, between missionaries and anthropologists, who admired the Lacandón religion and hoped it would survive (Perera and Bruce 1982:17).

During the 1940s the price of tropical hardwoods rose, and the Mexicans became interested in harvesting them from the Lacandón forest. The Department of Health spent several years eradicating malaria from the area, and settlers and lumbering interests arrived in force. Vast jungles were destroyed, leaving the Northern Lacandón of Najá the last Lacandón group with their forests and customs relatively intact. By the late 1980s, however, their forests were gone, too.

Ethnography

The explorers Alfred P. Maudslay (1899), Desire Charnay (1863, 1887), and Karl Sapper (1891)) left useful information on the Lacandón as they were during the latter nineteenth century. Then, anthropologist Alfred M. Tozzer lived with the Lacandón in 1901 and 1903, leaving a report that continues to be of considerable value (1907). The next anthropological work was done by Jacques Soustelle, who published a series of notes on Lacandón religion and other aspects of their lives (1933, 1935, 1937). During the 1940s and 1950s Frans and Gertrude Blom explored and wrote about the Lacandón and their country (Blom 1954, Blom and Duby 1955, Duby 1944, 1955, 1959, 1961), and they founded a center for Mayan studies in the Lacandón forest. Linguistic missionary Philip Baer took up residence among the Northern Lacandón in the 1940s and began work among the Southern Lacandón some 15 years later (Baer and Baer 1949). Baer and William Merrifield, a linguistic anthropologist and missionary, prepared a study of Southern Lacandón history and culture (Baer and Merrifield 1971). American anthropological linguist Robert Bruce lived and studied among the Lacandón from time to time from the middle 1950s into the 1980s, concentrating on their language and dream symbolism (Bruce 1965, 1968, 1974, 1975). The prominent Mexican anthropologist, Alfonso Villa Rojas, also worked among the Lacandón, emphasizing economic, social and religious aspects of their lives (Villa R. 1967, 1968).

Several other anthropologists have worked among the Lacandón since 1970, including population anthropologist James Nations (1979), Virginia Davis (1978) and Michael Rees (1977). Anthropologist Didier Boremanse spent 20 months among the Lacandón between 1970 and 1979 and has published a number of valuable reports on various aspects of their lifeway (1977-78, 1978, 1979, 1981a, 1981b,

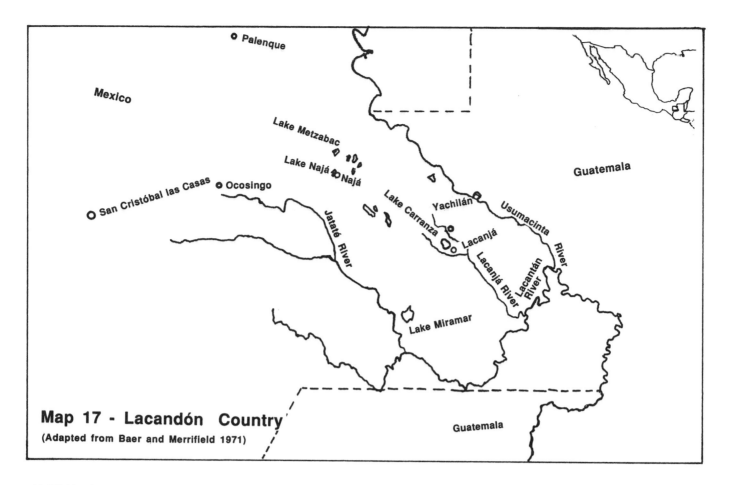

Map 17 - Lacandón Country
(Adapted from Baer and Merrifield 1971)

1982). During the 1980s, anthropologist R. Jon McGee made repeated visits to Lacandonia, concentrating on religious ritual (R. McGee 1984, 1987).

Lacandón Country

Lacandón territory lies in the jungles of Chiapas in the southeastern portion of Mexico not too far from the Guatemala border. The Usumacinta River angles from southeast to northwest along the edge of Lacandón country and the border between Chiapas on the Lacandonia side and Guatemala and Yucatán on the other. In 1970 the Northern Lacandón lived in a relatively small area, 15 miles or so in diameter, about 30 miles due west of the ancient Mayan ruins at Yachilán on the Usumacinta and less than 15 miles southwest of the Usumacinta where it flows past Piedras Negras. They lived around and near Lake Najá, which lies at 2,700 feet above sea level. The Southern Lacandón occupied a somewhat smaller territory just to the north of the Bonampak ruins on the Lacanjá River. A still smaller group was found near where the Azul River entered the Jataté River, but the Jataté group had moved away by 1980.

At the altitude of Lake Najá typical tropical vegetation prevailed, but pine forests covered the surrounding hills. Shady places were always cool, though it became uncomfortably hot in the open at noon (Perera and Bruce 1982:9). But increasing areas of the Lacandón jungle hardly fit this description by the 1970s and 1980s, since lumbering inter-

ests were cutting the forests and peasant farmers using slash-and-burn agriculture in its most destructive form were turning the oak, pine, and mahogany forests into sterile eroded hills.

The animals of the Lacandón jungle included spider monkeys, black howler monkeys, deer, peccaries, tapirs, jaguars, cougars, raccoons, coatis, grisons, rabbits, gophers, agoutis, cavies, nutrias, squirrels, porcupines, armadillos, frogs, turtles, iguanas, crocodiles and many more. Among the birds were ducks, eagles, hawks, grouse, pheasants, doves, owls, goatsuckers, parrots, toucans, motmots, woodpeckers, grackles, cuckoos, curassows, owls, blackbirds, crows and many others (Baer and Merrifield 1971:242). At least ten varieties of fish inhabited the lakes and rivers of Lacandón country. At one time the jungle around Najá teemed with animals and birds, but many forms became scarce as deforestation continued. A major exception is the deadly viper, the fer de lance. It had always been a danger to people, but it thrived in even greater numbers in the brush that replaced the forests.

Language

When anthropological linguist Robert Bruce studied Lacandón speech he discovered 27 different *phonemes*, which included twenty consonant phonemes, six vowel phonemes, and one phoneme consisting of vowel lengthening (Bruce 1968a:19). One of the phonemes consisted of four alternative sounds, which means the people could use any of the four sounds in a given word or other utterance without changing or destroying its meaning. Actually, each of the four was used in a slightly different sound environment, so the utterance would sound odd to the people if a speaker failed to employ the customary sound. But the meaning would be retained. English speakers would probably think of the four sounds as different kinds of *k* or say that there was a /k/ phoneme (slashes indicate a phoneme) in Lacandón made up of four slightly different sounds. Other Lacandón phonemes consisted of either one, two, or three alternatives, and Bruce recorded approximately 40 different sounds in Lacandón speech. The meaning of any utterance is destroyed or altered only when a speaker switches to a sound not in the phoneme in question. For example, if a Lacandón said *mab* instead of *kab*, which means "honey", the utterance would no longer mean "honey."

A society's language is part of its culture, since linguistic customs are learned and shared among the members. Moreover, linguistic customs, like all cultural traits, must be seen as linked to other customs of the culture. According to anthropology's doctrine of *functionalism* every culture is a *system*, which means that its elements are interconnected to form a larger configuration. Language is connected to the rest of the culture partly as the main vehicle by which customs are communicated from person to person and generation to generation. The grammar also reflects and affects various other aspects of life. Bruce found that the customary poise of the Lacandón was built into their language (Perera and Bruce 1982:15). Maya grammar, he noted, emphasized possession and location. Everything had an owner and a position in relation to everything else. This is consistent with their building of harmonious, well-balanced pyramids, with every stone in its correct place, though it cannot be concluded from this that prehistoric Lacandón were among those who built pyramids. The ancient Maya also excelled in astronomy and mathematics, which interrelated the features of the universe and defined where each belonged. Though the astronomy, mathematics, and pyramid-building were gone, twentieth century Maya, including the Lacandón, continued this emphasis on position and harmony.

While the languages of the Northern and Southern Lacandón were mutually intelligible, the people could be as *ethnocentric* about their speech as any people. Ethnocentrism is experiencing and/or judging the customs of another culture by reference to the categories and standards of one's own culture. Members of the two Lacandón groups often misunderstood one another's peculiar terms and deplored their allegedly outrageous pronunciation. Bruce noted that when groups from the northern and southern divisions interacted with one another there would always be at least one person who would refuse to understand the speakers of the other dialect and who would declare their speech "totally unintelligible" (Perera and Bruce 1982:8). Some Mexican speakers of Spanish express similar contempt for the speech of Texan and other Spanish-speaking groups in the United States.

Personality and Behavior

The Northern Lacandón held that all things, especially important matters, should be treated with calm and poise. Anthropologist Robert Bruce described this as a kind of confidence of being in one's proper place and in correct relation to whatever might come (Perera and Bruce 1982:15). When Bruce's friend Victor Perera once threw his pen to the table in frustration while trying to compose a letter to President López Portillo, his Lacandón companions reacted with embarrassed silence, since such emotional outbursts were offensive to them (Perera and Bruce 1982:135). Their poise sometimes made them seem shy to outsiders, but they were not. Bruce and others have observed that the Lacandón were as confident and relaxed with jet setters, Mexico City crowds, or the president of Mexico himself as with their own people, so much so that they sometimes appeared arrogant to outside observers. When the young Lacandón K'ayum went to Mexico City to talk to the President about the destruction of Lacandón forests, he quickly made himself known to Mexico's chief executive and confidently stated his case with no apparent awe.

While the Lacandón were confident in their relationships with others, they did not like unpleasant confrontations. They simply gave way in the face of unwanted intrusions, and when the disrupting stimulus was withdrawn or ran its course, things fell into proper place again. This provided the people with an often effective way of surviving brash tourists. The Hach Winik also had a way of turning the tables on outsiders. Bruce has noted that a kind of reversal or mirror imaging is an important element of their storytelling and dream interpretation. This has manifested itself in their relationships with tourists, anthropologists and other aliens.

In addition to their poise and avoidance of confrontation, the Northern Lacandón exhibited a propensity for carefree, cheerful conversation and joking. They enjoyed good fellowship, visited one another a good deal, gossiped, told jokes, laughed a lot, and played tricks on one another (Blom 1969:290). Perera noted that many of the conversational exchanges among the men participating in a drinking ceremony were pointed and rather crude, but there was no evidence of malice. Everybody laughed together, and tension was reduced and the men brought closer together (Perera and Bruce 1982:80).

Clothing and Personal Appearance

In some Lacandón groups both sexes dressed alike and wore their hair the same, making it difficult for outsiders to tell who were men and who were women. Both the men and women of the northern group wore the long, loose tunic of white cotton with elbow-length sleeves. The men wore tunics extending to just below their knees. But the women had bright red underskirts that hung to their knees, and their tunics were so short that they left several inches of skirt exposed. And while Lacandón women in other places wore their hair long and loose like that of the men, the northern women worked their long hair into a single braid or pigtail in back. The married women tied toucan or parrot feathers to the end of this tress. The women completed their costume with beads about the neck and earrings. Both sexes went barefooted. Some of the people kept their tunics clean and white, while others permitted them to remain rather grimy most of the time. The men commonly carried a deerskin pouch over the shoulder and a machete and/or gun.

Anthropologists normally practice *participant observation* as they collect field data, which means they live as much like the people as seems feasible according to several considerations and, while participating, observe the people's customs. This sometimes includes using the native costume. Accordingly, Robert Bruce lived as much as he could like a Northern Lacandón while studying their language and culture full time, wearing the cotton tunic, permitting his hair to grow halfway down his back, and carrying the machete, deerskin pouch, and other items the Lacandón men normally kept with them. To this he added his notebook and pen (Perera and Bruce 1982:4).

Houses and Other Structures

The Northern Lacandón built their traditional houses by setting strong posts in the ground to form the corners of a rectangle and support the framework for a double-pitched roof. They set taller poles in the middle at each end to support a ridge pole and ran beams from post to post along the sides to support the lower ends of the rafters. Then they lashed a number of light horizontal poles to the rafters to support the thatch. At each end they set a semicircle of poles to support a rounded roof framework, so that each end of the structure was covered by a rounded sloping roof shaped like a segment of a low cone and extending from the gables of the double-pitched roof. They thatched both the double pitched and rounded roof sections with palm leaves and built walls of vertical sticks bound with vines or wound with large sheets of bark (Blom 1969:285). The rectangular portion of a house described by Bruce was about thirty feet long, with the rounded ends making a total length of about forty feet. The walls were made of rough upright planks of light balsa wood, and several openings in the walls served as doors (Perera and Bruce 1982:9). As time went on the people were also building houses with board walls and sheet-iron roofs, some of them having concrete slab floors.

The only furniture consisted of items such as small wooden stools, cupboards, old boxes for storing valued possessions, platform beds for sleeping, and hammocks for daytime use. The floor was usually littered with rubbish, since the Lacandón seldom swept the earthen floors, and the underside of the roof was black with soot from the fire. They kept dried beans and other foods in baskets or large bowls made from squash rinds, both of which they suspended from the roof. Sheaves of tobacco also hung from the rafters.

Like so many other Mesoamerican groups, the Hach Winik of Najá prepared food in a separate structure, a small shack near the main house. Some compounds also had small thatched doghouses and chicken coops of sticks propped against one another in a pyramid shape (Blom 1969:285). The best constructed building in the compound was the ceremonial house, which had no walls and was furnished only with a few stools. The people kept the clay offering pots on a board under the roof and suspended various other items of ceremonial use from the roof.

Usually a residential compound was occupied by a man, his wife, and unmarried children, and, sometimes, a married offspring with his or her family. Sometimes there were from two to five of these compounds clustered in a forest clearing and sometimes only one. The clearings were widely scattered, some of them being over a day's walk apart. By sometime during the 1970s this settlement pattern was disrupted among the Northern Lacandón by the encroachments of lumbering enterprises and peasant farmers, and Lacandón families established larger hamlets or villages near Lake Najá.

Livelihood

Like the ancient Maya the Northern Lacandón obtained most of their food through slash-and-burn agriculture, and they were known as fine farmers. Lacandón farmers cleared an area of rain forest by cutting the trees and brush with their machetes and axes, allowing the vegetation to dry, and burning it. They then planted the seeds among the charred remains of the trees in holes made with their digging sticks. Perhaps ninety percent of a *milpa*, as people called the field, was planted in maize (Indian corn), and the rest was planted at the appropriate times in sweet potatoes, beans, squash, onions, tomatoes, mint, cabbage, tobacco, and a large variety of other crops (Boremanse 1982a:71, Perera and Bruce 1982:102). The milpa had to be weeded from time to time, and the people checked it almost daily to protect it from destruction by deer, peccaries, birds, gophers, and other forms. Lacandón families cooperated to prepare and care for their milpas.

The Lacandón rain forest was one of the world's richest, but it grew on some of the world's poorest soil (Perera and Bruce 1982:25). Only a few inches of topsoil covered by several inches of rich leaf mold lay directly over sterile limestone. The Lacandón obtained excellent yields immediately after clearing a milpa, but they could get no more than two years of acceptable corn and tobacco crops from a given milpa because of the thin soil. At this point they established a new milpa, though they used the old one for a third year for sweet potatoes, onions, and other root crops. After that they left it to grow back to weeds and second growth jungle twice as high as a tall man. This took about five years, by which time the soil was good enough again for a couple of years of maize crops. Under this arrangement each Northern Lacandón family could get along with three milpa sites, all of which continued to produce excellent corn (Perera and Bruce 1982:179).

The Najá Lacandón built a shed in each milpa for the storage of their maize. The women picked the corn and threw the ears on a pile. Then they pulled up the stalks, making another pile, and burned them. After the men cleared the grass and weeds with their machetes, they planted tobacco, going through this corn and tobacco cycle perhaps three or four times a year. They stacked the maize in the storage shed in neat high rows, forming a wide bed. Najá husbands and wives enjoyed sexual companionship on these beds of corn, commonly during a work break in the late morning.

The Hach Winik were also excellent hunters and, until recently, took a good deal of their food supply this way. They shot some animals, deer and peccary for example, when they threatened their crops, but they also went on hunting excursions. They took a variety of kinds of birds, including curassows, turkeys, and partridges. Peccaries were especially important to them among the animals, but they also took deer, monkeys, armadillos, tapirs, and a variety of kinds of rodents. By the 1970s the weapon of choice was the 22-caliber rifle. A number of the men had rifles, but they were unable to use them a great deal because it was difficult to obtain ammunition. The Lacandón were excellent marksmen with both rifles and bows and arrows. They apparently went on special hunting trips, lasting part of a day, approximately once a week (Baer and Merrifield 1971:233).

Lacandón hunters also took animals of all sizes with snares. They would bend a sapling and attach a noose to it and arrange the bait and a release device so the animal would be caught when the trap was sprung. For large game they placed the bait in a hole so the animal had to extend the neck well down into the noose before triggering the device.

Fish were abundant in the Lacandón forest streams, and the people made considerable use of them. They were expert fishermen, using spears, hook and line, traps, poisons, and lures (Baer and Merrifield 1971:245]. They sometimes attracted fish to where they could take them more easily by placing berries, bits of termite nest, or other substances in the water to attract minnows, since the minnows attracted larger fish. Sometimes, they staked a gourd with an opening in it and bait inside in the bottom of a stream. When fish entered, the fisherman covered the hole with his hand and tossed the fish ashore. Some of the fish spears were 20 feet long. Poison to stun fish was taken from the *barbasco* vine as well as other plants.

The Lacandón knew of many edible fruits and plants in their forests and took them as opportunity afforded. Perera's impression was that there was hardly any tree, shrub or weed that the people did not use for something, but anthropologists consistently find that people fail to use some of the edible products in their environments. The Lacandón prized the honey from stingless bees and used it for making their alcoholic beverage, *balché*. They ate breadnuts, wild cloves, cress shoots, *mamey* fruit and its seeds, mushrooms, tamarinds, nettle fruits, vine berries, several parts of the various palm trees, and much more. They also planted extensively a variety of ornamental and fruit plants near their houses or in their corn fields, though they gave them little care. These included orange, lemon, grapefruit, cherry, avocado, banana, mango, papaya, guava, plum, and sugar cane.

The Hach Winik enjoyed eating fresh corn on the cob when it was available. Their main foods, however, were maize tortillas, corn drinks, black beans, and meat. The women prepared these and other foods over the hearth of three stones on the ground that is so characteristic of the Mesoamerican culture area. They baked the round thin cakes known as tortillas on a round clay griddle, and the griddle rested on the three stones, with the fire on the ground among the stones. For preparing corn drinks and heating or boiling other food mixtures they placed clay pots on the three stones.

Like other Mesoamericans they cooked the dried corn kernels in lime water to soften them and separate the skins from the kernels in preparation for grinding them into dough with the *metate* (stone grinding base) and *mano* (hand stone). To make lime they fired a pile of freshwater snail shells and slaked the resulting ash with water (Baer and Merrifield 1971:153). Traditionally, the women spent many hours grinding the kernels, but by the 1970s most of them had acquired hand corn mills for the preliminary grinding, using the metate and mano to work it into fine dough.

The people made tamales from corn dough also, sometimes placing fish or meat and other items on a patty of dough before folding it and baking it. Some tamales were boiled rather than baked, and some were of corn dough with nothing added. The people roasted, boiled, or fried bananas and plantains and boiled or roasted sweet potatoes. Though the Lacandón grew several varieties of squash, they were not as fond of them as many other Mesoamericans (Baer and Merrifield 1971:198).

This provides only a few glimpses of some of the main Lacandón foods. They consumed such a variety of items and prepared them in so many different ways that even a minimal, well-balanced description would require several dozen pages. The Hach Winik took their food mainly at a regular evening meal after their work was done and ate at irregular times the rest of the day (Blom 1969:281).

Crafts, Tools, and Techniques

Like groups all over the world throughout history the Lacandón quickly substituted metal for stone tools when they became available. Since the late nineteenth century they have used steel axes, machetes, and knives for their clearing, cutting of firewood, weeding, and similar tasks (Blom 1969:285). They used the *adze*, which has a blade running at right angles to the length of the handle, the ax, and the machete to fashion their mahogany and cedar dug-out canoes. The people traveled mostly on foot but used canoes to get to their fields if they lay across a body of water. As the result of the government sponsored cutting of hardwoods, it was becoming increasingly difficult for the Hach Winik of the early 1980s to find good trees for their canoes. The people also made most of their furniture from mahogany, as well as the ceremonial "canoe" in which they fermented balché, their ceremonial liquor. The men carved stools for sitting and for forming tortillas, as well as wooden spoons for making food offerings to their deities.

The Northern Lacandón also used bark for several purposes. The men sometimes made and wore ceremonial shirts of bark cloth, and they decorated their incense burners with bark (Blom 1969:285). To obtain the bark they felled the desired tree and cut the bark loose. They then placed the bark on a log and beat it with a wooden mallet until the fibers shifted so that they crossed one another to make a kind of cloth. The women made nets from bark which had been soaked for a month and worked into strings.

The men also produced the clay pots and incense burners. To shape the vessels they used a piece of gourd with teeth cut into it. Their leather bags were made from the skins of deer, alligators, and other animals, which they tanned with a preparation made from mahogany bark. They raised gourds in their fields for containers for water and food substances and other purposes.

The women of the Northern Lacandón traditionally wove cotton fabrics on the *backstrap loom*, also referred to by some as the *belt loom*. By 1970, however, only a few of them had a loom. A weaver stretched the warp threads between two cross members, attaching one of them to a post or tree and the other to a belt around the waist so they could maintain tension on the threads without having a frame. The women spun cotton thread for the loom by twirling the fibers on a spindle in a bowl made from a squash rind. They made tunics by weaving two strips of cloth and sewing them together, leaving a space open at one end for the head. For this they used needles of either steel or bone. The women also made string from *agave* (*maguey*) fiber by fastening one end of a length of fibers to the big toe, stretching them toward them with one hand, and rolling them into string on the knee with the other hand.

The Lacandón made a few baskets. The women obtained vines about an eighth of an inch in diameter, cut them into lengths about 16 inches long, divided a bunch in half, tied them together in the form of a cross, and spread them out to form radially patterned warp elements. Then they plaited lengths of vine in a circle through the warp members, working from the center outward so as to form a gentle upward curve. At the outer edge they doubled the strands over the last weft, tucked them into the checkerwork, and lattice-twined a double strand around the edge to complete the rim (Baer and Merrifield 1971:150). This resulted in a shallow basket with flexible bottom and sides, which they used for washing corn and sweet potatoes and storing food. Blom says they also used baskets for catching fish and small birds (Blom 1969:286).

Lacandón men made their bows from a strong, flexible, resinous wood. They heated a length of wood with fire so they could make it as straight as possible, making it almost as long as the bowman was tall. Then they attached a bowstring of agave fiber. The arrow shafts were made of a flowering wild cane, and the points were of wood for fish and small game and flint for birds and larger animals. In most cases the point was attached to a hardwood foreshaft. The Northern Hach Winik fletched their arrows with feathers from toucans, jays, or other forest birds. During the late 1970s and early 1980s most of the bows and arrows were made for sale to tourists, since game for hunting had become scarce and people preferred to use 22-caliber rifles.

Social Organization and Relationships

The monogamous or *polygynous* family was the basic social and economic unit of Northern Lacandón society. In many nonliterate societies polygyny, marriage of a man to more than one woman, is the ideal arrangement. The sex ratio, of course, nearly always prohibits more than a few polygynous combinations, and this was the case among the Northern Lacandón. In 1975 13 of the 50 families were polygynous, most of the men with more than one wife having only two. There were 67 married females at that time (Boremanse 1977:133). Looking at the situation in terms of individual counts rather than marital combinations affords another perspective. Eighty, or 68 percent, of the 117 married individuals were involved in polygynous combinations.

The co-wives lived in the same house and worked together some, though they normally had separate fires and ate separately with their children. Sometimes, apparently, some of them lived with their children in separate kitchen buildings.

The wives were commonly of different age groups. For example, while it was unusual, a teenage male might begin his married life by marrying a little girl, who would not enter into full wifehood until she was mature enough. When Perera and Bruce were with the Northern Lacandón in the late 1970s a fifteen year old young man and a five year old girl were about to become man and wife. The girl's father expressed pleasure with his prospective son-in-law as one who worked hard and took good care of his daughter. The aged headman at Najá in the 1970s and early 1980s had three wives. One was close to his own age and had her private kitchen separate from the family kitchen, and there she cured tobacco and rolled cigars for the family. His third wife, however, was only twenty-two at the time and was the headman's chief sexual partner and the bearer of his youngest children. The second wife was intermediate in age and had her own special and affectionate relationship with her husband. She said she gladly agreed when her husband wanted to marry a third woman, since the first wife had taken that attitude when she married the headman and she felt that, as leader of the society, her husband should have many children (Perera and Bruce 1982:123). She had given her husband ten children herself and recognized the legitimacy of a younger wife's status as her replacement in this respect.

This is not to say there was no tension among Lacandón co-wives. There was. The point is that we as outside observers are in danger of ethnocentrically misunderstanding situations of this kind. Actually, interpersonal stress often emerged in both polygynous and monogamous marriages. Women, in fact, often seemed to relieve their stress by venting their anger on the family dogs, throwing things at them and cursing them with a passion that often seemed unwarranted by the occasion. In polygynous families this could be partly related to tensions among wives, but it also seemed to be a product of the strongly patriarchal character of the Lacandón family. The father was definitely the head of the family, and the women were subservient to him (Boremanse 1982:94). In both monogamous and polygynous families he might exercise his authority in ways that weighed heavily on a wife. Not only did women sometimes take their feelings out on the dogs, they were prone to frame sarcastic remarks at the expense of their husbands (Perera and Bruce 1982:296)

There was one case of *polyandry*, marriage of a woman to two or more husbands, when Perera and Bruce were among the Hach Winik. In this instance a middle-aged woman who had already had other husbands was married to two young men. It was a temporary marital combination, however, and the woman was the wife of one man by 1981 (R. McGee, personal communication). Polyandry is much less frequent in human society than polygyny, but it has probably occurred with greater frequency as a temporary and minority arrangement than scholars formerly realized.

In many tribal societies marriages were brittle, and this was the case among the Northern Lacandón in spite of the stability of the headman's family. At Najá it was easy to get married and easy to divorce, and many of the people had been married to several others. By the 1980s this had become more difficult because of the shortage of eligible women.

Lineal descent units are common ancestor groups whose members trace their ancestry through one person in each generation. In *unilineal* societies the ancestral links are of the same sex in each generation for all members—females only in *matrilineal* societies and males only in *patrilineal* societies. Such groups tend to be *exogamous*, the members finding their spouses in a kinship group other than their own. This results in a father and mother belonging to different groups, and children in patrilineal societies are assigned to the father's group, while children in matrilineal societies are assigned to the mother's group. Much of Mesoamerica lacks unilineal descent, but there is a high incidence of patrilineal descent and patrilineal kinship groups in Mayan societies.

Some have reported patrilineal descent groups for the Lacandón of the early and middle twentieth century, but several students hold that they lacked them. Each member of Northern Lacandón society inherited one of two identi-

ties called *onen*, and the onen were inherited patrilineally. Onen is translated as "that by which one is known," and it functioned rather like a surname (Bruce 1975:20). A Lacandón, man or woman, was identified either with the wild boar or the spider monkey, with the result that the society consisted of two categories. At one time the categories probably were exogamous, but the rule had lost much of its force among the Northern Lacandón by the 1970s and 1980s. Some still preferred to marry a person of the other onen. The headman at Najá, Chan K'in, for example, had the spider monkey as his onen, while all three of his wives had the wild boar as their onen.

Though the two categories of Northern Lacandón did not function as the unilineal common ancestor groups known to anthropologists as *clans* or *lineages*, they were patrilineal descent categories. All the children were identified at birth and for life with the onen of their father. All of the elderly Chan K'in's children, for example, were identified with the monkey (R. McGee 1987:48). Though the Lacandón categories do not qualify as full fledged clans or lineages, their existence undoubtedly reflects the fact that such groups have existed in Mayan societies. The ancestors of the Lacandón may have had clans and/or lineages.

Bruce found that the onen were linked with certain kinds of deities. The monkey onen was associated with solar deities, while the wild boar onen had to do with earth deities. The Hach Winik held that each member of other societies had an onen, too. They concluded that anthropologist Robert Bruce had the puma for his onen, and they identified R. Jon McGee with the partridge.

Bruce and McGee agree that it is misleading to try to identify the Lacandón onen concept with similar concepts in other cultures. *Totemism*, broadly defined, refers to belief in a mystical relationship between a common ancestor group and a kind of animal, plant, or other category of nature. But the traits that are associated with totemism in so many of the world's societies, such as the notion that the group descended from the totem, were not part of Lacandón belief, nor did the people have taboos against eating their onen animal (R. McGee 1987:48).

Many Mesoamerican cultures include belief in a *nagual*, which is a human transformed into an animal by his or her own power, but a Lacandón could not change into an animal. Another common Mesoamerican notion is the belief that a person has a counterpart animal somewhere in the countryside and that whatever happens to that animal will happen to the individual. This is the *tonal*, but the Hach Winik were not directly associated with an animal in this fashion.

When Bruce studied Northern Lacandón culture in the 1970s, the only strong function of the onen in Lacandón life related to dream interpretation, a matter they were keenly interested in. The subject is so involved that Bruce was able to produce a two volume work on it. The people considered their dreams carefully and drew conclusions from them about their lives. For example, if a person dreamed that someone with the boar onen attacked him with a knife or a machete, this might indicate that he would be attacked by a boar clearly showing his tusks (Bruce 1975:25). The Hach Winik had alternative interpretations of dreams and had to evaluate their elements with some care to come up with the right interpretation. One possible interpretation of dreaming of being very hungry was simply that the dreamer would see an animal of his onen that was very hungry, but it could also mean that the person would eat very well for the next several days.

Anthropologists anchor much of their attention to kinship terms around those a person uses for his or her siblings and cousins and those used for the parents, aunts and uncles. The Northern Lacandón used an *Iroquois* system for siblings and cousins. This means that there was one set of kinship terms for brothers, sisters, and male and female *parallel cousins* and another for male and female *cross cousins*. People are parallel cousins to one another if they are children of two brothers or two sisters (siblings of the same sex), and they are one another's cross cousins if they are children of a brother and sister (siblings of opposite sex). Iroquois terminology tends to occur frequently with unilineal common ancestor groups (clans or lineages), which is consistent with the possibility that the Hach Winik once had functioning descent groups.

Within the context of the Iroquois terminology, the Hach Winik also distinguished younger from older siblings and parallel cousins. The Lacandón used the term *sukun* for older brothers and older male parallel cousins (i.e., older father's brother's or mother's sister's sons). They used the term *kik* for both older sisters and older female parallel cousins (Boremanse 1978:134). If the siblings or parallel cousins were younger, they called them *itsin*, whether they were male or female. Note, then, that the terms distinguish the sexes if the relative is older than the speaker, but not if he or she is younger.

Lacandón addressing or referring to a mother or mother's sister used the term *na'* but they used a different term, *ixkit*, for the father's sister. So they used the term for mother for both the biological mother and her sister, (the maternal aunt), but excluded the father's sister from that category. Anthropologists often call this *bifurcate merging* terminology, a mode of classifying parental generation relatives they have found in many societies. This lumping of the sibling who is the same sex as one's parent under the term for the parent applied only on the *matrilateral* (mother's side) of the family among the Lacandón. On the patrilateral (father's) side they restricted the term *tet* to the biological father and called the father's brother *yum*. The mother's brother was called *akan*, differentiating him both from a person's biological father and father's brother. Anthropologists call terms that differentiate the father, father's brother, and mother's brother from one another *bifurcate collateral* terminology. So the Northern Lacandón used bifurcate merging terminology for the mother and her siblings but bifurcate collateral terminology for the father and his siblings.

Anthropologists do not study kinship terminology to enable them to afflict their students. The terms are often important in the life of the society whose culture an anthropologist is trying to understand, since people tend to behave toward those they use the same term for in similar ways. Boremanse has pointed out that it is essential to study the relationship system of the Lacandón carefully if one wishes to understand their social life, since it is the only system they had to classify their social experience (Boremanse 1978:134). To know how to behave toward another individual, a Lacandón had to know what term to use for that person. The first thing that people who were unacquainted did when they met was to find out what kinship terms they should use for one another.

Kinship terms acquired special significance among the Hach Winik because they used so few personal names. All Najá men were Nux, K'in, Bol or K'ayum, while all women were named either Nuk or Koh (R. McGee 1987:46). Parents addressed their children by their names, but everyone else used kinship terms.

Actually, there was far more to Northern Lacandón kinship terminology than I have indicated. I have not mentioned a number of terms for other relatives, and the terms for siblings, cousins, parents, and aunts and uncles were extended to include more remote relatives. A Lacandón used the term *itsin* not just for younger brothers and sisters and younger parallel cousins but also for his or her sister's sons and daughters, younger mothers brother's sons wives, younger father's sisters son's wives, and younger wive's sister's husbands. The implication for social behavior is that the Lacandón would behave toward all of these relatives in somewhat the same ways they interacted with their actual younger sisters.

A Northern Lacandón woman usually continued her regular tasks until giving birth. The men prayed a good deal during the pregnancy, and there were certain tabus to be observed. For example, a man should not kill a jaguar or make an arrow for killing one during the pregnancy (Blom 1969:296). Another woman attended the mother during delivery, which took place in the forest near the house if it was daytime or in the house at night. Meanwhile, the men remained in the ceremonial house and prayed over the god pots. The husband then took a palm leaf blackened by the incense and waved it over his wife. The mother assumed a kneeling position during the delivery. After birth the people used a reed to cut the umbilical cord. If the baby was especially feeble or deformed, it might be smothered immediately or allowed to starve, since people felt it would not survive the difficult forest life (Perera and Bruce 1982:148). For the same reason, if twins were born, one was usually allowed to die. Both the umbilical cord and the placenta were buried outside the house.

For several days after the birth a mother rested in a hammock protected from wind by a wall of palm leaves, and a large fire was kept burning nearby. She drank warm beverages and ate meat and other strengthening foods, but she avoided pork and armadillo meat, since they were thought to cause hemorrhage and death. She took a bath the fourth day, and she avoided strenuous work for several weeks. This avoidance of physical strain for a long period after parturition is common in Mesoamerica and contrary to the popular notion that women in traditional societies return to heavy work immediately after childbirth.

Mothers nursed their children for about two years. By the time they were weaned they were expected to be toilet trained. The adults seldom scolded or punished their small children, and they seemed to be well-behaved. They generally played around the house with things like tops made from large acorns. The boys played with miniature bows and arrows and wooden airplanes, while the girls had dolls of clay or soft wood. They learned mainly by watching their parents and helping with adult tasks.

Both young men and young women were initiated into adulthood in a two day ceremony. First, offerings were made to the gods in appreciation for their preservation of the young person since birth. For both a girl and a boy certain objects were placed before the god pots in the temple. For a girl these objects were spindles of cotton, thread, loom parts, a net bag containing a water gourd, a wooden comb, a gourd bowl, a broom, and a table on which tortillas were made. These, of course, were things the woman would use as an adult. The next day, in a ritual of instruction, a woman selected as the girl's sponsor showed her how to sweep, fetch water, locate the woman's latrine area, weave, and wash her hands and cooking implements before preparing food. These were ritual teachings, since the girl already knew these things. Finally, she received a gourd of ceremonial liquor (balché) to drink, and her father chanted over her (R. McGee 1987:153).

The items involved in a boy's ritual instruction were bows and arrows; a leather pouch; a net bag; a machete; a gourd bowl; and flints, feathers, a knife, and a cord on a gourd plate (R. McGee 1987:147). The boy was ritually taught how to escape a dangerous animal by climbing a tree, how to sweep the floor and the shelves where the god pots rest, how to use the bow and arrow, where the men's latrine area was, how to get to the family corn field (milpa), and where to find the trees from which the family's copal was taken. Again, these were matters the young person already knew about.

When this instruction and the variety of rites, not described here, that preceded, accompanied, and followed it were concluded, the young person was ready to assume adult roles and responsibilities. The ceremony is very similar to the *hetzmek* ritual of the Yucatec Maya, although the hetzmek took place in infancy rather than at adolescence.

Young Lacandón were expected to avoid sexual intercourse before marriage, and the people carefully kept all violations secret. They were especially condemnatory of childbearing outside the marriage bond (Nations 1979a:194).

A Northern Lacandón female, as we have already seen, might acquire a young man several years her senior as a husband while she was still a small girl. This seems to have been related partly to the shortage of women due to polygyny, which was also reflected in marriages between young men and middle-aged or aged widows. The previously mentioned marriage of two young men to a middle-aged woman also seems to fit here. When a man married a small girl, she would move to his house as soon as she was able to make tortillas. In some cases a man who already had a wife much older than he would be given a girl for a second wife. These kinds of practices account for the various cases of a man being married to wives of greatly different ages.

When a man sought a girl as a wife his father normally petitioned the girl's parents. He was expected to bring gifts with him, and the parents might not accept until after several visits, which might be up to a year later. The marriage ritual took place at dusk, when the boy went to his bride's house and the father of the girl placed their hands together (Blom 1969:297). The husband served his wife's parents for a year or two after the wedding, and took up residence in the same clearing. *Matrilocal residence* is the practice by which a married couple resides in the same household as the bride's parents, or near them. Residence among the Northern Lacandón in the 1970s and early 1980s pertained to whether the couple would reside in the same settlement as the bride's father or the groom's father, and it was sometimes matrilocal and sometimes *patrilocal* (Boremanse 1982a:91). If a young man moved into his wife's parents' settlement, his father lost the authority over him that he had enjoyed when the boy was unmarried, and he no longer profited from his labor. But even if the young man brought his wife into his father's clearing, he still gained considerable independence from his father's authority when he married.

Najá Lacandón still living in the latter 1970s remembered when, with the approval of all involved individuals, they were allowed to arrange sexual intercourse with partners other than their spouses. One arrangement, for example, was for an exchange of spouses for an afternoon. A man also might offer his wife to a visiting single man. People occasionally entered into sexual sharing arrangements as recently as 1949 (Baer and Baer 1949:105).

By the 1970s the Northern Lacandón had forgotten most of their healing practices, including the administration of herbal remedies. They had accepted Western medicine by then and allowed a French physician to minister to them. They also prayed to the gods for those who became ill, but it was important to know which gods might be disposed to cure the sick person. Both gods and people, they held, were associated in some special way with an animal and had an animal name (the onen), and there were certain ways in which one animal was considered incompatible with another. Therefore, they should pray to gods whose animal names were compatible with that of the sick person. If a person had the Spider Monkey for the onen, the prayers should be addressed to solar deities. And if the patient was identified with the Boar onen, the prayers should be made to to earth deities. They also considered the sick person's recent dreams as well as the dreams of anyone associated with him or her. Dreams revealed tendencies, potentials and realities not yet apparent, so the people analyzed them for clues useful in approaching the gods for healing (Perera and Bruce 1982:17). Usually the family head offered prayers for a sick person in his family, but in especially serious cases all the men of a compound assembled to pray, chant, and burn incense before the proper gods until the sick person died or recovered.

The Lacandón believed that the soul of a person near death would leave the body and wander about, visiting places and people he or she had been familiar with (Perera and Bruce 1982:170). A Lacandón approaching death used these visits to inform others of his coming demise.

Until well past mid-century the Northern Lacandón buried their dead in their clothing, wrapped in a hammock, with the body facing the east. With the body they buried a dog made of palm leaves, a lock of hair, a bone, a bowlful of corn, and certain tools. They also constructed a little hut with a thatched roof over the grave. The hut's special geometric design was meant to help the soul on its trip to the next world. On its journey to the afterworld, they held, the soul had to pass through the evil realm of Metlá'an. There it was confronted by vicious dogs, and the bone was to be thrown to them. The hair was thrown to swarms of lice, and the corn fed to bands of chickens that barred the way. The palm-leaf dog represented the man's most faithful hunting dog, who would take pity on his former master and carry him across a river full of alligators, after which he entered the house of Sukunkyum, the older brother of Our True Lord. While in Metlá'an bad souls were alternately roasted and frozen by the evil deity, Kisin, but good souls escaped this. When they reached their destination the good souls were told by Our True Lord's elder brother that the dogs, lice, chickens, and alligators were all illusions and that the river was the stream of tears wept for him by wives, brothers, and friends. The soul then resided in an underworld or went to one of five heavens, depending on what kind of person he was and the manner of his death. The headman of Najá during the 1970s and early 1980s, some thought, might be the last Lacandón there to receive a traditional burial.

Though the soul was in another world, the Lacandón felt that a ghost emerged from a corpse. After burial the blood vessels, especially the veins of the legs, developed into a ghost which left the grave and haunted the places the person had lived, frightening the living (Boremanse 1982a:87).

Government and Social Order

Political mechanisms among the twentieth century Lacandón were extremely informal. Such civil authority as there was during the 1970s and early 1980s rested in the hands of an elderly, well-respected, conservator and teacher of Lacandón traditions named Chan K'in. He was a "great one" and might be referred to as a *headman*. Headmen normally lead by virtue of their personal qualities and their capacity for influencing others, which brings them enough

respect that people allow themselves to be influenced by them. The Northern Lacandón emphasized the headman's knowledge of the traditions, especially religious matters. They also recognized that one of the sons should succeed a "great one" though there was some question in the early 1980s as to which son, if any, would qualify to replace the elderly Chan K'in. He himself sometimes denied that he was a true "great one," in the tradition of those of the past, but he clearly was the spiritual leader and guardian of the traditions at Najá (Perera and Bruce 1982:102). He also assumed responsibility for seeing that all land, property, and gifts were distributed equitably among his people. Though feeble, Chan K'in was still alive in 1986.

In spite of Chan K'in's influence and the respect he enjoyed, he was not an authority figure. McGee stressed that the Lacandon remained "extremely egalitarian." They were having to deal regularly with commercial and political questions resulting from the increased contact with the outside world, and these decisions were made in community meetings where issues were discussed until unanimity was reached. The Hach Winik were aware of the notion of authorities with power over others lives, but it was something they chose not to adopt. Najá had a *presidente* during the 1980s, elected by the other men of Najá. But he was only a person who could represent Najá in business and political matters because of his ability to read and write some Spanish and do elementary mathematics (R. McGee 1987:30).

Art and Play

The art of the Northern Lacandón was not highly developed, yet they exhibited considerable skill in a number of ways. During the 1970s and early 1980s a few were producing well-made traditional arrows for the tourist trade. They also decorated various religious objects, such as the gourds with which they served their ceremonial liquor, balché, and corn drinks. The designs on the balché gourds were rather intricate.

The people also made rattles, flutes, and guitars. The rattles were also nicely decorated and had bark streamers dyed with soot at the tips. They made the flute of a hollow reed and fastened a feather quill at the tip with beeswax.

All the people, including small boys and girls, smoked cigars. The balché was for ceremonies, but some adults had learned to drink the liquor brought in by aliens. The people of the 1980s were enjoying radios, tape recorders, harmonicas, and the like. They also had a fund of stories they liked to tell. As noted earlier, they also enjoyed witty, humorous conversation and gossip.

Religious Beliefs and Practices

Scholars have been especially interested in Lacandón religious beliefs and rituals, partly because of the widespread perception that many of them are survivals of ancient Mayan civilization. For that reason there is probably a good deal more information available on this aspect of Northern Lacandón culture than any other. As recently as the late 1970s and early 1980s observation and recording of Northern Lacandón religion continued to show significant similarities to what we know of ancient Mayan supernaturalism. Robert Bruce maintains that the Northern Lacandón are the last people to practice the ancient Maya religion (Perera and Bruce 1982:13).

The Lacandón of the 1970s and early 1980s retained a truly polytheistic religion, since they believed in some 30 major deities. The supreme being, creator and father of the gods, was K'akoch. Anthropologists have found that the people of many societies around the world regard supreme deities of this sort to be remote from the people and quite uninterested in human affairs. This applied to K'akoch. Though he created everything, the Hach Winik made no offerings or prayers to him and had no god-pot representing him in their temples. According to one of their myths the Lacandón did not even know K'akoch. However, they did believe that he watched over the rest of the Lacandón gods and that the gods made offerings to him (R. McGee 1987:91).

The most important god for the Lacandón was Hachäkyum or "Our True Lord," who was also known as "Our Lord" and "Lord of Heaven." Hachäkyum was all-powerful, lived in many places at the same time, walked the Milky Way at night, and was embodied in a god pot or incense burner. The people spoke of Hachäkyum often and prayed to him and burned incense before him. He made the earth fit for life and created the jungle, animals, and people (R. McGee 1984:182). He also made the stars, which the Lacandón regarded as the seeds of plants belonging to him (Blom 1969:295). Yet there was a remoteness in Hachäkyum also, since, according to the religious leader at Najá, he was attacked by the evil god of one of the underworlds and had to take refuge in his heaven. His spirit was no longer able to come to earth, and the people had to approach him through other gods who acted as mediators (Boremanse 1982a:86). The bravest and best of all Lacandón went to Hachäkyum's realm when they died and there associated with the souls of eagles, jaguars, and large serpents (Perera and Bruce 1982:176).

Another important deity was Hachäkyum's older brother Sukunkyum, a benevolent supernatural who presided over one of the underworlds. At night Sukunkyum took the sun into his domain, fed him, carried him on his back through his realm, and protected him from the evil deity, Kisin, until morning, when he returned to the sky for his daily journey. Sukunkyum judged the souls of the dead and sent those who had lived normally good lives through the underworld and on to live in the house of the god of rain, Mensäbäk. Sunkuyum sent bad souls to Kisin, who alternately burned them with hot iron and froze them in cold water (R. McGee 1987:106)

Kisin, the evil god who presided over the other underworld, Metlá'an, was Sukunkyum's opposite. Kisin was Sukukyum's brother-in-law, an animal-like and even dog-like being. To attack Hachäkyum he followed him by smell, and his food was tree mushrooms and maggots (Boremanse 1982a:92). He spent his days lying in the warm ashes of a fireplace, like an old dog, but at night he was out to try to destroy the sun and the whole world. He was always angry, and he would shake the poles of his house in fits of temper, causing earthquakes (Blom 1969:295). In addition to roasting and freezing the bad souls sent to his realm, he had special tortures for those who had committed certain sins and might boil a soul in a caldron so it returned to earth as a parrot, coatimundi, dog, pig, mule, or other animal. He boiled the souls of murderers until they ceased to exist (Perera and Bruce 1982:176). Kisin was the god of deaths and earthquakes.

Six of the Northern Lacandón supernaturals were assistants to Our True Lord, Hachäkyum. The principle assistant was the guardian of the stone pillars in the underworld that supported the earth. The other five included the gods of balché, music, and poetry, as well as the sweeper of Hachäkyum's home, the Sun himself, and White Jaguar.

Another especially important deity to the Lacandon was Mensäbäk, the god of rain. He, too, had assistants, each of which was associated with a direction. Four of them were associated with the cardinal directions and the colors red, white, black, and yellow, while the other two were related to the northeast and southeast. Each of the six were known as chacs. The chac of the east was associated with red; white was the color of the chac of the north, and the chacs of the west and south were connected with black and yellow (R. McGee 1984:185). Mensäbäk, whose name might be translated "Powdermaker," made rain by making a black powder that he gave to his assistants, who spread the powder through the clouds with wands made of macaw feathers.

In addition to the supernaturals already mentioned, there was a moon goddess (the childbirth deity), a maize deity, a fire god, a guardian of the jungle, a god of commerce and foreigners (also created before Hachäkyum), a milpa deity, a god of art and writing, a hail god and guardian of lakes and alligators, and a god of the forest.

Bruce mentioned a whirlwind god, one of Hachakyum's assistants, who would gather the ashes from newly made god-pots and newly burned milpas and carry them up to Hachäkyum in his heaven. Bruce and his companions in ceremony witnessed the dark cloud of ashes, smoke, and flashing sparks moving across a clearing and into the forest, which, to his Lacandón friends was the whirlwind god bearing the god-pot ashes to Our True Lord (Perera and Bruce 1982:31).

Jaguar was a minor god that figured importantly in Lacandón stories. The headman of Najá was full of jaguar stories, a jaguar itself being the god in disguise. A jaguar, according to a story sung and chanted by the "great one," once followed a mother and her small son, intending to make a meal of the little one. But the boy was one of the elect of the gods, and the mother had magical powers, so she turned her boy into a sweet potato and hid him in her milpa. The jaguar ascended a tree and surveyed the field, trying to determine which sweet potato was the boy. The story continued until, partly because the Lacandón alerted the gods through their prayers, the boy was delivered from his pursuer and elevated to the upper heavens (Perera and Bruce 1982:86).

Another time the headman chanted a story about a drunk man who was eaten by a jaguar. The jaguar became drunk from the balché in his victim's blood, dressed himself in the man's tunic, went to his house, and presented the remains to his widow as monkey meat from the day's hunt. He took the husband's place at the table and consumed tamales the wife had prepared, unknowingly using her husband's flesh for the filling. The jaguar went to sleep in his chair and the wife spotted his tail under her husband's tunic. So she got an axe and chopped off his head. Since he was actually a god, the jaguar woke up during the night, put his head back on, and looked for the woman's small son. She had hidden the boy in a pot of chiles so the jaguar could not smell him. Then she climbed a zapote tree and threw unripe fruit at the jaguar, and the jaguar pursued her. As he climbed the tree, she chopped off his front claws with her loom shuttle, and the jaguar fell to the ground to heal his injuries and wait for morning. But Our True Lord's son-in-law, the god of maize and protector of people, learned of the woman's predicament, helped the woman down from the tree, and ordered the jaguar not to eat people any more (Perera and Bruce 1982:98). It turned out that the woman was the moon goddess, and the other gods did not know of her trouble because her face was hidden by an eclipse. This is why the Lacandón prayed and made offerings at the beginning of an eclipse, so the gods would defend the moon goddess from the jaguar. Were the Lacandón to fail to pray and alert the gods to the moon's trouble, she would be reluctant to help a woman suffering a difficult childbirth. Around the world, anthropologists have found, myths serve an explanatory and validating function. This story explained eclipses and validated the Lacandón custom of praying to the gods when eclipses occurred.

Many religious systems include a variety of beliefs in spirits, monsters, demons, and other supernaturalistic entities having various characteristics and functions. In many parts of Latin America the Xtabay is a beautiful woman who lures men into the bush or forest with her beauty and the promise of physical love, then harms or destroys them. The Northern Lacandón held that beautiful women who had been the consorts of minor gods once wandered in the forest. They would choose certain of the Lacandón ancestors as their sexual partners, after which a man so lucky should go to the house of the guardian of the forest, spend the night there, and receive his blessing. From then on, all he had to do to see the Xtabay was to light incense to the forest guardian. But a man who neglected this would never see an Xtabay again, finding only barren rock where they had spent time together. The headman said his grandfather knew the Xtabay and had seen them and minor gods walking in the forest (Perera and Bruce 1982:160). He further

noted that the Xtabay were hiding in caves because of the many foreigners in the forests.

There were also cannibal beings in the forests as late as old Chan K'in's childhood, since one tried to carry him away when he was a small boy. They were giant, ugly beings with green warts, who covered their bodies with jaguar skins. If a female cannibal being caught a man, she made him cut wood all day long and have intercourse with her all night until he died of exhaustion. Then she cooked and ate him in one piece.

The various Lacandón groups differed some in what gods they believed in, some were more important to some Lacandón than others, and many deities were local and minor. A deity accepted by the Lacandón of Najá during the 1970s and early 1980s was Jesus Christ, but he was taken to be a god of the whites that they need not concern themselves with.

The Hach Winik believed their gods were concerned with human conduct and punished them when they misbehaved. Therefore, a good deal of their religious practice was concerned with establishing and maintaining the proper relationships with the gods. People who had committed a fault expected that the gods would make them or members of their families sick or, perhaps, destroy the crops. If trouble struck they knew that they had done something wrong and would have to beg the angry gods for mercy and promise them some kind of reward. They resorted to divination to learn what they had done, which gods were angry, what kind of ceremony the gods wanted them to perform, and which gods were willing to serve as mediators (Boremanse 1982a:86)

The concept of mediation was basic in Northern Lacandón religion, since an offended god was too angry to approach directly. It might be necessary to have a neighbor conduct the divination, and when a man had discovered what to do and through whom, he burned incense in the god-pots of the mediating deities, asking them to appease the angry gods and promising them an important ceremony, usually the balché ceremony. Analysis of dreams was an especially important type of divination.

The Lacandón made their ceremonial drink, balché, by submerging dry bark strips from the balché tree (*Lonchocarpus longistylus*) in a mixture of water and sugar cane juice or honey for 24 hours. This produced the fermented drink that they used in their several kinds of balché ceremonies. During the early 1980's McGee found that the Northern Lacandón preferred to sweeten their balché with honey. They used a ceremonial dugout canoe for the container.

The day preceding a ceremony a man prepared the balché in the dugout outside the ceremonial hut or god house. The headbands to be placed on the god pots during the ceremony were made by cutting the pieces of bark, beating them, and boiling them with the lining of seeds from the achiote tree to give the bands a bright red color. The people also prepared achiote dye for painting themselves and their clothing and offerings of tamales and beans.

The next day the host blew a conch shell trumpet in his god house to inform the gods that they were going to be fed and announce to the neighbors that the ceremony was about to begin. The ceremonialist made a fire by rubbing sticks together, put copal in the censers, and lit the copal with a stick from the fire—all this accompanied by chanting. He then removed the headbands from the dye and hung them up, and later he wrapped them about the god-pots and the balché pot, which bore the image of Bor, the god of balché. He then filled the gourd bowls from the balché pot and placed them in front of the many censers, by then aflame from the burning copal. Each god-pot had the face of the god it represented molded to one side. After the offerings were set before the god pots the men who were present were served balché. Following a long period of drinking, they gave balché to the women outside the hut. Later during the ceremony the leader and an assistant removed the headbands from the pots and wound them around the heads of both the men and the women and painted achiote on their foreheads, cheeks, chins, wrists, and ankles. They also spotted their tunics with red and painted the balché dugout and house poles with large red circles. As the men, sitting on the low mahogany benches, became pleasantly inebriated from the balché, smoked cigars, sang, and swapped jokes and good natured taunts, the ceremonial leader offered the prayers to the gods in a low guttural chant. It was both a social and religious occasion. At various points during the ceremony the leader might add incense to the pots, burn maize in them, dribble balché on them, or apply gruel to the lips of the god faces on the sides of the pots. When a ceremony was over, the officiant removed the ceremonial offerings from in front of the god pots and distributed them among the participants, who were not free to refuse to consume them.

Alien participants have reported that the effects of the balché are rather different from those of the white man's drinks and from substances such as peyote and marijuana. Bruce found that perceptions of normal physical realities remained but were sharpened and intensified. He experienced no nausea and no depression, and little or no hangover. Sometimes, he reported, the experience was somewhat like taking hallucinogenic mushrooms (Perera and Bruce 1982:31). Jon McGee, who had participated in more than twenty balché rites by 1987, was aware of no such effects on himself, even when he drank several quarts at a time (personal communication).

The longest, most intense Northern Lacandón ceremony was the renewal of the incense burners. After a solar eclipse or some great or unnatural disaster the people made a new set of god-pots, discarded the old ones at some forest shrine, and held the renewal ceremony (Perera and Bruce 1982:29). If nothing special happened they nevertheless renewed the burners every few years, at least every eight years according to the headman at Najá. For a month or two the participating men devoted their days and nights to the renewal. The 1970 ceremony, the last to have been held until at least the late 1970s, lasted 45 days. The men either made new

benches, hammocks, clothing and other personal effects for the occasion or carefully scrubbed or refinished them, and no one not participating was to even touch them. The participants ritually isolated themselves from the rest of the community, avoiding sexual intercourse and the eating of chili peppers. The women prepared their food, omitting the chiles and leaving the containers of food at a neutral place where the men could pick them up after the women had departed. In the open-sided temple the men were exposed to the weather and insects, and the sleeping was so uncomfortable and the ritual duties so intense that they slept an average of only two or three hours out of every twenty-four. In 1970, when Robert Bruce participated in the ceremony, none of the men suffered physically in any way, and all, he reported, felt an augmented consciousness and perception.

The Northern Lacandón were careful to offer the first fruits of their crops to the gods, also using the copal censers. They considered all food to be a gift from the gods, especially maize. When the green maize was ready in August it was offered to the god-pots, and more ceremonial offerings of maize in various forms took place from time to time during the season.

Scholars have been much impressed by a collection of Quiché Maya creation stories and legends found in the town of Chichicastengo, Guatemala, dated A.D. 1560 and, perhaps, written at the Quiché capital of Utatlán by the Quiché Lords (Carmack 1981:7). This is the famous *Popol Vuh*, or *Book of Counsel*, so widely used by students of Mayan civilization. Robert Bruce has collected and published the stories told him by the "great one" of Najá, Chan K'in, under the title *El Libro de Chan K'in*.

In 1976 one of Perera's students in a Central American literature course compared four stories from the two books, showing impressive correspondences between them. In both accounts, for example, the first truly human beings were especially intelligent and farsighted. They could see all of the heavens and the earth and the activities of gods, including their sexual encounters. People felt gratitude toward their creators and sang praises to their gods. The creator gods were pleased but concerned that men might challenge their power some day. Hachäkyum, Our True Lord, removed peoples' eyes and burned them in a hot earthen pan so they could no longer see what the gods were doing, but those who observed the rituals and presented their offerings to the gods retained their memories of the heavenly worlds. The gods of the *Popul Vuh* created people three times, obtaining the kind of beings they wanted only the third time. True men, according to the *Popul Vuh*, were fashioned from sacred corn. According to the Northern Lacandón only their teeth were made of kernels of corn, the rest of their bodies being formed from clay and sand (Perera and Bruce 1982:17, 179).

Westerners, with their emphasis on specialized knowledge, have become accustomed to looking at life in fragments and seem to find it difficult to see life and the universe as an integral whole. Tribal and other traditional societies often seem to find it easier to see relationships and whole configurations. One of the main emphases of anthropologists has been what they often call the *holistic approach,* by which they mean the attempt to understand human behavior by tracing and examining the relationships among all the elements that affect that behavior. They try to consider both genetically transmitted and socially learned elements of human life and how they are related to one another. They seek to unearth and interpret the significance of the total range of human characteristics and cultural developments, wherever they are found on the face of the earth and whenever they have appeared. Thus they study tribal and peasant cultures as well as urban-industrial lifeways, and, through archaeology and human paleontology, reach back through time to the beginnings of humanity. Yet, the habit of looking at things in fragments is so deeply ingrained in our history that anthropologists constantly struggle to live up to their holistic ideals and seem to have to exert great effort to keep their diverse discipline from flying apart and being absorbed by a dozen neighboring fields.

Accordingly, anthropologists feel a special appreciation of cultures, such as that of the Northern Lacandón, that embody an integrative world view. Bruce found that life was one continuous stream of experience to the Lacandón, who viewed other people as extensions of themselves and set no artificial barriers between their conscious and unconscious lives (Perera and Bruce 1982:88).

Moreover, as the "great one," Chan K'in, taught, the roots of all living things were intertwined, so that whatever happened to one affected the others. Following a parallel thought, anthropologists teach that the customs that comprise a culture are interdependent, changes in one element precipitating changes elsewhere in the lifeway. Further, they have stressed the interdependence of human custom with biological, population, and habitat features as well as the interdependence of cultures with one another. If this seems obvious to some, the observation of human events reveals that Europeans and Americans find it difficult to remember and apply. The Northern Lacandón exhibited an awareness of interdependence seldom found in the modern world. Chan K'im held that Hachäkyum made the trees and the stars from the same sand, clay, ashes and lime, that a star fell from the sky each time a mighty tree was felled, that one should ask permission of the forest guardian before cutting down a mahogany tree, and that when many of the great trees were cut, the rain would end and the forest turn to weeds and grass. Hachäkyum would be displeased by all this and the Hach Winik and all other men would die. His view is not far removed from the awareness of some scholars that the entire world climate may be disastrously altered by the onrushing destruction of the Lacandón and other tropical rain forests of the planet earth.

Cultural Change

Even before the Spanish came the Maya of southeastern Mexico abandoned their ceremonial centers, continuing their traditional lives in their jungle homes. It is impossible to know how long they preserved knowledge of their mathematics, the calendar, writing, and other elements of their ancient civilization. Many of the Mayan cultures of Mexico and Guatemala experienced additional and extensive alteration at the hands of the Spanish and Mexicans. But the Lacandón Maya, whether they came mostly or entirely from the Yucatán Peninsula or whether they descended mostly from Mayan groups of what is now Lacandonia, lived relatively isolated and undisrupted lives for an extended period until about 1940.

Modern developments have placed ever increasing demands on the world's resources, partly because new scientific and technological advances require additional materials and partly because of the world population explosion. When missionaries, lumbermen, chicle hunters, anthropologists, and tourists finally descended on Lacandonia, they profoundly altered the culture in the space of a few decades.

Anthropologists, with their special appreciation of cultures as creative responses to the issues of human existence, tend to be upset over anything that greatly undermines a traditional lifeway. They tend to be upset with some missionaries, a number of whom have shown little awareness of the far-reaching and sometimes destructive consequences of induced change. They are also upset with those who, for whatever reason, destroy habitats important to maintaining cultures so meaningful to their carriers, in this case the Lacandón. Though the number of Lacandón had increased to nearly 500 in the early 1980s, their culture was under heavy pressure to change.

Much of this consisted of events similar to those in many other places around the globe. As the demand for timber and mineral resources expands, the tentacles of industrial exploitation move into the remotest areas of the earth. Those who regard themselves as civilized feel they need the resources so abundant in the jungle forests and obtain government approval to cut the forests. When they clear an area droves of peasants needing land to grow their crops follow, clearing and burning the remaining vegetation. The rich tropical forest soil soon becomes too depleted of nutrients to produce acceptable crops, and the peasants move on to other newly lumbered areas. Then come the cattlemen, who plant the remaining soil to grass and produce meat for the world market. The grass soon exhausts the soil completely, so the cattlemen move on. The forest is gone and the life forms that were abundant before are destroyed, seriously reducing the possibility of maintaining the indigenous tribal cultures.

Just before the midcentury mark the price of tropical hardwoods such as mahogany, red and white cedar, *bari,* and sapodilla rose high enough to motivate lumber interests to enter the rain forests of southeastern Mexico to obtain them (Perera and Bruce 1982:25). The Mexican Department of Health virtually eliminated malaria from the zone, and during the 1960s the lumber companies were building roads into Lacandón country. Soon the sequence of destruction just described got under way. The road reached the Lacandón around Lake Mensäbäk first, and countryside once covered with oak and pine forests and abounding with game and wild fruits was turned into a dry and sterile desert. Each mahogany that fell took with it three or four smaller trees, and the cutters made corridors through the forest for the bulldozers to drag out the trees. The destroyed areas quickly became choked with thorns and vines that the Lacandón hunters could hardly get through, and deadly poisonous vipers multiplied in the newly provided cover. After Mensäbäk the roads were extended to the Southern Lacandón community of Lacanjá.

The Lacandón, while disturbed by the destruction of their country, enjoyed the large payments of money the headmen received. They spent it on gas stoves, automobiles, trucks, wrist watches, radios, phonographs, tape recorders, sheet iron, and other items, many of which they either did not know how to use or discarded when in need of repair. The women were afraid of the gas stoves and continued making their tortillas on the clay griddle set on three stones over a wood fire. When the brakes failed on a Volkswagen Safari, the Lacandón shoved it into a ditch and abandoned it (Perera and Bruce 1982:26).

The Mexican government intended the money to go for water systems, schools, clinics and other modern benefits, but a few Lacandón who had learned to manipulate such things managed to commit the whole Lacandón tribe and control most of the funds. The Northern Lacandón knew that the funds were being mishandled but were unsure how it was being done or what to do about it, and most of the money was squandered.

The Northern Lacandón headman was most concerned about the destruction of the environment, which he viewed as destructive of the whole lifeway, and he refused at first to permit cutting around Lake Najá. But a southern Lacandón leader granted permission in 1977 for a count of the trees at Najá, and the Najá Lacandón acquiesced to the cutting a year later. By February 1979 four hundred giant mahogany trees had been felled at Najá and a road was extended through Najá and some distance beyond it. The Hach Winik of Najá had concluded they could not continue to resist successfully and that they might as well have the payments for the trees. With money in hand, various new developments were possible, including one Najá Lacandón's practice of hiring Tzeltal Indian laborers to work in his fields, since he was afraid of the snakes.

The unsurfaced road was impassable during rains, and one of the headman's sons, who was president of Najá and had opened a store there, persuaded the lumber company to use payment money to gravel the road and put in culverts and ditches. In addition, an airstrip was put in near Najá, and Bruce and Perera used it on a trip to Lacandón country in 1978. In 1979 the old headman moved his house to high ground where it would overlook the airstrip and the new road, and most of the community moved with him.

The time since the last renewal of the incense had extended beyond the eight-year period the headman had said was the longest time that should go by since the previous ceremony, and Bruce was unable to ascertain the reasons for the delay. The most often used pots were full of cinders, rising in some cases above the rims, and the effigy faces of the gods were encrusted with the black residue of food and drink offerings. A new temple would have to be built in the new location, and Chan K'in might have been waiting for that. Or he may have been hoping the logging activity would run its course, the road would be abandoned, and fewer visitors would be coming in after awhile. Another possibility was that the will to continue the ancient ways and the peoples' commitment to them were weakening (Perera and Bruce 1982:30).

Besides the destruction of habitat essential to the traditional Lacandón lifeway, the increased number of tourists and other visitors was destructive. Around the world Western tourists have tended to treat tribespeople almost as though they were animals in a zoo, entering their homes and trampling on their sacred places without permission and with little sign of respect for the peoples' feelings and welfare. During one of the Northern Lacandón ceremonies three camera-laden tourists arrived by plane while a ceremony was in progress. The old headman continued to drink his balché and smoke his cigar while the tourists snapped their pictures. When they had used up their rolls of film the pilot thanked the headman, who shook hands unenthusiastically with the tourists and returned to the ritual. But the mood had been shattered, and the participants soon stopped for lunch.

Intermarriage leading to rather unanticipated consequences has been another effect of the presence of whites. A Spanish rancher had fathered one of the most respected patriarchs at Najá, as well as about twenty others, and the old headman's son was married for a time to a Canadian young woman. The increased incidence of light-skinned individuals in the Najá population and the presence of foreign women from all over the world in the area led to a preference for light-skinned wives. The Northern Lacandón believed that Hachäkyum had originally created them with light complexions and curly hair and that the evil deity, Kisin, had darkened them and straightened their hair with a stick while Hachäkyum was not looking. It became a matter of prestige and modernity to have a light-skinned wife.

Commercial ventures also developed from contact. Young Chan K'im, son of old Chan K'im, the headman, had a store, and a Lacandón in another Najá settlement built a guest hut. It had walls of mahogany, was furnished with two cots, three pillows, and a sleeping bag, and the charge was less than a dollar a night, including the meals cooked by the owner's wife. The owner built himself a house with walls of sheet iron and mahogany planks with a roof of tar paper. In one room of his house he stored clay drums and sets of bows and arrows for the tourist trade. Drums and arrows were flown to the city of San Cristóbal at least weekly.

In 1978 K'ayum, the same Najá Lacandón who paid Tzeltal Indians to harvest his maize and tobacco, lived in a spacious hut with mahogany siding and a wide reed cot covered with mosquito netting. He also had a typewriter, an accordion, enamel pots, plastic cups and saucers, a hammock, a clothesline, a plastic laundry hamper, a plastic bathtub for his eighteen month old boy, toy cars and trucks of plastic, color pictures on the wall of himself and his family, a pop poster showing lounging university students, and stacks of bows and arrows. But he was one of the few who owned no radio or record player. K'ayum was also a painter of water colors, though his technique had not matured. He was responsive to the idea of going to art school in Mexico City. He tried to sell his paintings in San Cristóbal de las Casas but eventually abandoned the project.

One of the crucial questions has been the fate of the Lacandón with the mahogany gone. They could have suffered the fate of thousands of other groups, reduction to the status of impoverished dependents on a fickle outside world. The Mexican government began exploring Lacandonia for oil, and the environment would be changed extensively if they began to drill there. There was still the possibility during the 1980s that Lacandón culture would be destroyed eventually and the people incorporated fully into the modern world.

It may be that the same pattern of exploitation in other places will complete the destruction of the world's rain forests and change the total world situation so drastically there will be no further need for oil, uranium, and the like. The Najá "great one" and other perceptive Indians understood that the changes would affect all mankind.

There were Mexican plans afoot in 1978 to persuade the Lacandón to relocate on a remote lake sixty some miles to the southwest in the Sierra Miramar. The area would have been a protected national park, with no logging activity to disrupt the Lacandón lifeway. The country lay 2,000 feet higher than Najá, was a good deal colder, had no streams, and had only a few mahogany trees. The Lacandón were to be provided with warm clothing. The old headman, Chan K'in, after hearing the proposal, responded in Spanish. He pointed out that the Hach Winik milpas and temples were at Najá, that his mother and uncles and others lay buried in the surrounding forest, that their graves were sacred to them, and that they would not leave Najá as long as he was alive (Perera and Bruce 1982:234).

In 1981 the Mexican government's Instituto Nacional Indigenista was operating a socioeconomic outreach center in Tani Perlas, which lies between Ocosingo and Bonampak. There they maintained a boarding school, clinic, store, and other facilities, but the northern Lacandón were maintaining their isolation. The government aimed to resettle them in places near the school and roads to break that isolation so the Lacandón could be integrated more effectively into Mexican national life (Anonymous 1981:15).

Anthropologists generally use the term *acculturation* to refer to all the changes in a culture that occur due to contact with another culture. This is what we have been talking about. The reduction of hunting due to deforestation, the scarcity of land for new milpas, the reduced enthusiasm for properly conducted ceremonies, the premium on

light-skinned wives, the making of drums and bows and arrows for the tourist trade, hired labor for milpa work, plastic toys and utensils, stores, the guest house business, automotive vehicles, tape recorders, and political power games in the Western manner. All of these and many more illustrate acculturation. The initiators of the contacts that produce such changes often fail to realize the consequences of their activity. They fail to realize that a culture is a fabric, as anthropologist Edward Spicer has reminded us (Spicer 1952:16), and that pulling on certain of its threads may well distort the shape of the whole piece. Unfortunately, some who know this care little, since they are more concerned with other goals. This is not to say that change should or can be avoided, but many would like to see change approached with the care and awareness that would limit consequences destructive to human welfare. Some feel that awareness and care will come too late to prevent extensive, worldwide depopulation and a return of humankind to premodern conditions.

The ultimate fate of the Lacandón Maya remained unknown in the late 1980s. The published pronouncements of a number of anthropologists and other observers have left the impression that Lacandón society was about to fall apart and disappear. But a different perspective has emerged from the work of R. Jon McGee, who was paying regular visits to the Northern Lacandón through the 1980s and carefully observing and assessing the course of cultural change there. He discovered that the Lacandón were maintaining their identity and basic aspects of their culture while adapting successfully to change. They were continuing to make money from their crafts and were experiencing extensive material changes, as mentioned previously.

McGee explored the change issue especially in regard to religion and religious ritual. He found, as other outsiders have, that the elders were complaining that the younger men were uninterested in the old ways and were forgetting them. The younger men themselves would grant as much in the presence of their elders, apparently out of respect. But more careful probing revealed that they knew much of the old ritual and the religious concepts underlying it, that they believed in the traditional Mayan gods, and that they were actually ready to take over ritual leadership as necessary. They were doing little at the time because it was not needed. The older men were still providing ritual leadership, and not as many ritual leaders were needed as before, since the people no longer lived in smaller, widely scattered communities and could combine their ritual activities. In addition, younger men were leading ceremonies in a small minority of cases. McGee found good evidence that some of the younger men were ready, both by knowledge and inclination, to take over ritual leadership when the older men were gone. Every married man at Najá still prayed and made offerings from time to time and attended the ceremonies.

McGee noted evidence that old Chan K'in himself was more like late twentieth century young Hach Winik than he granted (1987:183). As a young man, he, too, had made bows and arrows for sale to outsiders. He may not have known Hach Winik ritual and lore much better than young men of the 1980s, and his ideas and concepts had grown and changed, even during the latter decades of his long life. This sequence of change in the lives of a society's members takes place in all groups, including those who are not so pressed by culture contact as latter twentieth century Lacandón.

The general picture during the 1980s seemed to be that the Hach Winik of Najá were quite realistically and productively combining customs from the modern world with traditional ideas and behaviors. They were accepting modern medicine but continued with traditional healing concepts and practices. They purchased and used machines and objects made of plastic, but they wore the traditional tunic and left their hair long. They were doing at least two things of basic importance. They were maintaining a sense of identity and esteem for themselves and their past by behaving in ways that set them apart from the modern world and the often demoralized, poverty-stricken Indians of other tribes. Second, by doing so, they maintained a favorable economic position for themselves, since outsiders would continue to purchase the bows and arrows, drums, and other traditional objects of Lacandón material culture the people crafted. McGee found that the men were keenly aware of these kinds of considerations and intentionally manipulated their lives and behaviors accordingly. McGee's informed judgement was that the Northern Lacandón might yet escape the cycle of destruction due to environmental and acculturation pressures that has engulfed so many peasant and nonliterate societies.

Another feature of this kind of situation, which is found all over the world, involves the distinction between underlying, persistent aspects of a culture and those that are more superficial in the sense of being more easily changed. Observers often conclude erroneously that a culture has expired because the people are living in modern houses, using modern machinery and appliances, using the services of Western medicine, and driving motor vehicles. Time and again anthropologists have found that such material changes can take place while the traditional ideologies and social and religious commitments survive relatively unchanged. This seems to be happening at Najá, and the Hach Winik appear to be fitting customs from the outside world into their traditional ideological system.

Chapter 16

THE QUICHE OF CHICHICASTENANGO, GUATEMALA

The Quiché town of Chichicastenango has long been one of the best known Indian places in Guatemala. Chichicastenango became famous partly because Fray Francisco Ximénez found there the valuable historical, ritual, and mythological book of the Maya known as the *Popol Vuh* (Carmack 1981:7). Also, several anthropologists studied Chichicastenango during the earlier decades of ethnographic work in Mesoamerica, making it the anthropologically best known community in Guatemala for some time. In addition, Chichicastenango has struck outsiders as an especially colorful place, and it has been visited regularly by tourists and featured in travel and other popular magazines. The Quiché (approx. kee-CHEH) number in the hundreds of thousands and occupy a large portion of Guatemala, and the Maxeños (Indians of Chichicastenango) serve as our example of a Quiché Maya community.

During the 1930s the 25,000 Quiché of Chichicastenango lived mostly in the 64 cantons that made up the *municipio*. Their homes were scattered about the mountains, hills, and small plateaus, only a few of them being close enough for people to call from one to the next. There they planted their Indian corn (maize), beans, and other crops, using the machete and hoe as tools. They lived mostly in rectangular adobe structures with double-pitched, clay-tiled roofs, one of the long walls being set back so the structure included a covered porch along the front. The people were devoted to the community, many of them having houses in the town itself as well as out on their lands. They went to town often for markets, fiestas, visiting, and to transact business. The men were traders, traveling to many portions of Guatemala and even beyond its borders at times. Both sexes, but especially women, wove fabric for their colorful clothing, mainly on backstrap looms. The men wore short trousers, tunics of black woolen fabric, and head cloths, while the women wore striped wrap-around skirts and embroidered blouses.

A newly married Chichicastenango couple took up residence with the groom's parents, producing the three generation *patrilocal extended family*. The couple established their own household as soon as feasible after the first child had arrived, which explains why there were both extended and independent nuclear families in the community. Patterns of authority were strong within Quiché families, submission was emphasized in all aspects of life, and intrafamily tensions were sometimes intense. There were no common ancestor groups, such as clans or lineages, but the *compadrazgo* system (godparent-godchild-coparent network) was present.

The community had a set of municipio officials headed by a *first alcalde*, and each canton had its own leader and a representative of the municipio government. The religion of Chichicastenango was basically pagan, with elements of Roman Catholicism here and there. The people conducted many of their complex pagan rituals in and around the church building and, also, at shrines scattered about the rural area. Religious brotherhoods, known as *cofradías*, conducted many of their ceremonies. Chichicastenango has long been a major tourist attraction, partly because of its accessibility, but also because of its colorful twice weekly market and the ease with which people can observe the rituals being conducted in and around the church.

Prehistory

Archaeologists have identified sites in the Quiché area that date back to late Paleo-Indian times. The Paleo-Indian peoples of North America lived by hunting and gathering, including the taking of large game such as mammoths, mastodons, and prehistoric bison. Evidence from New Mexico and other places in the United States and, also, from the Valley of Mexico, indicates that Paleo-Indian cultures prevailed from at least 12,000 B. C. until around 8,000 B.C., and highland Guatemalan campsites have been dated between 9000 and 8,000 B. C. (Gruhn, Bryan, and Nance 1977:11). Brown has found Paleo-Indian types of artifacts in the Quiché region (Brown 1980:314). Presumably, then, humans have lived in the Quiché region for over ten thousand years, though the evidence fails to reveal just when they first entered the area.

The Quiché highland, at least during the centuries before Quiché became a separate language around 1000 A.D. and for a couple of centuries more, was somewhat isolated from the major cultural developments of Mesoamerica (Carmack 1981:52). From about A.D. 700 until 1200 cultural change was quite slow. The area was well populated during this time, but the people were mostly rural and the communities rather evenly scattered rather than concentrated anywhere. The largest political units during this period were small chiefdoms, each usually limited to a small plateau within that rugged mountainous region.

The millennium before Spanish conquest was a time of major civilizations in many Mesoamerican groups, a number of which had cities, monumental architecture, highly-developed pottery, intricately carved stone statuary, and other complex developments. One of the major cultural phenomena of these times was the flow of influences back and forth between the non-Mayan tribes of Central Mexico and the Mayans of Yucatán and adjacent regions. Archaeologists have evidence that the Toltec Civilization, which dominated Central Mexico before the Aztecs came along, was influenced by the Mayan cultures. They believe that several elements combined to form the Toltec civilization of early Postclassic times (about A. D. 900-1200) and one of them was an immigration of skilled, refined Maya from southern Veracruz and Tabasco (Weaver 1981:360). During the Postclassic Toltec culture seems to have heavily influenced the Maya of Chichén Itzá in the northern part of the Yucatán Peninsula, and still later, the Mayans of the southern Veracruz-Tabasco region along the southern coast of the Gulf of Mexico.

The Valley of Mexico cultures also seem to have influenced several portions of the Guatemalan highlands between A.D. 900 and 1200, but this apparently changed the highland Maya cultures very little. The settlements remained small, and architecture, pottery, and stone statuary remained relatively simple. The people raised square temple mounds and a few rectangular buildings but none of the large and intricate structures of so many other places. Their pots and stone statutes were crudely done as compared with those of other Mesoamerican regions. Basically, the area was a cultural backwater until outsiders arrived approximately 1200 A.D.

The final major impact of the Toltec resulted from the destruction of Tula, the Toltec capitol (some 75 miles to the northwest of what is now Mexico City), in A.D. 1156. The Toltec then moved into various other parts of Mesoamerica, including the southern coast of the Gulf of Mexico, that is the southern Veracruz-Tabasco region. It was from these places of Toltec influence on the southern Gulf Coast that bands of warlords brought a more complex, more militaristic civilization into the Quiché region. Carmack indicates that small military bands using Nahua speech moved from the Tabasco-Veracruz area along the Usumacinta River and into the Guatemalan highlands, where they established small defensive centers as bases from which to attack the surrounding Quiché-speaking peoples. They entered the Quiché region around 1250, bringing a superior military technology, human sacrifice, monumental buildings, I-shaped ball courts, urban life, a dynastic line going back to the mythological priest-king of Tula, Quetzalcóatl, and other features of Postclassic Mesoamerican civilization.

While the invaders dominated the Quiché and changed them, the new culture was a blend of foreign Toltec-Maya customs with the native lifeway. Significantly, one of the native elements that prevailed in this blend was the Quiché language. The conquerors were unable to impose their own speech on the natives, having no choice but to learn and use Quiché themselves. Nevertheless a significant number of Quiché words are of Nahua origin, manifesting the Toltec influence on the language as well as other aspects of the culture.

Such blending of cultures is what usually happens when one society conquers another. The Aztec, who entered Central Mexico around A.D. 1250, seem to have had a relatively simple culture until then, perhaps originally living the hunting and gathering lifeway of the northern Mexican tribes known as Chichimecs. The Aztec conquerors in large part learned and lived the lifestyles of the people they conquered, though they also contributed their own ways to the new cultural configuration that endured until the Spanish arrived in the Valley of Mexico nearly three hundred years later. The Aztec Nahua began to dominate Central Mexico about the same time that Toltec Nahua and Maya from the Tabasco-Veracruz region imposed much of their lifeway on the native Quiché. As we noted, the conquerors lost virtually all their language except some of their Nahua vocabulary. Then, during the last few years before the Spanish arrived, the Aztec, too, were beginning to influence the Quiché.

When the Spanish troops under Pedro de Alvarado arrived in 1524 they were confronted by the armies of a Quiché state known as Utatlán, a kingdom that had extended its influence over most of what is now Guatemala (Carmack 1981:3). The nucleus of this kingdom was a confederacy of three adjacent towns near the modern community of Santa Cruz de Quiché and lying nearly seven miles to the north and slightly west of Chichicastenango. One of the towns, Utatlán, dominated the other two, and the state was known as Utatlán to the Aztec well before the Spanish arrived. This tripartite nuclear confederacy governed the peoples of the Quiché plateau, the population of which was organized into coordinated territorial subdivisions that participated in the governmental process (Carmack 1981:6). Fundamentally, this was the Quiché state of Utatlán, though in its later history it extended its control to incorporate provinces culturally different from the Quiché and from one another and only weakly integrated into the kingdom. This larger sphere of influence included the Cakchiquel and Tzutujil to the south, the Aguacatec and Uspantec to the north, some of the Mam to the west, and some of the Pipil, Pokomam, and Kekchí to the east and northeast. Chichicastenango, known then as Chuwila, lay within the core territory of Utatlán.

Carmack's analysis suggests that the supreme ruler of Utatlán was a king, who was a member of and selected by the highest ranked Quiché lineage. He was assisted by an assistant monarch, also a member of the highest lineage, and a judge and a speaker chosen respectively by the members of the other two main lineages (Carmack 1981:170). Utatlán had a complex *segmentary lineage system*, composed of *major*, *principal*, and *minimal* lineages, and the lineages furnishing the four top governmental officials were three of these lineages.

The Aztec sent spies disguised as traders into the areas they wanted to dominate. The Quiché king had ordered these merchants out of his country in earlier years, but by 1510 the Mexica (Aztec) were powerful enough to demand and receive tribute from the Quiché—gold, precious stones, cacao, cloth, and quetzal feathers (Carmack 1981:142). Later the Aztec ruler, Moctezuma, gave two of his daughters in marriage to the king of Utatlán, and representatives of the Aztec nation were present at Utatlán most of the time.

After the Spanish arrived in the Valley of Mexico, Moctezuma warned the Quiché of the impending Spanish invasion. The Quiché rulers campaigned to organize the peoples for an effective defense against the Spaniards, and many groups responded favorably. But the Spanish defeated the Guatemalan tribes in one battle after another and took Utatlán and its rulers in 1524. The invaders burned Utatlán, but it was reoccupied and renamed Santa Cruz. In 1540, tradition has it, members of the Quiché nobility fled Santa Cruz Utatlán to escape the ruthless exploitation of the conquerors and established at Chuwila the settlement that became Chichicastenango.

Ethnography

The American anthropologist Ruth Bunzel and the German anthropologist Leonard Schultze-Jena did the first comprehensive field study of Chichicastenango culture. Bunzel studied under the "father" of academic anthropology in the United States, Franz Boas. She was one of several women who entered anthropology under Boas at Columbia University, Margaret Mead, Ruth Benedict, and Gene Weltfish being among the others. She did her work between 1930 and 1932, and her ethnography gives special attention to social structure and ritual and religious aspects of the culture.

Schultze-Jena, who entered Chichicastenango a few months after Bunzel, collected ethnographic texts there and analyzed them for their cultural content. He also studied the culture of Momostenango and, in his ethnography, failed to consistently distinguish between Momostenango and Chichicastenango customs. His data are valuable for understanding Quiché culture (Carmack 1981), but they are less useful for constructing a picture of specifically Chichicastenango lifeways. The two ethnographers did not collaborate, which Bunzel credits to their widely different training, theoretical orientation, methods, interests, and temperament (1952:xiii).

But she takes note of the close agreement between her results and those of Schultze-Jena and offers it as a demonstration of the objectivity of anthropological field work.

The prominent Mesoamerican specialist, Sol Tax, studied land tenure and family structure in Chichicastenango for six months during 1934 and 1935, and O. G. Ricketson, N. Rodas, F. Rodas and L. F. Hawkins also did important work there. Various others have studied selected features of the Chichicastengo lifeway.

Chichicastenango Country

The Quiché referred to their country as "the mountains and plains." Human events have altered the countryside's appearance considerably since pre-Spanish times, but basic features, of course, persist. To the south of the Quiché region, beyond the Sierra Madre range, lie the broad lowlands of the Pacific coast. The rugged Sierra Madres run east and west, extending into El Salvador and Honduras, to the east of Guatemala. The Sierra Madres include 33 volcanoes, the highest, Tajumulco, rising to 13,846 feet. In spite of the height of the Sierra Madre, there are canyons through the range so deep that, on the clearest days, properly positioned highland observers can see through them to the Pacific shore (McBryde 1971:6).

Quiché country is a hilly, mountainous plateau region between the Sierra Madre on the south and the Sierra Chuacas range to the north. These highlands consist of a number of small plateaus among the heights and deep gorges, a larger central plain containing the site of the town of Utatlán, and the lower ridges and valleys of the Sierra Madre and Sierra Chuacas ranges. The eastern part of the Quiché region is also an area of ridges, hills and tiny valleys, and the plain to the east continues until suddenly dropping off into the Motagua River Basin. The municipio of Chichicastenango lies in a hilly, gorge interrupted area. The town itself, in fact, is bordered on three sides by gorges (Bunzel 1952:1). One of the Quiché names for Chichicastenango means "town of the gorges." The central square or plaza is about the only level area to be found.

Quiché country was once heavily wooded with oak and pine, but, due to slash-and-burn cultivation through the centuries, only small tracts of forest remain. Fields of maize and grassy and bushy areas now extend over great areas, even the steep mountainsides. In the higher elevations pines and tufts of giant bunchgrass prevail, and groves of cypress top the higher mountains. The territory of Chichicastenango in the early 1930s was made up of interspersed corn fields, grassy, brushy pastures, and woodlands. Small patches of forest were scattered among small areas of corn fields and grassy, brushy lands that had once been cultivated and would be in the future. There were small forested areas on the steep sides of the gorges and on nearby hills. Most of the higher hills were relatively heavily wooded, but a few fields interrupted the forest there as well. Much of the woodland was park-like, with large trees and no undergrowth, due to

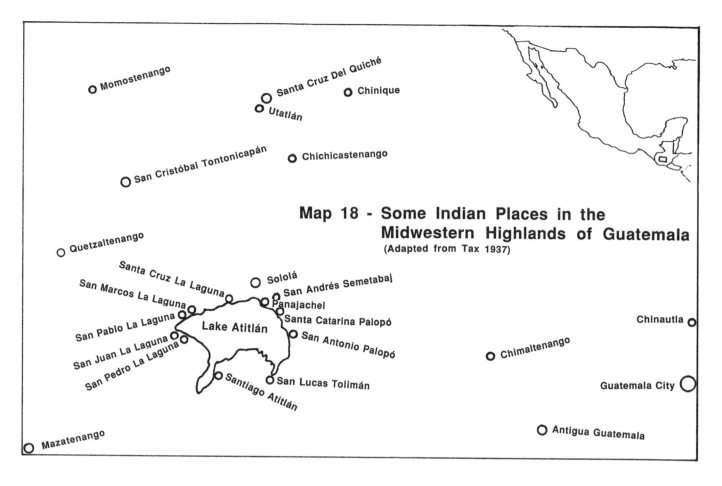

Map 18 - Some Indian Places in the Midwestern Highlands of Guatemala
(Adapted from Tax 1937)

Momostenango

Santa Cruz Del Quiché

Chinique

Utatlán

San Cristóbal Tontonicapán

Chichicastenango

Quetzaltenango

Santa Cruz La Laguna

San Marcos La Laguna

Sololá

San Andrés Semetabaj

Panajachel

San Pablo La Laguna

Santa Catarina Palopó

Chinautla

Lake Atitlán

San Antonio Palopó

San Juan La Laguna

Chimaltenango

San Pedro La Laguna

Santiago Atitlán

San Lucas Tolimán

Guatemala City

Mazatenango

Antigua Guatemala

the cutting of firewood over the generations (Bunzel 1952:16).

The destruction of so much of the vegetation over the years altered the wildlife situation considerably in Quiché country. Deer, important game in earlier times, are seldom seen, and rabbits and quail and other edible birds are scarce (Carmack 1981:94). The pre-Conquest Quiché were very interested in eagles and hawks, but few are left. Buzzards, doves, and hummingbirds are about the only wild avian forms still common. Coyotes, snakes, squirrels, rats and mice seem to be the most common twentieth century animals.

Chichicastenango lies 6,900 feet above sea level. The wet season extends from April to November, with the rains normally coming daily in the afternoons. The rain falls for days on end during portions of the rainy season, and during other periods the weather is clear and sunny with occasional brief showers (Bunzel 1952:47). In December, the beginning of the dry season, the days are clear and the nights cold, and things begin to bloom. From January through March it is hotter, and the atmosphere becomes more oppressive, though the nights remain cool. The people are ready for the rains to change things. The atmosphere becomes oppressive at this time partly because of the heat and lack of rain but also due to volcanic activity and the brush fires due to the burning of vegetation in preparation for the coming planting season.

Language

The Quiché language, which the conquering warlords from the Gulf Coast had to learn and use in spite of their dominance over the native people, belongs to the Macro-mayan language stock, and Longacre includes it as one of 33 languages of the Mayan family (Longacre 1967:120 facing).

Most anthropologists distinguish cultural from other human characteristics as learned rather than biologically inherited and social or shared rather than solely individual. They further treat speech characteristics as cultural along with social life, religion, subsistence practices, and other aspects of life. Any group, then, such as the Quiché, differs from others in its cultural-linguistic features. These pertain to their speech sounds, which of the differences among their speech sounds express differences in meaning and which do not, how the sounds are combined to form units of language that have meanings, how those units with meaning are used to make words, and how words are used to construct phrases, clauses, sentences and other larger linguistic configurations.

The sound classes in a language that make a difference in meaning when one sound class is used rather than another are called *phonemes*. The linguist who studied the Quiché dialect of San Cristóbal Totonicapán, not far from Chichicastenango, found 28 Quiché phonemes (Fox 1966:60). He found that they used some of the same phonemes as English. (We are talking about speech, not writing.) The sounds British and Anglo-Americans designate with the letters *m*, *n*, and *o*, for example, are presumably quite similar to those the linguist uses the same symbols for in writing Quiché. But in a number of ways the Quiché divide the sound spectrum differently from English speakers. Quiché speakers have two kinds of *k*, so to speak. They pronounce one of them, [k], with little or no air puffing through the mouth. The same sound is found in English as the sound in skin. But both English speakers and Quiché speakers also use a k sound with the puff of air, written phonetically as [kʔ]. The difference between English and Quiché on this point is that, in English, whether or not the puff or air is present makes no difference in meaning. If the English-speaker pronounces skin with an air puff accompanying the k ([kʔ]), the word will sound unusual, but the meaning will be the same. But if a Quiché uses the k with the puff of the air it changes the meaning of whatever utterance it is used in. If the Quiché were to say *sakʔaric* instead of sakaric ("hello!") it would no longer mean "hello!" The use of [kʔ] instead of [k] would destroy that meaning. We could say that, at this point, the Quiché have two phonemes (units that affect meaning) where we have one. There are many other ways that the sound system of Quiché differs from that of other languages.

Languages also differ in a variety of other characteristics. Fox's summary of the major features of Quiché grammatical structure takes up 27 pages (Fox 1966), but it is, as he notes, only a concise description of this complex language, with much of the grammatical detail omitted. One of his more interesting points is that the clauses that make up Quiché sentences commonly include components which duplicate the elements of the larger clause. For example, the utterance *quebuluc'am lok* in the clause, *Manuel quebuluc'am lok ri xila chque pa ri ja chanim* duplicates the features of the larger clause of which it is a part. Both *qu* and *chanim* indicate present time. Both *eb* and *ri xila* specify the object, them. *Manuel* is the subject, but so is *u*, which signifies "he." Both *lu* and *chque* indicate "for." *C'am* means "bring in both," and *lok* in the smaller unit and *pa ri ja* in the larger indicate "this way." Accordingly, many Quiché clauses include an element within them which is kind of a miniature of the clause it is part of. This feature is absent from English and many other languages.

Personality and Behavior

The Maxeños (people of Chichicastenango) of the 1930s manifested personality and behavior traits widely found in other Mesoamerican groups. They tended to be reserved and formal in their relationships with one another. Like other groups, they recognized the possibility of interpersonal hostility and witchcraft and tended to keep their feelings under cover as a defensive measure.

Tax and Hinshaw (1969:93) make the point that both social relations and religious observances among the Quiché were impersonal and secularized. The people engaged in complex social and religious ritual, faithfully and conscientiously performed, as though they were meeting their obligations with a minimum of intimacy and authentic concern. Reina noted the same thing for the Pokomam people of Chinautla when he characterized their relationships as contractual. The people fulfilled their obligations as they would a formally drawn contract rather than as expressions of personal regard (Reina 1966:287). This, of course, is only a relative matter. It would clearly be wrong to say that the people had no sense of affection or concern for one another. But these seem to have been inhibited and hidden by the formal aspects of their behavior. Some have said that the Quiché are very religious, but this has to be understood in terms of their observance of ritual obligations rather than inner commitment to the supernatural. Tax and Hinshaw point out that there was a relative lack of domestic religious observances, most being confined to service in the ceremonial religious societies.

There appears to be more ethnographic comment about Quiché attitudes toward land and toward the earth than there is for some other Mesoamerican groups. This may be related to commitment to the local community, which is strong throughout Mesoamerica but seems especially powerful in much of Guatemala. The Quiché felt a debt of gratitude to the earth, to their own lands, and especially the *milpa* (corn field). They felt deeply committed to the family lands, and they normally did not sell them. If something happened to necessitate selling, the male members of the family would exert every effort to buy them back, and others were sympathetic to the effort. Bunzel noted that love of the land was one of the most deeply felt emotions in Chichicastenango and that it was, in fact, the foundation of family life and social structure. If one bought land, he had to apologize to his ancestors and to the ancestors of the former owners of the newly purchased property.

Apparently, there was no area of Mesoamerica where people were more loyal to the village or town where they were born, which was expressed in part by the clothing differences among communities, especially in women's clothing. In Guatemala the sense of community distinctiveness has long been so strong that some believed a kind of plant that thrived in one community would not thrive in the soil of a different place. They believed that the soil itself, as well as stones. plants, trees, animals and other objects of nature had guardian spirits. Quiché would not complain when climbing a steep hill, for the hill might be offended and send illness (Tax and Hinshaw 1969:91).

In a number of North American Indian tribes, the Pawnee and the Fox, for example, as well as in a number of other societies around the world, nothing was more demeaning or resented than being given orders. In those societies, people developed a keen understanding of their social responsibilities and a well-honed sensitivity to the needs and desires of their associates and carried out what was expected without direct orders. It was different for the Maxeños. Submission to authority, Bunzel tells us, was the cornerstone of the social system, and receiving and carrying out the orders of those with the authority to give them was no threat to ones pride (Bunzel 1952:31). Children learned to obey their parents, and adults unquestioningly obeyed the town, religious, and other authorities.

Clothing and Personal Appearance

Many observers have been impressed with the strength of a Guatemalan Indian's identification with his or her community, and one of the chief marks of identification has been clothing. Those who know the costumes of the country have long been able to identify an Indian's village by clothing style. This applied to both men and women, but the costumes of the men began to change until only the women's clothing served to reveal their home town. By the early 1930s Chichicastenango was one of the few villages left in the area where both the men's and women's costumes were distinctive (Bunzel 1952:60).

At that time the Maxeñas wore a short wrap-around skirt of blue and white striped cotton held in place by a long, narrow woolen belt several feet long. This was topped by a blouse, a *huipil* in Spanish, of either white or natural brown cotton with complex designs in red wool, red cotton, or purple silk woven into the fabric. The belts were solidly embroidered in bright silk thread for several feet from one end. After folding the skirt around them, the women folded the cloth extending above the waist inside the part below the waist and wrapped the belt very tightly. The seamstress sewed three sections together to make the huipiles (blouses)—a broad center section for the front, shoulders and back, and smaller side sections. She cut a round hole in the center section for the neck and sewed an applique design of silk ribbon around it. The designs woven into the front and back of the garment and four ribbon rosettes on the chest and shoulders represented the world. The round neck opening was the sun and the bordering ribbon its rays. The rosettes represented the four directions. Stripes woven into the material represented corn fields, zigzags stood for mountains, and diamonds indicated corn. The main color in these designs was red, though purple prevailed in a very few. All the Maxeñas wore blouses of this design with the exception of those in two of the sixty-four cantons, where the women wore solid white huipiles.

The huipil was so large that the women folded it on the sides toward the back and tied it in place with a cord. Godmothers at the baptism of a godchild and the wives of members of the religious brotherhoods at important ceremonies wore the ceremonial huipil over the regular one. It was white with bands of red on the front, back and shoulders.

The large number of elaborately decorated cloths carried by each women and used for a variety of purposes may well be included as part of the costume. They were of various sizes from very small to very large and decorated in a variety of designs. Many were red with narrow stripes of yellow, green, and black arranged in different ways. The designs might be almost anything--simple stripes; figures of birds, spiders, galloping horses, and the like; or, perhaps, scenes of dog fights or elopements. The women carried their babies slung on their backs in at least two large square cloths, and baskets and bundles were always wrapped in one or several cloths. The women spent several hours a day weaving their garments and cloths, though the men wove their belts for them.

The Maxeños wore short trousers and tunics of black wool, red or white head cloths, and, sometimes, leather sandals or straw hats. They often went barefooted around the house, and they wore hats, usually over the head cloth, only when working or traveling. The trousers, tunics and head cloths were richly embroidered in silk and had fringes. The head cloths were large squares with heavy silk tassels at the corners. The men folded them diagonally and tied them at the back of the neck, two tassels hanging down the back and the others above the shoulders. The Maxeños held their trousers in place with a wide, fringed, red sash several feet long. Male weavers living in the mountains wove the cloth for men's clothing. In the early 1930s the only clothing fabric not woven by the Indians of Chichicastenango was that for the women's skirts, which was made by and purchased from two Ladinos.

A young child in Chichicastenango wore a single loose-sleeved shirt extending to the ankles, but from about age five on both sexes wore adult clothing.

Houses and Other Structures

The Ladinos, culturally non-Indian Guatemalans of mixed ancestry, lived along the streets nearest the plaza, or central square, in houses typical of Latin America. Entry doors and barred and shuttered windows interrupted the walls along the streets. Inside, a short passage led to the patio, around which the rooms of the house were situated. The rooms opened into each other and into the columned corridor that surrounded the patio. One room on the street side was generally used for a store or other business.

The Indian houses, both those in the town and those on their lands, were quite different from Ladino dwellings. A narrow opening, sometimes closed by a low wicket of corn-stalks, led into a courtyard with small buildings grouped here and there. The main building was often a rectangular structure of adobes some four inches thick and up to four-teen by twenty-four inches long, topped by a double-pitched clay-tiled roof (Tax 1947:764). The peak of the roof ran lengthwise, and along one side the wall sat back several feet so the roof covered a long open porch, the front edge of the roof being supported by several wooden pillars. The door was in this wall. Other buildings might include a sleeping room, kitchen, chicken house, storeroom and, possibly, a workshop. In many households the sleeping room and kitchen were in the same building, and there were few, if any, separate buildings. Some of the secondary structures were attached to the main house, some were thatched rather than tiled, and one or more walls might be made of cane or some material other than adobe. The floors of the houses were usually of packed earth, though a small number had tile floors. The main houses were furnished with benches and, perhaps, low tables and small wooden chairs. The family altar, which might be a table with carved images of the saints on it, stood against one wall in the bedroom. The most unique structure was a beehive-shaped sweat bath. On the edge of town the yard was a corn field, but even in town there would be some corn plants growing in the courtyards. The great majority of the Maxeños spent most of their time living on their lands away from the town, so some maintained both town homes and rural homes.

Livelihood

As with other Mesoamericans, the Maxeños set a high value on making milpa. The milpa, basically, was the corn field, though it was also the corn plant itself and the activity of growing corn and other plants in the plot. Milpa in Chichicastenango of the early 1930s was largely garden horticulture, as it was in all other Quiché municipios. The garden plots were allowed to lie fallow for several years under the slash-and-burn cultivation system that is so common in so many parts of the world. After several years of cultivation the soil became so exhausted the land could no longer be used for making milpa. Then the gardener had to either clear fallow land of its grass and brush or cut and burn some forest. The fields near the village were located on the slopes of the gorges and were so steep that the men had to position themselves sideways to maintain a foothold and had to zigzag back and forth when moving up and down the field.

The fields of the gorge slopes were good land, and along with some more remote areas to the north and east below 7,500 feet, were part of the temperate lands. In the fields of the temperate zone the people could plant corn, beans, squash, fruit trees, and potatoes, while in the higher cold country, which lay along a certain ridge to the south and southwest, they planted only corn, wheat, and potatoes. The Maxeños also distinguished between fertile and barren land, the latter having a good deal of red clay. Much of the land near Santa Cruz de Quiché, adjacent to the site of Utatlán, was of this kind, and only corn could be raised there.

The Maxeños burned the first fields, in the higher altitudes, in February; and when Bunzel was there in April of 1932 they were still burning fields (Bunzel 1952:50). They used mainly the machete and the hoe. The machete was useful for clearing a field of previous years' growth as well as for cutting the corn. They planted with the hoe, pacing through the field and, at each step, digging a hole and dropping several maize (Indian corn) kernels in each before moving on. They also added some beans and, if the field was to be manured, seeds of the large green squash known in Spanish as the *chilacayote*. They never planted white and yellow corn in the same field and, in fact, kept the two separate during all phases of the agricultural operation to avoid speckling. To fertilize a field they added manure of sheep, goats, or burros. About two months after planting the white corn they cultivated it with the hoe, and the yellow corn was cultivated two-and-one-half months after planting. They hilled the corn twice, a month after cultivating it for the white corn and five weeks later for the yellow corn and, again, two months after the first hilling for both kinds. During the first hilling they planted a second type of beans in the furrows between the hills of corn. They planted the first corn in February and the latest in April. Potatoes were planted in April and wheat in May. The first potatoes were ready in July and the first squash in August. They harvested the earliest corn in September and continued harvesting corn from time to time until the corn planted in the high, cold regions was harvested in January. In October they broke and bent down the stalks of nearly mature corn so that the rain would run from the ears rather than accumulating there and rotting them. The wheat was threshed in February.

The Maxeños cut the corn with the machete, husked all or most of it in the fields, and packed it to the village in large net bags. They tried to bring in the whole harvest at the same time, hiring extra laborers if they could. If the corn had to be carried some distance, the carriers ran and shouted the whole way. They were met at the house by the owner and his wife, and the seed corn was put aside in a safe place and the rest spread out in the patio to dry for a few days. After drying it was stored in raised, closed bins with grated openings at the front. While the cultures of all Mesoamerican communities are basically similar, it is in specific ways like harvesting customs that they often vary from one another. In the Zapotec town of Teotitlán del Valle in Mexico, for example, the ears were removed from the stalks by hand rather than with the machete. They were not husked in the fields, and they were transported to the village in ox drawn carts. (R. Taylor 1960:67). The Maxeños of the early 1930s did not use oxen and lacked plows or carts.

Only the men of Chichicastenango worked in the fields, while in some Mesoamerican communities women sometimes helped with planting and harvesting. A women often went to stay with her husband in fields far from the house, where she cooked and wove cloth; but the two returned home at night or, if the field was especially remote, after a few days. Men with much land or who had other work might hire laborers for major jobs like planting and harvesting. But relatives did not help one another, not even brothers, since hostility, rivalry, and mutual suspicion were so strong. Also, women were to have almost nothing to do with their families after they married, so the families of husband and wife never cooperated economically. This isolated each household. Men available for wage work were those who had inherited little or no land, had no trade, or who had voluntarily left their parents and thereby forfeited their rights of inheritance. Such men worked for their neighbors or left the municipio to work on the plantations. An employer paid the laborer a small wage and fed him three meals a day; and when he left for home each evening the woman of the house gave him a couple of tamales. At harvest time an employer gave a feast for the laborers and family and friends of the household.

The doctrine of *functionalism* states that every culture must be understood as a system. Each culture is most usefully viewed as a configuration of interrelated, interdependent customs, each custom having its part in the ongoing cultural system. One of the implications of functionalist doctrine is that, when we divide a culture into aspects such as religion, subsistence, family life, art, folklore, political organization and the like, customs in different aspects may be as tightly interdependent as customs in the same aspect. To illustrate the point, we will follow Bunzel in noting a few connections between agricultural customs and religious beliefs and practices.

When earthquakes struck, a woman would knock on the door of the corn bin, calling to the corn so that its spirit would not be frightened and run away. On the day 8 *qanil* in the 260 day Mesoamerican calendar the people of Chichicastenango had to perform or participate in religious ceremonies, for the day was sacred to corn. These included a mass for planting and cultivating; offerings of candles, incense, roses, and liquor at mountain shrines; offerings in the church to the ancestors and to Santiago and San Martin; and offerings to the corn itself in front of the corn bins.

The Maxeños observed a number of other calendrical ceremonies for agricultural purposes, but their ritual did not accompany the activities themselves. They performed no ritual in the fields when they planted or harvested, and the planting ceremonies were performed at scheduled times whether or not the planting actually occurred at those times. For example, on one occasion in a neighboring village the priest blessed the seed corn for the people for the day 8 *qanil*, even though that day did not occur during the planting season that year.

Most Maxeño families of the early 1930s had sheep and pigs. They used sheep manure for fertilizer, and they sold wool to weavers in the mountains or turned it over to them to weave into fabric for the owner (Bunzel 1952:59). Nearly every family had at least one pig, and large numbers of pigs were a sign that the owners had a surplus of corn to feed them. People sold piglets to outsiders or to Maxeñas (Chichicastenango women) who fattened them to sell in non-Indian markets. The sheep were herded daily by children, mainly girls, and pigs wandered in the patios and kitchens and along the roadsides and in the forests. The women and children were responsible for their care. The people also had some goats, but no cattle, which do poorly in the highlands. Each family also raised a few chickens, which they killed as needed. Hunting and gathering were so unimportant in Chichicastenango that Bunzel wrote nothing on it.

As in all of Mesoamerica, the food staple at Chichicastenango during the early twentieth century was maize, or Indian corn. The Maxeños consumed a variety of other items, however, including beans, potatoes; many kinds of fruit and greens; and sometimes eggs, meat, or fish. They also used chile and other condiments.

The tortilla was the main corn food. To prepare the corn a woman heated it in lime water in a clay pot until the skin would peel off the kernels when she pressed them. Then she removed the pot and added fresh water to rid the corn of the lime taste. The next morning she washed the corn well and ground it three or four times on the grinding stone. She would then pat the resulting dough into thin, flat cakes and bake them on a griddle to make tortillas.

To make tamales a woman dipped either green corn leaves or dry corn husks in warm water for a moment and wrapped corn meal in the husks. Then she cooked the tamales in water for about a half hour. This was the simple everyday tamale, but a number of more elaborate kinds were also made. Women sometimes wrapped the corn meal in aromatic leaves; combined it with chicken or other meat; added raisins, cloves, chile, or other condiments; or sweetened it with brown sugar.

Another major maize food was *atole*, found throughout Mesoamerica and made in a variety of ways in different places and for different occasions. The Maxeñas made everyday atole by grinding the corn into meal and mixing it with water. They made atole for fiestas by baking a corn cake on the clay griddle, followed by grinding the cake and mixing it with water, spices, toasted and ground cacao seeds, and a condiment known as *sapuyul*. After mixing the product with more water, heating it, and whipping it until the cocoa butter foamed on top, it was ready to drink.

The Maxeños also used beans, their second staple, in a variety of ways. They considered meat a delicacy and bought small quantities in the market. They ate chicken at many of their fiestas and ceremonies. They consumed a number of locally produced vegetables and fruits, such as squash, cabbage, turnips, potatoes, chard, peaches, quince, cherries, guavas, and avocados. They also bought a number of tropical fruits brought in from the outside, such as bananas, oranges, mangos, and papaya, and several local wild berries were used.

Food was cheap and plentiful in Chichicastenango, and no one went hungry. Different households had their meals at different times, depending on residential and occupational situations. Those living and working in their fields went to work without food and had coffee and tortillas at about nine o'clock, ate their major meal at about three in the afternoon, and took a drink of atole before going to bed. There were some that had their main meal just before bedtime. Those Maxeños who lived and worked in town ate three meals a day like the Ladinos--after arising in the morning, at noon, and around six in the evening. The consumption of foods of one kind or another was of central importance in all Maxeño ceremonies.

One of the most noteworthy features of Mesoamerican life is the extensive occupational specialization of the towns and villages and the system of markets where the products of this specialization are exchanged. The Maxeños did not have a major technological specialty like most Mesoamerican places. Their specialty was trade, and their market was one of the most important in the highlands (Bunzel 1952:67). Their colorful, picturesque, and widely used twice-weekly market is one of the major reasons the place has been so popular among tourists. People from neighboring towns brought their products to sell in the plaza of Chichicastenango. Onions and turnips came from Sololá, the potters of Totonicapán brought in great loads of ceramic ware, and women from Santa Cruz del Quiché sold the hats they had made. But there also were all kinds of items from more distant places, brought from all parts of Guatemala over dangerous mountain trails by the traveling merchants of Chichicastenango. Bunzel called them the "middlemen of Guatemala." (Bunzel 1952:69) The Maxeños transported foodstuffs, notably eggs, beans, and potatoes, as well as small quantities of corn, wool, and woolen fabric, to other towns. There they sold them in their markets or other places and picked up items produced in those towns for transport to still other communities. Traders, for example, would leave for the coast with loads of eggs, potatoes, and beans, arriving in Mazatenango for the Wednesday market. There they would sell their goods and purchase cotton, cacao, coffee, fruit, rope, baskets, gourds, hoes, and other items available in that region, returning with them in time for the Sunday market in Chichicastenango. The traders went to Chiníc to obtain mats and Cobán to purchase ropes and take them and the things they had gotten elsewhere to other parts of the country to sell. The list of places and their products could be expanded almost indefinitely, including items such as rice, cotton, shrimp, fish, matches, machetes, paraffin, incense, wash basins, imported china, clay jars, salt, sugar, anise, silk, and hammocks. The traders sometimes went as far as Tapachula in Mexico and to San Salvador, and some of the longer trips took them from the community for up to forty days.

They always traveled by foot, carrying loads that to North American Anglos are incredibly heavy and unwieldy. Occasionally, some of the men took animals with them, but they always carried a burden themselves and used the animals for additional loads rather than riding them. They carried baskets and bags of products on their backs, held there by the strap across the forehead known as the *tumpline*. Some of the loads reached 200 pounds, and 100 pound loads were common (Tax and Hinshaw 1969:83). Outside observers, including anthropologists, are tempted to report the loads unbelievably heavy, but this is an ethnocentric and potentially inaccurate reaction. *Ethnocentrism* is perceiving, interpreting, and judging the customs of other cultures in terms of our own society's values and ways of looking at things. Ethnocentric reactions, while natural and largely inevitable, nearly always distort matters. To the Maxeño the loads were not unbelievable; they were familiar, expectable, and understandable. In fact, a Maxeño might find it incredible that a modern American would be unwilling and/or unable to carry such loads.

Crafts, Tools and Techniques

Many of the Indian towns of Guatemala had a major industry that brought in cash, but the Maxeños had only home industries. The most important craft specialty was weaving, done mainly by the women. They wove to provide fabric for clothing and for the all important cloths they used for so many purposes. The importance of weaving was evident in its interdependence with Chichicastenango religion. At a girl's birth and at her baptism the people prayed that she would be a skillful weaver, and they always mentioned weaving in prayers about a person's destiny. Again, we have an illustration of how customs in one aspect of life are linked to those in another aspect.

Older women spun brown yarn and some of the white, using cotton purchased from native merchants from the coast. They twirled the *spindle*, on which a ball of sealing wax or hard rubber served as the *whorl*, or weight, in a gourd shell and drew the thread out with their fingers. Most of the yarn imported from other towns and countries was bought in the plaza. The yarn was wound onto a revolving frame from which it could be reeled off in preparing the warp.

A weaver formed the *warp* for a *backstrap loom* by winding the threads around pegs driven into a board around four feet long. A basic objective in preparing the warp was to prepare two sets of alternate threads that crossed one another at two places so there was space between the sets to insert weft or cross-threads (Sperlich and Sperlich 1980:17). The warp threads extended between two horizontally positioned cross-bars, one attached by a cord to a house post, tree, or anything else convenient, and the other to a strap or cord that passed around the weaver's waist. There were no side bars, so there was no frame. Tension was maintained as the weaver leaned back. The work was slanted, since the weaver sat or kneeled on the ground and the other end was fastened in a higher position than the backstrap end. Visualizing the work directly from the side, the warp threads had to be prepared so that they went around the end bars and alternate threads crossed one another twice between the end bars. A device for changing the positions of the two sets of threads is known as a *heddle*. The weavers of Chichicastenango made a heddle by preparing a slender cross-bar slightly longer than the width of the fabric they intended to weave, say about 14 inches. They tied a series of yarn loops to the crossbar, one for each even-numbered warp thread, extended the loop several inches and looped it around one of the even-numbered threads on the lower side of the end bars. The crossbar was above the work, and by raising it the weaver pulled the set of even-numbered threads upward between the set of odd-numbered threads. While they were in that position, a weft or cross-thread was inserted, and the even numbered threads were lowered between the others in readiness for insertion of the next cross-thread.

When the weaver had wound the warp threads around the warp board pegs in the proper way, he or she inserted the end bars, a thick crossbar to hold the alternate sets of threads far enough apart to insert a bobbin holding the weft thread, and smaller sticks across and between the two sets of threads and closer to the weaver than the larger bar to help keep the threads in order. The next step was to tie the threads loosely in position where needed, remove the warp from the board, and dip it in a bowl of fluid which, when it dried, stiffened the threads so they stayed in order better than they would otherwise. Then the weaver attached the heddle, and the loom was ready for placing.

The *batten*, often called the sword, was the most actively used part of the loom. This was a flat, wide stick sufficiently longer than the width of the work to make it easy to manipulate. The weaver (1) rapidly inserted the batten, (2) placed it on edge near the place where the weft thread was to be inserted to hold the warp threads well apart, (3) inserted the weft thread, (4) turned the batten on its side and drew the edge of it firmly against the just-inserted thread to pack it in place, (5) withdrew it, (6) alternated the two sets of threads by means of the heddle, (7) and inserted the batten again. The weft yarn was wound endwise on *bobbin sticks*, which were mounted in *shuttles* unless the work was so intricate that shuttles would be in the way.

While weaving was a major occupation for all the women, it was a specialty for the men. The men who wove woolen fabrics used the European *frame loom*, except when they wove the women's belts. They washed the wool, carded it on wire cards and spun it, usually on a spinning wheel. Occasionally they used the spindle whorl instead of the wheel. The loom had a horizontal warp wound on rollers, and the heddle was operated by pedals. The cloth, woven from natural black wool, was both used in the men's garments and traded to other places.

The other crafts found among the Maxeños were leather working, brick and tile manufacture, candle making, and four milling. The leather workers had stalls in the town plaza, where they made sandals, belts, pack straps and other items. Their leather came from a tannery on the edge of town. In a ravine not far from town others made sun dried adobes, bricks, and tiles. The members of one of the cofradías (religious brotherhoods) had a butchering business and made tallow candles from the fat of the animals they slaughtered. There also were several people making candles of paraffin, which they imported from Guatemala City.

Social Organization and Relationships

When Chichicastenango Quiché married they usually took up residence with the man's parents, a practice included under what anthropologists call *patrilocal residence*. When the couple had children it extended the family to three generations, producing a *patrilocal extended family*. If more than one son brought his wife into the household, it consisted of the elder parents, sons and their wives, the sons' children, and possibly unmarried adult sons and daughters.

The Maxeños held that the new wife naturally entered the new family situation unwillingly, and she was expected to be touchy during the first days of her marriage. But she was also expected to obey her husband's parents as she would her own—in fact, to behave as their daughter. She used the same kinship terms for them as for her own parents. At the first signs of pregnancy, she would turn to her mother-in-law rather than her own mother, and her father-in-law arranged for her care and performed the ceremonies for her protection (Bunzel 1952:119).

The elder father commanded his wife, sons, and daughters, and the elder mother exercised absolute authority over the work of the younger women. Moreover, younger brothers were expected to defer to their older brothers, and the wives of older brothers had priority over the wives of younger brothers. A young married couple had no privacy in the household, and other members of the extended family knew about and commented jealously and maliciously on their most intimate relationships. The members of the extended family got on one another's nerves, and the atmosphere was tense. But there was little open quarreling, because the Maxeños adhered to the ideal of the sanctity of the home. The ancestral spirits and other supernaturals were watching and would punish them for harsh words or coming to blows. Accordingly, their overt interaction was governed by an elaborate etiquette, a set of rituals that manifested their ideals of self control. Those in authority commanded, and their subordinates responded respectfully. Bunzel tells us that a superficial calm prevailed in all households, the bitterness and hostility covered by a sullen and unsmiling formality. People from a society in which independent nuclear families prevail might ethnocentrically assume that this tension was due to physical closeness, but this would be incorrect. Bunzel, in fact, comments on the contrast between Maxeño extended family life and that of the Zuni Indians of New Mexico. When Bunzel lived with the Zuni to study their lifeway, she found their extended family life marked by harmony and evident good will (Bunzel 1952:119).

There were also many independent nuclear family households in Chichicastenango. When the first child arrived, the Maxeños regarded the couple as fully adult for the first time and granted them new respect. The couple might remain with the man's parents after having children, but usually the time would soon come when the man wanted to set up a separate household. This meant that his father had to grant him his share of the inheritance. If the man's wife agreed and supported him, the move would normally be accomplished, though not without tension. In their new home the man and wife entered into a new and stronger relationship with each other. They had endured the difficult early years together and now experienced a higher level of interdependence and mutual respect. The Maxeño ideal was one of unity between husband and wife, although that ideal was not always fully realized. In fact, a number of marriages did break up, but those that survived their time as part of an extended family usually endured.

Many of the world's peoples have or have had *unilineal descent groups*, commonly referred to by anthropologists as *lineages* and *clans*. With *bilateral descent* people trace their ancestry through both parents, both sets of grandparents, and on back through the generations as far as they have any concern with it. But with unilineal descent, people trace their ancestry through only one person in each generation. In unilineal societies that are *matrilineal* people trace their ancestry through a line of mothers, while in *patrilineal* societies they trace it through a line of fathers. In societies with unilineal descent groups, the groups are usually *exogamous*, which means a person obtains a spouse from a unilineal group other than ones own. The result is that husband and wife belong to different groups, and under unilineal descent rules, all children belong to only one of the two groups. In a society with patrilineal descent groups, all the children belong to the father's group. Apparently, many of the Mayan tribes once had patrilineal descent groups, and Bunzel found evidence that the Quiché of Chichicastenango formerly had patrilineal clans.

Bunzel discovered that the Maxeños did not define very clearly who could marry whom. They indicated that one could not marry relatives, which seems to have meant parents, siblings (brothers and sisters), half-siblings, uncles and aunts, and first cousins (Bunzel 1952:111). They also told her they could marry more distant relatives "if they come from far away" and as long as they had different names. This she interpreted as a survival of earlier patrilineal clan exogamy, since members of the same clan would share the clan name. Her interpretation is reasonable in terms of the description of the marriage system by a famous missionary of colonial times, Bartolomé de las Casas. Bunzel also notes that the Maxeños of the 1930s preferred to marry someone from a different canton among the 64 that made up the municipio of Chichicastenango, and she found an especially strong emphasis on patrilineal inheritance.

By the early twentieth century the kinship terminology was essentially what anthropologists call *bifurcate collateral* and *Eskimo*. The terms were bifurcate collateral in that the Maxeños used *terms of reference* reserved for their parents only, and they also had terms separating their maternal from paternal uncles and aunts. By contrast modern American society lumps uncles and aunts from both sides of the family together. The people of Chichicastenango had no kinship terms for uncles and aunts other than descriptive terms, i.e. "my father's brother," "my father's sister," "my mother's sister," and "my mother's brother."

For a person's own generation level they used Eskimo terms, terms reserved only for biological brothers and sisters rather than including some or all kinds of cousins under the sibling terms. They also lacked special terms for cousins, simply referring to them as the "arms of brothers" (Bunzel 1952:411). Their terms for referring to their brothers and sisters, however, made distinctions consistent with the Maxeño emphasis on age and sex difference. They had a general term for all brothers and sisters but also terms for older and younger siblings. They had a term, used by both

men and women, that meant "my elder sibling of my sex" and another term, again used by both males and females, meaning "my younger sibling of my sex." And they had still a third term meaning, simply, "my youngest sibling," whether the sibling was a brother or a sister. Many other societies around the world also distinguish between older and younger brothers and sisters in their terms of reference. *Terms of address* are usually more variable than reference terms.

The compadrazgo system has long been important in many Mesoamerican communities. This is a system of fictive kinship through which parents select godparents for their children at baptism and various other occasions, which initiates a lifelong set of relationships between parents and godparents as well as between children and their godparents. The system was present in Chichicastenango, but Bunzel gave it slight attention. In most Mesoamerican places the parents request someone they respect and who can benefit their children and themselves as a godparent. But being a godparent, or *padrino*, was a profession in Chichicastenango, and the parents apparently selected a professional padrino, who could be a man or a woman, to sponsor their child at his or her baptism (Bunzel 1952:81). They compensated the padrino with food, and he or she presented gifts to the godchild and accepted a measure of responsibility for the child's welfare. There was a long civil ceremony conducted at the church, which signalized the child's acceptance into the community and the conferral of the obligations of citizenship. The Maxeños baptized a child only after they felt it was going to live.

When a Maxeña noticed she was missing menstrual periods, she was to let her husband's and her own mother know. When they had agreed that she must be pregnant and had decided about how far along she was, the mother-to-be let her husband know. He in turn reported formally to his father, who then arranged a protection ceremony. Ceremonial offerings were prepared which, according to one of Bunzel's informants, included a package of copal, five wax candles, incense, flowers, *aguardiente* (an alcoholic beverage), and twenty tallow candles. On the selected day the couple went to the father and knelt before him while he conducted the ritual. He first placed the offerings on the woman's head, adjured his son to be industrious and think well of the offerings, and placed them on the table. He then pleaded for the woman's protection and welfare before the World, the saints, and Jesus Christ, and recited the Ave María and other formulas in the Quiché language (Bunzel 1952:94).

The father next arranged for a midwife for his daughter-in-law. The midwife would visit the woman and instruct her and the family about the balance of the pregnancy. When her time to be delivered came, the woman and the midwife went into a separate room. If the mother had difficulty the family might call a diviner to determine the reason. They would be concerned that she was being punished for sins she had committed, and if the diviner confirmed it the husband would be called in to whip her to free her from her sin.

When the child was born the parents named it and the midwife bathed it. The new father notified the two sets of parents, who impressed upon him, if it was the first child, that he and his wife were no longer children, that living was going to be expensive from then on, and that he must be industrious to bring in money. They also made offerings and performed ritual for the child's protection. Then began what they called "the days of the mother," a ten day period during which she remained in bed and the midwife brought her food daily. A part of modern North American culture is a commitment to the idea that peasant and primitive mothers are up and back at work immediately after giving birth, but Mesoamerican women generally undergo a period of complete rest for a period much longer than in North American society.

The birth of the first child had special importance because it confirmed the marriage and brought the couple to full maturity. If a woman had no children she might be divorced. The marriage would be in jeopardy, in fact, until she had borne a child, and the husband's parents would continue to treat him as a child. Parents were not interested in large families, but they accepted the coming of all children as a gift of God, gave them good care, and felt guilty if their little ones became sick. Infanticide was totally out of line with their moral standards and, presumably, never took place.

The people of Chichicastenango, while they watched their infants carefully and attended to their needs well, did not play with or talk to their children much. Bunzel found no evidence of lullabies, stories, or games that adults played with infants and children. Mothers carried small children in two cloths on their backs on longer excursions, and a father might carry an older child. Older sisters of the child might also carry and help care for an infant. The parents apparently did not wean their children suddenly and toilet trained them gently and without scolding or physical punishment. In fact, Bunzel seldom saw children slapped or scolded.

Both fathers and mothers often took their children with them on their business excursions, including those to other towns. They treated them well and allowed them to help in various ways they could. Fathers apparently did little or nothing to discipline young children, leaving it up to the mother. The children Bunzel observed played relatively quietly with their brothers and sisters and seldom quarreled. They seldom played with children of other families and had no organized or competitive games. She noticed no evidence of sibling hostility among young children, even though bitter rivalry would develop when they became adults.

The Guatemalan government maintained three schools in Chichicastenango in the early 1930s—the main school in town and two branches in the rural areas. The children began to attend school at about age eight, but, as is usual throughout Mesoamerica, many of the parents were reluctant to send their children to school. Many of them had to go too far to get to school to suit the parents, and they needed the children to help care for the animals or help their mothers. The Quiché highly respected literacy but did not think it was for everybody. The majority of the people at that time knew no Spanish and saw no need for it. In 1931 or 1932, Bunzel found that neither the first alcalde nor the first principal de pueblo were able to use Spanish. In 1932 three Indian children attended the town school regularly, and two of them were the sons of secretaries.

The transition to adulthood among the Maxeños was gradual, and full independence often did not come until people had been married for years. When boys and girls reached about eight years of age their parents began to have them care for their small flocks of sheep. They also taught girls to weave at about that age. Most of the boys were conscripted for either public or church service at fourteen or fifteen.

When a boy reached puberty his parents began to think about marriage for him, and when they decided to find him a wife, they entered into a series of complex negotiations. If the young man was grown he had probably become acquainted with a young woman that he liked, and the parents might consult him about who he wanted them to get for him. Sometimes a youth would go to his father and ask him to get a girl he was interested in. The father and son performed ceremonies to ensure the success of their petitions, all to overcome any objections the girl's father might have. The girl's father and the girl herself would always refuse at first, which gave the father a chance to look into the advisability of the marriage. Both parties consulted a diviner during the process. When they petitioned the girl's father they always availed themselves of the services of a marriage spokesman or *chinimtal* and observed many formalities and rituals. The father and the marriage spokesman might visit the girl's father four or five times over a period of weeks before the matter was concluded. If the girl's father finally accepted the marriage, the petitioners returned several times at two month intervals with a series of food gifts. After five or six visits from the boy's parents they went to tell the girl's parents they were ready to take the girl, and they gave a feast if they were rich enough. A month later, with the boy along for the first time, they came to receive the girl, again bearing gifts.

When the couple had children, and especially when they had set up an independent nuclear family household, the relationships between husband and wife took on a partnership quality. Men occasionally beat their wives, but this was out of line with their ideals. Normally, both husband and wife were glad to get away from the parents and other members of the extended family because of the tension and hostility. Fathers and sons would almost come to blows, and brothers disagreed over the household work, their status, and their inheritance rights. If something went wrong or seemed to be about to go wrong, they suspected first of all the hostility of a member of the family. They were afraid a brother or some other relative would work sorcery against them, and when the men got drunk their suspicions often erupted into quarrels.

Between brothers the issue was land, which was all important to the Quiché. Fathers thought of their eventual displacement from their land by their sons, and the sons were anxious about whether or not the father would give them the land they wanted. So brothers were rivals for land, the symbol of life and power (Bunzel 1952:142). The eventual result was that all but the oldest brother left with their inheritance, leaving the old parents and the one son with his wife and children as a small extended family. The departed nuclear families thereby escaped the tensions of the larger unit, and the spouses enjoyed their newfound freedom to be real partners. Of course, as their sons grew up and took wives, new cycles of extended family hostility began.

Humans have developed two especially widespread explanations for what is wrong with the body of a sick person--soul disorder or loss and intrusion of something alien. The second explanation prevailed among the Maxeños. They believed that evil substances entered the body as supernatural punishment for sin, neglect of ceremonial obligations, sorcery, or because someone asked the ancestors to send it. In the immediate sense all sickness was sent into the body by the powerful Lord of Sickness, and all responses to an illness involved petitioning him through burning incense, offering food and drink, prayer, and similar measures. They also took medicines, purges, and emetics and used the sweat bath. They used the sweat bath to treat smallpox, for example. A special herbal infusion served for bloody dysentery, and an infusion of eucalyptus leaves was sometimes used for fevers. The people used magical techniques, too, *magic* being a formula which, if followed properly and nothing interferes, will have its result. When children had stomach trouble, for example, they might rub the stomach with a pitchpine stick and say, "Go to our neighbor, José" (or whatever the neighbor's name was), and then throw the stick into the middle of the road. In other cases the Lord of Sickness sent disease because the person had unconfessed sin, and illness also could come because of a fright.

If the disease symptoms were vague or the usual treatments were not working the Maxeños might call in a *diviner*, the most important kind of professional in Chichicastenango. There was a fairly large number of diviners in Chichicastenango, most of them men. They were more than diviners, they were also, with respect to their divinatory powers, *shamans*. A shaman has a special individual relationship with the supernatural and, therefore, is able to accomplish things the ordinary person cannot. The Maxeño diviners had special power to view and interpret the combination of forces that ruled the days of the Maya calendar, so their services were often necessary. But they were not shamans with respect to healing. They knew the ritual for bringing about healing, but once the cause of the disease was known, the patient could conduct the healing ritual. The advantage in using the diviners lay in their more extensive knowledge of what to do and how to do it, not in their special power. The power of their divining was in themselves, but the healing power lay in the ritual rather than the ritualist. In most societies with shamans their main power is healing power, but not among the Maxeños.

Once the diviner had determined the cause of the sickness, which often was an unconfessed sin, the patient or the diviner conducted the healing ritual, which was long and complex and involved magic, offerings, and often extensive prayers to those powers able to do something about the situation. Often, the diviner would learn that someone had asked justice of the ancestors or had worked sorcery against the patient. The Maxeños held that the dead continued to practice the same occupations and had the same loyalties and responsibilities that they did on earth and that the ancestors could discipline any living relative against whom apparently just complaints had been made. An enemy could lodge a complaint with the dead alcaldes, who would demand that the ancestors of the accused person bring him to justice. A person could get sick, then, as the result of a complaint against him through the ancestors. The cure was to confess and make penance for the offence or establish innocence. This people did by addressing the ancestors in prescribed ways so they could render a decision.

The complaint via the ancestors could be handled in public, just like a court case not involving ancestors. But sorcery was evil magic done in secret—at night in the cemetery, on a river bank or precipice, or in a field (Bunzel 1952:295). Acts of sorcery involved a variety of procedures of *sympathetic* magic, such as reciting familiar prayers backwards, damaging crosses inscribed with a victim's name, and digging up bones and reburying them near the victim's home. Only under great pressure would anyone admit to practicing sorcery, but the fear of it was a powerful force for social control in Chichicastenango life. The possibility of becoming a victim kept many a person conforming to the moral ideals much of the time. Doing sorcery was also dangerous, because a diviner might identify the sorcerer, who could become a victim of counter sorcery.

The Maxeños manifested little grief when someone died. Often, as funeral processions passed, many of the onlookers would be unaware of who had died and, perhaps, would care less. The people felt grief when someone close to them died, of course, and their funerals were elaborate enough to evidence their concern over their loss. But death did not horrify them, and they had no fear of touching or being in the presence of dead bodies. A funeral and the events that followed were times of merriment, with plenty of liquor available to help obliterate sorrow. After the burial the people sped the spirit on its way by firing rockets, and the mourners drank by the grave to relieve their grief. Shortly afterward the diviner met with the relatives at the church to introduce the dead person's soul to his ancestors, and the relatives were already staggering drunk. After that they resorted to a tavern to continue their drinking.

Government and Social Order

The town of Chichicastenango was the central place in the municipio of Chichicastenango, which was divided into 64 rural subdivisions known as cantons. Each canton was headed by a *Principal de Canton* selected by the canton citizens. Each canton also had an *auxiliare*, who represented the municipio government.

The smallest canton contained nine households and the largest fifty-eight. The homesteads were scattered over the hills and mountains, either isolated from one another or clustered into three or four within calling distance, but there were no hamlets, villages or towns. The town itself was what Mesoamerican specialists call a "vacant town." Though most of the Indians of Chichicastenango felt great loyalty to the town itself, they did not live there most of the time. Only those with occupations or administrative responsibilities that required them to live in town resided there, which was only about 400 people in the early 1930s. The other nearly 25,000 Indians lived in the rural areas. There were about 75 Ladino families in Chichicastenango. Many of the Indians maintained houses both in town and country, and unless a fiesta or other occasion brought them to town, the village presented a picture of a place with many vacant homes. Bunzel first entered the town chauffeured by an Indian driver. As he sped through the streets the only people she saw were a few Ladinos lounging at the doors of their shops (Bunzel 1952:5). When they got to the plaza they saw three old women sitting with baskets in front of them and Indian municipal officials on the benches in front of the court house, spinning and embroidering. There were also two boys playing dice on the church steps. No one could be seen at the Indian homes and the doors were locked.

The Indians enjoyed going to town for markets, fiestas, or business. Sunday was a market day, and the roads to town early in the morning were filled with Indians carrying burdens. The day's activities included ceremonies of the religious brotherhoods, buying and selling in the plaza, the reading of official proclamations, baptisms, marriages, complex individual religious rituals and prayers in and before the two churches, divination ceremonies, drinking in the *estancos*, and, in the evening, dancing and more drinking by some. By evening most of the houses were locked again until the following week. Maxeños without town homes stayed in the homes of others when they went to town.

Not all of the Guatemalan communities are vacant towns. In many places the people live in the village or town, going to their fields in the morning and returning in afternoon or evening. The towns around Lake Atitlán to the west, for example are of this type, the so called *nucleated towns*.

The 64 cantons of Chichicastenango were grouped into five districts, each headed by a *Principal de Pueblo* selected by the district leaders of the cantons in the district. These five men were the most powerful authorities in Chichicastenango. They named the Indian alcaldes and removed employees that did not serve well, and they were in charge of all kinds of public work. They also were in charge of the municipio title and map.

In 1932 the main official in Chichicastenango was the *Ladino alcalde*. There was also a secretary, a treasurer, two *Indian alcaldes*, a literate Indian who served as official in-terpreter, a treasurer, and a collector of market fees. The only other Ladino official was the *Comandante*, who policed the town with the aid of three or four soldiers. The Ladino alcalde handled minor disputes among Ladinos, performed civil marriages, and received and executed orders from higher governmental levels. If any of the latter concerned the Indians, he passed them on to the Indian alcaldes to be enforced. The Ladino alcalde was formally elected by the citizens of Chichicastenango, though the *Jefe Político* of the Department of Quiché, the next higher level of government, informally approved a list of candidates in advance. In matters that concerned only the Indians the Ladinos and higher levels of government interfered very little.

In addition to the two Indian alcaldes (first alcalde and second alcalde), there were eight *regidores*, five *mayores*, two *fiscales*, and a number of *alguaciles* and *chajales*. The first regidor was the *Síndico*. The five principales de pueblo selected the alcaldes, Síndico, regidores, mayores and fiscales, while the First Alcalde named the auxiliares to represent the government in the cantons. This took place at the fiesta of the Concepción on December 8. All the officials carried staffs or *varas* as symbols of their authority when going about on public business. The alcaldes participated in the ritual of the religious brotherhoods, settled disputes, handled minor criminal matters, and carried out orders from the non-Indian officials. The regidores summoned defendants for all complaints, going to the various cantons to locate them and, while there, dealing with some of the minor disputes and executing decisions made by the alcaldes. They also worked with the auxiliares to prepare lists of youths eligible for public service as alguaciles or chajales and helped bring them in. In fact, much of the time of the regidores was spent in bringing people to town as required.

Four of the mayores were old men responsible for supervising the alguaciles, who were young men engaged in community service. Another mayor was responsible for reading public proclamations around the town. The alguaciles were about 200 boys around 14 years old who swept and cleaned the streets after markets and fiestas, carried messages or baggage, provided essentials for travelers, served as guides, and performed other community work. Each alguacil served about one week out of six, about 35 being on duty at a given time.

The fiscales were in charge of the chajales, who were about thirty young people that worked at the priest's household, tending his gardens, house, horses, and livestock, and carrying messages, helping in the kitchen, etc. They worked every fourth week, six on duty at a time, and others on reserve as substitutes. The fiscales also kept track of the convent revenues. They served alternate weeks, sleeping in a room behind the convent kitchen while on duty.

As in other parts of Mesoamerica the political organization of Chichicastenango was part of a civil-religious hierarchy of offices. Each man was expected to participate in this hierarchy, moving to ever higher levels as he alternated between religious positions and political office. Only a few, of course, rose to the top echelons. In portions of Mesoamerica the religious offices are those of the religious brotherhoods called cofradías, which are organizations devoted to the cult of a saint. Chichicastenango had fourteen cofradías in the early 1930s, each of which owned a saint's image kept on an altar in the first mayordomo's home. Other sacred objects on the altar might include creche figures, a figure of the cock that rebuked Peter when he denied Christ, images of the sorrowing angels that accompanied María Dolores, and so on. Candles burned on the altar on Sunday and fiesta times, and there were fresh flowers in the vases. The officers of the cofradías were called *mayordomos* in Spanish, and two remained at the cofradía house constantly for a week at a time. Some of the cofradías had six mayordomos, so they had to serve one week in three, while those with eight mayordomos had to serve once every four weeks. Those on duty kept the house in order and watched the candles to prevent fire. All the mayordomos were to be present on Sundays and fiesta days.

Each mayordomo had special duties, some being responsible for ritual and prayer, another for administration and leading ceremonies, and one each for sacramental food, care of the house, and selling drinks at the drinking and dancing parties. Each of the mayordomos' wives also had special assignments. Each cofradía had its round of ceremonies, which culminated annually in the fiesta to the saint. At this time they selected and installed the next year's mayordomos. The first and second mayordomos of six of the cofradías made up an executive council to handle all church matters. They appointed the new mayordomos for all the cofradías and officiated at their installation. The First Alcalde of Chichicastenango made the installation speeches, one of the linkages between the religious and governmental components of Chichicastenango life. Also, the council of 12 mayordomos met with the two alcaldes and the five principales to consider public issues. The alcaldes and principales also attended the cofradía fiestas and walked at the head of cofradía processions, carrying their canes of office on these and other cofradía occasions.

The first step in climbing the civil-religious hierarchy was to serve as an alguacil, something that was expected of all young men by about fourteen years of age. Before holding a higher responsibility in the municipal system, a man had to serve as one of the lower ranking mayordomos. There were only 48 such positions annually, so the opportunities were limited. A man would be considered for such a position about four years after completing his alguacil service. It took a great deal of time and money to be a mayordomo, so only those from economically well-off families able to spare an active male would be chosen. The income from the drinking and dancing parties called *zarabandas* paid only part of the cofradía expenses, so much of the money for masses, incense, food, musicians, cooks, and so on, had to come out the mayordomo's pocket. But when the service was completed, providing he had acquired other knowledge and experience, the man might be chosen for a governmental position. A man chosen to be a regidor had to have become expert in contracts, domestic relations, and

legal matters by serving in those respects in the cantons. Only after being a regidor would a man be eligible to serve as First Mayordomo in one of the less important cofradías. The alcaldes were chosen from among the relatively small group of men who had served as First or Second Mayordomo, and some held those positions three or four times before being selected.

During the pre-Spanish days of Utatlán Quiché society was divided into the noble class, the descendants of the conquerors from the coast of the Gulf of Mexico, and the common people (descendants of the native Quiché). Bunzel guessed on the basis of her observations that the influence of this social distinction still affected affairs in Chichicastenango, though the people denied all rank differences. She found that the chief mayordomos were chosen only from wealthy families that owned or had access to town houses. All of the five principales de pueblo, the ruling body of the community, came from this group. They had lands in different rural portions of the municipio and were placed in power and kept there by the principales de cantones in their areas. The five principales de pueblo chose the mayordomos and the alcaldes from the members of their own class. Bunzel also noticed that all of her informants who wore the sunburst design embroidered on the fronts of their tunics belonged to the wealthy families. These things, she hypothesized, reflected earlier times.

Art and Play

A great deal of human custom is expressive in the sense that it involves the use of skill to manifest sentiments or values. Under this heading fall drama, music, dancing, plastic and graphic arts, folklore, and pastimes. While these can be and often are separated as distinct areas, skilled expression of sentiments permeates all aspects of life. Weaving and, especially, the weaving of complex patterns into the cotton and woolen fabrics and the silk embroidery of designs that have meaning was a part of the expressive culture of Chichicastengo in the early 1930s. Dozens of pages could be written describing the artistic techniques involved and the sentiments and meanings expressed.

Some ethnographies devote hundreds of pages to the texts of folktales, but this would not be possible for Chichicastenango. Contrary to the situation in many other Mesoamerican communities, perhaps most, the Maxeños exhibited a poverty of folktales. The German anthropologist Schultze-Jena went to Chichicastenango to make a collection of their folktales, but he obtained almost nothing (Bunzel 1952:264).

Moreover, the people of Chichicastenango simply did not have the competitive games and sports so important in other societies. They engaged in activities for the sake of enjoyment and to symbolize important values largely within the context of their work and religion. The town officials, for example, embroidered elaborate designs on garments while they were on duty at the municipio headquarters. The women found the backstrap loom convenient for passing the time, since they could fold their work, carry it with them, and quickly and easily attach it to a shrub, post, or whatever was handy to weave for awhile if they had to wait somewhere with nothing else to do.

As in many other Middle American communities, the people enjoyed certain aspects of their religious ritual and the activities connected with them. The speeches to the supernaturals made by the diviners could well be considered works of art the composers themselves enjoyed delivering. Certainly, people enjoyed watching the diviners arrange their seeds and interpret the forces of the world.

If, as full length ethnographies often do, we were to give a full account of the ceremonial calendar of Chichicastenango and the rituals involved, we would find many elements of drama, music, dance, and simply passing the time enjoyably. Though we do not explore these elements here, it is important to be aware that religious ceremonial took up a great part of the time in Maxeño life. The fiestas, which involved masses, processions, drama, dancing, fireworks, drinking, and other elements, were highly complex, focusing many aspects of their complex social life (Bunzel 1952:192). Bunzel commented that many people attended the fiestas simply for the pleasure of it. She reported in some detail on the Fiesta of María del Rosario from October 2 to 5, the fiestas of All Saints and All souls days from October 28 through November 3, the exciting Holy Week ceremonies from March 20-27, and the rituals of the cofradía of San Sebastián. She devoted some 55 pages of small print to the descriptions of these three ceremonial periods, and in one of her book's appendices she listed nearly 30 additional scheduled ceremonies she did not describe. Some months were heavier with ceremonies than others, but none were without any. When one combines these with the ongoing unscheduled ritual activity, it is clear that there was plenty to do in Chichicastenango.

Outsiders find the Volador or Flying Pole ritual, performed by a number of Mesoamerican tribes, of considerable interest. In Chichicastenango a diviner began the preparation for the ritual by making prayers and offerings to the World and the ancestors, most likely on a ceremonially important hill known as Pokojil (Schultze-Jena 1954:116). After a week of sexual abstinence four dancers went into the hills and slept for the night beneath the tree selected to be made into the pole they were to descend from. The next day people from town arrived, and the diviner conducted more ritual. The cutters stripped the tree of its branches and bark and cut a smaller pole, too, for the flyers to practice on. They left the pole to be used for the actual ceremony in the mountains until shortly before the time. The diviner also conducted ceremonies near the hole that had been dug in the ground before the church to receive the dance pole. The flying was dangerous, and the people sought to forestall accident through the prayers and offerings. A square framework was constructed so that it could rotate at the top of the pole, and ropes were attached to the corners of the framework and wound around the top portion of the pole. The flyers climbed to the top, slipped into loops at the ends

of the ropes, and started the platform spinning. They launched themselves into the air, swinging around the pole at the ends of the unwinding ropes until they descended to the ground. In some Quiché groups only two people actually swung at the ends of the ropes, while the other two men danced atop the framework, guided the rotation, and slid down a rope to the ground after the others had descended. If all descended without accident the diviner thanked the supernaturals. This dramatic spectacle was especially popular, and thousands of spectators enjoyed it on each occasion until it was forbidden because of the occasional injuries and deaths.

Sol Tax observed three flying pole dances in April 1935 in the Chichicastenango canton of Quejol. The pole was 45 feet long and sat in a three foot deep hole, where it was held in place by sticks. In this case two men would descend on the ropes, and sometimes there was a third man who remained on the framework (Tax 1947:424).

Another event that illustrates the expressive and recreational aspects of Maxeño ceremonies was the zarabanda, the dance put on by the cofradías to raise money for their activities. They hired a marimbist to play and sold beer and liquor in the room where their patron saint was kept. The room was cleared of everything but the altar and benches around the walls. A zarabanda began about midafternoon Sunday, about when the market began to break up, and lasted through the next night and day and, sometimes through a second night. Not many danced, and most of the dancers were young men. The emphasis was on the drinking. There were always more men than women present, and people laughed, shouted, and engaged in erotic behavior.

Religious Beliefs and Practices

Though Roman Catholic personnel, ritual, and material symbols were present in Chichicastengo, it would hardly be accurate to describe the people as Catholics. In many Mesoamerican places the people have long been so sensitive about criticism of pagan ways that they are hidden. They have been made part of what anthropologists call *covert culture*, which consists of customs that are not readily detectable by outsiders, either because the people keep them hidden or they are ideological customs not often expressed in language and bodily movements. But in the early 1930s anthropologist Ruth Bunzel had no difficulty observing the rituals of the diviner and learning about many non-Catholic elements of their religion. She lived in the convent while she did her field work, and as she walked with the Catholic priest on one occasion they came across a diviner swinging his censer before a shrine on a wooded knoll and praying loudly to the supernaturals. He greeted the priest and Bunzel briefly and continued with his ritual. Moreover, the people felt free to conduct many of their rituals on the plaza before the Catholic church and in the building itself. In fact, the Indians owned the building. These aspects of the religion, then, may be considered overt culture.

During Bunzel's visits there the Maxeños believed in and interacted with a wide variety of supernaturals, which they invoked during the course of their elaborate religious rituals (Bunzel 1952:266). There was the World, commonly the first supernatural addressed. The Quiché word is not clearly translatable into English. Mountain-plain would be closer, but it seems to have to do more with "the multiple manifestation of the universal essence," to use Bunzel's words. There were also the natural phenomena—the sun, the directions, the cloudy sky, the cold wind, and volcanoes. The saints included the Eternal Father, Christ in various contexts, the patron saints of the village and the cofradías, and the patrons of midwives, angels, and other figures of basically Christian origin. The idols were the carved stones from ancient sites, wherever they were found or used. The forces of destiny consisted of time, destiny, the days of the sacred calendar, and the peoples counterpart soul-animals, known elsewhere in Mesoamerica as *tonales*. The death-bringers included the Lord of Sickness and gods of special sicknesses like poisoning, alcoholism, violent death, and physical torture. Masters of useful activities were the gods of agriculture, weaving, business, midwifery, sorcery and other such things. The Lords of Justice were deceased alcaldes and other such officials. Finally, there were the ancestors--the souls of the dead. The religion of the Maxeños was essentially pagan and polytheistic like those of other Mesoamerican communities.

When the ritualists or the common people of Chichicastenango prayed and made offerings to the supernaturals they often invoked many of them in a single ritual, but only those they regarded as having some relevance to the purpose of the moment. Also, it was appropriate to address them in the proper place. For example, the Maxeños usually did not pray or make offerings in the church to natural phenomena and the ancestors. The various powers were relatively neutral rather than friendly or hostile, but some could be more destructive than others. It was also possible to fool, bribe, or threaten some of them. The main protectors among them were the saints and the masters of useful activities, and the idols and the death-bringers were especially destructive.

The ancestors were the most constantly present and influential supernaturals in daily life. They were largely the same as living humans, and they maintained an ongoing concern with what happened in the lives of their descendants. As previous owners of the homes and lands, they insisted on order within the home. In fact, the people considered them the real owners of the houses and land, and ancestors could oust people who misbehaved. They were greatly offended by family quarrels and displeased by adultery, theft, drunkenness, and neglect of ritual obligations, as well as a number of other things. The Maxeños lived in fear of their ancestors, since they would punish misbehavior by sickness, death, or property loss. Much of their daily religion was concerned with keeping the ancestors satisfied and seeking their protection. As noted before, a person could complain to his or her ancestors about an enemy, and the

ancestors would pass the complaint on to the authorities in the other world for trial. If the decision went against the defendant, he or she could be called through death to appear before that court of the other world.

In spite of their fear the people were not afraid of ghosts. In fact, they confidently and even joyfully interacted with the dead on many occasions. One of the main ones was All Souls Day on November 2, when they offered candles and flowers to the ancestors at the church. The preceding evening they decorated their homes and set food, flowers, and candles out to receive the ancestors, who, during the night, entered their former homes to feast and be with their descendants.

A tonal (confused with a *nagual* in some descriptions) was a person's counterpart soul in some wildlife form or sacred object. It could be a snake, deer, or bird, for example, or a stone idol buried in the earth. The tonal was a person's destiny in the sense that what happened to the tonal would happen to the person. Most people never met the tonal, though some did, and this was good luck. The animal would signal a person somehow, so that it would not get shot, and it might talk to the person. If the tonal was killed in the woods the person would die immediately. If it was wounded the individual would feel great pain in the corresponding place. The Maxeños believed that such occurrences accounted for many accidents and sudden, unexpected deaths.

The days of the 260 day sacred calendar were also supernaturals. Like other Mesoamerican calendars, the Quiché sacred calendar involved the combining of 20 day names with 13 day numbers so that the period was divided into 20 thirteen day units. Each day was designated by a name and a number. The first day of the period was 1 Thread, which stood for ritual continuity with the past. The thirteenth day was 13 Darkness, symbolic of evil in the human heart, and on the fourteenth day the day numbers began over again with number one while the day names continued. The fourteenth day was 1 Qat (no translation given), symbolizing evil in general. The twentieth day was 7 Dog, standing for sexual and other sins; and with the twenty-first day the day name cycle began over again while the day numbers continued. The twenty-first day was 8 Thread. It took 260 days until the cycle was complete, and on the 261st day the cycle began again with 1 Thread.

Each day was either good or bad and had a number of implications which only diviners were specially gifted to interpret. The diviners had bundles in which they kept a hundred *maguey* seeds and an ancient sacred stone. A diviner arranged the seeds in positions that related to the sequences of days, interpreting divine forces, continuity, evil, regeneration, arbitrary cruelty of the universe, and so on according to principles that only he or she was empowered to understand.

Religion permeated the culture of Chichicastenango in a way and to a degree foreign to most modern North Americans and Europeans. This is one of the great differences between Euroamerican cultures and many peasant and tribal societies.

Culture Change

As with all Mesoamerican communities the early twentieth century culture of Chichicastenango was much different from pre-Spanish and colonial times. No culture ever stops changing, which is always apparent in anthropological community restudies. Ruth Gruhn lived in Chichicastenango for two months in 1969, almost 40 years after Bunzel and Schultze-Jena were there. She was intimately familiar with Bunzel's ethnography and found that the 1969 culture was enough like that of the early thirties that she could use Bunzel's description as a reliable guide to understanding a great deal of what was going on around her (Gruhn 1973:231).

Anthropologists and others have often observed that cultural elements with material manifestations change more readily than so-called nonmaterial culture, and this was apparent in Chichicastenango. Gruhn heard portable radios playing in the remotest cantons and found that many people owned bicycles and wrist watches and that all households owned metal and plastic utensils. The great majority of the men had abandoned the traditional male costume, the exceptions being the oldest men and those holding political or religious office (Gruhn 1973:243). But all of the women and girls still used the complete traditional female costumes. A similar situation prevails in other Guatemalan Indian communities, and it is common in other parts of the world, too, for women to be conservative with regard to clothing. This is often connected with the fact that the men have more contact with the outside world, which has always been the case in Chichicastenango. The clothing worn by Ladinas was available to the Maxeñas in the market, but they did not buy it.

Gruhn found the Maxeños economically quite well off. Several, in fact, were relatively rich. Indian farmers had taken to using chemical fertilizers since the 1930s and had gotten considerably improved yields. However, they continued to hold that only the traditional varieties of corn were suited to their lands. They continued to get most of their food from maize cultivation, but at least one family in each canton had acquired a small mechanical corn mill that served the people of the canton. All over Mesoamerica Indian women have been relieved of many hours of grinding at the *metate* by the coming of corn mills, commonly motor powered. Gruhn also noticed that the Indians had become willing to buy and sell milpa plots and did so, whereas this rarely occurred in the early 1930s.

By 1969 there had been a considerable increase in the number of Maxeños in commercial and business activity. Many were butchers or bakers, and a number of Indians owned taverns and stores, including a pharmacy. Gruhn was told that one of the Maxeños still living in a rural canton of Chichicastenango owned a restaurant in Guatemala City. Maxeños owned and operated at least one of the bus lines serving Chichicastenango, and a number of Indians had cargo trucks. In a number of instances Ladino wage laborers worked for Indian businessmen. A number of families in the rural cantons maintained small stores or taverns in their homes, and vendors sold soft drinks and food from stands along the major roadways. Gruhn and her husband, archaeologist Alan Bryan, were able to circulate among the cantons, something that the people would not allow Bunzel to do in the 1930s (Gruhn 1973:233, Bunzel 1952:xi).

One of the outstanding changes was the increased school attendance. There were several well-attended schools in the town, and most of the cantons had their own school. Most of the young people had become bilingual and knew how to read and write Spanish. The largest Indian school had 800 students and had a medical clinic adjoining it, supported in part by philanthropic groups in the United States.

There were fewer changes in the family, governmental, and religious aspects of life. Apparently, people of the same name still avoided marrying one another, families still lived on their lands most of the time instead of in town, and the relationships within and among extended and nuclear families were much as they were before. The political system operated much as it did before, though there were only two principales de pueblo instead of five, and public service for boys had been eliminated. Each canton had a military commissioner responsible to the Quiché departmental government, but the Ladino government still had no direct control over the rural cantons, especially since the political-military offices, held by local Indians, were responsible directly to the department government at Santa Cruz del Quiché. The campaign for the Guatemalan elections of 1970 was on during Gruhn's time in Chichicastenango, and she observed that all national political parties had functioning organizations both in the town and the cantons, and many of the Indians voted in the March elections.

In 1969 the organization Catholic Action, whose members were known as *catequistas* (catequists), was providing the greatest force for change. The main purpose of the organization was to convert the people from the paganism in Catholic trappings that dominated their religion to orthodox Roman Catholicism. Their approach was to discredit and actively attack traditional paganism. In 1957 a group of catechists went to one of the most important pagan shrines and broke the image, tore the stones from their places and threw them down the hillside, and set the woods on fire. The Indians responded by rebuilding the shrine. The priest at Chichicastengo at that time had come from Spain in 1960 and was very different from the former curate. In earlier times, including Bunzel's stay there, the priest was tolerant of traditional religious beliefs and practices, but the new priest supported the catequistas actively. He took strong measures to stop the practice of pagan rituals in and around the church, and a rumor that he was going to abolish the cofradías circulated. In response to this a multitude armed with clubs attacked the church one night, and the priest fled to Guatemala City. The Indians then sent a delegation of prominent citizens to the president of Guatemala to protest the priest's activities. The priest took steps to pacify the people, and, after several months, returned with police guards, who remained for some time. From then on he avoided attacking the traditional religion openly and directly. When Gruhn was there the old customs were being practiced as openly and vigorously as ever within and around the church. Catholic Action continued, however, concentrating on converting family heads. In 1969 the population of the municipio of Chichicastenango had increased from the 25,000 of Bunzel's time to 40,000, and probably about 4,000 of those had become catechists.

The diviners were still active in 1969, a number of them being relatively young. The cofradías were as much in evidence as ever, though some of the less important groups appeared to be having difficulty finding people to serve as mayordomos.

Chichicastenango lies just two hours by paved road from Guatemala City and has been a place of major interest for tourists for many years. They have always been attracted by the colorful markets, the throngs of Indians in town for a fiesta or market, and all the ritual activity going on in plain view in and around the church. In 1969 almost every travel agency of importance in Guatemala City included Chichicastenango in its tours, private cars with English-speaking Ladino guides arrived regularly, and there was a luxury hotel in town should people wish to stay over. On a given market day there would be 50 or more tourists present.

Many anthropologists have been concerned about the possibly deleterious effects of tourism on traditional societies. Often, the people themselves gain little or nothing from the presence of tourists, and in Chichicastenango the hotel owner and the Ladino guides apparently were the only ones profiting from their visits. In many places around the world the tourists are a nuisance, but worse than that, the impressions of the local cultures they take away with them are erroneous and may contribute to cross-cultural misunderstanding. Gruhn noted that most of the tourists visiting Chichicastenango were ignorant nuisances. They took pictures everywhere with little concern for the feelings and interests of the Maxeños, including within the church itself. Their comments about what they were seeing revealed a profound misunderstanding of it and a high degree of prejudice against Indian ways. The guides themselves imparted a great deal of misinformation and thereby reinforced the tourists' prejudices. The Indians ignored the tourists and went about their business, but the Quiché word for tourists, "cannibals," reflects how they feel about them. If anything, Gruhn felt, the Indian reaction to tourism has strengthened Maxeño commitment to their traditional ways. But she also noted that this is certainly not the only explanation for the strong conservatism in Chichicastenango.

All in all, the Maxeños were continuing to manifest a strong pride in their indigenous culture as late as 1969, and fragmentary, informal reports indicate the continuation of this pride and conservative orientation through the 1980s.

Chapter 17

THE AGUACATEC MAYA OF GUATEMALA

Many modern North Americans have heard of the Maya, and some realize that Guatemala is Maya country. A few may have heard of the Quiché, since they are one of the largest Mayan groups, but the Aguacatec (approx. ah-wah-kah-TEHK; Aguateca in Spanish) occupied only a small area and in 1972-1973 numbered only about 10,000 (Brintnall 1979:62). Anthropologists consider the Aguacatec one of the Mamean-speaking peoples of northwestern Guatemala. who, including the Mam proper, the Aguacatec, and the Ixil, may number around 300,000. Anthropologists conventionally intend only the Mam proper when they refer to the Mam. The *municipio*, or township, of Aguacatán lies in the Guatemalan Departamento of Huehuetenango, which occupies a nearly 3,000 square mile northwestern corner of that part of Guatemala that juts westward south of part of the Mexican state of Chiapas.

The Aguacatec were residents of the municipio of Aguacatán, which also included some Quiché, Mam, and Ladinos. During the 1970s there were a number of Aguacatec who still lived by the traditional customs, but a sizable percentage of the others had rejected them in favor of a way of life characterized by schooling and literacy, participation in organizations, cash-crop agriculture, pride and confidence in their abilities to cope with the larger world, and either standard Roman Catholicism or evangelical Protestantism.

Many of the people lived in rectangular adobe brick houses with clay tiled, double-pitched roofs. The front wall of the house was usually inset to provide a covered porch, with posts supporting the front edge of the roof. A woman usually wore a blue wrap-around skirt held in place by a long sash, a decorated blouse, a shawl, and a head band in which she wrapped her hair and formed it into a tiara-like arrangement. A man wore white cotton trousers held in place by a sash, a white shirt, a blue jacket, a felt or straw hat, and sandals. The people planted corn and other crops by slash-and-burn agriculture or plow culture without irrigation or produced garlic cash crops on irrigated land. Many of those who produced garlic were wealthy or at least fairly well-off economically. Corn dishes such as tortillas and *atole* (a sweetened corn drink) were important elements of the diet. The people also kept livestock. Though the women wove some of their own garments on the *backstrap loom*, crafts were unimportant among the Aguacatec.

The three generation *extended family* of parents and married sons and their families was important. There were also many independent nuclear families, some of them formed when the patriarchal family head gave a portion of his land inheritance to a married son and set him up in a separate home. Other independent nuclear family households were those of men who had rejected dependence on periodically doled-out land from the father and had managed to get into garlic production. There were no unilineal common ancestor groups such as clans or lineages in Aguacatán, and available sources describe no ritual kinship system. There were a number of schools in Aguacatán, both in the town and in the rural hamlets. Agricultural cooperatives, political parties, and Peasant Leagues were important organizations with active memberships. Both Ladinos and Indians held political office in Aguacatán, the alcalde being the top official. There were also councilmen, treasurers, a police chief and others.

There were three religious groups in Aguacatán, the Christo-pagans, the Roman Catholics, and the evangelical Protestants. The Christo-pagans were formerly the only group, the main religious belief being that the ancestors were concerned with how the living behaved, wanted to be consulted about important matters, and would punish people who misbehaved or ignored them. The people also believed in many nature deities and the saints. They observed an extensive complex of rituals and fiestas prescribed by the ancestors. The Roman Catholic group resulted from the work of Maryknoll missionaries and the Protestant Church from the efforts of linguistic missionaries associated with the Summer Institute of Linguistics. Neither group participated in the Christo-pagan fiestas.

Prehistory

Hunters of big game seem to have ranged through Guatemala during Paleo-Indian times. Elephants, mastodons, and horses were there, and near the city of Huehuetenango, about fifteen miles west of Aguacatán, someone living around 11,000 years ago used crude stone tools to butcher horses and mastodons (Weaver 1981:32). From then on the people of the northwest highlands must have participated in the cultural developments typical of the area, though archaeological research is too sketchy to provide anything like a complete picture. Archaic cultures, which emphasized collection of wild plant foods, undoubtedly succeeded Paleo-Indian lifeways in the highlands as they did elsewhere in Mesoamerica. Sometime during the Archaic, pottery and plant cultivation appeared, though gardening provided only a small fraction of the total food supply. This is not to say that ceramics and domesticated plants originated in the northwestern highlands, since they could have been invented elsewhere and spread by diffusion. Wherever they began, the evidence for them is earlier elsewhere than here.

As cultivated plants came to dominate collection of wild forms and the cultures of Mesoamerica became more complex, the people entered a phase archaeologists commonly call Preclassic. Beginning around 2500 B.C. (4,500 years ago) the basic patterns developed that led to the great Classic civilizations that emerged after the time of Christ. Archaeological evidence is too sparse to provide more than rare glimpses of these times in northwestern Guatemala. One such glimpse comes with the suggestion of diffusion of certain pottery techniques during Middle Preclassic times from southern Chiapas in Mexico eastward and, eventually, through the northwestern highlands of Guatemala. The evidence comes from the headwaters region of the Río Negro, which lies a bit to the east of Huehuetenango and, accordingly, close to Aguacatán. There archaeologists have found a good deal of orange pottery identical to that in probable centers of origin to the west (Lowe 1978:372).

By the late Preclassic highland peoples around what is now Guatemala City developed impressive temple pyramids, artistically crafted pottery, intricately carved and monumental stone objects, and a number of other items indicating complex cultural development. These were found at the famous Mayan site of Kaminaljuyú, where evidence indicates a highly stratified society with wealth, power, and prestige in the hands of an exclusive elite (Weaver 1981:138). Kaminaljuyú lies around 65 miles southeast of Aguacatán.

The Valley of Guatemala continued to be important during Classic times, reaching an especially complex level of development four to five-hundred years after Christ. One of the most interesting developments is the presence of large numbers of people from the great Valley of Mexico city of Teotihuacán, who apparently did not rule the Guatemalan kingdoms but exercised major commercial and architectural influences. By Postclassic times, beginning around A.D 1000, the situation had changed in the Valley, and the people were living in well-defended communities on hilltops. By 1400 the Quiché had conquered much of the Guatemalan highlands, making their capital at Utatlán, but the Cakchiquel and other groups revolted successfully within a

hundred years (Weaver 1981:477). Zaculeu, situated at Huehuetenango, was a Mam city-state during Postclassic times. Aguacatán was known as Chalchitán in pre-Columbian Postclassic times. There are many unexcavated mounds just to the northwest of town and within a mile or two to the east (H. and L. McArthur 1966:140).

History

After Cortés vanquished the Mexica, he dispatched Spanish forces in various directions to subdue other parts of New Spain. The ruthless Pedro de Alvarado explored and conquered Guatemala with the assistance of Mexican (Aztec) and Tlaxcalan warriors. He moved into the highlands of the Mexican state of Chiapas and western Guatemala in 1524, where he was obliged to overcome strong resistance in spite of the cholera and smallpox epidemics which had already ravaged the region. With the destruction of the Quiché capital of Utatlán and the subjugation of the Cakchiquel, the sequence of post-Conquest cultural development characteristic of Mesoamerica got underway in this part of Central America.

In 1940 anthropologist Oliver LaFarge published his description of the cultural sequence that followed the conquest of the Maya, a scheme that has been accepted as valid for Mesoamerica in general. He based his contribution on the evidence from the western highlands of Guatemala, where he had conducted field studies in the Jacaltec community of Jacaltenango, around 30 miles northwest of Aguacatán, and in Santa Eulalia, a Kanhobal community nearly 30 miles north of Aguacatán. La Farge suggested that during the Conquest, from 1524 until around 1600, the Indian cultures were shattered by the violence of Spanish oppression. Under the *encomienda* system the Spanish government granted certain territories and the Indians that lived there to conquerors and other prominent persons. The *encomenderos*, as the grantees were known, were to have the right to the Indians' labor and tribute in return for teaching them Christianity and looking after their welfare. The encomienda was actually used to enslave and cruelly exploit the people, and agony and resentment ran deep. The *repartimiento* gave village and higher governments of New Spain the right to the labor of both Spanish and Indian citizens on various public works projects, and it, too, was used to exploit the Indians. In many places the Indians fought back, but to no avail.

During the Colonial Period, from about 1600 until around 1720, the destruction of Mayan elements and introduction of Spanish and Christian institutions continued. Spanish control was vigorously maintained during this time and change was great, but Indians who had experienced pre-Conquest life were gone. There was no chance of returning to the old order even if revolt had proven successful. Resentment and hostility remained strong and trouble broke out occasionally in places, but the Indians for the most part had been crushed. Only a few had adjusted to and

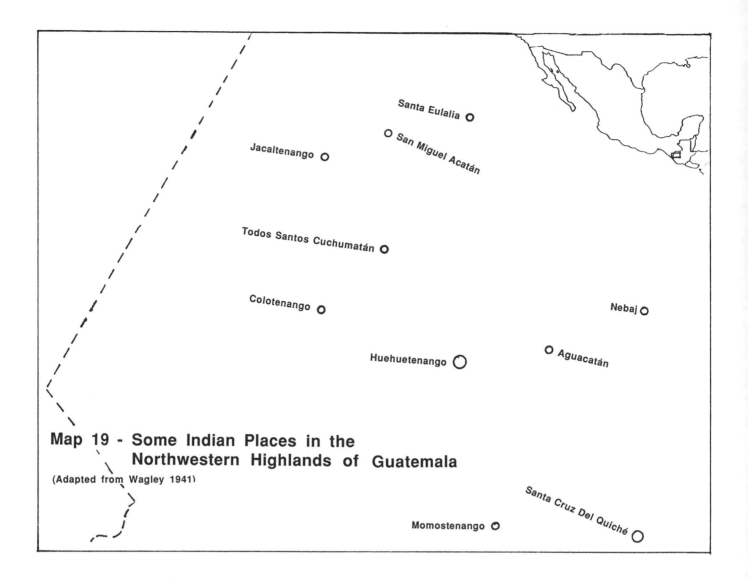

Map 19 - Some Indian Places in the Northwestern Highlands of Guatemala

(Adapted from Wagley 1941)

Santa Eulalia ○

San Miguel Acatán ○

Jacaltenango ○

Todos Santos Cuchumatán ○

Colotenango ○

Nebaj ○

Aguacatán ○

Huehuetenango ○

Santa Cruz Del Quiché ○

Momostenango ○

embraced the new order. It was a time when much was mangled or lost and much added to Indian lifeways. The result was artificial because it was largely forced, basically resented, and largely unintegrated. Much of the old culture was practiced clandestinely.

The First Transition, from approximately 1720-1800, was a period of gradual relaxation of Spanish control. As La Farge has indicated, new exploitation necessitated increasingly stronger efforts for declining yield, and Spanish administration in New Spain was internally weakened. Troops to support priests and outlying Spanish settlements were reduced, and both the encomienda and repartimiento systems were gone. The Indians enjoyed a greater measure of freedom to live as they wanted, and they kept Spanish ways they liked, adapted them to their needs, returned to some of the pre-Spanish culture, and gradually developed new and distinctive patterns.

During the Recent Indian I, the Indians lived by relatively well integrated life patterns with which they had become comfortable. A new and distinctive culture type had emerged in Middle America, a syncretism of Spanish and pre-Columbian ways, and Indian life was relatively stable. This state continued from roughly 1800 to 1880.

After that the machine age Spanish-American cultures began to disrupt the newly stabilized patterns. The process was much less destructive than the Conquest, and Indian cultures were changed much more in some places than others. This is what LaFarge calls Recent Indian II, which continues to the present.

Perhaps the greatest and most destructive influence for change during the early decades of Recent Indian II in Guatemala was the development of the coffee export industry and the enactment of various official and unofficial ways of forcing large numbers of Maya to work on the coffee plantations. The Guatemalan Ladinos (culturally non-Indian people of Spanish Indian descent) dominated the Aguacatec and other Maya until things began again to change in the Indians' favor after 1944, the year dictator Jorge Ubico was overthrown. The Indians suffered heavily under this domination, and those who tried to avoid plantation work were jailed, whipped, subjected to hard labor, and made to go to the plantations, too (Brintnall 1979:103). During his time in Aguacatán in the 1970s Brintnall found that stories of their mistreatment and misery under the traditional regime remained plentiful among the Aguacatec. The accounts emphasized themes such as separation from loved ones, sleeping without shelter in the open, and beatings.

This order collapsed in Aguacatán after 1944. The stranglehold of the Ladinos was broken, a road to Aguacatán was put in, the traditional political and ritual systems were largely abandoned, and the Indians entered into new kinds of political and organizational activities. This set the stage for Mayan participation in national efforts to break the oppression of the Ladino elite in Guatemala and the violence that was continuing to plague Guatemala during the 1980s.

Ethnography

The Aguacatec culture before Brintnall studied there during the 1970s can be known mostly through its apparent similarities to other western highland communities studied by anthropologists during the 1930s and 1940s. Linguistic missionaries Harry and Lucille McArthur of the Summer Institute of Linguistics/Wycliffe Bible Translators took up residence in Aguacatán in 1952 and have translated the New Testament into Aguacatec as well as making several ethnographic contributions (H. and L. McArthur 1965, 1969; H.McArthur 1972, 1973). Douglas Brintnall's field study in 1972 and 1973 and in 1975 was the first major field investigation of Aguacatec culture by a professional anthropologist (Brintnall 1979). Anthropologist Mary E. Odell resided in Aguacatán for several periods from 1972-1976, giving special attention to the family, systems of production, and demographic change (Odell 1978, 1982, 1984). This chapter draws heavily on Brintnall's ethnography and, secondarily, on the work of Odell and the McArthurs.

Aguacatec Country

The main geographical feature of the department of Huehuetenango is the rugged Cuchumatán Mountains, a large L-shaped portion of which lies 8800 some feet above sea level. Nearly all of the rivers of Huehuetenango begin in the Cuchumatán Mountains, some of them flowing westward into Mexico where their waters converge in the Grijalva River and flow into the Gulf of Mexico. The others run eastward into the Ixcán River, which turns northward and joins other rivers to form the Usumacinta, which flows northwestward along part of the border between Guatemala and Mexico and eventually joins the Grijalva 15 or 20 miles before it debouches into the Gulf of Mexico.

The base of the L-shaped Cuchumatán range runs east and west, and a parallel east-west range of volcanic mountains lies to the south, the two bars of mountains enclosing a highland territory with its lower elevations around 3300 feet above sea level. Much of the municipio of Aguacatán lies in this area, but it extends into the high Cuchumatán country. The town of Aguacatán lies in a valley along the Buca River in the lower elevations of the municipio. Some of the municipio's outlying hamlets are in the lower regions while others lie in the mountains. The northern part of the municipio is a high, cool, wet, rainy area of mountain tops, high plains, and pine forests. At a somewhat lower level scrub trees rather than pines are found, the country is hot and rocky, and few houses or fields are to be found. The valley, by contrast, is a lush, irrigated area of well tended fields.

The town of Aguacatán is laid out in a grid pattern, but it is crowded between the hills to the north and the Buca River to the south, resulting in a long main street with many side streets at right angles to it and only a few parallel streets. To the south, across the river, is a pine-covered, partly mountainous, mostly unirrigated, arid section (Brintnall 1979:59).

The Language

Aguacatec was not the only language of the municipio of Aguacatán. The people of the northern high mountains were Quiché who had migrated from other municipios, some of them being relatively recent immigrants and others having arrived over a century earlier. Though both Quiché and Aguacatec belong to the Macro-mayan linguistic stock, they are mutually unintelligible. Ladinos, who spoke Spanish only, lived in the town itself, and many of the Indians were unable to carry on ordinary conversations in Spanish. About one percent of the people of the municipio spoke Mam, which is not mutually intelligible with either Aguacatec or Quiché. Finally, the Aguacatec who lived east of the town plaza spoke a slightly different dialect from those that lived to the west.

According the MacArthurs' analysis of Aguacatec, the language consisted of 33 *phonemes* (Brintnall 1979:xix). There are more sounds (*phones*), than phonemes in a language, which derives from the fact that some phonemes are comprised of two or more alternative sounds. Aguacatec-speakers, for example, could pronounce *l* either with voice or without, and it made no difference in meaning. But they had two kinds of *k* sounds that belonged to separate phonemes because the difference between them made a difference in meaning. A word including a *k* accompanied by lung air meant one thing while an otherwise identical word using a *k* accompanied by pharyngeal air would mean something else. English-speakers, by contrast, do not distinguish among different kinds of *k* sounds. Languages differ from one another in the sounds they use and what sound differences they use to alter meanings.

They also differ grammatically, that is in what units having specific meanings they use and how they arrange them in relation to one another to form messages. Syntax or sentence construction is one major aspect of grammatical variation between languages. A free translation of one Aguacatec sentence is, "When a baby dies he is not buried like an adult." But if Aguacatec sentence structure was adhered to it would read, "When dies a baby, no like is-done to-him as is buried an old-one his-stomach." (H. and L. McArthur 1966:165.)

Personality and Behavior

The Aguacatec Indians of the 1970s shared the widespread Mesoamerican feeling of mistrust toward those outside their own family, community, and tribe. Whatever there might have been of this in pre-Columbian times, much of it undoubtedly developed out of mistreatment by Europeans and Guatemalan nationals. Brintnall suggests that the Ladino domination of the Aguacatec during the twentieth century had great psychological and behavioral impact. Outwardly, the Indians were very submissive toward the Ladinos, and they lived in fear of them. They were afraid of being ridiculed, failing to understand commands given in Spanish, or being whipped or beaten (Brintnall 1979:103). It is hardly surprising that the people distrusted not only outsiders but fellow Indians who might have been pressured by Ladinos to betray them. Brintnall hired an intelligent, well educated Aguacatec Catholic to teach him the language, but he found him deeply suspicious at first. It took months of association before the man became sufficiently open with Brintnall that he could discuss the culture with him freely. Brintnall's ability to speak and understand Aguacatec, his treatment of individual Indians either as his equals or his superiors, and his uncritical participation in certain aspects of the lifeway contributed significantly toward overcoming some of the peoples' mistrust.

Though no systematic study of Aguacatec psychology is at hand, it is enlightening to look at their personalities in terms of how they differed from the stereotypes held by Spanish-speaking and other outsiders. Brintnall heard such stereotypical views from small town Guatemalans, wealthy Guatemalans of the national elite, a U.S. businessman, and "hippie" tourists (Brintnall 1979:xxii). Contrary to the stereotypes, he found, the Indians were industrious, intelligent, open and cooperative with those they came to trust, definitely interested in improving their living conditions, and frequently willing to experiment with alternatives that would free them from subjugation and poverty.

Clothing and Personal Appearance

In much of Mesoamerica people can identify an Indian's home village by his or her clothing, and in some places clothing is rather colorful and, to outsiders, picturesque. This seems especially so in much of Mayan Guatemala, where weaving has long been highly developed and clothing often intricately designed and brightly colored. The traditional Aguacatec women's costume, still in use by a number during the 1970s, consisted of a blue cotton skirt, a white blouse decorated with ribbons and embroidery, three inch wide headbands, sandals, and a shawl, or *rebozo*. Others wore multicolored skirts and blouses with ribbons braided into their hair, and a few wore factory-made dresses. The women wove the heavy blue skirts of cotton on their backstrap looms. They wrapped the skirt high around the waist in such a way that there was one thickness of cloth in front

and three in back, with the excess falling in a fold at the right front (H. and L. McArthur 1966:141). The skirt, which extended almost to the ankles, was held in place by a woolen sash around two-and-a-half inches wide and long enough to pass around the waist three or four times. The colors were natural whites, browns, and blacks. The short blouse was similar to an inverted sack with an opening cut for the head and slits in the sides for the arms (Brintnall 1979:68). It hung loose rather than being tucked in and was decorated with horizonal bands of ribbon and rows of embroidered animal figures. Ladina seamstresses made most of the blouses and sold them to the Indian women. The Indian women usually made their own headbands, which were approximately three inches wide and six feet long. They wove them mainly in red designs representative of birds and animals, though younger women often used more blues and greens and geometric designs. They wrapped their long black hair in the headbands in such a way as to bring all of it to the top of the head in a turban-like arrangement. They also wove many of their shawls, which usually had widths of black, yellow, green, and white on a red background. Many of the women put on sandals made of automobile tire treads for going to market or traversing the trails.

Women's costumes differed both among towns and villagers and between Eastern and Western Aguacatec. The Eastern women, for example, used silk threads of various colors to embroider the necklines of their blouses, while the Western women limited themselves to red thread. For the headbands the Eastern women wove designs of many colors into a red background, while the Western women made red head bands with a narrow white stripe along each edge (H. and L. McArthur 1966:141). The Quiché women wore blouses that were easily distinguished from those of the Aguacatec, and other elements of their costume differed as well.

By the 1970s the Aguacatec men were using manufactured clothing similar to that of the Ladinos. They wore cotton shirts that buttoned in front. trousers with leather belts, jackets, either straw or felt hats, and, usually sandals. The Indian men often wore jackets and pants of a characteristic dark blue, and the shirts were white. In earlier times the men wore a red loincloth instead of pants, and a few of them still wore the cloth around the top of their trousers instead of a belt (Brintnall 1979:71).

Houses and Other Structures

The Aguacatec built their houses near the fields. Sometimes, mostly in irrigated valley land, two or three families placed their houses near one another. In other places houses were usually several minutes walk from one another. Typically the Aguacatec lived in rectangular, windowless dwellings of adobe brick with double pitched roofs covered with red tiles. The front wall was usually set back and the edge of the roof supported by posts, thereby forming a porch running the length of the structure. The women did much of their work there and harvested crops were stored there temporarily. The people had their cooking fires inside the house, however, allowing the smoke to escape between the tiles. Some of them whitewashed the adobe, especially the wealthier Indians. The wealthy also tended to build larger houses and put in concrete floors.

The Aguacatec used very little furniture. They made most of their beds of several wooden planks raised about a foot above ground level, with a palm mat (*petate*) for a mattress. The entire nuclear family slept on the same bed, covered by a couple of woolen blankets and, in some instances, by sheepskins. If there was too little room for everyone, some slept on a mat on the floor. Families kept their clothing in a large wooden chest hung on the wall with strong nails (Brintnall 1979:75).

Nearly every house had a small sweat bath hut nearby, where people bathed one to three times weekly. They made steam by throwing water on very hot stones on the hut floor. A bather crawled through the tiny door, dropped a curtain over it, and remained as long as desired. Someone usually remained nearby and called to the bather occasionally to be sure he or she had not fainted.

The people sometimes made chicken pens from cornstalks and sticks and corrals for holding sheep, goats, or cattle.

Livelihood

The people of Aguacatán raised more corn and beans for food than anything else, though squash was grown most everywhere, and various other items were produced in house gardens. On the steepest slopes the farmers used their digging sticks to loosen the soil and make holes in which they dropped the kernels, and where it was not too steep they made furrows by means of ox-drawn, Spanish-colonial plows. A planter deposited several kernels together at intervals in the furrows and raked dirt over them with the foot. The Aguacatec grew some of their corn on dry land, depending only on rainfall for moisture, but they irrigated many of the fields near town north of the Buca River. Owning land which could be irrigated was a distinct advantage, since the farmers could produce two or three crops a year rather than letting the fields lie fallow part of the time. They could also save their crops in times of drought (Brintnall 1979:107). Beans require even more water than corn, so more beans were produced on irrigated lands than on dry lands.

The people also grew a variety of minor food crops such as lettuce, tomatoes, onions, carrots, beets, tomatoes, and chili peppers in their gardens. At appropriate elevations they kept fruit trees in their yards, raising oranges, limes, mangos, avocados, bananas, peaches, plums, apples, and other tree products. They used sheep and goat manure and vegetable garbage as organic fertilizers, thereby doubling their yields over what they would be otherwise. Those who could afford to used chemical fertilizers. They ate some of the vegetables and fruits and sold the rest at markets in neighboring towns. In spite of irrigation most families failed to meet their food needs on their own lands and purchased corn brought in from other areas. In some cases the people had to purchase corn because their land was too poor and/or they owned too little, but even those with larger tracts of irrigated land might have to purchase corn because they devoted their fields to the production of garlic, an especially valuable cash crop.

Though irrigation made larger yields of corn and beans possible, the main reason for the large number of irrigated fields was to earn money through garlic production. Only a few people had grown garlic early in the twentieth century, possibly learning about it from a local Ladino, so the relatively large scale irrigated garlic production was a later development. Irrigation on a large scale required considerable labor and a good deal of cooperation among many people, so there had to be an especially good reason for going to the necessary organizational and physical effort. The Indians had to tap streams at points several miles from some of the fields and found it necessary to build and maintain long, shallow ditches, sometimes in solid rock (Brintnall 1979:112). During the early decades of the twentieth century most of the irrigated lands near the town were owned by Ladinos, and the Indians were forced to spend too much time working on the coffee plantations to undertake the tasks of bringing water to the many more lands that were irrigable. By 1973, however, around half of the Western Aguacatec owned irrigated fields, a third of the Eastern group had some, and the irrigated area was still being enlarged while Brintnall was there during the 1970s.

Garlic was raised for money, some of which was used for purchasing corn, the main Indian food. The Aguacatec used corn mainly in the form of tortillas, which they made the basic part of every meal. They also prepared atole, the thick drink made by mixing corn dough with water and adding a sweetener. As in other Mesoamerican groups, they made tamales for special occasions. For cooking they placed their round tortilla griddles of clay or metal and their pots on the typically Mesoamerican three stone ground hearth, making the fire among the stones. The people normally ate with their fingers, skillfully using the tortilla to retrieve food and convey it to the mouth. Some families used spoons and enamel cups and bowls (H. and L. McArthur 1966:142).

We have to consider latter nineteenth century developments to understand how irrigated garlic production became so important to the Aguacatec. International commercial developments and the concern of the Central American countries to progress economically combined to bring about a change from hacienda to plantation agriculture (Helms 1975:244). The far more productive plantation system of henequen, coffee, or banana production promised to bring great profits from selling export crops to markets usually found in industrializing countries that imported raw materials and foodstuffs for their own economic purposes. The plantations required capital investment, which was often provided by foreign corporations. Foreign businessmen also financed the building of roads and rail facilities for efficient product transportation.

The plantation owners needed both land and labor, but the large numbers of highland Maya preferred to continue to work their *milpas* (corn fields). To undermine the Indians' agricultural self-sufficiency the nation abolished communal land ownership, and many Indians lost their lands to plantation estate developers. The Guatemalans also legalized several forms of debt peonage, and laborers were encouraged to assume debts for foods and other items they purchased. This kept them bound permanently to the estates. Aguacatán, of course, though located in the highlands, was one of the communities from which the coastal plantations to the south drew their laborers. The Guatemalans also used the *mandamiento*, though the people of Aguacatán do not remember it. They simply conscripted labor in the Indian communities, paying local Ladinos to round up the Indians. The Ladinos often enticed the Indians with liquor, money, or other things they desired, getting them in debt, after which they would force them to work on the plantations to pay off obligations actually too great to repay before they had to assume new debts. When a man died, his children inherited his debts, and the process continued. Ladino labor contractors employed *caporales*, who were often bilingual Indians, to hunt down any who attempted to hide (Brintnall 1979:109). At the plantations the workers lived under miserable conditions for weeks or months at a time, not only men, but women, children, and barnyard animals. There were times when the countryside around Aguacatán was almost empty. It was out of this kind of situation that a sequence of events was set in motion that led to what has been happening in Aguacatán since the middle of the century.

Brintnall identifies population growth, new national labor laws, the building of a road to Aguacatán, and improvement in agricultural technology as major factors changing the economic situation of the Aguacatec (Brintnall 1979:110). Population increased slowly during the nineteenth century, but it increased rapidly all over the country during the twentieth. Before 1945 this seems not to have been from medical advances, and Brintnall suggested that, with so many people working off debts on the plantations, the Indians may have felt a need for larger families to have enough children to care for the home fields. He also points to the availability of food on the plantations, which reduced starvation in times of crop failure. If these notions are correct, the Ladino elite's oppression of the Indians created the very conditions that led to the relaxation of that oppression. Whatever the reasons, the population increased until there were too many people for the land and many of them sought relief through plantation employment. With the necessity for coercing the Indians to work removed, the Guatemalans rescinded the oppressive labor laws, and forced labor was ended by 1944. More of the Aguacatec began to turn to irrigation and growing onions and garlic to get the most from their land. Garlic prevailed because it brought more money. Cash cropping became even more feasible in 1943 when the all weather road to Aguacatán was completed, making marketing easier and reducing the cost. The com-

ing of chemical fertilizers during the 1950s was still another contributor to greater production (Odell 1984:11).

Brintnall identifies two major economic effects of garlic cash cropping. One is the wealth it brought to the owners of irrigated land. Though growing garlic requires intensive labor, the profits are great. One of Brintnall's studies showed a return of over 200 per cent in only four months (Brintnall 1979:113). The second is the greatly increased availability of work for the poor and landless, since garlic requires so much more labor than corn and other crops in soil preparation, planting, irrigating, and post-harvest processing (Brintnall 1979:114. Brintnall noted that each morning during the garlic production season the paths into the garlic zone were crowded with day-laborers from the poorer, rainfall dependent sections of the municipio. Though hundreds of Aguacatec continued to work in the coffee harvests, the people were no longer so dependent on the plantations and the poor could work for the newly wealthy Indians rather than for Ladinos and plantation owners.

Livestock production was also important to the Aguacatec. They raised chickens, turkeys, pigs, cattle, sheep, goats, horses, donkeys, and mules, which provided them with meat, draft power, transportation, and organic fertilizer. They also realized cash gains, since the value of animals increases as they grow (Brintnall 1979:107).

Aguacatec women of the 1970s collected some of the firewood, maintained the fire, and prepared the meals. They had to get up at four or five o'clock each morning to get the fire going and prepare food, and husbands sometimes remained in bed for a time. The women could take their corn, which they had soaked overnight in lime-water, to be ground at one of the several small corn mills, but many of them still spent several hours a day grinding the corn with the stone *metate* and *mano* (grinding base and cylindrical hand stone). They also cared for their children, washed the family clothing, took care of the fowl and other animals, bought and sold in the market, and helped with the agricultural work. They washed clothes in springs, rivers, or irrigation ditches—soaping them, beating them on rocks, rinsing them, and laying them out on grass or draping them over bushes or tree branches to dry. Travelers in Mesoamerica witness similar clothes-washing scenes repeatedly.

The women also fed garbage to the pigs, and they and the children took the sheep and goats to pasture each day. On market days most of the buyers and sellers were women, who sat in rows with eggs, fruits, vegetables, and other small items for sale. They might work in the fields to help clear rocks, work the ground with the hoe, plant, water, weed, and harvest, but usually only when extra help was needed.

The men did most of the agricultural work; cared for the cattle, horses, and other large animals; helped collect firewood; and sold potatoes, corn, beans, and animals on market days. More men than women worked for wages.

Aguacatec land was generally owned by men and inherited patrilineally (by sons). They doled out the land to their sons in installments, the first typically being either when a young man married or soon thereafter (Brintnall 1979:83). A father was expected to divide his lands equally among his sons, and they tended to become hostile toward one another over the question of land inheritance. When the first son married and received land, for example, the younger sons were often envious. The pressure increased as more sons married and began to put pressure on their father for additional land. A father strongly dominated his sons, however, since he could delay providing them with land if they did not submit to his authority. This applied mainly to families of average land ownership. The sons of land-poor men had to work on the coastal plantations, work for richer families, get an inheritance by marrying a woman from a family with no sons, or rent some land for cash cropping and hope to get ahead. Those who were successful with the last option managed to escape both poverty and the father's domination. In wealthy families sons might inherit enough land early in life to become relatively free of paternal authority, and they, too, might have the resources to farm by irrigation and multiply their wealth. Those who owned or managed to obtain access to irrigable land, of course, had a major advantage. There were both very wealthy and very poor Aguacatec, depending on whether or not they had irrigable land and the cash crop wealth that resulted. There was a class of wealthy men relatively free of patriarchal authority and Ladino domination and a class of men as poor and as dependent on their fathers or plantation owners as ever.

The Ladinos were also an important part of the town's economic life, concentrated as they were in either the town itself or adjoining hamlets. The rural Ladinos differed little from the Indians, but those in town specialized in making something for sale. Brintnall listed 35 economic specialties, including basketmaking, storekeeping, carpentry, marimba playing, sewing, and baking (Brintnall 1979:102). Many of the occupations served the needs of both Indians and Ladinos, while others served mainly wealthy Ladinos.

Social Organization and Relationships

Approximately two-thirds of the Aguacatec families were independent nuclear units—husband and wife and two or three children. Most of the other households were composed of extended families, usually an older couple, one or more married sons with their wives and children, and unmarried children, if any. In a few cases the extended family consisted of the older parents and a married daughter with her husband and children. Many anthropologists denote such three or more generation units when they refer to extended families.

Extended families are one kind of *composite family*, made up of two or more nuclear families. *Patrilocal* extended families, the most common type among the Aguacatec, result from patrilocal residence, which is the residence of a man and his wife and children with his parents. If only one married son resides with his parents the extended family is composed of two nuclear families linked by the membership in his father's nuclear family and his own. Of course, if there are other married sons in the household, it consists of more than two nuclear families. During the 1970s there were also a very few *joint families* in Aguacatán, which consist not of three generations but two or more nuclear families of the same generation functioning as a single unit. In Aguacatán joint families developed when brothers or sisters with their spouses and children resided together. A few households were occupied by a nuclear family plus a widowed or divorced parent, and others consisted of widows or divorcees living by themselves or with their unmarried children.

The patrilocal extended families of the Aguacatec commonly developed when sons married and brought their wives to live with their parents. As mentioned before, tensions usually developed among the sons over whether the father was favoring or would favor one or another as he doled out his land to them in stages. Brintnall noted that the fathers were not free of either conscious or unconscious favoritism, and the sons and their wives were very sensitive to the slightest suggestion of it (Brintnall 1979:83). The sons were under a father's heavy authority, and many of the young wives felt exploited by their parents-in law. The women bore their children and worked under the mother-in-law's supervision, and they felt the burden of it. As time went on and tensions increased, sons pressured their fathers for more land and separate houses. When a son finally moved away from his parents and siblings he thereby established an independent nuclear household, the most common type in Aguacatán. The father was usually reluctant to let a son go and might withhold some of the inheritance. Some chose to hold the final installment from a son until death.

The extended family was clearly a stage in the family cycle. Nearly all Aguacatec lived in extended families during their early marriage, independent nuclear households during their middle years, and extended families again when their own children married and took up residence with them.

Some Aguacatec fathers dominated their sons during most of their lives, the inheritance of land by installments giving them the necessary leverage. Anthropologists customarily emphasize the *systemic* nature of cultures, which means that the various elements making up a group's lifeway are interdependent; they are functions of one another. Age consciousness and respect for elders were strong values in Aguacatán, and they were clearly interdependent with the custom of land inheritance by installments. Other specific customs were involved in this network of interconnected beliefs and practices. Male friends only a year or two apart might address one another by terms reflecting the age difference. The younger would use the formal address form, while the older employed the informal term. This could be dropped only if the friendship lasted several years. Also, when using kinship terms a man could not refer to his brother without specifying whether it was an older or younger brother. Moreover, there was a special term by which parents referred to their youngest son, which may have reflected the circumstance that youngest sons often remained in the family and cared for their aged parents.

There were also a number of couples not so heavily dominated by the husband's parents. More than before there were men who had become relatively independent of the father's dominance through garlic cash-cropping. By irrigating their land and growing a crop with such a high monetary return they freed themselves from having to depend on additional installments of inherited land. If they inherited land they could irrigate, they could declare a measure of economic and social independence early in their economic careers rather than having to wait to inherit more land.

Still others got by without receiving even an initial inheritance. The son of one of the most important Western Elders defied his influential father to turn to Catholicism. He was the first important Westerner to convert, and his father punished him by ejecting him from the family and leaving him with only a tiny parcel of land. The intelligent young man was already experienced in garlic marketing and had speculated some in commodity futures, so he knew how to speculate on garlic price fluctuations. He made enough money to rent some irrigated land and made a profit his first year. Each year he rented more land and made more money, succeeding economically without his father's backing (Brintnall 1979:135). He also convinced his brothers to refuse land from their father, who was left without sons to inherit from him. By the 1970s the increasing irrigation cash-cropping had seriously undermined the patriarchal extended family, and the process was continuing.

Aguacatec males referred to their close kin by what anthropologists call *Eskimo* and *lineal* terms. Eskimo terms are a type some societies, including modern North America, use to designate their siblings (brothers and sisters) and cousins. In both Aguacatec and modern American society a man referred to his brothers and sisters by one set of terms and lumped his cousins under another term or set of terms. Some other societies use terms that separate different kinds of cousins from one another or lump brothers and sisters under the same terms of reference as some or all of the cousins. Though the Aguacatec and modern North Americans used Eskimo terms, there was a difference between the two systems. An Aguacatec male referred to an older brother by one term (*wutzicy'*) and his younger brother by another (*witz'in*), which reflected the stress on age differentiation mentioned previously. He did not distinguish between his older sister and younger sister, however.

At the parental level the Aguacatec used lineal terminology, which keeps parents separate from all aunts and uncles and lumps the latter under the same set of terms for both sides of the family. This is like the modern North American system except that the Aguacatec speaker did not differentiate aunts and uncles from one another and referred to them as older brothers (Brintnall 1979:86).

By the 1970s a substantial portion of the Aguacatec population was Protestant, and a number had left the traditional Christo-paganism for a more standard brand of Roman Catholicism under the leadership of the Maryknoll missionaries. These converts no longer practiced all of the traditional life cycle customs. Traditionally, the family called in a ceremonial specialist before a child was born to offer candles before an image in the church and pray for the child's safe arrival. About a month before the child was expected they arranged for a midwife. The mother kneeled on a mat to give birth and might be given a steam bath if she had difficulty. After birth the baby was washed and given a steam bath, and both mother and child rested for at least a week on a low board heated by a fire of coals beneath it. A ritualist used sacred beans to divine the child's future. About twenty days after birth the baby was presented to its protector, which was the spirit of a hill, river, cross, or something else of sacred significance. The child was supposed to return to the spot where the ritual was conducted every nine months to renew the relationship with the spirit and feed it. The people also performed special rituals, including a feast, over the umbilical cord, and someone took it far away and left it in the top of a high tree or threw it in the river so the child would be protected when climbing trees or crossing rivers (H. and L. McArthur 1966:147). Contrary to the widespread idea that the women of tribal societies return to normal activity immediately after birth, it is characteristic of Mesoamerican mothers to rest for a prolonged period after parturition. The same is true of many other societies around the world.

Aguacatec women carried their children on their backs, wrapped in a shawl, almost constantly during the first two years. They were quick to put the child to the breast whenever it fussed and might nurse a little one until it was five unless another child arrived. They weaned most of their children by age three, however. As children grew up they were gradually taught various adult tasks, boys helping their fathers in agricultural work and daughters working with their mothers at home. The Aguacatec seldom punished their children physically, and they were generally obedient. Brintnall saw a parent threaten a child only once, though he heard stories of older children being beaten (Brintnall 1979:80).

Aguacatec men usually married in their late teen years, while the women usually married several years younger. Girls made themselves as attractive as they could, keeping themselves and their clothing clean and neat. They also wove their own headbands to demonstrate their feminine abilities. They put on their best appearance for the Sunday markets, where they moved about with their mothers or other girls. The boys began to try to save money toward marriage costs when they reached about fifteen or sixteen, and on market days they walked about in small groups. Sometimes young people met and talked briefly while walking along trails or when a girl was herding the family animals. Young men also got to meet the daughters of farmers they worked for, and daughters of wage workers who worked alongside their fathers might get to meet the employer's sons. Boys sometimes tried to seduce girls. Apparently, the girls were generally reluctant, and parents might punish a daughter who became pregnant and/or demand a payment from the boy.

A male wanted to marry a girl who was attractive, industrious, and honest; while girls were interested in the same characteristics plus the boy's prospects for obtaining land. As in other Mesoamerican communities marriage arrangements were usually made through an intermediary, though some young men directly approached the girl first. When a girl agreed the parents were informed, and if the father approved the families entered negotiations for a *bride price*.

Bride price is among the most widespread marriage ratification devices around the world, others including *bride service*, *brother-sister exchange*, *elopement*, and *gift exchange*. Many Westerners suppose that the bride price involves purchasing a wife as property, but this is hardly ever the case. Commonly, it is a tribute to the woman's value to her family, who should be compensated for the loss by a payment. During the 1970s in Aguacatán the bride price consisted of money the boy had saved plus money from his father. It was commonly between twenty and thirty dollars in 1973, but it approached a hundred dollars in some cases (Brintnall 1979:81). Sometimes a father opposed to a marriage would demand an extremely high price.

During the 1970s the marriage was finally ratified by a small ceremony, traditionally involving certain rituals performed by a shaman, the exchange of flowers and incense, the burning of candles, and the payment of the bride price. Protestants and Maryknoll Catholics had church weddings instead.

The wife continued to reside with her parents for two or three weeks after the ceremony, with the husband visiting her each evening and spending the night. After that he took her to his home. The people emphasized faithfulness between spouses and traditionally believed that sexual infidelity and the resulting disturbance of relationships among neighbors made the dead angry. Anthropologists find that there are discrepancies between people's ideals and their performance in every society. In harmony with this, Brintnall learned of many cases of adultery during his field study. There were also a fair number of divorces, indicated by households composed of divorced persons living alone or with their children.

Formerly an adult male gradually gained influence and prestige by participating in an age-graded hierarchy. He occupied positions of low responsibility as a young man and advanced through a series of graded political and ritual positions until, during his forties or fifties, he became an Elder. But during the early 1950s the age grade system of the Eastern Aguacatec suddenly collapsed, which precipitated a series of public confrontations between traditionalists and Catholics for some years. By 1972 twenty-three percent of the Easterners were Catholics and were not participating in the traditional age grade system. Many also had been converted to Protestantism and no longer participated. The system also collapsed among the Westerners before too long. Nearly one-third were Catholics by 1972, and many others had converted to Protestantism, constituting over one-fifth of the Westerners.

Instead of participating in the age grade system many of the young men accepted roles in new religious organizations, either Catholic or Protestant. Easterners and Westerners, who formerly had nothing to do with one another,

found themselves working together in the same groups. They were also relatively free of the dominance of the Elders and occupied positions in accordance with their abilities and the tide of events. They also found outlets for themselves and avenues of service in savings and loan cooperatives, agricultural cooperatives, political parties, peasant leagues, and educational organizations. Their prestige and influence developed within the context of these new organizations and the new economic order rather than under the dominance of the age grade hierarchy. Men of various ages found it possible to fill leadership roles such as political party candidate, peasant league secretary, church catechist, or president of an agricultural cooperative (Brintnall 1979:168).

Specific information on illness and healing among the Aguacatec is scarce, but characteristic Mesoamerican concepts were undoubtedly present to one degree or another. Wagley mentions the concept of the evil eye and illness from a fright as typical Northwestern Highland notions (Wagley 1969:63). People believed in the possibility of witchcraft as well as evil magic (sorcery) everywhere in the Cuchumatán region. *Witchcraft* is practiced through the power of the witch to manipulate circumstances supernaturally to bring misfortune or illness, while *sorcery* is a *magical* procedure that has power to cause evil. In witchcraft the power is in the witch, while the power is in the formula or procedure in magic. The Aguacatec may or may not have distinguished between witchcraft and sorcery. Probably a more important notion in Aguacatán was the belief in illness as punishment from the dead. When people did things that displeased their ancestors many expected illness, disaster, or death to overtake them. Many others, however, especially the Maryknoll Catholics and the Protestants, felt that their new religious faith protected them from the anger of the dead.

Healing in the highlands of northwestern Guatemala was accomplished by either shaman-priests or healers. A shaman-priest divined the cause of the illness by scattering beans on the ground and picking them up in a prescribed manner while reciting the twenty day-names of the ancient Mayan calendar. Then he carried out the rituals necessary to appease the dead or other supernaturals. The healers (*curanderos*) used herbal remedies, charms, incantations, and procedures such as bleeding and cupping (Wagley 1969:65).

When someone died traditional families called the shaman-priest in to divine the cause. Friends and relatives usually came in the evening with candles, flowers, or money, and the women busied themselves carrying water and preparing food for a feast. The people did not go to bed, though they might nap briefly, and they drank a good deal of liquor. Young men dug a grave early the next morning, and the people ate a last meal in the dead person's presence. They placed the body in a wooden box and took it to the cemetery, where they placed food, drink and a few personal possessions in the box before burial. The shaman burned incense and candles while preparations were going on. The soul left the box through a hole in the side and remained in the area for some days. It had to be fed daily with candles, and the shaman-priest determined its departure time by means of divining beans. Protestants and Catholics normally followed the rituals appropriate to their respective religious beliefs.

The traditional Aguacatec believed in no heaven or hell based on how people had lived. Instead they felt that the welfare of the dead depended on how their living descendants behaved. When people behaved well and got along well with one another the dead were contented. If someone was victimized he or she could hire a shaman-priest to transmit the complaint to the dead. The Elders among the dead would then put a close relative of the wrongdoer in jail, perhaps a dead father, mother, or grandparent. Upon being jailed, the ancestor would make his misbehaving descendent ill, or bring him some other kind of trouble (Brintnall 1979:92). The only way out was to get a shaman-priest to divine what was going on and to have him make a sacrifice to the dead Elders to get them to free the ancestor from jail.

Government and Social Order

The Aguacatec of the 1970s had done away with the traditional political system. Previously the municipio had been governed by Ladinos, and the Indian political hierarchy was an instrument through which the Ladinos controlled the Indians and bent them to their will. Beginning at about age fifteen, each male was required to hold political and religious positions at the lowest levels of responsibility. They were appointed for one year terms and, then, rested a year, though at the higher levels cargo holders rested four or five years between positions. There were nine age-graded levels among the Eastern Aguacatec and ten among the Westerners. It took a man at least 25 years to advance to the levels of highest responsibility and be recognized as an Elder.

But the Indians were not actually free to govern themselves. Few spoke Spanish well enough or were otherwise well enough educated to cope with national Guatemalan society, so the Ladinos took care of such things for them. Indian welfare was dependent on the Ladinos who, of course, took advantage of their favorable position. Neither did the Ladinos permit the Indians to acquire the education or knowledge required to effectively represent themselves.

The Indian government was subordinate to the official Ladino-controlled government (Brintnall 1979:99). The subordination was manifested in two ways. The Indian leaders relied on Ladino authorities to enforce their decisions in difficult cases, and the Ladinos required the Indians occupying civil positions in the hierarchy to work for them, building roads, hauling loads, carrying messages, and similar menial tasks. With regard to the Indians' position relative to the Ladinos, Brintnall describes the Indian hierarchy as a government of weakness.

By the 1970s, however, the Aguacatec were participating in the municipio government and had both the knowledge and power to represent themselves in Guatemalan society. The chief elected officer of Aguacatán was the alcalde, who was a Ladino when Brintnall began his fieldwork in the early 1970s. Below him were four elected councilmen, a secretary, two treasurers, a recorder, a police chief, and several lesser officials. The first Indian alcalde, an Eastern Protestant of the Christian Democratic Party, was elected in 1969. But revolutionary violence was wracking the relatively non-Indian eastern part of Guatemala, and the government declared a state of siege. This meant that the local military commissioner took power, but the eloquent new Indian alcalde and his associates defied him. Through a series of misunderstandings and incidents, troops were sent to Aguacatán. Officials were ordered to arrest many Indian leaders, but Indian law enforcement officials defied the orders and allowed many to escape to the mountains. A few were captured and imprisoned for various periods of time. The Indian alcalde remained in office but had been rendered almost totally ineffective. Many of the Indians held him responsible for the course of events.

In 1974 both the Christian Democratic Party and the National Liberation Movement put up Indian candidates for alcalde, and the Christian Democratic candidate won. The president of Guatemala at that time belonged to the National Liberation Movement and declared the newly elected candidate defeated. Similar actions were taken for many Guatemalan municipios. After negotiations the National Liberation Movement candidate, a Western Aguacatec Indian, became alcalde in Aguacatán.

During the late 1970s the Maya of Aguacatán found themselves grouped into two political parties. The Easterners were associated with the Christian Democratic Party, while the Westerners controlled the National Liberation Movement. The Ladinos no longer completely dominated the municipio government, and a new class of intelligent, educated Indians stood ready to fill important elective and appointive offices. Many battles remained to be won, however, since most of the power remained in the hands of the Ladino municipal secretary and the town council (Odell 1984:12).

The stage for these developments and the organized Indian action against the oppression of Guatemalan national governments was set largely by the work of the Summer Institute of Linguistics linguistic missionaries and the Roman Catholic Maryknoll missionaries on one hand and the development of irrigation and garlic agriculture on the other. Both the Protestant and Maryknoll missionaries arrived in 1952, the Protestants to translate portions of the Bible into Aguacatec and teach the people how to read it and the Maryknoll Catholics to bring the people into standard Roman Catholicism and enable them to supply their own clergy. When some of the people sought to follow the new religions the possibility of economic freedom through garlic production gave them the means to defy the patriarchs.

The Eastern Aguacatec age-graded hierarchy collapsed in 1953 and 1954. The Eastern Elders fell into a dispute among themselves, and at least three elders actually commanded their oldest sons to become Catholics, apparently as a way of antagonizing their opponents (Brintnall 1979:121). This illustrates well how a major cultural change can come about as the result of a very specific event. Students often ask anthropologists how certain customs or complexes of customs came into being in one culture or another. Often the only possible answer is that specific circumstances there is no possibility of learning about led to the change.

In this instance the action of the Elders backfired, since the young converts were influenced by the missionary priest to stay away from an important organizational meeting for a fiesta. This was serious, since the men were the leaders of their age-grades and their presence was necessary for matters to proceed. This intensified the row among the Elders, and the fathers of the converts, the most powerful men among the Easterners, led many into the Catholic church. Still others who had wanted to become Catholics but were afraid to felt free to join them. These events precipitated a series of confrontations between Traditionalists and Catholics, and the latter finally prevailed. They gained control over the church, ritual objects, and other sacred places, and the Traditionalists could no longer function as they had. They still held their processions and fiestas, but only old men and women with a smattering of very young people participated when Brintnall was last there.

The Westerners watched the events of 1953 and 1954 closely. A few of them had responded to the work of the linguistic missionaries, but the conversion of the son-in-law of one of the most influential Elders in 1953 had been the first notable breakthrough. A number of other members of the convert's hamlet followed his lead.

In 1955 the sons of important Western Elders rebelled, one of the most charismatic and otherwise able young men becoming a Catholic. He clearly saw his action as a way to strike at Ladino domination and exploitation and said so (Brintnall 1979:133). Others followed him into Catholicism, and within two years the hierarchy was crippled. Young men were no longer willing to enter it, and the Elders could no longer force them to. By 1964 the hierarchy was completely disbanded. The Catholics did agree to celebrate fiestas with the Traditionalists, the planning to be in the hands of a joint committee composed of people from both factions. Also, by 1972, a large percentage of the Easterners had been converted to Protestantism.

A significant element in these changes was the literacy and knowledge brought to the Aguacatec by the missionaries. Both the Catholics and the Protestants wanted the people to know how to read. During the late 1950s and early 1960s the missionaries succeeded in getting a few rural public schools built, and both Protestants and Catholics were quite interested in sending their children. In 1964 the priest established a parochial school in the town, and Indian children were taught to read in both Aguacatec and Spanish. During the late 1960s and early 1970s Peace Corps workers successfully encouraged people in poorer, more conservative hamlets to establish their own schools. Schools also hired some very intelligent Indian graduates of the parochial school as teachers, and the Summer Institute of Linguistics missionaries trained Aguacatec Protestants to be bilingual promoters for the public schools. These people were highly regarded by the Indians in the hamlets where they worked, not only because of their literacy but because they represented the hamlets to Ladino officials in the municipio and at the department capitol. Both school children and Indians who had never attended school were becoming literate. In fact, Brintnall referred to it as an educational revolution (Brintnall 1979:153).

Along with the new wealth and education came a growing Indian pride and sense of independence. The cultural dominance of the Ladinos was broken, and a new order continued to develop. The Indian ethnic groups of Aguacatán had acquired the institutions necessary for sustained political cooperation against Ladino domination and, even, institutions for cooperating with other tribes to work against the continuing domination of the national Ladino elite. These kinds of developments among the Aguacatec and other Indians underlay the ferment of opposition to the oppressive Guatemalan governments of the late twentieth century. Some top Guatemalan officials, including at least one president, were inclined to bring Indian leaders into national decision-making processes, but none of them were able to shake the military power of the national Ladino rulers.

Religious Beliefs and Practices

The Aguacatec religion of the 1970s was also part of the changed cultural life pattern. Anthropologists commonly include *cultural integration* and *social integration* among the outstanding functions of religion in traditional and small-scale societies. When religious elements permeate every aspect of life they can be viewed as tying them together-- integrating the culture. Traditionally, Christo-pagan concepts and rituals permeated the political life. The ancestors were thought to want people to live by the principles of the age-graded hierarchy, and participation in the hierarchy was a religious and ritual obligation for all men. This also meant that the religious beliefs and political and ritual organization were linked to the high valuation of age. The religion of the Aguacatec emphasized the power and rightful influence of the old by extending their power beyond the grave, since the dead were concerned with and could influence the experience of the living. They were involved in the coming of illness as well as the healing of disease. Whether modern Catholicism and Protestantism tied the people's lives together with the same power that the old religion did is unclear. In modern North America both Protestant and Catholic clergy have complained about Sunday only Christians.

Social integration refers to feelings of unity and belonging among a society's members and the question of how effectively they cooperate with one another to realize shared goals. If there is just one configuration of religious patterns in a community people are bound together by their sharing of those patterns. If there is more than one and the religions conflict the religious situation may be divisive instead of integrative. The commonality of belief in traditional Aguacatán promoted unity, but other factors undermined that unity. The Easterners and Westerners held negative attitudes toward one another in spite of their religious similarity. Moreover, some of the Easterners and Westerners found themselves bound together by new institutions as the traditional order faded, notably through the Maryknoll brand of Catholicism. There was obvious conflict between the Traditionalists and the Catholics, sometimes intense, yet the Traditionalists and the Catholics of the Eastern Aguacatec managed to cooperate to stage their fiestas. Protestants, of course, set themselves apart from both the Christo-pagans and the Catholics by refusing to participate in religious processions and fiestas.

Like other Mayan groups the traditional Aguacatec were polytheistic, believing in supernatural owners of mountains, rivers, springs, trees, and rocks as well as regarding the sun, moon, stars, and the earth as supernaturals. The days of the ancient Mayan calendar were also supernaturals and had to be fed and placated by offerings of incense, candles, and liquor (H. and L. McArthur 1966:143). The saints, which were the statuettes that occupied the church, were also regarded as supernaturals. In the religions of many other Mesoamerican communities the nature deities and/or the saints were the most important supernaturals, but among Aguacatán traditionalists and among quite a few other Mayans the ancestors were the most important supernaturals. When Aguacatec died they continued their concern with and intervention in the lives of their children and grandchildren, helping them when they behaved properly and punishing them when they did not. The people believed them to be especially desirous that everyone continue to respect and practice the special cultural traditions known as *costumbres*. In addition, they wanted their descendants to interact with one another harmoniously. They also wanted the living to consult with them on all important affairs, such as naming children, selecting spouses, selling land, the inheritance of land, and so on. The shamans acquired much of their importance through this belief, since people hired them to divine what the ancestors were doing and what they wanted. They often found the ancestors were involved in bringing illness because people were not following the traditions, were not getting along with one another, or were not consulting the dead about important matters. As mentioned earlier, a victim of mistreatment might hire a shaman to complain to the Elders among the dead, who would jail a dead relative of the troublemaker, and the distraught prisoner would send sickness or other trouble. Having divined the source of the affliction, the shaman was paid to make a sacrifice, often of a turkey, that would free the imprisoned ancestor. According to Brintnall's analysis the keystone of the traditional Aguacatec ideological order was the "wrathful power of the dead." After many Aguacatec defected to Catholicism and Protestantism and prospered,

many were uncertain about the power of the dead, but continued to be concerned about their wrath. It was obvious that the defectors had seldom suffered the punishment that should have come, but many thought the ancestors would yet bring disaster.

The costumbres were manifested mainly through the public ritual life—the annual cycle of fiestas. Each lasted for a week and consisted of parading the statues of saints through the streets, becoming intoxicated on hard liquor, listening to marimba music, and dancing. The shaman-priests were paid to conduct many special rituals for the community during these periods (Brintnall 1979:92). Various groups and families were responsible for different ritual elements. There were ritual dance groups, the obligation to dance being inherited from father to son and mother to daughter. Various families had responsibilities of setting off rockets along a parade route, playing a flute, beating a drum, carrying candles, burning candles before saints, and so on. The McArthurs list eight fiestas regularly celebrated by the Christo-pagans (H. and L. McArthur 1966:143).

The Catholics were known as those who studied doctrine. They rejected the ancient beliefs and no longer offered incense, candles, and liquor to the supernaturals. To them the costumbres had become not only unnecessary but evil as well. The Catholics honored the Aguacatán patron saint, María Encarnación and observed Easter and Christmas. Much of their belief and practice was similar to that of Catholics in other places.

Protestantism in Aguacatán was of the theologically conservative kind communicated by the Wycliffe Bible Translators, who are also organized as the Summer Institute of Linguistics for the purpose of their scientific and educational work in various countries. The linguistic missionaries stressed belief in the Bible and use of scripture in the people's spoken language. This is why they translated the New Testament into Aguacatec and taught people to read.

In several basic ways the doctrines of the Protestants and Catholics were similar. But those who left Christopaganism commonly lacked effective understanding of or commitment to those doctrines, since they usually changed in revolt against the old religion and its validation of the age authority system and because they wanted the economic and socio-political freedom they associated with the two new religions. The Easterners who ordered their sons to become Catholics had little or no concept of what they were getting them into, and the linguistic missionaries commented that those who became Protestants commonly failed to understand the implications of their new commitment at first. This illustrates a common influence for acceptance of alien customs. People may accept new ideas or practices because they perceive them as accomplishing what the change agents define as their purpose. But in many cases, the reason is that accepting the change serves as an instrument by which the respondent can realize some advantage other than the novelty's conventionally understood purpose (Barnett 1953:361). So it was that many Aguacatec turned to Protestantism or Catholicism not for Christian salvation but to gain the economic and social freedom they desired or as a device for gaining an advantage over those with whom they were in conflict.

Social and cultural integration have been mentioned before as major functions of religion. Another is *validation* of various nonreligious components of the culture. Christopaganism validated the costumbres and economic and social dominance of the old over the young. When young members of the society came to see the age hierarchy based on inheritance of land by installments as a burden they could escape from, they rejected the religious system that validated it. As Brintnall indicated, it was a "revolt against the dead" (Brintnall 1979:117). Both Protestants and Catholics tended to retain their belief in the wrathful power of the dead but felt the new religions would protect them from it.

Cultural Change

The changes that occurred in Aguacatec culture during the middle twentieth century were similar in several basic ways to those taking place in a number of other Guatemalan places, and this accounts in some measure for the ongoing pressures for national change during the latter twentieth century. Anthropologists have often discussed whether changes of these kinds are ultimately founded on the culture's material base or on social and ideological factors. *Cultural materialists* regard the material base as primary. This consists of the ecology, technology, and economy as a system of interrelated elements. Their argument is that social and ideological changes stem from the material base more than vice versa. Brintnall, probably like most anthropologists, stresses the reciprocal relationship of the three in change (Brintnall 1979:177). The changes in the national

labor laws (social structure) made possible agricultural developments on Aguacatán's irrigable lands (material factors), which prepared the way for the development of rich and poor classes, revolt against age domination, and escape from dependence on Ladino mediation (all social structural factors). Yet those social changes could be effected only through acceptance of Protestantism or Catholicism and rejection of the power of the dead (ideological changes). More ideological changes (bilingualism and education) came with the new religions, making it possible for the Indians to do their own labor contracting for the cotton plantations, a matter of social arrangements. Through agricultural cooperatives, another social arrangement sponsored by the new religions, another material factor, chemical fertilizer, was brought in. The network of interdependent changes continued, since the increased profits from chemical fertilizer, irrigation cash-cropping, and the resulting wealth made possible various other developments. The Indians gained new pride in themselves, hostility between them and the Ladinos became open, and political activism emerged on both the local and national levels.

In 1977, when a mining company in the Mam community of Ixtahuacan closed down and fired its 300 employees, 71 miners and their families began a march from village to village through the highlands of Guatemala. As they moved along, thousands of peasants supplied them with food, water, clothes, and money. They finally arrived at Guatemala City to participate in a protest involving tens of thousands. This could never have happened in traditional Mayan Guatemala. It was the outgrowth of a network of interrelated changes, not only in Aguacatán and the department of Huehuetenango, but in many Guatemalan places. A configuration of major cultural changes had taken place, and there was no turning back.

PART IV   CIRCUM-CARIBBEAN CULTURES

Chapter 18

CULTURES OF CIRCUM-CARIBBEAN CENTRAL AMERICA AND THE WEST INDIES

Middle America includes not only the gathering-hunting areas of northern Mexico, horticultural Northwestern Mexico, and Mesoamerica but, also, the remainder of Central America and the islands of the West Indies. Along with the northern coast of South America, lower Central America and the Caribbean islands form an oval ring around the Caribbean Sea. The part of Central America we are now concerned with includes most of El Salvador and Honduras, Nicaragua, Costa Rica, and Panama, while the Caribbean area includes Cuba, Haiti, the Dominican Republic, Jamaica, Puerto Rico (together known as the Greater Antilles) and the many small islands of the Lesser Antilles—the Virgin Islands, Antigua, Guadeloupe, Dominica, Martinique, St. Lucia, Barbados, St. Vincent, Grenada, Tobago, Trinidad and others. Culturally, Lower Central America was influenced heavily by both Mesoamerican and South American groups, while the West Indies cultures were affected mostly by South America. Anthropologists sometimes refer to these areas as the *Circum-Caribbean culture Area.*

Circum-Caribbean Central America (which excludes Guatemala and Belize, since they are culturally part of Mesoamerica) is bordered by lowlands along much of both the Pacific and Caribbean coasts, with ranges of mountains and interior plateaus and basins, all intersected by a number of rivers, between them. The Pacific coastal lowland is generally narrower and drier than the Caribbean lowland, but there are places on both coasts where mountains rise abruptly from the sea or close to it. The Pacific lowlands are seldom over 15 miles wide, and the most extensive areas are around the Gulf of Fonesca where a small portion of Honduras extends to the Pacific, on the Nicoya Peninsula in northwestern Costa Rica, and on the Azuero Peninsula along the southern Pacific coast of Panama. In some places the lowlands are wet and forested, and in other places there are drier grasslands interspersed with more limited forests of different type. A strip of lowland cuts across mainland Nicaragua at its border with Costa Rica, following the course of the San Juan River to the Caribbean coast. For some years the British were interested in building a canal across Central America at this point.

The Caribbean strip of lowlands extends 150 miles or more inland at some points, and much of it is rainy, heavily forested, intersected by inlets, and swampy. The widest part is the famous Mosquito coast, which begins in northeastern Honduras and takes up much of the Caribbean east coast of Nicaragua. The rest of the Caribbean strip, through Costa Rica and Panama, is narrower and at places interrupted by mountains or hills approaching the sea.

The mountains vary from low ranges about 2,000 feet high to high ranges containing peaks over ten or eleven thousand feet above sea level. Some of the peaks, high and low, are active volcanoes. The mountains in the northern and western parts of Central America are generally higher and more rugged than those closer to South America. Knife-like ridges, deep valleys, and steep slopes are typical. In central Panama, where the canal crosses, the mountains give way to a hilly area. Between and within some of the ranges are large and small plateaus and flat basins ringed by mountains.

There are a number of rivers important to the inhabitants. The largest lake of the region is Lake Nicaragua. Lake Managua is nearby, and Gatún Lake intersects the Panama Canal.

Though the Caribbean islands vary greatly in size most of them consist of a mountain spine or conical peak surrounded by a rim of coastal plains. Cuba is more variable than most, since it makes up around half the land mass in the Indies. The northeastern (windward) slopes of the islands are typically covered with dense tropical rain forests, while the opposite sides are drier. Trinidad, which is close to the South American mainland, is also somewhat different from most, since it is covered with lush tropical vegetation.

The Aboriginal Cultures

The cultural prehistory of Circum-Caribbean Middle America has not been worked out nearly so well as that of

Mesoamerica. And, though archaeologists may now be in process of abandoning the traditional five period scheme for Mesoamerica, it would be difficult to know what alternative sequence would be generally acceptable until the change is accomplished.

There are sites in the Circum-Caribbean that can be called Paleo-Indian, Archaic, Formative or Preclassic, Classic, and Postclassic.

Archaeologists would assume a Paleo-Indian time here simply because of the evidence of ancient big game hunting in South America. One of the better examples is the Fell's Cave site in Tierra del Fuego. There the association of Paleo-Indian artifacts with the bones of horses, guanacos, and the extinct mylodon has been dated as over 9,000 B.C. (Lynch[Jennings] 1983:117). Anthropologists generally assume that humans first came to the Americas through Alaska, so Paleo-Indians or earlier peoples would have to have passed through Central America. But there is also direct evidence of Paleo-Indians there. Snarksis, for example, found 18 Paleo-Indian artifacts at Turrialba in Costa Rica (Snarksis 1979).

There was no big game in the Caribbean Islands, and the earliest known presence of humans there is estimated to be about 5,000 B.C. (Rouse and Allaire 1978:437).

Around seven or eight thousand B.C. cultures emerged in the Americas that relied more extensively than the Paleo-Indians on plants and a greater variety of animals. Archaeologists have usually referred to these as Archaic cultures. During later phases of Archaic times, some groups domesticated plants and began to make pottery. There were pre-horticultural, preceramic Archaic cultures in Circum-Caribbean Middle America, but, because the evidence is so sparse, archaeologists are finding things difficult to interpret in terms of broad schemes. On the island of Hispaniola archaeologists have found evidence of people living an Archaic type of life by at least 1450 B.C. (Rouse and Allaire 1978:467)—possibly much earlier. Archaeologists have evidence from Costa Rica and Panama of both preceramic and ceramic (pottery-making) Archaic cultures. The ceramic cultures date back to more than 3,000 B.C.

We hear regularly of the Aztec and the Inca and, very occasionally, other civilizations of Mesoamerica and South America but civilizations also developed in Circum-Caribbean Middle America. Though agriculture and pottery were present during much of the Archaic, the people remained basically nomadic gatherers and hunters. But between 2,000 and 500 B.C. people here and there began relying primarily on domesticated crops and adopted a more sedentary life, developing in these and other ways toward the complexity that marked the civilizations of that region.

For Mesoamerica, Circum-Caribbean South America, and the Andean region archaeologists have used the Preclassic, Classic, and Postclassic epochs to classify periods of civilization's development. During the Preclassic, villages increased in size; mounds of increasing height appeared; people built civil-religious centers; complex pottery and other arts developed; and social classes, established states, intersocietal trade patterns, religious cults, and cities appeared.

Classic civilizations were marked by large ceremonial structures, complex ritual and religious art, highly developed priesthoods and religious organizations, and theocratic governments. Archaeologists viewed the Postclassic civilizations as more secular and militaristic than the Classic cultures and, sometimes, somewhat inferior to Classic societies in their aesthetic and intellectual accomplishments. But some archaeologists have turned away from this scheme for Mesoamerica and South American areas, and it has hardly been used for Circum-Caribbean Middle America.

Investigators have found a number of similarities with neighboring areas, notably in some of the pottery types, so the developments in Circum-Caribbean Central America and the Indies could be correlated with the three stages of civilization on that basis. These similarities reflect the strong influences from both Mesoamerica and South America, both by diffusion and by the arrival of outside groups. So variability within the region has been great, and late twentieth-century archaeologists have deemed it most useful to classify cultures as Lithic, Archaic, and Ceramic.

The Lithic Age is the time of stone tool-making by chipping. The Archaic Period begins when ground stone and/or shell tools appear, and the Ceramic Age begins with the first pottery-making. In this scheme foodgetting patterns are not taken into account, the latter part of the Archaic as used by other archaeologists is assigned to Ceramic times, and all of the civilizations fall in the Ceramic Age. For Circum-Caribbean Central America the Ceramic Age began a little before 3,000 B.C. in places, and ceramicists and agriculturalists from the South American mainland moved into the Caribbean islands during the first centuries after Christ (Rouse and Allaire 1978:478). The most impressive manifestation of Circum-Caribbean civilizations is the great variety of well-made items of fired clay (ceramics), many of which were done in several colors (polychrome).

Circum-Caribbean Central Americans spoke languages mainly of the Macro-Chibchan phylum and the Chibchan family. The Macro-Chibchan languages are South American rather than Mesoamerican. They were spoken by the Indians of Panama, most of Costa Rica and Nicaragua, and parts of Honduras and El Salvador. Most of the Indians of Panama and Costa Rica spoke languages belonging to the Chibchan family, while most of the Macro-Chibchans of Nicaragua, Honduras, and El Salvador used languages of the Misumalpan family. Several other Central American Circum-Caribbean societies used languages belonging to the Uto-Aztecan phylum, which allies them linguistically with many of the peoples of Mesoamerica, Northwest Mexico, and North American culture areas. The Uto-Aztecan languages of this area belong to the Aztecoidan family, and the tribes speaking Aztecoidan languages arrived from Mesoamerica and settled mainly along the Pacific coast of Nicaragua and Costa Rica from two to four centuries before the Spanish Conquest. Oto-Manguean is a third phylum represented here, the families represented being Chorotegan and Xinca-Lencan. Many of the major languages of Mesoamerica were Oto-Manguean, and a few Chorotegan languages were found there. A major Xinca-Lencan language is Lenca, spoken by an important tribe of Honduras and El Salvador. A fourth phylum represented in Circum-Caribbean Central America is Hokaltecan, which includes a couple of languages in El Salvador and Nicaragua belonging to the Supanecan family and the Jicaque language of the Jicaquean family in Honduras.

The vast majority of Circum-Caribbean island tribes spoke languages of the Arawakan and Cariban phyla. Representatives of the Arawakan group in the islands spoke languages of the Taino family, which includes the languages of most of Cuba, the Bahamas, Jamaica, Haiti, the Dominican Republic, Puerto Rico, and the Virgin Islands. The languages of the Lesser Antilles, except those of the Virgin Islands, belonged to the Carib group. There were many Carib-speaking groups on the South American mainland, and the Caribs of the islands had been there only since about A.D. 1400. They apparently were in process of conquering the Arawakan groups and might have moved on into the Greater Antilles had the arrival of the Spanish not interrupted them.

We learn about the protohistoric cultures (those that prevailed just before the Spanish arrived) through the researches of archaeology and ethnohistory. Ethnohistorians examine the records of the explorers, missionaries, administrators and others who wrote of Indian customs soon after the Spanish entered the area. Such records include information gotten from Indian informants as to what their lifeways were like before the Spanish arrived as well as the records of what the Spanish observed of Indian behavior. To the extent their observations are accurate, the latter may be assumed to reflect in large part what the Indians were like during the immediately previous decades. We also consider Indian customs practiced generations and centuries after the conquest when they are clearly not European in origin, since they may be survivals of pre-Conquest ways.

Most of the Circum-Caribbean groups farmed intensively, maize, *yuca* (a root crop known also as sweet manioc or sweet cassava), beans, and peppers being especially widespread staples. The Indians of Middle and South America domesticated well over a hundred plants, and this is reflected in the variety of crops in protohistoric Central America and the West Indies. Some were found only in certain parts of the area, and others were secondary to the staples. Pineapples, coconuts, cacao, maguey, papayas, almonds, alligator pears, guavas, potatoes, *yautia* (a tuberous root plant), the arrowroot, and peanuts are a few of them. In much of the northern-western part of the culture area, maize was the chief crop and sweet manioc secondary or absent, while manioc was the main item in many of the places closer to South America. Some groups were raising bitter manioc (poisonous manioc which had to be leached before being used for food) during colonial times, but most schol-

ars think it was probably introduced following the Spanish Conquest (Steward 1948:4).

The Circum-Caribbean Indians farmed by the slash-and-burn technique, which is common among small-scale cultures in all parts of the world, but a number of their fields were larger and better maintained than in other slash-and-burn areas. They moved their fields either annually or every few years, cutting and burning a new area when the soil in existing gardens became unproductive. In many places they were able to secure adequate yields in the same place for relatively longer periods by adding soil; fertilizing with urine, ashes or other substances; and by irrigating. Some groups brought soil from other locations to build and maintain mounds in which they planted their crops. The Circum-Caribbeans, like most other tribal farmers, used the pointed digging stick to work the soil and make holes for planting. In general, the men of the Circum-Caribbean did a good deal more agricultural work than Mesoamerican men. The women did most of the crop work in a few Circum-Caribbean groups, while the men did most of it in the others.

The people also hunted, fished, and collected wild plant and animal foods. They used the bow and arrow, with arrow poison in most places. Some groups used blowguns, spears, lances, axes, or various kinds of traps to take deer, monkeys, birds, tapirs, peccaries, iguanas, squirrels and other fauna. The people fished with nets, hooks, spears, harpoons, traps, and stupefying drugs. Judging from the great lack of information, the people must have made only limited use of wild plants. They gathered several wild fruits and roots and collected forms such as lizards, snakes, spiders, and insects. Domesticated turkeys and Muscovy ducks were present in a few places, and dogs may have been kept for eating.

Sweet manioc was the main food item in the islands and those parts of Central America closest to South America, while the people closer to Mesoamerica emphasized maize. They roasted or boiled both or made them into beer. Central American women ground maize with the *metate* and *mano* (grinding stone and hand stone), mixed the meal with water, and made a loaf they boiled or roasted. The Nahua tribes brought tortillas into their part of the area. At least some of the island groups did not have metates and manos and may have used only the soft green maize in soup, but Carib groups ground corn and made loaves as the Central Americans did. The Circum-Caribbeans roasted sweet manioc, yautia, arrowroot, and the other tubers they grew. They often chopped or ground the tubers, meats, fish, peppers, fruits and other items to make soups or stews. The Taíno of Hispaniola, for example, characteristically kept a clay bowl of stew (commonly known as the *pepperpot*) simmering over a fire, adding items from time to time as they became available and eating from it as desired. These were some of the main foods, but a good variety more were prepared by one group or another—from roast frog to raw cacao beans.

All of the Circum-Caribbean Indians prepared fermented beverages from maize and sweet manioc, and many made both fresh and fermented drinks from the juice of the *pejibaye* palm. Chocolate and other drinks were important from place to place, too. Smoking cigars and taking snuff were also general in the area.

A Circum-Caribbean woman generally wore a cotton apron, while a man in many tribes wore a breechcloth of cotton. Both sexes used various kinds of mantles and cloaks, commonly of bark cloth. The different groups varied some in clothing. Women in some tribes wore the wrapped skirt, which was absent in other tribes. Skin garments, sandals, and the penis cover, for example, were found in some places, but not in others. All over the area people wore headbands, ear rods, nose pendants, bracelets, necklaces, rings, and other ornaments for appropriate occasions, and gold ornaments were widely used. Tribes in Panama and part of Costa Rica produced gold and traded gold objects to the other tribes. The people also used ornaments of teeth, bone, shell, jade and other stone, and feathers. They painted the body for special occasions in all groups, and scarification, chipping of teeth, removal of body hair, and other forms of ornamentation were found in places. One widespread custom was deforming the head by flattening it in front or both in front and back. Different tribes used different hairdos, from long hair tied in back for both sexes in some places to partial shaving of the head in others.

The people of this area built their dwellings mostly of cane or poles for walls and grass or leaves for the roofs. In some places their houses were rectangular and in other places round or oval. A few groups built at least some of their houses on piles or in trees. Some tribes had single family dwellings, while others used large multifamily structures. In parts of Honduras they coated the house walls with mud, and peoples of eastern El Salvador built flat-roofed buildings of adobe. In many groups the chief's house was of a different size or style than those of his subjects and/or built on a higher level, perhaps on a mound. Among the Taíno of Hispaniola the chiefs lived in large rectangular houses, while others lived in smaller, round structures.

In some areas people slept in hammocks of cotton cloth or netting secured to the house posts, while in others they slept on mats of cotton, leaves, or other materials or on platforms of various kinds. Many groups used wooden stools and headrests of wood or stone. They hung their baskets, tools, and other equipment on the walls and from the ceilings.

The people grew cotton and wove cotton textiles on looms, often painting designs on the cloth. All but the Lenca of El Salvador and Honduras made cloth from the inner bark of certain trees. They had a variety of kinds of often well made baskets and used several kinds of weaves, though coiling was uncommon.

The people of this area produced highly crafted ceramic items in a variety of animal, human, and tripod forms, decorating them with modeled appendages, incised designs and applied substances. The pottery of many groups was both complex and colorful.

The people of Panama, part of Costa Rica, and possibly some other places mined and smelted gold and copper and produced gold alloys with copper and silver. Some Circum-Caribbeans also produced nicely made objects of stone, wood, shell, or bone. Groups in Costa Rica produced elaborate metates, carved jade pendants and other stone objects, and the Taíno of Hispaniola made various stone items such as bowls, daggers and axe heads. The Taíno were also outstanding woodworkers, making well polished bowls and carved stools among other things. They also fashioned ax heads from shells and picks from bone or shell. Different tribes emphasized different crafts, but archaeological and ethnohistorical reports demonstrate that many of the protohistoric Indians of the West Indies and Circum-Caribbean Central American were outstanding craft workers.

Watercraft of various kinds were important here, especially in the Antilles and those parts of Central America closest to South America. Indians of Hispaniola (Haiti and the Dominican Republic) made dugout canoes, some of which carried seventy to eighty people. They used them both to move along the coasts and from one island to another. Some Carib groups used cotton sails on their large dugouts, though paddles seem to have been more common. Some Central American groups also used seagoing craft, and 45 foot long canoes moved along the San Juan River, now the border between Costa Rica and Nicaragua. Some tribes had log rafts and small bark canoes. In much of the Circum-Caribbean the people used the *tumpline*—a strap across the forehead to carry baskets or other back burdens. In some places people used a *balance pole* across the shoulders, with the burdens suspended from each end. Most of the people traveling on land made their way on foot, but in many places a chief rode on a litter, which might be a hammock, carried by several men.

The Circum-Caribbeans valued trade highly (Stone 1966:229). Most communities and tribes lacked markets, however, the exceptions being the tribes that had come from Mesoamerica, where markets were of considerable importance. In most of the Circum-Caribbean traders transported a variety of goods large distances either in canoes or carried by slaves. Anthropologist Doris Stone found pottery, raw cotton, cotton thread, woven and painted cloth, shell beads, gold figurines, hammocks. slaves, dogs, salt, wild pigs, feathers, birds, cacao, maize, resin, and shields among the trade items mentioned in the works of early European writers (Stone 1966:229). The traders bartered rather than using money. The main objects of barter in Hispaniola, where groups of Indians traveled from village to village to trade, and even from island to island, were manioc, pepper, stools, wooden bowls, pottery, gold, and carved stone objects (Rouse 1948a:530).

A number of tribes had *matrilineal clans*, in many places at least localized in a single multi-family dwelling. Husband and wife commonly or always belonged to different clans, and each person was assigned at birth to the mother's rather than the father's clan. A localized matrilineal clan consists of a core of males and females related to one another through the clan's women, plus the men who, under *matrilocal residence* have married into the group. This produces a collection of families tied to one another through matrilineal descent, and this may well have been the unit that lived in large multifamily dwellings in some places. Stone's ethnohistorical studies reveal matrilineal clans to have been common in Panama, part of Costa Rica, Nicaragua, and elsewhere. Some of the Arawak and Carib of the Antilles may have had matrilineal clans, but information is too sparse to be sure. Apparently, many Circum-Caribbean tribes had no clans or lineages.

There seems to be little specific information about protohistoric Caribbean families, but *matrilocal extended* (three or four generation) *families* were undoubtedly important in areas with localized matrilineal clans. *Patrilocal residence* has been reported for Hispaniola and other places, but it is difficult to know whether this means a couple lives in the household of the husband's parental family or whether they simply live in the same village or neighborhood as the husband's family. Many groups allowed *polygyny* (having more than one wife), especially for chiefs. Inheritance of property seems to have been through the maternal line in many places.

Most of the tribes appear to have had well developed social classes, sometimes four and sometimes three. Some groups were divided into chiefs, nobles, commoners, and slaves, but in most chiefs and nobles were not distinguished. Warfare contributed strongly to class differentiation, since it strengthened the position of the elite, and war captives might form a slave class

The Circum-Caribbean was an area of many large communities, commonly of several hundred to several thousand inhabitants. In many tribes the houses were arranged along streets and around plazas and surrounded by palisades, though neighborhood communities, composed of scattered homesteads, have been reported for some places.

A chief ruled over the community. Characteristically, he lived in a larger house, had several wives and many retainers, wore distinguishing adornments and insignia, was carried on a litter, and received tribute. When he died, his body was either dried or mummified, and it might be placed in a special structure or buried along with wives and servants who were stupefied and interred alive (Steward 1948:3).

In some areas villages were combined under a district or tribal chief, and there were cases where a high chief presided over a hierarchy of district chiefs and village headmen (Steward, 1948:3). The Spanish reported five provinces for Hispaniola, each ruled by a chief, a number of district subchiefs under each provincial chief, and headmen over the each of a district's villages. In other cases, as among the Carib of the Lesser Antilles, each village was independent of any higher authority.

In Circum-Caribbean Central America some of the tribes were governed by a council of elders who elected a chief from among themselves to rule for a specified term of office. Many of the chiefs in this culture area inherited their positions but, as elsewhere in the world, other factors might be brought into play, too. Generally, both chiefly position and property were inherited matrilineally. There seems to

have been a high incidence of rulers with dictatorial powers in the Circum-Caribbean. The chiefs on Hispaniola controlled much of the their subjects' lives and enjoyed a great many privileges. They were supposed to have the power to order a subject's death, though not all exercised that power. Commonly, chiefs received tribute, which they used to maintain their privileges, to carry out their administrative responsibilities, and look after the peoples' welfare. In some other places both councils and chiefs were elected and subject to recall by those who elected them. Some writers have reported female rulers for certain groups.

Warfare appears to have been important in some tribes and unimportant in others. In some groups, at least, a man could improve his social status considerably by high achievement in war, even advancing from commoner to noble status. Circum-Caribbean groups commonly fought over land and, in some tribes, to demonstrate their military ability or obtain slaves or victims for sacrifice (Stone 1966:229). War to obtain sacrificial victims was especially important in Costa Rica. The Carib of the Lesser Antilles fought out of pride and glory, raiding other villages for human flesh to eat, male captives to torture to death, and female and child captives to become slaves (Rouse 1948b:559). In contrast, the Taíno of Hispaniola were relatively peaceful. They fought over hunting or fishing rights, murders, and other matters, but they lacked the military prowess to defend themselves well against Carib raids (Rouse 1948a:532).

Most of the Indians of the Circum-Caribbean seem to have believed in a supreme deity of some sort, who was usually so remote that they paid little if any attention to him. They were regularly concerned with various other deities, who were celestial beings, animal deities, or reptilian gods. The sun, moon, and certain stars were often fairly important deities. The Circum-Caribbeans were especially concerned with a multitude of spirits associated with or living within natural and artificial objects. They were similar to the Mesoamericans in believing that mountains, pools, trees, rocks, and woodlands were indwelt by spirits that could affect human welfare. In some groups they prepared *fetishes*, or idols, sometimes in large numbers, for spirits to dwell in. The Indians of Hispaniola had what have been called *zemis*, or cemis, usually human-shaped idols of wood, stone, bone, shell, clay, cotton, or gold, which they made and kept in their homes, special structures, sacred caves, and elsewhere.

The people worshipped their zemis, made offerings to them, and received power from them. Many groups were also concerned with their ancestors and the ghosts of the dead. Chiefs became gods or temple idols in a number of places. Many groups centered their worship around a temple, a special building in which they kept their idols. In a few places the temples were situated on mounds.

Priestly organizations were rare. Instead, shamanism was especially strong in the Circum-Caribbean, and the shamans conducted the religious ceremonies at the temples and elsewhere, served as oracles of the gods and spirits, and made offerings and sacrifices. Functionally, then, they were *shaman-priests*. The people held them in high pres-

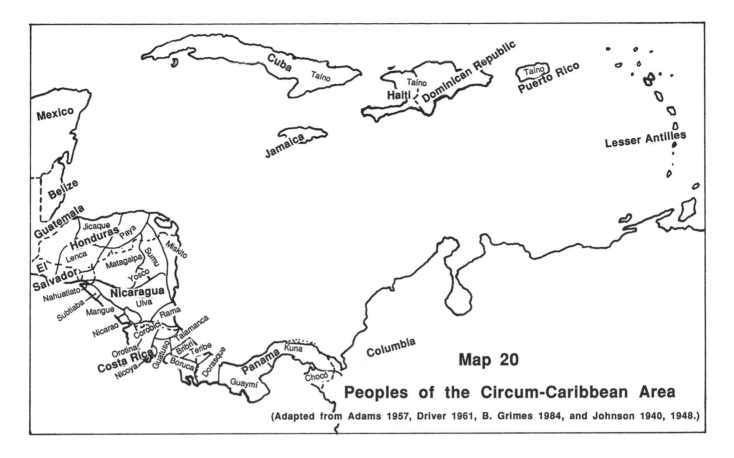

tige, and many were wealthy and powerful. Among the Hispaniola Indians the chiefs may have been shamans. They kept their zemis in temples and presided over ceremonies in which the villagers brought offerings to his zemis.

The shaman-priests of Circum-Caribbean America also diagnosed and cured diseases by the same kinds of techniques used by shamans around the world. Many were specialists in removing disease-causing items from the sick person's body by sucking them out or similar means. Some of them could transform themselves into their animal familiars and, in some instances, performed witchcraft. Some communities had different kinds of shamans, depending on the kinds of activities they engaged in.

Anthropologists know less about Circum-Caribbean cultures and peoples than they do about most other culture areas. The tribes of the Indies lived on islands, and it is a relatively short distance from coast to coast in much of Central America, so many groups were located close enough to the coasts that they were quickly overrun by the Spanish. Their cultures and often the people themselves were extinguished before qualified observers could study their pre-contact ways. Also, during much of the earlier history of anthropology fieldworkers stressed recovering data on aboriginal cultures about to be extinguished by European contact and neglected cultures that had already been greatly changed, and many of the surviving societies of the Circum-Caribbean had already lost most of their distinctively Indian ways. Finally, those parts of the culture area where Indian groups still retained much from pre-Spanish days lived in places that had the reputation of being rather unhealthy for most Europeans. It is understandable that more ethnographic work has been done in environmentally agreeable and readily accessible areas than in difficult places.

Twentieth Century Circum-Caribbean Tribes

The results of contact varied from one place to another, depending on its intensity and nature. The Taíno (approx. tah-EE-noh) of the Bahamas, Cuba, Hispaniola, Puerto Rico and nearby islands have long been gone, and there are no Indian communities there for anyone to study. Most surviving groups are so changed that their cultures are generally like those of the nationals of the country in which they are found. This is the case with the Lenca (approx. LEHN-kah) of Honduras, for example, though traces of Indian ways can be detected. Other groups have developed cultural blends easily distinguishable not only from that of the nationals but from the culture of their pre-contact ancestors. This seems apply to the Miskito (approx. mee-SKEE-toh) culture of eastern Nicaragua and Honduras and to the San Blas Kuna (approx. sahn blahs KOO-nah) of Panama. The Miskito culture is a unique configuration of customs derived primarily from the precontact background, African black cultures (through contact with communities of former black slaves), and English pirates and colonists.

The history of Central America is such that is difficult to portray the twentieth century tribes. Only remnants of some groups are left, and most of those have been heavily acculturated. In the early 1940s Doris Stone indicated that the Lenca of the southwest highlands of Honduras were being slowly eliminated as a distinctive cultural group, though some of them were trying to maintain some aboriginal ways. She found that the Lenca differed both physically and culturally from place to place (Stone 1948:205). There were also Lenca in El Salvador in aboriginal times, and twentieth century groups known as Indians in that country may have been descendants of Lenca forebears. Some anthropologists would object to calling the Lenca Indians, since their culture, at least since the middle of the twentieth century, was very much like that of other rural groups of Honduras and El Salvador. But at the midcentury mark there were still Lenca who thought of themselves as Indians and who were called Indians by others. Only a handful of them spoke Lenca, however. Just before 1950 there may have been 78,000 some persons in Honduras known as Lenca (Adams 1957:606). But thirty years can make considerable difference at twentieth century change rates in Central America, and by the 1980s the language was extinct (Helms 1984:59). Linguists assign the Lenca language to the Macro-Chibchan phylum but have not associated it with a family (Voegelin and Voegelin 1977:112).

There were also twentieth century remnants of the Jicaque (approx. hee-KAH-keh) people of the northern lowlands of Honduras. According to Von Hagen there were many fully hispanicized Jicaque living in Yoro department in Honduras, but only a small group, found in the Montaña de la Flor, retained much of the ancient lifeway in 1937 and 1938 (Von Hagen: 1943:2). In the 1950s there were at least 8,400 people identified as Jicaque in northern Honduras just to the west of the north-south midline, some of whom still spoke Jicaque at that time. Another 5,000 people living to the north of the Lenca might have been descendants of Jicaque ancestors, but they no longer used or remembered an Indian language and could not be identified. By the 1980s only a handful of Indians in the high cloud forests and isolated mountains of north central Honduras could be identified as Jicaque (Helms 1984:59).

The Paya (approx. PAH-yah), another lowland group just to the east of the Jicaque, were culturally almost identical to the Jicaque when Kirchoff wrote about them during the 1940s, though the two groups probably were more culturally distinct in aboriginal times (Kirchoff 1948:219). Only 600 were identifiable as Paya at midcentury (Adams 1957:607). They were undoubtedly gone by the 1980s.

Still another group thought to be Indian spoke Matagalpa (approx. Mah-tah-GAHL-pah), which linguists have assigned to the Misumalpan family of the Macro-Chibchan phylum (Voegelin and Voegelin 1977:230). Around 1950 there may have been from fifteen to twenty thousand Matagalpa in the northern highlands of Nicaragua, around fifteen thousand more across the border in Honduras, and a handful in northeastern El Salvador. They no longer spoke the language at midcentury, though some of them remembered a few words (Stone 1957:256). Noticeable differences between their culture and that of non-Indian peasants existed at that time. By the 1980s, though some still referred to Matagalpa Indians, their customs were virtually indistinguishable from those of Ladinos (Helms 1981:72).

Various twentieth century groups known as Sumu (approx. SOO-moo), Miskito, or Miskito-Sumu lived in east-

ern Honduras and the eastern lowlands of Nicaragua. The Sumu and Miskito may have been the same people in aboriginal times, with the Atlantic lowland people becoming the Miskito as the result of their contacts with non-Spanish Europeans. Tens of thousands of Miskito maintained their largely non-Hispanic culture into the twentieth century, mostly in the coastal and lower riverine areas of eastern Nicaragua but also in eastern Honduras. By 1980 there may have been over 75,000 Miskito, most of them in Nicaragua, but a fair number in Honduras. During the 1980s many moved to Honduras. Miskito was still the main language. A few Sumu still lived in villages along the upper reaches of some of the rivers, and there was a small number of Rama (approx. RAH-mah) near Bluefields, Nicaragua. Linguists have suggested that Miskito and Sumu are best viewed as dialects rather than separate languages. They have assigned Miskito and Sumu to the Misumalpan family of the Macro-Chibchan phylum (Voegelin and Voegelin 1977:230). Rama is Chibchan.

During the last half of the twentieth century there were several thousand Indians of the Bribri (approx. BREE-bree) and Cabecare (approx. kah-beh-KAH-reh) groups in Costa Rica (I. Kaplan 1983:92). They have sometimes been referred to as Talamanca (approx. Tah-lah-MAHN-kah). There may have been 1,500 to 2,000 Boruca (approx. boh-ROO-kah) Indians in Costa Rica as well. The Bribri, Cabecare, and Boruca spoke Chibchan languages. Less than 200 so-called Guatuso (approx. wah-TOO-soh) Indians lived in the northern part of Costa Rica, where they maintained much of their Indian lifeway at that time.

The Guaymí (approx. y-MEE) of western Panama numbered about 25,000 persons in 1950, but they had increased to almost 36,000 by 1960 (Young 1977:80). They survived over the centuries primarily by withdrawing into territory non-Indians were relatively uninterested in. They actually have descended from several aboriginal and colonial Indian groups, only some of which have been identified. Best evidence indicates that there were two Guaymí languages surviving into the twentieth century--Murire (approx. moo-REE-reh) and Ngawbere (approx. ngah-BEH-reh), both of which consisted of two or more dialects (Young 1977:21). These languages belonged to the Chibchan family of the Macro-Chibchan phylum.

Most of the Kuna were found along the Atlantic coast of eastern Panama, where they lived on the offshore San Blas Islands and commuted to the mainland to work their fields. A very small number of Kuna lived somewhat inland. There were between twenty and thirty thousand Kuna at midcentury and around forty thousand by the late 1970s (Nyrop 1980:62, 64). The Kuna language has also been assigned to the Chibchan family.

The several thousand Chocó (approx. choh-KOH) lived in extreme eastern Panama, where they had intermarried extensively with blacks. Very little is known about them. Chocó belonged to a separate grouping within the Macro-Chibchan phylum.

Chapter 19

THE MISKITO INDIANS OF NICARAGUA AND HONDURAS

In all parts of the world tribalistic groups have suffered from their contacts with the representatives of modern nations. For most of their history, however, the Miskito (approx. mee-SKEE-toh; sometimes Mosquito) of eastern Nicaragua and adjacent Honduras have benefited from contact. For several centuries they and the English maintained mutually advantageous relationships, and from the time Nicaragua and Honduras incorporated them within their territorial boundaries until recently, they continued to have little do with people of Spanish descent. They took on a number of the cultural characteristics of the English rather than the Spanish, and the Nicaraguans, particularly, have found it difficult to make them a functioning part of their nation. The Miskito have experienced a series of difficulties with the Nicaraguans, beginning in the latter days of the dictator Somoza's regime and intensifying under the revolutionary government of the Sandinistas. They had a way of life that, in spite of periods of economic difficulty, was satisfying to them, but their future has become increasingly uncertain.

The Miskito of the nineteenth and early twentieth centuries lived either along the coast, where they fished, took the green turtle, and engaged in slash and burn agriculture, or in the interior, where they were primarily slash-and-burn farmers. Hunting, fishing, bartering and selling natural products, and working for wages have also been important to the Miskito from the beginning. They lived in small, rectangular single family dwellings with steep roofs. The walls were built of bamboo, and the roofs, supported on posts, were thatched with palm leaves. In some places some of the Miskito lived in houses of more modern materials. Traditionally-dressed men wore a breech cloth and poncho, but shirts and trousers were replacing them. The people made a large number of objects from wood and bamboo and wove cotton fabric. They also made crude storage baskets and bags, hammocks, and the like from bark fiber.

The Miskito reckoned kinship relationships *bilaterally*, that is through both males and females on both sides of the family. They had no government for the tribe as a whole, the largest governmental unit being the village or town.

Shamans have remained important among some Miskito into the twentieth century , but Moravian Christianity became the prevailing religion. Though reports disagree, it appears that there may have been more than 75,000 Miskito in 1984.

Prehistory

Though limited archaeological work has been done in the Miskito area, notably by Richard Magnus, no synthesis of the prehistory of specifically Miskito territory is available. Magnus was unable to find cultural evidence from either pre-ceramic or early ceramic times (Magnus 1974:220), and a number of later pottery forms seem to have originated outside Miskito country. It is clear also that the Atlantic coast of Nicaragua and southeastern Honduras was heavily influenced by South American cultures during most of its prehistory. Mesoamerican influences were apparently absent there, though they were strong on the Pacific side. So far, archaeologists have been unable to develop a sequence of prehistoric cultural stages specific to the Atlantic side of the area.

History

Neither the Miskito nor their Sumu neighbors are physically and culturally what they were before the Europeans came. Helms flatly states that neither tribe existed as such until after contact (Helms 1971:16). In fact, the name Miskito seems to be of post-contact origin, and Helms looks with favor on historian Charles Gibson's suggestion that the name developed from the fact that the segment of the indigenous population that eventually became the Miskito were armed with muskets, spelled *mosquete*, *musket*, and *mousquet*, respectively, in Spanish, English, and French (Helms 1971:16). Scholars generally reject the idea that there is any connection between the group's name and the insect. The Miskito, then, appear to be those Indians of the area that came into close contact with the English and, since they obtained arms, dominated the unarmed Indian groups. Before that they probably were culturally and linguistically indistinguishable from some of the other tribes of the area.

The Miskito people appear to have formed from those Indians of that area who came into closest contact with the English, French, Dutch, and Blacks. The lagoons and reefs of the Mosquito Coast made a good place for English pirates to base their raids on Spanish shipping, and English and Indians joined in attacking Spanish ships and traveling up the rivers to raid Spanish settlements well into the interior. The Indians also fought alongside the British colonial army in their Central American operations of the 1700s. Miskito political leaders, crowned by the British, served as middlemen between the British and the Indians of the area beginning in 1640 and continuing until 1894 (Dennis and Olien 1984:720). The British and their slaves withdrew from the area in 1740 but continued their contacts with the Indians from nearby Belize. In 1848 Moravian missionaries began intensive work among the Miskito, which transformed the culture considerably. So the people who associated with the English and their slaves along the coast became culturally different from the other Indians of the area and were soon known as Miskito.

Biologically, the Miskito became a mixture of Indian, Black, and White. Culturally, perhaps they combined mainly Indian and European customs with a smaller admixture of African elements. Since we do not know precisely what their Indian ancestors were like culturally, it is difficult to classify customs by their origins. We know the circumstances by which this new cultural blend developed, but not specifically much of what happened and how. We know that the Indians associated in work and war with the pirates. We know that many moved to the coast or closer to it so they could be in contact with European colonists. We know that they lived next to communities of Blacks.

Helms alludes to one series of events that illustrates the kinds of situations that developed. In 1631 English Puritans colonized Providence Island 150 miles from the Mosquito Coast, and they soon brought in a large number of Blacks. The Spanish conquered the island only ten years later, and many hundreds of the blacks escaped to the mainland. As the years passed more Blacks joined them as they escaped from Spanish mines and English plantations. The result was that the Mosquito region was already mixed before 1700 (Helms 1983:179).

The Miskito Indian culture developed out of this kind of contact ferment, a culture marked above all, perhaps, by its flexibility and adaptability. As their history moved on, the Miskito faced new developments creatively, forging an ever changing culture that became one of the most vital in the region. They developed the capacity for incorporating many foreign items and making them distinctively Miskito (Dennis 1981:276).

The Miskito were not only adaptable, they became basically anti-Spanish. They had a history of fighting against the Spanish with the buccaneers and raiding their Spanish neighbors, and the Miskito of Nicaragua did not become part of the country until 1894. According to the Treaty of Managua in 1860, the Miskito were to govern themselves within the Miskito Reserve, but the Nicaraguans deposed the last king in 1894 and took over. Even so, the Mosquito region remained geographically and culturally isolated from the rest of the country, and the Miskito more or less continued to go their own way.

In the latter part of the nineteenth century the Miskito men increasingly entered wage work for European and American fruit, lumbering, and mining enterprises. With cash available the Miskito became accustomed to having manufactured tools, foods such as flour sugar and coffee, and medicines, clothing, and similar items. Wage labor became the male area of exploitation, while the women continued their traditional concern with agriculture. Dennis noted that the people seemed to acquire a sense of well-being from being able to earn good money and having well-stocked stores from which to buy what they wanted (Dennis 1981:279).

Moravian Christianity became stronger than ever during the same time. The Moravians learned the Miskito language and translated the Bible, and a mass religious conversion known as the Great Awakening took place in 1881. The missionaries introduced many technological items that remained important in Miskito life, such as board houses, new varieties of rice, and breadfruit trees, and they managed to eliminate much of the shamanism, ritual drunkenness, and other elements deemed incompatible with their faith. Eventually, the Miskito took over the Church, and it became an integral part of Miskito life.

Ethnography and Ethnohistory

For many groups around the world the ethnohistorians have been able to provide us with basic information about the nature of indigenous cultures at the time of first contact with Europeans. Missionaries, adventurers, explorers, and the like have often left written records describing the lifeways of the people they contacted. Ethnohistorians are specialists, some in history and some in anthropology, who reconstruct earlier lifeways by locating and studying early written records for data about given cultures. There are a few reports by traders and missionaries, but not nearly so much as for some other societies. The result is that our knowledge of their pre-contact culture is severely limited.

The first ethnologist to study Miskito culture was Eduard Conzemius, who spent time with both the Sumu and the Miskito early in the twentieth century for the Smithsonian Institution. Other anthropologists had entered the area earlier, but only briefly to collect artifacts or study physical types. Then, in the mid 1960s, anthropologist Mary Helms studied the culture of Asang, a Miskito community that lies 200 miles inland on the Nicaragua side of the Río Coco. Also, geographer Bernard Nietschmann has made major contributions to our knowledge of Miskito culture of the coastal regions in relation to the habitat. Anthropologist

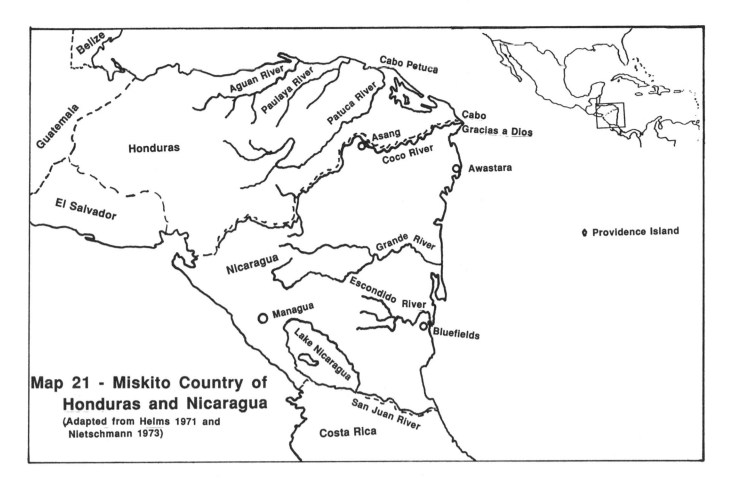

Map 21 - Miskito Country of Honduras and Nicaragua
(Adapted from Helms 1971 and Nietschmann 1973)

Paul Kirchoff contributed a summary of Miskito, Sumo, Paya, and Jicaque cultures to Julian Steward's *Handbook of South American Indians*, Volume 4. In addition, Philip Dennis studied the culture of the coastal community of Awastara in 1978-79.

The following cultural description depends primarily on the work of Conzemius, who emphasized traditional customs. Essentially, it depicts the culture as it was during the nineteenth and early twentieth centuries, though I indicate later changes as information is available.

The Country

The countries of Honduras and Nicaragua form a bend in the direction of Central America. The Atlantic coast of Honduras runs basically from west to east, while the Atlantic coast of Nicaragua runs almost due south from the mouth of the Río Coco. The Mosquito Coast extends from Cabo Honduras eastward and southeastward to the Río Coco and the Cabo Gracias a Dios, and from Cabo Gracias a Dios southward to the Río San Juan, which is the border between Nicaragua and Costa Rica. From the coast it extends inland about 200 miles in some places.

The elevation is seldom more than 600 feet above sea level, though the land rises gradually in a series of terraces (Conzemius 1932:2). Low hills begin generally from 100 to 150 miles from the shore. Pine savannahs interrupted by occasional stands of hardwoods extend over most of the area. In the west secondary forest and other regrowth gradu-

ally replace the savannah (Helms 1971:12). Several rivers of goodly size run from the highlands and rain forests to the west across the Mosquito Coast to the Atlantic. The Aguan, Tinto and Patuca Rivers flow to the northern coast of Honduras, while the large Coco, Grande, Escondido and San Juan Rivers extend across the Nicaraguan section of the Coast. The Atlantic shore itself consists of extensive beaches and hills of sand interrupted by a large system of lagoons interlaced with mangrove swamps. Beyond the shore lies a system of coral reefs and large numbers of cays.

It rains heavily in the Mosquito region—100 inches and more annually. From the River Patuyo eastward and southward most of the rain comes in May through December, though there are sunny days without rain during that season and occasional rainy days during the dry season. The rains characteristically come in great torrents lasting only part of a day, after which the sun makes its appearance again. During the summers the temperatures seldom rise above 90 degrees Fahrenheit and usually do not go below 65 degrees in the winters. Along the shore pleasant sea breezes blow regularly. Conzemius noted that many Europeans have found the Coast a relatively healthy, pleasant place to live.

South American wildlife characterizes the Mosquito region. The larger mammals include the tapir, the manatee, jaguars, and cougars. Several kinds of monkeys inhabit the area, and there are ocelots, deer, peccary, anteaters, armadillos, opossums, sloths, agouti, porcupines, squirrels, rabbits, racoons, coatis, weasels, skunks, kinkajous, alligators, river turtles, the green sea turtle, iguanas and other lizards, and many poisonous and harmless snakes. Sharks and sawfishes enter the lower courses of the streams. There are many kinds of birds, many of the winter species being migrants from North America. Insects are various and abundant, including the malaria mosquito.

Language

Linguists classify the Miskito language under the Misumalpan family along with the closely similar Sumu language of interior Nicaragua and Honduras and Matagalpa of the highlands of those countries. The Misumalpan family is affiliated with the Macro-Chibchan language phylum, most of the Macro-Chibchan languages being found in South America.

The various societies of the world do not differ in language because of genetic differences. Anthropologists have concluded that the newborn of all societies are equipped to learn any other language. They accordingly regard languages as composed of linguistic customs—learned and socially standardized just as surely as religious, technological, social, and other customs. The *phonological* (sound system) and grammatical differences among languages, then, are cultural differences. Heath has noted, for example, that Miskito lacks the English labio-dental sounds *f* and *v*, with the result that they change words they borrow from English accordingly. The word "beef," for instance, becomes *beep*, and "heaven" becomes *heben* (Heath 1913:54).

These examples illustrate projection of familiar cultural elements into alien configurations, a process common to all humans. Barnett has pointed out that this kind of occurrence is psychologically but another type of innovation—a process that takes place whenever something is borrowed from a culturally different society (Barnett 1953:210). Innovation occurs whenever people identify something familiar to them with something different, as when the Miskito identified the English *f* with their *p* and the English *v* with their *b*. They made this identification because *p* and *b* were the closest sounds to *f* and *v* that they had in their native language. Making those identifications made it possible for them to substitute one sound for another, in these examples by projecting it into the alien words to form new combinations— including *beep* meaning "beef" and *heben* meaning "heaven." People also innovate by assimilating foreign cultural elements into configurations familiar to them instead of projecting. Again, genetic factors do not determine this specifically. Many Miskito, in fact, have learned to pronounce English words with English sounds.

Miskito also differs grammatically from English in many ways. For example, the Miskito do not modify words to form plural meaning but add the word *nani* to indicate plural number. *Upla* is the Miskito word for a person, with *nani* added to denote people, yielding *upla nani*. Also, verbs are usually placed last in a sentence.

Personality and Behavior

No in depth analysis of the personality orientations and world and life view of the Miskito is available. Conzemius suggests that they were generally frank and outspoken, honest and reliable (Conzemius 1932:104). But he also expresses himself in a somewhat patronizing way, noting what he sees as a tendency to laziness, ingratitude, and shyness. This seems to conform to a tendency of many outside observers in earlier generations to react rather impressionistically and ethnocentrically to the behavior of tribal groups rather than understanding that behavior by carefully relating it to its whole cultural-situational context.

Conzemius notes that the Miskito tended to be rather reserved in their relationships with one another, even their own relatives. They also emphasized generosity and strongly condemned stinginess. He also indicates that patience, endurance, and self-control were strongly developed. The people exhibited this patience and self-control when hunting and fishing, keeping carefully at their tasks over long periods to realize the fruits of their labor. They also exhibited it in their relationships with one another, keeping control of their emotions and hiding resentment and anger rather than quarreling much, or fighting.

Conzemius also characterizes the Miskito as "noisy, bold, daring, adventurous, self- assertive, arrogant," and domineering in their relationships with culturally different Indian groups (Conzemius 1932:105). He suggests that this is a change in character due the large admixture of Negro blood and their association with foreigners and traders. Modern anthropologists would say that the biological mixture with Blacks had nothing to do with a character change but that the Miskito might change in personality as the result of associating with the culturally different Blacks of the Mosquito coast.

In the absence of the right kind of properly collected data, it is difficult to account with certainty for the fact that the Miskito exhibit more aggressive personalities than other Indians of the area. They could have been more self-assertive and responsive to outside opportunity before the Europeans arrived, and this could help account for their domination of other Indian groups and their ready and effective collaboration with the British. On the other hand, maybe they developed their aggressive qualities because they lived where they came into closer and more frequent contact with the Europeans and acquired the arms to dominate their neighbors. We also can characterize the Miskito as largely conservative, anti-socialist, anti-Spaniard, and somewhat capitalistic. Most of them do not fit well into the Sandinista revolution.

Clothing and Personal Appearance

Conzemius describes the Miskito men of an unspecified earlier time as wearing the loin cloth, usually of bark cloth but sometimes of cotton. The cloth was eight or nine feet long and twelve to fifteen inches wide, and they wrapped it around their hips several times and tucked it in so that the ends hung down in front and back. Later they made shirts and trousers from imported cloth, usually wearing the shirt-tails outside.

A woman wore a wrapped skirt extending from the waist to the knees and held in place by tucking it in at the waist. The skirt was of bark cloth in earlier times, but the women began to use brightly colored imported cloth when it became available and also added open-cut blouses or frocks. Both boys and girls wore loincloths differing from the men's garments in that the ends were wider than the rest to form aprons in front and back.

Clothing universally functions to mark social status, even if no more than sexual status. High ranking Miskito men added a sleeveless cotton tunic that extended to their knees. These tunics were beautifully embroidered with muscovy duck down and dyed with vegetable juices. They completed the outfit with a six inch wide sash around the waist. On festive occasions the men wore cotton bands with bright feathers attached on their wrists and around their legs above and below the knees, painted their faces and bodies, and added other ornaments on the breast, between the shoulders, or in perforations in the nasal septum and lower lip. Ordinarily the people went without headgear, but many of the men wore purchased hats for special wear. The women always went barefooted, and some of the men occasionally made and wore moccasins or bought shoes.

The men cut their hair short, and the women cut their hair just above the eyebrows and back to the temples, letting it hang long elsewhere. Both men and women used oil made from palm seeds to keep their hair in good condition. Their combs were bundles of small sticks that tapered to a point at each end.

The men blackened their faces and bodies with pine soot and coats of turpentine. In earlier times a woman painted her husband's body, but later all applied their own pigments. The women used a reddish to yellow or brown pigment prepared from the seeds of the annatto shrub or tree. They obtained a waxy material from the seeds by boiling them, coagulating the mixture with the aid of certain leaves or other seeds, and storing it in calabashes or bottles for future use. When ready to use it they added vegetable oils and applied the paint with small wooden sticks, making lines, dots, dashes, and, sometimes, geometrical designs on the nose, cheeks, chin, and forehead. They sometimes painted their legs to match the designs on their skirts (Conzemius 1932:25). In earlier times the people tattooed themselves—mainly on the face, arms, or breast—by piercing the skin and rubbing in pine soot. They used various kinds of thorns, splinters of flint, agouti claws, or fish teeth to pierce the skin. Later they took to using steel needles instead, and gunpowder replaced pine soot. Most of the designs were geometric.

Houses and Other Structures

The Miskito usually built their villages by rivers, lagoons, or the sea, usually on high banks for protection against flooding. They built oblong structures, usually with each end rounded, though some were elliptical, especially in more recent times. They supported the steeply-pitched roof on four posts and thatched it with palm leaves. The eaves extended to at least four feet above the ground, making it necessary to stoop to get inside. Inside the structure they built a floor about seven feet above the ground to form a loft, which they had to use a notched tree trunk ladder to get to. There they slept and stored their food. The fireplace was on the dirt floor below the loft. After contact with the Europeans the people added walls of split bamboo and a bamboo floor about three feet above the ground. The indigenous Miskito houses were large, multiple-family structures with separate compartments for the component families. The Miskito traditionally slept on layers of bark spread on the floor or ground, but later they began to build split bamboo sleeping platforms about three feet above ground level. The men rested in hammocks made of cotton, bark, or *Briomelia* fibers during the day or used them for sleeping when traveling. Only unmarried boys and girls slept in them at home at night, and that rarely. Women never used them. The women either sat on the ground or on low wooden stools.

The Miskito stored clothing and valuable items in wooden chests. They illuminated the house with pinewood torches or candles of beeswax or tree gum and cotton thread. They stored various items inside the roof by hanging them from the rafters, putting them on crude racks, or sticking them in the thatch. Bags and bottles of various substances also hung from the inside of the roof. They protected food from crawling insects by suspending it from the rafters on small shelves.

Livelihood

Each year the Miskito men cleared new fields, using axes and machetes, and burned the slash. The women then planted and cultivated with the digging stick and harvested the crops. They planted some fields to a single crop such as sweet manioc or another root plant, and in other fields they combined crops. Sweet manioc was especially important to the Miskito in general, but bananas were the staple crop in many interior Miskito groups. The Miskito also raised sweet potatoes, yams, pumpkins, squash, the *chayote* (a fruit), tomatoes, beans, maize, *pejivaye* palms, sugar cane, pineapple and a variety of other fruit trees, chili peppers, peanuts, cotton, and other plants (Conzemius 1932:64).

The Miskito have long taken much of their food from the rivers, lagoons, and the ocean, using harpoons, hooks, nets, and bows and arrows (Conzemius 1932:65). A harpoon, by definition, has a detachable point with a line attached to it, so the harpooner can dispense with the staff in order to pull in the animal. The Miskito used harpoons with detachable metal points to take large fish such as tarpon and snook. Two men would work together, one to handle the boat and the other to harpoon the fish. They caught the manatee, or sea cow, with a slightly different type of harpoon, and they took the green sea turtle with still a third kind. Some of the Miskito captured the turtles with nets or, sometimes, simply caught them when they came ashore to lay their eggs. They built corrals for turtles in shallow areas, where they could keep them alive until they wanted them for food. Harpoons and spears, by definition, are thrown, while lances are thrust while retained in the hand. Conzemius reported that the Miskito used at least two kinds of lances for taking fish (Conzemius 1932:690. The men did most of the fishing, but women, children, and old men used fish hooks, which they baited with worms, spiders, grasshoppers, or certain fruits. The Miskito also used various kinds of nets for taking fish, and sometimes would stretch a net across a stream to trap fish. They also took them with substances that stupefied fish when added to small creeks and pools. They obtained some species of fish by paddling their canoes along a stream bank while rocking them violently and beating on the bank with the paddles. This kind of thing so terrifies some kinds of fish that they leap out of the water, and many of them landed in Miskito canoes. For several kinds of river fish they used the bow and arrow, a method of fishing that is fairly common among tribal groups. The women gathered lobsters, crabs, and a variety of kinds of shellfish. Several kinds of charms were in use to aid the fishing efforts.

Apparently, at one time all the Miskito maintained their permanent villages away from the ocean and went to temporary fishing stations to take sea life. Later, when they began to take sea forms for the commercial market, many Miskito moved permanently to the coast.

Miskito men have long been skilled hunters, taking peccary, deer, monkeys, tapirs, birds, lizards, jaguars, puma, *pacas* (a kind of rodent), alligators and other animals. They were excellent stalkers, imitated bird and animal calls to attract their prey, drove game into water, set dogs on them, set fire to the bush to drive out the animals, shot them with bows and arrows or guns, clubbed them, or trapped them. They took alligators with large hooks.

The Miskito either boiled their meat, fish, sweet manioc, bananas, and other foods in water or roasted them in hot ashes. They preserved flesh by drying and smoking it over a fire for several days. Sometimes they buried green bananas, plantains, or other foods between layers of leaves and earth, which preserved them for up to six months as a kind of ensilage. They usually prepared it for eating by boiling it with water to make a beverage or baking it between leaves to produce a breadlike cake. They also made maize dough, sometimes soured, into a cake by wrapping it in leaves and baking it over an open fire. Sometimes they boiled food in coconut milk instead of water, and they sometimes fried fish in coconut oil. Apparently they ate whenever ready rather than at regular times, beginning the meal with

some sort of broth or soup. The women served the men in their hammocks, and the women and children sat on the ground together apart from the men.

The Miskito used a variety of beverages, alcoholic and nonalcoholic, mostly while traveling. *Wabul* was a drink made from green bananas that had been peeled and boiled in an iron pot. After pouring off the water, they mashed the bananas with a short wooden stick, adding water a little at a time. They served wabul in a calabash, usually between meals and when strangers arrived. They made an oil palm and banana beverage by passing the pulp that surrounds the palm seeds through a calabash colander and mixing it with wabul. Like the Indians of Northwest Mexico, the Miskito roasted maize and pulverized it with the *metate* and *mano* (stone grinding base and hand stone). They sometimes mixed the maize powder with water and added sugar cane syrup or wild honey to make a refreshing beverage. They produced two other maize drinks by sieving grains of green corn and by mixing maize paste with water. They were especially fond of several kinds of soured vegetable drinks, especially those made from sweet manioc, *tania* (a root plant), sweet potatoes, yams, and *pejivaye* fruit. They made paste from these items, wrapped it in leaves, and allowed it to sour. When travelling, they only had to add some water to have a refreshing, nutritious drink.

To prepare alcoholic beverages the Miskito mashed the item; put it in a large container such as a cask, earthenware pot, or even a canoe, added water; and allowed it to ferment. They made fermented drinks from sweet manioc, sweet potatoes, yams, maize, palm sap, and other substances.

Crafts, Tools and Techniques

In earlier times the Miskito produced fire with the *fire drill*, which consisted of a hard-wood stick and a notched piece of cane. They placed the end of the stick in the notch and twirled it until the friction got the wood hot enough to ignite the cotton fibers they used for tinder.

The fire drill is one of three basic friction methods widely used in nonliterate societies. Some societies use the *fire saw*, which involves drawing one member (flexible or rigid) back and forth across the grain of another piece of woody material. With the third method, the *fire plow*, the end of a stick is rubbed back and forth in a groove in the same direction as the wood grain. A given group commonly uses only one of the three techniques, and the Miskito used only the fire drill. Like other peoples of the world, they took to using matches when they contacted Europeans.

Two main devices for pulverizing or mashing grains, fruits and other substances are common among nonliterate peoples, and the Miskito had both. One device is the *mortar and pestle*, which consists of a container (the mortar) for the substance to be pulverized and a smaller elongated member (the pestle) to pound or mash the material. The Miskito had large wooden mortars, probably a short section of log excavated from one end, and two types of pestles. The most common was a hardwood member with the end that is applied to the substances larger than the handle end. They also used a cylinder shaped pestle, either end of which could be applied to the substance in the mortar.

The second device is the grinding stone and muller, which consists of a relatively large base stone and the hand stone, or muller, that the operator moves over the surface of the base stone. In Spanish, these are called the *metate* and *mano*. The Miskito metate was a flat-topped river boulder shaped with a stone chisel, and the mano was a rounded water worn stone. The Miskito used both devices to pound or grind maize, cacao, fruits, and berries.

At one time the Miskito cooked in clay pots, but iron pots replaced them. They continued for some time to use large clay vessels, some of which were four feet high, to ferment beverages in. Eventually, they ceased to make even this type of pottery. Archaeological finds indicate that Miskito women of precontact times were quite skilled, but their postcontact pottery was less well-made than before.

Though the Miskito made and used objects of stone and metal, most of their precontact tools and utensils were of clay, wood, shell, bone, and the like. After contact several kinds of European metal tools became important to them. When they obtained the machete, a cutlass-like knife about two feet long, they made it their most important tool. They carried it with them wherever they went, using it to clear small trees, shrubs, brush, vines, weeds, and the like for house sites and fields and to obtain construction materials. They also used it to defend themselves from animals and snakes and sometimes used it on one another. They also acquired metal axes, which replaced their stone axes. Both men and women used the ax. They also acquired metal adzes, woodworking tools that have the blade running crosswise to the long axis of the handle rather than a blade in line with the handle like axes. They used adzes in shaping canoes and other wooden objects. Metal knives and hoes also became important to them.

Formerly, the Miskito made and used a coarse brownish cloth made from the inner bark of a certain tree. People make bark cloth by pounding the bark until its fibers crisscross one another to form a fabric. The Miskito used bark cloth for their clothing and for bed blankets. After soaking the inner bark of the *tunu* tree in water for several days, they scraped the sticky gum from it and dried it in the sun. Then they placed the bark on a log and pounded it with a grooved wooden mallet. Occasionally. they made white bark cloth from a different species.

Cotton was a precontact crop in the Americas, and the Miskito cultivated it, spun it into yarn or thread, and wove it into cloth. Their spindles were slender hardwood shafts twelve to eighteen inches long and tapered to a point at both ends. The whorl of stone was flat on one side and cone-shaped on the other. It was one to one-and-a-half inches in diameter by three-quarters of an inch to one inch thick. It encircled the spindle about two inches from the lower end, where it served as a flywheel. A woman formed a thread

with her fingers from a strip of cotton and attached it to the spindle just above the whorl. Then she set the spindle upright in a calabash and twirled it so it would continue rotating about half a minute. She then drew a strip of fiber from a pile of cotton in her lap and worked it into yarn, which was twisted by the action of the spindle. She allowed it to wind onto the shaft above the whorl until the spindle was full.

The Miskito wove their cotton fabrics on a device found widely in both the Old World and the Americas—the *tension-type*, or *backstrap, loom*. They passed the base or *warp* threads around and between two beams and attached one beam to a house post about six feet above ground level and the other beam to a cord around the waist. This placed the work in a downward slope from the house post to the weaver's waist and made it possible for her to maintain tension on the warp threads by leaning back. There were no side members to the loom, so it was not a frame. With the proper tension on the warp threads she could insert the cross-threads, the *woof* threads, with her fingers. Undoubtedly, the weaver used *heddles*, sticks to which every other warp thread was attached, to alternate the two sets of warp threads so the woof threads could be inserted so they passed over one warp thread and under the next. They also must have used a *batten*, a wooden member for packing woof threads against one another as their work progressed.

The Miskito made their fish lines, nets, bowstrings, and similar items from silk-grass fiber. They scraped the sticky pulp from the fiber, washed it, and rolled it into cord between the hand and thigh. People in many parts of the world have used the hand and thigh technique for making cords.

The Miskito used machetes and the adze to carve three-legged wooden stools, walking sticks, or scepters, house posts, cradles, and various domestic utensils. They carved the stools from solid blocks and decorated the legs with elaborate carvings. The handle of the scepter, the insignium of political office, was a carved human head, and the house posts were richly elaborated with animal and human heads and geometric designs.

The Mosquito Coast provided considerable material for making baskets, but the Miskito did not make many. They made round baskets for storing small kitchen utensils, but they used carrying bags made of silk-grass fiber more than baskets. They used calabashes as containers a good deal and often engraved them with triangles, circles, zigzag lines, parallelograms, and other geometric figures. They learned from whites to make leather and used it for drumheads, sandals, belts, and the like.

The women made a number of ornaments from the small, colored, glass beads they obtained from the whites, red and yellow beads being their favorites. They used needle and white thread to prepare necklaces, bands for their wrists, ankles, and the legs just above the knee, as well as hatbands and watch fobs for men.

Dugout canoes were of major importance to the Miskito. They had two types, one for navigating the lagoons and the ocean and the other for the rivers. They made both types from large single lengths of tree trunk, shaping and hollowing them by charring them with fire and cutting the charred material away with an adze. They widened the canoes by filling them with water for several days and inserting a series of increasingly longer sticks until they got them the desired shape and width. Some of the ocean-going canoes, which had keels, were about five feet wide and forty feet long. The river dugouts, called *pitpans*, had thick, flat bottoms so they could withstand being pulled over rocks in the river. Each end of the pitpan ended in a flat platform a man could stand on. In shallow waters the boatmen poled their craft, and they used paddles for deeper water and as rudders. The Miskito used cotton sails and, later, sails of imported cloth to some extent. They also had light wooden rafts for descending rivers. The Miskito used their canoes for fishing, traveling to hunting spots, and for military and trading expeditions.

Women used a widely found device called the *tumpline* to carry back burdens. The tumpline is a cord or strap fastened to the burden and passed around the forehead.

Social Organization and Relationships

The Miskito had two types of families, one being the *matrilocal extended family* and the other an *independent nuclear family*. At the beginning of their marriage a couple took up residence in the bride's parents' household. The arrival of children extended the family beyond two generations, forming the three generation matrilocal extended family. If some of the woman's sisters and their husbands already had children, the newer couple's children would simply be an addition to an already existing third generation.

As the extended family grew the home became crowded, and second generation couples and their children would move out to establish separate nuclear family households. The Miskito practiced not only household matrilocal residence but, also, village matrilocal residence, which means the couple established the household in the village of the woman's parents. This continued relatively close relationships with the man's in-laws after the couple left the extended family household. Helms points out that this resulted in Miskito communities consisting of a core of related women (mothers, sisters, and daughters) and their families. She also notes that this is functionally congruent with the frequent absences of Miskito men for hunting and fishing, trading, and warfare (Helms 1971.25.) The group of related women provided for cultural continuity and stability through agricultural cooperation, child socialization, and other functions that make social life meaningful. It would be different in a patrilocal society, since the women would be unrelated and unlikely to relate to one another so effectively.

A few Miskito men had more than one wife, a practice known in anthropology as *polygyny*. In such cases each wife had her own hearth, where she prepared food for herself and her children. Often the wives were sisters, which many societies consider good on the grounds that the sis-

ters have already learned effective ways of interacting with one another. Jealousy can be a problem in polygynous families, and *sororal polygyny*, as anthropologists call it, can reduce the problem. Among the Miskito non-sororal polygyny resulted when an already married man took his just deceased brother's wife as his own, a custom known as the *levirate*.

The ties of the men to their communities and families were somewhat weaker than those of their wives, partly because they were away some of the time and partly because of the pull of their parents and sisters in the villages they grew up in. During the couple's time in the woman's parents' household a husband who became ill went to his parent's home to be treated. Sometimes the wife and in-laws of a lazy, cruel or otherwise deficient husband refused to take him back, and the marriage ended. Couples might also divorce by mutual consent. The children always remained with the mother. Actually, there is a large proportion of tribal societies in which the divorce rate is quite high.

Though the Miskito practiced matrilocal residence and there was some emphasis on the matrilineal line for inheritance and other purposes, they were *bilateral*, not *unilineal*. This means they considered the children to be related to others through both mother and father. Accordingly, they lacked the common ancestor groups that result from lineal descent reckoning.

Most societies consider barrenness to be the woman's fault, and so did the Miskito. Most Miskito husbands abandoned their wives if no children arrived. The Miskito used herbal preparations to prevent conception or bring about an abortion.

When a Miskito mother was about to give birth her husband built her a special hut just outside the village, and she and a female relative or friend stayed there for about two weeks. She was considered impure, and it was considered important that neither she nor her child be seen by the shaman. She was also under certain food taboos for both her own protection and that of the community. At birth one of the midwives cut the umbilical cord with a sharp bamboo or wood piece and tied it with a cotton thread. The woman who did this became a special friend to the child and his or her parents. This illustrates the widespread custom of *institutionalized friendship*, a kind of *fictive kinship*, in which non-kin enter into the kinds of intimate relationships that ordinarily obtain between blood relatives.

One of the women buried the afterbirth and the umbilical cord so animals would not eat it, which could make the baby ill or bring death. For several days the father stayed out of the bush, avoided hard work, and abstained from certain foods. This is a mild form of the *couvade*, which in some societies involves labor pains for the father and a period of complete rest and recovery. The Miskito considered the mother impure for another week or two. They did not bathe the baby until the third day of life.

The people practiced female infanticide to a certain extent, leaving the baby exposed to die. They preferred male babies. Formerly, they buried deformed children alive, and they also left twins in the bush to die. They held that both could not be the father's and regarded twins as evidence of the mother's unfaithfulness.

The women carried their children in a long cloth slung over the back with the ends tied across the breast. Parents were patient with their children and did not punish them much. Rarely, they beat them severely with a whip. Parents told their little ones all kinds of stories, but they seldom sang to them. Apparently, they did not wean their children until the next child came along, and the last child was not usually weaned until four years of age or older.

Miskito fathers took their boys on hunting and fishing journeys as soon as they were strong enough. They also made toy canoes and paddles and small bows and arrows for them to become familiar with. A girl learned by helping her mother in the home and going with her to the fields and when she fished with hooks.

Sometimes parents betrothed their children during infancy or within the first few years of life. In such cases a girl and her fiance married when she reached puberty. Until then, the boy would occasionally give her and her parents small presents and help them with their work. This is a form of marriage ratification anthropologists refer to as *bride service*. As noted before, the boy went to live in his parents-in-law's home. In most cases, after the girl's father had assured himself that his daughter's lover would be a satisfactory husband and son-in-law, he accepted payment of a cow or a gun (a *bride price*) from the boy's family and had the young man clear a field for his wife-to-be. After a simple ceremony the boy took up residence with his wife and in-laws.

The Miskito considered menstruating women impure and had them live in a special hut during their periods. They had to cleanse themselves before returning to the house.

The Miskito generally kept themselves very clean and took twice daily baths in the river. They did have some trouble with fleas in their houses, however, since the dogs and pigs entered freely.

According to the Miskito, diseases, accidents, and deaths resulted from evil spirits who were sent into the body or in some other way afflicted the victim. A *shaman* was called on to make the cure, and the measures he used to exorcise spirits included administration of herbal preparations. The shaman would diagnose the illness by going into trance, during which time he was in contact with spirits who revealed to him the cause of the sickness and how it could be stopped. He usually healed in the dark. He had the patient fast or avoid certain foods. He might tie a knotted cord around parts of the body and, for himself, abstain from food and sex. He would whistle over the patient, blow tobacco smoke over him, massage him, and suck on the afflicted body parts. He stuck four black sacred sticks in the ground around the sick person's bed to keep evil spirits away. He danced, sang, and talked to the spirits. If one set of ritual efforts failed he would try others. If the patient never got better or died the shaman usually ascribed the

failure to disobedience of food restrictions. If he successfully expelled the evil spirit and the patient got better he organized a feast, which the patient had to pay for.

In earlier times the Miskito would starve people thought about to die, assuming that there was no point in feeding them any more. When the person died his female relatives tried to injure themselves by knocking their heads against the house posts or trying to hang or drown themselves. Others always prevented them from succeeding. Then they cut off their hair. From death on the person's name was never to be mentioned in the presence of relatives. The people were afraid of spirits of the dead, which hovered near their former homes and might materialize if they heard their names.

The evening of a death the whole village had a feast, with plenty of alcoholic drinks and food served. For two weeks after a death, a little before daybreak and again for awhile before sunset, female relatives took turns, one at a time for about a half hour, lamenting the person's death. Each woman sat near the body with a cloth over her head and cried a song or dirge lamenting the death. She improvised the words. When she was done she dried her tears and went back to her usual activities, and another woman took her place. The men did not cry or mourn in this fashion, but they might break out in soft lamentations at times.

In earlier times the Miskito wrapped the dead in bark cloth, but later they dressed the body in the person's best clothing and placed it in a canoe cut in half, one half serving as the cover. They carried the body to the burial ground, not far from the village, and they used to bury all the person's personal property with the body to provide a livelihood in the next world. They also included a pine torch and a small canoe to help the dead get there. Eventually, they took to placing only useless items in the grave, the family keeping the rest of the property. They also killed a dog at burial time, since the dead person had to cross a river with the dog's help. They erected a small hut over the grave, and the women lit a fire there every day for a period and prepared food and drink for the dead person.

The spirit always wanted to hang around the house, so the shaman had to catch it and take it to the grave. Sometimes it took him more than one night to catch the soul. The journey to the next world was difficult, but it was worth it, since the hereafter was much better than this life. Only Miskito went there, since it was not open to Sumu or other tribes or foreigners.

About a year after a death the people held a festival of the dead. They prepared a special intoxicating beverage from sweet manioc. All of the villagers put on their best clothes for the occasion, arriving at about sundown on the first day. They continued feasting and drinking until all was gone, which took two or three days. They danced and sang to some extent, though these were not prominent elements of the feast. The young men played drums and flutes or flageolets, and two or three old men played on long bamboo flutes during the middle of the night. There was also additional mourning at the festival and a good deal of drunkenness.

Government and Social Order

Most scholars believe the aboriginal Miskito lacked the highly stratified societies and despotic political leaders characteristic of much of the pre-contact Circum-Caribbean, but the issue has not been fully resolved. Undoubtedly, the most important political unit was the village, most of which seem to have ranged from a hundred to five-hundred people. The village chief or headman was often chosen by an assembly of elderly men. Sometimes a chief's nephew or son-in-law succeeded him.

Scholars have been unable to agree on how powerful the chiefs were. Some think they usually were not especially powerful and functioned more or less like those in many other societies in settling disputes and otherwise providing rather democratic leadership. Others think their power was supreme (Kirchoff 1948:224). For at least a part of Miskito history a chief's office was signified by the scepter or walking stick he carried and a metal breastplate suspended from the neck.

From 1660 until 1894 the Miskito had an unbroken succession of 16 kings, most of whom were educated by the British and coronated by them in England, Jamaica, or Belize. These kings served as middlemen to facilitate trade between the British and the Indians and maintained order in Miskito society so the British could carry out their desired activities. They wore fancy uniforms and otherwise behaved in ways that appeared to outsiders as vain and ridiculous, and a number of writers have commented on how little real power they had over the Miskito.

Top scholars have long insisted that the kings were created entirely by the British and hold that there was no foundation for such an institution in the precontact culture. But anthropologists Philip Dennis and Michael Olien question this interpretation as the result of their recent ethnohistorical research. They found that one of the kings manifested impressive power to marshall a labor force of Miskito to build an English fort (Dennis and Olien 1984:727). Another king ordered a hanging for a man convicted in a Miskito court of murder and general miscreancy and made the sentence stick in spite of violent protests from the criminal's relatives. They also note that some observers commented on the despotic power of the Miskito kings. There is evidence that each Miskito village had a "king's house," which the king would stay in with his assistants and attendants in periodic visits to the villages. He would then hear and settle cases and resolve other community issues presented to him. When a king visited a community crowds of villagers turned out to see him and hear news about him and his family. The village chiefs often urged their people to obey the king and used his visit as an occasion to solve various local problems. In the 1800s, when the Spanish captured and spirited away an English trader, the king ordered the Spanish to release him or suffer Miskito attack on their settlements. The king appeared to have the power to order Miskito forces into the field against the Spanish. Finally, visitors with direct experience with the kings found

them intelligent, knowledgeable, and highly regarded by local Miskito.

In addition to ethnohistorical evidence of this sort from Miskito country Dennis and Olien have looked at the situation in other parts of Central America, particularly in Panama. Although the British did not create kings in Panama the Panamanian chiefs manifested characteristics parallel to those of the Miskito kings. Dennis and Olien suggest that Miskito kingship conformed to a pattern of leadership common to the societies of lower Central America. These include training for office by powerful, wise foreigners; control over a useful secret language (English or other European languages for the Miskito kings); facilitation of long-distance trade; and fine clothing and other material symbols of their knowledge and authority. If Dennis and Olien's allegations are correct it seems that the kings, though backed by the British, were accepted as legitimate by most of the Miskito and were so effective in promoting British interests because they conformed to already familiar cultural patterns. Since 1894 village government has again prevailed, with the chief officers being representatives of the Honduran or Nicaraguan national governments.

The Miskito were a warlike people. Miskito villages often attacked both settlements of neighboring tribes and Spanish places. The people admired and honored brave warriors. The Miskito may not have been more warlike than other tribes but perhaps could dominate them because their location enabled them to acquire European arms before those of places more remote from the coast. The Miskito participated in a number of military missions with the British and accompanied the buccaneers on their raids. Companies of Miskito warriors helped England put down several slave rebellions during the early 1700s.

Though they were warlike, the Miskito do not seem to have been a highly criminal people. They seemed somewhat aggressive and individualistic, but they respected authority and conformed reasonably well to the cultural standards. Both the chiefs and the local shamans exerted considerable influence toward order in Miskito communities.

Art and Play

The Miskito enjoyed telling and hearing stories. Many tribal groups have a large fund of much enjoyed stories, and the Miskito used them especially to fill the evening periods of darkness before time to sleep. Miskito men related at length and in great detail accounts of their fishing, hunting, military, and other adventures, and they also had a goodly fund of myths and legends. Many of these were tales about animals and birds that ate, drank, loved, hated, and died just like people (Conzemius 1932:169). Like stories and fables in societies around the world, these carried a lesson reflecting culturally approved behavior.

The people sang some, their songs seeming soft and plaintive to European observers. Apparently, they enjoyed instrumental music more than singing, though most of the instruments were used in ceremonies or for signaling. The mens' favorite instrument after contact was the common English drum. They made the drums themselves and used them on drinking occasions and to announce a feast to neighboring villages. They also had an upright drum, goblet-shaped and carved from a solid block of mahogany or cedar. It was about three feet high, and the head was a piece of animal skin stretched across the top. They beat this drum with their hands and used it only for their festival of the dead. The women made rattles by removing the pulp from a calabash tree fruit and introducing pebbles, seeds, or beans. The Miskito also had several kinds of flutes and flageolets, some of which they used only at the festival of the dead. The shamans used a six foot long bamboo flute. The Miskito had no panpipes. They used conch shells for trumpets, and, since contact, they have enjoyed playing the Jew's harp. Their only stringed instrument, played by the women, was the musical bow. The women placed the string against the mouth to get resonation and plucked it with a wooden pick. In some places the Miskito have used violins, guitars, accordions, and harmonicas, mostly of German manufacture.

Dancing appealed to the Miskito, though it was confined mostly to their festivals. Most of the highly merry dancing was introduced by Blacks and Creoles.

Apparently, most of the Miskito graphic and plastic arts consisted of the designs they engraved on calabashes; tatoo and body paint designs; the color and design of their beadwork; the figures they carved on their house posts; walking sticks, stools and the like; figures on their clothing; featherwork decorations; and similar work already mentioned in other contexts.

Religious Beliefs and Practices

All known cultures have included beliefs and practices concerning supernatural entities and phenomena. Many cultures also include a belief in a supreme deity, who is usually too remote and uninterested in human affairs for people to exhibit much interest in return. The Miskito believed in a supreme deity they called "Our Father," but he was too unconcerned with people for the Miskito to pay much attention to him. He created the world and lived in heaven. But he was neither dangerous nor beneficial, and they directed no ritual toward him. In fact, there was no way to get into contact with him. Similar attitudes toward supreme deities have been reported for many societies and from many parts of the world.

The Miskito also regarded the sun, moon, and stars as deities, especially the Pleiades, and also the rainbow, thunder, and wind. Many of these deities formerly lived on the earth as men, and some of them presided over departments of nature. The god of wind and air, for example, sent hurricanes and floods. The Miskito also believed in a large number of spirits, many of them evil. Some of them possessed animals, and many lived in conspicuous hills, trees, and

other plants and haunted various spots. Many mischievous spirits were thought to have been set free by the dissolution of dead human bodies, and they caused trouble until a shaman directed them to the hereafter (Conzemius 1932:128).

The Miskito held that many aspects of the natural world had specific owners or masters. Each plant and animal had one, including medicinal plants. Possessions, such as houses, fruit trees, and canoes, also had owners. It was incumbent on a Miskito to know who something belonged to and take whatever measures were necessary to acknowledge that ownership. A medicinal plant's owner, for example had to be paid money before the plant could be picked. Dennis and Olien suggest that the Miskito king represented the ultimate extension of the master-owner concept (Dennis and Olien 1084:731). This would illustrate how cultural elements in different aspects of life are interdependent, since the suggested linkage is between a religious and a political concept.

The shaman was most important to the Miskito. The word comes from Siberia, and anthropologists have used it on a cross-cultural scale because they have found basically similar religious personages to be important in most other cultures. A shaman has special power and knowledge to deal with supernatural persons such as spirits or gods. He or she uses those powers mainly for healing but also for a variety of other things. The fact that healing is usually the main shamanistic activity accounts for the widespread use of the term medicine-man for a shaman. Most Miskito villages, especially the larger ones, had one shaman.

The Miskito shaman not only healed, but he divined, made rain, conducted ceremonies, did magic, and served as teacher and counsellor. He was usually of above average intelligence, and village leaders consulted him about many matters. His power was the ability to communicate with and influence the spirits, both good and evil. He learned from the spirits what had made a person ill and used his power to heal. Shamans were to use their powers for good, but they could abuse them. In cases of abuse they were functioning as witches, since witchcraft includes the ability to do evil by drawing on the knowledge and power of spirits. The ability to change into animal form is a common characteristic of witches around the world, and some Miskito shamans could change into a snake or jaguar to harm someone. People sometimes called on a shaman to damage an enemy. The Miskito shamans had an unusually wide range of functions and abilities.

Shamans were picked for their office by the spiritual world, though sons, nephews, and sons-in-law tended to inherit the office. Whether they inherited it or not, they had to be trained. They fasted, held vigils, avoided sexual intercourse, etc. while a tutelary spirit of a person, animal, plant, hill, cloud, star, or something else, instructed them. This same spirit was to become his permanent guardian. During his career he had to go through repeated periods of self-denial to maintain and strengthen his powers.

The Miskito also had a high shaman, one at a time for the tribe as a whole. He was said to be a special representative of the thunder god or the god of the air. The high shaman received his powers while unconscious from a lightning strike. He could make prophecies and do other things that demonstrated his ability, and he was a much more powerful healer than the village shaman. The last true high shaman died around 1895. He designated a Moravian Christian as his successor, and the man reluctantly yielded to pagan pressure that he assume a high shaman's responsibilities. Though excluded from the Moravian Church, he attended services and performed his pagan duties half-heartedly.

The Moravian missionaries, who arrived in 1848, converted many of the Miskito, and by the 1980s Christianity had been the dominant religious system among the Miskito for over a hundred years.

Contact and Change

Like tribal cultures in every part of the world the Miskito have continued to change since the time Conzemius was with them, but we had no anthropological description of the changes until Mary Helms begain her work among them. The interior Río Coco village of Asang as she found it in the mid-1960s and Awastara, the coastal village where anthropologist Philip Dennis lived for ten months in 1978–79, exemplify the mid to late twentieth century Miskito. The Miskito of Asang formerly enjoyed greater opportunity for wage labor than they did in the 1960s. They could no longer work for the large fruit and lumber companies, since the 1960 fixing of the Río Coco as the border between Nicaragua and Honduras put those companies in Honduras, and many firms closed or significantly curtailed operations. When Helms was with them the people felt poor and were supporting themselves as best they could with slash-and-burn agriculture, hunting, fishing, gathering, craft production, raising domestic animals, and a small amount of wage labor. The main source of cash, though limited, was growing rice and beans.

The village, with a population of 665, is located on the Río Coco river bank on the Nicaraguan side. In the 1960s it consisted of ninety dwellings, a school, a commissary, and two churches. Some of the rectangular dwellings were made of bamboo and others of lumber, but all sat on posts, which raised the floor about four feet above the ground. They were furnished with a combination of manufactured and more traditional items—bark cloth and purchased cotton bedding, a few tables and stools, maybe a sewing machine, benches, wooden shelves, enameled dishes and cups, cans, boxes, bottles, calabashes, clay stoves or raised board boxes filled with clay to cook on, iron pots, machetes, stirrers for the traditional boiled banana and water beverage described earlier, and so on (Helms 1971:50).

Most of the villagers were related through at least one parent to the five sisters and two brothers of a family that settled in Asang about the time it was founded in 1910. Most of the rest were descendants of a second pioneer fam-

ily. Independent nuclear families prevailed, though sometimes more than one lived in the same dwelling. Matrilocal residence had become unimportant to these Miskito, and many younger couples took up residence either near the husband's parents or in locations removed from the households of both sets of parents. Young people tended to marry someone from their own village.

The people of Asang wanted as little as possible to do with Nicaraguans, and Nicaraguan officials looked down on the Miskito and regarded assignment to a Miskito town or village as almost like exile (Helms 1971:174). The Nicaraguan government had police stations in several of the Río Coco towns and villages and appointed a Miskito resident of each community as headman and government representative. He was required to keep records of all births, marriages, and deaths; provide for civil marriage ceremonies; maintain the public schools staffed by Spanish-speaking Nicaraguans; and instill a feeling of being part of Nicaragua. The Nicaraguans did not require the Miskito to serve in their armed forces and did not tax their land or property.

The Moravian Church was of fundamental importance in Asang. Some of the oldest residents remembered with pleasure some of the pagan festivals, but those were gone. Funeral and other life crisis occasions and holidays were observed basically as Christian occasions. The lay pastor and his assistants were politically important in their roles as settlers of disputes. Major announcements about village life were made in church, and it provided recreational opportunities through Young People's Association meetings, choir practices, and drama rehearsals (Helms 1971:191). In these and a number of other ways the Moravian Church provided village unity in ways typical of other Miskito places.

A series of troubles between the Miskito and the Nicaraguans followed the victory of the Sandinista movement in 1979. The Nicaraguans were still the Spanish to the Miskito, and the people still valued highly their relationships with Europeans and Americans. Miskito and English remained the main languages in the area. Also, the Sandinistas liked to de-emphasize ethnic differences in favor of the solidarity of the poor against those who exploited them, so they were not strongly oriented toward respecting and aiding Miskito nationalism. Moreover, Sandinista Marxist socialism was anathema to the Moravian and somewhat capitalistically oriented Miskito. Some of the Miskito, unrealistically, still hoped for a separate Mosquito Coast nation.

There are more complicating factors, the Miskito relationship with the Somoza dictatorship being one of them. Many of the Miskito were uncomfortable with some of Somoza's policies but admired him as a successful strongman. As noted before, the Miskito were not democratically oriented, and they have long admired a king or other leader with the charisma and aggressiveness to command a following and enforce his rule. Somoza used the Miskito in various ways to advance his own interests. Dennis believes he managed to recruit a large number of Miskito into his Guardia Nacional de Nicaragua, which was founded by the United States Marines in 1927 and, after the assassination of Sandino in 1934, became an effective personal army of the Somoza dynasty (Dennis 1981:291-2). Miskito service in the Guardia, he suggested, fits well the proud military tradition the Miskito had maintained since the days of the pirates, and they were quite willing to serve in a military unit that would be fighting against some of their traditional enemies—in this case, Somoza's Nicaraguan enemies.

After the Sandinistas took over Nicaragua they forced many Miskito communities to abandon their villages. They displaced many Miskito by burning their villages, and, reportedly, committed many atrocities. Large numbers of Miskito fled to Honduras, where they lived in refugee camps and, to some extent, cooperated with Contras and others trying to topple the Sandinista government. Within the Miskito Coast it seems clear, the material level of well-being

for the Miskito declined. Since the Miskito also had a reputation for committing atrocities against "Spaniards," including Nicaraguans in this century, it is not difficult to understand that many in the Sandinista forces would not be above a little revenge.

Scholars have been divided on the merits of different points of view concerning the Sandinista-Miskito situation, and it has been difficult to establish the facts. By the middle 1980s the Sandinista government was trying to establish better relationships with the Miskito, allowing them to reestablish a measure of the independence they had before, but much damage was already done. In the late 1980s the then current circumstances and probable future of the Miskito, both those that remained in the country and those who had fled, remained rather unclear.

Chapter 20

THE TAINO OF PUERTO RICO, HISPANIOLA, AND EASTERN CUBA

The cultural worlds of the American Indians have been disappearing since the Europeans reached American shores just before the turn of the sixteenth century, and one of the cultural types to disappear the soonest was that of the islands where Christopher Columbus first landed. Though the Taíno (approx. tah-EE-noh) culture impressed many observers as relatively sophisticated the people were unable to resist the ruthless treatment by the Spanish, and they were soon gone. Narrowly defined, they occupied the eastern portion of the island of Cuba, most of the large island of Hispaniola, where Haiti and the Dominican Republic are found now, and Puerto Rico. Latter twentieth century scholars held that evidence failed to justify distinguishing the Taíno from the Sub-Taíno, Lucayo, and other horticultural peoples of the Greater Antilles and the Bahamas, which means that essentially Taíno people were found through most of the Bahamas, Cuba, Hispaniola, and Puerto Rico. The Taíno may have been named that by outsiders after the Taíno word for noble or class (D. Taylor 1977:18)

The Taíno were Arawak-speaking townsmen and villagers who provided themselves a livelihood by producing the root crop known as manioc, corn, and several other crops; hunting iguanas, rodents and a few other forms; and fishing. The married women wore skirts of various lengths, while males and unmarried females wore nothing. Their houses were round with cone-shaped thatched roofs and were grouped irregularly in settlements ranging up to possibly 3,000 people. Their main crafts were the carving of stone, wood, bone, and shell, and they fashioned large and small dugout canoes, the larger ones being used for coastal and inter-island trade journeys.

Taíno villages were ruled by despotic chiefs and grouped into districts ruled by higher chiefs. Their society was stratified into classes, though the number is uncertain. The everyday religion largely involved a complex of relationships with spirits of nature and ancestors which resided in *fetishes*, most of which were carved of stone, wood and other materials. The shamans, who divined the causes of illness and cured people, and the chiefs, had especially powerful zemi spirits. The people enjoyed the many ceremonies of dancing and singing, the rubber ball games they played

on the courts that were located near the chief's houses, and several other sports. The Spanish viewed them as a generally peaceful people with gentle, amiable personalities, and they took note of their hospitality among themselves and to outsiders.

Prehistory

Archaeologists have learned less about the Greater Antilles (Cuba, Hispaniola, Puerto Rico and associated islands) than many other parts of the world. For a long time they had no evidence of human occupation on Hispaniola before 2000 B.C., but they now have a radiocarbon date of about 2500 B.C. for Lithic (stone) Age culture and assume that there may have been people there by as early as 5000 B.C. (Rouse and Allaire 1978:465). They are uncertain where they came from, but both Central and South American origins have been under consideration. Radiocarbon dates indicate that Puerto Rican peoples were making pottery by the first or second century B.C., and pottery came into Hispaniola about the same time. Non-agricultural Lithic peoples persisted in the Greater Antilles until Columbus arrived in the islands, these being the so-called Ciboney people of western Cuba and the narrow peninsula extending westward from the southwestern part of Hispaniola.

History

Christopher Columbus first contacted New World Indians in the Bahamas. From there he was guided by Bahaman Taíno (sometimes called Lucayo) to Cuba, following their 300 mile canoe route (Augier 1960:9). After failing to find evidence of sufficient wealth there he continued to the northern coast of Haiti, where he established the first American settlement of Europeans. An inexperienced tiller had allowed the Santa María to go aground on a sand bar, and the sea swells lifted it and dropped it on the bar until it was broken to pieces. The Spaniards had already found the Taíno Indians there peaceful, amiable, and hospitable, and the Indians helped them pick up the pieces from their great disaster. The people also had gold, which they had panned from streams, and they apparently were physically attractive to the Spaniards (Clarke 1952:309). The Indians willingly assisted Columbus and his men in building a fort from the timbers of the Santa María, and Columbus named it La Navidad (Nativity). He left 44 men at La Navidad, instructing them to search for gold while he was gone, and returned to Spain.

The following year seventeen ships carrying some 1500 men left Spain for La Navidad, but when they got there they found only broken tools and crockery and scraps of clothing. There is no way of knowing what happened. The Spaniards may have behaved abusively toward the people, who may have lost patience and killed them. Whatever happened, it set the stage for centuries of interaction between the Indians and people of European descent throughout the Americas, repeatedly marked by misunderstanding that led to ethnocide (cultural extinction) or genocide for many groups.

Soon after the trouble at La Navidad the Spaniards turned most of their attention to the American mainland, where they found the gold and large, wealthy cities they were searching for, but this did not save the island peoples from death and cultural destruction. Columbus founded a new community at a place he called Isabella, but the people were unable to discover much gold or other wealth, and the colonists failed to thrive in the new environment. As Columbus explored the islands, armed bands of disillusioned settlers prowled the area, troubling the Taíno and arousing hostility and active opposition. Columbus returned; organized a campaign against the Indians; sent five hundred of them to Spain as slaves; and imposed a tribute of food, gold dust, or spun or woven cotton every three months (Augier 1960:10). He returned to Spain again, leaving one of his brothers in charge. Discontent grew, the Spanish sent an emissary to right things, and he sent the Columbus brothers to Spain in chains. Though Columbus was soon freed he made only one more voyage and never recovered the position and honor he once enjoyed.

The Spanish appointed Nicolás de Ovando as Governor of the entire Indies, and he arrived in Hispaniola in 1502 with 2,500 colonists. But to prosper, the Spaniards needed labor, and a new royal policy sent to Ovando in 1503 provided it. It was the establishment of the *encomienda system*, which awarded a colonist land and the Indians on it to work for him. The colonist was to look after the Indians' general welfare and teach them Christianity. In 1514 the Spanish added the *repartimiento system*, which provided that citizens could be forced to work for wages on necessary government projects. This, too, was abused by the Spanish, and between the encomienda system and the repartimiento requirement the Indians were enslaved and nearly exterminated within fifty years.

There may have been two or three hundred thousand Taíno on Hispaniola in 1493, and, possibly, not more than 500 by 1548. The Spanish forced the people beyond their endurance. Their cattle destroyed the Indians' manioc crops, manioc being the Indian staple. Sometimes they tortured, imprisoned and killed them, and many died from smallpox and other European diseases. Investigators have established reasonably well that, under such conditions, people are both unable to meet their physical needs and become so demoralized that they lose the will and talent to survive.

Within a few years the Spanish also conquered Cuba and Puerto Rico, and they overran all of Taíno country within a couple of decades. Ponce de León made peaceful contact with the Taíno of Puerto Rico, but things soon degenerated for the same kinds of reasons as on Hispaniola. After the Indians of the Puerto Rican coastal plains were crushed, a number of groups apparently survived for an unknown time in the mountainous interior, but they eventually intermarried with Spaniards and lost their Indian lifeway. Though the Taíno culture is gone, Indian physical features can still be observed in portions of the population.

Ethnohistory

Specialists called anthropologists did not exist in the sixteenth century, so we rely on archaeology and ethnohistory for our knowledge of Taíno culture. Ethnohistory, as a specialty in the twentieth century disciplines of history and anthropology, studies the cultures of extinct societies that have existed during historical times by examining governmental, travel, missionary, and other reports written by individuals who observed or heard about the peoples whose cultures they wish to reconstruct. One of the most important ethnohistorical documents was written by Fray Ramón Pane, who was with Columbus when he returned from Spain to find La Navidad wiped out. Columbus, wanting to understand Taíno religion, ordered Pane to live among them and tell him about their beliefs (Arrom 1975:15). Modern anthropologists stress the importance of living with the groups whose cultures they are studying to obtain the most adequate picture of their lifeways, so Pane was conforming to one of the basic principles of modern data collection. His data should be of considerable value, provided he was a competent observer. He completed a manuscript on the Taíno about 1498, titled *Relación acerca de las antiguedades de los indios*. Columbus apparently took it back to Spain in 1500, where scholars judged it an important contribution. The famous Friar, Bartolomé de las Casas, who devoted so much effort to trying to get the Spanish to treat the Indians of the New World justly and who wrote so much about the Indian cultures of Middle America, abstracted portions of Pane's manuscript and included them in his *Apologetica historia de las Indias*. Moreover, the entire report was included in Fernando Colón's biography of Columbus, his *Vida del almirante don Cristóbal Colón*, which became available only when Alfonso de Ulloa translated it into Italian and had it published in Venice in 1571 (Arrom 1975:15). Historians and anthropologists have also drawn on the writings of several others who lived in Hispaniola

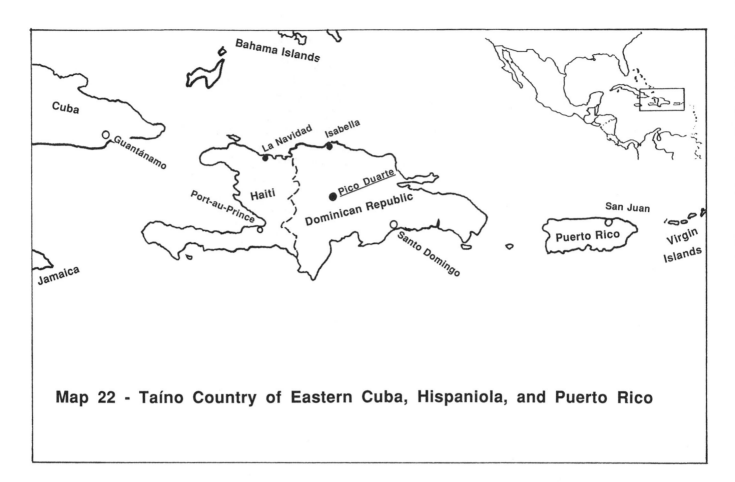

Map 22 - Taíno Country of Eastern Cuba, Hispaniola, and Puerto Rico

during early colonial times, but Pane's work, since he lived among the Taíno, seems to be the best source.

Relatively recent summaries available in English include Jesse W. Fewkes' work on Puerto Rico (1907), Roth's account of the Indians of Hispaniola, Lovén's book on the Taíno (1935), Stewart Culin's report on Cuban tribes (1902), and Irene Wright's history on early Cuba (1916). The most readily available summary of the culture of the Taíno of Hispaniola, which draws on the foregoing and other sources, is anthropologist Irving Rouse's work in the Handbook of South American Indians (1948). Another summary in English is a museum guide prepared by Julia Tavares (1978). Finally, during the 1980s Samuel M. Wilson did considerable ethnohistorical research on Taíno sociopolitical organization.

Late twentieth century scholars have been much impressed by Taíno art and religion and have been drawing on recently productive archaeological and ethnohistorical research to provide us with more information. José Juan Arrom's book on the mythology and art of the Taíno (1975) and Mela Pons Alegría's article on Taíno art (1980) are examples. Especially useful is a collection of articles on the Taíno prepared for a special edition of *Revista/Review Interamericana* by guest editor Ricardo Alegría (1978).

Taíno Country

Eastern Cuba, Hispaniola, and Puerto Rico, the regions of most highly developed Taíno culture, are basically simi-

lar to one another in topography, climate, and fauna and flora. All three include several mountain ranges, with large and small valleys interspersed and lowlands in the coastal regions. Climate and rainfall vary considerably with altitude and location. Tropical rain forests prevail in many places, whereas others are arid with cactus and various kinds of scrubby vegetation. Some of the lowlands are swampy. In Eastern Cuba two mountain ranges run east and west, with the large Guantánamo Valley between them and lowlands along the coasts. The mountains are low, as in the rest of Taíno country, and the highest peak in eastern Cuba reaches 6,476 feet. Most of the mountain country is considerably lower than this.

In Hispaniola a number of mountain ranges run in various directions, enclosing a large number of valleys of various sizes, many of them quite small. Again, the mountains are generally low, though Pico Duarte, the highest mountain of the Antilles, rises to 10,417 feet, and in one of the ranges a number of elevations reach eight or nine thousand feet above sea level. Some of the valleys are deep, and in places there are extensive swamplands.

Puerto Rico has fewer large valleys than eastern Cuba and Hispaniola, being a jumble of low mountains with many small valleys and relatively narrow coastal lowlands often broken by mountains.

Greater Antilles wildlife differs from that of the mainland in its lack of large animals and poisonous snakes. Birds and marine life are especially abundant, and there are many insects, rodents, and lizards. Iguanas are common, and there are crocodiles in some of the lowlands.

Language

As in other ways the Taíno belonged linguistically with the Indians of South America. Taíno speech is classified as Arawak. In one widely accepted system of classification, Arawak belongs to the Equatorial subfamily of the Andean-Equatorial family (Greenberg 1960:794). According to Loukotka, another classifier of South American languages, Arawak is a stock consisting of several languages spoken in the Islands and northern countries of south America. He lists five Arawak dialects, those of Hispaniola, Cuba, Puerto Rico, and the Bahamas. Since the people speaking these dialects were exterminated before linguistic science was fully developed no one has the complete information desirable for effective comparison and classification.

Personality and Behavior

Some descriptions of the Taíno depict them as savage and animal-like, but these reflect the stereotype that so-called primitives are always like that or, perhaps, encounters with Taíno who had become hostile because of Spanish greed, duplicity, and cruelty. Columbus and his associates found the Taíno friendly, trustworthy, cheerful, and hospitable, and this seems to be a more apt characterization of their orientation toward life. When the Spaniards indicated they wanted gold the people cheerfully gave them objects it had required years for them to obtain enough gold for. After the ocean swells pounded the Santa María to pieces on a sand bar the Taíno expressed great sympathy; made two large houses available to the Spanish, saying that they could have more if needed; and they supplied canoes and men to bring the contents of the wrecked ship to shore. Columbus testified that not even a needle disappeared during the process.

People can be quite gentle among themselves but vicious to enemies, and the Taíno may have been effective war-makers in their relationships with enemies. They seem to have been initially friendly to the Spanish, but when hostilities developed they were not up to resisting the Spanish effectively. At any rate they failed to survive Spanish abuse.

Clothing and Personal Appearance

Before puberty Taíno females normally went without clothing, but they began wearing a net over the genitals at that time. When they married they began to wear skirts or aprons of cotton, grass, or leaves. High ranking women apparently wore skirts extending to the ankles, while other women wore them shorter. Males of all ages, however, used no clothing.

Both sexes wore their hair in many tufts, with the areas between the tufts shaved. Both also painted their bodies for festivals and war. Red, white, black, and yellow were common, though the men, who painted themselves more often than women, favored red. The women preferred white. Sometimes Taíno used a combination of colors. Some painted figures of their *zemis*, or cemis, on their bodies, a zemi being a small idol in which a spirit resided. Some also tattooed themselves with zemi shapes. Another aspect of their physical appearance was their flattened foreheads, which they considered attractive. Apparently, the mothers held their hands against the forehead or used boards (Fewkes 1907:29). The Taíno also pierced the nasal septum and the ear lobes for pendant ornaments of stone, bone, shell, gold, and possibly silver. Many of the ornaments were shaped like zemis. Some, mainly high ranking persons, commonly wore necklaces of clay, shell, bone, stone, or gold. Various other ornaments were worn on special occasions such as dance ceremonies or war. Chiefs wore neck pendants of gold-copper alloy and apparently had gold crowns and feather headdresses. Their women wore wreaths of gold and turbans.

Houses and Other Structures

The basic Taíno house was round and polygonal with a steeply-pitched, cone-shaped roof. The builders set several posts of rot-resistant wood in a circle, each four or five paces from the next, as well as a center post several feet higher than the others. They fixed connecting beams between the tops of the posts and ran rafters from the beams to the top of the center post, where they lashed them together to form a peak. They bound cane stalks horizontally from rafter to rafter and thatched the roof with leaves, cane stalks, or other material. They formed the walls by running canes vertically from the cross beams at the top into the ground and lashing the canes against one another with fibers. The door was in one of the wall panels, and there were no windows. These were strong houses which resisted the severe Caribbean windstorms well, though they had to be rethatched every two or three years.

The chiefs lived in larger rectangular houses. These were built in basically the same way as the round houses, except that there was a tall pole at the center of each end of the rectangle of wall posts to support a ridge pole. The rafters ran from the ridge pole to the wall posts, and the builders caned and thatched the double-pitched roof in the same way they did cone-shaped roofs.

All of the houses had just one room, and the floors were of earth. For sleeping most of the Taíno suspended hammocks of cotton netting between house posts, though some of the chiefs had raised platform beds. The people hung household equipment from the roof and placed various kinds of gear along the walls. They had platforms on four posts for storing manioc bread and other food items, but we are not told whether these were in the dwellings, a structure of their own or, perhaps, in a chief's storehouse. The Taíno also kept one or more zemis (idols or fetishes) in each house. Many of the high ranking Taíno had carved stools of wood or stone in their houses.

The Taíno lived in villages that varied considerably in size, but Columbus said some had as many as 3,000 inhabitants and up to a thousand houses (Lovén 1935;336). They located their houses irregularly, and their villages usually had no streets, though there was at least one that had two streets intersecting to form a cross. Larger towns, at least, had a ball court in front of the chief's house, which also served as a plaza.

Livelihood

Basically, the Taíno obtained most of their food through agriculture, though they also took fish, small animals, birds, and wild plants. Their staple food was manioc or cassava (*yuca* in Spanish), the root plant from which we get tapioca. The men cleared and burned the fields, and the women planted, tended, and harvested the crops. In many places, especially on flatter land, they planted the manioc roots in mounds several feet across and a foot or two high (Lovén 1935:353). They prepared the mounds simply by throwing up the dirt with digging sticks, which had fire-hardened points. The digging stick is the most widespread of all agricultural implements around the world, and hardening the point by burning it is also common. The women of parts of Hispaniola prepared extensive plantations of mounds, and in a few places the fields were ditch irrigated. Lovén suggests that the mounds of loose earth, with ashes mixed in, retained moisture better than ordinary soil and mounding was the most effective way to prepare and maintain a loose, clod-free growing medium (Lovén 1935:357). On the mountainsides the Taíno did not use the mounds. Fewkes does not mention the use of mounds in Puerto Rico, which may reflect the relative scarcity of flatlands there. The Taíno of Hispaniola, and perhaps elsewhere, also fertilized the mounds with urine (Rouse 1948:522). The people grew two kinds of manioc, bitter and sweet. We find both types in Central and South America, also, and in general the bitter manioc was grown. The people had to remove the poison from the bitter manioc before using it.

The Taíno also planted a good deal of corn, though not in mounds. They always planted it on the hill and mountain slopes rather than flat areas. They cleared and burned their fields and used their digging sticks to make the holes a step apart for the seeds. A planter carried the kernels in a bag hanging from her neck, dropped four or five in each hole, and carefully pressed the soil over the kernels with her feet so the birds would not take it. They planted corn during the new moon, since they held that corn grew along with the moon. They also preferred to plant when the ground was damp from rain so that it was easy to make the holes and press the soil into them firmly. To further protect the corn from parrots and other birds, they had children keep watch on the fields from covered platforms in the trees or on scaffolds.

In addition to manioc and maize (Indian corn) the Taíno cultivated a number of other plants. They grew a good many sweet potatoes and, apparently, had several varieties (Fewkes 1907:51.) Other root plants cultivated by the Taíno include the age-root, *yahutia*, and the arrowroot (Lovén 1935:368). They also had beans and peanuts and cultivated and gathered several spices. The Taíno ate quite a variety of fruits, some of them planted in orchards near their houses and others wild. Wild roots gathered by the Taíno included varieties of arrowroot, peppers, and a kind of turnip.

The Taíno hunted iguana, a small rodent called the *hutia*, birds, and snakes. When they found an iguana they wanted they tormented it by imitating its call and stuffing something in its mouth when the irritated lizard opened it (Lovén 1935:437). To take the hutias they built large pens of poles standing upright next to one another and bound together with vines. To drive the animals into the pens they set fire to the vegetation in the appropriate places or drove them in at night with torches and dogs. The animals could be kept there until wanted for food. There are references to taking hutia and other game on the run by "beating them up," which presumably means that they clubbed them. Apparently, they used neither spears nor bows and arrows for hunting, though they used spears in war and knew of the bow and arrow.

Outsiders are often puzzled that people fail to apply knowledge readily at hand, but the failure is universal. It is common for people, whether individuals or groups, to fail to discern relationships and possibilities if they lack the predisposing orientations or frames of reference. The people of South Asia, for example, lined wells with stones fitted together by shaping them so that the inner side was shorter than the outer surface. In this they had the principle of the arch, but it did not occur to them to visualize the curves in their well walls in an upright position, and they did not use the arch for building. Similarly, the ancient Indians of Mexico had wheeled toys but did not make and use carts or other wheeled vehicles. In some cases people may be aware of alternatives but see insufficient merit to them to justify using them. If it occurred to a Taíno to hunt with spears he may have concluded that driving and penning game would be more productive, more enjoyable, or something else. Outsiders who conclude that people are stupid or overly conservative because they fail to apply what to them seems obvious are likely to have ethnocentrically misjudged the true situation.

In all cultures we can find evidence of considerable technological ingenuity. In fact, Euroamericans often lack the knowledge to survive in the habitats of culturally different societies. The Taíno, for example, were among the widely scattered groups who took water fowl by going under water and grabbing or snaring their legs. They would remove the seeds from a number of calabashes, stop the holes, and allow them to float about on a lake frequented by geese. When the geese had become accustomed to the calabashes a man would put a calabash with eyeholes in it over his head, wade into the lake, and get close enough to a goose to pull it under the water. Supposing it had dived, other geese would approach and get caught in the same fashion (Oviedo Vol 1,

p. 500–Lovén 436). Lovén's statement that this is a curious way to catch geese is ethnocentric, that is, it seems curious only from the points of view of European culture. Were the custom part of European culture, it would not seem so curious.

The Taíno also used pet birds as decoys. One writer told of how a ten or twelve year old child would climb into a tree with a parrot on his head. The hunters camouflaged themselves in leaves and did something to make the bird cry out. All the parrots in hearing would flock to the pet bird, and the child would snare some of them one by one with a noose, choke them, and throw them to the ground (Fewkes 1907:50). Taíno often clubbed birds they could get close enough to by one means or another, but they did not use the bow and arrow. Sometimes, for example, they chased flightless birds with their dogs until they tired and they could club them. The dogs were mute.

The people used a variety of fishing techniques—hook and line, stupefying them with the juice of the liana or other vines, harpooning, netting, catching them in baskets or stationary weirs, and shooting them with bows and multi-pointed fish arrows. Columbus saw the Indians of Cuba use the remora, a sucking fish, to take turtles. They attached a line to several remoras, which attached themselves to a turtle or a shark, after which the Indians could retrieve it (Lovén 1935:425). Apparently, the Taíno of Hispaniola did not use the bow and arrow for fish as much as the Lucayo of the Bahamas (also Taíno) and some other Indian groups. The fish arrows were used mainly for large fish. The Cuban Indians also would dive for shellfish.

It is clear that the Taíno had a variety of foods. They ate at least three times a day. They kept a *pepperpot*, a bowl in which they prepared and maintained a kind of stew consisting of a variety of items, both flesh and vegetable, on the fire continuously. The liquid base for the stew was a product of removing the poison from bitter manioc.

The Taíno scraped the manioc root's skin off with a piece of shell or stone and shredded the root on a grater. Commonly, this was a board with pieces of flint or other hard stone set in it, though the people apparently made some of their graters with sharp pieces of wood rather than stone. They removed the juice, and the poison with it, by squeezing the pulp in a large palm-fiber basketry or cotton tube. The walls of the tube would contract considerably when it was stretched. They made the tubes with loops in each end, suspended them by one end from branches, and placed stone weights in the lower loop to extend and constrict them. Another way of constricting a tube was to fasten one end of a pole to the ground and extend it through and beyond the lower loop. A woman then sat on the outer end of the pole to stretch and constrict the tube. They placed a container below the tube to catch the bitter liquid, then rendered it harmless by boiling it.

The liquid resulting from this process, in combination with the fruit of the *aji* plant, formed a mixture used in the pepperpot as a stabilizing base for adding all kinds of meat and vegetable items. Instead of having to consume perish-

able items before they spoiled, the Taíno simply added them to the pepperpot mixture. When they were ready to eat they only had to dip into the pot. The pots themselves were often fairly large boat-shaped containers.

After the juice was squeezed from the shreds the women took the remaining pulp, shaped it into a cake, and baked it on a disk-shaped clay griddle. The cakes were rather hard, and diners commonly dipped them into the pepperpot mixture to soften them for eating.

The Taíno harvested their corn green and used it mainly to make a soup. They also may have made it into loaves of corn bread. They used both corn and manioc to make beer. They prepared meat and fish both by boiling and roasting on a spit, and both, of course, were among the variety of items added to the pepperpot.

Crafts, Tools, and Techniques

The Taíno produced a good deal of pottery in a variety of shapes. They made many bowls—including the boat-shaped pots commonly used for the pepperpot, round shallow bowls, globe-shaped bowls, bottle-shaped vessels, platters, and disk-shaped griddles with low rims. In the absence of the pottery wheel pots can be shaped by applying the clay to a mold, hand-shaping it according to a model in one's mind, or coiling strips of clay. The Taíno made theirs by coiling. They incised designs on some of the pots before firing them in an open hearth, painted some of them, and left others unpainted. Some of them had faces shaped onto the surface or representations of bird, animal, or human heads attached. Sometimes a whole vessel would be shaped to represent a life form.

The Taíno had baskets for carrying salt and other food items, carrying offerings to zemis, storing small objects, etc.; but there is virtually no information on their techniques. They made a good deal of cord, using agave fibers, cotton, hemp, and a certain kind of grass. They apparently used the whorl-weighted spindle to spin cotton thread, but there is no evidence they had looms. They made women's clothing, hammocks, bags, and the tubes for squeezing manioc pulp, but all of these could have been made by basketry and netting techniques (Rouse 1948:527).

Most of the Taíno did not emphasize working in stone, wood, bone, or shell. But in view of their need for effective tools and utensils and the availability of the materials in their habitat it is not surprising that they produced some well-made objects of each material. They made and used ground and polished stone axes of various shapes, stone knives and chisels, pestles with the forms of animal or human heads on the ends of the handles, metates or flat surfaced grinding stones, mortars (bowl-like containers for pounding substances with the pestle), and bowls. They also had shell axes and wedges and picks made of shell or bone. Their digging sticks were made of wood, as were fire drills, paddles, ceremonial batons and stools, idols, and a variety of other items. The people of western Hispaniola were especially good at working wood, making fine stools and polished bowls. Zemis were made of stone, wood, bone, shell, or fired clay.

To obtain gold for their ornaments the Taíno panned it from streams or dug it from dry river beds or other deposits. They were unable to meet Spanish demands for large quantities of gold, since they were able to extract it only in small amounts. They did not know how to smelt gold ore but shaped their gold by hammering it on chunks of stone. They may have obtained their gold alloy ornaments from South American groups.

The Taíno made their most outstanding transportation device, the seagoing dugout canoe, from the single trunk of a cedar or cottonwood tree. They killed a tree by building a fire around the bottom and left it to season. After felling and trimming the tree they placed coals of fire on the log to char it and removed the charred wood with their axes. They continued this process until the log had been sufficiently hollowed. To widen the vessel they buried it in wet sand and wedged staves between the sides (Fewkes 1907:208). They then formed the bow and stern by inserting triangular pieces of wood in the open ends. The sides were built up further with sticks and reeds lashed together with fiber and pitched with gum to make the structure watertight. They painted the craft and ornamented it with carved figures. Their paddles were spade-shaped, each with a cross-bar on the handle. The largest seagoing dugouts held 50 to 80 persons (Roth 1887:280), and with the kinds of paddles they used and their paddling skill the canoes traveled faster than the racing rowboats the Spanish used (Lovén 1935:416). The Indians polished their paddles with sharkskin.

The Indians of the Antilles used small one or two man canoes on inland waters and bays, but they traveled along their coasts and from island to island in the large ones. Their longer journeys included trips between Cuba and Jamaica, Cuba and the Yucatán Peninsula, and through the Lesser Antilles to Trinidad and South America. The trip between Cuba and Jamaica was a nonstop voyage of over 110 miles. The voyagers took food and water with them and whatever they intended to use for bartering. The Indians of Hispaniola may have taken gold to Cuba and the Bahamas (or the Cubans and Bahamans may have gone to Hispaniola for gold). The Taíno of Gonave Island off the western coast of Hispaniola bartered their well-crafted items of wood for other things. Wooden bowls, stools, pottery, carved stone objects, gold, manioc, and pepper seem to have been the main things bartered (Rouse 1948:530). The people from different Taíno villages on the same island also traded extensively with one another, sometimes traveling along the coast by canoe and sometimes by land.

Social Organization and Relationships

There is a shortage of information about family and kin among the Taíno, though this is one of the most important aspects of the life of any society. We know little about who could marry whom. Siblings surely could not marry, nor could parents and children, since nearly all societies we have information for have held to the family incest taboo. Ancient Hawaiian and Egyptian and some other societies had brother-sister marriage within a royal family, but that is usually a permitted or required exception rather than the rule most people are expected to live by. We also are told that a Taíno man could not marry his sister's daughter. Beyond that there seem to be few data on how kinship and residence affect marriage rules.

There was a tendency for people of the same rank to marry one another, not just within a village but between politically distinct groups. Wilson's analysis of ethnohistorical sources has led him to conclude that the chiefly families of different Taíno groups were cementing alliances with one another through marriage, and this may include intermarriage between the elite of groups on Hispaniola and groups on Puerto Rico (Wilson n.d.:3)

The lack of data means we do not know all the kinds of families the Taíno had. The information from Pane in Las Casas' work indicates that a single house could contain 10-15 nuclear families (Lovén 1935:339). We also know that some of the houses contained several families, and we are told that those families were related. Apparently, at least some of the Taíno families were *avunculocal extended families*. Extended families consist of at least three generations—a senior married couple, a related junior couple, and the children of the younger man and wife. Avunculocal extended families result when a man's sister's son takes up residence with his uncle and aunt, bringing his bride with him into the family and producing children, thus forming a three generation unit. Some avunculocal families include unmarried children of the older couple and/or unmarried sister's sons. We do not know whether or not the Taíno had independent nuclear families or other kinds of three generation families.

We also know that at least some of the Taíno chiefs practiced *polygyny*; that is, they had more than one wife. One Puerto Rican chief is supposed to have had thirty wives. In some societies each wife with her children lives in a separate dwelling or apartment, but Taíno houses had only one room and all the nuclear families were in that room.

Anthropologists judge that the Taíno did not have clans, though they did practice matrilineal inheritance, that is, inheritance of political office and property through females.

Like other Circum-Caribbean societies the Taíno had a class system. The fact that the Spanish supplied so much information on Taíno classes and so little on their kinship arrangements illustrates again how our *ethnocentric* tendencies influence our observations. *Ethnocentrism* includes perceiving, interpreting (or misperceiving and misinterpreting), and evaluating the customs of other cultures in terms of our own. The Spanish themselves had a class system and, therefore, easily noticed Taíno classes and, also, interpreted them in terms of their own. Lovén remarked that when the Spaniards negotiated with Indians who directed any community activity, whatever it was, they saw a nobleman (Lovén

1935:498). Also, since the Spanish had most to do with the chiefs, they reported more about their lifeways than they did those of the common people.

Some have reported a four class system—chiefs, nobles, commoners, and slaves. The chiefs (which the Spanish called *caciques*) and their relatives comprised the upper class. The noble class, the *nitainos*, assisted the chiefs in leading the people and exercised certain judicial functions. The commoners did the village work—the farming, hunting, fishing, craft work, etc., and the slaves or *naborias* may have attended the chiefs and nobles. They may not have been true slaves, though the Spanish called them slaves. Scholars have only been able to determine that they existed, not just how one became a naboria or what the person's position might be in the society. Recent analysis by Samuel M. Wilson has led him to conclude that it is more accurate to view the Taíno as having two classes—the elite and commoners. This could indicate the Spanish, with their bias toward emphasizing class distinctions, saw more divisions than there actually were.

Apparently, the Spanish left no record of Taíno birth customs. The mother bathed her baby immediately after its birth. On Puerto Rico, and probably elsewhere, there was a naming ceremony for a chief's son immediately after his birth.

The Spanish noted that the people allowed premarital sexual intercourse. In fact, it was reported they looked with favor on a young women with wide sexual experience. Also, Taíno chiefs offered their wives and young women to the Spanish leaders, and there is evidence that a chief might offer his wife to another chief. In spite of these customs adultery was a serious offense.

The widespread story that the Spaniards introduced syphilis to Europe as the result of their sexual contacts with the Taíno, thus explaining the great outbreak of syphilis in Europe in the late sixteenth and early seventeenth centuries, does not fit the facts. It has been shown that syphilis was known in Europe long before 1492 (Clarke 1952:317).

There is only a little information on marriage arrangements. Among the chiefs, and probably among others, too, the husband's family made some kind of petition to the bride's family involving gifts. The groom's family also had to pay a bride price or, possibly only among the common people, the groom performed bride service to ratify the marriage (Fewkes 1907:48). It is almost impossible to generalize with certainty as to which islanders and which classes practiced the various customs mentioned. Scholars have noted that the Spanish reported more about the lifeways of the upper classes than they did about the commoners. Among chiefs the bride price is said to have been strings of stone beads and plates of gold-copper alloy. The bride price was paid in installments over a period of a month, during which the bride's family kept her secluded, allowing her to see only the young women that brought her food. At the end of the period the girl's hair was cut, the people feasted and danced, and the bride's father gave gifts to the groom. Apparently, only members of the bride and groom's own class

attended the ceremonies, and the male guests were allowed to have intercourse with the bride before the husband did (Lovén 1935:527). There were a few *berdaches*, men who dressed and behaved as women, in Taíno society, but specific information on their customs and social status is lacking.

The sources also offer relatively little information on sickness and death. Zemis apparently sent something foreign into the body if their owners did not care for them properly, and sorcerers might also send something into the body. The idea that intrusion of something foreign accounts for disease is one of the two most widely found theories of what is wrong with a sick person's body. The other is soul disturbance or loss. Curing techniques reflect these theories, and the main task of a Taíno shaman was to remove the foreign item from the body. Shamans by anthropological definition have special individual power to deal with the supernatural to do what they do, which is most often divining the causes of illness and healing the sick. A shaman commonly has a familiar spirit through which he can influence the supernatural world. Among the Taíno the shamans worked through the spirits in their images or zemis. A Taíno shaman called on to heal a sick person would first divine the cause of the sickness by taking snuff, a means of getting a vision from his zemis. He would then blacken his face and purify himself by taking an herb that caused vomiting, vomiting being a widely found ceremonial purification technique. After that the shaman would begin singing and shaking a rattle. He ran his hands down the patient's legs and seemed to be pulling something out of his body through his feet. Whatever it was, he took it to the door and blew it away, telling it to go to the mountain, the ocean, or somewhere else. Then he would suck on various parts of the body and soon began to cough and make faces and immediately took an object from his mouth. Sucking is one of the most used shamanistic techniques around the world, and it harmonizes well with the intrusion theory of sickness. If the object was a stone, the shaman might give it to his patient and tell him to keep it as a zemi (Fewkes 1907:63).

Many societies distinguish between diseases to be treated supernaturally and those that taking herbs can cure. Sometimes, however, the taking of an herbal infusion is considered to involve the supernaturals. Taíno shamans as well as some of the old women treated sickness with herbal preparations. Bathing and purgatives have also been mentioned.

The Taíno abandoned dying people. Sometimes the person was forced to leave the house; other times they placed a patient in a hammock between trees and left some food and drink. Sometimes on Hispaniola a dying person was strangled, either on the initiative of his relatives or by order of the chief (Lovén 1935:540). A dying chief, especially, was strangled. In some societies political leaders are killed if they become seriously ill because they in some sense embody the health of the society they govern and, for the good of their subjects, should not endure poor health. The reason the Taíno strangled their chiefs does not seem to be available.

If the sick person had been abandoned the relatives would collect and bury the bones later. If a person died at home they might burn the building with the corpse inside. The Taíno opened the body of their chief, dried it by a fire, and made it a zemi. Others might keep the heads of their dead relatives in baskets in the house for the same kind of reason. Some buried their dead in caves, leaving some bread and a gourd of water with them. Sometimes people were buried in underground graves, with the body flexed and bound with cotton. Lovén thought this was the most common disposal of corpses before the Spanish arrived. In Puerto Rico some people, apparently wealthy, were buried flexed in earth mounds (Fewkes 1907:83). The Taíno also had some cemeteries.

The souls of dead Hispaniolans went to a paradise in some remote valley on the island, where they feasted and danced and suffered no illness. They returned at night to obtain a kind of fruit they especially liked and to visit the living. The Taíno seemed to have considered the ghosts dangerous and moved about in groups at night to avoid them. Ghosts would sometimes rape people, so a woman would make sure her sexual partner had a navel before going further.

Government and Social Order

Each Taíno village was ruled by a chief, but the villages were also grouped into larger governmental units, each ruled by a higher chief. The Spanish also thought that Puerto Rico and Hispaniola each had a king or paramount chief. The Spanish described Hispaniola as made up of five Taíno provinces, each having a paramount chief, or cacique. They indicated that each province in turn was divided into districts, perhaps around 30, with the chiefs of each district under the province chief. There may have been 70 or 80 villages within each district.

One of a village chief's responsibilities was to organize the daily hunting, fishing, and farming activities. Chiefs also are said to have judged disputes among their subjects and imposed punishments for crimes. A third responsibility was to host people from other places and conduct relationships with other villages. A chief greeted visitors, presided over events staged in their honor, and represented the village in dealings with chiefs of other villages and with district and provincial chiefs. This could include leading the village in battle against another village. Fourth, the chief presided over the feasts and dances, including directing the singing. Finally, he was a religious leader. He had the most powerful zemis or idols, and the people considered him closer to the supernatural world and more knowledgeable in that area than his subjects.

Chiefs were supposed to have had absolute power over the villagers and the perquisites that go with that power. A chief apparently could order people put to death. The people always addressed him by five inherited titles; and he ate special food, lived in a special house, wore special clothing and ornaments, traveled on a litter carried by his subjects, and had the largest canoe.

The wearing of special attire, the display of fine possessions, and the other privileges of the chief constitute *rituals* reflecting Taíno sentiments about their leaders. We can define ritual as symbolic affirmation of values by means of culturally standardized utterances and actions. Anthropologists have noted that ritual behavior not only expresses people's sentiments but also reminds them of what they believe important and strengthens their commitment to their values. Politically, the ritual strengthen's the governmental system, so we can say that the ritual surrounding the Taíno chief strengthened his capacity to lead effectively.

In spite of his supposedly great power the chief met with his associates when confronted with major decisions such as war and peace. These meetings involved the taking of snuff, consulting the supernaturals, and, apparently, some voting.

In Hispaniola the office and all that went with it apparently went either to the chief's son or his sister's son. If no one else was available a female relative could become chief. Women also became chiefs on Puerto Rico, but we lack information on how they performed and people's attitudes toward them. If a chief had no surviving relative, the people chose the man they deemed most qualified.

The district and provincial chiefs apparently could requisition agricultural and military services through the chiefs below them, but scholars do not seem to have been able to determine their precise responsibilities and degree of power.

Scholars view human governmental systems as having two major functions, maintaining internal order and conducting relations with other governmental systems. The former includes the settling of disputes and the system of justice, and the latter embraces diplomacy and warfare.

There is little information on Taíno legal matters and social control, but several sources mention that thieves were punished severely, even by death. Adultery is another crime that seems to have been punished by death. The chiefs tried and sentenced criminals, and those of small villages may well have been in a good position to do so in view of their close interaction with their subjects.

The systems of relationships among the various Taíno chiefdoms is somewhat unclear, but Wilson's investigations suggest a high level of interaction among the rulers of Hispaniola and other Taíno areas. He identifies several channels of interaction—the exchange of prestige goods, the ball game, intermarriage of members of elite families, and warfare (Wilson, undated manuscript:2)

As previously mentioned, Taíno village chiefs represented the village in dealings with other villages, including serving as master of ceremonies when they received and entertained visitors. Such occasions were marked by the exchange of prestige gifts such as finely woven cotton textiles, feathers, elaborate ceramic objects, and finely carved wooden items (Wilson undated manuscript:1).

Wilson and others hold that competition between villages was manifested in the rubber ball game so important to the Taíno and that the game was an important aspect of Taíno diplomacy. Perhaps there is a parallel between Taíno ball games and twentieth century Olympic games in this respect, though careful analysis should proceed without making too much of the comparison. When teams from different villages opposed one another, the chiefs sometimes offered prizes, and they observed the contests from their carved wooden stools.

Wilson has suggested that the political organization of the Taíno was becoming more complex about the time the Spanish arrived, primarily through intermarriage of elite from different political units and the practice of political succession by sister's sons. The frequency of such intermarriage seems to have been so high that the ruling classes of different chieftainships were more closely related to one another than they were to the common classes of their own communities. This was accentuating the differentiation between elite and commoner, strengthening the class system considerably. One of the ways chieftainships combined with one another to form larger political units was through the intermarriage and succession systems. Due to intermarriage the sister of a chief might be the wife of the chief of another political unit, and it would be possible for her son to inherit both his father's chieftainship under the father-son succession practice and his mother's brother's chieftainship under the sister's son succession provision. Wilson cites evidence that this actually happened.

Occasionally, chiefs led their villages into warfare because of disputes over hunting or fishing rights, marriage arrangements, or a murder, but villages were usually at peace with one another. The chief led all the men of the village into battle. They fought with spears, javelins, clubs or digging sticks, and stones. They propelled their spears with a spear thrower, which consisted of a stick with a fish bone peg projecting from the top at one end and a loop of braided cotton at the other. They placed the end of the spear parallel with the stick and the base of the shaft against the bone peg and grasped the other end of the thrower with their fingers through the loop. When they threw the spear the device acted as an extension of the arm, giving greater distance and force. Spear throwers have been used in many parts of the world. Taíno painted their bodies red, hung small stone images of their zemis on their foreheads, and did a war dance before going into battle. In battle they relied heavily on ambush and surprise. They also had a victory dance.

Art and Play

Art consists of the exercise of skill to express and symbolize sentiments, whether it be painting, carving, bullfighting. story telling, dancing, gymnastics, or something else. Some artistic or expressive activities result in objects of art such as paintings and carved images, and some do not. The Taíno were highly skilled in producing the religious art objects known as zemis, carving them from stone, bone, shell, and wood. Careful examination of their zemis reveals their expertise in this area, and art and archaeology scholars have been much impressed with Taíno art (Pons Alegría 1980:8). Some of their ceramic work—the paintings and designs on their pots—was also artistically done, as were the pieces of gold jewelry they made. There are probably other aspects of Taíno expressive life that students can no longer appreciate because there is nothing left to examine, such as the designs painted on their bodies, the tattooed designs some of them made, and the melodies they sang. As cultures pass, much of the richness of human creativity is lost.

The Spanish records indicate that the Taíno combined dancing and singing in events of considerable importance. They held these events, known as *areitos* in Spanish, in connection with various other functions, such as the annual ceremony in honor of the chief's zemis, ball games, weddings, funerals, war, and receptions for honored visitors. At least some, perhaps many, of the areitos took place on the ball courts, and some were held in houses. A chief presided, beating a wooden gong. The people wore rattles and strings of shells that jingled with their movements, and they used maracas in some of their dances. Some of the girls used castanets in one of them. Usually men and women danced separately. In one type the people formed a circle with their arms around one anothers shoulders or waists, and in some instances they lined up opposite one another. As the chief went through the often vigorous dance movements, the people repeated them. Much of the dancing was highly dramatic, depicting things appropriate to the occasion. In war dances, for example, they dramatized the departure of the warriors, ambushes, the surprise of the enemy, combat, and the warriors' return (Fewkes 1907:64) The people sang as they danced, led by the chief. After he sang a passage, the people repeated it in a higher tone. The songs lasted three or four hours and dealt with topics such as zemi power, the exploits of the ancestors, love, and war.

The Taíno also got drunk during their areitos, and some took snuff. To prepare for a dance the people bathed, decorated themselves, and purified themselves by vomiting.

Apparently, the Taíno also had informal secular dances at times, which the chief did not lead and with no wooden gong beating. People also sang at times independently of dancing, the singing of the women as they scraped manioc roots being an example (Lovén 1935:523).

The Taíno enjoyed athletic contests, including races, wrestling matches, mock battles, and especially a rubber ball game. Their ball courts, located adjacent to a chief's house or, sometimes, on the outskirts of a village or town, were rectangular and lined with upright blocks of stone, and at least some of the courts seem to have been nearly 50 feet long. It seems that the teams were composed of up to 20 or 30 players, and they played from side to side rather than end to end. They were required to keep the ball, which was apparently soft and spongy, in the air without knocking it out of the prescribed playing area or touching it with their hands or feet. Whenever they failed, the ball went dead and the opposing team gained a point. Usually, men played men and women played women, though a team of young men and one of young women sometimes played one another. Sometimes, teams from different villages opposed each other, and we have already noted the diplomatic significance of the ball game. The chiefs sat on their carved stools while the rest of the spectators, presumably, sat on the stone blocks

The Taíno probably made snuff by grinding the seeds of the Piptadenia plant in mortars, though one observer thinks it was made from tobacco leaves (Rouse 1948:534n). At any rate they used it for religious reasons rather than taking it for recreational purposes. They made and used cigars, fashioned by wrapping a dried tobacco leaf in a corn husk. The Circum-Caribbean region, then is the part of the world where cigars originated. However, the Taíno used them in a way seldom if ever seen in Anglo-American places. They placed one end of the cigar in a nostril and inhaled. It seems that intoxication from beer took place only at festivals.

Religious Beliefs and Practices

Many Circum-Caribbean groups had large numbers of small fetishes, that is, objects indwelt by spirits, and the Taíno belief in the fetishes called zemis, or cemis, seems to have been a central part of their religion. The Taíno believed in many spirits, which occupied, trees, stones, and other objects of nature. They held that both nature spirits and spirits of the dead would, under various circumstances, take up residence in different kinds of objects, which were the zemis. The Taíno were interested in having zemis because this gave them control over the spirits that resided in them and brought them supernatural power. A shaman, of course, had zemi spirits that were especially powerful, and so did a chief.

Many kinds of objects could become zemis, but most of them were made by the Taíno for that purpose. They made them of wood, stone, shell, bone, fired clay, gold, cotton, or painted or incised designs. They kept them in their houses, caves, niches in walls, or carried them around with them. The zemis had names, and the people knew stories about how they came into being, the kinds of power they had, and their temperament. They put many of these stories to song. A Taíno liked to think that his or her zemis were superior to those of others.

The Taíno had a great variety of zemi shapes, but different classes are recognizable. Most of them were small, grotesquely shaped, humanoid figures, many with prominent male or female sexual characteristics.

A large number of them, especially from Puerto Rico, have been called "three pointers." They were small, somewhat elongated images with their bases slightly concave from front to back. On the top side, opposite the base, the back of the image came to a rounded point; the sides (viewed from the top) were slightly wider than the ends; and one end was carved as a head or face. To some people they might resemble large hunch-backed slugs with faces. Viewed from the front or from the side, they showed a somewhat triangular outline, but since they were commonly longer than they were wide the base of the triangle as viewed from the side might be much broader than that of the triangle as seen from the front.

Other zemis were simply cone-shaped, and many represented animal or vegetable forms such as frogs, birds, turtles, lizards, potatoes, manioc, and so on. As previously mentioned, bones of the dead might also be zemis, and petroglyphs and images of cotton could be zemis, too. A zemi's form reflected its history and nature. The people believed that one animal zemi would escape into the forest at night, a male zemi was sexually unfaithful, and other human zemis ate food offerings set before them.

The zemi spirits had various powers, such as helping women during childbirth, affecting the weather, improving hunting and fishing, bringing victory in war, foretelling the future, and so on. Three pointed stones were often related to manioc and had power to improve its yield. A person who wanted to draw on his zemi spirit's power placed snuff on its head and sniffed it through a forked tube. This caused visions through which the spirit revealed its will or gave information. Petitioners might fast for five days before approaching the zemi or purify themselves by vomiting. The Taíno induced vomiting either by taking a paste made from a certain herb or swallowing a portion of a curved stick made for that purpose. The vomiting sticks, sometimes called swallowing sticks, commonly had carved heads at the handle end. The Taíno also held an annual village ceremony for the chief's zemis—organized and led by the chief and conducted at the special hut where he kept his zemis. If a zemi's owner didn't give it food regularly it would make him or her sick. One way of feeding it was to rub it with manioc.

In their daily lives the Taíno seemed most concerned with their relationships with the zemis and, within that context, the divining and healing activities of the shaman. But they also had a variety of other supernaturals, even though some of them were matters of belief more than behavior.

They shared with a large number of other societies around the world the belief in a rather kindly but remote supreme being, a sky god (Arrom 1975:19). And, although there is no evidence that the Taíno were directly concerned with the sky god, linguistic analysis of the names for this being suggest connections with manioc. The three-pointed zemis were representative of manioc, and the Taíno buried them in the manioc mounds to increase the yield. This suggests the possibility that the Taíno regarded these zemis as lithic representations of the sky god (Arrom 1975:22). Full confirmation of this would have to come from careful observation by an anthropologist or other field investigator in direct contact with the Taíno, which is obviously not possible. Things of this kind are often *covert* aspects of a cul-

ture, that is, they are not easily discovered by outside observers. Moreover, for the Taíno themselves, this may well
have been a relatively *implicit* aspect of their belief, something that they themselves did not grasp clearly enough to
express effectively to others. This is the case with large
portions of all cultures. Conceivably, the Taíno could have
related to the three-pointed zemis only slightly conscious of
their connection with the sky god, which means that they
would say little or nothing about it. An investigator, therefore, could ascertain the matter only by careful conversational exploration or by making inferences from their behavior. Yet, for all anyone actually knows, if the zemis
were manifestations of the sky god the Taíno may have had
the connection clearly in mind and might have been able to
clarify the matter quickly for an inquiring anthropologist.

Taíno mythology also reveals belief in supernaturals
connected with the sun, rain, wind, the land of the dead,
dogs, and other phenomena, many or all being manifested
in one or more zemis. If someone were able to study living
Taíno religion more carefully than did the untrained Spanish missionaries, they might well have found that the zemi
religion was the concrete expression of a more abstract system of religious belief.

Culture Contact and Change

Since Spanish greed and misunderstanding soon erased
from the face of the earth groups that could be identified as
biologically or culturally Taíno, there is little to say about
the events of change. We can observe that change always
goes on, whether contact occurs or not. If the Spanish had
arrived fifty years later than they did Taino culture would
have been different, at least in small ways. If the political
and stratification systems were, in fact, becoming more
complex, the situation would have been different later. The
course of change in the Greater Antilles also provides food
for meditation about the capacity of human groups for troubling one another.

We can also observe that, though no purely Indian individuals remain and though no system of customs constituting a Taíno culture remain, Taíno biological and cultural
characteristics have probably influenced twentieth century
American cultures. In some of the rural areas, for example,
observers have noticed individuals with physical features
similar to those of Indians still living in Central and South
America. For an example from the cultural arena, it has
been suggested that the *bombas*, danced by rural Puerto
Rican blacks (descendants of slaves brought from Africa),
are associated with song words and music that incorporate
survivals of Taíno areito music (Fewkes 1907:69). If this
sort of thing is true, perhaps twentieth century life reflects
in little ways the richness of Taíno culture.

Chapter 21

THE KUNA OF THE SAN BLAS ISLANDS, PANAMA

Some of the world's small scale societies have developed reputations among the citizens of large modern nations, and the Kuna people of the San Blas Islands off the Atlantic Coast of Panama are among them. Outsiders have been especially interested in the colorful, intricately designed women's blouses they make, known as *molas*. They are also noted because of the unusually large number of albinos among them, which is probably one of the sources of rumors about so-called "white savages." Moreover, most outsiders who contact or learn about them find them rather colorful in several other ways.

When using the Kuna language among themselves, the twentieth century Kuna refer to themselves as *Tule* or *Tulemala*, but they have no objection to being called Kuna by outsiders (Howe, 1986). The terms Kuna or Cuna, of course, are firmly established in the literature of the outside world, but the San Blas people prefer that it be spelled with a *K*. Tule means person, people, or Indians as opposed to non-Indians, and Kuna as opposed to all other kinds of people. It is common around the world for societies to designate themselves by words that mean people. Almost as commonly, the names most known to outsiders are not used by the people for themselves.

The Kuna of 1940 lived on the islands closest to the shore. Their dwellings were rectangular houses with cane walls and double-pitched thatched roofs. They commuted daily to the mainland to work their fields, since the islands lacked suitable soil for agriculture. Using the slash-and-burn system they grew plantains, bananas, yams, manioc, sugar cane, corn, rice, and a number of other crops. Their main foods were iron pot stews and thick drinks made of plantains and other items. The women wore wrapped skirts, colorful reverse-appliqued blouses, headcloths, beaded wrist and ankle bands, gold nose rings, and earrings, while the men dressed in short shirts, trousers, and felt hats.

A household was a *matrilocal extended family* of three or four generations—basically, the oldest couple, their unmarried children, their married daughters with their husbands and children, and sometimes married granddaughters with their husbands and children. There were no lineages or clans. The main unit of government was the village, the village chief being the main official. The villages were divided into two confederacies in 1940, with a high chief over each.

The people strongly believed in countless evil spirits that had to be dealt with by chanting in several ceremonial contexts, including the healing activities of the shamans.

Prehistory

Though the Kuna were utilizing the resources of the San Blas Islands, no one lived there when the Spanish arrived. Humans, of course, had to pass through the Isthmus of Panama to get to South America from the north, and archaeological investigation shows that people were in Panama at least by 10,000 years ago (Haberland 1978:418). A lot of archaeology has yet to be done to obtain a clearer picture of what happened in Panama over the millennia and reveal who were the ancestors of the Kuna. One of the most productive archaeological efforts there is in the province of Coclé in western Panama, to the west of the Panama Canal and Kuna territory, and some have suggested that the ancestors of the Kuna lived in Coclé. Those most intimately familiar with the data during the late 1970s and early 1980s, however, rejected this connection, holding that twentieth century Kuna of eastern Panama are descendants of pre-Columbian peoples living in eastern Panama (Helms 1981:20). Since archaeologists have yet to accumulate enough data for a synthesis of the prehistory of eastern Panama, there is no point in reviewing the archaeology of that area here. It is worth noting, however, that pre-Columbian similarities to modern Kuna culture have been found. For example, a grave excavated in the Bayano region, just to the south of the San Blas Islands, shows that modern Kuna have burial practices identical to some of those of pre-Conquest peoples, and urn burials mentioned by the sixteenth century Spanish were found in pre-Columbian sites in Darién, the easternmost province of Panama (Linares 1977:79).

History

The culture of the twentieth century San Blas Kuna was the result of a series of realistic and productive responses to the coming of the Spanish. The Spanish wiped out the Taíno and others of the Greater Antilles, the people of Central Panama, and a number other American groups, but not the Kuna. The culture of the twentieth century Kuna is much different from that of their pre-Spanish ancestors, but over the centuries the San Blas Kuna and their forebears have adjusted to acculturation pressures by "rolling with the punches," so to speak, accepting much, rejecting much, retaining customs from their past, and making do quite well with changes forced on them.

The Spanish explorer Bastidas landed on the San Blas Coast of Panama in 1501. There, he reported, the men wore no more than penis covers of gold, which would be a far cry from the full costumes of today's Indians. The Spanish established the first colonies on the American mainland in the Gulf of Urabá region where the Caribbean coast of Panama joins the South American mainland (Nordenskiold 1938:2). In 1510 Balboa established the first successful mainland community, Santa María del Antigua, near the Tarena River just to the west of the Gulf of Urubá (Helms 1975:138). They abandoned Santa María in 1524 and made what is now Panama City the capital. The Indians there at the time treated the Spanish well at first, but the Spanish raided them for gold, took slaves, made them farm and build for them, and took them away to work in the mines. This established Indian hostility toward the Spanish, which eventually was directed toward the Panamanians as well. After the Spanish moved to the area of Panama City, they colonized the Pacific side, and Kuna migration toward the north and the San Blas Coast may have been a result. The Spanish also brought in black slaves, many of whom escaped over the years and lived near the Kuna. The Indians resented the blacks and did not intermarry with them until the twentieth century.

Early in the 1600s the Spanish sent a powerful expeditionary force to bring the Kuna under their control. But the Kuna repelled them, and for several decades the San Blas region was relatively free from heavy Spanish pressure. It was during the seventeenth century that Dampier and other English pirates associated with Kuna of the San Blas Coast. The Scots established a colony in Darién, the easternmost part of Panama, in 1698. It failed, and the people survived only with the help of the Kuna, after which the Spanish allowed them to return to Scotland. Then, at the end of the seventeenth century and the beginning of the eighteenth, largely Calvinist Frenchmen settled among the Kuna, marrying Kuna women and establishing families. Kuna sailed here and there around the world with the pirates, learning a few things about European cultures in the process.

In the early 1700s the Spanish again tried to bring the Kuna under their control, and when this failed they made a treaty with them, including the French. By that time many of the Kuna were able to use the French language.

The French also had participated in Kuna attacks on the Spanish. The Kuna killed all the French in 1757, however, possibly at the prompting of Englishmen who had provided them with arms. Toward the end of that century the Spanish occupied a portion of Kuna territory, but they were forced to leave in 1790.

During the 1800s American, English, and French engineers looking for a canal route came into contact with the Kuna, who were friendly but sometimes refused to let them cross their territory. Around 1850 the Kuna began to settle on the islands, and this continued over the next generations until most of the tribe had moved. Trade in coconuts and tortoise shell with American and other ships plying the San Blas Coast had become important by 1850, and for those purposes it was an advantage to live on the islands. The islands were also freer of insects and disease (Stout 1947:54). The Isthmus of Panama went to Colombia in 1826, but the Colombians failed to subjugate the Kuna. Kuna country came under the dominion of Panama when it declared its independence of Columbia in 1904. The Americans finished the canal in 1914.

In 1925 Kuna of one confederacy killed a number of the Panamanian policeman assigned to their villages and allowed other Panamanians to escape, and the Panamanians left the Kuna to themselves until 1930. An American explorer and adventurer assisted them with their rebellion, which significantly strengthened the already favorable Kuna attitude toward North Americans.

A significant number of Kuna traveled to other countries and even lived there, returning to exercise leadership and influence among the Panamanian Kuna. Since the late 1930s many tourists have visited the San Blas Islands.

The Spanish managed to provoke enduring hostility among the Kuna. The Indians survived the early abuses to enjoy the relatively positive contacts with English pirates, the Scots, and French colonists; and, later, the Americans and other Europeans at home and abroad. They drew to a limited degree on the cultural inventories of a number of societies—especially Spanish, African Black, English, Scottish, French, and American. The Kuna have not experienced the deculturation of so many tribal cultures but have repeatedly reformulated their lifeway over the centuries, retaining some pre-Columbian elements, and they continued to do so through the twentieth century.

Ethnography

In 1927 Erland Nordenskiöld of Sweden became the first cultural anthropologist to work among the San Blas Kuna. His countryman, Henry Wassén, spent several weeks among the Kuna in 1935 and compiled and published material brought to Sweden by a Kuna named Pérez Kantule as well as information sent by another Kuna by the name of Guillermo Hayans.

Between 1939 and 1941 David B. and Ruth Stout accumulated about five months of field time among the Kuna

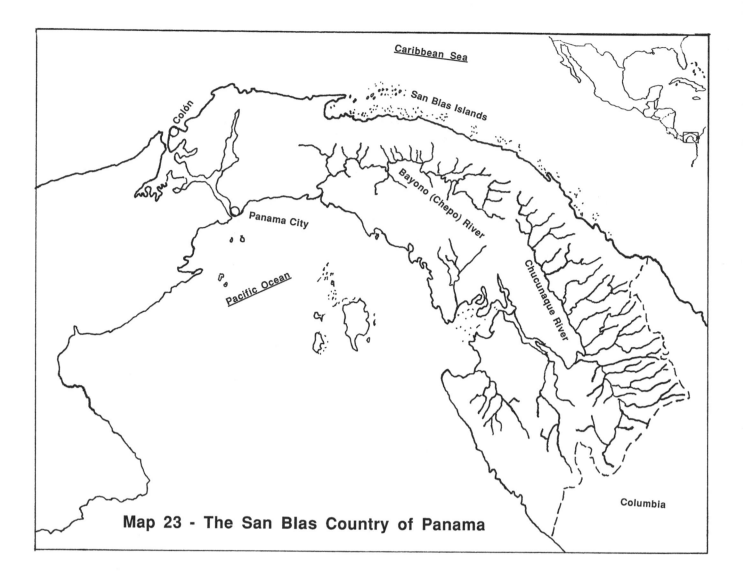

Map 23 - The San Blas Country of Panama

and compiled a report on the culture which has been widely used. Linguist Nils Holmer analyzed their language (1947), and Manuel Puig (1948) worked among them in the 1940s. Other anthropologists who have worked among the San Blas Cuna are Reina Torres and Manuel Reverte, both of who spent time there during the 1950s and 1960s, and Regina Holloman, who did research there in the late 1960s. Several scholars have studied among them since then, including Mac Chapin (1970, 1976, 1980 with Howe and Sherzer, 1983), Lawrence Hirschfeld (1976, 1977a, 1977b, 1981 with Howe), Regina Holloman (1969, 1975, 1976), James Howe (1974, 1976a,1976b, 1977, 1978, 1979, 1980 with Sherzer and Chapin, 1981 with Hirschfeld, 1982, in press), Sandra Smith McCosker (1974), Alexander Moore (1981, 1983), Cameron Nickels (1981), Mari Lyn Salvador (1975, 1978), Joel Sherzer (1974, 1976 with Dina Sherzer, 1979, 1980 with Howe and Chapin, 1983), Frances Stier (1982, 1983), and Reina Torres (1972, 1980).

Kuna Country

The San Blas archipelago is a string of about 375 islands distributed over a distance of some 150 miles along Panama's northern coast east of the Canal and lying from within a mile or so of the shore to around ten miles out. All of the islands except a few at the eastern end are formed of coral, and most of them are less than three feet above sea level at high tide. In 1940 the San Blas inhabited about 35 of the islands closest to shore, having their fields on the mainland. Much of the shoreline consists of salt marshes and mangrove areas covered with semi-aquatic vegetation. The elevation gradually rises to drier areas where palm, coconut, mango, avocado, balsa, mahogany and other trees grow. The fields are on the foothills above these forests, and the San Blas range rises beyond. Most of the higher elevations are less than 4,000 feet above sea level. A few Kuna lived along the coast, but most of the mainland people were found along the upper reaches of the two main rivers emptying into the Pacific, the Bayono, or Chepo, River and the Chucunaque River. There were also a few Kuna in Colombia.

The few inhabited San Blas islands in 1940 lay within a mile of the coast and near the mouth of a river, since all of them lack sweet water sources and soil suitable for farming. The islands closest to shore have mangroves on them, and the Kuna seldom visited them. Most of the rest of the islands have coconut groves, and about half have beaches.

A variety of wildlife inhabits the mainland, such as tapirs, agoutis, peccaries, iguanas, monkeys, several kinds of cats, deer, sloths, armadillos, anteaters, and other forms characteristic of South America. The sea contains tarpon, sharks, red snapper, sting rays, turtles, and many other kinds of fish, and alligators and crocodiles frequent the river mouths and coastal waters. Birds are abundant, and herons, brown pelicans, parrots, and parakeets are much in evidence. A number of life forms, including plants, are venomous. On the San Blas Islands, however, except for marine birds, many forms, both harmless and poisonous, are absent.

The rainy season begins around the end of April and continues until the end of December or early January, though there are variations in the amount of rain during that season. Apparently the annual rainfall is lighter in at least parts of the San Blas area than in other parts of Panama and the rainy season not so well defined. The humidity is generally high.

Language

Linguists have classified Kuna as belonging to the Chibchan family and the Macro-Chibchan stock.

A *phoneme* is a sound or class of similar alternative sounds. The alternative sounds of which many phonemes consist can be substituted for one another without changing the meaning of the utterance in which they are used. But if some sound outside the phoneme is used, it either changes or destroys the meaning of the utterance. The native speakers of a language are normally unaware that the phonemes they combine with one another to form words or parts of words that have meaning consist of alternative sounds. They automatically use the alternative that fits the sound environment in which the phoneme is used, or they use a range of similar sounds in the same speech contexts without realizing it. There are, for example, different *k* sounds in English, though most English speakers do not realize it. Sometimes we use an aspirated *k*, with a puff of air, and sometimes an unaspirated *k*, with little or no air. Which we use normally depends on the sound environment. If we say "skill" there is little air with the *k*, but if we use the word, "kill" there is marked aspiration involved. When the *s* sound precedes the *k* in English, there is little aspiration. If someone aspirates the *k* in "skill," "skim," "sky," or other such words, it sounds unusual but leaves the meaning intact. Both *k* sounds function as alternative sounds (*phones*) within the same phoneme or sound category. Of course, if the speaker switched to *t* instead of *k*, it would change the meaning, since the *t* sound belongs to a different phoneme.

The phonemes of Kuna include the vowels /i/ (ee), /e/ (like the second *a* in English vacation), /a/ (ah), /o/ (oh) and /u/ (oo). The consonants are represented by the symbols, /p/ ([b] or [p]), /t/ ([d] or [t]), /k/ ([g] or [k]), /kw/ ([gw] or [kw]), /s/ ([s] or [ch]), /m/, /n/, /l/, /r/, /w/, and /y/ (Sherzer 1983:36). The slashes enclose phonemes and brackets the component phones.

The differences between the sound systems of different cultures is nicely illustrated by the Kuna /p/ phoneme.

In the Kuna language it is possible to use either the voiced bilabial stop [b] or the voiceless bilabial stop [p] without changing a word's meaning. In other words. the sounds [b] and [p], which belong to different phonemes in English, belong the same phoneme in Kuna (Sherzer 1983:893). The alphabet prepared for the language of the Kuna uses a symbol for each phoneme, as indicated in the previous paragraph. When a Kuna reads a word with the letter *p* in it, he or she uses either the *b* or the *p* sound, whichever is appropriate at the moment in that context.

Kuna grammatical customs also differ from those of many other societies. We cannot use the space for an extensive description of them, so a couple of examples will suffice. The Kuna form many of their words, especially many of their verbs, by attaching a string of suffixes to the stem, which is also a word. The suffixes have a variety of meanings, such as "plural," "negative," "again," "want to", "sitting," and so on. One Kuna verb is *antaysasurmoka*, which means "I did not see either." It consists of five *morphemes*, a morpheme being the smallest unit of a language having a specific meaning. A morpheme can have just one phoneme in it, or it can be a combination of phonemes. In this Kuna word, the stem morpheme "too see" that is used in combination with affixes (prefixes or suffixes) is *tay*. *An* is a first person prefix morpheme. *Sa* is a suffix morpheme indicating the past. *Sur* is a suffix meaning "negative." And *moka* is a suffix meaning "also" (Sherzer 1983:40). Transliterated it would be "*I-see-past-not-also.*" This example illustrates for English-speakers how utterances that require a sentence in some languages require no more than a word in others and, also, that the sequence of meanings differs in various languages. The Kuna use the same sequence of meanings in sentences as they do in words. *Tule ome taysa*, ("The man saw the woman."), would be transliterated "Man woman saw."

Kuna culture of 1940 also differed from some others in the degree to which the people used different *phonological* (having to do with phones and phonemes) and grammatical customs for different situations. There were four kinds of Kuna speech, everyday Kuna, chiefly language, stick doll language, and *kantule* language. The chiefly language was used by chiefs in certain settings for certain topics. Stick doll language, named after figures with hats and long noses that represented tree spirits, was used in healing chants. And kantule language was used by the director of girls' puberty rites in addressing the spirit of the flute during puberty ceremonies. The vocabulary differences among these four varieties of Kuna were considerable, and a variety of prefixes and suffixes were added to distinguish them. For example, *mola* meant blouse in everyday Kuna, while in stick doll language the term was *uumola* and in kantule language *ilukkamola* (Sherzer 1983:27).

These fragments illustrate interdependence in cultural systems between linguistic customs and social and religious customs, and Sherzer has contributed a major analysis of such interdependence. Linguistic anthropologists call such analyses "the ethnography of speaking." In reference to the Kuna this is a description of how the Kuna said they used their language and how they actually used it in both ordinary and ritual situations (Sherzer 1983:11).

Personality and Behavior

Every culture includes a number of ideals, values, ways of viewing the world and experience, and reacting to life that are especially important to the people and enter into many aspects of life. Anthropologists have called these *cultural themes*, and Morris Opler, who coined the term, made the point that themes stimulate activity and control behavior (Opler 1945:198). Stout found in 1940 that the San Blas Kuna highly valued cooperation, sexual modesty, modesty concerning personal achievement, industriousness, wealth, and hospitality and generosity (Stout 1947:47). They expected every man to cooperate with others by helping build houses, helping his relatives in the fields, supporting village projects with work or money, and donating food and fuel for ceremonies. Kuna culture included very little provision for individuals to become wealthy at the expense of others. Even business enterprises were few. There were some storekeepers, and that was about all. Kuna concern with not injuring others seems consistent with their belief that they should be hospitable and generous.

The Kuna were said by some to be prudish about sex, but it is more accurate to say they were generally modest about bodily functions and sexual matters. Adults were careful to keep their genitals covered in public, and joking about sexual or excretory functions was limited. They avoided teaching their children and young people about sex and reproduction and prevented them from engaging in sexual play. They drew on a large supply of euphemisms to refer to birth, menstruation, and the like in their myth-telling and ceremonies. So they were more modest in this respect than many groups, but the matter is relative. Men often bathed naked in the open, keeping their genitals tucked between their legs, and women bared themselves to the waist when washing clothes. There were also certain contexts in which the Kuna would joke about sexual and excretory matters, though their public statements and behaviors often sounded quite puritanical to many outsiders.

A Kuna was also expected to be modest about his or her personal achievements, and bragging would lower one's position in the eyes of others. As in all societies, however, there were ways for Kuna to let their achievements be known to others without overt bragging. This modesty about achievement was combined with an emphasis on achievement through hard work and learning. They kept all avenues of achievement open to all men, including albinos, and for women to some extent also. They had very few inherited statuses, and even those who inherited status had to validate their positions by extensive study and training. Kuna interest in acquiring wealth functioned within these contexts.

Stout also lists a number of other major interests in Kuna life (Stout, 1947:896-7). They highly valued cleanliness, age, Kuna biological purity, individual freedom of movement, political democracy, property, and English-speaking whites. They also valued pleasant odors, and Howe mentions their sensitivity to both pleasant and unpleasant odors.

Clothing and Personal Appearance

In 1940 Kuna women wore two skirts, a short, solid-colored underskirt and a calf-length, wrapped skirt of figured dark blue cloth, held in place by rolling it around the waist (Stout 1947:20). They covered their upper bodies with the short-sleeved, richly appliqued blouses known as molas, which have greatly impressed tourists and students of textiles and which, consequently, have been widely studied and featured in magazine articles and books. On her head each woman wore a rectangular red cloth, which hung down to the shoulders in back. Nearly all the women wore tight wrist and ankle bands of small, colored glass beads, as well as gold rings in their noses. Many of the women colored their cheeks red with paint prepared from *achiote*, or *bixa*, fruit. and a few painted a black streak down the forehead and nose and a few dots on their cheeks (Stout 1947:69). They bobbed their hair and had bangs in front. They wore nothing on their feet. On special occasions a women wore gold ear pendants and a breast plate or beads. The Kuna put no clothing on girl babies until they were two years old, when they put them in molas and gold rings. Later they used the full adult costume. A small number of women on one of the islands, who had occasion to visit the outside world frequently or who were wives or daughters of highly westernized men, wore dresses.

Helms has compared the mola designs with those on pre-Columbian pottery and metal objects. On this basis she has suggested that the twentieth century designs reflect preferences for certain kinds of visual forms and styles which have endured in that region for many centuries (Helms 1981:2), though her allegation has been questioned. The molas had a rectangular, appliqued panel in front and one in back. Red and black were basic in most, with one color used as background and the figures outlined in another color. The women used yellow, orange, green, blue, and white in the figures, but not brown or grey (Sherzer and Sherzer 1976:34) The designs depicted elements of Kuna life, such as canoes, cooking pots, jungle animals or birds, and human figures. Western objects of all kinds, such as crosses, coat hangers, and American flags were also depicted. They also added geometric fill-in designs, including small squares, triangles, diamonds. spirals, circles, chevrons, and many others.

Kuna men wore trousers, often rolled up to the knee, and short shirts. They cut their hair in European style and wore felt hats, but they used nothing on their feet. Sometimes they would wear gold ear disks. Boys were nude until six to nine years of age, at which time they donned adult clothing.

The Kuna believed it important to keep clean. Everyone took a shower from a calabash bottle the first thing in the morning and bathed several times during the day as opportunity afforded. They built special enclosures used for bathing and other such things. The women bathed when they went to wash clothes in the rivers, and the men stopped to bathe on their way back from their fields. Children spent several hours wading or swimming each day.

Housing and Other Structures

The San Blas lived in rectangular structures from 25 to 50 feet long, 15 to 40 feet wide, and 12 to 15 feet high (Stout 1947:19). They made the walls of upright posts connected by beams at the top and panels of cane or palmwood slats. The double-pitched roof consisted of the ridge pole running from one end post to the other, rafters running from ridge pole to the beams along the tops of the walls, and a thatch of palm leaf sheaves. They lashed the framework together with split vines. Packed earth served as the floor. They made a door but no windows. They placed stools, benches, tables, wooden chests, and storage platforms against the walls and in the corners, leaving the central portion of the house bare. People slung their hammocks at various places in the open space and pulled them high during the day to get them out of the way. At night they used kerosene lamps and lanterns.

Most families also had a cook house, which was smaller than the main dwelling. Its main feature was a fireplace of radiating logs; and firefans, wooden tongs, calabash sieves and dippers, and cooking containers lay near by. The people kept water bottles, jugs, and cans in one corner and wood and corn husk fuel in another. They kept their dishes and other utensils on packing box shelves, wall pegs, or the floor.

Livelihood

The Kuna of 1940 tended coconut groves on the islands and grew the rest of their crops on the mainland. This, of course, was one of the main reasons they lived on islands close to shore, since they commuted daily between their homes and fields. They left before dawn, got to their fields about sunrise, and returned to the islands about noon. During that same time the women washed clothing in the river and got a new supply of fresh water.

Some people had fields two or three miles from the river banks or five or six miles from the ocean shore. Those with fields so far away sometimes stayed in temporary dwellings on their land several days at a time rather than commuting so far (Stout 1947:21). Each man usually had holdings in various places rather than together. Some of the villages had communally owned chicken farms on uninhab-

ited islands, and each man had to take his turn tending the chickens for several days at a time.

A man established a field in virgin forest by marking a path around the area he intended to clear. In some villages that was enough to preserve his claim, but in most it was necessary for him to clear and plant the land to establish permanent rights to it. Established fields had rows of straight trees along the boundaries or occasional trees with marks on them. The Panamanian government did not allow the Kuna to sell land to non-Kuna, but a field or coconut grove sometimes changed hands among Kuna. By 1940 some of the Kuna were less interested in agriculture than those of earlier generations.

Groups of male relatives or friends worked together in the fields. They cleared their fields during the dry season, using machetes, and when the rains were about to begin burned them in preparation for planting. They planted a variety of crops, plantains and bananas being the most important for food, and coconuts for cash. They also grew yams, sweet manioc, sweet potatoes, rice, corn, sugarcane, hot peppers, coffee, garlic, pumpkins and several more. In addition to their coconut palms they tended orange, lime, mango, papaya, cacao, and avocado trees.

They worked the ground with an iron dibble and used the machete for the various cutting tasks. The dibble was an iron implement about three feet long with a flat, spade-like point. Another important agricultural tool was a long, plier-like implement for opening coconut shells.

Men of all ages fished, though Stout noted that, during his time there, some of the young men were reluctant to fish. Young boys used seine nets in the shallow waters around the islands to obtain minnows for bait. The men would then fish with hook and line from any spot that was convenient and productive. Groups of men owned nets in common and occasionally fished in groups. Those who didn't participate in a given fishing project received somewhat smaller portions than the rest.

Groups of men also built weirs out from the shore and harpooned tarpon there. A weir consisted of stakes driven into the bottom in a horseshoe pattern, with a gate on the seaward side that could be closed after the tarpon had entered. The fisherman also built a catwalk so they could get to the gate without entering the water and from which they harpooned the trapped tarpon. The harpoons were of *chonta* palm, some being up to 18 feet long (Marshall 1950:106).

In shallow streams the Kuna formerly shot fish with the bow and arrow, using a single, iron wire point. For shooting fish in deeper waters they had a multi-pronged arrow. By the 1940s only boys were using bows and arrows to take fish. The Kuna also used drag and throw nets, a stunning narcotic, and their hands. Sometimes they fished from a canoe at night with palm leaf torches. Flounder, dorado, snapper, jacks, jewfish, lobsters, crawfish, and oysters and other molluscs were among the many other forms they took. They caught turtles by netting them and, also, by turning them upside down when they came ashore to lay their eggs.

The Kuna spent much less time hunting than farming and fishing, using shotguns to take peccaries, tapirs, agoutis, iguanas, squirrels, monkeys, deer, and birds. Groups of men took peccaries by surrounding and shooting them. The Kuna also constructed pitfalls for tapirs near their corn fields, fixed sharp stakes in the bottom, and covered the opening with leaves. This was the only trapping they did in 1940 (Stout 1947:22). They sometimes used their dogs for hunting. They used blowguns for hunting in earlier times, and, Howe notes, some individuals still owned one in 1970.

The Kuna raised pigs and chickens, occasionally killing a pig for food but selling most of both to traders. They ate eggs only on one ceremonial occasion and chicken only at funerals and the girls' puberty ceremony. Some families kept cats, dogs, birds, or monkeys as pets.

The basic foods of the Kuna included a fish stew incorporating coconut juice and oil squeezed from shredded coconut meat; green bananas and plantains; ground crops such as yams and manioc, and, occasionally, corn dumplings (Howe:personal communication). The Kuna usually removed the fish from the stew and ate them from a separate vessel or with the fingers, and the plantains and bananas were also pulled out and eaten with the fingers.

A widespread Circum-Caribbean trait of pre-Spanish times was the preparation and maintenance of an ongoing stew in a pot. Commonly, peppers were a significant element of these stews, and other meat and vegetable items were added as available. When people were ready to eat they could dip into this nutritious stew. Such a pepperpot stew has been reported for the San Blas Kuna of 1940 (e.g. Marshall 1950:148), but there was no such preparation by the early 1970s. The report of the pepperpot for the 1940s may have emerged from the fact that the Kuna prepared several kinds of stews, soups, and drinks, one special kind containing peppers. But by the time Howe studied among the Kuna during the 1970s peppers were nearly always prepared separately, frequently after being roasted in a fire. It seems doubtful, therefore, that the people maintained an ongoing pepperpot stew in the 1940s.

Drinks reported for the 1940 Kuna include one made of sugarcane juice, roasted corn meal, cacao, and water. Another was prepared from mashed bananas or plantains with cacao and water. People took these at breakfast and as snacks at other times and ate their main meal after returning from the fields at noon.

The Kuna also roasted bananas and plantains and ate them with a little boiled or smoked fish and, sometimes, some broth or hot sauce. Though they valued game meat highly, they had very little. They either smoked it or boiled it in the fish stew.

The men usually ate before the women and children. They sat on their personal wooden stools around a table covered with banana leaves, and the women placed the food they had prepared on the table. Each man ate from his individual bowl. After making sure the men were well served, the women fed themselves and the children.

The Kuna were fond of sweets. One of their concoctions was a loaf made of cornmeal, grated coconut, and sugar cane juice, baked on an open griddle. They also had "sugar plums" of corn meal and sugar cane juice, and they liked to drink sugar cane juice. They enjoyed coffee with an infusion of cocoa beans, as well as corn and plantain beer. The corn beer, known as *chicha*, was widely found in South America. In earlier times the women masticated the kernels of corn, spit the mixture into a gourd or pot, and allowed it to ferment. By 1940 very few Kuna chewed the corn for chicha, and the drink was nearly always consumed before it fermented much. The people used fermented chicha made mainly from sugar cane juice in puberty ceremonies.

The islanders traded with foreigners who came in schooners. They obtained iron pots, china, enamel ware, large clay beer pots, tools, fish line, hooks, shotguns and shells, cloth, hammock string, needles and thread, soap, salt, sugar, kerosene, tobacco, glass beads, and other things in return mainly for their coconuts, though they sometimes traded oranges and eggs. Several goldsmiths operated their own schooners, and the Kuna paid for the gold items with pigs. Each month small groups of mountain Kuna came to the eastern part of the San Blas coast to trade twine, rope, resins, red paint, cacao beans, rare woods, magic stones, medicinal items, and other products of their areas.

There were small stores on most of the inhabited islands, which got most of their stock from the trading boats. The people also went to Colón to obtain things and sold items from their own fields or from the fields of others who had surpluses. They took coconuts and eggs in payment and, also, sold them to the traders or in Colón.

Crafts, Tools, and Techniques

Kuna women wove hammocks on the vertical *roller loom*. Some were better weavers than others and made hammocks for sale. They also made the molas, using manufactured cloth, and some of the boys' and men's clothing. Sewing was a major craft that took a good deal of their time.

The men did the woodworking, making canoes and paddles, one piece stools, fish spears and harpoons, wooden fetishes, and other items. They also worked in groups to build the houses. Only the men made the baskets and firefans. Both men and women made the fired clay braziers used in funerals, though only the women made them in one community. The men also made the nets.

Most households had a mechanical corn mill and a large *mortar and pestle* of wood. A number also had stone *metates* (grinding stones) and *manos* (mullers), but the Kuna of 1940 made nothing of stone. Often two women used the wooden mortar at the same time, alternating strokes with their pole-like pestles.

Several households shared a sugar cane press. This consisted of an upright post with a hole just large enough for two heavy poles to be inserted through it, one atop the other. The bottom pole extended from the opening for a foot or so, while the top one extended several feet beyond the lower one. One woman stood on the long top pole near its end, using a light pole to balance herself, and bounced up and down as other women fed the sugarcane between the two poles (Parker and Neal 1977:109). They caught the juice in a wooden trough.

Kuna men fashioned calabashes into dippers, rattles, water bottles, and sieves. They used a *pump drill* to make the sieve holes. The pump drill had two cords attached to the top of the drill stick and twisted around it, with the other end of each cord secured to a horizontal crossbar. The bar was worked up and down to wind and unwind the cords and turn the drill. The owners of the calabash water bottles marked them so that, when one woman took bottles belonging to several people to get water for them, they would be returned to their proper owners. This apparently reflects the Kuna sense of property.

Kuna women carried most things in large baskets held on their backs by the *tumpline*, a strap around the forehead, while the men used *balance poles* across their shoulders. Some of the San Blas used narrow dugout canoes with platform ends for travel on the rivers and seagoing dugouts with sails for inter-island travel. They developed the twentieth century craft as the result of their nineteenth century move from the mainland to the islands.

Social Organization and Relationships

The San Blas Kuna were *matrilocal* in the sense that newly married couples took up residence with the bride's family. This created matrilocal *extended families*, that is, families of three or more generations consisting of the older pair, their daughters, the husbands of their married daughters, their daughters' children, and, perhaps, the husbands and children of their married granddaughters. This three or four generation unit was the basic kind of social group living under the same roof.

Some households were different, however, since, for example, a son-in-law with an especially large family in a crowded house might move out and establish a new household. Also, if one or both of the oldest pair died, the composition of the household would be changed in that respect and, in a number of cases, the unit divided into two or more smaller households. When households divided, a socially functioning unit consisting of two or more related households came into being. A household commonly included foster, step or illegitimate children in addition to the regular family members

When a groom joined his wife's household he came under the authority of the household head, who was usually his father-in-law but might be another older male. When he joined, the family might already include sons-in-law, all of whom had to obey the household head and who were ordered by age. Each evening the head told each of the other men what they would work at the following day. One might fish, another hunt, and others gather agricultural products; or all of them might cooperate to clear trees, plant, or harvest crops (Stout 1947:25). If they went ashore together in the same canoe the head sat in the stern and each of younger

men in order by age in front of him, the youngest in the bow. When they got to land they walked single file in the same order. The same arrangements applied to the women, the wife of the head being in authority. A man maintained a number of obligations to his father and returned to his father's house to work for him occasionally after having gotten the household head's permission.

If a household head became tyrannical or exploitive other Kuna would object, and the fathers of the sons-in-law would censure him. If a the father-in-law got too far out of hand a son-in-law might divorce his wife, and his services to the family would be lost without monetary or other compensation. Actually, men often quarreled with their in-laws and frequently divorced their wives. The children remained with their mother. Studies show that, in the United States, at least, marital disruption stresses people severely (Naroll 1983:51). Divorced North Americans are especially subject to mental disorder, death by automobile accidents, murder, alcoholism, and other misfortunes. For small scale societies like the Kuna the picture is unclear, but, in general, the divorce rate is higher than in modern North America. One study showed that divorce was easy to arrange in 74 percent of a sample of 117 small scale societies, while it was extremely difficult to bring about in eight percent (Minturn, Grosse, and Haider 1969:312). The ease and frequency of divorce in Kuna society, then, is in line with the situation in most other small-scale societies, but we do not know whether divorce stresses them more or less than modern North Americans.

Kuna households that were related to one another as a result of the divisions that took place would continue to cooperate with one another. The same kind of cooperation would be established when a man in one family married a woman in a nearby household. In either case men from the different households might cooperate in agricultural tasks, especially in clearing and burning. The women from the related houses often went for water together and used the same sugar cane press. They helped one another in preparing for and during ceremonies for girls. The related households also shared cemetery plots and helped one another keep them in repair.

Some societies have common ancestor groups such as *clans* or *lineages* that permeate their lives extensively. Other societies have common ancestor groups of minor importance or which function only in specific areas of life. A member of a *matrilineal descent group* only a few generations deep can trace his or her relationship to the common ancestor through just one person in each generation, always a woman. Members of *patrilineal descent groups* trace the relationship through one male in each generation. In still another type of descent group each member traces the relationship to the common ancestor through one person of either sex in each generation. That is, in some generations the connecting ancestor may be a male, in others a female. These are *ambilineal*, or *cognatic, descent groups*, and the Kuna appear to have developed such social units in the late nineteenth century as a way of controlling and profiting from their widely scattered coconut plantations. This came about because Kuna inheritance rules provided that land was inherited by dividing it equally among the children. Consequently, a coconut grove was owned jointly by a number of people, and many had an interest in several widely scattered groves. The joint owners rotated in harvesting the groves, each taking a month at a time, since the groves produced the year around. If children of the ambilineal descent group's founder were alive, each had his or her month at harvesting the grove. If any or all of these were dead, each of their children got a turn. And if any of the grandchildren were dead, the same rule applied to the next generation. Accordingly, there was a group of people with rights in the same coconut grove who possessed those rights by virtue of having descended from the same ancestor. These groups overlapped, so that many Kuna belonged to more than one ambilineal descent group. Their operation, however, was limited to coconut plantation ownership and exploitation (Howe 1976a:161).

In 1940 the Kuna addressed one another by both kinship terms and personal names for one another. A Kuna female referred to her parents and aunts and uncles by *lineal* terms, the same kinds of terms used by modern North Americans. She used special terms for her parents, and lumped her aunts together and her uncles together regardless of whether they were her mother's siblings or her father's. A man also used lineal terms for his parents, aunts and uncles.

For a Kuna's own generation things were a bit more complex, since they classified siblings and cousins of the opposite sex of the speaker differently from those of the same sex. A Kuna female referred to all her brothers and male cousins by just one term, but when she referred to her sisters and female cousins she distinguished her older sisters and female cousins from those younger than herself. To generalize in a different way, she included all cousins under the same terms as those for brothers and sisters, distinguished older from younger sisters, and failed to distinguish older brothers from younger brothers.

The men followed the same pattern in reverse, including female cousins under the same term they used for their sisters without distinguishing older sisters from younger sisters. They included male cousins under the terms they used for their brothers, and used terms separating older brothers or cousins from younger brothers or cousins. Anthropologists call terms that lump all cousins with brothers and sisters Hawaiian terms.

A person's status in his or her society consists of a set of rights and duties—a set of roles expected by other members of the society. Sex, age, albinism, and being born in a caul affected a Kuna's position in life. The Kuna of San Blas felt that men were a little more intelligent than women, and more occupations were open to them. Age determined one's rank in a household, and the elderly were respected for their experience unless they were dull or stupid (Stout 1947:31). However, the Kuna emphasized achievement rather than age as the primary basis for change of status during a person's lifetime.

Completely albino persons enjoyed special status. The Kuna believed that they were more intelligent than brown people and would occupy a better place in heaven. They held that they were special to God and especially free from sin. Only albino Kuna could scare off the demon who devoured the sun or moon during eclipses. However, the Indians did not allow the albinos to marry one another, though they could marry brown Kuna. They regarded them as poor workers because they were unable to see well in the daylight and sunburned very easily. Some families killed an albino at birth.

The highest ascribed status among the Kuna was that of *nele*, which was open to anyone born in a caul. If a parent did not want his child to become a nele, he could use certain medicine to neutralize the innate potential it was born with. Even if they did not eradicate the power the person had to go through a special course of learning and development to become a nele, the process concluding with a special eight day ceremony. In 1940 ten of the San Blas Kuna were neles (Stout 1947:32). They were theologians, disease diviners, seers, and unmatched in their ability to relate to the supernatural world.

For the most part Kuna women grew up to do what other Kuna women did—cook, wash clothes, fetch water, and care for children. A few gained reputations as especially good hammock weavers or seamstresses, but these were spare time activities at best. Sometimes a shaman's wife became a midwife, which would bring her limited remuneration. Also, a few women on each island specialized in cutting girls' hair for their puberty and coming-out ceremonies.

By contrast, male Kuna could occupy many statuses. They might become known as good hunters, fishermen, canoe-builders, or basketmakers. They could hold various political offices or become a shaman, a mass healer, a ceremonial chanter, a grave digger and pall bearer, a marriage-maker, a chanter's assistant, and more. In many societies with matrilocal extended families the women enjoy considerable power, but not among the Kuna. Kuna daughters did inherit property, just as much as the sons, and enjoyed income from their coconut plantations. But the men often delayed the women's marriages, they were allowed little personal freedom before marriage, they did not participate in government, and they enjoyed very few opportunities to vary their lifestyles.

Anthropological restudy of the Kuna has not been able to confirm Stout's conclusion that Kuna were divided into two relatively weak social classes (Howe 1986:28). As in all societies there were prestige and wealth differences, but not the ranked categories social scientists refer to as social classes. Some Kuna were more wealthy than others in coconut groves, large canoes, fine clothing, and jewelry and cash. Some of them were generally less responsible than others and failed to conform very well to the society's moral standards, but these kinds of differences were individual and family matters rather than forming a basis for class distinctions.

Kuna women gave birth in special temporary huts from which men and children were excluded. A midwife attended the mother, while a shaman chanted outside and provided the various medicines as she needed them. The baby was born into a canoe full of water placed beneath the mother's hammock, a hole in the hammock having been made for this purpose. The midwife retrieved the baby and removed its umbilical cord and buried the cord beneath the house floor.

The *couvade* is strong in several South American societies, but the notion that a woman's pregnancy and parturition affects her husband is detectable in many cultures. In a full couvade the husband takes to his bed, experiences birth pains, and has to recover from childbirth. With the mild couvade of the Kuna the husband remained in his house for three days after his child was born.

The Kuna kept their infants in hammocks and sometimes carried them astride the hip. They gave them a good deal of attention; and older brothers and sisters, grandmothers, and sometimes aunts got into the act. The little one was normally born into an extended family, and anthropological studies are showing that extended family life has quite different effects on children than independent nuclear family life. Rohner, for example, has found that parents are warmer toward their children when mothers get child care help from other adults in the home (Rohner 1975), and this is what happened in Kuna families. The Kuna not only wanted children, they were very affectionate toward them, seldom punished them physically, and trained them to respond quickly to verbal discipline. Rohner's studies also suggest that children who are treated coldly in the family tend to think less of themselves all their lives, are more dependent on others and, yet, more hostile toward others.

During an infant girl's first year the Kuna pierced her nose and ears. They weaned their children when the next child was born, and a child might nurse for up to six years. Kuna boys played with small canoes, bows and arrows, and fish spears, and sometimes balls. The adults gave small boys the responsibility of catching bait minnows, and they soon learned to swim and to handle their canoes expertly. They were free to roam the whole island and its waters. By contrast, the Kuna kept their girls close to the house, where they took care of younger brothers and sisters. They rocked the hammock-cradle, sang improvised lullabies to the infant, and amused it by shaking calabash rattles. Some of the islands had schools, which emphasized speaking, reading, and writing Spanish. Attendance was voluntary at private English schools and compulsory at government schools.

There were no puberty ceremonies for boys, but the Kuna had ceremonies for girls at their first menstruation. The ceremony leaders and as many of the village men who would volunteer built a special enclosure. The Kuna confined the girl to this enclosure for four days, where her female friends and relatives frequently poured large quantities of both sea and fresh water over her head and shoulders. On the fourth day a female ceremonial hair-cutter bobbed her hair and made bangs. After that she was painted

black with *Genipa* fruit and freed. The fruit was gathered by a special male who knew the proper chants. While the girl was being doused two men dug up a male and female land crab on the mainland to foretell the girl's future. If they had to dig deep to find the crabs, they predicted she would experience hard labor with her first child. If the crabs fought vigorously it meant she and her husband would quarrel a lot. And which crab died first indicated whether she or her husband would die first (Stout 1947:35).

While these things were going on the chicha brewer and his pupils made the beer from sugar cane juice and corn or bananas and plantains. It took about ten days to ferment, and they resumed the ceremony when it was ready. The ceremonial leaders conducted a day long ceremony of drinking chicha and smoking long ceremonial cigars. At the end of the day, the girl served chicha to her male relatives, the ceremonial leaders, and all the men who helped build her enclosure. Then she served her female relatives, the haircutter, and the women who doused her. That night there was a public dance, during which the chanters and their pupils played flageolets and sang songs about the origin of the puberty ceremony.

Before a Kuna girl could marry she had to undergo a second ceremony, usually from one to five years after the puberty ceremony. This was an expensive four day ceremony for which the family had to accumulate what they needed for months ahead of time. The whole village helped by contributing fuel wood, sugar cane, and bananas. The chicha brewer and his assistants made chicha, and when it was fermented the ceremony could begin. The ceremony was complex and directed throughout by the chanter. It involved the confinement of the girl in an enclosure; chicha drinking; smoking long cigars; making rattles; preparing materials for flageolets; painting balsa wood planks and hanging them in the ceremony house; applying red paint to the faces, palms and soles of all present; making special ropes for the ceremonial hammocks; an imitative agouti dance; removal of all the girl's hair; constant burning of cacao beans to keep evil spirits away; and, finally, a public dance. Though eligible from this time on some girls remained unmarried for several years more.

The Kuna considered males adults as soon as they were able to work on the mainland for a full day without supervision. Boys usually achieved this between the ages of fifteen and seventeen, though they usually did not marry until several years later.

The Kuna manifested modesty concerning sex, as noted before, and tried to keep their children ignorant of sexual things until they were married. Young people talked about sexual matters, so they were not entirely ignorant of them, but many young persons had no premarital sexual experience. Young Kuna women were often quite embarrassed for some time after marriage and stayed in their homes as much as possible. The Kuna used euphemisms for menstruation or birth in their myths and chants. They felt most of their medicines and ceremonies would not be effective unless they were preceded with a chant telling of the copulation of

God with his wife, but they avoided chanting it aloud. Instead they went through it in thought or chanted in such a low voice that people could not grasp the content. The Kuna tended to confine sexual relations to nighttime, though, in more recent times at least, there was some daytime copulation. They also tabooed sexual relations during pregnancy and menstruation.

Kuna parents arranged the marriages of their children. When two fathers had come to an agreement they notified the marriage-maker, who chose several people to help him get the man and carry him to the girl's house. The whole thing was supposed to be a surprise to both bride and groom. They put the man in a hammock and the girl on top of him. After a few minutes, they both went to bathe. The couple was put in the hammock several times, and the fifth time they stayed in the hammock all night. They were not to sleep or engage in sexual relations, however. The next morning the young man sealed the marriage by making a trip to the mainland for firewood. Sometimes a young man would run away and would have to be brought back, though he might be allowed to forego the marriage if he went to another village and did not return for several weeks. In societies where matrilocal extended families are strong marriage may be hard on the young men, since they have to conform to the will of the wife's father and other members of the family. The same tends to be true for brides in patrilocal extended families, since they must adjust to leaving their parents and living under the husband's mother and daughters-in-law already there. There is some indication that suicide rates are higher in societies where marriages are arranged by people other than the bridal couple themselves (Naroll 1983:328), though Howe reports that suicides were uncommon in San Blas. He notes that a San Blas man's parents were actually nearby and that men visited, took meals with, and worked with their own parents some. This reduced much of the tension between a man and his in-laws (Howe: personal communication).

According to the Kuna most illness and death was the result of one's soul being stolen by an evil spirit (Stout 1947:42). They felt that a few diseases, including malaria and diarrhea, were not due to soul theft, but they still assumed that evil spirits caused them. To recover a stolen soul a shaman secured the help of a spirit of a carved wooden fetish. He held it in his hands and addressed it in a chant, telling it where to go to find the soul and bring it back. The spirit would then leave on a journey to the fourth layer of the underworld, argue the chiefs of the evil spirits into giving up the soul, and return with it.

When an entire village was suffering from a disease a mass healer took over. Assisted by his pupils, he conducted chants for eight nights, with assistants smoking long cigars and burning cacao beans in braziers to repel evil spirits. He called on the spirits of a large number of carved balsa wood fetishes to help him track down the evil spirits causing the trouble.

At death the Kuna washed the body with warm water and dressed it in the person's best clothing. They left the corpse in a hammock with a sheet over it while close relatives mourned for a full day and night. The mourners chanted the story of the dead person's life and character and the rewards and punishments awaiting the person in the underworld he or she had to pass through on the way to heaven. Sometimes they employed a death chanter to describe the soul's journey. The second morning two gravedigger-pallbearers tied up the hammock and carried it on a pole to the funeral canoe, and the closest relatives rode in the canoe with the body. The gravediggers prepared the grave at the cemetery during the day, while the relatives continued to mourn by the suspended hammock. About nightfall they suspended the hammock on two stakes in the grave, covered it with staves and leaves, and filled it in with dirt. They buried personal possessions and models of various objects with the body and placed broken furniture and other objects on the grave. Some were for the person to use in the next world, and others were gifts to relatives who died earlier. The objects were broken so they would not be stolen. After the mourners left, the gravediggers attached a string to one of the staves, strung it across the river, and fastened it on the other side. The first person going up or down the river in a canoe was to cut the string, and the dead person's soul would travel to heaven along the spirit of the string. They also placed a small model of canoe with paddles in the water at the river's edge. The souls of good persons went directly to heaven, while those of the bad were punished in the fourth layer of the underworld before going on to heaven.

Government and Social Order

Kuna tribal government, if it could be called that, was quite weak in 1940. There were confederacies during the early decades of the twentieth century, but the chiefs who headed them were unable to overcome the strong village autonomy that characterized Kuna political organization. The village chiefs selected confederacy chiefs from among their own number. They elected them for lifetime terms, but they remained village chiefs also. As high chiefs, they led delegations to Panamanian officials on matters of tribal concern, presided at tribal congresses of delegates from each island, confirmed the results of village elections, and had veto powers over them.

The Kuna exercised their main governmental functions at the village level. They elected village chiefs and other officials, who held office until they were either too old to continue or were asked to resign. They filled the village offices or made other community decisions at two kinds of public gatherings. One was a *talking meeting*, only the men attending, and the other was a *singing meeting* that included the women. The Kuna had these meetings several times a week, holding them either in a large house or a special building. At a talking meeting the officials and male citizens in attendance discussed whatever was brought before them. At a singing meeting the village chief delivered allegorical chants in the chiefly language, and interpreters repeated his songs in everyday Kuna so the people would understand. A second chief accompanied him in these chants and sometimes substituted for him. There was also a third chief, who might accompany the second chief when he substituted. A chief had to have a good knowledge of the tribal myths and legends, since he based both his sermons and his allegorical chants on them.

The Kuna had a number of other village positions, some villages more than others, and one man sometimes held several offices at the same time. There were elder advisors, treasurers, police, and officials in charge of communal enterprises such as housebuilding, transporting half-completed canoes, communal farming, path maintenance, preparation for girls' ceremonies, chicha brewing, and handling communal turtle and fish nets.

The nineteenth century Kuna frequently dealt with legal violations and disputes outside the formal governmental context, but by 1940 the old system was virtually gone and disputes were settled by governmental action (Howe 1986:219) Village authorities tried to handle as many violations and disputes at that level as they could, though they were expected to submit serious matters, such as major thefts, homicides, etc. to higher authorities. Village officials adjudicated or arbitrated disputes either at the village gatherings or, occasionally, elsewhere.

When community cooperation was in order the people worked together. *Reciprocity, shame, affective reinforcement,* and *logic* may be considered widespread mechanisms of social control in human culture (Taylor 1980: 194). Under reciprocity people who do not conform find that others withhold needed help. Shame may be evoked by public ridicule or other ways. With affective reinforcement people are praised or otherwise rewarded for conforming. And logic is applied when deviants or potential deviants are reminded that they are or would be violating their own standards, which they share with the rest of the society. There were undoubtedly elements of all four in Kuna social control. The Kuna expected all, regardless of status, to cooperate, to carry their part of the load in community projects, and anyone who shirked found himself cut off from help when he needed it. Stout reported that a shirker was likely to find himself publicly shamed at a singing meeting, where the people would sing an allegory about him based on their myths and legends. But Howe, who studied Kuna political institutions of the 1970s in depth, found no examples of such specific shaming at the village meetings.

It is clear that the sacred singing meetings comprised an important aspect of Kuna social control, since the chiefs chanted about various aspects of Kuna behavior in rather specific terms, even if they were not directed at specific individuals. The chiefs chanted about the "Father's Way," so called because the meeting house belonged to God, the Kuna were His people, and much of a chant recounted relations between the people and their chief deity. Chants dealt with the nature of the universe, the world of the spirits, and Kuna history. Within this sacred context the chant-

ers admonished the people, perhaps urging the women to keep their houses clean or advising how people should behave toward their relatives (Howe 1986:47).

Art and Play

The aesthetic and recreational activities of the San Blas Kuna included their folktales, carving of fetishes and other objects, the mola applique work, the chants, the music and dancing associated with their ceremonies, and the lullabies the women and older girls sang to their little ones. Besides the myths and legends that formed the basis for much of their ritual and governmental activity, they told a number of stories simply for enjoyment. A number of the stories told of pairs of animal adversaries, one of whom vanquished the other, often through trickery. One tale told how the people tried to cut down the World Tree, but each night a giant frog would undo their day's work by healing the cut. After two failures, the culture hero asked the frog's brother to kill him, after which fresh and salt water, crop lands, plants, animals, fish and birds emerged from the top of the fallen tree. When someone told an audience a story, someone was to act as a respondent. The respondent ratified each line of the story with an affirmative grunt, a repetition of a word or phrase, a comment, a laugh, or a question (Sherzer 1979:146).

Many of the men carved religious figures of wood, and women fashioned the mola designs as described on page 276. The wooden figures were usually human, though some were shaped like animals and birds. The knees of the human forms were bent and the clothing was European, including modern suits, an eighteenth century uniform, and a nun's habit (Stout 1947:103). Each carver followed his personal tastes in designing a fetish, since the kind of wood it was made of determined its power rather than the actual shape. It seems likely that the Kuna learned the bent knee position from seeing African fetishes.

Kuna chanting corresponds with the definition of *art* as the exercise of skill in the expression and communication of sentiments. When the chief chanted at singing meetings, for example, he sought to innovatively and aesthetically integrate various themes (Hirschfeld 1976:46). He developed this skill partly through careful study of the chanting of other chiefs on his own and other islands. The aesthetic nature of the chiefly chanting based on mythological episodes illustrates the interdependence among customs in different aspects of life, in this case among aesthetic, administrative, and religious elements. Anthropologists emphasize that no custom or aspect of life can be adequately understood without examining how it relates to the cultural configuration of which it is a part and within which it functions.

The Kuna used music in connection with their ceremonies and just for enjoyment. The puberty ceremony chanters and their apprentices, for example, played flageolets during the chant telling of the ceremony's origin. The Kuna also played their instruments on other occasions, the only reason being enjoyment. Kuna dancing often involved the imitation of animal movements.

The Kuna enjoyed getting drunk on chicha, but they limited their drinking to ceremonial occasions. They had no competitive games and athletic contests. In earlier times tobacco was used only in ceremonies in the form of cigars, but the Kuna of the 1940s smoked pipes and cigarettes for pleasure.

Religious Beliefs and Practices

In 1940 Kuna believed that God, or the Great Father, created all things, including his own wife; and everything came from their union. They held that God personally directed the punishment of sinners and admitted souls to heaven, but they did not pray to him.

In addition to God and his wife they believed in a lesser deity, the female spirit, Muu, who supervised the formation of human fetuses and supplied them with their characteristics.

The people believed that God sent a great *culture hero*, Ipeorkun, to earth on a bar or plate of gold, and he taught the Kuna how to behave, what to call things, and how to use them. He had a number of disciples, also culture heroes, who spread his teachings. After the culture heroes came ten great neles, who taught the people much and made many journeys to the underworld and heaven, returning to teach the people what they had learned there. They apparently taught chiefs and various heroes, some of whom eventually led the San Blas Kuna down from the mountains and onto the islands. The Kuna chiefs and chanters drew upon and recounted these stories in their sermons and chants.

Kuna held that the earth was a plane on which people lived, that heaven consisted of eight invisible layers above the earth, and that there was an underworld of eight layers below it. The chiefs of the evil spirits lived on the fourth layer of the underworld. They thought of the sky as a hemisphere and believed that the sun, along with certain evil spirits, traveled about in a ship. The moon and some of the stars traveled in another ship.

God also created evil spirits, according to the Kuna, and they were literally everywhere. God had them do things for him, and they also caused a good deal of disease, death, and other trouble on their own. They felt that evil spirits were especially abundant on mountain tops and in caves, whirlpools, old trees, and swamps. They most often appeared in human form, but some appeared as monsters. They also took the shape of dead individuals and appeared to people in their dreams. As noted, the Kuna attributed all sickness and death to the work of evil spirits, usually soul theft.

The people maintained that every person and object was indwelt by souls, citing shadows, echoes, reflections, and similar phenomena as proof. They felt that humans had many souls, one for each part of the body, though they were united into one at death. An evil spirit apparently stole only one soul at a time. Some souls were better than others, and the stealing of the best soul, according to some Kuna, resulted in certain death. A person's soul could also leave during sleep, which explained dreams of being somewhere else. The ideas of soul absence causing sickness or death and soul travel explaining dreams are found in all parts of the world.

The Kuna also believed in a kind of life principle existing in all animate things and, some of them thought, in rocks, water, and metal, too. It left the body at death, though most were unable to say where it went.

People were born with a power that grew as the person grew and which could be augmented or decreased by medicines. It was manifested in bravery and industriousness and was associated with sexual potency, too. Too much sexual activity would weaken this power, and the evidence of its weakness would be high susceptibility to being scared by strange forest noises.

Still another quality was predisposition and talent, which was centralized in the brain. There was one of these qualities for every activity or ability—hunting, meeting snakes, associating with spirits in dreams, and so on.

With regard to the daily religious life of the Kuna, the concern with evil spirits and the rituals and ceremonies of the chanters and religious personages who dealt with them were paramount. Every island had several healers in 1940. They had to study for years to learn all the medicines and chants, nearly always under the tutelage of an older practitioner. They did not obtain their position through revelations or vision quests as shamans do in so many societies, though evil spirits sometimes revealed specific medicines to them while they were alone in the forest.

Kuna healers used chants extensively in combination with medicines to heal their patients. The curing chants were effective only if the healer first chanted the story of the medicine's origin and sang all the chants in the correct order. They were very repetitious and contained a great many names and figures of speech not used in every-day communication. The healer used various kinds of voices and modified the chants further by holding the hands in various positions over the mouth. Many of the healers recorded their chants in colored picture-writing, usually with crayons and in cheap notebooks, to ensure that they sang them in the right order. Each had his own writing system, and it was mnemonic writing rather than representing units of speech. Before the Spanish came the Kuna had no system for reading and writing their language.

The healers used a great variety of powdered medicines as well as red paint, resins, cacao beans, pepper pods, magic stones, carved wooden figures, wooden staffs, and many pieces of wood, vines, and thorny branches (Stout 1947:44). The medicines involved magical imitation. For example, the healers made medicine for fever from plants gathered by a river, since rivers are cool. They put most of their medicines in water and had people drink it or bathe in it, which applies the principle of magical contagion. They chanted to the spirits that occupied the wooden fetishes to get them to bring stolen spirits back from the fourth underworld. They thrust the staffs into the ground beneath a patient's hammock while chanting and addressed their spirits as they did those of the carved images. As they administered medicines and performed chants, cacao beans and peppers were burned to repel evil spirits. The Kuna held that red paint on fetishes and over house doors would repel spirits, too. The healers also used the magic stones, found in rivers by mainland Kuna and traded to the islanders, for curing fevers.

Only the Kuna neles could divine, since they had specially developed power to associate with the evil spirits in dreams. Since the neles were the only practitioners with the power to deal with the spirits, they fit the common anthropological definition of a *shaman*, a person with special individual ability to contact the spirit world, most often for the purpose of healing.

If a Kuna healer was unsuccessful he would give the patient a carved figure to hold and have him take it to a nele. The nele's soul would then contact the spirit occupying the figure in a dream, and the spirit communicated with the evil spirits to find out why the cure was failing. If it was the wrong medicine the nele would prescribe something else, or if the person was going to die anyway the nele simply reported that fact. The people also consulted neles to locate lost objects. Neles were supposed to know much more about the supernatural world than anyone else. There were six male neles and four female neles when Stout was with the Kuna (Stout 1947:46).

Contact and Change

The culture of the San Blas Kuna was far different in 1940 from what it was when the Spanish arrived. It has continued to be influenced by the modern world, though even in the 1970s and early 1980s the people continued many of the customs mentioned in this summary. During the 1970s Sherzer found the singing meetings, shamanistic curing, puberty rites for young girls, slash and burn farming, cooperative agricultural labor, exchanges with trading boats, hunting and fishing, gathering of medicinal plants, sleeping in hammocks, the making of molas, and many other traditional cultural complexes still in place.

At the same time it was clear that the Kuna had not turned their backs on the outside world. They were changing while trying to control that change in their own best interests, an approach they have taken practically from the beginning of their contact with Europeans (Hirschfeld 1977b:164). Somehow the Kuna developed a talent, as Breslin and Chapin remark, "to search through the warehouse of Western culture, pick out those ideas and techniques they consider useful, and then adapt them to their traditional structures" (Breslin and Chapin 1984: 86, 6:40-43).

Many observers would be interested in learning how they developed this ability. There may have been some-

thing in their pre-Columbian culture that was relevant. The particular kinds of experiences they had with Europeans and the kinds of Europeans they were most intensely in contact with may have been involved. And they may have had more freedom than some to develop their capacity to cope with alien societies because of the relative remoteness of their location. A comprehensive and definitive set of specific answers to the question would have required expert observers on the scene for something like a thousand years. Unfortunately, anthropologists have no choice but to give evasive answers of this kind to many a question about how given cultures have come to be what they are.

Since 1938 the Panamanians have allowed the Kuna to largely govern themselves within the territory set aside for them, the reserve known as La Comarca de San Blas (Stier 1982:519). During the 1980s the Kuna General Congress changed the name of the Comarca to Kuna Yala, which means Kuna Land/Mountain (Howe 1986:xiii).

There were about 30,000 Kuna in 1980 (Howe and Hirschfeld 1981:297). Most of them still lived on the islands in villages of many sizes ranging from about 20 people up to some 3,000 (Stier 1982:519). About thirty eight of the islands were inhabited in the middle 1970s, with 11 communities remaining on the mainland (Howe 1978:539). In 1970 about 34 percent of the Kuna over 10 years of age could read and write, but literacy varied greatly from community to community. On one island of 647 people over 80 percent were literate, whereas in another place with 96 people less than 10 percent were literate (Howe 1979:2). The easternmost islands remained most conservative in this and other respects, partly because the western islands were closer to urban areas and were visited more often by tourists. Two of the island communities, Nagarna and Corazón de Jesús, were especially progressive in the late 1970s, many of their citizens being highly acculturated (Moore 1981:261). In 1984 there may have been about 4,000 Kuna living in Panama City, attending school or working (Hallowell 1985:30).

The number of students studying at the National University and in other countries and the proportion of professionally qualified was steadily increasing. In line with Kuna interest in understanding the world they lived in and responding productively to forces for cultural change, a number had taken degrees in anthropology. By 1988 quite a few Kuna had bachelor's degrees in anthropology; several had earned master's degrees, and at least one had earned a Ph.D. (Howe: personal communication).

Nearly all of the Kuna continued to live in rectangular, cane-walled houses with thatched roofs. The streets were more regular in some communities, but in many the houses were still irregularly laid out. Small islands tended to be crowded with houses from shore to shore. Many of the households were still matrilocal extended families, and, as before, independent nuclear and other types of families came into being as men decided to separate from their fathers-in-law. Most of the women continued to make their molas and wear the traditional costume, including the gold nose rings. The men's clothing, however, was changing as that of the outside world changed. Craft work for sale to tourists had become increasingly important, especially the making of molas. Tourists filtered through the islands, the number of cruise ships arriving annually continued to climb, and there were four Kuna owned and operated hotels. As in so many other changing tribal societies, portable radios were abundant.

Kuna experience with tourism, as reported by anthropologist James Howe, illustrates their pattern of response to the outside world. They have had a fair amount of trouble with outside commercial interests and have learned to keep a close watch over things and to keep developments under their own control. In the middle 1960s an American obtained a permit from the three inter-island chiefs to build a fancy resort, but the chiefs angered many Kuna by failing to bring the issue before the General Congress. The community nearest the resort made some money, but the American was abusive in some ways. Eventually, an argument developed over alleged underpayment of rent and nonpayment for work, and the American would not yield. In 1969, someone burned the entire resort to the ground. The American rebuilt it and began to bring in parties of homosexual tourists, which offended the Kuna considerably. He also wrote a malicious article about the Kuna that was published in a major American newspaper. Kuna got a copy of it, and it was read at one of the meetings of the General Congress. In 1974 the resort was burned again, and the Panamanian government forbad the American to return.

In 1973 the Panama Tourism Institute presented the General Congress with a major plan for tourist development, including a 686 room hotel, a museum, a dock for cruise ships, and a small jet airport. While some communities near the proposed site supported the plan, the Kuna were seriously divided over the matter. In 1974 Kuna wielded clubs to drive away a party of officials and technicians who had arrived to survey the airport site. The Tourism Institute reduced the size of the project, but by 1977 sentiment against it had become so strong the Panamanians gave up.

In another case a Kuna owner leased his hotel to a Panamanian, who proved to be unable to get along with local leaders. At one point the operator brought in an electronic band, and the music blared across the tiny island, disturbing the people. When the Panamanian wouldn't cooperate, Kuna students threw rocks and coconuts at the hotel, and the next day the authorities cut off part of the hotel's water supply on grounds of well contamination. The following day, Panama national guardsmen removed the manager and told him not to come back. After that, the Kuna ran the hotel themselves as a communal venture.

Another American had operated a resort on one of the islands but finally ran into trouble with the Kuna in 1981, when he was shot in the foot, beaten, and driven off the island. Kuna clashed violently with one another over this incident, but the Panamanian government barred the American from returning. Howe's judgement is that the Kuna actually showed restraint, resorting to violence only when

it became clear that laws would not be enforced. The ultimate result of this kind of thing is that the Kuna became careful to watch outside interests and developed plans for their own tourist enterprises (Howe 1982:17)

Although the Kuna of the 1970s and 1980s had become more involved with nonagricultural occupations, traditional slash-and-burn agriculture was still strong, and fishing remained important as well. There are examples of Western-educated Kuna who had lived in urban areas returning to the traditional agricultural lifeway, apparently with satisfaction. Actually such cases are known from all parts of the world. Wage work away from San Blas had become an important way for sons-in-law to escape the tension of working under the authority of their fathers-in-law within the matrilocal extended family. But the absence itself was sometimes a source of tension, since the wife would either have to get help from her husband's relatives or her grown children or work in the fields herself. Sometimes a father-in-law would refuse to release his son-in-law, in which case the village authorities sometimes denied him a travel permit (Stier 1983:18). In many cases, however, there was too little agricultural work to keep all the men busy, and temporary absences were no problem. In spite of some tensions, periodic absence of males to work elsewhere became a usual part of the male life cycle in San Blas (Holloman 1976:145). Several anthropologists have concluded that extended matrilocal families are ideal for psychologically and economically supporting women and children whose husbands often leave them for periods of work. This may well be one reason that matrilocal extended families have survived such male absences in a number of societies.

Kuna government of the 1970s and 1980s exhibited its roots with the past while having adjusted to changing circumstances. Each village continued to have its chief, chief's spokesman, and policeman, the three main officials at that time (Howe 1978:540). Also, the Panamanians had earlier divided the islands into three groups and had the people select three chiefs, one for each. The Kuna had three representatives in the Panamanian national legislature and exerted influence on Panamanian national policy.

The people still met several evenings a week for their talking or singing meetings, using the village meeting house. Quite a few of the Kuna had become restive about devoting the evening, after a day of work, to this kind of activity. The leaders reacted by keeping attendance records, one of several ways they have integrated writing into the traditional system. In this instance they used a modern development to enforce the traditional system (Howe 1979:3).

The meeting houses traditionally were larger versions of the dwellings housing extended families, but the town of Nargana built a modern congress house in the *basilica pattern* (Moore 1981:261). The basilica arrangement is familiar to Euroamericans. The audience, subordinate in the meeting situation, sits or stands in ranks facing the front, with an aisle maintained for movement back and forth by authorities and supplicants. The authorities are at the front, facing the audience, often on a higher level and often behind tables, etc. that supplicants may approach. The social implications of this arrangement had little relevance to traditional Kuna political-ritual contexts, and this lack was expressed while Moore was in Nargana by a movement on the part of some of the people to construct a traditional building. The traditional meeting house had center posts and other parts from which the chiefs slung their hammocks for the meetings, and the chiefs delivered chants from their hammocks recounting the founding of the meeting house by one of their cultural heroes as well as his instructions as to how such a house should be built. The basilica type structure, then, did not fit the traditional mythological and ritual context still so important to so many of the people. In fact, in Nargana the chiefs no longer delivered chants at the meetings. Actually, they were so highly acculturated that they had never learned them or the lore on which they were based.

Kuna healers were still active in the 1970s and 1980s in many of the same ways they were before. They still went into the mainland forests to gather the medicinal substances they needed, and people still called on them to heal their diseases. This is one aspect of the culture that would be severely affected were development enterprises to clear the forests for commercial agriculture put into effect.

Hirschfeld reported that the three remaining verbal art forms in the middle 1970s were the chief's chants, the puberty ceremony chants, and the chanting of the shamans (Hirschfeld 1977a:105). He indicated that the woman's art of lullaby singing had declined, though another observer claimed that they remained important (Nickels 1981:553). Apparently the people seldom if ever used the traditional musical instruments in recreational contexts, since they had adopted Western instruments.

No one can predict that the pressures for change will not at some point become so powerful that Kuna culture will crumble, but the Kuna of the 1980s clearly continued their selective and integrative responses, perhaps even strengthening their ability to survive change. A road can be one of the most damaging developments. In 1973 the government of Panama began to build a road from the Pan American Highway to cross the mountains and reach the San Blas Coast. Some of the Kuna were interested in easier access to the outside, but many were wary.

In Panama and other places in the world, peasant slash-and-burn agriculturalists have been increasingly displaced by large scale cattle ranching. Cattle ranching is highly profitable because of the great demand for meat in North America and some other places. Peasants turn their exhausted land into pasture, sell it to ranchers, and move into virgin forest to establish new fields. The easiest way to do this is to follow the roads and highways, and as a road is built through the rain forests, the displaced peasants follow, clear their fields, farm them until the soil loses its fertility, and turn it over to the cattle operations for pasture. The cattle ranchers keep moving, too, because the rains wash the shallow soil away within a few years so the ground will not even produce grass. This is the situation that was moving ever closer up the Pacific side of the San Blas mountains.

The Kuna decided they should have a hand in what was going on, and from 1975 to 1981 they experimented with agricultural and ranching operations near the crest of the San Blas range where the road was to enter San Blas territory. They quickly found that such enterprises were incompatible with the rain forest habitat and developed a deeper appreciation of the need for saving their forests. They then decided to set aside the entire top of the mountain ridge at that spot as a 5,000 acre reserve to save the forest and provide a scientific research facility. The reserve was to be patrolled by Kuna forest rangers. It was the first institution in the world of its kind created and operated by an indigenous tribal society (Breslin and Chapin 1984:41).

As development enterprises are rapidly destroying our tropical rainforests the world is threatened with the loss of indispensable botanical and other resources as well as the destruction of weather patterns necessary to the survival of agriculture in the world's breadbaskets. It will be interesting to see if the Kuna can make a significant contribution to avoiding such a disaster and, at the same time, continue to maintain their lifeway in the face of destructive change pressures.

References

Acheson, James
    1972 Limited Good or Limited Goods?: Response to Economic Opportunity in a Tarascan Pueblo. American Anthropologist 74:1152-1169.

Adams, Richard E. W.
    1977 Prehistoric Mesoamerica. Boston: Little, Brown and Company.

Adams, Richard N.
    1957 Cultural Surveys of Panama - Nicaragua - Guatemala - El Salvador - Honduras. Washington: Pan American Sanitary Bureau.

Alegría, Ricardo E. (ed.)
    1978 The Taínos: Anthropological, Historical and Cultural Perspectives. Revista/Review Interamericana VIII(3).

Anales del Instituto Nacional de Antropología e Historia 18 (1965):93-108).196

Angulo, Jaime de
    1932 The Chichimeco Language (Central Mexico). International Journal of American Linguistics 7:152-194.

Armillas, Pedro
    1971 Gardens on Swamps. Science 174:653-661.

Arrom, José Juan
    1975 Mitología y Aretes Prehispánicas de las Antillas. México: Siglo Veintiuno Editores, S. A.

Ascher, Robert
    1962 Ethnography for Archaeology: a Case from the Seri Indians. Ethnology 2:360-369.

Aschmann, Homer
    1959 The Central Desert of Baja California: Demography and Ecology. Berkeley: University of California Press.
    1966 The Natural and Human History of Baja California: From Manuscripts by Jesuit Missionaries. Homer Aschmann, trans. & ed. Los Angeles: Dawson's Book Shop.

Augier, F. R. and S. C. Gordon, D. G. Hall, and M. Reckord
    1960. The Making of the West Indies. London: Longman Group Limited

Baer, Phillip and Mary Baer
    1949 Notes on Lacandón Marriage. Southwestern Journal of Anthropology 5:101-106

Baer, Phillip and William R. Merrifield
    1971 Two Studies on the Lacandones of Mexico. Summer Institute of Linguistics

Bamonte, Gerardo
    1977 Agricoltura di un gruppo di pescatori Huave, golfo de Tehuantepec, Messico. Société des Américanistes Journal, Paris, N.S. 64:115-122.

Bandelier, Adolph F.
    1890-92 Final Report of Investigations Among the Indians of Southwestern United States, Part 1. Papers of the Archaeological Institute of America. American Series, 3.
    Publications in Linguistics and Related Fields, Number 33. Norman: Summer Institute of Linguistics of the University of Oklahoma.

Barnett, Homer G.
    1953 Innovation: The Basis of Cultural Change. New York: McGraw-Hill Book Company, Inc.

Barry, Herbert III, Irvin L. Child, and Margaret K. Bacon
    1959 Relation of Child Training to Subsistence Economy. American Anthropologist 61:51-63.

Basauri, Carlos
    1940 La Población Indígena de México: Etnografía. México: Secretaría de Educación Pública.

Beals, Ralph L.
    1932 Aboriginal Survivals in Mayo Culture. American Anthropologist 34:28-29.
    1943a The Aboriginal Culture of the Cáhita Indians. Ibero-Americana 19.
    1943b Northern Mexico and the Southwest. In El Norte de México y el Sur de Estados Unidos. Tercera Reunión de Mesa Redonda Sobre Problemas Antropológicas de México y Central America. México. D.F.
    1945a The Contemporary Culture of the Cáhita Indians. Ibero-americana 14:1-86.
    1945b Ethnology of the Western Mixe. University of California Publications in American Archaeology and Ethnology. Volume 42, No. 1. Berkeley: University of California Press.
    1946 Cherán: A Sierra Tarascan Village. Smithsonian Institution. Institute of Social Anthropology. Publication No. 2. Washington: United States Government Printing Office.
    1968 [1952] Notes on Acculturation. In Heritage of Conquest: the Ethnology of Middle America. Sol Tax, et. al., eds. pp. 225-232. New York: Cooper Square Publishers
    1969 The Tarascans. In Handbook of Middle American Indians, Volume 8, Ethnology, Part 2. Evon Z. Vogt, ed. Austin: University of Texas Press.

Beals, Ralph L., Pedro Carrasco, and Thomas McCorkle
    1944 Houses and House Use of the Sierra Tarascans. Smithsonian Institution, Institute of Social Anthropology, Publication No. 1. Washington: U. S. Government Printing Office.

Belshaw, Michael
    1967 A Village Economy: Land and People of Huecorio. New York: Columbia University Press.

Benítez, Fernando
    1975 In the Magic Land of Peyote. John Upton, translator. Austin: University of Texas Press.

Bennett, Wendell C. and Robert M. Zingg
    1935 The Tarahumara, an Indian Tribe of Northern Mexico. Chicago: University of Chicago Press.

Blom, Frans
    1954 Ossuaries, Cremation, and Secondary Burials among the Maya of Chiapas, Mexico. Journal de la Société des Américanistes, Paris 43:123-135.

Blom, Frans and Gertrude Duby
    1955-57 La Selva Lacandona: Andanzas Arqueológicas. México: Editorial Cultura.

Blom, Gertrude and Frans Blom
    1969 The Lacandón. In Handbook of Middle American Indians, Volume 7, Ethnology, Part 1. Evon Z. Vogt, ed. Austin: University of Texas Press.

Bloomfield, Leonard
    1933 Language. New York: Henry Holt and Company.

Boremanse, Didier
    1977/78 Northern Lacandón Relationship Terminology. Folk 19-20:133-149.
    1978 The Social Organization of the Lacandón Indians of Mexico. Doctoral Dissertation. Oxford University.
    1981a A Comparative Study of Two Maya Kinship Systems. Sociologus 31(1):1-37.
    1981b Una Forma de Clasificación Simbólica. Journal of Latin American Lore 7:191-214.
    1982a A Comparative Study of Lacandón Maya Mythology. Journal de la Société des Américanistes Paris. 68:71-98.
    1982b Tomorrow: Latin American Indian Literatures 6(1):1-8.

Bowen, Thomas and R. Felger, E. Moser, and M. Moser
    1970 Figure 1. Map of the central coast of Sonora.... The Kiva 05:140.

Bowen, Thomas and Edward Moser
    1968 Seri Pottery. The Kiva 33:89-132, 167-8.
    1970a Seri Headpieces and Hats. The Kiva 35: 168-177.
    1970b Material and Functional Aspects of Seri Instrumental Music. The Kiva 35:178-200.

Brand, Donald D.
    1971 Ethnohistoric Synthesis of Western Mexico. In Handbook of Middle American Indians, Volume 11, Archaeology of Northern Mesoamerica, Part 2, Gordon F. Ekholm, and Ignacio Bernal, eds., pp. 632-66. Austin: University of Texas Press.

Breslin, Patrick and Mac Chapin
    1984 Land-Saving, Kuna Style. Audubon Magazine 86, no. 6:40-43.

Brintnall, Douglas E.
1979 Revolt Against the Dead: The Modernization of a Mayan Community in the Highlands of Guatemala. New York: Gordon and Breach.

Brockway, Earl
1979 North Puebla Nahuatl. In Studies in Uto-Aztecan Grammar, Volume 2, Modern Aztec Grammatical Sketches. Ronald W. Langacker, ed., pp. 141-198. Arlington, Texas: Summer Institute of Linguistics and University of Texas at Arlington.

Brown, Kenneth L.
1980 A Brief Report on Paleoindian-Archaic Occupation in the Quiché Basin, Guatemala. American Antiquity 45:313-324.

Bruce S., Roberto D.
1965 Jerarquía Maya entre los Dioses Lacandones. Anales del Instituto Nacional de Antropología e Historia 18:93-108).
1968a Gramática del Lacandón. México: Instituto Nacional de Antropología e Historia.
1968b Términos de parentesco entre los Lacandones. Anales del Instituto Nacional de Antropología e Historia 19 (1966): 151-157.
1974 El Libro de Chan K'in (Textos Lacandones). Serie Científica Número 10. México: Instituto Nacional de Antropología e Historia.
1975 Lacandón Dream Symbolism. México: Ediciones Euroamericanas.

Bunzel, Ruth
1952 Chichicastenango: A Guatemalan Village. Publications of the American Ethnological Society. Locust Valley, New York: J. J. Augustin Publisher.

Burckhalter, David
1976 The Seris. Tucson: University of Arizona Press.
1982 The Power of Seri Baskets: Spirits, Traditions, and Beauty. The American West 19:38-45.

Cancian, Frank
1965 Economics and Prestige in a Maya Community. Stanford: Stanford University Press.

Carmack, Robert M.
1981 The Quiché Mayas of Utatlán: The Evolution of a Highland Guatemala Kingdom. Norman: University of Oklahoma Press.

Carrasco, Pedro
1957 Tarascan Folk Religion. In Synoptic Studies of Mexican Culture by Munro S. Edmonson, Pedro Carrasco, Glen Fisher, and Eric R. Wolf. Middle American Research Institute Publication 17., pp. 1-64. New Orleans: Tulane University.

Cassa, R.
1974 Los Taíno de la Española. Santo Domingo: Editora de la Universidad Autónoma de Santo Domingo.

Castile, George Pierre
1972 Cherán: The Adaptation of an Autonomous Community in Michoacán, Mexico. Ann Arbor: University Microfilms.
1974 Cherán: La Adaptación de una comunidad tradicional de Michoacán. México, D. F.: Instituto Nacional Indigenista, Serie de Antropología Social (26).
1981 On the Tarascanness of the Tarascans and the Indianness of the Indians. In Persistent Peoples: Cultural Enclaves in Perspective, Eds. George Pierre Castile and Gilbert Kushner. Tucson: The University of Arizona Press.

Cerda Silva, Roberto de la
1941. Los Huave. Revista Mexicana Sociología. 3(1):81-111.

Champion, Jean René
1963 A Study in Culture Persistence: The Tarahumara of Northwestern Mexico. Doctoral Dissertation. University of California.

Chapin, Mac
1970 Pab Igala: Historias de la tradición Kuna. Panama City: Universidad de Panama.
1976 Muu Ikala: Cuna birth Ceremony. In Ritual and Symbol in Native Central America, University of Oregon Anthropological Papers No. 9, Philip Young and James Howe, eds., pp. 57-65. Eugene, Oregon: Department of Anthropology, University of Oregon.
1983 Curing among the San Blas Kuna of Panama. Doctoral dissertation, Department of Anthropology. Tucson: University of Arizona.

Charnay, C. J. Desire
1863 Le Mexique: souvenirs et impressions de voyage, 1851-1861. Paris: E. Dentu.
1887 Ma derniere expedition au Yucatán, 1886. Tour du Monde 53:273-320.

Cheney, Charles Clark
1976 The Mareños: Tradition and Transition in a Huave Community Organization. Vanderbilt University Publications in Anthropology No. 15. Nashville: Vanderbilt University Press.
1979 Religion, Magic, and Medicine in Huave Society. Kroeber Anthropological Society Papers No. 55-56, 59-73.

Clarke, Charles Walter
1952 Columbus, Charles VIII and the Serpentine Disease. Journal of Social Hygiene. Volume 38, pp. 306-336.

Colby, Benjamin N.
1967 Psychological Orientations. In Handbook of Middle American Indians, Volume 6, Social Anthropology, Manning Nash, ed., pp.416-431. Austin: University of Texas Press.

Conzemius, Eduard
1932 Ethnographical Survey of the Miskito and Sumu Indians of Honduras and Nicaragua. Washington: United States Government Printing Office.

Coolidge, Dane and Mary Roberts Coolidge
1939 The Last of the Seri. New York: E. P. Dutton and Co.

Covarrubias, Miguel
1946 Mexico South: The Isthmus of Tehuantepec. New York: Alfred A. Knopf, Inc.

Crosby, Harry
1984 The Cave Paintings of Baja California, rev. ed. San Marcos, California: Copley Books.

Crumrine, Lynn S.
1961 The Phonology of Arizona Yaqui. Anthropological Papers of the University of Arizona 5. Tucson: University of Arizona.

Crumrine, Lynn S. and N. Ross Crumrine
1965 Ancient and Modern Mayo Fishing Practices. The Kiva 33:25-33.

Crumrine, N. Ross
1964 The House Cross of the Mayo Indians of Sonora, Mexico: A Symbol of Ethnic Identity. Anthropological Papers of the University of Arizona 8. Tucson: University of Arizona Press.
1968 The Easter Ceremonial in the Sociocultural Identity of Mayos, Sonora, Mexico. Doctoral dissertation, Department of Anthropology. Tucson: University of Arizona.
1969 Capakoba, the Mayo Eastern Ceremonial Impersonator: Explanations of Ritual Clowning. Journal for the Scientific Study of Religion 8(1):1-22.
1970 Ritual Drama and Culture Change. Comparative Studies in Society and History 12:361-372.
1973 The Earth Will Eat You Up: A Structural Analysis of Mayo Indian Myths. America Indígena 33:1119-1150.

1977 The Mayo Indians of Sonora: A People Who Refuse to Die. Tucson: University of Arizona Press.

Crumrine, N. Ross and Lynne S. Crumrine
1969 Where Mayos Meet Mestizos: A Model for the Social Structure of Culture Contact. Human Organization 28:50-57.

Crumrine, N. Ross and B. June Macklin
1974 Sacred Ritual vs. the Unconscious: the Efficacy of Symbols and Structure in North Mexican Folk Saints' Cults and General Ceremonialism. In The Unconscious in Culture, Ino Rossi, ed., New York: E. P. Dutton & Co.

Culbert, T. Patrick
1983 Mesoamerica. In Ancient South Americans, Jesse D. Jennings, ed., pp. 25-85. San Francisco: W. H. Freeman and Company.

Culin, Stewart
1902 The Indians of Cuba. In Bulletin of the Free Museum of Science and Art, University of Pennsylvania, Volume 3, pp. 185-226.

Davis, Edward
1965 The Seri Indians. In Indians of the Southwest United States and Northwest Mexico, Charles Russell Quinn and Elena Quinn, eds., pp. 139-224. Downey, California: Elena Quinn.

Davis, Edward H. and E. Yale Dawson
1945 The Savage Seris of Sonora. The Scientific Monthly 60:193- 202, 261- 268.

Davis, Virginia Dale
1978 Ritual of the Northern Lacandón Maya. Doctoral Dissertation. Tulane University.

Dawson, E. Yale
1944 Some Ethnobotanical Notes on the Seri Indians. Desert Plan Life 16:132-138

De Grazia and Ted Ettore with William Neil Smith
1970 The Seri Indians: A Primitive People of Tiburón Island in the Gulf of California. Flagstaff, Arizona: Northland Press.

Del Barco. Miguel
1973 Historia Natural y Crónica de la Antigua California. Miguel Leon-Portilla, ed. México: Universidad Nacional Autonóma de México.
1981 Ethnology and Linguistics of Baja California, Froylan Tiscareno, tr. Baja California Travel Series, No. 44. Los Angeles: Dawson's Book Shop.

Dennis, Philip A.
1981 Journal of Interamerican Studies and World Affairs 23:271-296

Dennis, Philip A. and Michael D. Olien
1984 Kingship Among the Miskito. American Ethnologist 11:718-737

De Rios, Marlene Dobkin and David E. Smith
1977 Drug Use and Abuse in Cross Cultural Perspective. Human Organization 36:14-21.

Díaz, May N.
1966 Tonalá: Conservatism, Responsibility and Authority in a Mexican Town. Berkeley: University of California Press.

Diebold, A. Richard, Jr.
1966 The Reflection of Coresidence in Mareño Kinship Terminology. Ethnology: An International Journal of Cultural and Social Anthropology 5:37-79.
1969 The Huave. In Handbook of Middle American Indians. Volume 7, Ethnology, Part I. Evon Z. Vogt, ed. Austin: University of Texas Press.

Di Peso, Charles C. and David S. Matson
1965 The Seri Indians in 1692 as Described by Adam Gilg, S. J. Arizona and the West 7:33-56.

Downs, James F.
1966 The Two Worlds of the Washo: An Indian Tribe of California and Nevada. New York: Holt, Rinehart and Winston, Inc.

Driver, Harold E.
1961 Indians of North America. Chicago: University of Chicago

Driver, Harold E. and Wilhelmine Driver
1963 Ethnography and Acculturation of the Chimichmeca-Jonaz of Northeast Mexico. Indiana University Research Center in Anthropology, Folklore, and Linguistics, Publication 26. Bloomington: Indiana University

Driver, Harold E. and Wm. C. Massey
1957 Comparative Studies of North American Indians. Transactions of the American Philosophical Society. XLVII, 165-456.

Duby, Gertrude
1944 Los lacandones: su pasado y su presente. México: Secretaía de Educación Pública.
1955 Los lacandones: el mundo y su influencia sobre ellos. Novedades, August14.
1959 Estado actual de los lacandones de Chiapas, México. America Indígena 19(4): 255-267.
1961 Chiapas indígena. México: Universidad Nacional Autónoma Mexicana.

Duby, Gertrude and Frans Blom
1969 The Lacandón. In Handbook of Middle American Indians. Volume 7, Ethnology, Part I. Evon Z. Vogt, ed. pp. 276-297. Austin: University of Texas Press.

Eger, Susan, in collaboration with Peter R. Collings
1978 Huichol Women's Art. In Art of the Huichol Indians. Kathleen Berrin, ed. San Francisco: The Fine Arts Museums of San Francisco/New York: Harry N. Abrams, Inc.

Fábila, A.
1949 Sierra Norte de Puebla. México, D. F.: Talleres Gráficos.

Felger, Richard S. and Mary Beck Moser
1970 Seri Use of Agave (Century Plant) The Kiva 35:159-167.
1971 Seri Use of Mesquite (Prosopis glandulosa var torreyana). The Kiva 37:53-60
1973 Eelgrass (Zostera marina L.) in the Gulf of California: Discovery of its Nutritional Value by the Seri Indians. Science 181[4096]:355-356.
1974 Columnar Cacti in Seri Indian Culture. The Kiva 39:257-275.
1976 Seri Food Plants: Subsistence Without Agriculture. Ecology of Food and Nutrition 5:13-17.
1985 People of the Desert and Sea: Ethnobotany of the Seri Indians. Tucson: University of Arizona Press.

Fewkes, Jesse Walter
1907 The Aborigines of Porto Rico and Neighboring Islands. In Twenty Fifth Annual Report of the Bureau of American Ethnology, 1903-04, pp. 3-296. Washington: United States Government Printing Office.

Fikes, Jay Courtney
1984 Huichol Indian Identity and Adaptation. Ann Arbor, Michigan: University Microfilms.

Flannery, Kent V.
1983 Divergent Evolution. In The Cloud People: Divergent Evolution of the Zapotec and Mixtec Civilizations, pp 1-9. Kent V. Flannery and Joyce Marcus, eds. New York: Academic Press.

Flannery, Kent V. and Joyce Marcus
1983 The Rosario Phase and the Origins of Monte Albán I. In The Cloud People: Divergent Evolution of the Zapotec and Mixtec Civilizations, pp. 74-77. Kent V. Flannery and Joyce Marcus, eds. New York: Academic Press.

Foster, Elizabeth A., translator and ed.
1950 Motolinía's History of the Indians of New Spain. Westport, Connecticut: Greenwood Press, Publishers.

Foster, George M.
1948 Empire's Children: The People of Tzintzuntzán. Smithsonian Institution, Institute of Social Anthropology Publication No. 6. Washington: United States Government Printing Office.
1965 Peasant Society and the Image of Limited Good. American Anthropologist 67:293-315.
1967 Tzintzuntzán: Mexican Peasants in a Changing World. Boston: Little, Brown and Company.

Foster, Mary LeCron
1969 The Tarascan Language. University of California Publications in Linguistics, Vol. 56. Berkeley: University of California Press.

Fox, David
1966 Quiché Grammatical Sketch. In Languages of Guatemala. Marvin K. Mayers, ed., pp. 60-86. London: Mouton & Co.

Fried, Jacob
1952 Ideal Norms and Social Control in Tarahumara Society. Doctoral Dissertation. Yale University.
1953 The Relation of Ideal Norms to Actual Behavior in Tarahumara Society. Southwestern Journal of Anthropology 9:286-295.
1961 An Interpretation of Tarahumara Interpersonal Relations. Anthropological Quarterly 34:110-120.
1969 The Tarahumara. In Handbook of Indians of Middle America, Volume 8, Ethnology, Part 2. Evon Z. Vogt, ed., pp. 846-870. Austin: University of Texas Press.

Furst, Peter T.
1967 Huichol Conceptions of the Soul. Folklore Americas 27:39-106
1969 To Find our Life: The Peyote Hunt of the Huichols of Mexico. (16mm. ethnographic film, sound and color) Los Angeles: University of California Latin American Center.
1972a Flesh of the Gods: The Ritual Uses of Hallucinogens. New York: Praeger.
1972b To Find Our Life: Peyote Among the Huichol Indians of Mexico. In Flesh of the Gods: The Ritual Uses of Halucinogens, Peter T. Furst, ed. New York: Praeger.
1977 The Roots and Continuities of Shamanism. In Stones, Bones, and Skin: Ritual and Shamanic Art. Anne Trueblood Brodsky, Rose Danesewich, and Nick Johnson, eds. Toronto: The Society for Art Publication.
1978 The Art of "Being Huichol." In Art of the Huichol Indians. Kathleen Berrin, ed., New York: Harry N. Abrams, Inc.

Furst, Peter T. and Marina Anguiano
1976 Myth and Ritual Among the Huichol Indians. In Enculturation in Latin America: An Anthology. Johannes Wilbers, ed. Los Angeles: UCLA Latin American Center Publications.

Furst, Peter T. and Barbara G. Myerhoff
1966 Myth as History: The Jimson Weed Cycle of the Huichols of Mexico. Anthropologica 17:3-39.

García Cook, Angel
1974 Una Secuencia Cultural para Tlaxcala. Fundación Alemana Para La Investigación Científica, Comunicaciones 10, pp. 5-22. Puebla.

Gibson, Charles
1952 Tlaxcala in the Sixteenth Century. Stanford, California: Stanford University Press.
1964 The Aztecs Under Spanish Rule: A History of the Indians of the Valley of Mexico, 1519- 1810. Stanford, California: Stanford University Press.

Gifford, Edward W. and Robert H. Lowie
1928 Notes on the Akwa'ala Indians. University of California Publications in American Archaeology and Ethnology 23:339-352.
1933 The Cocopa. University of California Publications in American Archaeology and Ethnology 16:257-334.

Gorenstein, Shirley and Helen Perlstein Pollard.
1983 The Tarascan Civilization: A Late Prehispanic Cultural System. Vanderbilt University Publications in Anthropology, No. 28. Nashville, Tennessee: Vanderbilt University.

Gortaire Iturralde, A.
1971 Santa Fé, Presencial Etnológica de un Pueblo-Hospital. México: Universidad Iberoamericana, A. C.

Graham, John A., ed.
1966 Ancient Mesoamerica: Selected Readings. Palo Alto, California: Peek Publications.

Greenberg, Joseph H.
1960 The General Classification of Central and South American Languages. In Men and Cultures: Selected papers of the Fifth International Congress of Anthropological and Ethnological Sciences. Anthony F. C. Wallace, ed., pp. 791-794. Philadelphia: University of Pennsylvania Press.

Griffen, William B.E
1959 Notes on Seri Indian Culture, Sonora, Mexico. The Latin American Monograph Series. Gainesville: University of Florida Press.

Grimes, Barbara F.
1984 Ethnologue: Languages of the World, 10th ed. Dallas: Summer Institute of Linguistics.

Grimes, Joseph E.
1955 Style in Huichol Structure. Language 31: 221-232.
1959 Huichol Tone and Intonation. International Journal of American Linguistics 25:221-232.
1960 Spanish-Nahuatl Monetary Terms. International Journal of American Linguistics 26:162-165.
1961 Huichol Economics. America Indígena 21: 281-330.
1964 Huichol Syntax. The Hague: Mouton.

Grimes, Joseph E., and Barbara F. Grimes
1962 Semantic Distinctions in Huichol (Uto-Aztecan) Kinship. American Anthropologist 64:104-114.

Grimes, Joseph E. and Thomas B. Hinton
1969 The Huichol and Cora. In The Handbook of Middle American Indians, Volume 8, Ethnology, Part 2, Evon Z. Vogt, ed., pp. 792-813. Austin: University of Texas Press.

Gruhn, Ruth
1973 Observaciones en Chichicastenango en 1969. Estudios de Cultura Maya 9:231-256.

Gruhn, Ruth, Alan Lyle Bryan, and Jack D. Nance
1977 Los Tapiales: A Paleo-Indian Campsite in the Guatemalan Highlands. Proceedings of the American Philosophical Society 121:235-273.

Gudschinsky, Sarah
1964 The ABC's of Lexicostatistics (Glottochronology). In Language in Culture and Society: A Reader in Linguistics and Anthropology. Dell Hymes, ed., pp. 612-623. New York: Harper & Row, Publishers.

Guiteras Holmes, Calixta
1968[1952] Social Organization. In Heritage of Conquest: the Ethnology of Middle America. Sol Tax, et. al., eds., pp. 97-118. New York: Cooper Square Publishers.

Haberland, Wolfgang
1978 Lower Central America. In Chronologies in New World Archaeology, R. E. Taylor and Clement W. Meighan, eds., pp. 395-430. New York: Academic Press.

Hallowell, Christopher
1985 A World of Difference. Americas 37:24-29, 62-63.

Heath, G. R.
1913 Notes on Miskito Grammar and on Other Indian Languages of Eastern Nicaragua. American Anthropologist, 15:48-62.

Helms, Mary W.
1971 Asang: Adaptations to Culture Contact in a Miskito Community. Gainesville: University of Florida Press.
1975 Middle America: A Culture History of Heartland and Frontiers. Englewood Cliffs, New Jersey: Prentice-Hall, Inc.
1981 Cuna Molas and Coclé Art Forms. Working Papers in the Traditional Arts, 7. Philadelphia: Institute for the Study of Human Issues.
1983 Miskito Slaving and Culture Contact: Ethnicity and Opportunity in an Expanding Population. Journal of Anthropological Research 39:179-197.
1984 The Society and Its Environment in Honduras: A Country Study. James D. Rudolf, ed. Foreign Area Studies. The American University, pp. 53-100. Washington: United States Government Printing Office.

Hinshaw, Robert E.
1975 Panajachel: A Guatemalan Town in Thirty-Year Perspective. Pittsburgh: University of Pittsburgh Press.

Hinton, Thomas B.
1959 A Survey of Indian Assimilation in Eastern Sonora. Anthropological Papers of the University of Arizona 4. Tucson: University of Arizona Press.
1964 The Cora Village: a Civil-religious hierarchy in Northern Mexico. In Culture Change and Stability: Essays in Memory of Olive Ruth Barker and George C. Barker, Jr., pp. 44-62. Los Angeles: University of California Press.
1969 Remnant Tribes of Sonora: Opata, Pima, Papago, and Seri. In Handbook of Middle American Indians, Volume 8, Ethnology, Part 2. Evon Z. Vogt, ed., pp. 879-888. Austin: University of Texas Press.

Hirschfeld, Lawrence A.
1976 A Structural Analysis of the Cuna Arts. In Ritual and Symbol in Native Central America. Philip Young and James Howe, eds. University of Oregon Anthropologica Papers No. 9, pp. 43-56. Eugene: University of Oregon.
1977a Art in Cunaland: Ideology and Cultural Adaptation. Man, New Series 12:104-123.
1977b Cuna Aesthetics: A Quantitative Analysis. Ethnology 16:147-166.

Holden, William C. et. al.
1936 Studies of the Yaqui Indians of Sonora, Mexico. Texas Techological College Bulletin 12(1). Lubbock: Texas Technological College.

Holloman, Regina E.
1969 Developmental Change in San Blas. Doctoral dissertation. Department of Anthropology, Evanston, Illinois: Northwestern University.
1975 Ethnic Boundary Maintenance: Readaptation and Societal Evolution in the San Blas Islands of Panama. In Ethnicity and Resource Competition in Plural Societies, Leo A. Depres, ed., pp. 27-40. The Hague: Mouton.
1976 Cuna Household Types and the Domestic Cycle. In Frontier Adaptations in Lower Centra America, Mary W. Helms and Franklin O. Loveland, eds., pp. 131-149. Philadelphia: Institute for the Study of Human Issues, Inc.

Holmer, Nils M.
1947 Critical and Comparative Grammar of the Cuna Language. Goteborg, Sweden Etnografiska Museum.

Honigmann, John J.
1963 Understanding Culture. New York: Harper and Row.

Horcacitas, Fernando
1972 Life and Death in Milpa Alta: A Nahuatl Chronicle of Díaz and Zapata. Norman: University of Oklahoma Press.
1979 The Aztecs Then and Now. México: Editorial Minutiae Mexicana, S. A. de C. V.

Howe, James
1974 Village Political Organization among the San Blas Cuna. Doctoral dissertation, Department of Anthropology. Philadelphia: University of Pennsylvania.
1976a Communal Land Tenure and the Origin of Descent Groups Among the San Blas Cuna. In Frontier Adaptations in Lower Central America, Mary W. Helms and Franklin O. Loveland, eds., pp. 151-163. Philadelphia: Institute for the Study of Human Issues, Inc.
1976b Smoking Out the Spirits: A Cuna Exorcism. In Ritual and Symbolism in Native Central America. Anthropological Papers No. 9, Department of Anthropology, pp. 67-76. Eugene: University of Oregon.
1977 Carrying the Village: Cuna Political Metaphors. In The Social Use of Metaphor, C. Croker and J. D. Sapir, eds. Philadelphia: University of Pennsylvania Press.
1978 How the Cuna Keep Their Chiefs in Line. Man, New Series 13:537-553.
1979 The Effects of Writing on the Cuna Political System. Ethnology 18:1-16.
1982 Kindling Self-determination Among the Kuna. Cultural Survival Quarterly 6, no. 3:15-17.
1986 The Kuna Gathering: Contemporary Village Politics in Panama. Austin: University of Texas Press.

Howe, James, Joel Sherzer and Mac Chapin
1980 Cantos y Oraciones del Congreso Cuna. Panama: Editorial Universitaria Panama.

Howe, James and Lawrence Hirschfeld
1981 The Star Girls' Descent: A Myth About Men, Women, Matrilocality, and Singing. Journal of American Folklore 94:292-322.

Hrdlicka, Ales
1904 Notes on the Indians of Sonora. American Anthropologist 6:51-89.

Iwanska, Alicja
1971 Purgatory and Utopia: A Mazahua Indian Village of Mexico. Cambridge, Massachusetts: Schenkman Publishing Company.

Ixtlilxochitl, Fernando de Alva
1952[1616] Obras Históricas. México, D. F.: Editora Nacional.

Jennings, Jesse D.
1974 Prehistory of North America, 2d ed. New York: McGraw-Hill Book Company.

Johnson, Frederick
1940 Linguistic Map of Mexico and Central America. In The Maya and Their Neighbors: Essays on Middle American Anthropology and Archaeology. Eds. Clarence L. Hay, Ralph L. Linton, Samuel K. Lathrop, Harry L. Shapiro and George C. Valliant.

Johnson, Frederick and Richard H. MacNeish
1972 Chronometric Dating. In The Prehistory of the Tehuacán Valley, Volume 4: Chronology and Irrigation. Frederick Johnson, ed., pp. 3-55. Austin: University of Texas Press.

Johnson, Jean B.
1950 The Opata. University of New Mexico Publications in Anthropology 7:1-50,

Johnston, Bernice
1968 Seri Ironwood Carving. The Kiva 33:155-166, 167-168.

Kaplan, Bernice
1965[1960] Mechanization in Paracho: A Craft Community. In Contemporary Cultures and Societies of Latin America. Dwight B. Heath and Richard N. Adams, eds., pp. 246-254. New York: Random House.

Kaplan, Irving
1983 The Society and Its Environment in Costa Rica: A Country Study. Harold D. Nelson. ed. Foreign Area Studies. The American University. pp. 71-129.

Kearney, Michael
1969 An Exception to the 'Image of Limited Good.' American Anthropologist 71:888-890.
1972 The Winds of Ixtepeji: World View and Society in a Zapotec Town. New York: Holt, Rinehart and Winston, Inc.

Kelley, Jane Holden
1978 Yaqui Women: Contemporary Life Histories. Lincoln: University of Nebraska Press.

Kelly, Isabel and Angel Palerm
1952 The Tajín Totonac. Part 1. History, Subsistence, Shelter and Technology. Smithsonian Institution. Institute of Social Anthropology Publication 13. Washington: United States Government Printing Office.

Kennedy, John G.
1963 Tesgüino Complex: The Role of Beer in Tarahumara Culture. American Anthropologist 65:620-640.
1969 La Carrera de Bola Tarahumara y su Significación. América Indígena 29:17-42.
1970 Bonds of Laughter among the Tarahumara Indians. In The Social Anthropology of Latin America. Walter Goldschmidt and Harry Hoijer, eds. Los Angeles: University of California.
1978 Tarahumara of the Sierra Madre: Beer, Ecology and Social Organization. Arlington Heights, Illinois: AHM Publishing Corporation.

Kennedy, John G. and Raoul A. López.
1978 Tarahumara Easter Ceremonies. Museum of Anthropology. Los Angeles: University of California.

King, Arden R.
1977 Mesoamerica. In The Native Americans: Ethnology and Backgrounds of the North America Indians. Robert F. Spencer, Jesse D. Jennings, et al. New York: Harper & Row, Publishers.

Kirchoff, Paul
1943 Los Recolectores-Cazadores del Norte de México. In El Norte de México y el Sur de los Estados Unidos. Tercera Reunión de Mesa Redonda Sobre Problemas Antropológicas de México y Central America. México D.F.
1948 The Caribbean Lowland Tribes: The Mosquito, Sumo, Paya, and Jicaque. In Handbook of South American Indians, Volume 4, The Circum-Caribbean Tribes. Smithsonian Institution, Bureau of American Ethnology Bulletin 143. Julian Steward, ed., pp. 219-225. Washington: United States Government Printing Office.
1954 Gatherers and Farmers in the Greater Southwest: A Problem in Classification. American Anthropologist 56:529-550.
1966[1948] Civilizing the Chichimecs: A Chapter in the Culture History of Ancient Mexico. In Ancient Mesoamerica: Selected Readings. John A. Graham, ed. Palo Alto, California: Peek Publications.

292

1968 Mesoamerica: Its Geographic Limits, Ethnic Composition and Cultural Characteristics. *In* Heritage of Conquest. Sol Tax, et. al. Viking Fund Seminar on Middle American Ethnology. New York: Cooper Square Publishers.

Klineberg, Otto
1934 Notes on the Huichol. American Anthropologist 36:446-460.

Kreger, Glenn, Albert Stairs and Emily Florence Scharfe de Stairs
1981 Diccionario Huave de San Mateo del Mar. Serie de Vocabularios y Diccionario Indígenas "Mar_ano Silva y Aceves." Num. 24. México D. F.: Instituto Lingüístico de Verano.

Kroeber, Alfred L.
1931 The Seri. Southwest Museum Papers 7:1-60. Los Angeles: Southwest Museum.

LaFarge, Oliver
1931 The Year Bearer's People. New Orleans: Tulane University Press.
1947 Santa Eulalia: The Religion of a Cuchumatán Town. Chicago: University of Chicago Press.
1977[1940] Maya Ethnology: The Sequence of Cultures. *In* The Maya and their Neighbors: Essays on Middle American Anthropology and Archaeology. Clarence L. Hay, et. al. eds., pp. 281-291. New York: Dover Publications, Inc.

Larson, Paul R.
1972 The Highland Chontal. New York: Holt, Rinehart and Winston, Inc.

Las Casas, Gonzalo de
1944[1574] La Guerra de los Chichimecas. México, D.F.: Vargas Rea. Laughlin, Robert M.
1969 The Huastec. *In* Handbook of Middle American Indians, Volume 7, Ethnology, Part 1, Evon Z. Vogt, ed., pp. 298-311. Austin: University of Texas Press.

Levy-Bruhl, Lucién
1923 Primitive Mentality. Lilian A. Clare, trans. New York: The Macmillan Company.

Lewis, Oscar
1951 Life in a Mexican Village: Tepoztlán Restudied. Urbana: University of Illinois Press.
1960 Tepoztlán: Village in Mexico. New York: Holt, Rinehart and Winston.

Linares, Olga F.
1977 Ecology and the Arts in Ancient Panama. *In* On the Development of Social Rank and Symbolism in the Central Provinces. Studies in Pre-Columbian Art and Archaeology, No. 17. Washington: Dumbarton Oaks, Trustees for Harvard University.

Linton, Ralph
1936 The Study of Man: An Introduction. New York: Appleton-Century-Crofts, Inc.

Longacre, Robert
1967 Systematic Comparison and Reconstruction. *In* Handbook of Middle American Indians, Volume 5, Linguistics. Norman A. McQuown, ed., pp. 117=160. Austin: University of Texas Press

Lopez, Raoul A.
1972 Tarahumara Ritual Aesthetic Manifestations. The Kiva 37:207-223.

Lovén, Sven
1935 Origins of the Tainan Culture, West Indies. Goteborg: Elanders Bokfryckeri Akfiebolag.

Lowe, Gareth W.
1978 Eastern Mesoamerica. *In* Chronologies in New World Archaeology. R. E. Taylor and Clement W. Meighan, eds., pp. 331-394. New York: Academic Press.

Lumholtz, Carl
1900 Symbolism of the Huichol Indians. Memoirs of the American Museum of Natural History 1. New York: American Museum of Natural History.
1903 Unknown Mexico: A Record of Five Years' Exploration among the Tribes Western Sierra Madre; in The Tierra Caliente of Tepic and Jalisco; and among the Tarascos of Volumes 1 and 2. London: Macmillan and Company, Limited.
1904 Decorative Art of the Huichol Indians. Memoirs of the American Museum of Natural History 3. New York: American Museum of Natural History.

Lupo, Alessandro
1981 Conoscenze astronomiche e concezioni cosmologiche dei Huave di San Mateo del Mar (Oaxaca, Messico). L'uomo 5(2):267-314.

MacNeish, Richard S.
1967 A Summary of the Subsistence. *In* The Prehistory of the Tehuacán Valley, Volume 1: Environment and Subsistence. Douglas S. Byers, ed. pp. 290-309. Austin: University of Texas Press
1978 The Science of Archaeology. North Scituate, Massachusetts: Duxbury Press. MacNeish.

MacNeish, Richard S., S. Jeffrey K. Wilkerson, and Antoinette Nelken-Turner
1981 First Annual Report of the Belize Archaic Archaeological Reconnaissance. Andover Robert F. Peabody Foundation for Archaeology.

Madsen, William
1957 Christo-paganism: a study of Mexican Religious Syncretism. Middle American Research Institute Publication 19. New Orleans: Tulane University.
1960 The Virgin's Children: Life in an Aztec Village Today. Austin: University of Texas Press.
1959 The Nahua. *In* Handbook of Middle American Indians. Volume 8, Ethnology, Part 2. Evon Z. Vogt, ed. Austin: University of Texas Press.

Magnus, Richard
1974 The Prehistory of the Miskito Coast of Nicaragua: Study in Cultural Relationships. Doctoral dissertation. Department of Anthropology. Yale University.

Malkin, Borys
1956 Seri Ethnozoology: A Preliminary Report. Davidson Journal of Anthropology 2, (pt. 1):73-83.
1962 Seri Ethnology. Occasional Papers of the Idaho State College Museum, 7.

Marcus, Joyce
1983 Topic 23: The First Appearance of Zapotec Writing and Calendrics. *In* The Cloud People: Divergent Evolution of the Zapotec and Mixtec Civilizations, pp. 91-96. Kent V. Flannery and Joyce Marcus, eds. New York: Academic Press

Marroquín, Alejandro D.
1957 The Situation of the Seri Indians of Sonora. Boletín Indigenista 17:332-343.

Marshall, Donald S.
1950 Folk: A Conceptual Scheme Involving the Dynamic Factors of Culture as Applied to the Cuna Indians at Darien. Doctoral dissertation. Harvard University. (HRAF Microform).

Marzotto, Lidia
1977 Osservazioni su alcune relazioni tra l'uomo e l'ambiente in una popolazione amerindiana dell Isto de Tehuantepec: gli Huave di San Mateo del Mar, Oaxaca, Messico. Société de Américanistes Journal, Paris, N.S. 64:123-134.

Mason, J. Alden
1948 The Tepehuan and other aborigines of the Mexican Sierra Madre Occidental. América Indígena 8:289-300.
1977[1940] The Native Languages of Middle America. *In* The Maya and Their Neighbors: Essays on Middle American Anthropology and Archaeology. Clarence L. Hay, et. al., eds., pp. 52-87. New York: Dover Publications.

Maudslay, Anne Cary and Alfred P. Maudslay
1899 A Glimpse at Guatemala, and some notes on the ancient monuments of Central America. London: J. Murray.

McArthur, Harry S.
1969 La estructura politico-religiosa de Aguacatán. *In* Cambio Político en Tres Comunidades Indígenas de Guatemala, Harry S. McArthur and Roland H. Ebel, eds, pp. 11-28. Guatemala: Editorial José de Pineda Ibarra.
1972 Los bailes de Aguacatán y el culto a los muertos. América Indígena 32:491-513.

McArthur, Harry S. and Lucille McArthur
1966 Aguacatec. *In* Languages of Guatemala, Marvin K. Mayers, ed., pp. 140-165. The Hague, Netherlands: Mouton & Co.

McBryde, Felix Webster
1934 Sololá. Middle American Research Series Publication No. 5, Studies in Middle America. New Orleans: Tulane University Press.
1971[1947] Cultural and Historical Geography of Southwest Guatemala. Westport, Connecticut: Greenwood Press, Publishers.

McCosker, Sandra Smith
1974 The Lullabies of the San Blas Cuna Indians of Panama. Etnologiska Studier Series 33. Goteborg: Etnografiska Museum.

McGee, R. Jon
1984 The Influence of Pre-Hispanic Jucatecan Maya Religion in Contemporary Lacandón Maya Ritual. Journal of Latin America Lore 10 (2):175-187.
1987 The Lacandón Maya. Unpublished Manuscript.

McGee, William J.
1898 The Seri Indians. Annual Reports of the Bureau of American Ethnology, 17, i, pp. 9-298. Washington: United States Government Printing Office.

McGuire, Thomas R.
1986 Politics and Ethnicity on the Río Yaqui: Potam Revisited. Tucson: The University of Arizona Press.

Meigs, Peveril
1939 The Kiliwa Indians of Lower California. Ibero-americana 15, pp. 1-114.

Mendelson, E. Michael
1967 Ritual and Mythology. *In* Handbook of Middle American Indians, Volume 6, Social Anthropology. Manning Nash, ed., pp. 392-415. Austin: University of Texas Press.

Merrill, William L.
1978 Thinking and Drinking: A Rarámuri Interpretation. Museum of Anthropology. University of New Mexico. Museum of Anthropology. Anthropological Papers No. 67:101-117.
1981 The Concept of Soul Among the Rarámuri of Chihuahua, Mexico: A Study in World View. Doctoral dissertation. Department of Anthropology. Ann Arbor; University of Michigan.

Minturn, Leigh, Martin Grosse and Santoah Haider.
1969 Cultural Patterning of Sexual Beliefs and Behavior. Ethnology 8:301-318.

Moises, Rosalio, Jane Holden Kelley and William Curry Holden
1971 The Tall Candle: The Personal Chronicle of a Yaqui Indian. Lincoln: University of Nebraska Press.

Monzón, Arturo
1943 Los dominios de Tata Rayo. México: Novedades, 23 de Mayo.

1952 La Estructura Social de los Seris. La Sociología en México 1:89-92.

Moore, Alexander
1981 Basilicas and King Posts: a Proxemic and Symbolic Event Analysis of Competing Public Architecture Among the San Blas Cuna. American Ethnologist 8:259-277.
1983 Lore and Life: Cuna Indian Pageants, Exorcisms, and Diplomacy in the 20th Century. 30:93-106.

Moriarity, James Robert III and B. F. Smith, translators and eds.
1970 The Cora Indians of Baja California: The Relación of Father Ignacio María Napoli, S. J., September 20, 1721. Los Angeles: Dawson's Book Shop.

Morley, Sylvanus G.
1946 The Ancient Maya. Stanford University, California: Stanford University Press.

Morley, Sylvanus G., G. Brainerd, and Robert Sharer.
1983 The Ancient Maya, 4th ed. Stanford, California: Stanford University Press.

Moser, Edward
1963 Seri Bands. The Kiva 28:14-17.
1973 Seri Basketry. The Kiva 38:105-140.

Moser, Edward and Mary Beck Moser
1965 Consonant Vowel Balance in Seri (Hokan) Syllables. Linguistics No. 16:50-55.

Moser, Edward and Richard S. White, Jr.
1968 Seri Clay Figurines. The Kiva 33: 133-54, 167-8.

Moser, Mary Beck
1964 Seri Blue. The Kiva 30:27-32.
1970 Seri: From Conception Through Infancy. The Kiva 35:201-216.

Motolinía, Toribio de Benavente
1914[1541] Historia de Los Indios de la Nueva España. Barcelona: Daniel Sánchez García.

Moya Pons, Fl.
1975 La Sociedad Taína. Santiago: Universidad Católica Madre y Maestra.

Muller, Kal
1978 Huichol Art and Acculturation. In Art of the Huichol Indians, Kathleen Berrin, ed., pp. 84-100. New York: Harry N. Abrams, Inc.

Murdock, George P.
1949 Social Structure. New York: The Macmillan Company.
1975 Ethnographic Bibliography of North America, 4th ed. New Haven: Human Relations Area Files.

Myerhoff, Barbara G.
1970 The Deer-maize-peyote Symbol Complex Among the Huichol Indians of Mexico. Anthropological Quarterly 43:64-78.
1974 Peyote Hunt: The Sacred Journey of the Huichol Indians. Ithaca, New York: Cornell University Press.
1975a The Huichol and the Quest for Paradise: Parabola: Myth and the Quest for Meaning 1:22-39.
1975b Organization and Ecstasy: Deliberate and Accidental Communitas Among Huichol Indians and American Youth. In Symbol and Politics in Communal Ideology: Cases and Questions, Sally Moore, and Barbara Myerhoff, eds. Ithaca, New York: Cornell University Press.
1976 Balancing Between Worlds: The Shaman's Calling. Parabola: Myth and the Quest for Meaning 1:6-13.
1977 Shamanic Equilibrium: Balance and Mediation in Known and Unknown Worlds. In American Folk Medicine, Wayland D. Hand, ed. Berkeley: University of California Press.
1978 Return to Wirikuta: Ritual Reversal and Symbolic Continuity on the Peyote Hunt of the Huichol Indians. In The World Upside Down: Studies in Symbolic Inversion, Barbara Babcock, ed. Ithaca, New York: Cornell University Press.

Nader, Laura
1969 The Zapotec of Oaxaca. In Handbook of Middle American Indians. Volume 7. Ethnology, Part 1, Evon Z. Vogt, ed., pp. 329-366. Austin: University of Texas Press.

Napoli, Ignacio María
1908 The Cora Indians of Baja California. American Anthropologist 10:236-250.

Naroll, Raoul
1983 The Moral Order: An Introduction to the Human Situation. Beverly Hills, California: Sage Publications, Inc.

Nash, June
1970 In the Eyes of the Ancestors. New Haven: Yale University Press.

Nash, Manning
1958 Machine Age Maya: The Industrialization of a Guatemalan Community. Glencoe, Illinois: The Free Press.

Nations, James D.
1979a Population Ecology of the Lacandón Maya. Doctoral dissertation. Department of Anthropology. Dallas: Southern Methodist University.
1979b Snail Shells and Maize preparation: a Lacandón Maya Analogy. American Antiquity 44:568-571).
1983 Tsmao; the Bows and Arrows of the Lacandón Maya. Archaeology 36(1):36-43.

Nelson, Cynthia
1971 The Waiting Village: Social Change in Rural Mexico. Boston: Little, Brown and Company.

Nickels, Cameron C.
1981 Singing a Lullaby in Kuna: a Female Verbal Art. Journal of American Folklore 94:351-369.

Nietschmann, Bernard
1973 Between Land and Water: The Subsistence Ecology of the Miskito Indians, Eastern Nicaragua. New York: Seminar Press.

Nordenskiöld, Erland
1938 An Historical and Ethnological Survey of the Cuna Indians. Henry Wassén, ed. Goteborg, Sweden: Goteborgs Museum, Etnografiska Avdelningen.

Nutini, Hugo G.
1968 San Bernardino Contla: Marriage and Family Structure in a Tlaxcalan Municipio. Pittsburgh: University of Pittsburgh Press.

Nutini, Hugo G. and Betty Bell
1980 Ritual Kinship: The Structure and Historical Development of the Compadrazgo System in Rural Tlaxcala, Volume I. Princeton, New Jersey: Princeton University Press.

Nutini, Hugo and Barry L. Isaac
1974 Los Pueblos de Habla Náhuatl de la Región de Tlaxcala Y Puebla. Instituto Nacional Indigenista, Serie de Antropología Social No. 27. Mexico, D. F.: Instituto Nacional Indigenista.

Nutini, Hugo and Douglas R. White
1977 Community Variations and Network Structure in the Social Functions of Compadrazgo in Rural Tlaxcala, Mexico. Ethnology 16 (4):353-384.

Nyrop, Richard F.
1980 The Society and Its Environment in Panama: A Country Study. Foreign Area Studies, Richard F. Nyrop, ed., pp. 51-86. Washington, D. C.: United States Government Printing Office.

Oakes, Maude
1951a Beyond the Windy Place: Life in the Guatemalan Highlands. New York: Farrar, Straus and Young.
1951b The Two Crosses of Todos Santos: Survivals of Mayan Religious Ritual. Bollingen Series, 27. New York: Pantheon Books.

Odell, Mary E.
1984 The Children of Conquest in the New Age: Ethnicity and Change among the Highland Maya. Central Issues in Anthropology. 5(2):1-15.

Olien, Michael D.
1983 The Miskito Kings and the Line of Succession. Journal of Anthropological Research 39:198-241

Oliveros, José Arturo
1974 Nuevas exploraciones in El Opeño, Michoacán. In The Archaeology of West Mexico. Betty Bell, ed., pp. 182-201. Ajijic, Jalisco: West Mexican Society for Advanced Study.

Opler, Morris Edward
1945 Themes as Dynamic Forces in Culture. American Journal of Sociology 51:198-206.

Owen, Roger C.
1959 Marobavi: A Study of an Assimilated Group in Northern Sonora. Anthropological Papers of the University of Arizona 3. Tucson: University of Arizona Press.

Padden, R. C.
1967 The Hummingbird and the Hawk: Conquest and Sovereignty in the Valley of Mexico, 1503-1541. New York: Harper and Row, Publishers.

Palerm, Angel
1967 Agricultural Systems and Food Patterns. In Handbook of Middle American Indians, Volume 6, Social Anthropology, Manning Nash, ed., pp. 26-52. Austin: University of Texas Press.

Parker, Ann, and Avon Neal
1977 Molas: Folk Art of the Cuna Indians. New York: Crown Publishers, Inc.

Parsons, Elsie Clews
1936 Mitla: of the Souls. Chicago: University of Chicago Press.

Passin, Herbert
1942a Sorcery in a Phase of Tarahumara Economic Relations. Man 42:11-15.
1942b Tarahumara Prevarication: A Problem in Field Method. American Anthropologist 44:235-247.
1943 The Place of Kinship in Tarahumara Social Organization. Acta Americana 1:360-383; 471-495.

Pastron, Allen G.
1977 Aspects of Witchcraft and Shamanism in a Tarahumara Indian Community of Northern Mexico. Doctoral dissertation. Department of Anthropology. Berkeley: University of California.

Pelliccione, Franco
1979 Il cambiamento culturale tra gli Indios lagunari di Santa María del Mar (Oaxaca, Messico): alcune osservazioni. Etnología: antropología culturale. Naples. 7:94-103.

Pennington, Campbell W.
1963 The Tarahumar of Mexico: Their Environment and Material Culture. Salt Lake City: University of Utah Press.

Perera, Victor and Robert D. Bruce
1982 The Last Lords of Palenque: The Lacandón Mayas of the Mexican Rain Forest. Boston: Little, Brown and Company.

Plancarte, Francisco M.
1954 El Problema Indígena Tarahumara. Memorias del Instituto Nacional Indigenista 5. México, D. F.: Instituto Nacional Indigenista.

Pons Alegría, Mela
1980 Taíno Indian Art. Archaeology, Volume 3, pp. 8-13.

Powell, Philip W.

1952 Soldiers, Indians, and Silver: The Northward Advance of New Spain, 1550-1600. Berkeley: University of California Press.

Puig, Manuel María
1948 Los Indios Cunas de San Blas. Panama City

Radin, Paul
1916 On the Relationship of Huave and Mixe. American Anthropologist 18:411-421,

Ravicz, Robert and A. Kimball Romney
1969 The Amuzgo. In The Handbook of Middle American Indians, Volume 7, Ethnology, Part 1, Evon Z. Vogt, ed., pp. 417-433. Austin: University of Texas Press.

Redfield, Robert
1930 Tepoztlán: A Mexican Village. Chicago: University of Chicago Press.

Redfield, Robert and Sol Tax
1968[1952] General Characteristics of Present-day Mesoamerican Indian Society. In Heritage of Conquest: the Ethnology of Middle America. Sol Tax, et. al., eds., pp. 31-39. New York: Cooper Square Publishers.

Redfield, Robert and Alfonso Villa Rojas
1934 Chan Kom: A Maya Village. Carnegie Institute of Washington Publication No. 448. Washington, D. C.: Carnegie Institute.
1941 The Folk Culture of Yucatán. Chicago: University of Chicago Press.
1962 Chan Kom: A Maya Village. Abridged edition. Chicago: University of Chicago Press.

Rees, Michael J.
1977 Mathematical Models of Lacandón Kinship. Doctoral dissertation. Department of Anthropology. New Orleans: Tulane University.

Reina, Ruben E.
1966 The Law of the Saints: A Pokomam Pueblo and Its Community Culture: Indianapolis: The Bobbs-Merrill Company, Inc.

Riley, Carroll L.
1969 The Southern Tepehuan and Tepecano. In Handbook of Middle American Indians, Volume 8, Ethnology, Part 2. Evon Z. Vogt, ed., Austin: University of Texas Press.

Rohner, Ronald
1975 They Love Me, They Love Me Not: A Worldwide Study of the Effects of Parental Acceptance and Rejection. New Haven: HRAF Press.

Romney, Kimball and Romaine Romney
1966 The Mixtecans of Juxtlahuaca, Mexico. Six Cultures Series, Volume I. New York: John Wiley and Sons, Inc.

Rorsheim. Ludwig
1928 Una visita a los indios huavis. Mexican Folkways 4:49-65.

Roth, Henry L.
1887 The Aborigines of Hispaniola. Journal of the Royal Anthropological Institute of Great Britain and Ireland, Volume 16, pp. 247-286.

Rouse, Irving
1048 The Arawak. In Handbook of South American Indians, Volume 4. The Circum-Caribbean Tribes. Bureau of American Ethnology Bulletin 143, pp. 507-546. Washington, D. C.: United States Government Printing Office.
1948 The Carib. In Handbook of South American Indians, Volume 4. The Circum-Caribbean Tribes. Bureau of American Ethnology Bulletin 143, pp. 547-565. Washington, D. C.: United States Government Printing Office.

Rouse, Irving and Louis Allaire
1978 Caribbean. In Chronologies in New World Archaeology. R. E. Taylor and Clement W. Meighan, eds., pp. 431-481. New York: Academic Press.

Roys, Ralph L.
1965 Lowland Maya Native Society at Spanish Contact. In Handbook of Middle American Indians, Volume 3, Part 2, Archaeology of Southern Mesoamerica, Gordon R. Willey, ed., pp. 659-678.

Sahagún, Bernardino de
1829-30[1590] Historia General de las cosas de Nueva España. México, D. F.: Impr. del cuidadano A. Valdés.

Sahlins, Marshall and Elman R. Service, eds.
1960 Evolution and Culture. Ann Arbor: University of Michigan Press.

Sanders, William T.
1981 Ecological Adaptation in the Basin of Mexico: 23,000 B.C. to the Present. In Supplement to the Handbook of Middle American Indians, Volume 1, Archaeology. Victoria Reifler Bricker and Jeremy A. Sabloff, ed., pp. 147-197. Austin: University of Texas Press.

Sapper, Karl
1891 Ein Besuch be den Ostlichen Landandonen. Ausland, 64:892-895

Schaeffer, Francis
1971 Pollution and the Death of Man: A Christian View of Ecology. Wheaton, Illinois: Tyndale House Publishers.

Schultze-Jena, Leonhard
1954 La Vida y las Creencias d los Indígenas Quichés de Guatemala. Biblioteca de Cultura Popular, Volumen 49. Guatemala: Ministerio de Educación Pública.

Service, Elman R.
1969 The Northern Tepehuan. In Handbook of Middle American Indians. Volume 8, Ethnology, Part 2. Evon Z. Vogt, ed., pp. 822-829. Austin: University of Texas Press.

Sheridan, Thomas Edward and Richard S. Felger
1977 Indian Utilization of Eelgrass (Zostera Marina L.) in Northwestern Mexico: The Spanish Colonial Record. The Kiva 43:89-92.

Sherzer, Dina and Joel Sherzer.
1976 Mormaknamaloe: The Cuna Mola. In Ritual and Symbol in Native Central America. Philip Young and James Howe, eds. University of Oregon Anthropological Papers, No. 9. pp. 21-42. Eugene: University of Oregon, Department of Anthropology.

Sherzer, Joel
1970 Talking Backwards in Cuna: The Sociological Reality of Phonological Descriptions. Southwestern Journal of Anthropology 26:343-353.
1973 Verbal and nonverbal deixis: The Pointed Lip Gesture Among the San Blas Cuna. Language in Society 2:117-131.
1975 A Problem in Cuna Phonology. Journal of the Linguistic Association of the Southwest 1:45-53.
1979 Strategies in Text and Context: Cuna kaa kwento. Journal of American Folklore 92:145-163.
1983 Kuna Ways of Speaking: An Ethnographic Perspective. Austin: University of Texas Press.

Signorini, Italo
1977 Padrino e compadre: analisi di un rapporto di scambio tra i Huave di San Mateo del Mar, Oaxaca, Messico. L'uomo 1(1):57-80.

Simpson, Lesley Byrd
1966 Many Mexicos. 4th ed. Berkeley: University of California Press.

Smith, William G.
1966 The People of La Pacanda: Social Organization and Social Change in a Tarascan Village. Doctoral Dissertation. Department of Anthropology. Berkeley: University of California.

Snarksis, Michael J.
1979 Turrialba: A Paleo-Indian Quarry and Workshop Site in Eastern Costa Rica. American Antiquity 44:125-138.

Snow, Dean R.
1976. Prehistory of the Valley of Tlaxcala. In The Tlaxcaltecans: Prehistory, Demography, Morphology and Genetics. M. H. Crawford, ed. University of Kansas Publications in Anthropology No. 7, pp. 9-12. Lawrence, Kansas: Department of Anthropology.

Soustelle, Georgette
1958 Tequila: un Village Náhuatl du Mexique Oriental. Paris: Institut d' Ethnologie.

Soustelle, Jacques
1933 Notes sur les Lacandón du Lac Pelja et du Río Jetzja (Chiapas). Journal de la Société des Américanistes Paris 25:153-180.
1935a Les idees religieuses des Lacandons. La Terre et La View 5:170-178.
1935b Le totemisme des Lacandons. Maya Research 2:325-344.
1937 La culture materielle des Indiens Lacandons. Journal de la Société des Américanistes Paris 29:1-95.
1961 Daily Life of the Aztecs on the Eve of the Spanish Conquest. Stanford: Stanford University Press. [English translation of La vie quotidienne des azteques a la veille de la conquete espagnole. Paris: Hachette, 1955].

Spencer, Robert F., Jesse D. Jennings, et al.
1977 The Native Americans: Ethnology and Backgrounds of the North American Indians. New York: Harper & Row, Publishers.

Sperlich, Norbert and Elizabeth Katz Sperlich
1980 Guatemalan Backstrap Weaving. Norman: University of Oklahoma Press.

Spicer, Edward H.
1940 Pascua, A Yaqui Village in Arizona. Chicago: University of Chicago Press.
1952 Human Problems in Technological Change: A Casebook. New York: Russell Sage Foundation.
1954 Potam: A Yaqui Village in Sonora. Memoirs of the American Anthropological Association 77.
1962 Cycles of Conquest: The Impact of Spain, Mexico, and the United States on the Indians of the Southwest, 1533-1960. Tucson: The University of Arizona Press.
1969 Northwest Mexico: Introduction. In Handbook of Middle American Indians, Volume 8, Ethnology, Part 2, Evon Z. Vogt, ed., pp. 777-791. Austin: University of Texas Press.
1976 Capturing the Feeling. In The Seris by David Burkhalter, pp. 5-12. Tucson: University of Arizona Press.
1980 The Yaquis: A Cultural History. Tucson: University of Arizona Press.

Spier, Leslie
1923 Southern Diegueño Customs. University of California Publications in American Archaeology and Ethnology 20:297-358.

Spores, Ronald
1965 The Zapotec and Mixtec at Spanish Contact. In Handbook of Middle American Indians, Volume 3, Part 2, Archaeology of Southern Mesoamerica. Gordon R. Willey, ed., pp. 962-987. Austin: University of Texas Press.
1967 The Mixtec Kings and Their People. Norman: University of Oklahoma Press.

Stairs, Emily F. and Barbara E. Hollenbach
1969. Huave Verb Morphology. International Journal of American Linguistics 35:38-53.

Stark, Barbara L.
1981 The Rise of Sedentary Life. *In* Supplement to the Handbook of Middle American Indians, Volume 1, Archaeology, Jeremy A. Sabloff, ed., pp. 345-372. Austin: University of Texas Press.

Starr, Frederick
1899 Indians of Southern Mexico: an Ethnographic album. Chicago: Frederick Starr.
1901-2 Notes upon the Ethnography of Southern Mexico. Proceedings of the Davenport Academy of Natural Sciences. Volumes 8 & 10. Davenport, Iowa.

Steward, Julian H.
1948 The Circum-Caribbean Tribes: An Introduction. *In* Handbook of South American Indians. Volume 4, Julian H. Steward, ed., pp. 1-41. Washington, D.C.: United States Government Printing Office.
1955 Theory of Culture Change: The methodology of Multilinear Evolution. Urbana: University of Illinois Press.

Stier, Frances
1979 The Effect of Demographic Change on Agriculture in San Blas, Panama. Doctoral dissertation, Department of Anthropology. Tucson: University of Arizona.
1982 Domestic Economy: Land, Labor, and Wealth in a San Blas Community. American Ethnologist 9:519-537.
1983 Modeling Migration: Analyzing Migration Histories from a San Blas Cuna Community. Human Organization 42:9-22.

Stone, Doris
1948 The Basic Cultures of Central America. *In* Handbook of South American Indians, Volume 4, Bureau of American Ethnology Bulletin 143, Volume 4, Julian H. Steward, ed., pp. 169-193. Washington, D. C.: United States Government Printing Office.
1957 The Archaeology of Central and Southern Honduras. Papers of the Peabody Museum, Harvard University, Volume 49, No. 3. Cambridge: Harvard University Press.
1966 Synthesis of Lower Central American Ethnohistory. *In* Handbook of Middle American Indians, Volume 4, Archaeological Frontiers and External Connections, Gordon F. Ekholm and Gordon R. Willey, eds., pp. 209-233. Austin: University of Texas Press.

Stout, David B.
1947a Ethnolinguistic Observations on San Blas Cuna. International Journal of American Linguistics 13:9-13.
1947b San Blas Cuna Acculturation: An Introduction. Viking Fund Publications in Anthropology No. 9. New York: Wenner-Gren Foundation for Anthropological Research.

Tannenbaum, Frank
1950 Mexico: the Struggle for Peace and Bread. New York: Alfred A. Knopf.

Tavares, Julia
1978 Guide to Caribbean Prehistory. Santo Domingo: Museo del Hombre Dominicana.

Tax, Sol
1947 Notes on Santo Tomás Chichicastenango. Micorfilm Collection of Manuscripts in Middle American Cultural Anthropology, No. 16. Chicago: University of Chicago Library.
1953 Penny Capitalism: A Guatemalan Indian Economy. Smithsonian Institution. Institute of Social Anthropology Publication No. 16. Washington, D. C.: United States Government Printing Office.

Tax, Sol, et. al., eds.
1968 [1952] Heritage of Conquest: The Ethnology of Middle America. New York: Cooper Square Publishers.

Tax, Sol and Robert Hinshaw
1969 The Maya of the Midwestern Highlands. *In* The Handbook of Middle American Indians. Volume 7. Ethnology, Part 1. Evon Z. Vogt, ed., pp. 69-100. Austin: University of Texas Press.

Taylor, Douglas
1977 Languages of the West Indies. Baltimore: The Johns Hopkins University Press.

Taylor, Robert B.
1960 Teotitlán del Valle: A Typical Mesoamerican Community. Doctoral dissertation. Ann Arbor, Michigan: University Microfilms, Inc.
1966 Conservative Factors in the Changing Culture of a Zapotec Town. Human Organization 25:116-121.
1980 Cultural Ways: A Concise Edition of Introduction to Cultural Anthropology, Third Edition. Boston: Allyn and Bacon, Inc. [Reissued as Cultural Ways: A Concise Introduction to Cultural Anthropology, Waveland Press, Inc., 1988]

Taylor, Walter W.
1966 Archaic Cultures Adjacent to the Northeastern Frontiers of Mesoamerica. *In* Handbook of Middle American Indians, Volume 4, Archaeological Frontiers and External Connections. Gordon F. Ekholm and Gordon R. Willey, eds. pp. 59-94. Austin: University of Texas Press.

Thompson, J. Eric S.
1966 The Rise and Fall of Maya Civilization. 2d. ed. Norman: University of Oklahoma Press.

Torquemada, Juan de
1943-44[1615] Monarquía Indiana. México D.F.: Chávez Hayhoe

Torres de Arauz, Reina
1980 Panama Indígena. Panama City: Instituto Nacional de Cultura, Patrimonio Histórico.

Torres de Ianello, Reina
1973 Le discours de la magie. L'Homme 13:38-65.

Tozzer, Alfred M.
1907 A Comparative Study of the Mayas and the Lacandones. London: Macmillan & Co., Ltd.

Turner, Victor
1974 Dramas, Fields, and Metaphors: Symbolic Action in Human Society. Ithaca: Cornell University Press.

Valliant, George C.
1950 The Aztecs of Mexico: Origin, Rise and Fall of the Aztec Nation. Harmondsworth, Middlesex: Penquin Books.

Van Zantwijk, R. A. M.
1967 Servants of the Saints: The Social and Cultural Identity of a Tarascan Community in Mexico. Assen: Royal VanGorcum Ltd.

Villa Rojas, Alfonso
1947 Kinship and Nagualism in a Tzeltal Community, Southeastern Mexico. American Anthropologist 49:578-587.
1967 Los Lacandones, su origen, costumbres y problemas vitales. America Indígena 27:25-54.
1968 Los Lacandones: sus dioses, ritos, y creencias. América Indígena 28:81-138.
1969 The Tzeltal. *In* Handbook of Middle American Indians, Volume 7, Ethnology, Part 1, Evon Z. Vogt, ed., pp. 195-225. Austin: University of Texas Press.

Voegelin, C. F. and F. M. Voegelin
1977 Classification and Index of the World's Languages. New York: Elsevier North-Holland, Inc.

Vogt, Evon Z.
1969a The Maya: Introduction. *In* Handbook of Middle American Indians, Volume 7, Ethnology, Part 1. Evon Z. Vogt, ed., pp. 21-29. Austin: University of Texas Press.
1969b Zinacantán: A Maya Community in the Highlands of Chiapas. Cambridge, Massachusetts: Harvard University Press.

Von Hagen, V. Wolfgang
1943 The Jicaque (Torrupan) Indians of Honduras. New York: Museum of the American Indian, Heye Foundation.

Wagley, Charles
1941 Economics of a Guatemalan Village. Memoirs of the American Anthropological Association No. 58. Menasha, Wisconsin: American Anthropological Association.
1949 The Social and Religious Life of a Guatemalan Village. Memoirs of the American Anthropological Association No. 71. Menasha, Wisconsin: American Anthropological Association.
1969 The Maya of Northwestern Guatemala. *In* Handbook of Middle American Indians, Volume 7, Ethnology, Part 1, Evon Z. Vogt, ed., pp. 46-68. Austin: University of Texas Press.

Wallace, Anthony F. C.
1956 Revitalization Movements: Some Theoretical Considerations for their Comparative Study. American Anthropologist 58:264-281.

Warman, Arturo
1974 Música de los huaves o mareños (#14) (Program Notes) México: Instituto Nacional de Antropología e Historia

Weaver, Muriel Porter
1981 The Aztecs, Maya, and Their Predecessors: Archaeology of Mesoamerica, 2nd ed. New York: Academic Press.

Weigand, Phil C.
1969 Modern Huichol Ceramics. Mesoamerican Studies No. 3. Carbondale: Southern Illinois University Museum.
1972 Cooperative Labor Groups in Subsistence Activities Among the Huichol Indians. Mesoamerican Studies No. 7. Carbondale: Southern Illinois University Museum.
1976 The Role of the Huichol Indians in the Revolutions of Western Mexico. Proceedings of the Pacific Coast on Latin American Studies. Tempe: Arizona State University Center for Latin American Studies.
1978 Contemporary Social and Economic Structure. *In* Art of the Huichol Indians. Kathleen Berrin, ed., pp. 101-115. San Francisco: The Fine Arts Museums of San Francisco/New York: Harry N. Abrams, Inc.
1987 Differential Acculturation Among the Huichol Indians. *In* Themes of Indigenous Acculturation in Northwest Mexico. Thomas B. Hinton and Phil C. Weigand, eds. pp. 9-21. Tucson: University of Arizona Press.

West, Robert C.
1948 Cultural Geography of the Modern Tarascan Area. Smithsonian Institution, Institute of Social Anthropology Publication 7. Washington, D. C.: United States Government Printing Office.

Whitecotton, Joseph W.
1977 The Zapotecs: Princes, Priests, and Peasants. Norman: University of Oklahoma Press.

Whiting, Beatrice B. and John W. M. Whiting
1975 Children of Six Cultures: A Psycho-Cultural Analysis. Cambridge: Harvard University Press.

Wilson, Samuel M.
1986 The Conquest of the Caribbean Chiefdoms: Sociopolitical Change on Prehispanic Hispaniola. Department of Anthropology, University of Chicago. (Unpublished doctoral dissertation)

296

n.d. Taíno Elite Integration and Societal Complexity on Hispaniola. (Unpublished manuscript.)

Wisdom, Charles
1940 The Chortí Indians of Guatemala. Chicago: University of Chicago Press.

Wolf, Eric
1957 Closed Corporate Communities in Mesoamerica and Central Java. Southwestern Journal of Anthropology 13:1-18.
1959 Sons of the Shaking Earth. Chicago: University of Chicago Press.

Wright, Irene Aloha
1916 The Early History of Cuba, 1492-1586. New York: Macmillan.

Young, Philip D.
1971 Ngawbe: Tradition and Change among the Western Guaymí of Panama. Urbana: University of Illinois Press.

Zantwijk, R. A. M. Van
1960 Los Indígenas de Milpa Alta. Instituto Real Trópicos, Amsterdam, No. 135, Secretaría Antropología Cultural y Física, No. 64.

Zingg, Robert
1938 The Huichols: Primitive Artists. University of Denver Contributions in Ethnography 1. New York: G. E. Stechert and Company. [Kraus Reprint Co., Millwood, N.Y., 1977]

Index

299